Tolley's Tax Planni
managed Business
2018–19

Tolley's Tax Planning for Owner-managed Businesses 2018–19

Twelfth Edition

Tolley®

Members of the LexisNexis Group worldwide

United Kingdom	RELX (UK) Limited trading as LexisNexis, 1–3 Strand, London WC2N 5JR
Argentina	LexisNexis Argentina, Buenos Aires
Australia	Reed International Books Australia Pty Ltd trading as LexisNexis, Chatswood, New South Wales
Austria	LexisNexis Verlag ARD Orac GmbH & Co KG, Vienna
Benelux	LexisNexis Benelux, Amsterdam
Canada	LexisNexis Canada, Markham, Ontario
Chile	LexisNexis Chile Ltda, Santiago
China	LexisNexis China, Beijing and Shanghai
France	LexisNexis SA, Paris
Germany	LexisNexis GmbH, Dusseldorf
Hong Kong	LexisNexis Hong Kong, Hong Kong
India	LexisNexis India, New Delhi
Italy	Giuffrè Editore, Milan
Japan	LexisNexis Japan, Tokyo
Malaysia	Malayan Law Journal Sdn Bhd, Kuala Lumpur
New Zealand	LexisNexis NZ Ltd, Wellington
Singapore	LexisNexis Singapore, Singapore
South Africa	LexisNexis Butterworths, Durban
USA	LexisNexis, Dayton, Ohio

First published in 2009

© 2018 RELX (UK) Limited.

Published by LexisNexis.
This is a Tolley Title

ISBN for this volume: 9780754555025

Printed and Bound in Great Britain by Hobbs the Printers Ltd, Totton, Hampshire.

Visit LexisNexis at www.lexisnexis.co.uk

Preface

Welcome to the twelfth edition of *Tolley's Tax Planning for Owner-Managed-Businesses 2018–19*.

I have been privileged to be involved in the production of the book since the first edition. Each year the challenge remains the same – to give clear practical guidance to practitioners wishing to help owner-managed business through the maze of UK direct tax legislation.

No two businesses are the same and the requirements of the business and their owners are constantly evolving. The taxes affecting owner-managed businesses are wide ranging, however, with the right structures in place running your own business can still be very rewarding.

Gabelle is an award winning independent firm of tax consultants who provide tax support to accountants and other advisers, as well as directly to clients. In January 2017, Gabelle was acquired by Abbey Tax to lead their tax consultancy services arm. By merging with Abbey Tax, Gabelle now has additional tax expertise and puts us in the fortunate position of coming across some really interesting tax problems on a regular basis.

As in previous years, the production of the book would not have been possible without the support of my colleagues whose insight is invaluable. The team are experts in their field, with many years of practical experience and are reputed in the marketplace for both their direct and indirect tax services. They are able to translate technical knowledge into practical ideas for advisers and their clients and this is evident when you work your way through the book.

Finally, thank you to the readers – we hope you enjoy the book and more importantly are able to take away some key learning points.

Paul Howard
London May 2018

Author Biographies

Paula Tallon

Paula Tallon is a Partner of Gabelle. A Chartered Accountant and Chartered Tax Adviser with an Advanced Diploma in International Tax, she has spent almost 20 years advising on tax. She has a broad range of tax expertise with particular emphasis on owner-managed-businesses and her particular areas of interest include property taxes, entrepreneurs' relief, business reorganisations and reconstructions, employment related securities and venture capital schemes. She regularly writes and lectures on tax issues affecting OMBs.

Paul Howard

Paul Howard is a Director at Gabelle. He is a Chartered Accountant and a Chartered Tax Adviser with 25 years in the profession, working for medium-sized accountancy firms where he specialised in tax issues affecting owner-managed-businesses, the owners and their families and covered a very wide range of issues. He has been advising accountants for over ten years and during that time has made regular appearances on the lecturing circuit as well as writing for the professional press.

Paul Bramall

Paul Bramall is a Partner at Gabelle. He is a Chartered Accountant and a Chartered Tax Adviser with over 30 years of professional experience. He specialises in advising non-domiciliaries on all tax aspects of immigration and emigration including residency issues and offshore corporate and trust matters. Paul has first-hand experience of the offshore industry having spent two years working in Guernsey. He is a regular face on the lecture circuit and contributes articles to various professional journals.

Vaughn Chown

Vaughn Chown is the Managing Partner at Gabelle. He is an Associate of the Institute of Indirect Taxation and has 30 years professional experience. He specialises in VAT. Vaughn spent nine years as a senior officer with HMRC. He has represented many cases in the VAT Tribunal including take away food, mixed and multiple supplies, VAT liabilities and VAT bad debt relief. He regularly lectures on all aspects of VAT and writes on the VAT issues facing OMBs and their advisers.

John Hood

John Hood is a Partner at Gabelle. He has over 20 years of professional experience in tax investigations. He specialises in representing owner-managed-businesses facing an investigation under either Code of Practice 8 or

9 involving Specialist Investigations of HM Revenue & Customs. John is experienced in dealing with the facilities offered by HMRC to allow people to bring their tax affairs up-to-date and can provide practical advice and guidance on all aspects of making the disclosure.

Kevin Offer

Kevin Offer is a Partner at Gabelle. He is a Chartered Tax Adviser and a Fellow of the ICAEW. Kevin specialises in private client tax and has a particular interest in the taxation of high net-worth individuals, sportsmen and entertainers. He is also a member of the International Tax Planning Association, the International Taxation of Entertainers Group, the VAT Practitioners Group, and a freeman of the Worshipful Company of Tax Advisers.

Martin Mann

Martin Mann is a Director at Gabelle. He is both a member of the Association of Tax Technicians and the Chartered Institute of Taxation with over 25 years of experience. His past roles have seen him advise on both business/corporate as well as personal tax issues and as a consequence Martin has developed a broad range of tax expertise. His particular areas of specialism are employment taxes (including share reward issues) as well as capital gains tax issues notably PPR.

Caroline Fleet

Caroline Fleet is a Director at Gabelle. She is a Fellow of the Institute of Chartered Accountants with over 15 years in the profession. Prior to joining Gabelle, Caroline worked at two of the 'Big 4' firms and for the last eight years has specialised in advising tax to clients within the real estate industry. Such clients have covered the whole spectrum of real estate ranging from institutional investors, developers to corporates, joint ventures and the collective investments. Caroline has particular experience in advising on trading vs investment considerations, permanent establishment and holding structures.

Thomas Dalby

Thomas Dalby is a Director at Gabelle. He is a Barrister and Chartered Tax Adviser with nearly 18 years in the profession. Prior to joining Gabelle, Thomas worked at Deloitte where, for the last 14 years, he was a member of the Specialist Employer Consulting and Opportunities team advising clients ranging from FTSE 100 multinationals, established family companies to start-ups on employee reward structures. He has worked with clients on the whole spectrum of employee share ownership, including EMI, growth shares, joint ownership shares, approved share plans, Employee Shareholder Status and bespoke share-owning arrangements. He has extensive experience in dealing with employee benefit trusts, including advising clients on mitigating their exposure to tax under the disguised remuneration rules and negotiating settlements with HMRC.

Kevin Hall

Kevin Hall is a Senior Consultant with Gabelle. After graduating from Oxford University, Kevin qualified as a Chartered Accountant. He has specialised in

VAT since 1998. He advises a wide variety of clients on VAT issues, including those related to property, international transactions, schemes for small businesses, financial services, yachts/aircraft, HMRC investigations and margin schemes. Kevin also writes and lectures on VAT and he has contributed to HMRC's VAT Manuals, specifically in relation to financial advisers.

Reshma Johar

Reshma Johar is a Senior Tax Consultant at Gabelle. She is both a member of the Association of Tax Technicians and the Chartered Institute of Taxation with over 10 years of experience. Her past roles have been within medium sized accountancy practices where she was involved providing bespoke advice to high net worth individuals, families and owner managed businesses covering a range of taxes. Reshma is also a committee member of the women in tax network, which provides both technical and soft skills training.

Sean Eastwood

Sean Eastwood is a Consultant with Gabelle. He is a member of the Association of Taxation Technicians and qualified as a Chartered Tax Advisor in 2014. Before working at Gabelle, he worked in general practice for over 13 years, starting out in audit and accounts, before making the move over to taxation. Sean's areas of interest revolve around the tax issues affecting private clients and owner-managed-businesses.

Reena Bhudia

Reena Bhudia is a Consultant at Gabelle. She is a member of the Association of Taxation Technicians and the Society of Trust and Estate Practitioners with an Economics degree. Prior to joining Gabelle, Reena worked within the Trust and Estates department at a leading Accountancy Practice and Trust Company. Reena's area of interest revolves around tax issues relating to Inheritance Tax, Trust and Estates.

Contents

Contents

Contents

Chapter 8   Reliefs Available to Businesses

Contents

Contents

Contents

Abbreviations

AIA	Annual-investment allowance
AIM	Alternative Investment Market
ASP	Alternatively secured pension
ATED	Annual tax on enveloped dwellings
BATR	Business Asset Taper Relief
BCE	Benefit-crystallisation event
BIM	Business Income Manual
BPR	Business Property Relief
BTL	Buy to let
CAA	Certified actuarial analyst
CGT	Capital Gains Tax
CIOT	Chartered Institute of Taxation
CSOP	Company share option plan
CTA	Chartered tax adviser
CVS	Corporate Venturing Scheme
EBT	Employee Benefit Trust
ECA	Enhanced capital allowance
EEA	European Economic Area
EIM	Employment Income Manual
EIS	Enterprise Investment Scheme
EMI	Enterprise Management Incentive
ER	Entrepreneurs' Relief
FHLs	Furnished Holiday Lets
FURBS	Funded Unapproved Retirement Benefit Scheme
FYA	First-year allowance
GAAP	Generally Accepted Accounting Principles
GAD	Government Actuary's Department
HMRC	HM Revenue & Customs

ICAEW	Institute of Charted Accountants in England and Wales
IHT	Inheritance tax
IHTA	Inheritance Act 1984
ITA	Income Tax Act 2007
ITEPA	Income Tax (Earnings and Pensions) Act 2003
ITTOIA	Income Tax (Trading and Other Income) Act 2005
LBTT	Land and buildings transaction tax
LLP	Limited Liability Partnership
LTT	Land Transfer Tax
NIC	National Insurance contribution
OECD	Organisation for Economic Cooperation and Development
PAYE	Pay As You Earn
PPR	Principle Private Residence
PR	Personal representative
PSC	Personal service company
QCB	Qualifying corporate bond
RCA	Readily convertible asset
R & D	Research and development
SIPP	Self-invested personal pension
SME	Small and medium-sized enterprise
SSAS	Small self-administered scheme
SSE	Substantial-shareholding exemption
TCGA	Taxation of Chargeable Gains Act 1992
USP	Unsecured pension
VAT	Value added tax
VCT	Venture Capital Trust
WDA	Written-down allowance
WDV	Written-down value

Table of Statutes

References on the right-hand side of this table are to paragraphs. References printed in **bold** type indicate where the Act is set out in part or in full.

Table of Cases

D

E

F

G

H

I

J

K

L

M

X

Y

Judgments of the European Court of Justice are listed below numerically. These judgments are also included in the preceding alphabetical Table.

Part I

Creating the Business

Chapter 1

Starting in Business

Introduction

[1.1] Numerous factors should be taken into consideration when an individual, or a group of individuals, sets up in business. Sometimes, the medium through which the business will be carried on is dictated by commercial practice, for example setting up an IT or commercial design business, where a corporate structure is usually required by customers and agents; or professional practices, which, historically at least, tend to be in an unincorporated form. Unfortunately, there are cases where not enough thought is given to the business entity when a business commences.

For example, a company may have been formed with no thought to the legal and practical implications. It is only when the individual engages the services of an accountant or solicitor or approaches their bank that they might consider whether a limited company is appropriate to their needs.

Determining which choice of entity must be guided by a range of commercial, practical and legal considerations, all of which are beyond the scope of this book. We will concentrate primarily on the tax considerations that are relevant to the decision on how to structure the business.

Natural progression in an individual's career, or as a result of redundancy or a 'life-style change' can often result in new businesses being formed. A new business could continue alongside the individual's 'day job', which, in itself, may have implications in relation to the chosen structure. This can be found particularly with property development, farming, or more 'life-style' activities.

Commencement of trade

[1.2] A number of cases, including the leading case of *Birmingham & District Cattle By-Products Co Ltd v IRC* (1919) 12TC92 considered whether and at what point a trade commenced.

In that case, the following were held to be preparatory activities:

- viewing other places of business of a similar character (business research);
- entering into a contract to build a factory and having the factory built;
- purchasing machinery and plant for carrying on the business;
- entering into agreements for the purchase of products;
- engaging a foreman of works.

The trade was deemed to have commenced when the company took delivery of the raw materials and turned out its product.

Retail shops and restaurants are usually regarded as commencing trade when they first open their doors for business. This follows the judgment in *J&R O'Kane & Co v IRC* (1992) 12TC303, 66 Sol Jo 281.

Some individuals may not appreciate that they have started a business that is subject to tax, for example Airbnb providers, or eBay users, where the individual has to determine whether there is sufficient commerciality in offering items for sale on the internet. Selling personal items is not likely to be regarded as trading, but if items are bought at a car boot sale and immediately offered for sale this would be regarded as a trading activity.

It is imperative to establish when a trade or profession has started to ensure that HMRC is notified of the commencement of the business activity and that appropriate National Insurance Contributions (NICs) are made at the correct time. Notifying HMRC can easily be overlooked among the burdens of starting and running a business, however, it should be done as a priority as penalties can be imposed for failing to notify on time. Failure to pay on time may also cause problems with future social security benefit claims. The HMRC website is helpful in this respect and provides guidance as well as download-able forms to complete the registration process. The guidance and forms can be found at www.gov.uk/topic/business-tax/self-employed.

The date of commencement of trade is important for unincorporated businesses to establish the fiscal year in which the commencement provisions apply, and to determine in which self-assessment tax return the trade should first be recorded.

For companies, the commencement of trade establishes the start of an accounting period, which will then run for 12 months or to the end of the period of account to which accounts are drawn up, whichever is earlier.

The commencement of trade will also be important in relation to the eligibility of valuable reliefs such as entrepreneurs' relief, substantial shareholdings exemption and business property relief, where a period of trading is a vital factor. These are considered in **CHAPTER 3** and **CHAPTER 5**.

VAT and starting in business

[1.3] It is important to ensure registering for VAT is made at the appropriate time, either on a compulsory or voluntary basis (VAT Act 1994, Sch 1).

- Penalties can be issued by HMRC for failure to register for VAT on a compulsory basis at the correct time (Notice 700/41).
- Businesses may apply under voluntary VAT registration to enable VAT to be claimed on business expenditure attributable to taxable supplies.
- If a business makes zero-rated supplies (VAT Act 1994, Sch 8) they should review whether they are required to notify their liability to be VAT registered, even if they will apply for an exemption from VAT registration.
- The making of supplies outside the scope of VAT, in certain circumstances, can enable a business to be registered for VAT and claim the VAT on attributable business expenditure (VAT Act 1994, Sch 1).

- Overseas businesses making supplies in the UK/EC should consider their liability to be registered for VAT and in which jurisdiction(s).
- Businesses may be required to register for VAT in respect of supplies or acquisitions from other member states (VAT Act 1994, Schs 2 and 3).

Eligibility for the use of special schemes should also be considered, eg:

- the flat rate scheme (Notice 733);
- cash accounting (Notice 731);
- annual accounting (Notice 732);
- retail schemes (Notice 727);
- tour operators margin scheme (Notice 709/5);
- second-hand margin scheme and global accounting scheme (Notice 718) etc.

Where a business has a VAT liability of £2.3m or more in any rolling 12-month period, it will be liable to make payments on account (Notice 700/60).

A business should consider pre-registration VAT that may be incurred. VAT on services incurred in the six-month period prior to setting up the business can be claimed and the VAT on stock and assets still on hand at the date of VAT registration can be claimed if the items were acquired within the previous four years. As always, there are some exemptions and criteria that need to be met for these claims to succeed.

Sole trades and partnerships

[1.4] Setting up as a sole trade or partnership is often used as the structure is easy to set up, requires little in the way of formalities, is easy to understand and if it does not work out, is easy to cease.

There are a number of advantages for tax purposes of an unincorporated business. Principally, losses of up to the greater of £50,000 and 25% of an individual's total income can be offset against an individual's other income, whereas although losses incurred by companies can be used very flexibly, the companies are initially unlikely to have any option other than to carry those losses forward to offset against future profits from the same trade.

An unincorporated business's profits form part of an individual's income for the fiscal year. This may be disadvantageous if that individual's total income is surplus to requirements, in which case it may be appropriate to form a company at the outset or move to a company structure by incorporating the business. The benefits of a company structure are covered in more detail in **CHAPTER 12**.

Levels of profits became particularly pertinent with a top rate of income tax of 45%, as personal income can be capped at £150,000 by using a corporate tax structure. Planning for the 45% rate is considered in **CHAPTER 6**.

Other important factors to consider when deciding whether to incorporate include the impact of the reduction of personal allowance for earners with income over £100,000 and a reduction in child benefit for those individuals earning over £50,000 per annum. The fundamental changes in how dividend income is subject to tax from 6 April 2016 will also alter the way of thinking when it comes to incorporation.

Individuals who are partners in a partnership or members of an LLP are subject to income tax on their share of profits as if they were carrying on a 'notional trade' (ITTOIA 2005, s 852).

The cash basis can be applied to small unincorporated businesses, introduced by Finance Act 2013, s 17. These provisions were introduced as a simplification for small businesses, although the details of the relief are complex. It is available to unincorporated businesses (not LLPs) with a turnover of less than the VAT registration threshold of £85,000. In addition, there are flat rate allowances for motor vehicles, use of home as office and use of commercial premises as a home, introduced by Finance Act 2013, s 18. It should be borne in mind that sideways loss relief is not available for losses incurred in a business that uses the cash basis. The business must stop using the cash basis when turnover exceeds twice the VAT registration threshold.

Loss relief for individuals

[1.5] There are a number of important restrictions that can apply on losses incurred by an individual, (as a sole trader, or as a partner or member of an LLP), which can be offset in the following ways:

- against general income (ITA 2007, ss 64–70);
- by carry back in early years of trade (ITA 2007, ss 72–74);
- by carry forward against profits from the same trade (ITA 2007, ss 83–88);
- as a terminal loss relief claim (ITA 2007, ss 89–94);
- by treating the loss as a capital loss (ITA 2007, s 71).

Against general income 'sideways relief'

A trade loss can be set off against an individual's general income under s 64 either for the loss-making year, or for the previous year, or for both years. The individual would need to specify which of the two years is to be used first.

Loss relief against general income is only available if the trade is 'commercial', which means that the trade must be carried out on a commercial basis and with a view to the realisation of profits (ITA 2007, s 66). It is sometimes difficult, therefore, to claim loss relief for activities that might be regarded as a hobby. The First Tier Tribunal has considered the approach to establishing whether a trade is carried on with a view to the realisation of profits in the case of *Beacon Estates (Chepstow) Ltd v HMRC*, First-tier Tribunal (2014) TC 3808, where hindsight was used to answer this question.

The number of cases in relation to tax schemes has increased, whereby HMRC has successfully argued that the business is not carried on on a commercial basis with a view to the realisation of profits. For example, in the case of *Seven Individuals v Revenue and Customs Comrs*: [2017] UKUT 0132 (TCC),

[2017] STC 874, the Tribunal concluded that a trade virtually certain to lead to a loss cannot be regarded as commercial. This decision was followed in the case of *Mills and Team Origin LLP v Revenue and Customs Comrs* [2017] UKFTT 378 (TC), [2017] SFTD 872.

Special rules apply to farming and market gardening, which aim to exclude hobby-farming losses from relief where losses continue for more than five years (ITA 2007, s 67). The Upper Tribunal decision in *Scambler (Bryan) and Scambler (Rebecca) v Revenue and Customs Comrs*: [2017] UKUT 0001 (TCC), [2017] All ER (D) 154 (Feb) highlights the subtlety of the operation of the restriction rules. The Tribunal concluded that the basic five year time-frame cannot be extended unless there is something in the nature of the farming activities means that the farm could not reasonably be expected to become profitable within that time-frame. These rules also extend to some equine activities.

In the first four years of a trade, an individual can claim to offset losses against general income in the three years prior to the loss year, taking the earliest year first (ITA 2007, ss 72–73). For the purposes of this relief, not only must the trade be carried on commercially, but also in such a way that profits could reasonably be expected to be made in the basis period or within a reasonable time thereafter (ITA 2007, s 74). HMRC tends to like to see an expectation of profit within a short period after commencement, even though the business model shows profits accruing over a longer timeframe.

Individuals will face restrictions to 'sideways' loss relief (ss 74A, 74C and s 74ZA). Losses are restricted to £25,000 where the individual carries on a trade (not profession) in a 'non-active' capacity. This applies where the individual spends less than 10 hours a week, on average, personally engaged in activities of the trade. The restriction, which was introduced to counter schemes that generated trading losses with no personal involvement by the individual claiming the loss, could be problematic for part-time traders, and at present for property developers in particular. Where an individual may be in this position, it is important to document their involvement in the trade.

Sideways loss relief is not available where the loss arises from arrangements where the main purpose is to obtain a tax reduction from sideways relief (s 74ZA).

Since 6 April 2013, there has been a restriction on total reliefs an individual can claim by applying a cap of the greater of £50,000 and 25% of an individual's total income on reliefs that are not otherwise subject to an upper limit. This cap will apply principally to sideways loss reliefs, loan interest, s 131 loss relief on shares, together with some other less common reliefs.

Other losses

Where trading losses are not used against general income, the loss can be treated as an allowable capital loss under ITA 2007, s 71, and TCGA 1992, ss 261B and 261C. The relief was introduced to assist traders who were forced to sell capital assets to fund trading losses. The amount of trading losses which can be used are restricted to capital gains less capital losses of the relevant year plus capital losses brought forward. A strict method of calculation has to be followed and this may mean wasting all or part of the annual exemption.

Where sideways loss relief cannot be obtained, relief for the loss will be given by carrying it forward and setting it against profits from the same trade (ITA 2007, s 83). If the trade has ceased or there is a change in activity, relief for the losses brought forward would be denied.

Should the trade cease permanently, the loss for the final year of trading, calculated in accordance with ITA 2007, s 90 can be set off against profits from the same trade in the previous three years, taking the latest year first. The full amount of any available overlap relief is included in the terminal loss.

Partnership loss restrictions

It is more complex for partners and LLP members in terms of the restrictions on sideways loss relief, and are contained in ITA 2007, ss 102–115. There are no restrictions for a full and active equity partner in a general partnership, whereas there are restrictions for an active member of an LLP. This may be an important aspect to deciding which entity to use for the trade. A summary of the main restrictions is as follows:

Loss restrictions	LLPs		General Partnership	
	Active	Non-Active	Active	Non-Active
Restricted capital contributions	s 107	s 110	None	s 110
Restricted to a maximum of £25,000	None	s 103C	None	s 103C

The restrictions only apply to trades and do not apply to professions. Restrictions under s 104 also apply to limited partners as defined in ITA 2007, s 103A.

Losses that cannot be relieved by 'sideways loss relief' claims can be carried forward to set off against future profits of the same trade.

NICs and losses

[1.6] The position of NICs in a loss-making situation should not be overlooked. Class 4 NICs are not due when a business makes a loss. If those losses are offset against other income (not trade profits) for income tax purposes, they are nevertheless available to carry forward and offset against future profits from the same trade for NIC purposes.

Furthermore, if the individual has income in respect of which maximum Class 1 contributions have been paid, it is possible to apply for deferment for Class 2 and Class 4 contributions in respect of the new business or for an exception for the Class 2 contributions if the business is expected to make a loss or a very small profit.

The Government had advised in November 2017 that there will be a delay until 6 April 2019 for Class 2 National Insurance to be abolished. It appears that the reform of Class 4 National Insurance has also been delayed.

Taxation of profits of sole trades and partnerships

[1.7] An unincorporated business's profits are subject to income tax and the results of the business are reported on the self-employment pages of the self-assessment tax return.

In the case of a partnership, the partners are treated as if they were each carrying on a business on their own account. The partners will decide how to allocate profits and losses. The allocation is reflected in the partnership tax return, which is the responsibility of the nominated partner to prepare and submit to HMRC. Each partner's share of profit or loss as shown on the partnership return must appear on his own return. The recent First-tier Tribunal decision in *King v HMRC* (2016 UKFTT 409) suggests that where a partner believes that the partnership tax return is incorrect, he can submit his own tax return with the figures he believes are correct.

Each partner is able to use losses as they choose, without reference to how the other partners utilise their share of losses. However, where the profits or losses of a partnership are allocated between the partners in such a way that some partners are allocated a loss and others a profit, the profits and losses are reallocated so that those partners allocated a profit make neither a profit nor a loss for tax purposes. As a result, the share of losses for loss-making partners is restricted.

Disposals by partnerships

[1.8] If a partnership disposes of a chargeable asset, each partner is treated as making a disposal of their own share of the asset for capital gains tax purposes. As with profits and losses, each partner's share of the gain must be reported on their own tax return.

Transactions between partners

[1.9] Statement of Practice D12, together with amendments to that Statement set out in Revenue and Customs Brief 03/08 provide useful guidance in dealing with transactions between partners. Transactions between partners, usually when a partner joins or leaves the partnership, or where the profit-sharing ratio changes, do not fit neatly into capital gains tax.

Strictly, when an individual joins a partnership, all the other partners make a disposal of their interest in the partnership assets. However, D12 will usually allow the partners to reallocate their base costs in the chargeable assets rather than record a disposal, except in the following situations:

- where actual consideration passes;
- where the assets are revalued in the partnership accounts;
- where the new partner is connected with the original partners, usually as a family member, and the new partner is introduced on such terms as would not have been entered into between unconnected persons;

- where one of the partners contributes an asset to the partnership (Revenue and Customs Brief 03/08)

Statement of Practice D12 also deals with the situation where a retiring partner is paid an annuity, ensuring that income tax relief for the payment is only obtained for an annuity that is commensurate with the profits earned by the partner before he or she retired.

Limited Liability Partnerships (LLPs)

[1.10] An LLP may be preferred by individuals rather than a traditional partnership because of the greater protection which is afforded by limited liability. There will usually be no tax consequences arising from the conversion of a partnership to an LLP. For most practical purposes, an LLP is taxed in the same way as a traditional partnership formed under the Partnership Act 1890.

An LLP, in most situations, is treated for tax purposes in the same way as a traditional partnership. However, when an LLP goes into liquidation, it ceases to be transparent vis à vis the members. On appointment, the liquidator acquires all the assets of the LLP at original cost, with a corresponding disposal by the members. This triggers a gain if the asset was originally acquired by the member under, for example, a hold-over or roll-over claim, where the CGT base cost is less than the original cost of the asset. Furthermore, the gain falls into charge on the member who made the original roll-over or hold-over claim.

During the liquidation process the LLP will, broadly, be taxed as a corporate entity.

Choosing a limited company

[1.11] There are many commercial reasons for choosing a company rather than an unincorporated business as a vehicle to carry on a trade. An analysis of these is beyond the scope of this book.

There are however, many tax considerations that have a bearing on this decision, not least of which is the differential between corporate and personal rates of tax. There is a substantial difference between the corporation tax rate of 19% and the top rate of income tax of 45%, and this difference is due to increase further when the corporation tax rate falls to 17% by 2020. It is therefore likely that most profitable businesses will want to consider trading in an incorporated form, although the recent changes to the taxation of dividend income will in some cases fundamentally alter the way of thinking when it comes to considering incorporation and profit extraction.

Notwithstanding the level of profitability of a business, a corporate structure provides greater flexibility in terms of ownership and participation, and offers a number of options for extracting profits and rewarding both proprietors and staff. There are also a number of reliefs that are available only to companies, which are considered in **CHAPTER 8**.

Incorporation is a more attractive option where the principals do not intend to draw all the post-tax profits out of the business. The profits can then be reinvested in the business or used for other ventures by the company. Where profits are largely withdrawn, either by salary or by dividend, the difference in tax rates between an unincorporated and an incorporated business may not be large. There are, however, other factors that make the decision an important one.

Once a business has been incorporated, it is no longer simply a matter of reporting profits or losses on the individual's personal tax return. A company is a separate legal entity with its own tax liabilities and reporting obligations. Money can be drawn from the company in a number of ways, all of which have their own tax and NIC implications.

A company pays corporation tax on its profits. The rate of corporation tax used to depend on the level of profits in a particular year and on the number of companies that are treated as associated with it; however with a uniform rate of corporation tax, this no longer applies. However, the number of companies comprising a group is still relevant for instalment payment purposes, where large companies are still required to pay corporation tax in instalments and the threshold for being a large company remains at £1.5 million (reduced by the number of companies in the group).

Losses can only be offset against a company's own trade profits, except in very specific circumstances.

Finance Act 2018 brought in the reforms being made to corporate losses being carried forward from 1 April 2017 onwards.

Profits may be paid to its shareholders or employees or retained in the company to provide working capital or for distribution in future years. The method of distribution of the profits can affect the corporation tax payable by the company.

Example

Assume a business makes taxable profits of £50,000. If the proprietor is already a higher-rate taxpayer, they will pay income tax of £20,000. He or she would also have a Class 4 NIC liability unless they had paid maximum Class 1 contributions, in which case Class 4 contributions can be eliminated. Class 2 contributions may also be payable, again dependent on the level of contributions on other earnings. If a single company makes those same profits, it would currently pay corporation tax of £10,000. If extraction of profits is not an issue, the conclusion is clear.

At this level of profits, the advantage of a corporate structure over an unincorporated business is only marginally evident if the whole of the profits are paid out by way of dividend and where there is a Class 4 NIC liability on the unincorporated proprietor.

However, this is usually only part of the analysis. A shareholder–director has a number of options. The company could pay the shareholder a salary or a dividend or both. The company could make a loan or provide a benefit to him.

The company must operate Pay As You Earn (PAYE) under Real Time Information (RTI) on any salary or bonus paid to directors or employees. The company will also have a liability to secondary Class 1 NICs, although this can be reduced by the

£3,000 Annual Employment Allowance unless the director is the only employee of the company in which case the company would not be entitled to the Employment Allowance. The total amount of salary, NICs and secondary Class 1 NIC paid by the company is deductible against profits for corporation tax purposes.

If, therefore, the company chooses to pay the whole of its profits (after basic salaries) of £50,000 as a bonus to the director, the tax position would be:

Salary		£	Dividend		£
Profits		50,000	Profits		50,000
Employer's NIC		(6,063)	Corporation tax at 19%		(9,500)
Gross bonus available		43,937	Net available for distribution		40,500
Income tax at 40%	17,575		Income tax at 32.5% (on net dividend)	13,162	
Employee's NIC	4,261				
Total deductions			Total deductions		(13,162)
Net pay		22,101	Net pay		27,338
Effective rate of tax		56%	Effective rate of tax		45%

Note that the above salary extraction calculation does not take into account the £3,000 per annum Employment Allowance or the new 0% band for dividends.

If salary was paid, as all of the profits have been expended by the company, there would be no corporation tax liability.

The company could choose to pay the whole of the profits to the shareholder as a dividend. The dividend is not deductible for corporation tax purposes, so 19% of the profits would have to be retained to cover the corporation tax liability.

Use of hybrid structures

[1.12] The past few years have seen an increase in the use of companies and partnerships together as business structures. The tax treatment of partnerships involving companies is dealt with in CTA 2009, ss 1256–1273.

The increase in corporate involvement in partnerships has led to the introduction of anti-avoidance rules on profit allocations to corporate members in a partnership, which are contained in ITTOIA 2005, ss 850C to 850E. The purpose of these provisions is to prevent excessive allocations of profit to a corporate member where an individual member is able to enjoy those profits. The corporate member's profit share will be restricted to what would be a reasonable return for their contribution to the business. The remainder of the profit assigned to the corporate for accounting purposes will be deemed to be distributed to the individual who is able to enjoy those profits for the purposes of calculating their income tax and Class 4 NIC liabilities.

Section 850C deals with the situation where there is an individual partner ('A') who has a share of profit or has neither a profit nor a loss, and there is a non-individual partner (usually a company) ('B') who has a share of profit in the firm. Where either Condition X or Condition Y applies, there is a potential reallocation of profits for tax purposes in accordance with s 850C(4) and (5).

Condition X

Condition X is that it is reasonable to suppose that—

- *amounts representing A's deferred profit are included in B's profit share, and*
- *in consequence, both A's profit share and the relevant tax amount are lower than they would otherwise have been. s 850C(2)*

Deferred profits are any amounts (such as remuneration and benefits) which are deferred or contingent upon the individual partner meeting any condition (however remote).

The 'relevant tax amount' is defined in s 850C(9) as the total tax which would be payable by A and B

Condition Y

Condition Y, is that:

- B's profit share exceeds an 'appropriate notional profit';
- A has the power to enjoy the profits of the corporate member;
- It is reasonable to assume that both A's share and the relevant tax are lower than they would have been in the absence of A's power to enjoy.

Appropriate notional profit is defined in s 850C(10) as the sum of the appropriate notional return on capital and the appropriate notional consideration for services.

The appropriate notional return on capital is defined in s 850C(11) as:

(a) *the return which B would receive for the relevant period of account in respect of B's contribution to the firm were the return to be calculated on the basis mentioned in subsection (12), less*

(b) *any return actually received for the relevant period of account in respect of B's contribution to the firm which is not included in B's profit share.*

(12) The return mentioned in subsection (11)(a) is to be calculated on the basis that it is a return which is –

(a) *by reference to the time value of an amount of money equal to B's contribution to the firm, and*

(b) *at a rate which (in all the circumstances) is a commercial rate of interest.*

Contribution to the firm is determined by reference to 'amount A' in ITA 2007, s 108, as amended by s 850C(14). For the purposes of s 850C, contribution means the amount contributed as capital, less any amounts drawn out or received back or which B is entitled to draw out or receive back.

The appropriate return on capital is a commercial rate of interest on the capital contributed. The commercial rate will reflect the level of risk involved.

The value of services should be calculated at arm's length and HMRC's view is that in almost all cases the notional consideration should be no more than the cost to the company providing the services plus a modest mark up.

The appropriate notional consideration for services is defined in s 850C(15) and (16) as:

(a) *the amount which B would receive in consideration for any services provided to the firm by B during the relevant period of account were the consideration to be calculated on the basis that B is not a partner in the firm and is acting at arm's length from the firm, less*

(b) *any amount actually received in consideration for any such services which is not included in B's profit share.*

It is important to be able to document and support B's profit share by reference to the appropriate notional profit determined in accordance with s 850C. Consequently, the partnership will have to ascertain an appropriate return on capital and to determine an arm's length price for any services provided by the non-individual partner to the partnership.

If B's profit share is deemed to be 'excessive', then whether or not the excess profits will be re-allocated to the individual partner depends on whether A has the power to enjoy B's profit share.

The power to enjoy provisions are set out in s 850C(18) and (19).

A has the power to enjoy B's profit share in two situations, first, where A is connected with B by virtue of ITA 2007, s 993, excluding subsection (4) which deals with connections through a partnership; and secondly where any of the enjoyment conditions set out in s 850C(19) are met.

Looking specifically at the situation where B is a company, A will be connected with B if:

(a) *A has control of the company, or*

(b) *A together with persons connected with A have control of the company (ITA 2007, s 993(6)).*

A will be connected with a spouse or civil partner, a relative, or a spouse or civil partner of a relative. A relative is defined in s 994(1) as brother, sister, ancestor or lineal descendant.

The enjoyment conditions in s 850C(19) are:

(a) *B's profit share, or the part, is in fact so dealt with by any person as to be calculated, at some time to enure for the benefit of A, whether in the form of income or not;*

(b) *The receipt or accrual of B's profit share, or the part, by or to B operates to increase the value to A of any assets held by, or for the benefit of, A;*

(c) *A receives or is entitled to receive at any time any benefit provided or to be provided (directly or indirectly) out of B's profit share or the part;*

(d) *A may become entitled to the beneficial enjoyment of B's profit share, or the part, if one or more powers are exercised or successively exercised by any person;*

(e) *A is able in any manner to control (directly or indirectly) the application of B's profit share or the part.*

This means that s 850C will apply whenever an individual partner, either alone or with relatives, controls or has the power to control the corporate partner. The section also applies where there are any arrangements in place such that the individual can enjoy the profits allocated to the corporate partner in whatever form.

Reallocation of profits s 850C(4) and (5)

Where either condition X or condition Y is met then A's profit share is increased by so much of B's profits as it is:

reasonable to suppose, is attributable to.

(a)   *A's deferred profit, or*
(b)   *A's power to enjoy,*

as determined on a just and reasonable basis. s 850C(4).

There is no statutory definition of reasonable. This test will involve looking at the motive and commerciality of arrangements between the partners, by reference to the substance of the matter and a realistic view of the facts.

Excess profit allocation – anti-avoidance ITTOIA 2005, s 850D

This section applies where an individual carries out work for a partnership, is not a partner, but is able to enjoy the profits of a non-individual partner in the firm. Section 850D(1) sets out the circumstances in which the section applies:

(a)   at a time during a period of account ('the relevant period of account') in respect of a firm, an individual ('A') personally performs services for the firm,
(b)   if A had been a partner in the firm throughout the relevant period of account, the calculation under section 849 in relation to A for the relevant period of account would have produced a profit for the firm,
(c)   a non-individual partner ('B') in the firm . . . has a share of that profit ('B's profit share') which is a profit . . . .,
(d)   it is reasonable to suppose that A would have been a partner in the firm at a time during the relevant period of account or an earlier period of account but for the provision contained in section 850C . . . , and
(e)   condition X or Y is met.

The provisions apply where, given the role performed by the individual, it would be reasonable to conclude that the individual would have been a partner in the firm were it not for the excess profit allocation provisions in s 850C.

This suggests that if a partnership comprising only corporate partners existed before these new provisions were announced in December 2013, and no new non-individual partners are admitted, these anti-avoidance provisions will not apply. This is because s 850C(1)(d) cannot apply to pre-December 2013 situations.

Conditions X and Y in s 850D mirror those in s 850C.

The effect of s 850D is set out in subsection (4), where:

A is to be treated on the following basis –

(a)   *A is a partner in the firm throughout the relevant period of account (but not for the purposes of section 863E),*
(b)   *A's share of the firm's profit for the relevant period of account is so much of the amount of B's profit share as, it is reasonable to suppose, is attributable to –*
       (i)   *A's deferred profit, or*
       (ii)   *A's power to enjoy,*
       as determined on a just and reasonable basis, and
(c)   *A's share of the firm's profit is chargeable to income tax under the applicable provisions of the Income Tax Acts for the tax year in which the relevant period of account ends.*

This means that A is taxed as if he were a partner in respect of the profit it is just and reasonable to suppose should be attributed to him from the corporate partner.

One consequence of these provisions is that, although they are headed 'partnerships with mixed membership', they can apply to partnerships set up after December 2013 comprising entirely corporate partners.

The relieving rule

Where profits are reallocated to an individual member, s 850E contains a relieving rule which exempts the reallocated profits from further tax when they are paid, directly or indirectly, by the corporate member to the individual so long as the payment is not made under any arrangements the main purpose, or one of the main purposes, of which is the obtaining of a tax advantage to any person.

Restriction for losses

There are provisions which deny an individual member of a partnership relief for losses from a UK or overseas business or trade where there are relevant tax avoidance arrangements. These are arrangements to which A (an individual) is a party, and the main purpose, or one of the main purposes, of which is to secure that losses of a trade are allocated, or otherwise arise, in whole or in part to A, rather than a person who is not an individual, with a view to A obtaining relevant loss relief (ITA 2007, s 116A(3)).

Relevant loss relief means:

(a)   sideways relief,
(b)   relief under s 83 (carry-forward trade loss relief),
(c)   relief under s 89 (terminal trade loss relief),
(d)   capital gains tax relief.

The loss relief restriction is wider than other anti-avoidance restrictions for losses, which usually focus on sideways loss relief and not carry forward relief. This is logical, however, as the focus of the legislation is to counter tax advantageous allocation of profits and losses.

Section 127C provides identical provisions to deal with losses from a property business.

Practical implications

These rules do not apply to genuine arm's length commercial arrangements that involve individual and non-individual partners. Nevertheless, for existing structures it will be necessary to consider:

- changing the profit allocation structure so that it reflects the commercial arrangements and is comparable to that which would exist were the corporate partner an independent third party;
- eliminating the corporate partners and installing an alternative business structure; or
- simply moving to full incorporation.

For property partnerships, for example, although the allocation of capital gains is not caught by these new provisions, the allocation of income would have to be considered to ensure that non-individual members receive a share of income that is commensurate with their contribution to the property investment. Also, ITA 2007, s 127C ensures that excess losses from a property business are not available to individuals who are partners in a property partnership.

Any adjustments arising under these provisions affect only the amounts subject to tax on the partners. It does not affect the allocation of profits for accounting purposes.

Corporate subsidiary of LLP

Where an LLP has different parts to its business, it could transfer one of the businesses to a company owned by the LLP. The tax benefits include: retaining profits in the company with low corporate tax rates, sale of goodwill at market value and possible liquidation when the business is finished. As the LLP is see-through for tax purposes the shares are treated as being held by the members of the LLP which could have favourable consequences in terms of entrepreneurs' relief and business property relief.

In using any of these structures the following should be considered:

- impact of employment related securities;
- provisions for incoming/retiring partners;
- drawings from the partnership;
- cost v savings of having two entities:
  - (a) valuation of goodwill if sold to the corporate member;
  - (b) potential exposure to a double layer of tax following a sale of assets held by the corporate member;
- possible loss of the annual investment allowance (AIA).

Pension contributions

[1.13] Instead of paying a salary or dividend, a company could make a pension contribution for the benefit of the shareholder-director. It is possible for a company to obtain a corporation tax deduction for a pension contribution without making a commensurate payment of salary to the individual. Deductibility is determined in accordance with the general wholly and exclusively principle.

In this respect, the company needs to demonstrate that the pension contribution has been incurred wholly and exclusively for the benefit of its trade. So long as the reward an individual receives from a company is demonstrably commensurate with the duties performed for the company, a corporation tax deduction should be available whether that reward is in the form of salary or pension contributions.

However, the employee's position must be considered, as the cap on pension contributions of £40,000 applies on the total of personal contributions and contributions made by a company for the benefit of that individual. If the aggregate contributions exceed £40,000, the individual will suffer an income tax charge on the excess. The limit is tapered down from April 2016 onwards for those that have adjusted income over £150,000. The reduction is £1 for every £2 of income over £150,000 and the minimum allowance is £10,000.

As pension contributions have their own cap, they are not taken into account for the purposes of the cap on reliefs (see **1.5** above).

Care and restraint must be exercised where pension contributions are proposed for the benefit of, for example, family members who may not participate fully in the company's business. The leading case in this area is *Copeman (Inspector of Taxes) v William Flood & Sons Ltd* [1941] 1 KB 202, (1940) 24TC53, where it was held that remuneration paid to family members for modest duties was not incurred by the company wholly and exclusively for the purposes of its trade, and therefore not deductible for corporation tax purposes.

Pensions are discussed further in CHAPTER 6.

Benefits provided by the company

[1.14] The position on benefits provided by the company depends on the nature of the benefit, both in terms of how the company gets relief and how the recipient is taxed. The provision of benefits has to be considered on a case by case basis, but as a general principle it may be advantageous to provide a benefit rather than pay a salary or dividend to enable the recipient to bear the cost of the item concerned. Further details on tax-efficient benefits are contained in CHAPTER 10.

Loans from the company

[1.15] Company law does not prevent a private company making a loan to a shareholder or director. Indeed, loans from private companies arise not uncommonly where the shareholder simply draws cash from the company without considering the nature of the withdrawal. There are serious tax implications, however, particularly for close companies.

Unless the loan is repaid within nine months after the end of the accounting year in which the loan is made, a liability to tax under CTA 2010, s 455 will arise, at 32.5% of the loan outstanding (25% for loans advanced before

6 April 2016). If the loan is repaid in a later year, the company can claim a repayment of the s 455 tax paid, but this can only be recovered nine months after the end of the accounting year in which the loan is repaid. Although a timing issue, the impact on cash flow cannot be overstated, especially if it is unexpected.

As the company cannot claim relief for the loan payments, it will also have a corporation tax liability on its profits. For example, if the company makes profits of £50,000, it will have a corporation tax liability of £9,500. If it lends what it believes to be its net profit to the shareholder, say £40,000, it will need to find a further £13,000 to pay the s 455 tax at the same time as it pays its corporation tax liability on its profits.

For an interest-free loan exceeding £10,000, the borrower will suffer a benefit in kind (BIK) charge from the date the loan is made to when it is repaid unless the loan is used for a qualifying purpose. The interest will be assessed at the Official Rate, currently 2.5%, which, on the above figures, would give rise to an annual benefit of £1,000. For a 40% higher-rate taxpayer, the BIK charge will give an income tax charge of £400. An employer Class 1A NIC charge will also arise on the benefit at 13.8% of the BIK.

If the borrower pays interest to the company at 2.5%, the benefit in kind will be extinguished, but the company will pay corporation tax on the additional profit of £1,000. Furthermore, the borrower is likely to have paid that interest out of post-tax income!

The tax paid under s 455 can also be recovered if the loan is written off. However, this will give rise to an income tax charge on the borrower, calculated as if the amount written off was a dividend. There will also be a Class 1 employer and employee NIC charge on loans written off. Loans to shareholders and close companies are dealt with further in **2.6**.

In most circumstances, loans to shareholders are not encouraged because of the cash-flow disadvantage resulting from the s 455 liability. Short term loans, however, have their place, although changes to the loans to participator rules introduced by Finance Act 2013 prevent bed and breakfasting, whereby loans are temporarily repaid. These provisions are looked at in detail in **2.6**.

Company losses

[1.16] As a company is a separate legal entity, it has its own tax liabilities and reliefs. If a company makes losses, those losses are not available to offset against the proprietors' income. Relief for corporate losses is set out in CTA 2010, Pt 4. Trading losses incurred by a company are, if possible, set off against other profits (of whatever description) of the same accounting period or of the previous accounting period under CTA 2010, s 37. In order to carry back the loss, the company must have been carrying on that trade in the previous accounting periods falling in the 12 months prior to the year of the loss. For this purpose, company profits include chargeable gains. It may be necessary to apportion profits for the purposes of the carry-back where more than one accounting period falls within the 12 months prior to the period of the loss.

Loss relief will not be available unless the trade is being carried on on a commercial basis and in a way so as to afford a reasonable expectation of making such a profit in the trade or in any larger undertaking of which the trade forms a part.

Where losses cannot be set off against other profits of the company, they are carried forward under CTA 2010, s 45 and set off against future profits from the same trade, so long as the company continues to carry on the trade. This gives rise to a potential problem when a company carries on more than one trade, either at the same time or consecutively. HMRC could argue that what looks like a single trade should be regarded as more than one trade. This might arise where a company has a number of outlets, where the question of whether they constitute a single trade must be considered on the facts.

When a company ceases to trade, CTA 2010, s 39 allows the loss accruing in the final 12 months of trade (using an apportionment, if necessary) to be set off against profits of the three years prior to the loss, starting with the later year first.

The F (No 2) A 2017 brought in changes on how losses post-1 April 2017 are carried forward (if in an accounting period beginning on or after 1 April 2017).

- Unrelieved losses can be carried forward to a later period for offset against profits of the trade, subject to a claim being made. The unrelieved losses are post-CTA 2010, s 37, 44, 48 or 52 or film/TV losses or it is a ring-fenced trade.
- The restrictions using the carried-forward losses will apply to an allowance of £5m (per group), plus 50% of remaining trading profits.

Loan relationships and losses

[1.17] Relief may be due in respect of losses arising out of a company's loan relationships. The way relief is given will depend on whether the loan relationships are of a trading or non-trading nature and whether or not the borrower and lender are connected. CHAPTER 7 covers loan relationships and the treatment of losses.

Change in ownership of the company

[1.18] As a company is a separate legal entity, its tax position is not affected in the absence of specific provisions to the contrary, by a change of ownership. However, losses brought forward may be affected by the provisions that seek to disallow losses carried forward by a company, if within any period of three years, there is both a change in the ownership of the company and a major change in the nature or conduct of a trade carried on by the company; or there is a major change in ownership at any time after the scale of activities in a trade have become small or negligible, and before any considerable revival in the trade.

conditions are met. The effect of this relief is to reduce the market value proceeds to an amount that produces neither a gain nor a loss, so that there is no capital gain chargeable on the donor but the donee's base cost will be equal to the market value of the shares less the held-over gain. The inheritance tax implications of gifting assets to individuals and trusts also need to be considered. These issues are discussed in CHAPTER 12.

Situations where gift relief is not available

[1.23] Gift relief is not available on the transfer of shares in an investment company.

Gift relief is not available where the donee is not UK tax resident. The gift relief is clawed back if, within six years of the gift, the donee becomes non-UK tax resident.

It is not possible to hold over the gain on any gift of shares to a company.

Gift relief is not available on disposals to most settlor-interested settlements or to settlements that become settlor-interested.

Formation of company by groups of individuals

[1.24] Instead of transferring shares to family members, the company could be formed by the family rather than by those individuals who are directly involved in running the company. Typically, this is restricted to husband and wife or civil partners, but wider family ownership or ownership by business associates may be appropriate. Care must be exercised with this type of arrangement, which has been challenged in the courts, usually by HMRC seeking to apply the settlements legislation. However, where the individuals subscribe for the shares in their own right and pay for them, this should not be an issue.

Settlements legislation

[1.25] The settlements legislation was originally enacted in the 1930s and is now contained in ITTOIA 2005, Pt 5, Ch 5. Over the years, there have been a number of cases that consider the application of the legislation, but until recently it was quite rare for practitioners to be faced with a challenge from HMRC.

Most commonly, HMRC invoked the settlements legislation where a company had issued, for example, A shares, usually carrying little in the way of rights apart from the right to dividends. Typically, these shares were transferred or issued to spouses or children, enabling dividends to be paid to those shareholders to cover their basic rate bands. The A shareholders usually had no involvement in the company, had invested very little for their shares and had no voting rights. This situation was considered in the case of *Young*

(Inspector of Taxes) v Scrutton [1996] STC 743, where it was held that the issue of such shares to wives constituted a settlement by the husbands. As a result, the dividend income was assessed to higher-rate tax on the husbands.

In recent years, with the proliferation of companies that were formed to take advantage of the favourable tax regime resulting from the introduction of the short-lived nil-rate band for corporation tax in large part, by IT consultants, HMRC has taken a much closer interest in the application of the settlements legislation to a wide range of situations.

What used to be regarded as a fairly academic area of tax law now has to be considered by every general practitioner advising owner-managed businesses.

The objective of the legislation is to prevent an individual from gaining a tax advantage by making arrangements to divert income to another person – usually, but not necessarily, another family member.

A settlement includes any disposition, trust, covenant, agreement, arrangement or transfer of assets. A settlor, in relation to a settlement, means any person by whom the settlement was made (ITTOIA 2005, s 620). It is clear, therefore, that a settlement includes much more than a trust, which is what one often associates with a settlor.

The expression 'arrangement' covers a very wide range of transactions. An arrangement could involve a single transaction or a series of transactions, and it is sometimes necessary to trace a series of seemingly unconnected transactions to establish the existence of an arrangement.

A person does not have to have been directly involved in the making of a settlement to be taxed on it, and the legislation covers situations where a person provides funds, undertakes to provide funds or makes arrangements with another person for that other person to provide funds or make a settlement.

HMRC looks closely at situations in which settlements for children exist where it appears on the face of it that persons other than close family are settlors. A settlement will be deemed to have been created for those children where there are reciprocal arrangements.

In principle, many transactions could come within the ambit of settlements. It is necessary, therefore, to consider the exemptions to the legislation.

Under ITTOIA 2005, s 624, where income arises under a settlement it will be treated as the settlor's income if it arises during the lifetime of the settlor and from property in which the settlor has an interest.

There are some exceptions to this rule, the most commonly encountered of which is under ITTOIA 2005, s 626, where outright gifts to a spouse or civil partner are exempt unless:

- the gift does not carry the right to the whole of the income arising; or
- the property given is wholly or substantially a right to income.

The settlor will be regarded as having retained an interest in a property if there are any circumstances in which the property or any related property is payable to or applicable for the benefit of the settlor or the settlor's spouse or civil partner, or will or may become so payable or applicable. There are certain exceptions in the case of bankruptcy or death of the parties to a marriage settlement.

ITTOIA 2005, s 627(2)(a) exempts annual payments made by an individual for bona fide commercial reasons in connection with his or her trade, profession or vocation. Commercial transactions which are entered into at arm's length are outside the meaning of 'settlement'. Following the case of *IRC v Plummer* [1980] AC 896, a settlement must include an element of bounty. Bounty is usually manifested as a gift or a transfer at less than full value.

Where a settlement is created in favour of unmarried minor children of the settlor, any income will be assessed on the settlor unless it falls below the de minimis annual limit of £100 (s 629). This was demonstrated in the case of *Bird v HMRC* [2008] SpC 720, where shares in a family run company were issued to three minor children of the controlling parents. The Commissioner, dismissing the parent's appeal that dividends on the children's shares should not be treated as their income, stated that the use of corporate structures to provide income to a minor child thereby reducing higher rates of tax was a settlement.

In summary, the settlements legislation applies where the settlor has retained an interest in property in a settlement, in which case the income arising is treated as the settlor's for all tax purposes. A settlement is likely to have been created where an individual enters into an arrangement to divert income to someone else, as a result of which there is a tax saving. This will apply where the arrangements are:

- bounteous;
- not commercial;
- not at arm's length; or
- in the case of a gift between spouses or civil partners, wholly or substantially a right to income.

The settlements legislation is not confined to situations where property is transferred to a spouse, civil partner or a child.

In RI268 (February 2004) HMRC set out the type of questions that are likely to be raised where the settlements legislation may be relevant:

- What has been invested?
- What assets, trade, profession have been placed in the company and by whom?
- Who does what to earn the income of the company?
- Is remuneration paid at a commercial rate for the job?
- Is someone getting a disproportionate return on the capital they have invested because of their relationship with the settlor?

The questions highlight the type of situations where HMRC may seek to establish whether the settlements legislation can be applied.

TSEM4210 makes it clear that one has to look at the whole arrangement. HMRC goes on to say:

'This could include a series of transactions, some of which may be commercial or involve outright gifts between spouses or civil partners. If the overall effect of the whole arrangement is to transfer income from one individual (the settlor) to:

- the settlor's spouse or civil partner; or
- minor children or step children of the settlor who are neither married nor in a civil partnership,'

the Settlements legislation is likely to apply. However, where the beneficiary of the arrangement is a spouse or civil partner you also need to consider whether the exemption for outright gifts applies (see TSEM4205). This exemption was the ultimate deciding factor in the well-known case of *Jones v Garnett ('Arctic Systems') (Inspector of Taxes)'*) [2007] UKHL 35, [2007] 1 WLR 2030, which is outlined at **1.26** below.

Example 1 — subscribed shares

'Mr U is a self-employed IT consultant. He reads an advert on a specialist website and as a result he decides to offer his services through a 'composite' company set up by another company specialising in taxation services. Under an agreement he will subscribe for a special class of share (a £1 'U' share) which has rights to all his earnings less a 'commission' paid to the organisers. The U shares have rights only to that income and repayment at par value. When the agreement is sent to him for signature there is a box to tick if he wants a share issued to anyone else. He ticks the box and asks for an additional share to be issued to Mrs U. Apart from subscribing £1 for the share, Mrs U takes no part in the business. During year one his efforts contribute income of £68,000 to the company. The company retains sufficient income to cover expenses and tax and the balance remaining of £54,000 is paid to Mr and Mrs U as dividends who each receive £27,000.

This is a bounteous transaction caught by the Settlements legislation. As the property given is wholly or substantially a right to income, the exemption for outright gifts to spouses and civil partners does not apply.'

HMRC gives numerous examples of where it considers that the settlements legislation may apply, in TSEM4215–4310.

TSEM4325 summarises the factors that may alert an Inspector to the possible application of the settlements legislation:

- Disproportionately large returns on capital investments.
- Differing classes of shares enabling dividends to be paid only to shareholders paying lower rates of tax.
- Dividends being waived so that higher dividends can be paid to shareholders paying lower rates of tax.
- Income being transferred from the person making most of the profits of a business to a friend or family member who pays tax at a lower rate.

There are a wide range of arrangements that can potentially be caught by the Settlements legislation which do not involve a trust. Each case will depend on the facts but some of the most common situations which we see are:

- Shares subscribed at par that carry only restricted rights.
- Shares given away that carry only restricted rights.

- A limited share in a partnership gifted or transferred below value.
- Dividend waivers. As highlighted clearly in the case of *SR Buck v HMRC* [2008] Spc 716.
- Situations where dividends are paid only on certain classes of shares.
- Dividends paid to the minor children or stepchildren of the settlor.

Arctic Systems (Jones v Garnett)

The facts

[1.26] *Jones v Garnett (Inspector of Taxes)* [2007] UKHL 35, [2007] 1 WLR 2030 was the catalyst that brought the settlements legislation to the attention of many practitioners who had previously never encountered this area of tax law. The facts of this case are by no means unusual. Mr Jones is an IT consultant, and in 1992 he and his wife decided to set up a company to run his own IT business. They each acquired one share in the company. Mrs Jones had some commercial experience and dealt with the bookkeeping and day-to-day administration, which took her about four or five hours a week. Mr Jones provided his services to the company as an IT contractor.

Mr and Mrs Jones took advice from their accountant, who advised them to take low salaries and to extract the rest of the company's profits by way of dividend. In some years, Mr Jones took a larger salary and Mrs Jones was unpaid because of worries that IR35 would apply to the services provided by Mr Jones, although this turned out not to be of concern.

HMRC position

[1.27] HMRC assessed Mr Jones on the dividends paid to Mrs Jones, arguing that they were income from a settlement created by him. Mr Jones appealed against the assessment, and with support from the Professional Contractors Group and others the case was heard in the House of Lords.

Special Commissioners and court decisions

[1.28] At the Special Commissioners, the two Commissioners came to opposing conclusions, but using a casting vote the decision went in favour of HMRC. Dr Brice decided that a settlement was made because Mr Jones allowed his wife to subscribe for shares and, through his work and the fact that he was the company director, enabled her to draw higher dividends than might otherwise have been the case.

The High Court also found in favour of HMRC but for different reasons. As Mrs Jones subscribed for her own share, there could not have been a gift, which means that the exemption in the settlements legislation for gifts between spouses could not apply. The whole arrangement was held to be a settlement, and that bounty was provided by virtue of Mr Jones's intentions with regard to the structuring of the flow of profits from the company.

The Court of Appeal found in favour of Mr Jones, concluding that there was no bounty because Mrs Jones paid for her share and the fact that a particular flow of funds from the company does not in itself create a settlement.

The House of Lords

[1.29] The House of Lords found in favour of the taxpayers, although their reasoning differs from the Court of Appeal decision. The House of Lords decided that there were arrangements that constituted a settlement, but that Mrs Jones, as a shareholder in the company had a bundle of rights that extended beyond a simple right to income. The taxpayers were not, therefore, caught by the settlements legislation.

The future

[1.30] The fact that these simple particulars have been interpreted in very different ways during the course of the case through the courts illustrates the inherent difficulty in applying the settlements legislation to any situation. The term 'arrangement' can catch a wide range of situations. There have been other cases involving settlements since the case of *Jones v Garnett (Inspector of Taxes)* such as the cases of *Bird* and *Buck* mentioned above. There has also been the interesting case of *Patmore v HMRC* [2010] UKFTT 334 (TC), [2010] SFTD 1124. In this case, a husband and wife had used a jointly held mortgage to raise funds for the acquisition of shares in a trading company in which Mr Patmore already held a stake. Despite Mrs Patmore contributing 50% of the capital outlay, in order to commercially protect her she only received 2% of 'A' shares and was issued with 10 non-voting 'B' shares. HMRC took the view that subsequent dividends paid on the B shares were income arising under a settlement and should be taxed on Mr Patmore.

In a surprising twist, the judge decided that the issue of shares did not fall within the settlements provisions and whilst the dividends did create a settlement, because Mrs Patmore contributed half the capital, the unfair allocation of A shares indicated that a constructive trust in favour of Mrs Patmore existed and that she was in fact entitled to 42.5% of the dividends. While this case is unique, it nonetheless demonstrates how complex such arrangements can be and it is very likely that this will not be the last case concerning settlements to make its way through the courts.

IR35

[1.31] The rules on IR35 need to be considered when deciding what type of entity to use as a trading vehicle, although in the arena of IT and other consultancy and business services, the service provider is often forced to use a company by client expectations.

The fundamental reason for this on the part of clients is to pass the self-employed risk to the contractor. Putting the limited company between the contractor and the end client ensures that the client does not get caught for

PAYE if the relationship turns out to be that of an employer-employee. Where there is a limited company and there is an employer-employee relationship with the client, the IR35 provisions will apply with the result that income received by the individual's company but not paid to that individual in the form of remuneration will be taxed as if it were remuneration. The Class 1 NIC position generally follows the income tax position.

Many agents will provide what are described as IR35-proof contracts, but these should be viewed with some circumspection and in light of arrangements between the client and the service provider.

It should be noted that for services provided to the public sector the IR35 rules have been changed, with the result that the onus on deciding whether the worker is in an employee relationship falls on the public sector body.

The application of IR35 needs to be considered carefully as, for the moment, and following the House of Lords decision in *Arctic Systems*, this will be the main focus of attention for Inspectors considering the tax position of similar companies. The End of Year Return under RTI (formerly P35) incorporates questions which enable HMRC to recognise more easily service companies which do not apply IR35. In addition, the personal self-assessment return requires details of 'dividends (including the tax credit) and salary (before tax was taken off)' that the individual has received from service companies. Guidance for taxpayers in applying IR35 is set out at www.gov.uk/topic/business-tax/ir35.

With effect from 6 April 2013 ITEPA 2003, s 49 has been amended so that where an individual holds an office with a company and provides his services to that company through an intermediary, IR35 will apply to fees paid to the intermediary.

HMRC does have a service online to check the employment status for tax purposes. It will check whether the intermediaries' legislation (IR35) applies to an engagement, the off-payroll working in the public sector rules or whether a worker should pay tax through PAYE for an engagement.

The BETs won't be taken into account for IR35 enquiries that HMRC opens on or after 6 April 2015. However, if HMRC opens an enquiry before then, and you can show that you have taken the BETs with an outcome outside IR35 or in the 'low risk' band, then HMRC will close the enquiry. They also won't open another IR35 enquiry for three years if the information provided is accurate and circumstances (in particular working arrangements) don't change in that time.

When HMRC has previously closed an enquiry based on a result of the BETs, then they won't open another IR35 enquiry within the three-year period previously notified to you.

Where HMRC closed an IR35 enquiry based on the BETs results, you should keep those results and any evidence relied on to take the tests for at least the three-year period involved.

Corporate residence

[1.32] An adviser could at some stage find himself having to advise on corporate residence in connection with overseas companies doing business in the UK or existing UK clients doing business abroad. It is beyond the scope of this book to go into the international aspects, but this section outlines the main points that the practitioner should be aware of.

Tax treatment of UK-resident companies

[1.33] UK-resident companies are taxed on their worldwide income. Subject to the election introduced in FA 2011, if a UK Company has an overseas branch, the profits from the branch are taxed as part of the Company's trading profits if the profits and losses are an extension of the UK trade.

Where the overseas branch is carrying on a different trade to that carried on in the UK, such that there is a separate trade carried on wholly outside the UK, the profits and losses will be treated as a separate trade.

Losses arising both in the UK and abroad can both be offset against profits in the Company in the same year. However, losses brought forward must be streamed, so that losses from the UK trade can only be carried forward and set against future profits from that same trade, and losses from the overseas trade only set against profits from that trade.

The Finance Act 2011 introduced a regime whereby UK companies could claim an exemption from UK corporation tax on branch profits. The election also means that branch trading losses can no longer be offset against other profits arising in the Company. Once made, the election relates to all overseas branches and is irrevocable. Such an election would be advantageous where profit making branches are operated in lower tax jurisdictions, however less so where those branches, particularly in the initial years of existence, are more susceptible to make losses.

Where interest is received by the overseas branch, this is taxed under the loan-relationship rules. It will be treated as a loan-relationship credit and will be grouped with the credits to the UK Company.

Foreign profits exemption

[1.34] Dividends received by a UK company from another UK company are normally not subject to corporation tax.

CTA 2009, ss 931A–931W set out the rules that apply to dividends received from overseas companies.

For small companies, dividends received from overseas companies are exempt from corporation tax so long as the payer is resident in a 'qualifying territory', no deduction has been allowed for the dividend in that overseas territory and the dividend has not been paid as part of a scheme to obtain a tax advantage.

The rules for medium and large companies are set out in CTA 2009, ss 931D–931Q. Dividends received from overseas companies are exempt so long as the distribution falls within an exempt class (set out in ss 931E–931Q) and no deduction is allowed for the dividend in an overseas territory.

The main exempt classes are:

(1)   where the recipient controls the payer;
(2)   where the recipient is one of two persons who, together, control the payer, and meet the 40% tests set out in ICTA 1988, s 755D(3)(4);
(3)   where the dividend is in respect of an ordinary irredeemable share;
(4)   where the recipient holds less than 10% of the issued share capital of the payer.

There are also a number of anti-avoidance provisions set out in ss 931J–931Q.

Tax treatment of non-UK resident companies

[1.35] Non-resident companies are subject to UK tax in a number of ways, depending on the activities carried on. If the non-resident company is carrying on a trade through a UK permanent establishment, the UK permanent establishment is charged to tax under CTA 2009, ss 19 and 20.

Diverted Profits Tax ('DPT')

[1.36] Consideration may also need to be given to DPT when structuring a UK business, particularly where there is an international element to the structure. This complex legislation originally dubbed the 'Google tax' was introduced in Finance Act 2015, Pt 3 and applies to companies in respect of goods, services and other property, including real estate. Although originally aimed at perceived artificial and contrived arrangements, its wide scope means that ordinary commercial arrangements could fall within its remit. Where the legislation applies, all taxable diverted profits arising since 1 April 2015 are subject to a 25% rate of tax, rather than the current 19% corporation tax.

This complex legislation will be applied in two scenarios:

•   A UK resident company (or a UK permanent establishment of a non-UK resident company) enters into arrangements with a related person where that person or the transaction's lack of economic substance results in a reduction of the UK company's (or UK permanent establishment's) taxable profits (FA 2015, ss 80 and 81 – 'Lack of Economic Substance scenario');
•   A person (whether or not UK resident) carries on an activity in the UK connected to the supply of goods, services or other property made by a non-UK resident company in the course of its trade in a way that avoids creating UK permanent establishment (FA 2015, s 86 ('Avoided Permanent Establishment scenario')).

Where the structure falls within the Lack of Economic Substance scenario, there must be a 'tax mismatch' and the 'insufficient economic substance' condition must also be met for the DPT rules to apply and additional tax to be charged. Where the structure falls within the Avoided Permanent Establishment scenario, a 'tax mismatch' or 'tax avoidance' condition must also be met.

There are some important exceptions to the application of this legislation, including:

- The effective tax mismatch outcome cannot be met as a result of a loan-relationship transaction.
- The effective tax mismatch outcome will also not be met because of expenses made by an employer to a pension scheme, payments to a charity, payments made to a person who is tax exempt by virtue of sovereign immunity or payments made to an offshore or authorised investment fund, which either meets a diversity of ownership condition or where at least 75% of its investors are certain tax exempt persons.
- All of the parties to the arrangements are SMEs (as defined by TIOPA 2010, s 172). It is worth noting that within HMRC guidance on the legislation, it is made clear that there is no 'grace' period provided for determining whether either party is 'large' for one year.
- In addition, the avoided Permanent Establishment provision will not apply if sales in respect of the UK activity carried on by the foreign company and connected persons do not, in aggregate exceed £10m or expenses related to the UK activity incurred by the foreign company and connected persons do not, in aggregate, exceed £1m.

In the event that a company believes that they may potentially fall within the scope of the legislation, they need to notify HMRC within three months of the relevant accounting period (six months for accounting periods ending on or before 31 March 2016). Following notification, HMRC will issue a preliminary notice detailing why HMRC considers the tax to apply and will include an estimate of the taxable diverted profits. Following receipt of the notice, the company has 30 days to make representations. Following receipt of these representations HMRC must then either issue a charging notice (DPT and associated interest would then be payable within 30 days) or confirm that no charging notice will be issued.

Given that the legislation is relatively new and was passed hastily through the legislative process, it is not clear how widely HMRC will apply this legislation going forward. However, in the context of OMB, the vast majority of structures, particularly given the SME exceptions, should fall outside its scope.

Permanent establishment

[1.37] A permanent establishment for UK tax purposes is defined in CTA 2010, s 1141. A company has a UK permanent establishment if it has a fixed place of business through which business is carried on in the UK, or an agent habitually carries on business activities on behalf of the company in the UK. Note that the definition of permanent establishment is different for VAT purposes.

The UK adopts the Organisation for Economic Cooperation and Development (OECD) model of what a permanent establishment is so that a fixed place of business includes:

(a)   a place of management;
(b)   a branch;
(c)   an office;
(d)   a factory;
(e)   a workshop;

(f)   an installation or structure for the exploration of natural resources;
(g)   a mine, an oil or a gas well, a quarry or any other place of extraction of natural resources; and
(h)   a building site or construction or installation project.

Many of the UK's double tax treaties have their own definition of permanent establishment, which may not be identical to that contained in CTA 2010, s 1141. For instance, Art 5(3) of the OECD model tax convention states that 'a building site or construction or installation project constitutes a permanent establishment only if it lasts more than twelve months'. In the standing-committee stage, there was a debate as to whether or not a 12-month period should be included in the UK legislation. However, it was felt that a 12-month time limit would not be appropriate in UK legislation. Tax treaties can override domestic law to provide relief from UK tax. However, they cannot create a charge in the UK if none exists. In some of the double tax treaties between the UK and other countries, a building site which exists for less than 12 months does constitute a permanent establishment. Therefore, to include a 12-month period in the UK legislation would have taken away some of the UK's taxing rights. Approximately 43 of the UK's current tax treaties include building sites with a period of less than 12 months.

A place of business includes any premises, facilities or other areas which can be used for carrying on the business of an enterprise, whether or not they are exclusively for that purpose. For example, a place of business could be a pitch in a market place or a certain area permanently used in a customs depot. Further detail on what can constitute a permanent establishment is contained in the OECD model tax convention.

An enterprise is treated as having a permanent establishment where it has a dependent agent. A dependent agent is one who has the authority to conclude contracts in the name of the enterprise and includes contracts which are binding on the enterprise even if those contracts are not in the name of the enterprise. Lack of involvement by the enterprise in transactions is often an indicative term of the grant of authority to an agent.

Where the agent is an independent agent, he will not have the authority to bind the enterprise. He needs to be independent of the enterprise both legally and financially and needs to act in the ordinary course of his business when acting on behalf of the enterprise.

A non-resident company, therefore, will be taxed on:

(a)   any trading income arising from the permanent establishment;
(b)   income arising from property used or held by the permanent establishment; and
(c)   any chargeable gains arising on the disposal of assets by the permanent establishment (TCGA 1992, s 10B).

The disposal of an asset is only charged to corporation tax if it is used in the permanent establishment at the time of the disposal. Where a permanent establishment ceases to trade in the UK, there is a deemed disposal and reacquisition of the asset under TCGA 1992, s 25. Roll-over relief is available to a permanent establishment provided the proceeds of the disposal are rolled into an asset which is used in a UK company or by a UK permanent establishment. The rules in respect of no gain/no loss transfers under TCGA 1992, s 171 also apply to transfers of assets between the UK permanent establishment and other UK companies.

A non-UK resident company with no permanent establishment in the UK can still be charged to UK income tax rather than corporation tax. The most common example is in respect of an overseas company which holds a UK rental property. The income tax rules apply in calculating the rental income, and any profits are taxed at basic-rate. Where the non-resident company receives any interest or dividends and tax is deducted at source, no further tax is payable.

A practitioner may be asked whether or not an overseas company should have its holding company in the UK. There are a number of reasons why the UK is a good place to have a holding company:

(1)   *Substantial Shareholding Exemption.* This facilitates the sale of shares in a trading company without giving rise to any taxable gain providing certain conditions are met.

(2)   *Taxation of dividend income.* For small companies, dividends received from foreign companies are exempt from corporation tax, so long as the paying company is in a country with which the UK has a double tax treaty which contains a non-discrimination provision.

The position for companies that are not small is more complex, although in most situations dividends would be exempt from corporation tax. However, each situation should be considered on a case by case basis (see CTA 2009, ss 931D–931V).

Where a UK company receives taxable dividend income from an overseas company of which it owns more than 10%, relief should be available for the underlying tax paid by that overseas company together with a credit for the withholding tax suffered. In some situations it may be appropriate to disapply the exemption by making an election under CTA 2009, s 931R allowing for an offset of foreign tax suffered. This election should be made within two years of the end of the accounting period in which the distribution is received.

(3)   *Transfer pricing and thin capitalisation.* The UK follows the OECD model convention on transfer pricing and thin capitalisation which looks at an arm's length pricing. This is in contrast to some countries which operate a more complex system.

(4)   *Deduction for interest payments for share acquisitions.* Under the UK tax rules, any interest paid for funds borrowed to acquire shares is deductible under the loan-relationship provisions.

(5)   *Low corporate tax rate.* The UK now has a corporate tax rate of 20%, lower than most other large European countries and is due to fall to 17% by 2020.

There are a number of other reasons, including relief for losses, or indeed tax credits, intangibles, etc, why overseas companies would want to locate their holding company in the UK.

Since 2013, a non-UK resident company may also be subject to capital gains tax if it holds UK residential property. However, if the property was held at

5 April 2013 and is subject to an ATED charge then the calculation of the gain can be based on the value of the property at that date. If no ATED charge is due then no liability arises. This rule has been extended with effect from 6 April 2015 to include all UK residential property owned by non-UK residents including companies. The calculation of the gain under these rules can be based on the original cost, the value of the property at 5 April 2015, if the taxpayer so wishes or on a time apportionment basis.

Determining UK residence

[**1.38**] In looking at whether a company is UK resident, there are two tests; incorporation and central management and control (CMC). Where a company is incorporated in the UK, it is treated as UK resident. Where the company is not incorporated in the UK, it is treated as being resident here if its CMC is in the UK.

The determination of CMC is based on case law. In the case of *De Beers Consolidated Mines Ltd v Howe (Surveyor of Taxes)* [1906] AC 455, it was found that 'a company resides where its real business is carried on . . . and the real business is carried on where the central management and control actually abides'. This case concerned a company established in South Africa which had a Board of Directors that exercised its powers in the UK. The company was found to be UK resident. In another similar case, *Bullock (Inspector of Taxes) v Unit Construction Co Ltd* [1959] Ch 315, the company had a constitution which gave control to the Board of Directors, who had to hold their meetings outside the UK. However, as a matter of fact, the real control in the company was exercised by the directors of the parent company, who were in the UK. Although this was unconstitutional, it meant that CMC was in the UK.

HMRC Statement of Practice 1/90 outlines the approach to determine whether a company is UK resident. This entails looking at the highest level of control to determine where CMC lies. CMC is distinguished from the place where the main operations are carried out. While the place where a board meets is important, it may not be conclusive, particularly now where conferences can be held by phone or online with each director in a different country.

Where a parent company has subsidiaries, the parent company will not be treated as controlling those subsidiaries provided the subsidiaries have decision-making autonomy on marketing, investment, production and procurement. The starting point is to establish who has control and once this has been established, to find out where that control is exercised. With the era of emails and teleconferencing, it is very important that where planning is carried out and meetings need to be held abroad, these meetings are indeed held abroad. No decision should be made by email while the parties are sitting in the incorrect countries.

More recently, there have been two cases concerning corporate residence, both of which HMRC has lost. These cases were *Wood v Holden (Inspector of Taxes)* [2006] EWCA Civ 26, [2006] 1 WLR 1393 and *News Datacom Ltd v Atkinson (Inspector of Taxes)* [2006] STC (SCD) 732. In both of these cases, the companies were found not to be UK resident.

The decision in *Laerstate BV v Revenue and Customs Comrs* (TC00162) [2009] UKFTT 209 (TC), [2009] SFTD 551, [2009] SWTI 2669 demonstrates that HMRC looks very closely at where important decisions regarding the company have actually been made, and rely on a wide range of evidence in establishing where a company is controlled. The main points which this case reminds practitioners of in advising on corporate residence are as follows:

• a company must be able to demonstrate where all important decisions are made and that all relevant information is made available to the decision makers;

• directors should attend the meetings and appropriate minutes should be taken recording all the decisions made;

• travel records and other documents supporting the place where meetings took place should be retained;

• the articles of the company should contain a clear reference to the person(s) who control the company and all persons dealing with the company should be made aware of the controlling parties (who may not be shareholders).

In advising clients on overseas matters, it is very important not to assume that other systems will be similar to the UK systems and to take local advice at the earliest opportunity.

Key points

[1.39] Key points to note are as follows:

• HMRC must be notified by 5 October following the tax year of commencement of any new business;

• watch out for the hobby-type activities which may become taxable, eg eBay traders;

• benefits of unincorporated businesses:
  – simple to set up and administer;
  – flexible;
  – losses can be set off against other income; and
  – no public disclosure.

• benefits of a limited company:
  – limited liability;
  – control flow of profit to individuals and thus timing of personal tax deductions;
  – easier to transfer shares; and
  – may give better business presence.

• consider the IR35 position;

• settlements legislation must be considered where shares are issued which confer a right to income or where there is a partnership interest with income rights;

• in setting up a business abroad consideration needs to be given to whether this is set up as a separate legal entity or as an extension to the UK business, bearing in mind the possible branch exemptions;

- consider where the CMC of a company resides in order to establish corporate residence; and
- the introduction of a foreign profits exemption in the UK makes the repatriation of profits attractive.

Chapter 2

Close Companies

Close companies and tax consequences

[2.1] Owner-managed companies will typically be close companies. A close company is one which is 'under the control (a) of 5 or fewer participators, or (b) of participators who are directors' (Corporation Tax Act 2010, s 439(2) (CTA 2010)). A non-UK resident company can never be a close company.

There are a number of consequences of close company status:

- Loans to shareholders are subject to a 32.5% (25% for loans and advances made before 6 April 2016) tax charge payable by the company (CTA 2010, s 455). This is in addition to the benefit in kind charge where the shareholder is an employee or a director.
- Benefits provided to non-working shareholders are treated as distributions (CTA 2010, s 1064).

With the increase in dividend rates from 6 April 2016, to counter the use of company loans as an effective way to extract funds from a company, the s 455 charge was increased, with effect for loans made on or after 6 April 2016, so it reflects the dividend higher rate (Income Tax Act 2007, s 8(2) (ITA 2007)), which is currently 32.5%. While benefit in kind rates remain low, there may be an advantage in extracting funds as a company loan where income tax at the additional dividend rate of 38.1% would be suffered on a dividend.

Despite the potential tax charges, there are some advantages to the shareholders of a close company, for example, interest relief is available where the shareholder has borrowed money to acquire shares in the close company or where the money has been lent to the close company for the purposes of its business (ITA 2007, s 392).

Participator

[2.2] A participator is defined in CTA 2010, s 454 as 'a person having a share or an interest in the capital or income of the company'. It specifically includes:

- a person who holds or is entitled to acquire share capital or voting rights in the company;
- a person who is a loan creditor of the company;
- any person who holds or is entitled to acquire a right to receive or participate in distributions of the company or in any amounts payable by the company (in cash or kind) to loan creditors by way of premium on redemption; and

- any person who is entitled to secure that company income or assets (whether present or future) will be applied directly or indirectly for their benefit.

Loan creditor

[2.3] A loan creditor (CTA 2010, s 453) in relation to a company is a creditor in respect of a debt incurred by the company in relation to:

- any money borrowed or capital assets acquired by the company;
- any right to receive income created in favour of the company;
- consideration the value of which to the company was (at the time when the debt was incurred) substantially less than the amount of the debt; and
- any redeemable loan capital issued by the company.

Normal trade creditors are not loan creditors. Neither are hire purchase creditors, as there would be no debt for capital assets acquired by the company. With a hire purchase, the assets remain in the ownership of the hire company until the final instalment is paid, therefore it is not a debt for the ownership of assets; the payments are more akin to a rent.

Director

[2.4] A director (CTA 2010, s 452) is any person occupying the position of a director by whatever name it is called. It also includes a person in accordance with whose instructions the directors are accustomed to act and a manager of the company who owns more than 20% of the share capital. In calculating the amount of share capital owned, the rights of associates are taken into account, as well as any shares owned indirectly.

Associate

[2.5] Associate (CTA 2010, s 448), in relation to a participator, includes:

- any relative — where relative means husband, wife or civil partner, parent or remoter forebear, child or remoter issue or brother or sister. Separated spouses are associated until they divorce. Half-brothers and sisters are associated, but step-brothers and sisters are not;
- business partner — where this means partners in a partnership or members in an LLP;
- the trustees of any settlement in relation to which the participator (or any relative living or dead) is or was a settlor;
- the trustees of a settlement or the personal representatives of an estate if the participator has an interest in any shares or obligations of the company which are the subject of a trust or form part of the estate of a deceased person; and
- any other company interested in shares or obligations, where the participator is a company and has an interest in the same shares or obligations which are subject to trust.

Settlements can lead to problems in looking at associates. For example, if a trust has 100 shares and the participator is one of five beneficiaries, are 20 shares counted or are 100 shares counted? The legislation directs that the rights of the trustee are counted, so this would cover the rights of the 100 shares. This can seem unfair if the beneficiaries are not associates. The same applies in looking at share rights under an estate.

In the case of *R v IRC, ex p Newfields Developments Ltd* [2001] UKHL 27, [2001] 4 All ER 400, Lord Hoffmann said:

> 'The effect of these cumulative definitions is that for the purpose of deciding whether a person "shall be taken to have control of a company" under s [450], it may be necessary to attribute to him the rights and powers of persons over whom he may in real life have little or no power or control. Plainly the intention of the legislature was to spread the net very wide.'

This concept has been considered recently in the case of *W Reeves v HMRC* [2017] UKFTT 192, where hold over relief was denied by virtue of attribution of rights over shares in a company where individuals to whom those rights were attributed had no interest in the company concerned.

Loans to shareholders

[2.6] Where a close company makes a loan to an individual who is a participator or an associate of a participator otherwise than in the ordinary course of a business, there is a 32.5% tax charge (25% in respect of pre-6 April 2016 loans). This amount is paid to HMRC where the loan is still outstanding nine months after the end of the accounting period. When the loan is repaid, the tax is returned to the company nine months following the end of the accounting period in which the loan is repaid.

Exceptions to the charge

[2.7] There are a number of exceptions to the charge to tax under s 455 and these are set out in s 456. They include:

- Loans in the ordinary course of the company's business of money lending;
- Money owed for goods or services supplied by the company in the ordinary course of its business under normal credit terms provided to external third party customers, as long as the credit period does not exceed six months; and
- Certain small loans made to full time employees or directors of the company.

Trade credit

The date that the debt is incurred is when the goods are delivered or the services are provided and credit runs from that time until payment, (CTM 61535).

Exception for small loans

A s 455 charge will not arise where a loan is made to a full-time director or employee of the close company assuming:

- the aggregate of the loans by the close company and its associated companies to that borrower do not exceed £15,000; and
- the borrower (together with his associates) does not have a material interest in the close company or any of its associated companies.

The £15,000 threshold

The following guidance and example in CTM 61540 are useful in determining whether the £15,000 threshold is breached.

'When deciding whether the limit of an individual employee has been reached, do not take loans to the spouse into account.

Where both husband and wife are directors or employees, they will each be entitled to a separate limit of £15,000.'

Cumulative loans total more than £15,000

'Where a participator who does not have a material interest in the company receives small loans over several periods, the aggregate may eventually exceed the £15,000 limit for exemption. For example, a director may receive £5,000 in AP1, £2,000 in AP2 and then £10,000 in AP3. In isolation each of these would qualify for the exemption, but in aggregate he has received £17,000. The two earlier amounts continue to meet the requirements for the exemption and therefore remain outside the charge.

However, we do not just charge the excess of the aggregate over £15,000 (£2,000) under CTA10/S455 in AP3. Rather the full amount of the £10,000 loan in AP3 does not meet condition A in S456 (4)). The S455 charge in AP3 is therefore on the full £10,000 loan in that period.'

Material interest

A material interest for these purposes (s 457) is more than 5% of the ordinary share capital or an entitlement to more than 5% of the assets of the company on a winding up or under any other circumstances.

If the borrower did not have a material interest at the time the loan was made, but later acquires one, the company is treated as making the loan at the time he acquires the material interest (s 456(6)).

Loans to acquire shares

[2.8] Where the loan is made before the individual becomes a participator – for example, if a loan is made to an individual and that individual subsequently becomes a shareholder – there is no charge under CTA 2010, s 455 provided there is no link between the loan and the individual becoming a shareholder. HMRC has been known to attack situations where a loan is made for the purposes of acquiring the shares. Some commentators would argue that there are no grounds for a s 455 charge in this situation as there is no legal entitlement to sue for the shares at the date the loan is made. HMRC's guidance at CTM 60120 states:

'The words "entitled to acquire" and "entitled to secure" introduce the concept of a potential participator. So, for example, a person is a participator if, by means of a contractual right or by rights arising under a trust deed, they can:

- require a shareholder to transfer shares to that person; or
- secure the issue to that person of unissued capital of the company; or
- secure that if the company makes a distribution or if a loan is redeemed by the company at a premium, that person has a share in the distribution or the premium.

Similarly, a person is a participator if by means of a contractual right or some other arrangement he can secure that income or assets of the company will be applied directly or indirectly for his benefit.

References to being "entitled to acquire" or "entitled to secure" apply where a person is presently entitled to acquire, etc., at a future date and where a person will at a future date be entitled to acquire, etc.'

If loans are made for the purpose of acquiring the shares, care needs to be taken with the documentation. It would be better, where appropriate, to have partly paid shares. Although partly paid shares give rise to a notional loan which is a benefit in kind, they do not give rise to a loan which can be taxed under CTA 2010, s 455. Further details on partly paid shares are provided in **CHAPTER 10**.

The FTT decision in *RKW Limited* (2014) TC03289 considered the position where a new investor (JG) subscribed for shares in a company, with an agreement to pay for the shares in four instalments.

The shareholder/directors of RKW Limited ('RKW'), a close company, identified a potential new investor, (JG). JG was not connected with any of the shareholders or directors in RKW.

RKW Ltd, its existing shareholders and JG entered into an agreement under which the existing shares were designated as A ordinary shares and JG subscribed for B ordinary shares, all issued on the signing of the agreement, giving JG voting control over the close company.

The terms on which JG would subscribe for a new class of B ordinary shares in RKW were recorded in an agreement between JG and the existing shareholders in RKW. The agreement stated that:

'20) JG shall subscribe for the "B" ordinary shares for cash at par and shall pay for that subscription in the manner and on the dates set out in Schedule 4. The "B" ordinary shares shall be fully unconditionally and irrevocably issued in consideration of the agreement of payments herein and as detailed herein within Schedule 4. ... The share to JG shall irrevocably be issued to JG immediately upon the signing hereof. ... the parties ... agree that JG is hereby acquiring a full 51% majority ownership of the Company ... '.

The subscription price referred to above (which was £2,170,102) was payable in four annual instalments with the first instalment becoming due one year following the signing of the agreement. Interest was payable on unpaid subscription amounts.

JG did not pay the subscription monies provided for in the agreement.

RKW recorded the subscription amounts in its balance sheet under the heading 'Debtors'. Under current accounting practices the inclusion of unpaid share capital within 'Debtors' is optional and in many cases it is not included until the amounts have been called up.

HMRC asserted that the arrangement was within loans to participators rules and that JG was a participator in RKW and the subscription amounts constituted a debt. HMRC first assessed RKW to tax under TA 1988, s 419 on the basis that JG was a participator in the close company who 'incurred a debt' of £2,170,102 on entering into the agreement.

HMRC later assessed RKW to tax on a different basis; that a liability to tax under s 419 in respect of a debt of £500,000 arose on 20 November 2001 when the liability to pay the first instalment payment in accordance with the agreement was not satisfied.

The FTT found that the subscription amounts did not constitute a debt for the purposes of section 419, ICTA 1988 (now CTA 2010, s 455). The FTT agreed that even if JG had incurred a debt, he was not a participator when he incurred the debt. JG only incurred a liability on signing the shareholders' agreement, which was the very action that made him a participator in RKW.

Consequently the appeal was allowed.

In another case, *Aspect Capital Ltd* UKUT (2014) 0081, the position where employees acquired shares with the benefit of a facility agreement was considered.

Aspect Capital Limited ('AC') operated an 'employee participation scheme', designed to give shares to 'selected key employees'. Employees wishing to participate in the incentive arrangement entered into a share acquisition agreement with AC.

Under the acquisition agreement, employees agreed to pay AC, the EBT trustee, or any other person as AC directed, the purchase price for the shares.

Employees entered into an arrangement known as a 'facility' to enable them to acquire shares without having to pay for them immediately. Once the acquisition agreement and the facility agreement had been executed, AC paid the facility amount to the EBT trustee, less the stamp duty due, and the trustee transferred legal title of the shares to the relevant employees.

HMRC asserted that the employees became indebted to the company at the time they entered into the facility agreement and acquired the shares and that the transaction was caught by the loans to participators rules.

AC argued that it had not made loans to the employees and cited the case of *Potts' Executors v CIR*, 32 TC 211 to support this.

The First-tier tribunal dismissed the appeal on the following grounds:

- The facility was both a loan to employees and a debt under ICTA 1988, s 419(2) (now CTA 2010, s 455) and not an advance.
- The definition of a 'loan' includes 'a payment by A to C at B's request where there is a legal obligation on B to reimburse A the amount paid'.

- The obligation for the employee to repay the facility amount arose at the time AC transferred money to the EBT, although the time the amount had to have been repaid was deferred until a contingency event.

The Upper tribunal agreed concluding:

- 'Although there was a possibility that the amount would not be repaid, or would not be repaid in full, that did not reduce the amount of the debt owed at the time it was created
- Tax was chargeable on the full amount of the facility made available to the employee.'

So why did these cases, both involving shares and outstanding amounts, have a different outcome?

The existence and use of the facility agreement is a key factor. The use of a facility agreement involved an extraction of profits, assets or value from the company - the exact mischief that s 455 is designed to counter.

Also *RKW* involved a subscription for new shares whereas in *Aspect* the employees purchased existing shares in the company.

Further details on employee shares and using partly paid shares are contained in Chapter 10.

Loans to relevant persons

Until 20 March 2013, a charge under s 455 applied where a loan or advance was made to a relevant person. A relevant person was defined in s 455(1) to include individuals and companies receiving a loan or advance in a fiduciary or representative capacity. In recent years, companies have used trusts and partnerships in structures to avoid a s 455 charge, while the participators still had the benefit or use of the funds.

If, for example, prior to 20 March 2013, a close company made a loan to a partnership in which all the partners were individuals and one of the partners was a participator (or an associate of a participator), HMRC would argue that there was a loan to a participator so that s 455(1) applied. However, where the partners were not all individuals, the loan was not caught as it was not to a relevant person, ie individuals.

Section 455(1) was extended by Finance Act 2013 and now applies to:

- trustees of a settlement where one or more of the trustees is a participator or an associate of a participator in the company;
- beneficiaries of an estate, where one or more beneficiaries (actual or potential) is a participator or an associate of a participator in the company; and
- an LLP or other partnership where one or more of the individuals is a participator in the company or an associate of the participator.

Example

Mr A is a 100% shareholder of B Ltd. Mr A and B Ltd set up an LLP where they are partners. If B Ltd makes a loan to the LLP the loan is chargeable under s 455.

Until the FA 2013 changes there was doubt about the application of s 455 to loans to a partnership whose members include the company itself. Where genuine partnership arrangements existed it was difficult for HMRC to contend that the loan was caught under s 455. However, if the loan was drawn out by the individual from the partnership HMRC applied s 459 so that a charge arose. This would be the case if the participator partner is also overdrawn on his own account with the partnership.

Where the loan is repaid relief will be available if the loan is repaid before the due and payable date (nine months and one day from the end of the accounting period). The usual exceptions also apply so that loans which are made in the ordinary course of a money lending business are not caught.

Generally, where a loan is made by the company to another company, even if this is controlled by one or more of the participators, no section 455 charge will arise unless the loan is in some way used to make a payment to participators. This is provided for in CTA 2010, s 459:

'Where, arrangements are made by any person otherwise than in the ordinary course of a business and:

a close company makes a loan or advance which, apart from this subsection, does not otherwise give rise to a charge to tax under section 455, and

a person other than the close company makes a payment or transfers property to, or releases or satisfies (in whole or in part) a liability of, an individual who is a participator in the company or an associate of a participator, s 459 will ensure a tax charge arises.'

Supposing the company makes a loan to an employee to buy shares from existing shareholders, s 455 will apply where the employee is already a shareholder, but if not, s 459 would apply following the acquisition of the shares. The same problem can arise in a situation where there is a takeover by a new company and part of the funding is from a loan from the target company. This loan finds its way out to the shareholders as a payment so the company gets caught with a loan to participator charge.

Repayment of loans

[2.9] The provisions at CTA 2010, s 464C address the issue of 'bed and breakfasting' and further provisions at ss 458 and 464B, prevent a repayment of tax arising under s 455 or s 464A, where loans effectively remain outstanding beyond the nine month window.

A restriction applies where a company has made a loan of more than £5,000 on which a s 455 charge arises (a 'chargeable payment'), repayments totalling more than £5,000 are made, and within a 30 day period new loans of more than £5,000 are made. In this case, the repayment is ignored (in whole or in part) for s 455 purposes.

Relief is denied on the lower of the amount repaid, and the amount of the new chargeable payment made by the company. The restriction does not apply where repayment is chargeable to income tax, for example where a dividend is used to repay the loan.

For example, assume that a company has previously made a loan of £10,000 to one of its shareholders, and it has paid tax under s 455 of £2,500 in accordance with its CTSA return for the year to 31 March 2014. On 31 March 2015 the shareholder repays the loan, the aim being to claim a refund of the s 455 tax on 31 December 2015. However, on 15 April 2015 the company makes a new loan of £8,000. In this case, the repayment will be restricted to (£10,000–£8,000) £2,000 x 25% = £500.

A further restriction applies where:

- immediately before a repayment is made, £15,000 or more is owed to a close company in respect of one or more chargeable payments made by the company to a person;
- **at any time** after the repayment is made, the close company makes a chargeable payment ('the new payment') to the person or an associate of the person; and
- at the time of the repayment any person intended that the new payment would be made, or arrangements had been made for the new payment to be made.

Relief is denied on the lower of the amount repaid and the amount redrawn. As with the 30 day rule, the restriction does not apply where a dividend, for example, is used to repay the loan.

There is no time limit on this restriction and it will catch any situation where there was an intention to draw money out of the company otherwise than by way of bonus or dividend. The objective is clearly to enforce compliance, especially bearing in mind the introduction of RTI at the same time, which requires a greater level of attention to PAYE obligations.

This restriction is intended to catch situations where a proprietor uses company money by maintaining an overdrawn loan account on which income tax is never paid.

Where dividends are used to clear loan accounts, the timing is crucial. There are two types of dividend: an interim and a final. The interim dividend is usually paid by the directors and they need to be authorised to do this in the Articles of Association. The interim dividend is treated as paid when the cash goes to the shareholders. Where it is credited against a loan account, it is treated as paid at the time it is credited to the loan account. This cannot be done retrospectively, so if a loan account is cleared with an interim dividend, this needs to be credited before nine months have elapsed since the year end to avoid a loan to participator charge. A final dividend is recommended by the directors, but it is approved by the shareholders at the annual general meeting. As it is approved by the shareholders, it is actually the shareholders who declare the dividend. It becomes due and payable at that point or such later date as may be agreed.

Where a number of loans have been made to an individual and these are subsequently repaid, the directors can decide which debt the repayment should be set against. In the absence of a specific allocation, the rule in *Clayton*'s case (1816) 1 Mer 572 applies so that the repayment is set against the earliest debt first.

Book entries can be used to make a loan repayment. These will be effective at the date the entry is made and so long as the entries reflect the underlying reality of a transaction and they are properly recorded in the company's books (CTM 61600).

Where a loan is written off or waived, the amount becomes taxable on the shareholder as a dividend under Income Tax (Trading and Other Income) Act 2005, s 415 (ITTOIA 2005). Where the participator is also an employee (or a relative of an employee), the charge under s 415 has priority over the charge on the employee under Income Tax (Earnings and Pensions) Act 2003, s 188 (ITEPA 2003) (HMRC CTM 61630). Therefore, any amount chargeable under ITTOIA 2005, s 415 is not also charged as income from employment. However, the amount released or written off will attract Class 1 NIC if it is remuneration or profit derived from an employment (Social Security Contributions and Benefits Act, s 3(1) (SSCBA 1992)).

Corporation Tax Act 2009, s 321A (CTA 2009) prevents a corporation tax deduction for the write-off. As CTA 2009, s 464 gives priority to the loan relationship provisions, it is unlikely that relief would be available under the 'wholly and exclusively' rules.

Arrangements conferring benefit on a participator

[2.10] Further provisions at ss 464A to 464B are aimed at catching other extractions of value by participators, such as capital contributions made by the company to an LLP where the participators are also members of the LLP.

For s 464A to apply there are two main conditions which must be present.

- A tax avoidance purpose. The main purpose or one of the main purposes is to avoid or reduce a tax charge or obtain relief from a charge under s 455 or to obtain a tax advantage for the participator or associate.
- Conferral of a benefit on a participator or an associate of a participator.

Using the facts of the example above where an individual, Mr A, who is a participator in B Ltd, forms an LLP with B Ltd. The profits of the LLP are allocated to B Ltd, B Ltd leaves the profits undrawn on capital account in the LLP. Mr A would draw on the capital amounts without triggering a s 455 charge.

Section 464A imposes a tax charge if during an accounting period a close company is party to arrangements which confer a benefit (directly or indirectly) on an individual who is a participator (or an associate) in the close company. 'Arrangements' is defined in s 464A(7) and includes 'any arrangements, scheme or understanding of any kind, whether or not legally enforceable, involving a single transaction or two or more transactions'.

Suppose that instead of making a loan in the example above B Ltd contributes capital to the LLP. There would be no charge under s 455, but if Mr A overdraws on his account with the LLP a charge will now arise under the new s 464A.

Section 464A is widely drafted and, in the absence of clearance from HMRC to the contrary, it would be prudent to assume that it will apply to the transactions of this nature.

Distributions

[2.11] Where a company is close, the meaning of 'distribution' is extended by CTA 2010, s 1064 to include certain benefits provided to participators. The benefits include:

- living or other accommodation;
- entertainment;
- domestic or other services; and
- other benefits or facilities of whatever nature to the extent that the expense is not made good to the company by the participator or an associate.

For corporation tax purposes, no deduction is available for the expenses incurred in providing the benefits to the participators which are included in the extended meaning of distributions.

The amount of the distribution is calculated using the same rules as for calculating the value of a benefit for employees. The provision of these benefits by reason of a person's employment will not normally be treated as a distribution.

Interest relief

[2.12] Interest relief is available under ITA 2007, s 392 where individuals borrow money and use it to:

(a)   acquire ordinary shares in a close company where the company is not a close investment holding company;

(b)   lend money to a close company (but not a close investment holding company) which is used wholly and exclusively for the purposes of the business of the company or an associated company; or

(c)   repay another loan on which relief is given under ITA 2007, s 392.

At the time the interest is paid, the company cannot be a close investment holding company (as defined in ITA 2007, s 393A). The legislation does not say that the company has to be a close company at that time. This is consistent with Statement of Practice 3/78, which states that TA 1988, s 360(2)(a) (the relevant provisions before the rewrite) does not require the company to be close at the time interest is paid.

SP 3/78 also states that at the time the interest is paid, the individual must hold some of the ordinary shares in the company and must have worked full-time in the company during the period from the use of the loan to the payment of the interest. Alternatively, the individual must have a material interest (5%) in the company. Both of these are considered in further detail in the sections on selling the business and management buy-outs in **CHAPTER 13** below.

The amount of relief will be limited by the cap on income tax reliefs (ITA 2007, s 24A). This cap restricts relief to the greater of £50,000 or 25% of an individual's income. The cap applies mainly to sideways income tax reliefs and qualifying loan interest.

There are some strict rules on the return of capital, the effects of which are outlined in ITA 2007, s 406. If the individual recovers any money from the company and this is not used to repay the borrowings, the individual is treated as if the amounts had been used to repay some of the borrowings, thereby restricting the interest relief. A recovery of capital occurs where:

- the individual sells or gives away some or all of his shares;
- all or part of the loan is repaid by the company; or
- the debt is assigned — this includes where it is converted into shares.

Example

Robert lent £300,000 to Bucolin Holdings from his own funds. He would like to have that money back and instead borrows money to lend to the company. If Robert simply borrows money and lends it to the company which repays his loan, he will not be eligible for interest relief. However, if Robert can arrange for the company to borrow money from a third party and that money is used to repay his original loan he can then borrow money and lend it to the company. The company will repay the third party loan and Robert will secure interest relief.

No interest relief

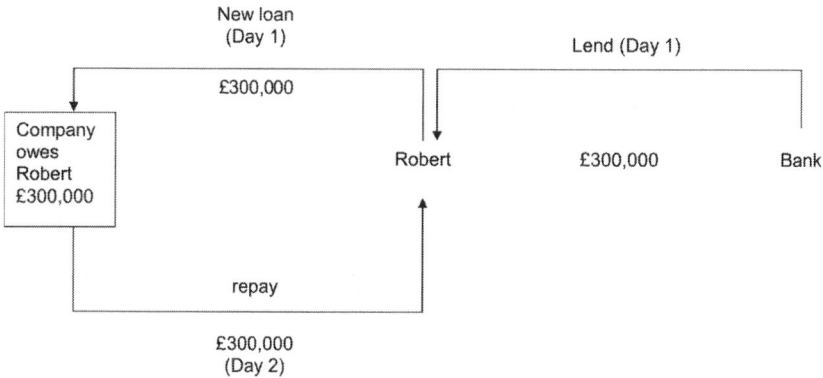

```
                    New loan
                    (Day 1)                          Lend (Day 1)

                     £300,000

 ┌──────────┐
 │ Company  │
 │ owes     │                Robert          £300,000        Bank
 │ Robert   │
 │ £300,000 │
 └──────────┘

                       repay

                     £300,000
                     (Day 2)
```

Full interest relief

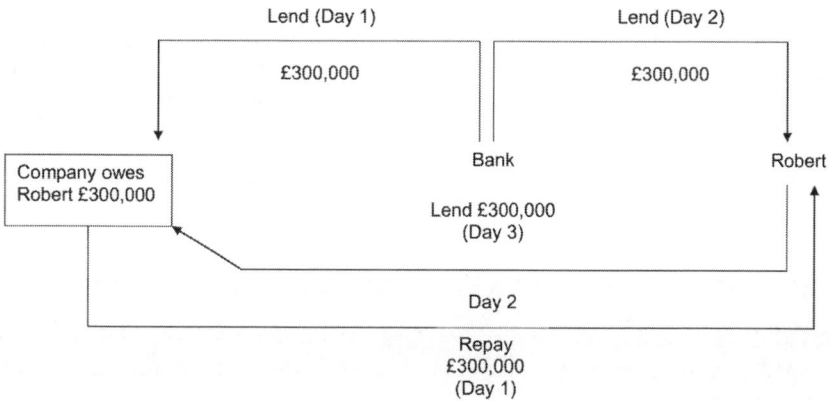

```
              Lend (Day 1)                        Lend (Day 2)

                 £300,000                            £300,000

 ┌──────────────────┐
 │ Company owes     │                  Bank                      Robert
 │ Robert £300,000  │
 └──────────────────┘           Lend £300,000
                                   (Day 3)

                                    Day 2

                                   Repay
                                  £300,000
                                  (Day 1)
```

Close investment holding company

[2.13] For the purposes of interest relief under ITA 2007, s 392, a company (candidate company) is a close investment-holding company unless through-out the accounting period it exists wholly or mainly for one or more of the following permitted purposes:

* for the purpose of carrying on a trade or trades on a commercial basis;

- for the purpose of making investments in land, or estates in land where let or intended to be let commercially to persons who are not connected to the candidate company or spouse or civil partner or a relative of the that person. For this purpose, relative means brother, sister, ancestor or lineal descendant;
- for the purpose of holding shares and securities or making loans to one or more companies which are either qualifying companies or companies which are under the control of the candidate company, directly or indirectly and exist wholly or mainly to hold shares in qualifying companies.

A qualifying company means a company which is under the control of the candidate company or of a company which controls the candidate company and exists wholly to carry out trading or letting of property to unconnected persons on a commercial basis.

Corporation tax relief

[2.14] Corporation tax relief is available for interest paid by a close company on a loan from a participator. When interest is paid more than 12 months after the end of the accounting period in which the interest would be accrued for accounting purposes, CTA 2009, s 373 sets out situations where corporation tax relief is delayed until the interest is paid. Where a close company borrows from an individual participator and interest is not paid within the period of 12 months following the end of the accounting period in which it would be treated as accruing, interest relief for the borrowing company, will be available on a paid basis, and the lender would be taxed on the interest when it is received.

The position for a corporate participator is set out in **CHAPTER 7**.

Transfers of value — IHT charges on participators

[2.15] IHTA 1984, Pt IV (ss 94–102) contains special rules for close companies which can give rise to IHT charges to the participators in two main circumstances:

- where there are alterations in share capital; and
- where the close company makes a transfer.

Alterations in share capital

[2.16] The rules relating to alterations in share capital are considered in **CHAPTER 15**, in relation to the discussion of the use of share reorganisations as part of a succession strategy.

Transfers by close companies — Employee Benefit Trusts (EBTs)

[2.17] The key principle here is that where a close company makes an IHT 'transfer of value', that transfer of value can be apportioned among the participators.

Historically it was believed that contributions to EBTs were immediately deductible for corporation tax purposes, as the assets held by the EBT had passed out of the legal ownership of the sponsoring company. This position was undermined by a combination of changes to the accounting rules, the decision in *MacDonald (Inspector of Taxes) v Dextra Accessories Ltd* [2005] UKHL 47, [2005] 4 All ER 107 ('Dextra') and rules introduced in FA 2003 (now found in CTA 2009, s 1290), which, in combination, led advisors to the view that contributions to EBTs were not deductible for corporation tax purposes unless and until there had been a payment made to an employee out of the EBT which constituted taxable employment income in his or her hands.

The significance of this view of the law is that a contribution to an EBT will not be automatically within the exemption in IHTA 1984, s 12, meaning that it would be potentially treated as a 'transfer of value' for IHT purposes: when a close company makes a payment to an EBT, it has reduced its own value by the amount transferred and therefore prima facie made a transfer of value for IHT purposes. If a company with two participators makes a contribution of, say, £1 million to an EBT, each participator can be deemed to have made an IHT transfer of value of £500,000 (IHTA 1984, s 94). Such deemed transfers are specifically defined by the Act not to be potentially exempt transfers (IHTA 1984, s 3A(6)). In these circumstances, therefore, the amounts deemed to be transferred by the participators in excess of their available IHT annual and nil-rate band exemptions may be treated as chargeable lifetime transfers and subject to an immediate 20% IHT charge.

This analysis has changed somewhat following the Supreme Court's decision in *RFC 2012 (in Liquidation) (formerly The Rangers Football Club plc) v Advocate General for Scotland* [2017] UKSC 45 ('Rangers', which is considered in more detail in **CHAPTER 10**), in which it was determined that contributions to an EBT that were made to remunerate an individual should be treated as the taxable employment income of that person; the redirection of the payment to the trustees of the EBT did not change the tax treatment of that payment.

On the basis of the Rangers decision, EBT contributions stand to be treated as taxable employment income when they are made and, following the principles set out in Dextra and CTA 2009, s 1290, should be deductible in the company's corporation tax calculations.

The IHT risks associated with EBT contributions are still relevant where the EBT is being used to warehouse assets or shares and is not being used to hold earmarked funds for particular employees.

Are all such transfers by close companies taxable?

[2.18] Clearly, not every transfer made by a close company will give rise to an IHT charge, otherwise the payment of a large salary or dividend could trigger the charge. The key exemptions to a charge on participators are as follows:

- *Taxable recipient*. If the amount transferred by the close company is taken into account in computing a person's profits or gains or losses for income tax or corporation tax purposes, no apportionment is made. This excludes capital gains tax.

- *Deductible expense in the company*. If the close company is entitled to a corporation tax deduction on the transfer, the transfer of value is not subject to IHT (IHTA 1984, s 12).

- *Restricted EBT*. If the terms of the EBT exclude participators holding more than 5% from benefiting (or do not exclude them entirely but limit the ways in which they can benefit) from the receipt of directly taxable payments and limit the class of all beneficiaries to employees and those closely connected with them (as defined in IHTA 1984, s 86(1)), the transfer of value is not subject to IHT (IHTA 1984, s 13).

- *Employee-Ownership Trusts*. Where a close trading company transfers property to the trustees of a qualifying employee-ownership trust, a specific exemption prevents that disposition from being treated as a transfer of value (IHTA 1984, s 13A). This is discussed in more detail at **[10.48]**.

- *'Commercial payments'*. If it can be shown that the transfer of value arose in circumstances where the close company did not intend to confer any gratuitous benefit and the payment was made at arm's length or was such as might have been made at arm's length, the transfer of value is not subject to IHT (IHTA 1984, s 10).

- *BPR*. Where the value transferred is attributable to relevant business property (IHTA 1984, s 105) relief from IHT should be available. This means that a cash payment made to an EBT may qualify for BPR provided it previously formed part of the transferor's business that qualified for relief (*Revenue and Customs Comrs v Trustees of the Nelson Dance Family* [2009] EWHC 71 (CH), [2009] STC 802, 79 TC 605).

When EBTs were established pre-*Dextra*, as mentioned above, there was anticipation of a full corporation tax deduction and no concern about a possible IHT charge on the participators because of the IHTA 1984, s 12 exemption referred to above.

Following the *Dextra* case, HMRC issued a statement indicating that, as there was no blanket IHTA 1984, s 12 exemption available, taxpayers should be on notice that IHT could now be due in relation to earlier contributions where a deduction had been invalidly claimed. In the authors' experience, HMRC has not embarked upon a universal attack on such EBTs, but selected companies have received letters requesting that an IHT account (form IHT 100) be submitted. How this position will change in the light of the Rangers case has yet to be determined.

In circumstances where there is now no clear s 12 exemption (because no direct payments to employees have been made by the EBT and therefore no corporation tax deduction is in point), it is necessary to consider whether the terms of the EBT fall within IHTA 1984, s 13, where 5%-plus participators have unrestricted rights to benefit from the EBT. If s 13 does not apply, the next line of defence should be to review whether the contributions can be said to come from the working capital of a trading company, in which case BPR should be available on the transfer.

Where BPR is not available, the circumstances of the establishment of the EBT would need to be considered to determine whether they might be considered sufficiently commercial in nature to satisfy IHTA 1984, s 10. In this context, the case of *Postlethwaite's Executors v Revenue and Customs Comrs* [2007] STC (SCD) 83 concerning the application of s 10 on a transfer to a Funded Unapproved Retirement Benefit Scheme (FURBS) is helpful.

In Revenue & Customs Brief 49/09, HMRC sets out a harsh and uncompromising policy line in relation to all of these statutory exemptions. This was updated in Revenue & Customs Brief 61/09 and reiterated more recently in Revenue & Customs Brief 18/11. On 1 July 2013, HMRC's manuals in relation to this area (IHTM 42901 – 42991) were comprehensively updated. The authors' experience has been that HMRC is far more ready to accept arguments on BPR where it is possible to establish the trading status of the contributor company.

Further points

[2.19] The following additional comments and observations will also be relevant in some circumstances:

- Where a participator is itself a close company, any amount apportioned to that close company is then further apportioned to its participators.
- Where a participator is a trust, special rules apply (IHTA 1984, s 99) but the effect is as one might imagine. Transfers of value apportioned to discretionary trusts, and trusts treated as discretionary trusts following FA 2006, trigger 'Exit Charges' in the trust. Where amounts are apportioned to pre-FA 2006-style interest in possession trusts (ie where the life tenant is treated as beneficially entitled to the trust assets), the trust is treated as coming to an end in relation to the amounts apportioned.
- There are special rules concerning the liability to tax contained in IHTA 1984, s 202. The transferee company is liable for the tax – which means that tax must be calculated on a 'grossed up' basis – and if the company doesn't pay within the appropriate timeframe, the participators can become liable personally.

- In Revenue & Customs Brief 18/11, HMRC has acknowledged for the first time that IHT BPR may be available in relation to the transfer to the EBT if the relevant BPR conditions are met.

Planning point

The position in relation to EBTs illustrates the operation of the IHT rule for close companies as well as providing some specific observations on the possible 'defences' to HMRC's attacks on the IHT position for EBTs.

In the majority of circumstances, of course, payments and transfers made by close companies will be entirely commercial in nature and will not trigger IHT charges for the participators. Where, however, the company is involved in any 'unusual' tax planning, designed, say, to avoid some tax other than IHT, it is always important to consider these IHT rules.

Key points

[2.20] Key points to note are as follows:

- A close company is a UK resident company which is under the control of five or fewer participators or of any number of participators who are directors.
- Loans to shareholders trigger a 32.5% tax charge on the company.
- Benefits to non-working shareholders are taxed as a distribution.
- FA 2013 has tightened the rules so non loans can also be subject to the 32.5% charge.
- Tax relief is available for interest on loans where the money is lent to a close company.
- There is a potential IHT charge on participators for transfers of value by a close company.

Chapter 3

Entrepreneurs' Relief, and Business Property Relief

Introduction

[3.1] Entrepreneurs' relief (ER) and business property relief (BPR) provide very valuable reliefs to the owners of businesses on the transfer of assets. Interestingly, the reliefs are very different, with their own unique set of rules. For advisers there is very often the conflict of preserving one relief while losing the other. If embarking on any planning for clients aimed at utilising these reliefs it is important to understand the clients' objectives. A client wishing to pass his business to his sons on death will not thank his adviser if the adviser has helped obtain ER but in the process loses BPR on part of the business. This chapter will examine both types of relief and will look at the planning and the pitfalls. It highlights the need to look at both reliefs together. Recent finance acts have introduced a number of changes to the ER rules in relation to associated disposals, goodwill and the definition of a trading company. These changes could impact on existing structures so structures should be reviewed regularly and well in advance of any sale. There is a table summarising the reliefs at the end of the chapter which is a useful guide for the adviser.

The Institute of Chartered Accountants in England and Wales (ICAEW) published TAXGUIDE 1/12 on 25 January 2012 which is a guidance note (Note) containing practical points on ER. The guidance is agreed with HMRC and includes technical questions to which HMRC has provided answers. This Note is referred to where relevant.

Entrepreneurs' relief (ER)

[3.2] ER applies to qualifying business disposals after 5 April 2008. Full legislative provisions are contained in Taxation of Chargeable Gains Act 1992, ss 169H–169SA (TCGA 1992). The relief is such that the first £10 million of gains arising on the disposal of qualifying business assets are charged to tax at 10%.

Qualifying business disposals

[3.3] ER is available for qualifying business disposals which are:

- a material disposal of business assets;
- a disposal of trust business assets;
- a disposal associated with a relevant material disposal.

Material disposal of business assets

[3.4] Within this there are two criteria which need to be met; 'material' and 'disposal of business assets'.

It makes sense to first look at the meaning of a disposal of business assets — it must be one of the following:

- a disposal of the whole or part of a business (this would exclude the disposal of individual assets unless the asset qualified as a going concern or business in its own right);
- a disposal of assets which were used for the purposes of a business which has since ceased but the assets must have been used in the business at the date of cessation (the disposal of an interest in such assets also qualifies);
- a disposal of shares or securities in a company (or an interest in shares or securities).

Disposal of the whole or part of a business

[3.5] Whether the disposal is material depends on what is being sold. For the sale of the whole or part of a business the individual must have owned the business throughout the year leading up to the date of disposal.

Whether a disposal amounts to a part disposal of a business for the purposes of ER, or a sale of assets, has been considered in the case of *Mr Gilbert t/a United Foods v HMRC* [2011] UKFTT 705 (TC) at the First-tier Tribunal. Mr Gilbert was a sole trader selling food on commission to wholesalers. He represented nine manufacturers. He sold part of his business to one of his suppliers, including the brands, trademarks, customer database relating to the business and all of the goodwill that went with it. Mr Gilbert claimed ER, but HMRC rejected this on the basis that he had not disposed of 'an identifiable part of the business which on its own was separately definable' therefore it was simply a sale of assets.

The FTT found that there were several factors that supported the fact that part of the business could be sold as a going concern.

- HMRC's manual at CG64015 is clear that a sale of a business as a going concern is a disposal of a business and the FTT could not see how this would not apply to part of a business.
- In the notes to the 2008 Finance Bill it says that the sale of a whole or part of the business must be as a going concern.
- In the retirement relief case of *Pepper v Daffurn* 66 TC 88, Jonathan Parker J held that a sale as a going concern is a sufficient but not necessary condition for the availability of the relief and this could extend to ER.

The tribunal found that the part of the business sold constituted a going concern as there was a disposal of both goodwill and a customer database. The FTT also considered HMRC's other assertion that there had to be a sale of a separate identifiable part of the business. The question is whether a purchaser would be able to carry on the business using only the assets transferred to it and the FTT agreed that in this case the purchaser could.

[3.6] For the disposal of assets of a business which has ceased the individual must have owned the business for one year immediately preceding the cessation and the disposal of the assets must take place within three years of cessation.

A question was raised in ICAEW's Note whether assets that are disposed of after the cessation of the trade qualify for ER. HMRC's opinion is that where the trade is carried on after the contract for disposing of assets has been made, it will still be possible to claim ER provided the business disposal is linked to the business cessation.

Pitfall

[3.7] Where a business occupies a valuable property, a developer may want to acquire the property and lease it back to the trader for a year or so while planning permission is being obtained. Given the continuation of the business it may be difficult to link the disposal of the business to the cessation of the trade. This would prevent the disposal of the property qualifying for ER. The trader needs to consider whether one year's additional trading profits will compensate for the loss of ER. In these circumstances, it can be better to have a longer period between exchange and completion thereby allowing the business to continue trading.

[3.8] The sale of a business asset following the cessation of a trade was considered in the case of *Jeremy Rice v HMRC* [2014] UKFTT 0133 (TC). Mr Rice operated as a sole trader, Performance Cars, selling used 'sporty' cars. He had a property at Fletton Avenue which consisted of a small showroom and a forecourt. At any given point Mr Rice would have about 40 cars in stock of which six would be in the showroom and the remainder on the forecourt. There was a small office and a small workshop on the premises where he carried out minor work to cars such as servicing, paintwork and valeting. Fletton Avenue was located on one of the four main roads into Peterborough. Mr Rice depended on passing traffic for business and did not advertise on the internet. Following problems with vandalism at Fletton Avenue, Mr Rice ceased trading there in May 2005 and sold his stock of cars at auctions or by newspaper adverts. He eventually sold the property in April 2008 to a property developer. He claimed ER on the disposal on the basis that the property was a business asset and it had been sold within three years of the cessation of the trade. HMRC disputed that the business had ceased on the grounds that Mr Rice continued to trade at his home address, Four Acres. Mr Rice had previously stored cars at Four Acres and at first he had intended to run the business at Four Acres in the same way as Performance Cars. However planning regulations prohibited this and in September 2006 he obtained planning permission to sell cars from the site but the conditions meant there could be no display of vehicles for sale to the general public and the number of vehicles which could be kept on site was restricted to 25. These restrictions meant that Mr Rice had to conduct his business by advertising on the Internet.

Potential customers would make an appointment to come and inspect a car. The type of cars sold at Four Acres Car Sales was four-wheel drive vehicles and family cars.

The FTT found that there was a very significant change in the business carried on by Mr Rice and concluded that there was a cessation of the trade carried on by Mr Rice at Fletton Avenue. As the asset was used in the trade in the twelve months preceding the cessation ER was available.

Partnerships

[3.9] Special rules apply to ensure that ER can be claimed where an individual carries on business as a member of a partnership:

- where an individual carrying on a business takes on a partner a disposal of interests in business assets contributed to the partnership are treated as a disposal of part of the business;
- where a partner disposes of all or part of his interest in partnership assets the disposal can be treated as a disposal of the whole or part of the partnership business.

Disposal of Goodwill to a close company

[3.10] Under s 169LA goodwill is not a relevant business asset for ER purposes where a person (P) disposes of goodwill to a close company (C), which is a related party as defined in CTA 2009, s 835. Under this definition, P is connected to C where he is participator or an associate of a participator in C.

The related party provisions only apply where P and any 'relevant connected person' together own at least 5% or more of the shares or votes in C. Changes have also been made to define who is connected for these purposes by the removal of 'associate', 'control' 'major interest' and 'participator' substituted by a relevant connected person which means:

(a)   a company connected with P; and
(b)   trustees connected with P.

The definition does not include individuals so it is possible that business interests could be passed onto family members who may be shareholders of the new incorporated company as long as the exiting shareholder does not hold 5% or more of the shares in the new company.

The introduction of sub-ss 1A, 1B and 1C allow ER in situations where P is required to incorporate into C before a sale to third parties.

Although a person may own more than 5% of the shares following incorporation they will not be caught by the related party rules where:

P and any relevant connected person dispose of C's shares to another company such that, immediately before the end of the relevant period, neither P nor any relevant connected person owns any shares in C. The relevant period for this purpose is 28 days from the date of disposal or longer subject to HMRC approval. As can be seen from the example below, this can help where a business is incorporate prior to a sale to a third party.

Example

> Bill has operated a qualifying ER trade since 2010 and received an offer for his business from a large group on the basis he incorporated and subsequently sold his shares. On 1 November 2017 he incorporated selling his goodwill to the new company for consideration left outstanding on loan account. On 20 November 2017, he sold his shares to the purchaser wholly for cash. As part of the deal the purchasers injected money into the company to repay the director's loan account.
>
> Although Bill will own all the shares and votes after incorporation as the subsequent sale of shares to the third party is undertaken within 28 days, Bill will be eligible for ER on the sale of goodwill to C.

Disposal of shares or securities

[3.11] For the disposal of shares or securities the individual must meet <u>one</u> of the following conditions (s 169I(5)–(7)(B)).

Condition A – s 169I(6)

[3.12] Throughout the year immediately preceding the disposal, the following conditions should be met:

- The company must have been the individual's <u>personal company</u>. A personal company is one in which the individual holds at least 5% of the ordinary share capital of the company and that holding gives him at least 5% of the votes;
- The individual must be an <u>officer or employee</u> of the company (or of companies that are members of the same trading group);
- The company must be a <u>trading company</u> or the holding company of a trading group.

Personal company

[3.13] The 5% of ordinary share capital test is measured in relation to the nominal value of the ordinary share capital rather than the actual value of the shares or the number of shares in issue. This follows the approach in the case of *Canada Safeway Ltd v Comrs of Inland Revenue* [1973] Ch 374. It has also been confirmed by HMRC in the ICAEW's Note and recent case law.

HMRC confirmed in the ICAEW's Note that if a shareholder's ownership drops below the 5% threshold due to holders of share options exercising their rights on the *same* day ie just before the sale of the business takes place, then this will not result in the disposal being ineligible for ER provided the other qualifying conditions are met throughout the qualifying period.

HMRC has also confirmed that there is no minimum disposal that constitutes a material disposal.

Once the shareholder meets the personal company test in the previous 12 months any shares or securities disposed of will qualify for ER eg non-voting shares.

Ordinary share capital is defined in ITA 2007, s 989:

> *'ordinary share capital', in relation to a company, means all the company's issued share capital (however described), other than capital the holders of which have a right to a dividend at a fixed rate but have no other right to share in the company's profits.*

For these purposes, non-voting preference shares with a variable rate of dividend, count as ordinary shares.

In the case of *Castledine v HMRC* [2016] UKFTT 145, the Tribunal found that the company's deferred shares were ordinary shares which meant that the taxpayer's shareholding was diluted to below 5% (to 4.99%) of the ordinary share capital making his disposal ineligible for ER. The taxpayer had argued that as the deferred shares did not carry voting rights or rights to dividends they were not ordinary shares but the tribunal rejected this accepting HMRC's argument that these shares were no different to ordinary shares.

The decision in the *Castledine* case is in contrast to the decision in *McQuillan v HMRC* [2016] UKFTT 305 (TC) where the First-tier Tribunal found in favour of the taxpayers. In the McQuillan case the issued share capital of the company at incorporation was 100 £1 ordinary shares of which the appellants each held 33 and two other individuals each held 17. The other individuals lent £30,000 to the company which was subsequently converted into 30,000 £1 redeemable non-voting shares. The redeemable shares were redeemed immediately before a sale. The tribunal had to decide if the appellants disposed of shares in their 'personal company' ie did the redeemable non-voting shares constitute part of the ordinary share capital of the company. The tribunal agreed with the taxpayer that a 'dividend at a fixed rate' includes shares which have no right to any dividend. Therefore, the McQuillans had disposed of shares in their personal company. HMRC appealed to the Upper Tribunal and the decision was reversed. The Upper Tribunal held that a right to a dividend of zero was not a right to anything at all. That type of share cannot be regarded as having a right to a dividend so therefore the shares constitute part of the ordinary share capital of the company.

At the time of writing, the Government has published a consultation document setting out proposals which are intended to allow ER where there is a dilution below 5% and that dilution is as a result of a new share issue and the funds have been raised for commercial purposes. It is proposed that the rules would work by allowing the individual to make an election to crystallise the capital gains that would be realised if there was a market value disposal immediately before dilution. The individual could then choose to defer paying the tax on this gain until the actual disposal of the shares. The consultation closes on 15 May 2018.

Officer or employee

[3.14] Employee and officer take their meaning from ITEPA 2003. Employment within ITEPA 2003, s 4 'includes in particular a contract of service' while office as per ITEPA 2003, s 5 is 'any position which has an existence independent of the person who holds it'. As the individual needs to meet this criteria throughout the 12 months prior to disposal the timing or resignation is critical. Resignation should be post sale of the shares.

This was considered in the case of *Corbett v HMRC*, [2014] UKFTT 298 (TC). Mr Corbett was a senior executive employed by Optivite International Limited ('Optivite'), and was involved in negotiations for the sale of the company to Kiotech International Limited ('Kiotech'), which took place in October 2009. Both Mr Corbett and his wife had shares in Optivite. Mrs Corbett was employed by Optivite, providing secretarial duties to her husband, for which she received a salary of £14,000 a year. Kiotech had a strict policy of not employing spouses of senior executives, and in order to avoid any problems with negotiations for the sale Mrs Corbett was removed from the company's payroll and received her P45 in February 2009. However, she continued to work for her husband, whose salary was increased by £1,200 a month to compensate them for the loss of her salary.

Mrs Corbett claimed ER on the disposal of her shares. HMRC argued that ER was not available as when Mrs Corbett received her P45 in February 2009 her employment ceased. After that date she was not employed by the company, as without remuneration there can be no employment. Mrs Corbett argued that she had remained as an employee of Optivite until October 2009. As the company operated a computerised payroll the only way of removing her was to produce forms P45 and P14, but this did not mean that her duties changed. She continued to do the same work as she had done previously.

HMRC's manuals confirm that remuneration is not required for eligibility to ER in CG64110. It could have been argued that because Mr Corbett's salary was paid into a joint bank account, Mrs Corbett continued to receive her salary.

Evidence was provided by Optivite's financial controller that confirmed the position described by Mrs Corbett and her advisers. The tribunal found that he was a credible independent witness, as it made no difference to the company whether she succeeded in her claim for ER. They were satisfied that, on the balance of probabilities, the company continued to remunerate Mrs Corbett by directing her salary to Mr Corbett and paying it into their joint bank account. The tribunal therefore allowed Mrs Corbett's claim for ER in respect of the sale of shares in Optivite.

While the decision in Mrs Corbett's case is surprising, and turns on facts that were corroborated by a credible witness better planning is to remain as an employee or officeholder until after the sale.

In order to claim ER on the sale of shares the shareholder has to be a director or employee of the company throughout the period of one year up to the date of sale. Where spouses or civil partners own shares in a trading company, and only one qualifies for ER, the usual advice is that, before the sale, the non-qualifying individual should transfer their shares to the individual that qualifies.

In a later case, *Hirst v HMRC* TC4038 [2014] UKFTT 924 (TC), [2015] SWTI 135, the FTT held that Mr Hirst met the employment condition in the 12 months prior to sale despite having resigned as a director 18 months earlier.

The tribunal firstly considered whether Mr Hirst was an officer of the company within the meaning of ITEPA 2003, s 5(3) in particular a de facto or shadow director. They drew upon statutory definitions in the Companies Act 2006 and the leading case of *HMRC v Holland* [2010] and concluded that Mr Hirst was not an officer of the company. However, the tribunal went on to consider Mr Hirst's employment status and concluded that there was an employment relationship. The work that Mr Hirst did was significant and went beyond that which might be expected of a shareholder or a former director with a significant shareholding.

Mr Moore was not as fortunate. In the case of *John Kenneth Moore v HMRC* [2016] UKFTT 115 (TC) the taxpayer, a founding shareholder and director of Alpha Micro Components Ltd, sold his shares back to the company. The agreement was reached in February 2009 but it was May 2009 before the sale of his shares was approved by a general meeting of shareholders and recorded in the company statutory records. On the same day, he signed a document confirming his resignation as a director effective from February 2009. His claim for ER failed as he was not a director or employee in the 12 months prior to sale. Both cases demonstrate the care that needs to be taken in dealing with the sale of shares if an ER claim is to be successful.

Trading

[3.15] A trading company for the purposes of ER is defined in TCGA 1992, s 165A as 'a company carrying on trading activities whose activities do not include to a substantial extent activities other than trading activities'.

Trading activities include:

'... activities carried on by the company:

(a)   in the course of, or for the purposes of, a trade being carried on by it,
(b)   for the purposes of a trade that it is preparing to carry on,
(c)   with a view to its acquiring or starting to carry on a trade, or
(d)   with a view to its acquiring a significant interest in the share capital of another company that:
  (i)   is a trading company or the holding company of a trading group, and
  (ii)   if the acquiring company is a member of a group of companies, it is not a member of that group.'

Activities in (b) and (c) are only qualifying activities if the company starts to carry on the trade as soon as is reasonably practicable. There is no statutory definition of what is meant by 'as soon as is reasonably practicable' but HMRC's manual at CG64075 states:

'Rather than impose a fixed time limit, the legislation allows companies whatever time is reasonable, having regard to the particular circumstances, to prepare to carry on a new trade or to acquire a trade or trading company. What is "reasonably practicable in the circumstances" will depend on the facts in each case. For example, a company may be in negotiations to acquire a trading company but owing to circumstances beyond its control the purchase is delayed. There might be, for example, a problem with the vendor proving title to the company's assets. Where this was the reason for the delay we would not suggest that the acquisition had not been made as soon as was reasonably practicable in the circumstances.'

In looking at a group, a trading group (TCGA 1992, s 165A(8)) is a:

'group of companies:

(a)   one or more of whose members carry on trading activities, and

(b)   the activities of whose members when taken together do not include substantial non-trading activities.'

Members of the group are any 51% subsidiaries. Where shareholdings in other companies are 50% or less, they could result in the company having investments. However, shareholdings of less than 50% can qualify under the joint venture rules.

In determining if the company or group is trading a qualifying shareholding in a joint venture company ('JVC') is one which is more than 10% and:

- in a company which is a trading company or the holding company of a trading group; and
- 75% or more of the ordinary share capital in the company is held by no more than five persons.

In using the JVC rules the status of the group is determined *by reference to the shareholder*. The same method is used where a company has an interest in a partnership. These rules are considered later in this chapter.

A company will not be a trading company if it has substantial non-trading activities. HMRC confirmed in Tax Bulletin 53 (TB 53) that substantial means 20%. Therefore, if a company has investments or other assets not used in the trade, these could disqualify the company as a trading company. In TB 53, HMRC gave guidance on how the 20% should be measured illustrating three bases of measurement.

This test requires that first a separate non-trading activity is identified and second, that a judgment is made as to whether that activity is substantial relative to the overall activities of the company.

Turnover from non-trading activities

[3.16] This examines the proportion of income from non-trading activities to that from trading activities. This is on a gross basis. For example, if there is interest arising on a bank account which holds cash not required for the business, this is compared to turnover. In the majority of cases, interest is unlikely to be more than 20%. Similarly, if the company has an investment property, the rental income should be compared to the turnover.

Expenses incurred by, or time spent by, officers and employees of the company in undertaking its activities

[3.17] This examines the time spent by officers and employees of the company on non-trading activities. Whether it is a property on a long let or cash in a bank account, in most cases it is difficult to see how such activity could take up more than 20% of the directors' and employees' time. The same holds true for the expenses test.

Asset base of the company

[3.18] For the majority of companies, this is the test that causes the most concern. Does the non-trading asset account for more than 20% of the company's assets? For an investment property the measurement will be relatively straight forward however if the non-business asset is cash this is not the case. This asset base test is considered later in relation to excess cash in the company.

These tests are a guideline and there is no requirement to meet three out of three. According to TB 53:

> 'The historical context of the company may be relevant. For example, it is quite possible that at an instant in time certain receipts may not be insubstantial but, if looked at on a longer timescale, they may. Looking at the historical context therefore a company might be able to show that it was a trading company at a particular point in time.
>
> It may be that some measures point in one direction and others in the opposite direction. We would weigh up the impact of each of the measures to balance the effects of measures that point in different directions in coming to a view.'

Advisers should remember that TB 53 is simply guidance. There may be other measures which are better suited to particular businesses, and advisers should not hesitate in using other measurements where these are appropriate.

Substantial cash in the company

[3.19] One of the most common problems faced by advisers in relation to the trading company definition is large cash balances held by the company. With the prospect of a 10% tax rate, many owner-managers build up cash balances in the business in the hope that there will be an eventual exit and a 10% tax rate will be available. This exit could be by way of a sale or perhaps a member's voluntary liquidation (subject to the TAAR which could prevent ER). Building high levels of cash in the business can be dangerous, because if cash is not required in the business and the amount is substantial, the company may not qualify as a trading company. The key issue is to determine what level of cash can be held in the business without a loss of ER. Remember for ER we are only concerned with a one year look back.

In deciding whether cash is excessive, the key measure is going to be the asset base of the company. It is unlikely that any interest is substantial in relation to turnover, and even if the director moved the money to a different bank account every day, it is unlikely to take up more than 20% of his time! Therefore, the practical basis of measurement is going to be against assets; what is the ratio of cash to the total assets? In calculating this ratio, it is back to basics and the use of a numerator and denominator test:

$$\frac{N}{D}$$

Where:

N = the excess cash in the company.

D = the total assets of the company.

This must be less than 20%.

Numerator

[3.20] The first point to remember is that it is only the excess cash that should be measured, not the total cash in the business. Therefore, any cash needed in the company should be excluded from the test. There are three main reasons why cash is needed in a company:

Working capital requirement — every business needs cash to finance its day-to-day activities. One way of looking at this is to work out the liquidity ratios for the company. These will provide information about the company's ability to meet its short-term financial obligations. The most common ratio is:

$$\text{Current ratio} = \frac{\text{Current assets}}{\text{Current liabilities}}$$

There could be a situation where the company has debtors who can control its trading, eg blue-chip companies, and creditors who can also control their credit terms. The company could find itself in a situation where it is waiting for money from a debtor and the creditor calls in its debts. To work out what cash would be required, the cash ratio could be used, as this is an indication of the company's ability to pay off its current liabilities if for some reason immediate payment were demanded:

$$\text{Cash ratio} = \frac{\text{Cash} + \text{marketable securities}}{\text{Current liabilities}}$$

For many owner-managed companies, this can pose a high risk.

Precautionary — all companies need a buffer of cash in their business for contingencies. While for many starter businesses the idea of contingent cash is a luxury, for established businesses it makes good commercial sense. Precautionary reasons include the reliance on a large contract, a possible downturn in the particular industry sector, a breakdown of machinery, a loss of key employees or anything else which poses a real threat to the company.

Future plans — a growing business will always want cash reserves to deal with future expansion plans. This could include the acquisition of a new property or new equipment. It is reasonable that a company would work towards building up a cash reserve for these purposes.

Whatever the reasons for holding cash in the business, it is important that these are documented. Even for very small family-run companies, HMRC places great reliance on board minutes. Any high levels of cash in the business should be discussed and considered and the reasons for holding the cash balances documented in regular board minutes. Detailed notes on the management accounts are also very helpful. The company should have evidence to back up its reasons for holding excess cash, and this should be maintained on an ongoing basis.

Having established what cash is required for the business, this should be deducted from the cash balance. It is this net figure which is used as 'N' in the above formula.

Denominator

[3.21] This looks at the total assets in the company and will usually be taken from the balance sheet. For the assets on the balance sheet, these should be adjusted to their market value. So, for the property that has not been revalued in a while, the market value should be obtained. Perhaps more importantly, many owner-managed businesses will not have goodwill on their balance sheet. However, if there is a sale of the business, the consideration is likely to be more than the net assets of the business. This means that there must be some goodwill in the business. This goodwill did not suddenly appear on the day of sale, it has been accumulating since the business started. So, in looking at the assets of the company, the value of goodwill should be included irrespective of the fact it is off balance sheet, because it is internally generated. This adjusted gross-asset figure should be included as 'D' in the above formula.

HMRC guidance

[3.22] Although HMRC appears to have a relaxed approach to cash in the company the following guidance is contained in CG64060:

'However, the long-term retention of significant earnings generated from trading activities may amount to an investment activity. The first point to consider is whether or not there is any identifiable activity distinct from the trading activity.

"Factors to consider include:

- whether the earnings are retained for the present and future cash flow requirements of the trading activity.
- the nature of the underlying investments used as a lodgement for the funds, for instance if the funds are locked into long term investments or the investments themselves are high risk that may suggest that they are not available for the trading activity.
- the extent of the company's (or group's) activity in managing the investments.
- whether the funds have been ear-marked for a particular use in the trading activity.

If a separate investment activity is identified then it will become necessary to determine whether that is substantial in terms of the overall activities."'

In practice where a company or group has cash which has been generated from its trading activities and a reasonable salary/dividend is extracted from the company HMRC would not seek to argue the ER position. Where large amounts of cash are retained in the business and there is a business purpose for this it is prudent to record the reasons and decisions in board minutes and other contemporaneous correspondence.

Joint venture structures

[3.23] The changes introduced by FA 2015 with the insertion of TCGA 1992, s 169S(4A), had an adverse impact on many genuine commercial JV structures. The provisions disregarded a corporate entity's interest in a partnership and changed the definition of 'trading company' and 'trading group' by removing TCGA 1992, ss 165A(7) and 165A(12).

These restrictions were eased by backdated provisions in FA 2016. Although not a total reversal of the FA 2015 restrictions they have nonetheless ensured that many genuine JV arrangements are not caught by the 2015 changes.

The new rules introduced in FA 2016 adopt a formulaic approach and are complex. The main restricting provision at s 169S(4A) has been removed and a new s 169SA inserted providing new definitions of trading company and trading group for ER purposes in TCGA 1992, Sch 7ZA, effectively reinstating s 165(7).

[3.24] Post-FA 2016, having established that a company qualifies as a joint venture member company, a JV company's (JVC) activities will only be attributable to that company holding the shares, now described as an investing company (IC), if the individual (P) claiming ER holds at least 5% directly or indirectly of shares and votes in the JVC.

The 5% tests are measured by two formulas as follows:

'Shareholding formula – R × S × 100, where:

"R = the fraction P has in IC;

S = the fraction of ordinary shares held by IC in JVC."'

'Voting formula – T × U × 100, where:

"T = the fraction of voting rights held by P in IC;

U = the fraction of voting rights held by IC in JVC."'

Where there are two or more investing companies, the percentages are added together. Where IC owns more than 50% of shares and/or votes, it is treated as owning the whole of the shares and/or votes.

Example [table 1]

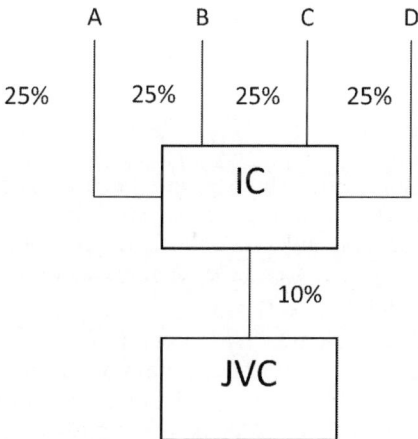

Shareholding: $0.25 \times 0.1 \times 100 = 2.5\%$

The example demonstrates that the formula still effectively blocks the use of a 'management feeder company' formed just to hold shares in a JVC. However, if one of the shareholders were to hold 70% of the shares and votes they would qualify for ER (0.70 x 0.10 x 100 = 7%) under the formula but the other three shareholders would not. The formulae therefore determine individual shareholder entitlement to relief rather than the overall trading status of the company. Shareholding and voting dilution could therefore have an adverse effect on ER entitlement.

Where a group exists, P's fractional share in IC is multiplied by the fractional ownership further down the structure by applying rules in CTA 2010, ss 1155–1157 as shown in example [table 2]. For these purposes a group takes its meaning from TCGA 1992, s 165A(4).

Example [table 2]

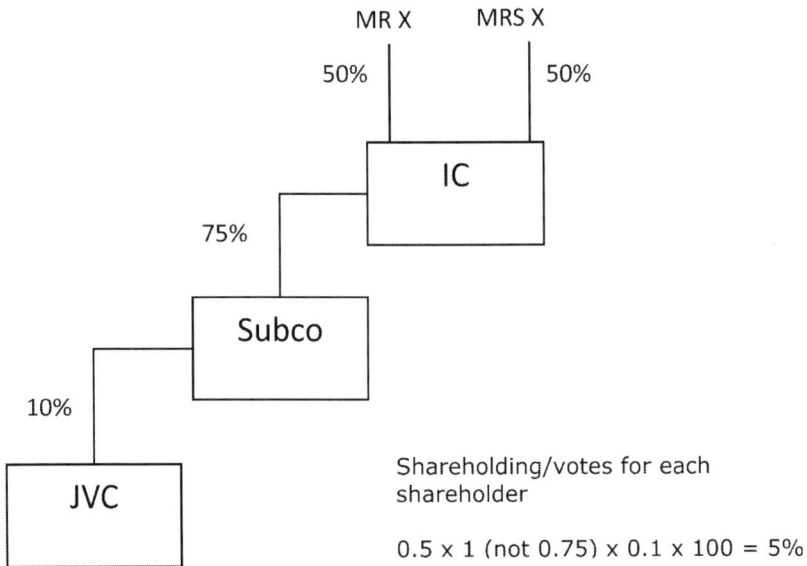

MR X   MRS X

50%   50%

IC

75%

Subco

10%

JVC

Shareholding/votes for each shareholder

0.5 x 1 (not 0.75) x 0.1 x 100 = 5%

Partnership structures

[3.25] Before the restrictions imposed by FA 2015, a corporate partner was treated as carrying on a proportion of the activities carried on by the partnership. The FA 2015 changes severed that link, so unless the company carried on a significant trade of its own, the shares held in the corporate partner company, would not be eligible for ER.

Again, changes have been made in FA 2016 to ease this situation. The new provisions of TCGA 1992, Sch 7ZA treat the activities of a company as trading activities where the company is a 'direct interest company' (DIC) or a 'relevant corporate partner' (RCP), in relation to P, who in turn must have indirect interest in at least 5% of the partnership profits/assets and votes. Further, the corporate partner must be a member of the partnership for a 12-month period for the activities to be attributed to it.

The indirect interest P holds is measured by the formula R x V x 100, where:

'R = the fraction P has in the DIC;

V = the lower of:

a. the fraction of profits in which DIC holds in the partnership; and
b. the fraction of assets of the partnership in which DIC has an interest.'

In relation to the voting tests, P's interest in the DIC will dictate the level of votes. If there are more than one DIC, interests are added together and where the DIC directly owns more than 50% of the shares, the DIC is taken to own the whole of the company.

Example [table 3]

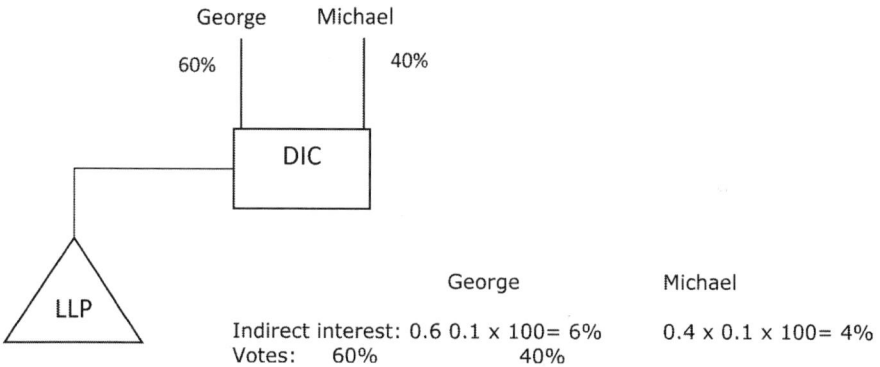

George   Michael

60% | | 40%

DIC

LLP

	George	Michael
Indirect interest:	0.6 0.1 x 100= 6%	0.4 x 0.1 x 100= 4%
Votes:	60%	40%

Table 3 example shows that although Michael has 40% of the voting rights, because the DIC's entitlement to assets is only 10%, his interest in the partnership is less than 5%. George conversely meets both 5% tests and would be eligible for ER.

Relevant corporate partners

[3.26] Where interests are held via a RCP, which is a company within the same group as the DIC, P's indirect interest is measured by the formula;

'R × V × W × 100, where:

"R = the fraction P has in the DIC;

V = the lower of:

a. the fraction of profits in which RCP holds in the partnership; and
b. the fraction of assets of the partnership in which RCP has an interest.

W = the fraction owned by DIC in RCP."'

Voting rights are measured by the formula T × X × 100 where:

'T = the fraction of voting rights held by P in DIC;

X = the fraction of voting rights held by DIC in RCP.'

Where the DIC owns more than 51% or more of shares and/or votes in another company, it is treated as owning the whole of the company.

Example [table 4]

Indirect interest: 0.5 x 0.2 x 100= 10%
Votes: 0.5 x 1 (not 0.51) x 100= 50%

The new rules, based around the various formulae mean that for ER purposes there is a greater emphasis on the interests individual shareholders have within the structure. The activities of the company itself should however not be overlooked when determining whether it is a trading company even after the attribution of the activities of the JV company or partnership.

Condition B – s 169I(7)

[3.27] Where the company ceases to be a trading company condition A must be met throughout the period of one year immediately before the cessation. The cessation date must be within the three years ending with the date of disposal.

Conditions C and D – s 169I(7A) and (7B)

[3.28] For shares acquired under an EMI option the rules are relaxed. Where shares are acquired under an EMI option and are disposed of after 5 April 2013 the 12-month qualifying period for ER will start from the date the options were granted. Also, there is no requirement for the holder of the shares to meet the 5% holding test.

Planning point

In cases where a company is sold and the shareholders receive shares in another company (AN Ltd) there is always a concern for ER. If the vendor receives 5% of the shares in AN Ltd how can he guarantee that he will not be diluted in the future thereby losing ER? One solution is for AN Ltd to create a new class of shares ('A' ordinary shares) that carry the right to rank pari passu with the existing shares but have no right to

---

receive dividends and only have a right to receive proceeds on a winding up or on a sale of AN Ltd up to par value. These shares could then be used to ensure that the 5% test is met.

Planning point

Where shares are held jointly by a husband and wife each is treated as having a 50% interest in looking at the personal company test. For example, if together a married couple hold 8% of the shares they are treated as holding 4% each in determining whether the 5% test is met. In this case neither would meet the personal company test. It would be beneficial for the couple to change their beneficial interests so at least the 5% test would be met by one party. The new arrangements would need to be in place one year before the benefit of ER is available.

A more efficient alternative is for one spouse to hold all the shares especially with the £10 million ER limit.

Planning point

In a husband and wife situation where both meet the 5% test but only one works in the business you could consider transferring the shares to the working spouse. The transferee spouse does not have to wait one year to dispose of the shares as the conditions above were met in respect of his existing shares. This means that this type of planning can be carried out shortly before a sale. For the vendors it's the difference between 20% and 10% tax so it is always worth considering.

Qualifying business disposals by trustees

[3.29] A trust is not entitled to ER instead it relies on using the ER qualifying status of a beneficiary. ER is available on the disposal of trust assets where all the following conditions are satisfied:

(1)   the trustees dispose of settlement business assets. These are assets (or an interest in assets) which have been used for the purposes of a business or shares or securities in a company;

(2)   an individual is a qualifying beneficiary in the settlement. A qualifying beneficiary is one who has an interest in possession (but not for a fixed term) in the whole of the settlement or the part that contains the business assets which have been disposed.

(3)   If the business assets are shares or securities the personal company conditions must be met by reference to the qualifying beneficiary's holding of shares and that individual must be an officer or employee of the company (or a group company). These conditions must be met

throughout a period of one year ending within the three years prior to the disposal. For the 5% test the beneficiary must meet this in his own right irrespective of what shares the trust holds.

(4)   Where the assets disposed are assets used in a business these must have been used by the qualifying beneficiary in a business carried on throughout a period of one year ending not earlier than three years before the date of the disposal and the beneficiary ceases to carry on the business at that time or ending three years before.

Point (4) indicates that the timing provision for trustees is more flexible and may be applied for a wider time frame. HMRC's view regarding the matter is that trustees may not have the same scope to determine when they dispose of their business assets as individuals would.

[3.30] Any references to an individual carrying on a business include references to where the beneficiary is a member of a partnership and the references to ceasing in business include the beneficiary ceasing as a partner or the partnership ceasing to carry on in business.

When calculating the total ER available to the trustees and any qualifying beneficiaries the £10m limit on gains is effectively shared (ss 169N(3)(7) and 169O). Trusts do not have their own ER limit; they are effectively given some of the beneficiary's limit subject to the trustees and the beneficiary making a joint election.

Qualifying associated disposals

[3.31] An associated disposal is the disposal of an asset owned by an individual and used for the purposes of a business carried on by a partnership in which the individual is a partner or a company which is the individual's personal company. A sole trader cannot have an associated disposal. Again there are some conditions to be met which are covered in s 169K.

(A)   The individual must dispose of all or part of his interest in the assets of a partnership or of shares or securities in a company which qualifies as a material disposal of business assets.

(B)   The disposal must be made as part of a withdrawal process from the business.

(C)   The assets must have been used for the purposes of the partnership business or company business throughout the period of one year ending with the disposal of the business or the cessation of the business if earlier. For assets acquired and disposed of on or after 13 June 2016, the asset must have been held for three years.

A withdrawal from the business is not linked to the amount of work done or time spent working in the business which has been confirmed by HMRC in the Note. For instance, if the individual sold his shares and a property which the company used, for the purposes of its trade, this would constitute a withdrawal from the business. Further commentary and some examples can be found in HMRC's manuals at CG63995.

For there to be an 'associated disposal' there needs to be a 'relevant material disposal' of business assets at or around the same time as the asset disposal.

HMRC acknowledges in their manual at CG63995 that it is quite possible that there may be an interval between the 'material disposal' and the disposal of the asset that is the subject of the 'associated disposal'. In such cases they will accept that a disposal qualifies as an associated disposal if the asset is disposed of –

- within one year of the cessation of a business,
- within three years of the cessation of a business and the asset has not been leased or used for any other purpose at any time after the business ceased,
- where the business has not ceased, within three years of the material disposal provided the asset has not been used for any purpose other than that of the business.

The relevant material disposal can be a gift of shares. HMRC interprets 'withdrawal' as meaning a reduction in shareholding. There is no requirement for the individual disposing of the shares to reduce their time spent working in the business or to sever all links with it.

Prior to 18 March 2015 there was no minimum shareholding reduction. The general professional opinion was that a disposal of 5% to 10% was sufficient. FA 2015 amended TCGA 1992, s 169K so that ER is only available for an associated disposal where the relevant material disposal is 5% or more. In addition, a restriction applied where there was no 'meaningful withdrawal' from the business and 'partnership purchase' or 'share purchase' arrangements existed to potentially allow the claimant to retain the assets in the future. This effectively ruled out disposals of assets to family members, which was detrimental when undertaken as part of the family's succession planning. To a large degree, the 2015 changes have been reversed with the provisions in FA 2016 which are effective from 18 March 2015.

Finance Act 2016 introduced a new condition 'ZA1' in TCGA 1992, s 169, backdated to 18 March 2015, which removes the 5% test for individuals in partnership. This allows those who hold less than 5% but wish to carry out a phased retirement to claim ER on an associated disposal as long as they:

- are disposing of the whole of their interests;
- have held at least 5% interest throughout a continuous period of at least three years in the eight years ending with the date of disposal; and
- do not enter into any 'partnership purchase arrangements'.

For associated disposals linked to the sale of shares, the 5% test remains.

In order to prevent transfers of assets to maximise relief, condition D imposes a condition at s 169 whereby assets acquired after 16 June 2016, have to be held for a three-year period ending with the date of disposal to be eligible for the relief.

Example

Jake held 8% in the family partnership since 2009. He disposed of 4% to a family member in 2014; and disposed of the remaining 4% on retirement in December 2015 along with his share of the trading premises acquired and held personally since 2009, but used entirely for business throughout ownership, rent-free.

Jake claimed ER on the material disposal in 2014 and can claim ER on the disposal of the remaining 4% stake on retirement. Finance Act 2015 rules made it ineligible for Jake to claim ER on the associated disposal due to the 5% test however, as Jake had held a 5% interest for three years in the past eight the backdated rules introduced in FA 2016 allow Jake to claim in respect of the property sale even though this occurred before the changes were announced.

The FA 2015 restrictions in relation to partnership purchase and share purchase arrangements, which were aimed at transactions where there was no meaningful withdrawal from the business have also been removed by FA 2016, but only where the arrangements were made before the material and associated disposals and without regard to either of them. This will make it easier to undertake transfers of the business interests to family members where there was always an understanding that assets would be passed to next generation however, plans should be documented well in advance of the disposals to prevent these restrictions applying.

Planning point

Where an asset is sold after the cessation of the business there is no restriction on how the asset is used between the cessation of the business and the date of sale where this is within one year. However the asset must have been in use in the business right up to the date of cessation. This gives a window of opportunity to obtain some income on the property.

Difficulties in claiming ER for an associated disposal will arise where the asset is disposed of before the material disposal. Where however the timing of disposals is as a result of commercial problems encountered and there is a clearly recorded understanding that both an asset and material disposal were desired, a claim for relief may be accepted. In some situations an adjustment will be required. These are outlined at s 169P.

Issue	Adjustment required
Asset only used for the purpose of the business for only part of the time owned	Adjust for the period of non-business use
Only part of the asset used on the business	Adjust for the part not used in the business
Individual involved in carrying on the business for only part of the period (personally, as a partner or as an employee or officer)	Adjust for the period not involved in the business.
Where rent was paid for the use of the asset post 5 April 2008	If rent was at market value no ER available. If the rent was less than market value the following proportion gets ER:

$$\frac{\text{MV rent} - \text{rent paid}}{\text{MV rent}}$$

Claims for ER

[3.32] To obtain ER a claim must be made by the first anniversary of the 31 January following the tax year in which the disposal is made. So for a disposal in 2016/17, the taxpayer has until 31 January 2019 to make a claim. For trust disposals the claim must be made jointly by the trustees and the qualifying beneficiary.

For a remittance basis user or a temporary non-UK resident, it is advisable to make a protective ER claim if a taxpayer has made a qualifying gain and there is a possibility that the gain will be remitted to the UK or that the taxpayer will return to the UK within five years of leaving. If the taxpayer has not made a protective claim and the statutory deadline for an ER claim has passed the ER would be lost. The applicable ER limit is the one existing at the time the gain arises not when the gain is remitted to the UK.

In dealing with a claim for ER by a trust there is no specific method for the joint claim. A joint claim should accompany the trustees' tax return. However, if the tax return is filed online the claim will have to be sent to the trustees' tax office separately. HMRC's Help Sheet 275 on ER contains a template claim which can be used for claims made jointly by the trustees and the qualifying beneficiary.

Where a trust ends due to the death of a beneficiary and the beneficiary met the conditions for ER, the representatives of the beneficiary can apply for ER.

Calculation of the relief

Step 1

[3.33] Calculate the relevant gains. These are gains arising on a qualifying business disposal.

Step 2

Deduct any relevant losses. These are losses arising on a qualifying business disposal.

Step 3

The net figure arising from the above two steps is taxed at 10%.

Allowable losses and the annual exemption may be deducted from gains in such way as is most beneficial to that person (TCGA 1992, s 4B). This assists in maximising claims for ER.

In ICAEW's Note HMRC has commented on aggregation issues regarding the disposal of shares and business assets. HMRC's view is that there is no reason to apply aggregation to shares of one company that are disposed of in separate years, so the disposals will qualify as separate material disposals.

In the example in the Note where a taxpayer sold his business and disposed of all the assets except for one which was sold separately to a third party, HMRC has taken the view that the fact that one of the assets was sold to a third party is not sufficient to treat the disposals as separate. The taxpayer sold the business, so the disposals should be treated as part of one deal.

Over-Riding Limit

[3.34] There is a lifetime limit of £10 million.

ER — Exchange for shares or loan notes on a takeover

[3.35] Where there is a 'paper for paper' transaction there are specific rules for ER. If the shares being exchanged would have qualified for ER and any subsequent gain will not qualify as the personal company requirement will not be met, the taxpayer can make a claim that the share for share rules (TCGA 1992, s 127) do not apply. This means the gain comes into charge in the year of exchange with the benefit of ER. The time limit for making such a claim is twelve months from 31 January following the tax year in which the exchange occurs.

Where shares are exchanged for QCBs, it is not possible to defer gains and claim ER. Vendors have to choose between claiming ER and paying 10% in the year of sale or paying tax at 18% or 20%/28% when the gain comes back into charge (TCGA 1992, s 169R).

Furnished Holiday Lets (FHLs)

[3.36] The ER legislation specifically provides for these to qualify for ER. The conditions to be met to qualify for FHL are set out in ITTOIA 2005, s 325. The rules changed in April 2012 so now criteria as to what qualifies changed from April 2012 – the availability of accommodation for letting as holiday accommodation and the actual letting of holiday accommodation during the relevant period (ITTOIA 2005, s 324) was increased to 210 and 105 days, respectively.

From 2011/12 the losses are restricted to offset against the same trade.

Planning Point

For businesses operating FHL, the qualifying conditions for ER have to be satisfied in a one-year period prior to the disposal. There is no restriction in respect of non-qualifying periods as is required for associated disposals. Therefore, if a long-held investment property starts to be used on a holiday-let basis, for at least 12 months prior to disposal, a claim for ER can be made reducing the capital gain from a worse case 28% to 10%.

ER — Interaction with deferral reliefs

Enterprise Investment Scheme (EIS)

[3.37] EIS deferral relief enables an individual to reinvest gains arising on the disposal of assets into shares in a qualifying company. When the new EIS shares are sold the deferred gain comes back into charge. Prior to 3 December 2014 any ER that would have been available on the original gain was not available.

From 3 December 2014 gains eligible for ER, which are deferred into investments that qualify for EIS or Social Investment Tax Relief (SITR), will benefit from ER when the gain comes back into charge.

This means that ER will not be lost as a result of investing in shares that qualify for EIS or SITR.

Incorporation relief (TCGA 1992, s 162)

[3.38] When an individual transfers a business to a company in exchange for shares the gain arising on the disposal of assets is rolled into the base cost of the shares where certain conditions are met. This treatment is mandatory if the conditions in TCGA 1992, s 162 are met. The amount of the gain rolled into the base cost is the gain before ER. If an individual wants to claim ER on the incorporation of a business an election should be made under TCGA 1992, s 162A to disapply incorporation relief. This means that the assets are treated as being sold to the company at market value and the gain is calculated in the usual manner with ER applied as appropriate. In this regard the changes introduced in FA 2016 in respect of the disposal of goodwill need to be considered, to arrive at the net gain. The date for making the claim to disapply TCGA 1992, s 162 is the second anniversary of the 31 January next following the year of assessment in which the transfer of the business takes place.

Business Asset Gift relief (TCGA 1992, s 165)

[3.39] ER applies after any claim for holdover relief under TCGA 1992 s 165 or s 260. Given the difference in the time limit between making an ER (one year from the normal self assessment filing date) and gift relief (four years after the normal self assessment filing date) claim this may cause difficulties in practice with planning.

Roll-over relief (TCGA 1992, s 152)

[3.40] Where an individual disposes of certain qualifying assets and spends the consideration on replacement assets any gain arising on the disposal can be rolled into the base cost of the new assets. ER is only available on any gain remaining after the application of roll-over relief.

BPR

[3.41] For an owner-managed business, inheritance tax BPR is a most generous relief. It reduces the value for inheritance tax (on death or in relation to a lifetime transfer) of certain business assets by sometimes 50% but more usually 100%.

In describing how the relief applies, it is useful first to set out an overview of the principal rules.

First (contained in IHTA 1984, s 105(1)), there is a list of the *types* of business asset which *could* attract relief. If an individual owns an asset on that list, there is a *possibility*, subject to the following provisos, that it will attract relief. If an asset is not on the list, any claim for relief falls at the very first hurdle.

Further, it is the *type* of asset which then determines the rate of relief as either 50% or 100%.

Next, there is a requirement as to the *nature* of the business with *investment* businesses and certain other businesses being denied relief. There are special rules for groups of companies, the holding companies of which would otherwise be denied relief as *investment* businesses.

There are then a number of rules which, while not completely denying relief to a business, would operate to *restrict* the level of relief available.

There are positive requirements concerning requisite periods of ownership – usually two years but with a number of exemptions.

Finally, there are also negative requirements in that *binding contracts for sale* need to be avoided if relief is to be available. Likewise, *liquidations* and *winding-ups* can have the same effect.

Each of these elements is considered below.

Qualifying types — 50% relief

[3.42] 50% relief (IHTA 1984, s 104(1)(b)) is available in relation to 'any *land* or *building, machinery or plant* which, immediately before the transfer, was used wholly or mainly for the purposes of a business carried on by a company of which the transferor then had control or by a partnership of which he was then a partner' (IHTA 1984, s 105(1)(d)). This is covered in more detail in **CHAPTER 4**. There is also a related rule providing 50% relief to 'any *land* or *building, machinery* or *plant* which, immediately before the transfer, was used wholly or mainly for the purposes of a business carried on by the transferor and was settled property in which he was then beneficially entitled to an interest in possession' (IHTA 1984, s 105(1)(e)).

50% relief is also available in respect of 'shares in or securities of a company which are *quoted* and which . . . gave the transferor *control* of the company . . . ' (IHTA 1984, s 105(1)(cc). 'Quoted' in this context means listed on a recognised stock exchange (see further below). This category is, of course, of no relevance to the vast majority of owner-managed businesses.

Qualifying types — 100% relief

[3.43] BPR is available at 100% in relation to property consisting of a business or interest in a business which is to say the assets of a sole trader or the partnership interest of a partner. (In this respect see also **CHAPTER 15** and the commentary on the *Nelson Dance* case.)

100% relief is also available in relation to any unquoted shares in a company, where 'unquoted' means *not* listed on a recognised stock exchange and which therefore includes shares listed on the Alternative Investment Market (AIM) or the OFEX or Euro Nasdaq markets and, more importantly, private company shares. It is important to note that the relief applies to *all* unquoted shares, regardless of the size of the holding and regardless of the rights attaching to the shares.

Finally, 100% relief is also available to 'securities' in a company that contribute towards the holder's control of the company (this is discussed further in **CHAPTER 12** in relation to the incorporation of a business).

The required 'nature' of the business: 1 — the desire for gain

[3.44] To qualify for relief, the business carried on by the sole trader, partner or by the company *can be* a business carried on in the exercise of a profession or vocation, but it *cannot be* a business carried on *otherwise than for a gain*.

Thus, a business carried on only with the intention of attracting BPR but with no intention to make a commercial return would be denied relief. Likewise, the authors have advised in cases concerning businesses that have been run for many years at a loss – more as a 'hobby' rather than a commercial enterprise – and these too are unlikely to qualify.

These situations need to be contrasted with the case of a business which is carried on with a view to making a commercial return but which is struggling and which therefore has a history of loss-making. Such a business should nevertheless fall within the definition of a business carried on '*for* a gain', even if none is actually being made.

The required 'nature' of the business: 2 — prohibited businesses

[3.45] BPR is specifically denied in relation to businesses consisting *wholly or mainly* of one or more of the following:

- dealing in securities, stock or shares (subject to certain exemptions concerning 'market makers' and discount houses) (IHTA 1984, ss 105(4)(a) and 105(7));
- dealing in land or buildings; or
- making or holding investments (IHTA 1984, s 105(3)).

The Special Commissioners case of *Piercy (executors of, decd) v Revenue and Customs Comrs* [2008] SWTI 1647 contains a useful statement on the distinction between a land dealing company and a property development company in this context;

' . . . a company whose business it is to acquire land with a view to promoting a development, and then realising the developed land once sub-contracted building work has been completed, is also not a "land dealing company" . . . The only type of land dealing company whose shares fail to qualify for relief is thus some sort of dealing or speculative trader that does not actively develop or actually build on land . . . '

It is the third of the above exclusions which is the most fundamental and far-reaching because it denies relief to all 'wholly or mainly' *investment* businesses.

When considering the application of this rule in practice, two important questions arise:

(1)   What is meant by 'investment' in this context?

(2)   How is the 'wholly and mainly' test to be applied?

The required 'nature' of the business: 3 — the meaning of 'investment'

[3.46] In recent years, a number of cases (mainly before the Special Commissioners) have tested what is meant by an 'investment' business.

In *Cook (Inspector of Taxes) v Medway Housing Society Ltd* [1997] STC 90, – a case not directly connected with BPR – Lightman J defined 'investment' as 'the laying out of money in anticipation of a profitable capital or income return', and this broad definition has been applied in a number of these BPR cases.

The holding of a portfolio of stocks and shares or an interest-bearing bank account would, prima facie, constitute 'investment' activities. The key element that has, in addition, emerged from the cases is that *holding land or property in anticipation of a 'rental' income* of some sort is also invariably considered to be an 'investment' activity by the Commissioners or the Courts. The decision of the Northern Ireland Court of Appeal in *McCall (Philip Norman) and Keenan (Bernard Joseph) (personal representatives of McClean (Eileen), (dec'd)) v Revenue and Customs Comrs* [2009] NICA 12, [2009] STC 990 illustrates this very clearly.

Beyond those clear-cut limits, however, it has proved difficult for HMRC to establish that a particular activity should be considered one of 'investment'.

In the case of *IRC v George* [2003] EWHC 318 (Ch), [2003] STC 468, for example, the Court of Appeal ultimately rejected HMRC's argument that services provided (eg gas, water, electricity) ancillary to a business of renting caravans should also be considered as part of the 'investment' business.

In the case of *Phillips (executors of Phillips, decd) v Revenue and Customs Comrs* (SpC 555) [2006] STC (SCD) 639, a company whose balance sheet consisted almost entirely of loan creditors qualified for relief because the Special Commissioner did not consider that the making of loans in these circumstances constituted the making or holding of investments.

The following list provides a quick summary of the application of the BPR rules in relation to a number of land and property based businesses.

- A property *dealing* business is specifically denied relief.
- A property *letting* company would not qualify as a result of the 'investment' proviso.
- A property *development* company would qualify because development is not 'investment'.
- A company operating a hotel or B&B would usually qualify because although, in one sense, it is letting land, the income comes from the provision of a much wider array of services than simply provision of land in anticipation of a 'rent'.

The position in relation to 'furnished holiday lets' has been subject to a relatively recent change in HMRC practice. Earlier versions of HMRC manuals stated:

'The HMRC Solicitor has advised the office that in some instances the distinction between a business of furnished holiday lettings and say, a business running a hotel or a motel may be so minimal that the Courts would not regard such a business as one of "wholly or mainly holding investments" for the purposes of IHTA84/s105 (3).'

The latest version (at IHTM 25278) states:

In the past we have thought that business property relief would normally be available where:

- The lettings were short-term
- The owner – either himself or through an agent such as a relative was substantially involved with the holidaymaker(s) in terms of their activities on and from the premises.

Recent advice from Solicitor's Office has caused us to reconsider our approach and it may well be that some cases that might have previously qualified should not have done so, In particular, we will be looking more closely at the level and type of services, rather than who provided them.'

At this point in the fifth edition of this book we stated as follows:

'In the author's view, it is likely to be difficult going forward – bearing in mind the *Farmer* criteria mentioned below – to persuade HMRC that the level and type of service provided with a furnished holiday let is such as to make it a "mainly" trading rather than investment business. In particular, it is considered that significantly more services than would typically be provided to a holiday-maker in a furnished holiday let will be required.'

This has proved to be the case to the extent that HMRC has now taken a case. In *Mrs M V Pawson (Deceased) v HMRC* [UKUT 050 (TCC)], decided in the Upper tribunal on 28 January 2013 (and reversing the First-tier decision) the BPR claim was rejected in relation to a furnished holiday letting where only the most basic services were provided to the holiday makers.

In overturning the decision of the First-tier tribunal Mr Justice Henderson concluded that the 'standard nature' of the services were 'all aimed at maximising the income'. To be trading there would need to be a level of services that enhance the holiday experience rather than simply providing it ie akin to a hotel or bed and breakfast.

For a full discussion and facts of the *Pawson* case, see the authors' *Beside the seaside in Taxation*, 23 February 2012.

Pawson concerned a small scale furnished holiday letting of a single property but scale has been dismissed as a factor. In the case of *Anne Christine Curtis Green v Revenue and Customs Comrs (TC041559)* [2015] UKFTT 334 (TC) there were five units but it was held that 'scale is not a relevant factor: the number of units and the amount of income derived from a property does not change the statutory analysis'.

In the 2013 case of *Trustees of David Zetland Settlement v HMRC* [2013] UKFTT 284 (TC) decided on 1 May 2013, the First-tier Tribunal relied upon the decision in *Pawson* to deny BPR to another land based business – that of a serviced office. Although the facts of the case were somewhat specific, the decision again turned on the fact that the business was mainly one of providing land in return for a rent and the level of service provided was insufficient to 'trump' this.

In the case of *Best v HMRC* [2014] UKFTT 077 (TC) decided in the First-tier Tribunal on 13 January 2014, BPR has been denied in relation to a 'trading estate'.

One important concept that has developed in recent years is that it is the view of the 'intelligent businessman' that is important. In McCall, Girvan LJ said:

'The term "business of holding investments" is not a term of art . . . the test to be applied is that of an intelligent businessman who would be concerned with the use to which the asset was being put and the way it was being turned to account.'

That the correct test is the 'intelligent businessman' test was also confirmed in *George*.

Even in the case of *Zetland* (which was decided against the taxpayer) it was acknowledged that:

'The tribunal must not start with the fact that the business consists entirely of the ownership of land giving rise to investment activity. It must be mindful of the broad spectrum of businesses and the fine distinctions between different businesses. The better approach is for the tribunal to have an open mind and not to pre-judge the issue at the start.'

In the author's experience, HMRC does not give sufficient (if, indeed, any!) weight to the 'intelligent businessman' test and while the First-tier Tribunal members in *Best* did acknowledge it, even they made no attempt to apply it! As both *McCall* and *George* are Court of Appeal decisions, this is very clearly an error.

The 'wholly or mainly' test

[3.47] BPR will be denied if a business is 'wholly or mainly' one of investment. Thus, a business which carries on both investment and trading activities will qualify for relief if it is 'mainly' not investment. In most cases, of course, if a business is not investment, it is trading and – although there is no positive requirement that a business has to be 'trading' to qualify for BPR – for ease of reference in the examples and commentary which follows, 'trading' is used instead of the more clumsy 'not investment'.

Quantitatively, the test is clear; it means more than 50%. Thus, a business which is 51% trading will attract relief, and a business which is 51% investment will attract no relief.

Qualitatively, the test is less clear, as there is no statutory guidance. It is unsurprising, therefore, that the question of how to apply the 'wholly or mainly' test has also been at the heart of a number of the important cases.

In the past, HMRC sought to place great emphasis upon net profitability as being the determining yardstick, so that only those businesses which generated less than 50% of their net profit from investment activities qualified for relief. This approach led to a detailed analysis of the source and nature of the income but also, and this was not always easy to determine, against which income the expenditure should be deducted.

By contrast, the Special Commissioners' decision in *Farmer (Executors of Farmer dec'd) v IRC* [1999] STC (SCD) 321 consolidated what has become known as the 'in the round' approach. The facts were that the deceased, who died in 1997, left a 449-acre working farm that included many properties which were surplus to the requirements of the farm and which were let to third parties. The executors claimed BPR on the let properties on the basis that there was a single business. The Special Commissioner stated as follows:

> 'It is now time to stand back and to consider the business in the round. Of the five relevant factors . . .
>
> • the overall context of the business;
> • the capital employed;
> • the time spent by the employees;
> • the turnover; and
> • the profit
>
> . . . four, namely, the overall context of the business, the capital employed, the time spent by the employees and consultants and the levels of turnover, all support the conclusion that the business consisted mainly of farming; the profit figures, and more particularly the net profit figures, on the other hand, support the opposite view. Taking the whole business in the round, and without giving predominance to any one factor, the conclusion is that the business consisted mainly of farming and not of making or holding investments.'

When considering the BPR position of a business with a mixture of trading and investment activities, it is usually helpful to consider the five elements set out in this case, and if, in relation to two or more elements, the trading activities predominate, there is at least the chance that HMRC may be persuaded to the view that the business is not, 'in the round', mainly an investment business (with, of course, the more trading elements the better). For a recent decision where these principles were applied in practice in favour of the taxpayer see the decision in the Upper Tribunal in the case of *Brander (representative of James (dec'd), Fourth Earl of Balfour) v Revenue and Comrs* [2010] UKUT 300 (TCC), [2010] STC 2666, 80 TC 163.

It should be emphasised that if the 'wholly or mainly' test is passed, the *entire value* of the business will potentially attract 100% relief. In other words, there is no automatic disqualification of relief in relation to the investment element of the business. Relief can be restricted only by the separate rules described below, and, as will be seen, these do not *automatically* apply to investments.

Holding companies and group structures

[3.48] When considering the position of an individual holding shares in a company constituting part of a group, it is important to remember that *strictly* it is only the BPR position in relation to the company directly owned by the individual that needs to be considered.

Thus, if an individual owns shares in a company which is the holding company of a group, what has to be considered is whether that holding company qualifies for relief or not.

Of course, a pure holding company is itself an 'investment' company because it does little but hold shares in its subsidiaries (assuming that it carries on no trade itself). Were it not for the following special rule, all holding companies would be denied relief on the grounds set out above. IHTA 1984, s 105(4), provides that the requirement that the business had to be 'not investment' does not apply to:

- 'shares in or securities of a company if the business of the company consists wholly or mainly in being a holding company of one or more companies whose business does not fall within that [investment] definition.'

The concepts of a 'holding company', 'group' and 'subsidiary' have the same meanings as for other taxes (as described in **CHAPTER 5**), and it is particularly important to understand which companies strictly form part of a group in determining the BPR position, as the following examples demonstrate.

Example 1

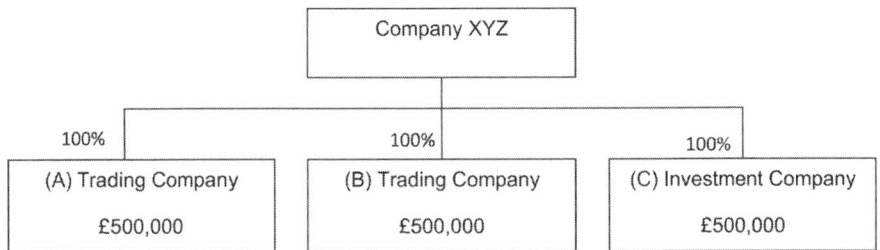

Here, all the companies are part of one group. Company XYZ is 'wholly' the holding company of group companies, and, to the extent that the value of the two trading subsidiaries exceeds that of the investment company, it is mainly a trading group. Thus, BPR should be available in relation to Company XYZ (but see below as to the restriction on the relief that would apply).

Example 2

If we assume the same structure as in Example 1 but with, this time, Company (B) as an investment company, Company XYZ would still be wholly the holding company of a group, but now the group would be mainly one of investment, so no relief would apply.

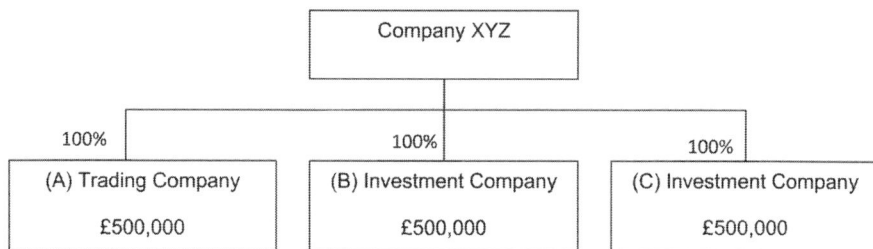

Company XYZ		
100%	100%	100%
(A) Trading Company	(B) Investment Company	(C) Investment Company
£500,000	£500,000	£500,000

Example 3

Finally, if we assume the same structure as in Example 1 but with, this time, the shareholdings in Companies (A) and (C) being 45% but worth exactly the same, only Company XYZ and Company (B) would (if we assume no unusual voting rights, etc) form a group. Thus, Company XYZ would then not be 'mainly' the holding company of a trading group; it would be 'mainly' a company holding investments (in Company (A) and Company (C)) and therefore, again (but for a slightly different reason), no relief would apply.

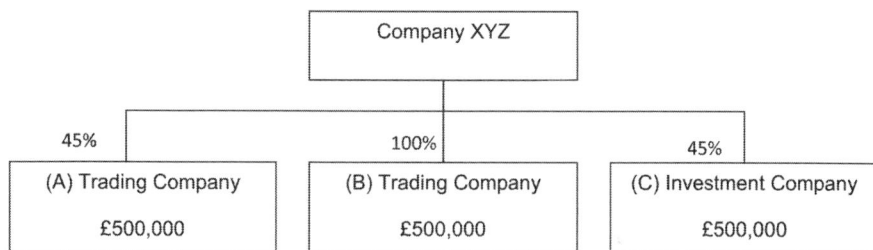

Company XYZ		
45%	100%	45%
(A) Trading Company	(B) Trading Company	(C) Investment Company
£500,000	£500,000	£500,000

There is no equivalent of IHTA 1984, s 105(4) where a general partnership or LLP holds interests in underlying trading companies. Likewise, a general partnership or LLP is not 'transparent' for IHT purposes. This has led HMRC - as noted in a joint technical release by ICAEW, CIOT and STEP (*Taxguide 1/14 (Tech 01/14 Tax)*) - to confirm that no BPR would be available in relation to a 'group' structure with a general partnership or LLP as the main holding entity (unless, of course, it was undertaking significant trade of its own). This view has been questioned by James Kessler and Oliver Marre in their article '*A Merry Dance*' which appeared in Taxation on 20 March 2014.

Restrictions on relief — 'excepted assets'

[3.49] Even if the requirements for BPR are met, an asset within a business or company will be denied BPR as an 'excepted asset' under IHTA 1984, s 112(2) if it is neither:

- used wholly or mainly for the purposes of the business during the previous two years or, if it has not been owned for two years, its entire period of ownership; nor
- required at the time of the transfer for the future use of the business.

The asset most commonly identified as an 'excepted asset' by HMRC is surplus cash within a business, and here there are parallels to the ER issues discussed above. HMRC will accept that every business requires a level of cash for day to day purposes – but the amount required will vary from business to business. In relation to any cash amounts held in excess of these requirements, HMRC will want to know for what 'future use' the cash is required.

In *Barclays Bank Trust Co Ltd v IRC* [1998] STC (SCD) 125, the executors failed in their argument that surplus cash within the business – which had in fact been used some seven years after the date of death to acquire an unrelated business – was *at the date of death* required for the future use of that business. It was held that whether an asset was so 'required' did not include the mere possibility that money might be required should an opportunity arise to make use of the money in the future, and that 'required implies some imperative that the money will fall to be used upon a given project or for some palpable business'.

In practice, HMRC will invariably refer to this case as authority for the denial of BPR where a company holds more than 'working cash' and where there are no definite future plans for the use of the excess. A close reading of the case is extremely helpful if faced with such a claim from HMRC as the facts were unusual and there may be good reasons to distinguish other cases from it.

In practice, as in relation to ER, it is imperative that evidence is always kept (ie in the form of board minutes, etc) as to why a business is holding cash not required for day-to-day business purposes.

An asset used wholly or mainly for the benefit of the owner of a business or of a person connected with him is deemed to be an excepted asset (s 112(6)) – for example, a property owned by the business but 'mainly' occupied by the owner as his home.

As mentioned above, the investment part of a mainly trading business is not per se treated as an excepted asset. An excepted asset cannot, by definition, be an asset used for the purposes of the business: however, the 'business' of a partly trading and partly investment business nevertheless includes an investment element. Thus, as the investment part is an element of the business, it cannot be an excepted asset.

It also needs to be remembered, however, that simply because a mainly trading company holds investments, this does not *necessarily* guarantee that those investments will attract relief. It always needs to be established that those investments constitute part of the 'business' of the company — ie by reference to the normal definition of what constitutes a 'business', discussed at **11.4** below.

Restrictions on relief — investment subsidiaries

[3.50] Where, within a group, there is a subsidiary company which is itself wholly or mainly carrying on an investment business, the *value* of that subsidiary is denied BPR (IHTA 1984, s 111). Thus, in Example 1 above, the value of Company (C) would not attract relief.

This rule is, however, subject to the caveat that if that investment subsidiary's main business is 'wholly or mainly' the holding of land for other group trading companies, its value will not be denied relief (IHTA 1984, s 111(b)).

Interestingly, this caveat appears – on a strict reading of the legislation – to apply only to subsidiary companies within a group and not to the holding company of a group. Thus, where a holding company owns a property which is let to one of its trading subsidiaries, that property could be considered as an investment of the holding company when identifying the holding company's main business. The counter argument would be that in these circumstances it would be wrong to think about the property as an 'investment' of the holding group – rather it is a property held to facilitate the trade in other parts of the group – and it is to be hoped, in any event, that HMRC would never seek to use such an anomaly to deny BPR to a bona fide trading group.

Planning point

If a trading group holds investments, if possible they should not be kept together in one subsidiary where the holding of those investments comprises that subsidiary's main activity. Instead, they should be distributed around the group and held in companies where the main activity is the undertaking of some non-investment activity. Provided the subsidiaries are not 'wholly or mainly' investment, then BPR should be available.

Planning point

It is the *value* of an investment subsidiary that is denied relief, and therefore any inter-group loans encumbering the subsidiary will reduce the amount of any restriction of relief.

Restrictions on relief — sole traders

[3.51] A similar but perhaps more fundamental issue arises in relation to sole traders in that it is only those assets 'used in the business' (IHTA 1984, s 110(b)) which can attract BPR.

An interesting example of how this issue applies in practice is the Special Commissioners case of *Ninth Marquis of Hertford (executors of Eighth Marquess of Hertford, dec'd) v IRC* (SpC 444) [2005] STC (SCD) 177. The Marquis' estate at Ragley Hall was run as a business, with 78% of the Hall itself open to the public and 22% reserved under a lease as private quarters. HMRC sought to argue that the living quarters constituted a separate asset which was not part of the business and which should therefore be denied relief. The taxpayer argued that the business asset was the entire Hall, which was not *mainly* put to personal use and that therefore BPR should be available in relation to it in full. After considerable head-scratching, the Special Commissioner sided with the taxpayer – principally on the basis that anyone coming to the estate would view the Hall as one asset – and relief was therefore available in full.

Similar conceptual issues concerning the identification of one or two businesses were discussed and found in favour of the taxpayer in the *Brander* case referred to above.

The order of events — using the limitations to advantage?

[3.52] The inheritance tax legislation does not state explicitly whether, when considering the availability of BPR, one should first undertake the 'wholly and mainly' test and then apply the restrictions only if the company is identified as mainly trading or whether the restrictions should be applied first with the 'wholly or mainly' test then carried out only in relation to the unrestricted assets. The difference between these approaches can be marked.

Take, for example, a company which is 40% trading, 30% investment and 30% excepted assets. At first blush, one might conclude that, as 60% of the company comprised investment or excepted assets, the 'wholly or mainly' test would be failed and therefore no relief at all should be available in relation to the company shares.

In fact, the position is a lot better than this. The 'wholly or mainly' test is used to identify the main business of the company. As explained above, an excepted asset cannot, by definition, be being used for the purposes of the business (ie it could not be an excepted asset if it were) and therefore, *before* applying the 'wholly or mainly' test, the excepted assets should be ignored.

When the 'wholly or mainly' test is then applied to the business, it is 40/70ths trading and 30/70ths investment. The business of the company is therefore mainly trading, so relief should be available in full (remembering that the investment part of a mixed but mainly trading business is not excluded from relief). The 30% which comprises excepted assets is denied relief, but a denial of relief in relation to 30% of the value is far better than no relief at all.

It is less clear that the same methodology can be applied when considering an investment subsidiary to which IHTA 1984, s 111 applies. This is because the legislation talks in terms of ignoring the *value* of the subsidiary. In the authors' view, it is arguable that the existence of an investment subsidiary should nevertheless be ignored when considering whether a holding company is 'mainly' the holding company of an investment group.

In relation to a sole trade, similar issues arise in determining which assets are comprised in the business. For example, trading premises with a let flat above it might be considered to be one business, which may or may not be mainly investment. Alternatively, it might be considered as two separate businesses, one of which is wholly trading and one of which is wholly investment.

If the trading element predominates, the taxpayer would be better to argue the former, as the investment element would then attract relief too. If circumstances are the other way around, it would be better to treat it as two businesses, so that at least the value of the trading would attract relief. The

Marquis of Hertford and *Brander* cases referred to above illustrate how difficult determining questions of this sort can be.

Planning point

Sometimes it is preferable from a BPR perspective to keep trading assets and investments together. Thus, in a business which is 60:40 trading and investment, the value of the investments will qualify for relief because they are part of a mainly trading business. Outside that business, of course, they would be fully chargeable to inheritance tax.

Alternatively, it is sometimes better to keep businesses apart. A company which is 40:60 trading and investment would get no relief as it is mainly investment, whereas in separate businesses at least the trading element would attract relief.

Often, in relation to mixed businesses like this – particularly where the investment element of the businesses grows relative to the trading elements – there comes a point where the business tips over the 50% barrier into being mainly investment.

In these circumstances, it may be sensible to suffer a tax charge on an extraction of some of the investments from the business, to restore the trading dominance. Alternatively, some form of reconstruction might be considered (see **CHAPTER 11**).

Minimum ownership period

[3.53] To qualify for relief, the owner must either have owned the business property throughout the previous two-year period (s 106) or be deemed to have satisfied that condition because of one of the following rules.

- Business property which has replaced other qualifying property can qualify for relief (IHTA 1984, s 107). This is explored more fully in **CHAPTER 12** in the context of the incorporation of a business.
- Those who inherit relevant business property from their spouse on death can add the deceased spouse's period of ownership to their own (IHTA 1984, s 108).
- Business property which was subject to an earlier transfer can qualify for relief if it, or the earlier transfer, is made on death (IHTA 1984, s 109). This is explored more fully in **CHAPTER 15** in connection with inter-spouse transfers of business assets prior to a death.
- In relation to unquoted shares, if new shares are identifiable with other previously owned shares for capital gains tax purposes – for example, in relation to a reorganisation – the period of ownership of the previously owned shares is included in relation to the new ones (IHTA 1984, s 107(4)).

It is important to note that the two-year requirement concerns only the *ownership* of the assets. In the authors' view, there is no specific requirement that the assets have to have qualified for relief during the entire two-year ownership period. As long as they have been owned for two years (or treated as such) and qualify for relief at the relevant time (ie death or the date of the gift), relief should be available.

Binding contracts for sale/liquidations

[3.54] If a binding contract to sell has been entered into in relation to business property, BPR will not be available pending sale. Thus, care needs to be taken if a lifetime gift of business assets is being contemplated around the time of a sale.

More importantly, however, if any shareholders or partnership agreement contains a clause *requiring* a deceased shareholder's shares or partner's partnership interest to be purchased by the surviving shareholders or partners, that will constitute a binding contract for sale as at the date of death, thus denying relief at precisely the moment it is required.

Planning point

The same problem does not arise if the surviving shareholders or partners have *options* to purchase or if the estate of the deceased has an *option* to sell.

Likewise, accruer provisions in partnership deeds will not constitute a binding sale contract.

Relief is also denied in relation to a company in the process of a winding-up or liquidation, with exceptions where this is carried out as part of a reconstruction or amalgamation (see further IHTA 1984, s 105(5)).

Liabilities incurred to acquire business property

[3.55] Finance Act 2013 introduced significant changes to the rules governing the deductibility of liabilities for inheritance tax purposes – including new rules in relation to liabilities incurred to finance property qualifying for BPR.

For deaths and chargeable transfers occurring on or after 17 July 2013, liabilities incurred *after* 6 April 2013 to finance the acquisition, maintenance or enhancement of property qualifying for BPR will first be deductible against such property.

Such loans were previously first deductible against property against which they were secured and the change blocks the common inheritance tax planning techniques of incurring debts secured on chargeable property to acquire BPR property, and of securing business loans on non-business assets.

Key points

[3.56]

Availability of relief	ER (capital gains tax)	BPR (inheritance tax)
Company's activities	The company must carry on trading activities, and the activities when taken together must not include substantial non-trading activities (a non-statutory business clearance application by a company permitted to determine whether the company is a qualifying trading company)	The company must not be wholly or mainly involved in dealing in securities, stocks or shares, or land or buildings, or making or holding investments
Measurement	80% test	51% test
Excepted assets	None. If the company qualifies, the relief applies to all assets	Excepted assets such as cash and assets used personally by the shareholders/directors must be excluded
Minimum holding requirement — unquoted company	The shareholder must have at least 5% of the ordinary shares and the entitlement to 5% of the votes by virtue of the shareholding and be an officer or employee of the company	No minimum holding requirement for an unquoted company
Minimum holding requirement — quoted company	The shareholder must have at least 5% of the ordinary shares and the entitlement to 5% of the votes by virtue of the shareholding and be an officer or employee of the company	The transferor must have control
	However where the individual has acquired the shares through the exercise of an EMI option there is no minimum holding requirement. In addition the ownership period starts on the date of the grant of the EMI options.	

Availability of relief	ER (capital gains tax)	BPR (inheritance tax)
Available in companies not meeting the activities test	No	No
Available to unincorporated businesses	Yes, where these are trading businesses and are carried on as a sole trader or in partnership	Yes, where these are an interest in a business which is not dealing in securities, stocks or shares, or land or buildings, or making or holding investments
Rates available	Gains of up to £10m — chargeable to CGT at 10%	100% on unincorporated businesses, unquoted shares and unquoted securities giving control
		50% on listed shares giving control, land and buildings or plant and machinery used by a company in which the transferor has control or a partnership in which he is a partner
Relief for assets used by unconnected businesses	No	No
Restrictions on trade	No	No, but not available for property dealing or share dealing
Look-back period during which the company must meet the activity test	One year leading up to the date of disposal	Minimum holding requirement of two years, but must meet the activities test at the date of the transfer

Chapter 4

Property and the Business

SDLT/LBTT and LTT

[4.1] Since April 2015, for transactions involving properties located within Scotland, and since April 2018 transactions involving properties located within Wales no longer fall within the scope of SDLT, although the ATED regime still applies. Instead these transactions fall within LBTT, as set out in Land and Building Transaction Tax (Scotland) Act 2013 and LTT, as set out in Land Transaction Tax and Anti-avoidance of Devolved Taxes (Wales) 2017. While much of the underlying principles of LBTT and LTT are derived from SDLT, there are a number of important differences. For the purposes of this chapter, the SDLT position is considered in more detail, however when dealing with a Scottish or Welsh property, it is important to obtain specific LBTT/LTT advice.

As part of the Finance Act 2016, there were some important SDLT changes made including increased rates of SDLT in respect of commercial property, applicable for all completion after 17 March 2016, and the introduction of an additional 3% rate for the acquisition of further residential properties. This latter change applies to all transactions completed after 1 April 2016 and have a number of detailed complex rules, which are beyond the scope of this book. However, as a general overview, a taxpayer will be liable to this additional higher rates of SDLT if they are a corporate or an individual who is purchasing a residential property for more than £40,000 and that for the individual this property does not represent the replacement of their main home.

Trading from home

[4.2] Many small businesses are carried on at the proprietor's home, with little or no modification to the premises or domestic arrangements. These businesses can usually claim capital allowances on expenditure on equipment used at the home, for example office equipment, storage shelves or other specialist equipment used in the business. Allowances can be claimed whether or not the business is carried on in an unincorporated form or through a company.

The owner can also claim a deduction as a sole trader for running expenses that are attributable to the business. The trader would have to show that the expenses are incurred wholly and exclusively for the purposes of his trade (Income Tax (Trading and Other Income) Act 2005, s 34 (ITTOIA 2005). BIM47820 gives some guidance on specific expenses that could be claimed for use of home, dividing expenditure into two categories; fixed costs and running costs. For fixed costs, such as insurance, mortgage interest, repairs, it will normally be appropriate to apportion these expenses by area and time if part of the home is set aside solely for business purposes. For running costs, the claim needs to be made by reference to the facts of that usage, although HMRC will usually accept modest claims.

The situation is slightly more complex for an owner managed company. The company can claim deductions for expenses paid to an employee, including the proprietor, which are wholly and exclusively for the benefit of its trade (CTA 2009, s 54). However, for the employee himself, to avoid a tax charge, the expense needs to be incurred wholly, exclusively and necessarily by him in the performance of his duties of employment (ITEPA 2003, 336). HMRC has recognised the importance of home working, and Tax Bulletin 79 and EIM 32760 sets out their position in this regard.

Where an individual sets aside part of his residence exclusively for business purposes, the principal private residence exemption from capital gains would be restricted by TCGA 1992, s 224, which says:

'If the gain accrues on the disposal of a dwelling-house or part of a dwelling-house part of which is used exclusively for the purpose of a trade or business, or of a profession or vocation, the gain shall be apportioned and section 223 shall apply in relation to the part of the gain apportioned to the part which is not exclusively used for those purposes.'

Where possible the business should be carried out in a part of the house that is also used for other domestic purposes, which should avoid the need to apportion the gain. Where part of the premises are used exclusively for the purposes of a trade carried on by the owner, any gain attributable to that use is likely to be subject to capital gains tax at 28% (or 18% when the gain does not bring total taxable income and gains above the basic income tax rate band). In some situations it may be possible to claim ER, for example if the property is sold when the trade ceases or is sold. However ER is restricted where rent has been paid by a company for use of home (TCGA 1992, s 169P).

Consideration will also need to be given to whether business rates apply. Broadly speaking, business rates will not apply where the room is not exclusively used for the business and it was not specifically built or adapted for use by the business.

Not all businesses remain sufficiently small to be run from the proprietor's home, although with modern communications it is feasible for sizeable businesses to operate without business premises. In addition, due to the planning permission required, there has been a rise in the development of specific live/work units, particularly in urban locations. There are also certain businesses, most notably farms or guest-houses, which are by their nature run from premises that form an extension to the proprietor's home. These will be considered later.

Since 6 April 2013, a new cash accounting scheme has been available for unincorporated smaller businesses with income less than £81,000 for fiscal year 2013/14 (or £162,000 if Universal Credits are being claimed). The scheme enables smaller businesses to opt to prepare accounts on the cash basis. These rules are independent of an 'opt in' to cash for VAT purposes.

As an alternative to claiming the allowable proportion of the actual expenses incurred (as described above) small businesses also have the option of either:

(a)   electing to use a standard deduction based on the amount of time spent working at home, where a home is used for business purposes. The rates are £10 for 25-50 hours a month, £18 for 51-100 hours a month, or £26 for 101 hours plus a month; or

(b)   making an adjustment based on the number of occupants using the premises as a home each month, where the premises are used as both a home and for business purposes. For 1 occupant the deduction is £350 a month, for 2 occupants it is £500 a month, and for 3 or more occupants £650 a month.

Taking on business premises

[4.3] The decision to take on business premises is driven by commercial considerations that are beyond the scope of this book, although tax issues should not be overlooked as part of that decision-making process.

Unless the acquisition of premises is part of a wider business or investment strategy, most businesses will, at least initially, rent premises. Whether the business is unincorporated or run through a company, the tax issues for rented premises are broadly the same, except where there is private use of part of the premises.

When acquiring premises, it is essential to consider whether capital allowances on fixtures are to be acquired with the building, particularly in light of the changes in April 2014. Where a property is acquired, part of the acquisition price will be in respect of fixtures within the building. Depending on the nature of these fixtures, capital allowances may be claimed either under the main pool or integral features pool. Since April 2014, the availability of the capital allowances that have previously been claimed by the vendor in respect of fixtures are conditional on (i) the seller having recognised the costs within his capital allowance pool and (ii) the value of the fixtures being formally agreed. Both of these conditions must be met within two years of the transfer. In determining the value of the fixtures transferred, there are two methods available; either applying to First Tier Tribunal unilaterally for a determination under the 'just and reasonable' apportionment method or under a joint election under CAA 2001 s 198 (s 199 for leasehold interests).

Planning point — Tax issues

In a number of situations, the contractual acquisition price is replaced by market value in determining the amount to be taken into account for both the vendor and purchaser in respect of capital allowances. Additionally, there may be subsequent disagreement between the vendor and purchaser when preparing their computations as to the value to use.

To fix the amount on which capital allowances are to be claimed, an election under CAA 2001, s 198 (or s 199 for leasehold interests) can be made. This should avoid disagreements between the parties and the need

---

to apply to the First Tier Tribunal for adjudication, which could lead to unexpected additional tax liabilities. See **CHAPTER 8** for further details on the form of the election. Although ss 198 and 199 elections can be made on both integral features and other fixtures, it should be noted that these elections do not extend to other forms of plant and machinery. As noted above any elections under ss 198 and 199 must now take into account the provisions of CAA 2001, s 187A, which was inserted by FA 2012. This means that an election under s 198 must be made within two years of the acquisition of the property, and must have been 'pooled' by the vendor.

Repairs

[4.4] One of the most frequent areas requiring consideration is whether the costs of repairs are allowable. In principle, repairs are allowable. However, where there is an improvement to an asset or the whole of the asset is replaced, then this is likely to be capital expenditure and not eligible for a revenue deduction.

HMRC accepts that repairs using the nearest modern equivalent are revenue expenses. For example, replacing single glazed windows with double glazing would not be disallowed as an improvement.

When acquiring second hand property, it is sometimes necessary to undertake repair work to those premises. Under normal circumstances, this type of work may be accepted as a revenue deduction, however where those premises could not be used in the state acquired or the cost of the property was reduced because of the repair, the associated costs may need to be treated as capital.

The timing of revenue deductions follows its accounting treatment. (ITTOIA 2005, s 25 and CTA 2009, s 46). In most cases such expenditure should be expensed as this provides an immediate deduction. If the expenditure is capitalised, the deduction will only be available as the asset is depreciated, thereby delaying any deduction.

Since April 2008, where expenditure of more than 50% of the initial cost to replace an integral feature is incurred over any twelve-month period, the expense is not eligible for an immediate tax deduction. A claim for capital allowances as an integral feature can however be made, giving an 8% annual deduction (CA 2001, s 33B). This effectively defers relief for the expenditure. The definition of integral features is provided in CA 2001, s 33A (see **CHAPTER 8**). It should be noted that the twelve-month period is not dependent on accounting periods but on actual dates on which actual expenditure is incurred.

> **Planning point**
>
> Subject to commercial considerations, it may be appropriate to delay or stagger expenditure on integral features over a period greater than 12 months.

Example

Brown Ltd has air conditioning which was originally installed into its headquarters in 2013. On 31 January 2016 the company paid £25,000 to repair the air conditioning. At the time, it would have cost £60,000 to replace the air conditioning.

In December 2016, the air conditioning needed to be repaired again for an additional £5,001. If this expenditure were incurred immediately, the full £30,001 would be disallowed as a revenue deduction. Delaying this repair until after January 2017 would enable revenue deductions to be made.

In the above example, it may be possible to delay the expenditure by a month, without having an impact on the business. If the initial expenditure was incurred in September 2015, and the system subsequently broke in July 2016, being summer, it may not be possible to delay its repair without impacting the business.

Renting premises

[4.5] Where premises are solely used for business purposes and a market rent is paid to an unconnected landlord, the rent paid will be deductible for income tax or corporation tax purposes.

Most leases for commercial properties tend to be tenant repairing leases. In general, repairs carried out by the tenant are deductible against profits. However, care should be exercised where the tenant has agreed to restore the premises so that they can be used, in which case the decision in *Jackson (Inspector of Taxes) v Laskers Home Furnishers Ltd* [1956] 3 All ER 891, may deny a deduction for those costs. If the tenant incurs costs fitting out the premises, full details of expenditure should be obtained, as, for tax purposes, the costs may include items that are either deductible as revenue items, capital costs to the building or items on which capital allowances could be claimed. As the deduction of revenue costs is based on the accounting treatment adopted by an enterprise, expensing these costs will accelerate their deduction, although this is subject to commercial considerations. In practice, only a small part of the costs is likely to be revenue expenditure. It is vital, therefore, to identify what items can be included in a claim for capital allowances (see **8.4** below).

Where a premium is paid by a trader under the terms of the lease, not exceeding 50 years, the revenue deduction in respect of this premium is determined by what amounts are treated as income for the landlord and this expenditure is spread over the term of the lease and not in line with cash flow (see ITTOIA 2005, s 277 and CTA 2009, s 217 for details). The balance is treated as a capital cost and may be deductible in determining the capital gain on a future disposal of the lease. As a short lease is a wasting asset, the amount to be brought into account on disposal will reduce over the tenant's ownership period (see TCGA 1992, s 240).

Where the trader is provided with a rent-free period the tax impact of this will follow accounting treatment. Under 'old' UK GAAP (broadly applicable to accounting periods commencing prior to 1 January 2016) this is usually spread until the first rent review or break clause. However the introduction of new UK GAAP, which uses IFRS principles, means this is likely to extend the period over which the rent-free is spread to the length of the lease. Under either accounting basis, it should allow for a tax deduction to be obtained in respect of rent before the rental is paid.

Care should be taken in respect of the form of any rental guarantees that are provided as part of the lease negotiations and who provides such guarantees, although it is acknowledged that this is often difficult commercially to vary. In *Howden Joinery Group v HMRC* [2014] TC03396, the First Tier Tribunal found that payments made by a parent company in respect of a trading subsidiary's rental guarantee were not allowable as management expenses. However, the costs incurred by the parent company in mitigating its obligations under the guarantees were allowable as management expenses.

If the tenant incurs legal expenses in connection with a new lease, they will not be deductible against profits, as they are considered to be a capital cost.

Legal expenses incurred to renew a lease for more than one year are likely to be capital. However HMRC accepts that these may be allowed on de minimis grounds. Revenue Officers are instructed to contend that expenditure on new leases is of a capital nature where the lease is for more than 50 years or where there are provisions in the lease for the payment of a premium to extend the lease (BIM46420).

Dilapidation expenses are allowable if they are in connection with repairs that a tenant is obliged to carry out during the term of his lease. This tax deduction is available in line with the accounting treatment and therefore appropriate provisions will accelerate the tax deduction (*Jenners Princes Street Edinburgh v IRC Commrs* [1998] STC (SCD) 196.

A dilapidation charge payable by the tenant on the termination of the lease will be deductible if it is in respect of revenue expenditure. However where it relates to capital expenditure (for example, the costs in connection with the demolition of a structure installed by the tenant), no deduction will be available.

A payment made by the tenant to the landlord for early termination of the lease is unlikely to be deductible. This would be a capital payment incurred by the tenant to remove an onerous obligation, and, in tax terms, would be a 'nothing'. It may therefore be preferable in such circumstances for the tenant to look at maximising payments made under any dilapidation provisions or look at sub-letting out the property.

If the landlord makes a payment to the tenant to vacate the premises before the end of the lease, in most situations the receipt would be treated as a capital gains transaction, usually with no base cost. An individual may be able to argue that ER should apply to the transaction, although in order to do so he would have to identify the asset being sold and demonstrate that that asset was used for the purposes of a trade and sold when the business ceases or is sold.

In certain circumstances, it could be argued that the compensation is statutory compensation under the Landlord and Tenant Act 1954, in which case it could be free of tax for the recipient. The recipient would have to demonstrate that the amount received was by virtue of the Act and nothing else. This issue was considered in the cases of *Davis v Powell* (1738) Cooke Pr Cas 146, 7 Mod Rep 249 and *Drummond (Inspector of Taxes) v Austin Brown* [1983] STC 506, 58 TC 67 in the context of agricultural holdings.

Buying premises

[4.6] From a wider commercial perspective, it may be preferable to buy rather than rent premises. There is an expectation of capital growth, and the property could be used in the future to provide collateral for borrowings. It may make sense economically and give greater flexibility in terms of use for the property. Often the purchase is dictated by the source of funds or the equity and conditions imposed by the lender financing the purchase.

Interest payable on personal loans to finance the acquisition of business premises is generally allowable in calculating taxable profits. However, since 6 April 2013 a cap has been introduced in relation to this relief. The cap is the greater of £50,000 or 25% of an individual's income. Income for the purposes of the cap will be net of pension contributions, but gross of any charitable donations. The effect of the cap is as follows.

2012/13	Personal loan (£)	Company loan (£)
PBIT	100,000	100,000
Interest costs	0	–60,000
Profit	100,000	40,000
Personal deductions	–60,000	0
	40,000	40,000
2013/14		
PBIT	100,000	100,000
Interest costs	0	–60,000
Company Profit	100,000	40,000
Personal deductions	–50,000	0
	50,000	40,000

Where an individual partner or director borrows money to acquire a business premises, which is then occupied by the partnership or company rent free and the partnership or company pays the interest on the loan taken out by the individual partners or directors, it should be possible to claim a deduction for the interest costs within the trading entity. Restrictions to this deduction would arise in the event that the interest rate was deemed excessive or if the property was only partly used for that business. The individual partners/directors would be treated as receiving rental income payable by the company which is then fully covered by the external interest payable, resulting in no property income.

Who should buy the premises?

[4.7] When the trade is being carried on by a company, the basic question is always 'who should buy the property?' Often the property is used to secure bank finance. Where the property is held by the company, the company may use it as security to obtain finance. Interest payments in relation to such finance will generally be available when calculating taxable profits. Where an individual buys the property, he may use it as security to take a personal loan, which he can then lend to the company. As mentioned above, a cap on income tax relief has been introduced, effective from 6 April 2013, whereby the interest relief in this scenario may be capped at £50,000 (or 25% of his income if greater). It may therefore be preferable for the company to take out the loan, albeit personal guarantees may be required. Alternatively, the company may hold the property in order to secure bank finance.

ER is available in certain circumstances, but not if the proprietors intend keeping the property after the company carrying on the trade has been sold. ER will be restricted on a 'just and reasonable basis' if the company pays rent for the use of the property.

Where the intention is to sell the premises with the trade, by holding the premises in the company, ER should be available on a disposal of the shares, the value of which would include the property.

For IHT purposes, where the property is owned by a company, full BPR should be available on the property when calculating any IHT exposure on the shares. Where the property is owned by the proprietor and let to the company, BPR is restricted to 50%.

Despite the interest relief, ER and BPR advantages of holding a property through a company, there are a number of reasons why it may be preferable to keep the property outside the company.

(1)   Rent can be paid to the proprietor/landlord. Assuming that the rent is no greater than a commercial rent for the property, the company should be able to claim a deduction for the rent paid. If the rent charged is greater than a commercial rent, the excess could be treated as a dividend (in which case no deduction would be due) or as remuneration (in which case, the excess should be subject to PAYE and NIC). The payment of a market rent is a convenient and acceptable way of extracting profit from the company without incurring an NIC liability. The recipient would pay income tax on net rentals from the company. It should be noted that where rent is paid to a proprietor, this will restrict the availability of ER. However from a commercial viewpoint, he may require this rent in order to fund his interest obligations.

(2) There is much greater flexibility when the business is sold or wound up on cessation. The property can be retained as an investment or sold to the purchaser. The purchaser can buy either the company or the business, and in the latter case the company can be wound up without the need to disturb the property, thereby avoiding two potential tax charges, firstly on the uplift in the property value and secondly on the distribution of the property.

(3) The property can be retained as an investment if the company needs to change premises, without turning the company into a hybrid trading/ investment vehicle, which could detract from its trading focus or create potential conflicts if shares or share options are issued to employees. ER for the shares could be jeopardised if the company ceases to be a trading company.

(4) The property is separated from the company's trading activities and protected in an insolvent liquidation of the company. This protection could be afforded by the creation of a group, with a separate property-holding company, but independent ownership may be seen as cleaner.

(5) If the property is sold for a large gain, perhaps because it is sold to a developer, the proceeds are locked in the company. If the proprietors wished to use the proceeds personally, the funds would have to be extracted from the company, either in the form of dividends or remuneration. In either case, income tax would be payable by the recipients in addition to the tax on the disposal of the property (albeit the company should be able to obtain a deduction for any remuneration payment).

The main reason premises are bought by the company is that the company has the funds to provide equity in the purchase and banks prefer to lend to companies because of the quality of the security. Additionally, although companies are chargeable to corporation tax at 19%, which may be higher than the rate suffered by individuals on their capital gains (depending on whether entrepreneurs' relief is available or whether the individuals are basic or higher rate taxpayers), companies historically enjoyed the benefit of indexation allowances, which over a period of time was valuable. Since January 2018, however, companies are no longer able to claim indexation allowance.

With a 45% rate of income tax, the tax implications of holding property directly may need to be reassessed. Proprietors will still need to consider whether their ongoing income tax liabilities outweigh the benefit of a relatively low capital gains rate of 10%/20% (if commercial property)/28% (if residential property).

VAT aspects of property and the business

[4.8] Businesses which lease or purchase commercial property for use in their business may be charged VAT on the supply according to whether the landlord or vendor has opted to tax or the building being purchased is a new building. Having confirmed that VAT is chargeable, checking any option to tax that may have been exercised, the business should consider whether the VAT can be attributed to the making of taxable supplies and reclaimed.

Fully taxable businesses will be entitled to reclaim any VAT charged in the appropriate VAT return period. If the business is partially exempt or makes non-business supplies, the VAT incurred may need to be apportioned and the appropriate amount claimed using a suitable partial exemption or non-business recovery method.

Where the property acquisition is £250,000 exclusive of VAT or more, the building is subject to the VAT capital goods scheme and adjustment to the VAT claimed may be required over the 10-year adjustment period. If the acquiring business remains fully taxable throughout the adjustment period no VAT adjustments are required. Where exempt or non-business supplies are made, adjustments to VAT claimed may be required over the 10-year capital goods scheme adjustment period. See Notice 706/2.

Sub-leasing part of their property is often considered by businesses which have too much space or wish to share their property with another business. Due consideration to the VAT on the lease should be made together with opting to tax in the appropriate circumstances to protect input tax recovery, as any rental income is generally exempt for VAT purposes subject to the option to tax. See Notice 742A.

Where a business is transferred as a going concern, any property or land forming part of the transfer must be considered. The vendor and purchaser may need to take steps to enable the property/land to be considered as part of the transfer of a business as a going concern and outside the scope of VAT. See Notice 700/9.

Extracting a property from a company

[4.9] This may not be an issue of immediate concern, but as the company develops and aspirations change, ownership by the company may become problematic for one or more of the reasons outlined above. The proprietors may then seek a way of extracting the property from the company and minimise its tax exposure.

For capital gains purposes, because the parties to the transaction are likely to be connected, the transaction will be treated as having taken place at market value regardless of the agreed consideration.

If the consideration payable on a transfer of property from the company is less than market value, the difference will be treated either as a distribution from the company or as a benefit in kind. This will give rise to an income tax charge on the acquirer of the property.

If the proprietor acquires property from the company but the consideration is left outstanding on loan account, the company will have a liability under Corporation Tax Act 2010, s 455 (CTA 2010) unless the balance is paid within nine months of the company's year end. Since 20 March 2013, additional measures have been enacted to counter arrangements under which close companies seek to avoid CTA 2010, s 455 charge. Therefore, care needs to be taken so as not to fall foul of the new 30 day rule to prevent companies arranging for loans to be repaid shortly before the 9 months expire and then make a new loan shortly afterwards. See paragraph **6.12** for detailed analysis of these new rules relating to loans to participators. Furthermore, the individual will have an income tax liability as a benefit in kind unless interest is paid to the company at a rate at least equal to the official rate of interest.

SDLT for properties based in England, Wales and Northern Ireland and LBTT for properties based in Scotland (applicable since April 2015) and LTT for properties based in Wales (applicable since April 2018) is payable on the acquisition of the property, unless the property is transferred by way of distribution in specie from the company, for which the recipient provides no consideration, for example does not take on any indebtedness in relation to the property.

Distribution in specie

[**4.10**] A distribution in specie may be an appropriate way to transfer a property from a company to the proprietor, as the purchaser does not have to raise funds to fund the acquisition. For example, assuming the taxpayer is paying tax at the additional rate:

	£
Market value of property	650,000
Cost	(200,000)
Indexation	(30,000)
Gain chargeable on company	420,000
Corporation tax at 19%	79,800
Distribution to shareholder	650,000
Tax at dividend additional rate 38.1%	247,650
Net cost to the individual and company (84,000 + 247,650)	327,450

Purchasing the property from the company

[**4.11**] Alternatively, the individual could purchase the property from the company, but this would require either raising a loan, which would have to be repaid out of (probably taxed) money. If the company were to pay a bonus to the individual to fund the purchase, the situation would be as follows, assuming the individual is an additional rate tax payer:

	£
Market value	650,000
SDLT at commercial rates	22,000
Net bonus required	672,000
Gross bonus	1,267,925

	£
Tax and employees NIC	(595,925)

Tax cost to company

Gross bonus	1,267,925
Employers NIC at 13.8%	174,974
Corporation tax relief at 19%	(274,151)
	1,154,319
Corporation tax on gain at 19%	79,800
Less proceeds for property	(650,000)
Net tax cost to the company	570,200

The total net tax cost to the company would therefore be £570,200, as compared to a total tax cost for the company and the proprietor of £327,450 for a distribution in specie.

Split expenditure

[4.12] A situation that commonly arises is where the premises are owned by the proprietor but significant building work has been carried out by the company that occupies the property, and the build costs have been debited to the balance sheet as leasehold improvements. The reason for doing this is usually that the company has the funds available, but if these funds are distributed to the proprietor, an income tax liability would arise.

The potential disadvantage arises when the property is sold, because it is usually not possible to include these costs in the company's balance sheet as part of the cost of the building for capital gains purposes. The company cannot get relief for these costs because it is not making a disposal for capital gains purposes. Under land law, it is likely that the building belongs to the freeholder, with no right of compensation for the leaseholder.

For example, assuming the build costs for a new extension were £100,000, the costs net of tax would be as follows. If the company incurs the cost, it would not obtain a deduction for corporation tax purposes as the expense is on capital account. On disposal of the property by the proprietor, the £100,000 would not form part of the base cost. As a result the proprietor's capital gains tax liability will be £20,000 greater for higher rate tax payers (or £10,000 if ER can be claimed on the disposal). However, as the company has incurred expenditure on an asset owned by the proprietor, who is a director and shareholder in the company, has the company provided a benefit in kind on which income tax and NIC is payable? This would not appear to be in point, as the expenditure is shown as an asset of the company on its balance sheet, but does this show a true and fair view of the company's results? The position that has been created is somewhat ambiguous.

Providing funds to the proprietor for build costs

[4.13] If the company provides funds to the proprietor to enable him to incur the build costs himself, the company has a choice between a dividend and remuneration. The former provides no deduction for the company and an effective 32.5% income tax liability for a 40% taxpayer (38.1% for a 45% taxpayer. A bonus should be deductible for the company but would entail employer's and employees' NIC to be paid as well as income tax under PAYE. It would be practicable to pay a dividend only if the shares are not held by a number of shareholders and the company has distributable reserves.

Although a deduction can be claimed for revenue expenses incurred by a proprietor, it is likely that build costs will be capital in nature. A deduction will therefore be deferred until the premises are sold if the work undertaken is still reflected in the state or nature of the property on disposal (TCGA 1992, s 38). Where it is no longer reflected in the property, no deduction will be available.

Roll-over relief

[4.14] Rollover relief enables both individuals and companies to defer the tax on the disposal of a business asset by 'rolling it over' into replacement business assets, in TCGA 1992, Pt V, Ch I.

This relief is available in full where the whole of the consideration from the disposal of 'old assets' used only for the purposes of a trade throughout the period of ownership is reinvested into 'new assets' that are brought into use for the purposes of the trade. Relief is scaled down if not all the consideration is reinvested or if the old asset has not been used only for trading purposes.

The relief is available for certain specified classes of asset set out in TCGA 1992, s 155, the main type of which is land and buildings.

A more limited form of the relief is available to defer gains where the new asset has a life of less than 60 years.

Property no longer used for the trade

[4.15] A situation that is quite common is where a trading company has bought premises but those premises have fallen out of use by the company, perhaps because the trade has grown too large or the premises are no longer suitable for the trade. The company decides to keep the premises rather than sell them and rents them out to a third party. Whenever this happens, the ER and BPR position for the shareholders must be considered, as well as any potential issues that might arise if the shareholders decide to sell the company. In hindsight, it often seems that it would have been better to get the property out of the company earlier, and often this does not happen because of the tax cost of doing so. We consider elsewhere reconstructions, as this is how the situation is often dealt with, but simpler options, such as selling the property at market value to the proprietors, should not be overlooked, notwithstanding the likely stamp duty land tax and corporation tax liabilities.

Planning point

If a proprietor is thinking of selling his company, but the disposal will not qualify for ER because the company holds an investment property of significant value, he may wish to distribute the property out of the company 12 months before the sale. If the company is a trading company for 12 months prior to the sale, the disposal may qualify for the 10% ER rate. If an individual has a property that was used for the purposes of a trade carried on by him or his company, but is retained after the trade ceases or is sold, entrepreneurs' relief will not be available when the property is sold. The gain will, therefore, be taxed at a rate of 20% for a higher rate taxpayer (assuming a commercial property).

Alternatively, the company may decide that rather than renting the surplus space out, it will convert the existing commercial building into residential dwellings, for example under the PD Rights planning provisions, which can then be sold off. As well as having potentially a significant impact on the VAT status and the recoverability of the associated VAT costs, the change of intention in respect of the property will result in an appropriation of the property from fixed assets to stock at market value, resulting in a capital gains disposal. Provided that an election under TCGA 1992, s 161(3) is made within two years of this appropriation, it is possible to roll this gain into the carrying value of the stock and defer the gain until the disposal of the property. See **CHAPTER 5** for further detailed analysis.

Planning point

If a proprietor is thinking of selling his company but not the (personally held) trading premises, he may consider gifting the premises to his adult children at the same time as the sale of shares. The children will acquire the property at an uplifted base cost. The gift should not suffer any SDLT (or LBTT/LTT) provided there is no mortgage on the property. The proprietor will pay CGT on the deemed gain at 10% if he qualifies for ER.

Inheritance tax

[4.16] For inheritance tax, the extent of BPR available (if any) will depend upon whether a property is held 'inside' or 'outside' the business.

100% relief

[4.17] Assuming that (for the sake of illustration) we are using the example of a business which is 'wholly' trading, that business could be carried on in one of the following three forms and qualify for 100% BPR:

- sole trader;
- partnership; or
- unquoted company.

In each case, if the premises from which the business trades are included:

- as an asset of the business of the sole trader;
- as a partnership asset; or
- on the balance sheet of the company,

then the value of those premises will qualify for 100% relief.

50% relief

[4.18] In the case of partnerships and unquoted companies, property held outside the business can qualify for *at most* 50% relief (IHTA 1984, ss 104(1)(b), 105(1)(d)).

In the case of a partnership, for 50% relief to be available, it is sufficient for an individual to own property which is 'used wholly or mainly' for the purposes of a business carried on by a partnership of which he is a partner.

In the case of an individual owning property outside an unquoted company, 50% relief is available only if the property is used wholly or mainly for the purposes of a business carried on by a company *of which he has 'control'* (defined by IHTA 1984, s 269 but carrying its normal meaning — and see further below).

In both cases, of course, it is a requirement that the underlying business must be one which itself qualifies for BPR.

Finally, it should be noted that there is no rule providing 50% relief for premises held outside the business of a sole proprietor. Such a rule would be nonsensical. For a sole trader, either a property is used in the business – in which case it is an asset of his business, qualifying for 100% relief – or it is not used for his business at all, in which case no relief should be available.

It is also worth noting that in a joint technical release by ICAEW, CIOT and STEP (Taxguide 1/14(Tech 01/14 Tax), HMRC has confirmed that where a property is held in a LLP owned by individuals and the property is used by a trading company controlled by some or all of those same individuals, BPR is nevertheless not available as it is necessary to look at the business of the LLP in isolation for IHT purposes. This is on the basis that the LLP is not 'transparent' for IHT purposes (see **3.41**).

Further points

[4.19] When considering whether an individual has control of a company, as well as counting the votes he himself owns, one would also count the votes:

- exercisable by the trustees of a settlement in which he has a qualifying interest in possession (IHTA 1984, s 269(3)); and/or
- owned by his spouse or civil partner (which would be 'related property' for inheritance tax purposes) (IHTA 1984, ss 161, 269(2)).

For example, if a husband and wife jointly own a property in equal shares and that property is occupied by a trading company which they also jointly own, one might be tempted to conclude that, as neither husband nor wife controls the company (each only controlling 50% of the votes), neither would be entitled to relief in relation to their share of the property. In fact, because the shares owned by the other are, in each case, related property for inheritance tax purposes, *both* are deemed to control 100% of the votes, and therefore both are deemed to have control. Each would therefore be entitled to 50% relief on his or her share of the property.

Of course, were the couple to divorce, the shares would cease to be related property and both would lose their 50% relief.

Planning point — tax issues

As described above, there are important tax and commercial reasons why an individual might *not* wish to hold land within a company:

- the lack of ER on the sale of shares in a company if the property is not used in the trade;
- the 'double' tax charge if, following a sale of the property, the shareholder wants to use the proceeds personally;
- the commercial advantage in separating the property from the risks associated with possible precarious trading activities and liability to creditors, etc.

Thus, other than in the case of very elderly owner-managers – where inheritance tax is of more immediate concern – it is unlikely that anyone would choose to hold a property within a company simply to attract 100% rather than 50% BPR.

By contrast, however, there are fewer down sides associated with holding land within a partnership as opposed to holding it personally. Particularly, the capital gains tax and income tax treatments are broadly equivalent. Thus, from a tax perspective at least, it often makes more sense to hold property as an asset of a partnership (rather than holding it personally) because the inheritance tax treatment is so much better.

This would be the case particularly where the owners of the property were identical with the owners of the business – eg an equal partnership between husband and wife.

Where the ownership of the business and the property is not identical – eg where one partner had purchased the property using his own funds and did not wish to 'share' ownership with his partners – there might be a more logical reason to keep the property out of the partnership.

Even in these circumstances, however, given the possibility of setting out in a partnership agreement preferential rights in relation to the property for the original owner (which would not necessarily undermine the property's status as an asset of the partnership), the possibility of holding the property within the partnership should not be ignored.

Planning point

One of the practical difficulties that frequently arises in relation to partnerships is identifying whether a particular property is *already* within or without the partnership. In other words, identifying whether a particular property is or is not *partnership property*.

The main practical difference between holding land inside and outside a partnership concerns the succession of the land on the death of the owner. If land is held outside a partnership, it passes under the terms of the owner's will in the normal way. If land is held as a partnership asset, what the owner owns is an interest in the partnership which passes under the terms of his or her will. Such a partnership interest includes rights in relation to the land but does not imply (necessarily) direct ownership of the land itself. Given the potentially significant advantage of obtaining 100% relief as opposed to 50% relief in relation to a plot of land used by a partnership, it is more frequently worth considering whether steps should be taken to transfer land into a partnership or, more commonly, properly document that land is already held within a partnership.

The rules concerning when land is or is not a partnership asset are somewhat involved, but it is sufficient to say here that if it is the intention of the parties who own the land that it should be a partnership asset, then that can suffice, and the key issue then, of course, is to ensure that intention is documented.

To avoid any uncertainty in this area and the risk of a possible argument with HMRC as to which rate of relief should apply, it is the authors' view that it is *always* sensible for the partners to draw up a partnership agreement which – if it does nothing else – confirms the identity of the partnership assets.

In the case of a company – given the duty to prepare statutory accounts – there is unlikely to be the same level of uncertainty. A property will either be shown on the balance sheet or it will not.

Even in the case of a company, however, care is needed. The authors have come across many cases where businesses have been incorporated, with accounts drawn up for the new company including a balance sheet showing trading premises as being comprised within that company. However, on more detailed inspection, it has been found that no *legal* property transfers (either by transfer of legal title or by declaration of trust) have taken place, and that the 'incorporation' was simply a paper accounting exercise. It is essential that care is taken to complete the legal formalities on an incorporation as well as the accounting ones and the case of *Colley and Hillberg v Clements (Inspector of Taxes)* [2005] STC (SCD) 633 is an example of how an incorporation can 'go wrong' if insufficient care is taken.

Finally, in relation to Scottish partnerships, individuals will need to consider the potential differences in Scottish succession law – particularly the 'forced heirship' rules – applying to land owned personally and land wrapped up in an 'interest in a partnership'.

Property Businesses

[4.20] The way that property businesses, whether these are trading businesses or investment businesses is increasingly subject to a separate tax legislation and requirements.

Fundamental to the tax profile of property businesses is whether that business is an investment business where the properties are held for long-term rental yield and capital appreciation or whether the business amounts to a trade for tax purposes, for instance property development or property trading company. Determining the nature of the business is critical in order to calculate the timing of profits, whether the return/gain is subject to income or capital taxes as well as the potential availability of reliefs such as ER.

Successive Budgets have over the last few years have sought to change the tax treatment of both types of businesses in particular the following changes have applied:

- The advent of the ATED regime, since FA 2013. Whilst reliefs should be available for property businesses from the impact of this regime, these reliefs have to be claimed and the threshold for a residential property to potentially fall within its scope is now a market value of £500,000.
- The introduction of the higher rates of SDLT on the purchase of additional residential properties.
- A higher rate of capital gains tax on the sale of residential properties. Whilst the main rate of capital gains tax was reduced for fiscal year 2016/17 to 10%/20% for basic and higher rate tax payer. An 8% surcharge was retained in respect of disposals of residential property and carried interests.
- The introduction of tax restrictions on the level of interest deduction available against their rental business (see **4.23** for further details).
- The introduction of a Property Income allowance for up to £1,000 income from April 2017.
- The withdrawal of the wear and tear allowance (see **8.25** for further details).
- The introduction of Property Development tax from July 2016 (see **4.25**).

[4.21] The ATED regime was introduced in Finance Act 2013 and is applied to a 'non-natural' person which owns an interest in one or more residential dwellings, typically this is a company or a partnership with a corporate member. Broadly, where ATED applies it has three main implications:

- A higher flat rate of 15% SDLT on acquisition of the property.
- An annual tax charge. The rate varying from £3,500 for properties valued at over £500,000 and less than a million to £220,350 for properties valued at over £20m for the year 1 April 2017 to 31 March 2018.
- A higher rate of CGT on disposal, currently 28%.

Since the introduction of the ATED regime, the threshold taxable value for the residential property to fall within the regime has reduced significantly from £2m (if held as at April 2012 or the date of acquisition if later) to a value of £500,000. Within the provisions, there is also a requirement for determining the taxable value based on the value at 1 April falling five years after 1 April 2012 and thereafter. This will mean in determining the value of the residential properties for the ATED year 2018/19, companies will need to obtain up to date valuations of their residential properties as at 1 April 2017.

Importantly, there are a number of exemptions from falling within the regime, including a qualifying rental business, property developers and trading businesses. However, these reliefs need to be claimed by 30 April in the year of charge, in order for no penalties or interests to be applied. Given the drop in value to £500,000, some companies will potentially be in charge and need to claim the appropriate relief.

[4.22] From April 2017, income tax payers who have rental income arising from residential properties will have restrictions place on them in respect of the level of tax deduction that can be claimed for interest payments. The only main exemption for these restrictions are if the residential properties are part of qualifying Furnished Holiday Letting business.

These new rules are set out in new clause ITTOIA 2005, s 272A and will be phased in a four-year period – broadly in 2017/18 75% of interest will be claimed as a deduction against the rental income as before and 25% will be subject to the new rules, in 2018/19 50% will be claimed as a deduction against the rental income and 50% will be subject to the new rules, in 2019/20 25% will be claimed as deduction against rental income and 75% will be subject to the new rules. From April 2020, all interest deductions will be subject to the new legislation.

In outline, this legislation means that no tax deduction will be available for the financing costs (principally interest but also any arrangement fees etc) against the net rental income. Instead income tax will be calculated on the gross rental income after other allowable expenses (eg repairs). Subsequently as a tax restrictor, relief will be available for the finance costs at the basic rate of income tax. The level of interest relief is restricted to the lower of the finance costs incurred in the year and the net rental income for the period. This could therefore particularly impact BTL landlords who have a portfolio which has a high repair costs so have lower net rental income. Although, it is possible to carry forward unutilised finance costs to offset future profits.

Clearly, higher rate taxpayers are most impacted by these interest restriction changes. Such taxpayers need to assess now the impact of these changes and may wish to consider mitigation techniques including where possible raising tenants' rents, selling properties to deleverage the debt on the remaining portfolio or for larger portfolios look at incorporating their business (see CHAPTER 11).

However due to the mechanics of the legislation it can also impact basic rate taxpayers as it inflates their taxable income. It therefore can alter the availability of child benefits, pension contributions as well as the amount of personal allowances provided. Given these changes, affected taxpayers should make sure that they have worked through the full implications of the change in rules and considered their options going forward.

Non-resident companies who pay income tax on their UK rental income are not currently impacted by these interest restrictions, as they only pay income tax at the basic rate of income tax. However, during 2017 HMRC issued a consultation announcing their intention to bringing such companies within the scope of corporation tax in respect of their rental income from April 2020. In the event that this was to take place, such companies could find themselves under the new corporate interest restrictions rules that have applied to UK companies from April 2017. In addition, HMRC has announced that it is intending to bring gains arising from the disposal of non-residential property held by offshore companies and gains arising from the disposal of 'property rich entities' within the scope of capital gains tax from April 2019. Based on the current proposals, there will be a rebasing to the April 2019 market value for affected companies.

[4.23] As well as BTL landlords, the tax regime for property developers has changed significantly in recent years, particularly for those based offshore. Initially these changes arose from the introduction of the Diverted Profit Tax. However in March 2015, HMRC announced a comprehensive suite of changes that could impact not only offshore property developers but also UK taxpayers who develop UK land and property.

The main components of the changes announced included:

- The amendment of existing Double Tax Treaty protocols with the Channel Islands and Isle of Man.
- Further provision to amend the impact of any treaty relief claimed where it is considered this was not the purpose of the treaty.
- The creation of a new Property Development Tax (see **4.24** below).
- The introduction of a Targeted Anti-avoidance section where structuring is undertaken to fall outside the scope of the new tax.
- Specific rules to prevent fragmentation and sales to related parties to avoid the new tax.
- Replacing the existing Transaction in Land legislation with a new 'Transactions in UK land legislation'.

The new Transaction in UK land provisions widen the scope of these historic anti-avoidance provisions, as it is no longer necessary to have as the sole or main purposes of realising a gain or profit and the rules no longer have the explicit purpose of preventing the avoidance of income or corporation tax. These new rules can be applied where one of the following conditions is satisfied:

- The main purpose, or one of the main purposes, of acquiring the land was to realise a profit from disposing of the land.
- The main purpose, or one of the main purposes, of acquiring property deriving its value (say shares in Property rich company) from the land was to realise a profit or gain from disposing of the land.
- The land is held as trading stock.
- Where land has been developed, the main purpose, or one of the main purposes of developing the land was to realise a profit or gain from disposing of the land when developed.

[4.24] From 5 July 2016, Property Development Tax has been introduced for both corporate tax payers, under CTA 2010, Part 8ZB and for income tax payers under Income Tax Act 2007, Part 9A. The legislation is, as noted above, aimed at offshore property developers and will apply to all profits realised after 5 July 2016. In outline, where it applies profits will be subject to either corporation tax or income tax and it seeks all profits realised from the development of UK property, regardless as to whether this development is undertaken through a Permanent Establishment or not.

However, this legislation is widely drafted and could result in bringing other profits within its scope. For the legislation to apply, one of four conditions must be met:

Condition A: the main purpose, or one of the main purposes, of acquiring the land was to realise a profit or gain from disposing of the land.
Condition B: the main purpose, or one of the main purposes, of acquiring any property deriving its value from the land was to realise a profit or gain from disposing of the land, for instance shares in a company owning land.
Condition C: the land is held as trading stock.
Condition D: (where the land has been developed) the main purpose or one of the main purposes of developing the land was to realise a profit or gain from disposing of the land.

There is therefore a concern that most businesses will acquire property with the purpose of selling at some point with a gain. HMRC have in their guidance indicated that the conditions will not be considered to be met where the capital appreciation is directly attributable to general market conditions. However, it can be applied where an investment property is redeveloped shortly before a sale. In such a case, under the legislation there would be an appropriation in the value and only the increase in value since the decision to undertake the redevelopment would fall within the scope of Property Development tax.

This legislation also contains an anti-fragmentation rule, which in outline seeks to calculate the profits of the Property Developer ignoring any relevant contributions from related parties. Such contributions could include services, finance or other group overheads. This provision is therefore again widely drawn. However the guidance provided by HMRC is useful in particular in relation to any intra group financing which states that provided that the terms of the debt is akin to senior lending then a disallowance would not be sought under these rules.

Key points

[4.25] Key points to note are as set out below.

- Avoid using a room or area in a home solely for business purposes, to reduce the possibility of a capital gains tax charge.
- If a business property is held outside a company, payment of a market rent enables NIC-free profit extraction (but there may be a cap on the income tax relief available in relation to any personal borrowings secured on that property).
- Personal, rather than company, ownership of a property avoids a potential double tax charge on disposal.
- Before making a payment to landlord to surrender an onerous lease, other options should be explored.
- Careful consideration should be made as to the form of rental guarantees provided and who provides such guarantees.
- For taxpayers who are an incorporated BTL landlord calculate the impact of the new interest restriction rules and consider appropriate mitigation techniques.
- If a company-owned property ceases to be used for trade purposes, consider taking this out of the company.
- Always ensure that the transfer of a property to a partnership or company is correctly documented.
- Ensure that the appropriate ATED relief is claimed for any residential properties held within companies.

Chapter 5

Groups

Creation of a group

[5.1] Under UK tax law each company in a group is treated separately, although there are specific reliefs that recognise the close relationship between group companies. Trading and capital losses can be passed between group companies, assets can be transferred between group companies on a tax neutral basis, and there are specific reliefs and exemptions for loan relationships, disposals of subsidiaries and certain group reorganisations, to name a few.

Before creating a group the proprietors should consider what they want to achieve by having a group, as it is much easier to create a group than it is to break one up, as we will see in **CHAPTER 11**, on reconstructions.

A group can be used to ring-fence activities. Risky activities can be run through a separate company so that if the venture is unsuccessful other companies in the group will be unaffected except for suffering bad debts on loans or settling any covenants made in favour of the failed company. Exposure can be controlled.

A group structure can be effective in controlling a business with diverse activities, giving a measure of autonomy to directors of a division and perhaps offering minority shareholdings in the subsidiaries to incentivise key employees or to offer investors a stake in a particular business, perhaps on a joint venture basis. This provides a more formal demarcation than divisionalising the activities of a single company.

A group can be used to separate valuable property from trading activities, for example by holding premises or intellectual property in the holding company.

A group may arise as a result of a reorganisation or management buy-out, where a holding company may have been required to acquire the target company.

On the other hand, if a proprietor has a number of separate business interests he may not want to join them together either in a single company or in a group. This would allow him to sell individual companies, probably with the benefit of entrepreneurs' relief, or to offer EMI share options to key employees in particular companies (EMI is not available in respect of shares in subsidiaries).

A divisional structure within a single company should not be dismissed as this could, for example, reduce administrative costs. It might be appropriate to have different classes of shares to reflect interests in the divisionalised activities.

IHT issues in connection with groups of companies are dealt with in **3.41** to **3.43**.

What is a group for group relief purposes?

[5.2] It is possible to have a group for accounting or company law purposes that is not a group for corporation tax purposes. This could happen, for example, where a company holds all the voting shares of another company, without having a 75% interest in the entire share capital of that other company. An interest in share capital is measured by reference to the nominal value of each class of share. Moreover, the definition of 'group' differs depending on whether one is looking at group relief for losses or capital gains reliefs. Special provisions that apply to certain loan relationships look at control rather than specifically group relationships. It is important to establish which rules apply in relation to a particular transaction.

For group relief purposes two companies are members of the same group if one is a 75% subsidiary of the other, or both are 75% subsidiaries of a third company (CTA 2010, s 152). A 75% subsidiary is defined in ss 1154 to 1157. A company ('B') is a 75% subsidiary of another company ('A') if at least 75% of the ordinary share capital of B is owned directly or indirectly by A. Ordinary share capital is defined in s 1119 as 'all the company's issued share capital (however described), other than capital the holders of which have a right to a dividend at a fixed rate but have no other right to share in the company's profits'. So preference shares with a fixed dividend would be excluded from the calculation.

Consider the following structure:

A GmbH

```
        ┌──────────────────────────────┐
   85%  │                         90%  │
        │                              │
  B Ltd                          C Ltd
        │                              │
   80%  │                         90%  │
        │                              │
  D Ltd                          E Ltd
```

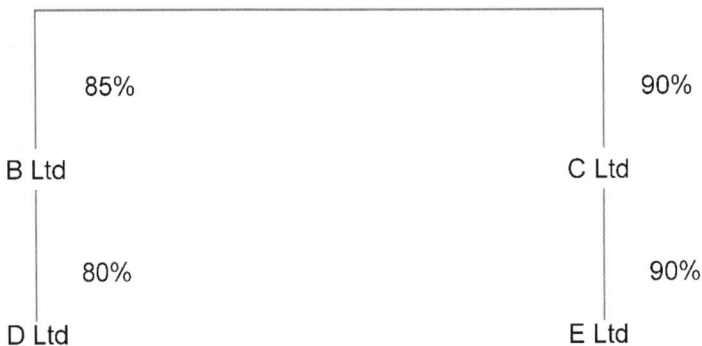

Even though A GmbH is a German company which is not resident in the UK a group relationship between two subsidiaries can be established. So B Ltd, C Ltd and E Ltd form a group (75% of the shares in E Ltd are owned indirectly by A GmbH as 90% × 90% = 81%). D Ltd does not form part of that group because the indirect holding by A GmbH is 85% × 80% = 68%. However, there is a second group comprising B Ltd and D Ltd. B Ltd is not prevented from being a member of two groups for group relief purposes.

Shares will not be counted in establishing whether there is a group relationship where those shares are held as stock in trade, or where those shares do not give the parent company a beneficial entitlement to at least 75% of the profits available for distribution or of assets available on a winding up of the subsidiary.

If arrangements are in place for a company to leave a group, for example where a sale is in progress, where there is a heads of terms, or a subsidiary company goes into liquidation, that company will no longer be treated as part of the group for group relief purposes (CTA 2010, s 154).

Group relief for losses

[5.3] Having ascertained the composition of the group the next step is to ascertain what losses are available to surrender and which companies are able to claim those losses in the most tax efficient manner.

Certain losses can be surrendered without regard to a company's other income; others must be offset against other profits within the company before being surrendered.

Losses that can be surrendered irrespective of other profits which the company may have include:

- trading losses;
- excess capital allowances; and
- non-trading loan relationship debits.

Losses that can only be surrendered after all other profits of the company have been extinguished include:

- charges on income;
- losses from a property business;
- management expenses; and
- non-trading losses on intangible assets.

For losses incurred before 1 April 2017 group relief is available only for the year in which the losses are incurred. Even though losses from a property business and surplus management expenses brought forward are treated as losses in the next accounting period under CTA 2010, s 62 and CTA 2009, s 1223, group relief is only available for current year losses.

However, losses incurred on or after 1 April 2017 can be carried forward and used in a group relief claim in future years. It will be necessary, therefore, to keep a record of when losses were incurred, as old brought forward losses will be available for offset only against future profits of the same company from the same trade. Companies can choose how and when to use the pre-1 April 2017 losses.

There are provisions to restrict loss buying. Broadly, where a company or group with losses is acquired, those losses cannot be group relieved against the purchaser's profits for a period of five years after acquisition.

Managing group relief losses

[5.4] If, for example, a company which is a member of a group has trading losses and property business profits, the trading losses can be surrendered to reduce the rental profits chargeable to corporation tax. This may enable group companies to avoid paying their corporation tax in instalments.

Losses can be surrendered so as to maximise the benefit of those losses around the group. A loss making company does not have to surrender all its losses to one company in the group, so in principle the position can be optimised so that more companies in a group can pay corporation tax on the normal due date nine months and one day after the end of the accounting period, rather than having some companies in the group paying corporation tax in instalments.

Dealing with overlapping periods

[5.5] Full relief is available where the accounting periods of the surrendering and claimant companies are coterminous. However, where this is not the case, only profits and losses in the overlapping period can be taken into account. Normally, the total profits of the claimant company and the losses of the surrendering company are apportioned on a time basis. However, where time apportionment would produce an unjust or an unreasonable result, either HMRC or the company can propose an alternative just and reasonable basis. HMRC states in its guidance (CTM 80260) that it would consider an alternative approach to apportioning profits or losses when:

'• there has been a significant change in the pattern of the company's results compared with previous periods. This applies particularly where there have been substantial disposals (of either circulating capital assets or fixed assets attracting a balancing charge or chargeable gains) which leave the company with a lower level of fixed assets or stock or both at the balance sheet date than in previous years; or

• a particular event, such as the acquisition of a major asset on which there are first-year or other enhanced capital allowances, or a financial transaction in respect of which there is a loan-relationship deficit, falls within or without the period to which profits or losses are to be apportioned; or

• the company's business is one in which disposals are otherwise large and 'lumpy' (such as property developers, for circulating capital assets, and shipping companies, for fixed assets attracting capital gains and balancing charges); or

• the company's business is both substantial and seasonal; or

• there is evidence of manipulation of the timing of relevant events within the accounting period.'

Whenever accounting periods are not coterminous, the possibility of an apportionment otherwise than on the basis of time should be considered. This could increase the losses or profits falling within the overlap period.

Overseas permanent establishment

[5.6] The availability of group relief for losses will also be restricted where a UK company has an overseas permanent establishment where any part of the overseas loss can be relieved elsewhere against non-UK profits, (CTA 2010, s 106). Usually, where a UK company trades in the UK and overseas, any losses in respect of the overseas trade will form part of the company's trading results and will form part of any losses available for group relief against other UK group companies.

Consortium relief

[5.7] Consortium relief is an extension of group relief, and allows a proportion of losses to be claimed or surrendered between consortium members and the consortium company.

Companies owned by consortiums and members of consortiums are defined in CTA 2010, s 153:

(1) '... a company is owned by a consortium if:

(a) The company is not a 75% subsidiary of another company, and
(b) At least 75% of the company's ordinary share capital is beneficially owned by other companies each of which beneficially owns at least 5% of that capital.'

Section 153(3) extends the definition to subsidiaries of a consortium company:

'If–

(a) A trading company is a 90% subsidiary of a holding company and is not a 75% subsidiary of any company apart from the holding company, and
(b) As a result of subsection (1), the holding company is owned by the consortium.

Then for the purposes of this Part the trading company is also owned by the consortium.'

Example of consortium relief

The ordinary share capital of D Limited is beneficially owned by the following shareholders:

A Limited	25%
B Limited	30%
C Limited	20%
Mr X	15%
Mr Y	10%

D Limited beneficially owns 100% of the ordinary share capital of E Limited.

A Limited, B Limited and C Limited are consortium members because between them they own 75% of the ordinary share capital of D Limited, and each of them hold at least 5% of the shares. D Limited is a consortium company, as is E Limited because it is a 90% subsidiary of D Limited.

Assuming that there have been no changes in ownership during the year and the year ends of the companies are the same, consortium relief can pass upwards and downwards between the members of the consortium and the companies owned by the consortium. The amount of relief available is apportioned in accordance with the ownership by each of the consortium members.

Where a company is both owned by members of a consortium and a member of a group itself, consortium relief is available only in so far as group relief is not available, whether or not maximum group relief claims are made. The group relief position between D Limited and E Limited would therefore need to be considered first.

Where there has been a change in the shareholdings between the consortium members the shareholdings are split on a time basis to establish what proportion of profits and losses can be offset by consortium relief. The relief is also affected where periods do not wholly overlap.

Group relief and consortium relief do not extend to capital losses, although both reliefs can be used to shelter capital gains made in the accounting year. There is also the possibility of using rollover relief, and the ability to make a notional transfer election to utilise a loss. Any capital loss incurred by a company can be carried forward and set off against future capital gains made by that company.

Payment for losses and surrender of tax refund

[5.8] The claimant company can pay for losses surrendered to it, and this is dealt with in CTA 2010, s 183. This is considered at CTM 80145:

'A payment which the claimant company in fact makes to the surrendering company up to the amount of the loss, etc surrendered is ignored. It is not taken into account in computing the profits or losses of either company, and is not treated as a charge on income or a distribution. The payment must be made under an agreement between the claimant company and the surrendering company. The maximum payment that can be treated in this way is the amount of the trading loss etc, not the amount of relief in terms of tax.'

Two companies in a group can jointly elect that a corporation tax or income tax refund due to one company can be paid to the other company, so long as the companies are members of the same group throughout the period starting with the accounting period to which the refund relates and ending with the date the election is made (CTA 2010, s 963).

Capital allowances

[5.9] A group of companies can claim only one annual investment allowance (AIA). If a number of companies in the group have incurred qualifying capital expenditure a claim for AIA can be made by one or more of those companies, and used, for example, to create a loss that can be group relieved, or to ensure that a company falls outside instalment payments (see **8.9** for details of AIA).

Where assets on which capital allowances are claimed are transferred between group companies, the actual consideration (restricted to original cost) is used for capital allowances purposes, unless the transfer of the assets is in conjunction with a transfer of the trade. In the latter case, the transfer is made at tax written down value (see CTA 2010, s 948).

Transfer of assets between group companies

[5.10] Where chargeable assets are transferred between group companies, the transfer takes place on a nil gain/nil loss basis for capital gains purposes. However, for this purpose, the definition of a group company differs from the one used for group relief purposes. A capital gains tax group comprises a 'principal company' and all its 75% subsidiaries. It also includes any company that is a 75% subsidiary of any of the 75% subsidiaries of the principal company, and so on down the chain, so long as they are effective 51% subsidiaries of the principal company (TCGA 1992, s 170). This means that a company could be a member of a capital gains group without being a member of a group relief group.

For example, where Company A owns 80% of Company B, they would be group companies for the purposes of group relief and capital gains. If Company B owns 75% of Company C, Company C would be grouped with Company A for capital gains purposes but not for group relief purposes.

Companies that belong to a capital gains group can pass chargeable assets between each other without giving rise to a corporation tax liability. The asset will pass at such a value as to give rise to neither a gain nor a loss, which means that in most cases the transferee company will be treated as having acquired the asset at its original base cost plus indexation to the date of transfer. It should be remembered, however, that if the transferee company subsequently sells the asset to a third party at a price which gives rise to a loss, that loss will be restricted in so far as it relates to indexation inherent in the base cost arising on the intra-group transfer.

Leaving the group — capital gains position

[5.11] If the transferee company leaves the group from which it acquired the asset within six years of the transfer and still owns the asset, a degrouping charge can be triggered. There are a number of situations that are considered in TCGA 1992, s 179, which contains exemptions to the charge and special charging provisions. As a result this section is long and complex, but can be broken down into a number of special rules that are set out in HMRC's manuals at CG45410.

Where an asset has been transferred between two group companies that form a sub-group, and both companies are sold by the group as a sub-group, a degrouping charge will not arise. This is because the transferor (Company B) and the transferee (Company A) companies remain members of the same group.

More complex company takeovers should be considered carefully. Usually where a group of companies becomes a member of another group of companies there will be no degrouping charge. However, if Company A subsequently ceases to be both a 75% subsidiary and an effective 51% subsidiary of a company that is a member of the acquiring group within six years of the takeover, a degrouping charge can be triggered.

Where a degrouping charge arises as a result of a disposal of shares, the gain that would have arisen on the original intra-group transfer is brought into charge by increasing the proceeds on the disposal of the shares. The gain forms part of the capital gains computation of the company selling the shares in Company A. Prior to the changes introduced in Finance Act 2011, Schedule 10 the gain came back into charge on Company A.

If the disposal involves an exchange of shares or securities the adjustment will give rise to a tax charge when the new shares or securities are sold. Furthermore, when the shares are sold the base cost of the property that was transferred intra-group will be increased to the market value of the property when the intra-group transfer took place. Company A will, therefore, benefit from an uplift in the base cost of the asset transferred to it.

If the disposal of shares is covered by substantial shareholding exemption, the adjustment to take the degrouping charge into account will also be covered by the exemption.

The commencement of the winding up of a company does not break the group relationship for capital gains purposes (TCGA 1992, s 170(11)). Neither does a degrouping charge apply where a company ceases to be a member of a group in consequence of another member of the group ceasing to exist (TCGA 1992, s 179(1)). HMRC's view, set out in CG45410, is that 'this exclusion applies only where a parent company ceases to be a member of a group on the occasion of its only subsidiary ceasing to exist on dissolution (or all its subsidiaries ceasing to exist simultaneously on dissolution).' However, the legislation does not seem to be so restrictive on this point.

HMRC accepts that a degrouping charge will not be triggered on assets transferred to the parent of a two group company which disposes of its only subsidiary, which was confirmed in CCAB Technical Release 386 dated 31 March 1980.

It is important to note that the provisions introduced by Finance Act 2011 apply only to assets that are chargeable assets for capital gains purposes. Where intangible assets are transferred intragroup and the transferee company leaves the group within six years of the transfer, the degrouping charge arises on the transferee company (CTA 2009, s 780).

Where a company in a group makes a gain or loss on a disposal or deemed disposal of a chargeable asset, that company and another company in the group may together elect under TCGA 1992, s 171A that all or part of the gain or loss is treated as accruing to the other group company. Prior to FA 2009, the effect of the election was to deem the asset to be transferred between group companies immediately before a sale to the third party. The new version of s 171A enables gains and losses to be transferred where they do not arise as a result of an actual sale, for example as a result of a negligible value claim. This relief is available only if a transfer between the two companies would have been treated as a nil gain/nil loss transfer under s 171.

The existence of a group is dealt with for roll-over relief in TCGA 1992, Pt V, Ch I by treating trades carried on by companies that are members of a capital gains tax group as if they were a single trade under TCGA 1992, s 175. This means that if one group company disposes of a chargeable asset that has been used for the purposes of a trade and a second group company acquires an asset that is brought into use for the purposes of a trade, the gain on the first asset can be rolled into the acquisition of the new asset. This is on the basis that the various requirements for replacement of business assets are met.

Where intangible assets acquired, or treated as acquired on or after 1 April 2002 are transferred between group companies, the intangible assets rules in Part 8 of the CTA 2009, and in particular CTA 2009, s 775, apply rather than the capital gains rules in TCGA 1992, s 171. Under s 775, intangible assets are transferred on a 'tax-neutral' basis, as defined in s 776. The broad effect of this section is the same as s 171, although in s 776, works by treating the transfer as not involving any disposal or acquisition of the asset. Rather, the asset is treated as if it had always been owned by the transferee company.

Where the transferor and transferee companies cease to be members of the same group within six years after the intra-group transfer, there is a deemed realisation and reacquisition of the intangible asset at market value (at the time of the original transfer) (s 780).

These provisions mirror the capital gains provisions, but they are not identical. There are some important differences, especially where assets are transferred between group companies and there is a subsequent group reorganisation. An important distinction is in relation to the operation of TCGA 1992, s 179(3D), which, in conjunction with TCGA 1992, Sch 7AC, para 15A can mean that assets can be transferred, for example, to a subsidiary, and if that subsidiary is sold a corporation tax charge may not arise. This is because s 179(3D) attaches the degrouping charge to the disposal proceeds for the shares in the subsidiary, but if substantial shareholding exemption is available (see **5.15**) that exemption covers the gain arising under s 179.

This does not apply where the asset in question is a post-1 April 2002 intangible asset, where a degrouping charge would arise under CTA 2009, s 780. The resulting gain would be chargeable to corporation tax in the transferee company.

Gift relief trap

[5.12] It should not be assumed, that for all tax purposes the activities carried on by group members are regarded as activities carried on by the group. For example, if an individual owns an asset which is used by a subsidiary of a holding company in which the individual owns all the shares, it might be assumed that if that individual gives away the asset, s 165 gift relief would be available, on the basis that it is an asset which is used for the purposes of a trade carried on by the individual's personal company. However, looking carefully at the definition of 'personal company' in TCGA 1992, s 165(8)(a), this does not always appear to be the case. A personal company is 'a company the voting rights in which are exercisable, as to not less than 5 per cent, by that individual'. The individual may have more than 5% of the votes of the holding company, but he does not exercise more than 5% of the votes of the subsidiary because the holding company has all the votes (*Boparan v Revenue and Customs Comrs* [2007] STC (SCD) 297).

Stamp duty and stamp duty land tax

[5.13] Finance Act 1930, s 42 provides relief from stamp duty where assets are transferred between 'associated companies'. Companies are associated for stamp duty purposes where one company is the parent of the other or another company is the parent of both companies. One company is the parent of another under s 42(2B) 'if the first body –

(a)   is beneficial owner of not less than 75% of the ordinary share capital of the second body;
(b)   is beneficially entitled to not less than 75% of any profits available for distribution to equity holders of the second body; and
(c)   would be beneficially entitled to not less than 75% of any assets of the second body available for distribution to its equity holders on a winding up.'

The ownership can be direct or indirect, but there must not be arrangements in existence at the time the relevant instrument is executed whereby other persons could obtain control of the transferee but not the transferor.

It should be noted that it is possible to treat two companies as associated for stamp duty purposes where they are both at least 75% owned by a partnership.

Stamp duty relief under FA 1930, s 42 must be claimed, which entails a formal adjudication under Stamp Act 1891, s 12.

Relief under s 42 does not apply where the instrument transferring the shares was executed '*in pursuance of or in connection with an arrangement where-under . . . . The transferor and the transferee were to cease to be associated within the meaning of section 42 by reason of the transferor or a third body corporate ceasing to be the transferee's parent (within the meaning of the said section 42)*' (Finance Act 1967, s 27). It should be noted, however, that this restriction to relief under s 42 only applies to transfers of assets down from the parent to a subsidiary.

Group relief for SDLT purposes is contained in FA 2003, Sch 7, paras 1 to 6 and applies to land transactions. Companies are members of the same group for SDLT purposes where one is a 75% subsidiary of the other or both are 75% subsidiaries of a third company. A company is, for this purpose, a body corporate, which means that for SDLT purposes companies owned by a partnership will not be treated as group companies, so the SDLT exemption will not be available.

Land transactions between group companies are exempt from SDLT, but there are provisions to withdraw relief if the transferor company leaves the group within three years of the transaction. It should be noted that, for this purpose the three-year period starts on completion rather than on exchange of contracts (which is usually the date of the transaction for CGT purposes).

There are a number of situations where the purchaser can leave the group without triggering a withdrawal of the relief, which are set out in Sch 7, paras 4 and 4ZA. Relief is not withdrawn:

- if the purchaser ceases to be a member of the group as a result of the winding up of the vendor or any other company that is above the vendor in the group structure;
- if the purchaser ceases to be a member of the group as a result of a reorganisation in respect of which stamp duty acquisition relief under FA 1986, s 75 applies and the purchaser becomes a member of the same group as the acquiring company immediately after the reorganisation;
- if the purchaser ceases to be a member of the same group as the vendor because the vendor leaves the group (see Sch 7, para 4ZA).

Group relief for SDLT purposes is not part of an adjudication process, but is claimed on the SDLT 1 form. A clawback event needs to be reported to HMRC Stamp Taxes within 30 days of the event.

51% group companies

[5.14] The 51% group company is relevant for the purpose of determining whether or not a company is a 'large' company obliged to pay corporation tax by instalments. For this purpose, the upper limit of profits which determine whether a company is large, £1.5 million, is reduced by the number of 51% related companies.

A company ('B') is a related 51% group company of another company ('A') in an accounting period if for any part of that accounting period:

'a)   A is a 51% subsidiary of B;
b)   B is a 51% subsidiary of A; or
c)   both A and B are 51% subsidiaries of the same company.'

A related 51% group company is ignored, if it has not carried on a trade or business at any time in the accounting period, or it was a related 51% group company for part only of the accounting period and has not carried on a trade or business at any time in that part of the accounting period.

A company is not treated as carrying on a business if it carries on a business of making investments in an accounting period and throughout the period the company:

'a)   carries on no trade,
b)   has one or more 51% subsidiaries, and
c)   is a passive company.'

A company is a passive company throughout an accounting period only if the following requirements are met:

'(a)   it has no assets in that period, other than shares in companies which are its 51% subsidiaries,
(b)   no income arises to it in that period other than dividends,

(c)   if income arises to it in that period in the form of dividends –
    (i)   the redistribution condition is met (see below), and
    (ii)   the dividends are franked investment income received by it,
(d)   no chargeable gains accrue to it in that period,
(e)   no expenses of management of the investment business are referable to that period, and
(f)   no qualifying charitable donations are deductible from the company's total profits of that period.'

The redistribution condition is that:

'(a)   the company pays dividends to one or more of its shareholders in the accounting period, and
(b)   the total amount paid in the form of those dividends is at least equal to the amount of the income arising to the company in the form of dividends in that period.'

If income arises to a company in an accounting period in the form of a dividend and the requirement in (c) is met in respect of the income:

'(a)   neither the dividend nor any asset representing it is treated as an asset of the company in that accounting period, and
(b)   no right of the company to receive the dividend is treated as an asset of the company in that period or any earlier accounting period.'

Fifty-one percent subsidiary is defined in accordance with CTA 2010, s 1119. A company is a 51% subsidiary of another company if it owns 50% or more of its ordinary share capital, directly or indirectly.

For accounting periods ending before 31 March 2015, the existence of associated companies may have an impact on the rate of corporation tax. A company is associated with another company if one of the two has control of the other or both are under the control of the same person or persons.

Control is defined in CTA 2010, s 450:

's 450(2)A person ("P") is treated as having control of a company ("C") if P–
    (a)   exercises,
    (b)   is able to exercise or
    (c)   is entitled to acquire,
direct or indirect control over C's affairs.
(3)   In particular, P is treated as having control of C if P possesses or is entitled to acquire:
    (a)   the greater part of the share capital or issued share capital of C,
    (b)   the greater part of the voting power in C; or
    (c)   so much of the issued share capital of C as would on the assumption that, the whole of the income of C were distributed among the participators, entitle P to receive the greater part of the amount so distributed; or
    (d)   such rights as would, entitle P, in the event of the winding-up of C or in any other circumstances, to receive the greater part of the assets of C which would then be available for distribution among the participators.

The remainder of s 450 and s 451 deal with the rights to be attributed to participators.'

In applying the tests, a person is treated as entitled to acquire anything he is entitled to acquire at a future date.

The control tests are mutually exclusive, so it is possible for more than one person or more than one group of persons to control a company. This introduces the concept of the minimum controlling combination.

Example

E Ltd is owned 100% by Mr A.

I Ltd is owned as follows:

Mr A	30%
Mr B	30%
Mr F	20%
Mr G	10%
Mr H	10%

Are the companies associated?

Mr A on his own controls E Ltd. Mr A, together with other shareholders as detailed below, controls I Ltd:

A + B	30% + 30%	= 60%
A + F + G	30% + 20% + 10%	= 60%
A + F + H	30% + 20% + 10%	= 60%
B + F + G	30% + 20% + 10%	= 60%
B + F + H	30% + 20% + 10%	= 60%

However, E Ltd and I Ltd are not associated, because the minimum controlling combination in E Ltd (ie Mr A) is not the same as any minimum controlling combination in I Ltd.

Substantial shareholding exemption (SSE)

[5.15] SSE was introduced in 2002 and can be found in TCGA 1992, Schedule 7AC. The relief was introduced to provide a form of participation exemption to make the UK attractive for holding companies when compared with groups in certain other jurisdictions where group transactions are largely exempted from tax. This relief applies to the disposal of shares by companies, so long as a number of requirements are met, relating to whether there is a substantial shareholding, the period the shares have been held for and the status of the investing and the investee companies.

A number of fundamental changes to SSE have been introduced in Finance (No 2) Act 2017, as a result of which the exemption will be more widely available.

Substantial shareholding

[5.16] A substantial shareholding exists if the investing company holds 10% or more of the investee company's share capital, is beneficially entitled to 10% or more of the profits available for distribution to the equity holders of the company and would be entitled to 10% or more of the assets of the company available for distribution to the equity holders on winding-up. Where different members of a group (which for this purpose means a holding company and its 51% subsidiaries) hold shares in a company, the group interest is aggregated to establish whether there is a substantial shareholding.

The investing company must have had a substantial shareholding throughout a 12-month period beginning not more than two years before the disposal takes place. This enables the company to dispose of its interest in the company piecemeal, so long as it disposes of all its shareholding within one year of its holding falling below 10%.

Where a company has acquired shares from another company on a nil gain/nil loss transfer (under TCGA 1992, s 171) the period of ownership by the transferee company will be extended by the period of ownership of the transferor company (Sch 7AC, para 10).

The investing company

[5.17] For disposals prior to 1 April 2017, the investing company must have been a sole trading company or a member of a qualifying group throughout the period beginning with the start of the latest 12-month period by reference to which a substantial shareholding existed and ending with the time of the disposal. Also, it must be a sole trading company or a member of a qualifying group immediately after the time of the disposal.

For this purpose, a qualifying group means a trading group or a group that would be a qualifying group if the activities of any group member that is not established for profit are ignored. A trading company is a company carrying on trading activities whose activities do not include, to a substantial extent, activities other than trading activities.

Trading activities include preparing to carry on trading activities and activities with a view to acquiring a trade or 51% or more of a company that is a trading company or the holding company of a trading group.

For disposals on or after 1 April 2017, it is no longer a requirement that the investing company is a trading company or the holding company of a trading group.

Disposal of sole subsidiary

[5.18] Before 1 April 2017, a common problem with obtaining SSE arose where, after the sale, the investing company was no longer a trading company. This might have arisen in the case of a small group comprising two companies where the subsidiary carries on most if not all the trading activities of the group. Before the sale, the investing company was the holding company of a trading group, but once the subsidiary was sold, the remaining company could not necessarily be treated as a sole trading company. This denies the company SSE.

TCGA 1992, Sch 7AC, para 3(3) was used to reinstate the relief so long as all the other requirements for SSE were met except for the requirement that immediately after the sale the investing company was not a sole trading company or a member of a qualifying group. This paragraph applied so long as the investing company was wound up as soon as reasonably practicable after the sale of shares in the investee company.

This provision was particularly useful for a small group comprising, for example, a holding company and a single trading subsidiary. After a sale of the subsidiary, the investing company would not be a trading company or the holding company of a trading group, so that SSE would not be available. More care would need to be exercised if, for example, the holding company owned the premises from which the trading subsidiary trades. In this situation, there would be a trade-off between the gain that would arise on a disposal of the property in the course of winding up the holding company and the gain that would be chargeable on the disposal of the subsidiary if the holding company is not wound up using the relieving provisions of para 3(3).

Paragraph 3(3) has been deleted with effect from 1 April 2017.

The investee company

[5.19] The investee company must also have been a qualifying company throughout the period beginning with the start of the latest 12-month period by reference to which a substantial shareholding existed and ending with the time of the disposal. The requirement that it must be a sole trading company or a member of a qualifying group immediately after the time of the disposal has been relaxed for disposals on or after 1 April 2017, except where there is a connected party disposal or the investing company is relying on the provisions of para 15A. Paragraph 15A applies where an asset has been passed to a group company and that company is sold within 12 months after that transfer.

There is no requirement that the investee company is a UK company.

Exclusions and interaction with other reliefs

[5.20] TCGA 1992, Sch 7AC, para 5 sets out specific exclusions to the exemption, and is aimed at 'tax-driven arrangements which are intended to exploit any of the exemptions' (SP 5/02). Paragraph 5 focuses on events that must occur in pursuance of arrangements designed solely or mainly to exploit SSE. These events are:

(1)   an untaxed gain accrues to a company (Company A) on a disposal of shares in another company (Company B); and

(2)   before the gain accrued, Company A acquired control of Company B or both companies were acquired by the same person or persons, or there was a significant change of trading activities affecting Company B while it was controlled by Company A or both were controlled by the same person or persons.

SP 5/02 considers when profits are 'untaxed', but approaches the question by stating that 'it is impossible to provide a comprehensive catalogue of all the situations where the gain will represent untaxed profits', and goes on to give examples of where profits will **not** be regarded as untaxed profits which include the following:

- 'a dividend is received by a holding company that is paid out of taxed profits of the subsidiary;
- where the profits in question themselves represent an exempt gain on disposal of a substantial shareholding;
- where no tax is payable on profits because they are covered by a specific relief (eg, loss relief).'

These examples suggest that 'normal' transactions are unlikely to be caught by the exclusions set out in para 5, but care should be exercised where steps are inserted into arrangements simply to engineer SSE status.

The interaction between SSE and other reliefs, particularly in connection with corporate reorganisations, is considered in para 4. Usually, where there is an exchange of shares for new shares or securities and TCGA 1992, s 116(10), or ss 127, 135, 136 apply, or there is a demerger under CTA 2010, s 1076, the transaction is not treated as a disposal, and new shares or securities acquired as a result of the transaction stand in the shoes of the old shares (see **CHAPTER 11** and **CHAPTER 13**). However, under para 4, to the extent that SSE applies to a transaction, the above provisions do not apply. This means that on a share for share exchange, for example, the old shares will be treated as sold with the benefit of SSE and the new shares will be acquired at market value. If there is a loss on the disposal of the old shares then that loss will not be an allowable loss and the value at which the new shares are acquired will reflect the loss on the old shares.

Sale of stock between group companies

[5.21] Transfers of stock between group companies may require careful consideration, especially where the stock has increased in value. This applies particularly to stock comprising freehold and leasehold property.

Where transfer pricing applies to the transferor company (either because in its own right, or by virtue of being a member group, it is large or medium-sized), transfer pricing rules take precedence over any other rules and reliefs that may otherwise apply. This means that any disposal of stock will be treated for corporation tax purposes as having taken place at an amount that would have been realised if the sale had been between independent persons dealing at arm's length.

Where transfer pricing does not apply, special rules can apply depending on the nature of the transaction. Where a company ceases to trade and transfers its stock to another group company which takes over that trade, the provisions in CTA 2009, ss 162, 164, 166, and 167 will apply.

As a result, where stock is sold at less than market value the companies can elect under s 167 that the sale takes place for corporation tax purposes at the greater of acquisition cost and the sale price. If no election is made the sale will be treated as having taken place at market value.

Where stock is transferred between group companies otherwise than on a cessation of trade in one company and the commencement of that trade in the transferee company, broadly the transaction will be treated as having taken place at market value unless the items in question are sold as stock and are treated as stock in the acquiring company.

This means that transfers of stock must always be treated carefully, as there is no equivalent of TCGA 1992, s 171 giving an automatic nil gain/nil loss transfer for such assets.

VAT – Groups Notice 700/9

[5.22] Two or more companies or limited partnerships may register as a VAT group – if they meet the following criteria:

- each body has its principal or registered office in the UK;
- they are under common control, for example each company is a subsidiary of a parent company;

If the turnover of the group of companies is over £10 million per year and the group is partly owned or managed by a third party, a group can only be registered as a VAT group if:

- no more than 50 per cent of benefits generated by the business go to third parties;
- the group uses consolidated accounting;
- no third party consolidates the group into its accounts.

A VAT group is treated in the same way as a single company registered for VAT. The registration is made in the name of the 'representative member'. The representative member is responsible for completing and submitting a single VAT return and making VAT payments or receiving VAT refunds on behalf of the group.

VAT groups have certain advantages such as VAT not being required to be charged between VAT group members and the completion of only one VAT return for the whole group. However, there are also disadvantages such as joint and several liability for VAT debts and the penalty limits applying to the group as a whole.

There are also VAT anti-avoidance provisions which apply to VAT groups detailed in VAT Act 1994, Sch 9A.

Key points

[5.23] Key points to note are as follows:

- Adding group companies will increase the number of associated companies.
- The definition of a group differs for trading losses, capital gains, stamp duty and VAT.
- Group relief must be claimed and the loss surrendered in the prescribed format.
- Group relief takes precedence over consortium relief.
- The surrender of losses can be done so as to maximise the use of small company limits.
- Care should be taken whenever assets have been transferred between group companies.
- SSE relies on a number of prescribed requirements being met.
- The existence of 51% related companies may have an impact on whether the company is large for corporation tax purposes and obliged to pay tax in instalments.

Part II

Running the Business

Chapter 6

Profit Extraction

Limited company

[6.1] Profits can be extracted from a company in a number of ways. At shareholder level this could be by way of dividend or capital distribution, in the form of capital reduction, a purchase of own shares by the company, or on winding up, or liquidation. The value of accumulated profits could be realised by the shareholders on a sale of the company.

At a proprietorial, director or employee level, profits can be extracted in the form of salaries, benefits in kind (including loans), dividends or pension contributions.

Profits could also be extracted by way of a loan to another company, for example.

Dividends v bonus

[6.2] The decision as to whether to extract profits from a company in the form of dividends or remuneration has been affected in recent years by a number of changes, which include a unified rate of corporation tax as well as the way dividends are now subject to income tax.

Where a bonus is paid, the company will obtain a corporation tax deduction for both the bonus and employer's NIC payable. When the top rate of corporation tax stood at 23% the payment of a bonus may have been preferable, however with the current rate of corporation tax at 19% and due to fall to 17% in 2020, although the payment of a dividend is more efficient as illustrated in the following example, the difference is not as significant as it was in prior tax years.

A company pays corporation tax at 19% and distributes £100,000 to a shareholder director. Ignoring the employment allowance of £3,000 for NIC and reductions of personal allowance, the comparisons for year ended 31 March 2019 are as follows:

	Higher rate taxpayer £	Additional rate taxpayer £
Payment of dividend of £100,000		
Corporation tax payable by company (taxable profits of £2 million)	380,000	380,000

	Higher rate taxpayer £	Additional rate taxpayer £
Income tax on dividend (after £2,000 exemption see below)	31,850	37,338
Total tax payable	411,850	417,338
Payment of bonus of £100,000		
Employer's NIC payable by company	13,800	13,800
Corporation tax payable by company	358,378	358,378
Income tax on bonus	40,000	45,000
NIC on bonus	2,000	2,000
Total tax and NIC payable	414,178	419,178

Changes to dividend allowance

[6.3] The Dividend Allowance will be reduced from £5,000 to £2,000 with effect from 6 April 2018.

Planning point

[6.4] Because of the impact of national insurance it is still marginally preferable to pay dividends rather than bonuses, however the increases in dividend taxation have narrowed the tax differential between bonuses and dividends as shown in the above example.

Income tax charge in relation to claw back of child benefit

[6.5] Child benefit is withdrawn for some taxpayers by way of an income tax charge. It applies to individuals who receive child benefit if they or their partner's income exceeds £50,000 a year. If both partners' income exceeds £50,000, the charge applies only to the partner with the highest income. For the purposes of these rules, the meaning of 'partners' includes a couple who are not married or in a civil partnership but who live together as if they were so.

For taxpayers with income higher than £60,000, the tax charge will match the amount of child benefit received. For taxpayers with income between £50,000 and £60,000 the amount of the tax charge is a proportion of the child benefit claim. The reason for this taper is to make withdrawal fairer (although not simpler). This is to avoid a situation where one family with income just over the 40% threshold lose their tax credits, while another just under the threshold keep their credits.

The charge is calculated as 1% of the amount of Child Benefit for each £100 of income in excess of £50,000. For example, if an individual whose income is £54,000 a year receives Child Benefit of £1,789 (the current amount for two children), the charge will be £715.60 (40% × £1,789). The charge on those whose income exceeds £60,000 will be 100% of the Child Benefit. Rather than paying the charge, taxpayers may elect not to receive Child Benefit. The election can be revoked to restore the benefit to cover situations where there is a fall in income.

'Income' for these purposes is calculated after a number of allowable deductions.

The charge is collected through self-assessment and PAYE.

Planning point

The impact of these rules must also be taken into account when considering the level of bonus or dividends drawn from a family company. If the clients have older children it may be worth delaying the payment of income to the following tax year. If possible, it would be preferable to pay husband and wife, say, £40,000 each rather than pay only one of them £80,000 and lose the child benefit credit (subject to the settlement rules).

Benefits in kind

[6.6] Profits can be used to provide benefits to the proprietors. A number of benefits are taxed in accordance with specific legislation, for example cars, vans or accommodation. The method under which these are taxed is beyond the scope of this book.

Where individuals have income approaching the 45% additional rate income tax threshold, the provision of benefits rather than salary or bonuses should be considered carefully, to ensure that the level of remuneration taxed at 45% is minimised. The use of an effective salary sacrifice arrangement covered further in **CHAPTER 10**, can provide tax and national insurance savings for both employee and employer.

As a general principle, where a proprietor wishes to acquire an expensive or high emission car, a comparison should be made between running the car personally, or running it through the company. There is no simple answer, as it depends on the benefit in kind charge on the individual as compared to the running costs and depreciation, as well as the level of business mileage. With an expensive car that is expensive to run, with comparatively low business mileage, it may be better to run the car through the company. On the other hand, with a more modest car with comparatively high business mileage, it may be better for the proprietor to run the car personally and charge a mileage rate for company business. There is no substitute, however, for doing the comparison on a case-by-case basis.

Low emission cars may be attractive, with 100% first-year allowances available for cars with emissions of not more than 50g/km, and a benefit in kind charge of 13% of the list price for cars with emissions up to 50g/km or less, or 16% of the list price for cars with emissions between 50g/km and 75g/km in 2018/19. The minimum percentage for benefit in kind charges will remain the same as 2017/18 from 1 April 2019 for cars with CO_2 emissions up to 50g/km.

It may also be worth considering a more expensive car with emissions of 130g/km or less (110g/km or less from 1 April 2018), as capital allowances could be available at 18% of WDV (which could be significantly more attractive than the former limit of £3,000 a year), and the benefit in kind charge would be based on carbon emissions and list price.

All benefit in kind charges are increased by 3% for diesel cars.

Vans

[6.7] Historically, the benefit in kind on vans has been modest in comparison to the charge on cars. Proprietors have been attracted to vehicles that fall under the category of van, even though they are of high specification. Even with a benefit in kind charge on vans of £3,350 in 2018/19 where private use is not limited to, for example, commuting, it may be worth considering this type of vehicle. Each case should be looked at on its merits to determine whether the vehicle is a car or a van. HMRC provides guidance in their Employment Manual at EIM 23110, which states

'In deciding whether or not a particular vehicle counts as a car for car benefits purposes, the starting point is the definition in Section 115(1) Income Tax (Earnings and Pensions) Act 2003 (ITEPA). This works by exception: every mechanically propelled road vehicle is a "car" unless it is

- (i) a goods vehicle (a vehicle of a construction primarily suited for the conveyance of goods or burden of any description),
- (ii) a motor cycle (as defined in Section 185 Road Traffic Act 1988),
- (iii) an invalid carriage (also as defined in that Act), or
- (iv) a vehicle of a type not commonly used as a private vehicle and unsuitable to be so used.

Exception (1)

This looks at the construction of a vehicle to see if it is primarily suited for the conveyance of goods or burden (note that "primarily" is crucial and that "goods or burden" does not include people). This means we must look to see if there is a predominant purpose of construction.

Actual use of a particular vehicle is irrelevant: the statutory test is a test of construction, not use.

The fact that the manufacturer or dealer describes the vehicle as a "commercial vehicle" is not conclusive.

If a vehicle is designed and marketed as a multi-purpose vehicle, it is unlikely to fall within this exception.

Exceptions (2) and (3)

It is normally obvious whether either applies.

Exceptions (4)

This exception can also be discounted in most cases. Irrespective of their use in practice, there is nothing that renders most vehicles inherently unsuitable for private use. Indeed the marketing of many whose status might otherwise be uncertain is aimed at illustrating how well fitted they are for private use.

It follows that, if a vehicle is to escape from being classified as a car, it will normally need to satisfy the first of the tests in Section 115(1).

Even if the preceding 2 paragraphs do not apply and neither purpose predominates with regard to the construction of the vehicle, the vehicle is not primarily suited for either purpose and this means that it does not escape from being a car. Clearly if its primary purpose is to carry passengers it will also remain within the company car legislation (unless it is so big that it is clearly a bus). It is only if the primary purpose for which the vehicle is constructed is the carriage of goods that it will escape from being a car.

If a vehicle has side windows behind the driver and passenger doors, it is also unlikely to fall within this exception. This is particularly so if it is fitted, or is capable of being fitted, with additional seating behind the row which includes the driver. This remains true whether or not those additional seats are in the vehicle at the time.

There is guidance on the specific type of vehicle known as double cab pick-ups at EIM23150, on other off-road vehicles at EIM23145 and on other specific types of vehicle at EIM23155.

Where a vehicle does escape being a car because exception 1 applies, the van benefit rules of Section 154 ITEPA will normally apply (EIM22700 for 2005/06 onwards, EIM22050 for years to 2004/05). Otherwise, unless the specific rules for heavy goods vehicles prevent a charge (EIM22990), the residual benefit rules of Section 201 ITEPA onwards will apply (EIM20000).

It is worth noting that Vehicle Excise Duty and VAT legislation are both different to direct tax legislation, so the same vehicle can be treated differently by the different agencies. For instance, VED is based on type approval at the time the vehicle is first registered, whereas VAT and the direct tax/NICs regimes consider the nature of the vehicle at the time of the transaction or in the relevant tax year.'

Accommodation

[6.8] An accommodation benefit can arise in situations where it may not be expected. For example, a company based in Leeds finds that it does a lot of work in London. The proprietor decides that, instead of spending money on hotels, he or the company should buy a flat in London, and he will stay there for three nights a week. HMRC will argue that, even though he only occupies the flat for three nights, it is available to him throughout the year, so he will be taxed on a benefit in kind for the whole year, based on the annual value, and on the excess of the acquisition cost over £75,000 multiplied by the official rate.

He decides, therefore, that he will buy the flat himself. He will provide the deposit, but the bulk of the purchase will be provided by way of mortgage. In order to fund the mortgage, he will charge the company a market rent. In this situation, he will still be charged a benefit in kind, even though he owns the property, but based on the rental paid by the company. This point was demonstrated in the case of *Revenue and Customs Commissioners v Tim Healy* ([2013] UKUT 0337 (TCC)).

Other assets

[6.9] Other assets provided by the company for the proprietor, for example a motorcycle, yacht or aeroplane, will be subject to the normal benefit in kind charge of 20% of the market value of the asset when first provided. Any running expenses paid by the company will be taxed as additional benefits in kind. The provision of assets that are expensive to run should be considered carefully. It may be possible to use these assets as part of a chartering business so as to mitigate the benefit in kind charge. Careful and bespoke planning would be required for this type of asset.

Dividend waivers

[6.10] Where a company's shareholders are spread, for example, across a family and not all the shareholders work in the company, the allocation of any distribution may be problematic. The company may wish to pay a dividend, but not necessarily in proportion to the shareholdings.

Despite the changes in dividend taxation there is still a potential advantage in paying a dividend rather than a salary or bonus, principally in terms of the NIC saving. Any perceived redirection of dividends could however be attacked by HMRC.

Dividend waivers need to be used with caution. The first step is to ensure that the dividend waiver is valid, because if not the shareholder will still be taxed on his right to the dividend. The dividend waiver is a gratuitous act and cannot be done in return for anything given or done by someone else. The dividend waiver must be effected by a deed and must be executed before the dividend is declared, or, in the case of an interim dividend, before the dividend is paid.

If the shareholder waives his entitlement after the dividend has been declared, that dividend will be treated as the shareholder's income for income tax purposes. He will be treated, simply, as having decided to give away his income.

To avoid any inheritance tax consequences, a dividend waiver should be effective for a period of less than 12 months.

As an alternative the company could consider issuing different classes of shares to different family members, although this should not be used as a way of replacing salaries with dividends. The settlement provisions are likely to apply, however, where some of the classes of shares have restricted rights the shareholders would have to consider implications under the settlements legislation.

Dividend waivers and settlements

[6.11] It is necessary to ensure that the dividend waiver does not remain the income of the waiving shareholder under the settlement provisions. A dividend waiver can be treated as a settlement within ITTOIA 2005, s 624 where there is an element of bounty. Therefore, if the waiver is executed to enable another shareholder to receive an increased dividend, this would be regarded as income arising under a settlement within ITTOIA 2005, s 624(1).

In this particular case, the person waiving the dividend would remain fully taxable on the whole of the amount waived. If a dividend of 40p per share is declared, the other shareholders must not receive more because some of the shareholders have waived their right. To back this up, there must be sufficient distributable profits. If there are insufficient distributable profits, the conclusion is that the waiver was intended to increase dividends to other shareholders, and on that basis the dividend would remain taxable on the waiving shareholders.

For example, assume a company has three shareholders with one third of the shares each, and one of the shareholders decides to waive his entitlement to the dividend that might be declared for the year to 31 March 2019. The company has distributable reserves brought forward of £70,000, makes profits in the year to 31 March 2019 of £85,000 and pays a dividend of £120,000 at the end of that year to the two shareholders (2 x £60,000) who have not waived their dividends. The total available for distribution is £155,000. If none of the shareholders had waived their dividend, the notional total dividend would have been £180,000 (3 x £60,000), for which there are insufficient reserves. The shareholder who has waived his dividend will be regarded as making a settlement in favour of the other two shareholders. This situation was confirmed by the Special Commissioners in 2008 in the case of *Buck (SR) v Revenue and Customs Comrs* (SpC 716) [2009] STC (SCD) 6.

If all the shareholders pay income tax at the same rate, there is no loss of tax. However, if the shareholders receiving the dividends pay tax at a lower rate than the individual waiving the dividend (or the rate that individual would pay if he had received his share of the waived dividend) an income tax advantage would have been obtained. It should be noted that the settlements legislation does not apply only to spouses and children. A settlement could be regarded as having been created in favour of any other person.

Keeping profits in the company

[6.12] Proprietors may be tempted not to extract profits from the company, so as to avoid the resultant income tax. If the company is profitable but does not need to reinvest those profits into the business, cash will accumulate, which may give rise to problems in the future with regard to the availability of entrepreneurs' relief on a sale or winding-up of the company.

Furthermore, following changes to the transactions in securities legislation, a winding up of a company is now treated as a transaction that could be caught by this anti-avoidance legislation. This means that if the winding up is effected with a view to obtaining a tax advantage the proceeds on a winding up could be taxed as a dividend. It is possible to obtain clearance from HMRC that these provisions will not be imposed.

Proceeds on a winding up of a company could also be taxed as a dividend if the TAAR in Income Tax (Trading and Other Income) Act 2005, s 396B (ITTOIA 2005), which was inserted by Finance Act 2016, applies. These rules counter phoenix operations, whereby the shareholders wind up a company, and within two years after the winding up are involved in a similar activity to the one carried on by the old company. There is no clearance procedure in relation to these provisions. Further details can be found in **Chapter 16**.

In certain circumstances, it may be appropriate for a company to make loans to the proprietors. The company is likely to have a liability under CTA 2010, s 455, and the borrower will have a benefit in kind charged at the official rate of interest. However, this should not be used with the intention of writing off the loan at a future date, as HMRC is likely to regard the initial loan as remuneration or a dividend from the company.

Those owner-managers who face a significantly higher tax bill from the payment of dividends may consider taking loans from the company as an alternative where the s 455 charge is currently 32.5%, which compares favourably with the higher dividend rate of tax of 38.1% even after taking into account the beneficial loan charge based on the current official rate of interest of 3%.

The rules relating to loans to participators were tightened with effect from 20 March 2013 when the following changes were introduced:

- Loans to various intermediaries were brought within the scope of the charge. An example would be a situation where a company and an individual who is a participator in the company are in partnership and the company makes a loan to the partnership.
- Loans to trusts where the trustees hold shares in the company or where the trustees are associates of a participator were brought within the s 455 provisions.
- The amendments targeted arrangements where close companies transfer value to participators other than by way of loan. This applies where, for example, an individual participates in a close company and they form a partnership with the profits allocated to the company. The company leaves the profits undrawn, leaving funds in the partnership which the individual draws down.
- A new 30 day rule was introduced to prevent 'bed and breakfasting' of loans of more than £5,000. This prevents participators repaying their loan just days within 9 months of the end of the company's accounting period and taking a new one shortly afterwards.

A loan may be useful where the borrower expects to receive, for example, proceeds from the sale of an asset (perhaps the company itself) out of which the loan can be repaid.

Using profits to fund other ventures

[6.13] The profits of a company could be used to fund another of the proprietor's ventures. Instead of extracting funds directly and paying income tax, the proprietor could form a new company, which could borrow funds directly from the old company. This could be a way of maximising the use of available funds, although the impact of legislation in connection with associated companies, loan relationships and entrepreneurs' relief in particular would need to be borne in mind.

This might be a suitable way of funding, for example, a company formed by the proprietor's children, which could be seen as a risky venture. With the introduction of one rate of corporation tax from 1 April 2015 and removal of the small companies' rate the impact of associated companies is removed. As the loan is not likely to be regarded as an asset held for the purposes of the parent's company's trade, the companies should not have a connection for loan-relationship purposes although the loan may have an adverse impact of the trading status of the parent's company for entrepreneurs' relief purposes.

This means that if the venture does not work and the loan has to be written off, the parent's company would obtain a corporation tax deduction for the write-off. If the proprietor had drawn money out of his company to lend to the children's company, he would have paid income tax and possibly NIC, and would only be able to claim a capital loss for the write-off of the loan under TCGA 1992, s 253.

It is important, therefore, to consider the whole picture before deciding how profits should be used by or extracted from a family company.

Unincorporated businesses and the 45% rate

[6.14] Once unincorporated businesses have become established and profitable, the question of incorporation arises, and this is considered in **CHAPTER 12**. With a 45% top rate of income tax the differential between incorporated and unincorporated businesses should be addressed, especially where the proprietors do not require all the profits for personal expenditure.

However, some types of business do not lend themselves to being operated through a company. Planning for the 45% rate needs to be addressed for this type of profitable business.

A solution that was becoming increasingly common was the introduction of corporate partners to shelter some of the profits of a partnership. The use of such structures has been curtailed by the introduction of anti-avoidance rules on mixed membership partnerships, the effect of which was to limit the corporate member's profit share to what it would have been entitled to on an arm's length basis. Despite the amendments in Finance Act 2016, the changes in Finance Act 2015 to the joint venture rules affecting entrepreneurs' relief entitlement further remove the effectiveness of corporate partner structures. A partnership or LLP can still include corporate members, but there must now be a commercial reason for having them and the impact on entrepreneurs' relief needs to be factored into any planning. It should also be noted that the anti-avoidance rules apply to income but not to capital gains.

Pensions

[6.15] Profit can be extracted from a business by the business making a contribution direct to a pension scheme. Likewise the business could also pay a salary or bonus to an employee or director and he or she could make a personal contribution to a pension scheme. There are differences in the tax treatment of the two approaches (which we explain below); however, the broad principle is that – within statutory limits on the *level* of contributions which should be made – income tax relief should be available on the transfer to the pension scheme.

Once the funds are in the pension scheme, they can grow free of income tax and capital gains tax until such time as any benefits are taken; however, there are strict rules governing the type of asset a pension fund can invest in.

When benefits are ultimately taken from a pension scheme, tax can be payable; however, there are certain beneficial rules which can apply and which can contribute to the overall tax effectiveness of an investment in a pension scheme.

The sections which follow are not intended as a comprehensive tax analysis of the use of pensions for retirement saving for individuals, nevertheless, an understanding of the underlying principles as they apply to owner-managed businesses is important and we therefore deal with the following issues below:

- The basic tax position in relation to pension contributions by businesses and individuals.
- The limits on tax effective contributions.
- The restrictions on pension fund investments.
- Taking benefits from a pension.

The sections will focus on the use of pensions in relation to the extraction of profits from an owner-managed business. As it would be very unusual for an owner-managed business to have a defined benefit scheme arrangement, the sections will predominantly cover the position in relation to defined contribution schemes. Interested readers wanting more detailed information on defined benefit schemes are referred to more specialist pensions' publications for further details.

These sections also cover the important changes to the pension regime over recent years. The A-day changes made in 2006 simplified pension taxation for the vast majority of individuals. These rules have since been modified as part of the general move toward restricting higher rate tax relief on contributions.

The taxation of contributions to a pension scheme

Types of pension

[6.16] There are broadly three types of pension to which contributions might be made:

- **Personal or stakeholder pension** – this is an 'off the peg' solution offered by an insurance company to a single individual, where the choice of possible investments is restricted to cash or a number of specific funds provided by the company.
- **Self-Invested Personal Pension (SIPP)** – this is a more bespoke option for a single individual, where the pension fund can be invested in any investment authorised by the tax rules.
- **Small Self-Administered Pension Scheme (SSAS)** – this is a form of occupational pension scheme where, unlike a SIPP, there can be a number of members. Typically, a SSAS would be used to provide pensions to the 'family' owners/directors of an owner-managed business although employees may become members too.

Auto-enrolment

[6.17] Automatic enrolment of eligible workers into a workplace pension began in October 2012. The arrangements had been phased in depending on the size of the employer with the largest starting first. By 2018, every employee working in the UK aged between 22 and state pension age, earning more than £10,000 per annum, will need to be enrolled in a workplace scheme.

There is a minimum total amount that has to be contributed by the employee and employer with the government topping up the contribution in the form of tax relief. This total minimum contribution is currently set at 2% (0.8% from the employee, 1% from the employer, and 0.2% as tax relief). In 2018 and 2019, the minimum contribution amounts will increase to 5% and 8% respectively of earnings.

The minimum contribution applies to qualifying earnings over £6,032 (in the tax year 2018/19) up to a limit of £46,350 including overtime and bonus payments.

Employees may opt out of the workplace scheme only after they have been enrolled. In doing so however employees will lose out on the employers' contribution plus tax relief. Depending on the timing of the opt out, it may be possible for contributions paid into the scheme to be refunded.

Auto-enrolment will inevitably lead to many more people accruing relatively small defined contribution pension pots. Changes introduced in the Pensions Bill 2014, allow the accumulation of small pension pots via auto-enrolment to be transported to new employer's schemes when the employee changes jobs. Others may be able to take advantage of the changes introduced in March 2014 in relation to the extraction of funds from small pension pots or the greater flexibility introduced in 2015, both of which are outlined below.

Since the rules for pensions were rationalised on 'A-day' the same tax rules apply regardless of the pension type. Thus, the commentary that follows will apply to contributions to each of the above pensions.

Contributions by individuals and companies – the personal tax position compared

[6.18] Let's assume that there is an amount of £10,000 (gross) which is to be paid by a company to an employee who is higher-rate (ie 40%) taxpayer and who would like to contribute this sum to a pension fund.

If the £10,000 is **paid to the individual** as salary or bonus, 40% income tax and 2% employee's NIC will be deducted under PAYE, and the individual will receive £5,800 (the company would also have an employer's NIC liability of £1,380). If the individual then contributes this £5,800 to a pension fund, the contribution will be made *net* of basic rate (20%) income tax (£1,450) which the pension fund will be able to recover from HMRC. Then, when the individual completes his tax return, he will show a gross contribution of £7,250 to a pension scheme and will be due a refund of a further 20% (£1,450) in relation to the higher rate tax paid. In this circumstance, therefore, there will be £7,250 in the pension fund and £1,450 in the hands of the individual.

To ensure that the full £10,000 is contributed to the pension fund, the individual would need to add £2,200 from his own resources to the £5,800 received from the company. The pension fund would then receive £8,000, and could recover £2,000 from HMRC. The individual could then show a gross contribution of £10,000 to the pension fund and could recover £2,000 via his own tax return to replenish his own resources. The individual could accelerate the relief by applying to HMRC to amend his coding notice for the current year.

The alternative approach is for the company to pay the £10,000 directly to the pension fund. In these circumstances, no PAYE is deductible; the pension fund receives the contribution *gross* so there is nothing to be recovered by the fund from HMRC.

In both cases, therefore, the full £10,000 has been extracted from the company to the pension fund free from any income tax for the individual.

It should be noted that tax relief can be claimed for a contribution only in the tax year that a contribution is actually made.

National Insurance Contributions

[6.19] One significant difference between these two alternatives is that the contribution made by the company out of earnings before tax will not give rise to any national insurance liability for the individual or the company, whereas NIC is a cost to both the company and the individual in relation to pension contributions made personally out of salary received.

The employer tax position

[6.20] Employer contributions to a pension scheme are deductible as an expense as long as they are incurred wholly and exclusively for the purposes of the trade or profession. In considering this test pension contributions will be looked at as part of the remuneration package of the relevant employee. This is a question of fact, and would be looked at particularly closely where contributions are made for family members. The leading case of *Copeman (Inspector of Taxes) v William Flood & Sons Ltd* [1941] 1 KB 202, 24 TC 53 is relevant here in determining the 'right' level of remuneration where this does not appear to be commensurate with the work done for the company.

As in relation to personal tax relief, a deduction can only be given for a period in which a contribution is actually *paid*. It is therefore not sufficient to simply *accrue* for a pension contribution.

Finally, if there is a large increase in the level of employer contributions from one chargeable period to the next, the tax relief may need to spread across a number of years. These rules cannot apply if the increase in contributions from one year to the next is less than £500,000 and they will therefore be academic in the majority of cases.

The limits on tax effective contributions

[6.21] There is no doubt that the A-day changes simplified pension taxation for the vast majority of individuals. However, changes introduced in FA 2009 and FA 2010, principally the restrictions applied to those with incomes above £150,000, aimed at addressing perceived unfairness within the pensions' tax relief system, added some complexity.

Apart from the general limit on employer tax relief imposed by the 'wholly and exclusively' test referred to above, from 6 April 2011 the effective limits on contributions by individuals, or employers on their behalf, are:

(1)   Rules limiting contributions to the 'relevant UK earnings' of the individual.

(2)   An *annual cap* on the contributions which can be made by an individual to all pension funds – subject to rules allowing unused annual amounts to be carried forward.

(3)   A *lifetime cap* on the size of an individual's pension fund(s).

Relevant UK earnings

[6.22] Subject to the other limits referred to above and discussed more fully below, a 'relevant UK individual', can claim tax relief on *the higher of*

• £3,600; or
• 100% of 'relevant UK earnings'.

For these purposes, an individual is a **relevant UK individual** for a tax year if he or she:

- has relevant UK earnings chargeable to income tax for that year;
- is resident in the UK at some time during that year;
- was resident in the UK at some time during the five tax years immediately before the tax year in question and was also resident in the UK when he or she joined the pension scheme;
- has for that tax year general earnings and overseas Crown employment subject to UK tax (as defined by ITEPA 2003, s 28); or
- is the spouse or civil partner of an individual who has for the tax year general earnings from overseas Crown employment subject to UK tax (as defined by s 28).

and **relevant UK earnings** mean:

- employment income such as salary, wages, bonus, overtime and commission, providing it is chargeable to tax under ITEPA 2003, s 7(2);
- income chargeable under ITTOIA 2005, Pt II, that is, profits derived from the carrying on or exercise of a trade, profession or vocation (whether individually or as a partner acting personally in a partnership) including furnished holiday letting;
- income arising from patent rights and treated as earned income under ICTA 1988, s 833(5B); and
- general earnings from an overseas Crown employment which are subject to tax in accordance with ITEPA 2003, s 28.

Where relevant UK earnings are not taxable in the UK due to TIOPA 2010 (double taxation agreements), those earnings are not regarded as chargeable to income tax and so will not count towards the annual limit for tax relief.

It should be noted that dividend income does not count as relevant UK earnings.

The annual cap

[6.23] Since A-day, there has always been a finite limit on the total annual contribution that an individual could make to his pension fund(s) and claim tax relief. By 2010/11 this had risen to £255,000.

As part of the drive to eliminate unfairness from the pensions tax system, this annual limit was reduced to £50,000 from 6 April 2011 and further reduced to £40,000 from 6 April 2014; however, for contributions on or below this amount, tax relief is available to *all* taxpayers, ie including those paying income tax at a marginal rate of 45%.

Effective from 6 April 2016, the annual limit was tapered where total adjusted income is over £150,000 by £1 for every £2 of income over £150,000 and the minimum allowance will be £10,000.

Any unused annual allowance can be carried forward for up to three years; however, it is only be possible for an individual to do this if he was a member of a registered pension scheme in the year for which the unused allowance is claimed.

Calculating whether the £40,000 cap has been exceeded is simple enough in relation to a 'money purchase' pension scheme – ie where the final pension receivable will represent a variable return – as (broadly) it is the absolute amount of the contributions made in a tax year (by either the individual or the employer) which needs to be within the limit.

In relation to a 'defined benefits' scheme – where a pension scheme guarantees benefits on retirement, usually related to period of service and final salary – the position is more complicated, with the 'contribution' calculated with reference to a multiple of the increase in the member's pension entitlement (over inflation) in the relevant period.

Where an individual has started to draw benefits from their pension, the annual limit will be restricted to £4,000 (£10,000 before 6 April 2017) for new contributions.

The annual cap operates by reference to 'pension input periods'. Each scheme of which an individual is a member has its own pension input period.

In considering whether the annual allowance has been exceeded, an individual is deemed to make *no* contribution to a scheme for a tax year in which the individual either dies or retires from the scheme on the grounds of serious ill health.

Where contributions to an individual's pensions fund(s) exceed the annual cap, there is an 'annual allowance charge'. This is taxed at the individual's *marginal* rate via the self-assessment tax return; however, it is not regarded as income for general tax purposes (and, therefore, cannot be reduced by allowances, losses or reliefs). In a UK Treasury statement issued on 3 March 2011, it was confirmed that annual allowance charges in excess of £2,000 can be met out of the individual's pension benefit where there are sufficient funds to do so.

The lifetime cap

[6.24] Since 6 April 2006, there has been no absolute limit on the level of benefits an individual can accrue within a registered pension scheme. However, there is instead a lifetime cap on the maximum amount that can be drawn from all registered pension schemes without triggering tax charges. The lifetime cap is expressed as a capital value.

The levels of this lifetime cap rose steadily from £1,500,000 in 2006/07 to £1,800,000 in 2010/11. It remained at £1,800,000 for 2011/12 but again as part of the 'fairness' agenda referred to above, it reduced to £1,500,000 from 6 April 2012 and further reduced to £1,250,000 from April 2014. From 6 April 2016 to 5 April 2018, the lifetime cap was reduced further to £1,000,000. From 6 April 2017, the Lifetime Allowance will increase annually in line with the Consumer Prices Index (£1,030,000). Unlike the annual cap, the lifetime cap does not operate to limit the tax relief *at the time the contribution is made*. Instead, there are points in time when the value of an individual's pension benefits will be checked against the annual cap and if it is exceeded, a 'lifetime allowance charge' arises. These points in time are known as 'benefit-crystallisation events' (BCEs).

A full list of the different types of BCE's can be found at HMRC's Registered Pension Schemes Manual at PTM088100. Broadly speaking, there will be a BCE when an individual takes a benefit from a pension fund, when 'lump sum death benefits' are paid out on the individual's death before 75, or where an individual reached age 75 without having taken any benefits. It can also be triggered if the pension is transferred to a qualifying recognised overseas pension scheme (QROPS). It is likely then that a BCE will arise at some point in the vast majority of cases; however, it should be noted that this point may be many years after contributions have been made.

When a BCE occurs, the pension scheme administrator checks to see if the lifetime cap has been exceeded. How this is done will depend upon the type of BCE but, for example, if the BCE occurs because the individual has taken only a partial pension benefit, it may be that only a proportion of the individual's lifetime allowance will have been used. The proportion of the individual's lifetime allowance being used up as a consequence of the BCE is added to any percentage used by the individual in previous BCEs. This applies whether the BCE has arisen from the same scheme or from a different registered pension scheme.

Where on a BCE the lifetime cap being exceeded, the lifetime allowance charge is calculated as a percentage of the excess as follows:

- In relation to any amount taken as a lump sum – 55%.
- In relation to any amount taken as a pension – 25%.

The reason for this difference is that any amount paid out as a pension will also be subject to income tax upon receipt.

Protecting the lifetime allowance

[6.25] Historically, some individuals may have an increased personal lifetime allowance if they had one of the previous 'Protections' in place. As the lifetime allowances have fallen over previous years, each year, various 'Protections' were made available.

With the reduction of lifetime allowances to £1,000,000 on 6 April 2016, 'Fixed Protection 2016' was made available for individuals to fix the lifetime allowance at £1,250,000. The FP 2016 is not available to individuals who already had a Fixed Protection in place as at 5 April 2016.

Individual Protection 2014 was introduced alongside Fixed Protection 2014 aimed at those with pension savings valued above £1,250,000. It protects the lifetime allowance at a level equal to the value of pension rights as at 5 April 2014, up to a maximum of £1,500,000. Further savings into the pension scheme can be made without losing this protection as long as the savings remain within the protected lifetime allowance. Those exceeding this limit will be subject to the 55% tax charge. This type of protection can be held while holding either Enhanced Protection or both forms of Fixed Protection.

Similarly, **Individual Protection 2016** was introduced in April 2016. Applications for Individual Protection 2014 can be made between August 2014 and 5 April 2017.

There is no deadline for applications for Fixed Protection 2016 or Individual Protection 2016. The applications will need to be made through an online portal which became available from July 2016, and no certificates will be issued by HMRC.

The restrictions on pension fund investments

[6.26] Pension schemes can invest in almost any kind of asset and the interest and gains on those investments will usually be free from income tax and capital gains tax.

Because HMRC was concerned that investment freedom would lead to the abuse of these tax privileges, measures were introduced by FA 2006 to deter investment in certain assets. The new rules, which were backdated to 6 April 2006, apply where 'investment-regulated pension schemes' invest in what is known as 'taxable property'.

An investment-regulated pension scheme is, broadly speaking, any type of pension scheme where a member has a say over the assets in which his pension fund is invested. Both SIPPs and SSASs are investment-regulated pension schemes.

Taxable property means:

- residential property (either in the UK or overseas); or
- tangible moveable property – meaning any asset that can be touched and moved, such as fine wine and works of art. However, it could also include items such as computers, machinery and photographic equipment.

Indirect investment in these assets via companies can also be caught.

All pension schemes are able to *lend* money to unconnected third parties; however, loans cannot generally be made to scheme members or those connected with them. An occupational pension scheme that satisfies certain requirements (which a SSAS is likely to meet) can make employer-related loans – ie to the sponsoring employer and those connected with it (eg associated companies). Such loans are, however, subject to strict rules – concerning eg their term, rate, repayment and their size relation to the scheme's net assets at the loan date.

There are likewise strict rules as to the amount a pension scheme can *borrow*, with the general limit being up to 50% of the scheme's value.

Where any of these investment limits are breached, punitive tax charges will arise. It is beyond the scope of this section to detail these charges; however, it goes without saying that specialist advice should be taken where pension funds are to be lent or taken out; or an investment is to be made in anything which might be considered to be 'taxable property'.

Drawing benefits

[6.27] This chapter is concerned with the tax effective extraction of profit from a business; however, the tax reliefs available on the 'extraction' of profits *to* the pension (ie the contribution stage) and the exemption from tax on the income and gains within the pension are only part of the equation. Ultimately the individual pension holder will want either himself or another member of his family to *personally* benefit from the pension fund and the taxation position when funds are ultimately 'extracted' from the pension also need to be considered in assessing the overall tax effectiveness.

Pension rules are complex and the following commentary is intended only as an overview. Specialist advice should always be taken in relation to the options available when considering how benefits should be taken from a pension.

There is no longer a requirement for an individual to actually retire before commencing to take benefits. The minimum age benefits can commence is currently 55.

The position prior to the 2014 Budget

[6.28] Prior to the announcements made in the 2014 budget relating to the UK pensions taxation system, an individual could deal with their pension pot in a number of ways. Whichever route is chosen, 25% of the fund can be drawn out as a tax free lump sum (ITEPA 2003 s 636B).

The traditional approach to taking benefits from a pension is for an individual to choose a date at which to start taking benefits and:

(a) To take the 25% tax free lump sum; and
(b) To use the balance of the pension fund to invest in an annuity which then guarantees the individual an annual income. The annuity itself can have various options attached to it, such as a spouse's pension on the death of the member, increases in payment each year and a minimum guaranteed term.

Where an individual has a pension pot totalling less than £18,000, the full amount can be withdrawn under the trivial commutation rules with the balance above the 25% tax free element chargeable at the individual's marginal rate.

For those individuals that hold £2,000 or less in two or less pension pots these can be extracted in full. Again amounts exceeding the 25% tax free lump sum would be taxed at marginal rates.

The ability to extract funds under the trivial commutation and small pot arrangements are only available to those aged 60 or over and are subject to the pension scheme rules which take precedence. The radical changes proposed for 2015, outlined below, will however provide greater flexibility where the pension pot exceeds the limit under the scheme rules.

Although an annuity can provide a guaranteed income for life, with interest rates at all time lows and increased longevity, annuity rates have been in decline for many years. As an alternative some individuals have extracted income from a pension in the form of a 'drawdown' of the fund itself and/or the income generated by it. The ability to drawdown from the pension fund has been around for some time but in April 2011, two forms of drawdown from a defined contribution pension scheme for those aged 55 and above were introduced.

The first of these is **capped drawdown**, which allows an individual to drawdown 120% of an equivalent annuity. The equivalent annuity is calculated by dividing the drawdown fund by £1,000 and then multiplying it by the appropriate rate taken from the GAD (Government Actuary's Department) which is based on the individual's sex, age and gilt yields. The maximum income under capped drawdown must be recalculated at least every three years until the individual reaches age 75 and every year thereafter.

The second drawdown facility is **flexible drawdown** which has no limit on the amount that can be taken out of the fund so no need to refer to the GAD rates. However, this flexibility is only available to those individuals who are able to satisfy the Minimum Income Requirement (MIR). The MIR imposes a condition that the individual must be able to demonstrate that they have at least £20,000 of secure lifetime pension income. This income can include income from certain pensions including pension schemes that have at least 20 members, state pensions, lifetime annuities and equivalent overseas pensions. It does not include drawdown pensions as the income is not secure for life.

From 6 April 2015, the MIR does not need to be met.

It is possible to withdraw the whole of the pension fund but the individual will suffer a 55% tax charge with the scheme itself suffering a 15% charge.

Where a pension fund is used to purchase an annuity, the pension fund will be exhausted and there will therefore usually be no funds left to be distributed on the death of the member. However, before an annuity is purchased or where a pension is still in 'drawdown', there could be funds still in the pension to be distributed to the beneficiaries of the deceased member in the form of a 'lump sum'. Finance Act 2011 removed the requirement for pension benefits to be taken on or before the age of 75 so these lump sums could now be paid out at any age.

Changes announced for 2014 and 2015

[6.29] The 2014 budget set out some radical changes to the UK pensions taxation system. Some of the changes took effect immediately with the more far reaching changes taking effect from April 2015. In addition, fundamental changes were introduced in the Summer Budget 2015 in respect of the lump sum death benefit charge, which will come into effect on 6 April 2016.

The immediate changes which took effect from budget day 27 March 2014 were as follows:

- The pension pot under which trivial commutation can apply has increased to £30,000;

- The small pots arrangement has been increased so that up to three pots with a value of £10,000 or less can now be taken in full;
- The age at which small pots and trivial benefits can be accessed has been reduced to 55;
- The amount which can be extracted by way of a capped drawdown has increased to 150%;
- The amount of guaranteed pension income needed to facilitate flexible drawdown has reduced to £12,000.

In addition, following the consultation on the pension reforms a permissive statutory override will be introduced to allow schemes to follow the tax rules relating to accessing small pots and trivial commutations rather than their own scheme rules should they wish to do so.

The age at which private pensions can be accessed will also be rising in line with the state pension age, such that from 2028 the minimum age will be 57.

The changes from April 2015

[6.30] The 25% tax free lump sum will remain but a summary of the other measures is as follows:

Members of defined contribution schemes:

- Individuals will be able to access any amount they require from the pension scheme in any one year. It is possible for the entire pension fund to be extracted at age 55. Any tax payable in respect of amounts exceeding the tax free lump sum will be charged at marginal rates not 55% as previously;
- Individuals will be able to access free independent financial advice on their options at the point of retirement. The advice will be provided by organisations such as the Pensions Advisory Service and the Money Advisory Service so that there are no potential or perceived conflicts of interest with the pension scheme providers. Pension scheme providers will be legally obliged to point their customers to the advice guidance service;
- The rules governing annuities will be relaxed to enable pension providers to create new types of annuity that more closely meet consumer needs, as well as creating products through the drawdown rules.
- It will still be possible to buy an annuity, which, for those individuals wanting a secure and regular source of income on retirement, may be the best option.

Members of defined benefit schemes:

- Members of private sector defined benefit schemes will continue to be allowed to transfer to defined contribution schemes to access the flexibility introduced in the 2014 Budget subject to obtaining independent financial advice and the trustees agreeing the transfer;
- The trivial commutation and small pots rules will remain for those in defined benefit schemes; and

- Members of unfunded public sector pension schemes will not be able to transfer out to a defined contribution scheme except in exceptional circumstances. Funded public sector schemes will continue to be able to transfer to defined contribution schemes.

The tax and other consequences arising from the changes

With a greater flexibility in the management of funds in retirement this will lead to an enhanced need for tax as well as investment advice in the future. For those not wishing to take an annuity, tax planning and compliance in retirement will become much more important, with the timing of drawdown becoming a major factor in minimising income tax liabilities. With the prospect of many pensioners being able to drawdown their pension how they wish, many may find themselves having to consider tax and file self-assessment tax returns. There could also be repercussions in respect of entitlement to means tested benefits.

In the light of these changes, the tax position in relation to the various ways in which funds can be extracted from a pension is broadly as follows:

- The pension commencement lump sum would typically be tax free and therefore these funds – which would also have attracted tax relief when they were transferred to the pension – would represent profits extracted very tax efficiently.
- Ongoing 'income' receipts from an annuity or under drawdown would be subject to income tax at the individual's marginal rate; however, there is no requirement that this rate has to be the same as the rate at which tax relief was obtained when the funds were originally contributed to the pension. Timing of drawdowns will be crucial in terms of minimising tax exposure.
- Lump sum benefits drawn down post 6 April 2015 will be taxable at the individual's marginal tax rates.

Under the current framework, rules prevent an individual in flexible drawdown from securing tax relief on further contributions to a pension scheme. Given that the conditions for flexible drawdown to apply (ie the MIR) were removed from April 2015, the government introduced specific provisions to maintain a similar restriction. Effectively, the rules create a cap so that those who have chosen to drawdown a pension worth more than £10,000 are restricted to a maximum relief on further pension contributions up to a maximum of £10,000.

Generally, given the ability to accelerate the payment of benefits this discrepancy in rates applied for relief going into a pension and that applied on extraction appears attractive and gives rise to concerns on how long tax relief at marginal rates will survive going forward. Currently, there are always a number of possible permutations and therefore possible tax rates that could apply – hence the need for specialist advice in all cases.

Key points

[6.31]

- The 0% rate on dividends is being reduced from £5,000 to £2,000 from 6 April 2018.
- It is more important to provide advice on a case-by-case basis as to how to extract profits from a company in the most tax efficient manner.
- No more MIR for pensions means there is more flexibility for the drawdown of pensions despite the new restriction on additional contributions. Clients need to budget exactly how much to drawdown as they will be unable to put excess over £4,000 back in the pension pot.
- Benefit in kind – expensive cars may now qualify for first year allowances if they are of sufficiently low emission.
- The lifetime cap has been further reduced to £1,030,000.

Chapter 7

Financing the Business

Introduction

[7.1] Raising money for OMBs can be difficult, but there are some valuable tax reliefs available. The Enterprise Investment Scheme (EIS) and the Seed Enterprise Investment Scheme (SEIS) help companies attract external investment by offering some fantastic tax breaks. In the case of SEIS the tax breaks can be as high as 78% of the money invested.

For borrowings, there is relief available to the owners where the amounts borrowed are subsequently used to acquire shares in a company or lend money to the business. From April 2013 aggregate tax reliefs have been capped to 25% of income or £50,000, whichever is greater. This affects loan interest relief and loss reliefs, and how borrowings are structured.

Although not usually part of the planning, there are also some welcome tax reliefs when it all goes wrong. This chapter will examine the different methods of financing and will then look at what happens in these worst-case scenarios.

Loans or equity

[7.2] In order to provide working capital or to grow the business, capital needs to be provided. For an unincorporated business, this is often provided by way of bank borrowings or by way of capital provided by the proprietors.

Unincorporated businesses

[7.3] Where a business is operated by a sole trader, interest paid to a bank or other lender should be deductible as an expense of the business for income tax purposes so long as the money has been borrowed wholly and exclusively for the purposes of the trade. Interest would not be deductible if, for example, the loan has been taken out to fund personal expenditure.

Where a loan is taken out by a partner in a partnership or by a member of a limited-liability partnership, interest paid by the partner or member should be deductible against his or her income so long as the loan meets the requirements set out in Income Tax Act 2007, s 398 (ITA 2007).

The loan must be used:

(1)   to purchase a share in a partnership;
(2)   to contribute money to a partnership, by way of capital or premium, that is used wholly for the purposes of the trade or profession carried on by the partnership;

(3)   to advance money to a partnership that is so used; or

(4)   to repay another loan that qualified for relief.

The cap on reliefs must be considered, and it may be appropriate for the partnership or LLP, rather than the individual, to borrow funds, so that loan interest becomes part of the computation of profits for the business. This would be suitable where the borrowings are used for working capital but not where borrowings are used by the individual to purchase an interest in the business.

Where the partnership borrows funds, interest would be charged to the profit and loss account, and would be deductible for income tax purposes so long as it is incurred wholly and exclusively for the purposes of its trade. Corporate partners would deal with interest paid under loan relationship rules.

Deduction of tax at source

[7.4] Usually, an individual does not have to deduct income tax from payments of yearly interest, except where the recipient's usual place of abode is outside the UK (ITA 2007, s 874(1)(d)). The meaning of place of abode is set out in HMRC's manuals at SAIM9080. Care needs to be taken when interest is paid to an overseas branch of a bank, as income tax may need to be deducted if the bank does not have a permanent establishment in the UK and so has a place of abode outside the UK. When an individual is in this position, income tax is usually accounted for under a direct collection mechanism (ITA 2007, s 963(1)(a)(ix)). In practice, the individual should write to his tax office, setting out the interest payment and the income tax to be deducted. The tax office will then raise an assessment, which enables the income tax to be collected (ITA 2007, s 963(3)). HMRC has consulted on the treatment of interest, and in the consultation it was proposed that the procedure for individuals accounting for income tax deducted on interest payments should be formalised by introducing a special form. To date this has not happened.

Financing a company

[7.5] With a company, the choice of finance is wider, and a proprietor of a limited company has the basic choice between share capital or loan capital. For a small or medium-sized private company with no outside shareholders, it is not common to have a large share capital. Typically, this type of company would be formed with, say, 1,000 ordinary £1 shares, with the balance of working capital provided by the proprietors or a bank in the form of loans. This structure minimises the lock-up of capital in the company and will be familiar to any adviser. A larger and more complex share structure may be required where venture capitalists or other outside investors are involved.

Now that it is easier to effect a reduction of share capital, a larger share capital should not be discouraged on the grounds of inflexibility. Indeed, when seeking external finance, share capital may be preferable to shareholder loans.

Loan capital

[7.6] There are a number of advantages for the proprietor in providing loan capital rather than share capital to his company. The loan can be increased or decreased easily as the company's needs change, and profits can be paid to the proprietor as a loan repayment so as to defer taxable payments, such as bonuses or dividends.

So far as the company is concerned, any payment of interest to the proprietor will be deductible as a loan relationship debit, which, on the basis that it is a trading loan relationship, will form part of the trading results of the company for corporation tax purposes. It should be noted that interest accrued but not paid within 12 months after the end of the accounting period is not deductible for corporation tax purposes (Corporation Tax Act 2009, ss 373 and 375 (CTA 2009)) where the loan is from a participator or an associate of a participator of a close company.

Where interest is paid at more than a commercial rate a corporation tax deduction can be denied under one of a number of anti-avoidance provisions in CTA 2009, ss 440 to 455A. Any amount paid in excess of a reasonable commercial return could be taxed on the recipient on the basis that it is a dividend (CTA 2010, s 1000(1) E).

Income tax deduction

[7.7] Interest paid by a company to an individual must be paid net of income tax at 20%, and the tax deducted must be paid to HMRC using a form CT61. This form must be submitted to HMRC together with payment, in respect of any quarter in which interest is paid under deduction of tax.

There are currently some exceptions to this rule, for example where the company pays short interest, which can be paid gross. The concept of short interest is based on case law which is summarised in HMRC's manuals at SAIM9075. Broadly, short interest applies to interest on a loan repaid within 12 months. HMRC will, however, challenge annual loans that are repeatedly renewed.

Interest paid to another UK company or to a UK bank can be paid without deduction of tax. If interest is paid to an overseas lender income tax must be deducted at 20%, although this may be reduced if an application has been made to apply the relevant treaty rate for the country of residence of the recipient of the interest.

Share capital

[7.8] A limited company can also raise capital through an issue of shares, which can comprise a number of classes, each of which have their own rights set out in the Articles of Association. Typically, an OMB will have a small amount of issued share capital, perhaps £1,000 or less. However, there are situations where a company needs to have a larger share capital. This might be because there are significant or multiple shareholders who are required to show their commitment to the company by introducing significant funds by way of share capital. A company issuing shares under the venture capital schemes will need to have more significant share capital, as relief for the shareholders is geared to the share capital they subscribe in the company. Significant share capital may arise as a result of a share for share exchange where the share capital issued in the holding company will generally match the value of that in the target company.

The company's bankers may wish to see a commitment in the form of share capital in the company. The company may need to have a larger share capital if it is tendering for large projects, in particular in the public sector or certain countries.

Shareholders may expect dividends from the company as a return on their investment. Dividends are not subject to withholding taxes, even if the recipient of the dividend is not resident in the UK. Dividends are never deductible for corporation tax purposes.

Preference shares

[7.9] The company could issue a mix of ordinary shares and preference shares. The advantage of preference shares is that they will usually carry a dividend rate, which can either be cumulative or non-cumulative, and may be redeemable. This may be attractive to investors who are prepared to put longer-term capital into the company but who require some comfort that they will get a return on their investment and that they can withdraw their capital in accordance with the Articles of Association of the company.

The redemption of preference shares at par value should not give rise to a capital gains tax charge on the shareholder, unless the base cost is reduced – for example, as a result of a previous reorganisation or takeover, or if the shares were acquired for less than par value from another shareholder.

The company should bear in mind that on redemption there will be a transfer from distributable reserves to a capital redemption reserve. There will, therefore, be a reduction in the amounts available to the ordinary shareholders as dividends following the redemption.

Shareholders should also bear in mind the potential impact on entrepreneurs' relief as preference shares can form part of the ordinary share capital of a company (see **3.12**).

Share capital v loan capital

[7.10] Investors must bear in mind that, unless they hold loan stock or redeemable preference shares, their capital will be locked into the company, unless the company decides to purchase shares back from the shareholders or carry out a capital reduction (which is subject to detailed rules dealt with elsewhere).

Company borrowings v personal borrowings

[7.11] Where capital needs to be borrowed from a bank, there is a further decision. Does the company borrow from the bank, or does the proprietor borrow and introduce the funds as loan capital or share capital? The decision on who borrows may simply hinge on who can borrow more cheaply. However, the decision is more likely to involve a number of commercial factors, such as how other investors can fund their contribution to the company, whether the company has other existing borrowings, the type of security required by the bank, and what the company's balance sheet will look like. However, the restriction on income tax relief also needs to be taken into account in this analysis.

The net of tax position for the company and for the individual should also be taken into account.

Example

The Bucolin Group requires a further £500,000 of working capital to fund new projects. Robert, the major shareholder, has decided to borrow the funds personally because he can get a better rate of interest with lower arrangement fees than the company could achieve for the same borrowing. He needs to decide whether the capital should be provided by way of loan capital or share capital. He wants a 5% return from the company on the capital so as to cover his borrowing costs and to reflect a commercial position in the company's accounts.

If the Group borrows £500,000 from Robert, it will incur an annual interest charge of £25,000. Income tax of £5,000 will be deducted and paid to HMRC, and Robert will receive net interest of £20,000. The paying company will obtain corporation tax relief, which will reduce the company's tax liability by £5,000.

If Robert subscribes for further shares, perhaps another class of ordinary shares, the company will pay him an annual dividend of £25,000. There will be no withholding tax, but no deduction for the company.

Robert should bear in mind that the company must have distributable reserves sufficient to cover the dividend, otherwise the dividend will be illegal and would be repayable to the company. The company would not need reserves to pay interest to Robert, and any loss arising as a result of the interest paid can be carried forward and set off against future profits of the paying company.

Robert's position would be as follows. For the purposes of this example, we will assume that Robert is a higher rate taxpayer, the additional income does not reduce his personal allowance and he has not used his 0% band of £2,000 for dividend income:

	Loan	*Dividend*
	£	*£*
Interest/dividend	25,000	25,000
Interest relief against other income	(25,000)	(25,000)
Net tax position:		
Refund of tax on interest	(5,000)	

	Loan £	Dividend £
Higher-rate tax on dividend		7,475
Refund of tax on other income		(10,000)
Net refund	5,000	2,525
Robert's cash flow:		
Other net income	60,000	60,000
Net interest/dividend received	20,000	25,000
Interest paid	−25,000	−25,000
Income tax refund	5,000	2,525
	60,000	62,575

At the personal level, therefore, it may appear more attractive to receive a dividend rather than interest. However, once one takes into account the company's position, and the corporation tax relief available at 19%, the combined position for Robert and the Bucolin Group is better by about £2,225 under the loan agreement.

If the company is unable to use the corporation tax relief, it may be better to fund the company by way of share capital, although one would have to ensure that reserves are available out of which dividends can be paid.

Income tax relief for interest paid

[7.12] In the above example, we assumed that Robert was able to obtain income tax relief for the interest paid to the bank. Relief is available under ITA 2007, s 392 where a loan is used to acquire any part of the ordinary share capital of a close company, or to lend money to a close company so long as the money is used for the purposes of the business of the borrowing company or any associated company. Income tax relief is not available where the loan is used to acquire shares in a close investment-holding company, or where the loan is used to make a loan to a close investment-holding company, or where the money is used for the purposes of the business of a company that is a close investment-holding company (ITA 2007, s 392(2)). A close investment-holding company is defined in ITA 2007, s 393A.

In most situations for owner-managed businesses, the company will be a close company, but this basic requirement must not be overlooked. Where the loan is used to acquire shares, those shares must be part of the ordinary share capital of the company. This means that Robert could subscribe for a new class of ordinary shares, but not for fixed-rate preference shares, which might be a temptation, as he stipulated that he wanted a return of 5% on the new capital provided by him.

Income tax relief is not available where the investor has claimed EIS income tax relief or deferral relief on the shares. Relief is also not available where the company's business is the occupation of commercial woodlands.

Relief for interest paid is subject to a continuous test, which must be applied at the time when interest is paid. The following must be satisfied:

(1)   the company must not be a close investment-holding company;

(2)   the individual has not recovered any capital from the company in the period from the use of the loan to the payment of interest, apart from any amounts treated as repayments of the loan;

(3)   the individual holds part of the ordinary share capital of the company and the greater part of his time is spent in the actual management or conduct of the company or an associated company; or

(4)   the individual has a material interest (more than 5% of the ordinary share capital or the assets on a winding-up) and, if the company exists mainly for the purpose of holding investments or other property, either the individual spends the greater part of his time in the actual management or conduct of the company or an associated company, or no property held by the company is used as a residence of the individual.

The restriction on income tax relief in ITA 2007, s 24A will also need to be considered. This section places a cap on the total of certain reliefs, which include loan interest relief, to the greater of £50,000 or 25% of adjusted total income. It may now be more appropriate for the company to borrow directly from a bank, rather than to borrow funds from the proprietor, who could suffer a disallowance of interest paid. When looking at how to finance a company in the longer term advisers should address the effect of an interest rate increase on any disallowance under the capping rules.

EIS and SEIS

[7.13] EIS relief is derived from a number of previous schemes that have been used to encourage and support new and growing businesses. Under the current scheme for individuals, two reliefs run in parallel: EIS relief, which provides relief against income tax and an exemption from capital gains tax, and EIS deferral relief, which enables the individual to defer capital gains tax liabilities on other gains. The two overlap in many respects but should be seen as separate reliefs. EIS income tax relief can be found in ITA 2007, Part V and EIS deferral relief in TCGA 1992, Sch 5B. The Summer Budget 2015 introduced a sunset clause, restricting EIS relief to shares issued before 6 April 2025 (ITA 2007, s 157(1)(aa)).

It has become apparent from a number of recent tribunal decisions that EIS and SEIS legislation is very prescriptive, and there is little latitude in the way in which the rules are applied. Extreme care must be exercised in relation to any issue of shares under EIS or SEIS, both in ensuring that the complex requirements can be met, and also that the implementation is meticulous.

EIS — Income tax relief

[7.14] Income tax relief is available where an individual subscribes for shares in a qualifying company and a number of requirements are met with regard to the nature of the trade carried on by the company, what the money raised is used for and some general issues pertaining to the company and the individual. In order to claim the relief, the individual must submit to HMRC the EIS3 certificate provided by the company.

An individual can claim 30% income tax relief for investments up to £1,000,000 in a tax year. ITA 2007, s 158 enables the individual to claim relief in the preceding year. Relief is obtained as a deduction from the individual's income tax liability, ie as a tax reducer.

Where an individual claims income tax relief, any gain on disposal of the shares is exempt from CGT. The FTT decision in *Robert Ames v Revenue and Customs Comrs (TC04523)* [2015] UKFTT 337 (TC) highlights that income tax relief must be claimed at least on some of the qualifying investment – investing in EIS shares without making the claim is not sufficient.

Qualifying conditions

The investor

[7.15] The investor must not be connected with the company at any time beginning two years before the issue of the shares and ending three years after the issue, or, if the money was raised for a company preparing to carry on a trade, three years after the commencement of trade. The rules for connection are contained in ITA 2007, Part V, Chapter II.

Connection is defined in terms of the individual's working relationship with the company and the individual's interest in the capital of the company. An individual's associates will be taken into account in determining whether any of the tests have been breached. An associate includes spouse or civil partner and blood relatives. Further detail on connection with the company is provided at **[7.17]**.

An individual is connected with a company if he or any associate is an employee or a partner of the company or of any subsidiary or partner of the company. A paid director will also be treated as connected with the company.

Section 164A introduces an existing shareholdings requirement which essentially prevents an investor from obtaining relief if he already holds shares in the company unless those shares are risk finance investments (ie EIS, SEIS or VCT investments) or are subscriber shares which have been held continuously by the investor.

Business angels

[7.16] There are special rules for directors who, in certain circumstances, can claim EIS relief. Such individuals are referred to as business angels. These rules recognise that individuals who invest in a company may be able to provide valuable expertise.

A business angel can claim EIS relief in the following circumstances, where adherence to the required sequence of events is crucial.

(1) An individual can subscribe for and be issued with EIS shares, then become a director of the company and receive reasonable remuneration for his services.
(2) An individual can become an unpaid director, with no entitlement to receive remuneration, subscribe for and be issued with EIS shares, and then become a paid director.
(3) An individual satisfying the criteria in 1 or 2 above can subscribe for further EIS shares so long as they are issued within three years of the first qualifying issue of shares, even if, in the meantime, he has become a paid director.

Connection with the company

[7.17] An individual is connected with the company if he directly or indirectly possesses or is entitled to acquire more than 30% of the ordinary share capital or voting power of the company or any subsidiary. Care must be taken to ensure that this limit is not breached at any time in the requisite period, for example where shares may be issued at different times. There is a relaxation where an individual has held only subscriber's shares in the company which mean that he breaches the 30% test, so long as the company has not carried on or made any preparations to carry on any trade or business. Again, care must be exercised here, and it is best for potential EIS investors not to form the company, so that the company cannot inadvertently make any preparations to carry on a trade or business before the individual's shareholding is reduced by further issues of shares.

Care must also be exercised to ensure that an investor's associates do not also hold shares so that the aggregate holding breaches the 30% test.

These provisions are illustrated in the following table, showing the availability of relief for various individuals who are considering an investment in an EIS company set up by Robert, who is related to the individuals in various ways (assuming Robert owns 30% of the shares):

	Income tax relief	Capital gains disposal	Capital gains deferral
Fleur (sister)	Y	Y	Y
Monica (employee)	N	N	Y
Edward (uncle)	Y	Y	Y
David (cousin)	Y	Y	Y
Candy (parent)	N	N	Y
Susan (spouse)	N	N	Y
Vincent (father-in-law)	Y	Y	Y
Belle (90-year-old great aunt)	Y	Y	Y

Planning point

For Belle, the investment could be very tax-efficient. Suppose Belle had a property portfolio worth £600,000 which is sitting at a gain of £300,000. If she dies holding the portfolio, inheritance tax of £240,000 would be payable (ignoring the nil-rate band). The assets would be uplifted to £600,000 for capital gains tax purposes. However, if Belle disposed of the portfolio now, she would realise a gain of £300,000. This gain could be deferred by reinvesting the proceeds into an EIS company. Due to the strict trading conditions for EIS, the company will also qualify for BPR at a rate of 100%. Therefore, after two years of ownership, no inheritance tax would be payable on death. As for the deferred gain, this gets washed out on death, so IHT of £240,000 is saved!

Linked loans

[7.18] There must be no linked loans made to the investor or any associate by any person in the period beginning with the incorporation of the company or two years before the issue of the shares, whichever is earlier, and three years after the issue of the shares or the commencement of trade, whichever is later. A linked loan is any loan which would not have been made, or would not have been made on the same terms, if the investor had not invested, or had not been proposing to invest, in the EIS shares.

Bona fide test

[7.19] The investor must subscribe for the shares for genuine commercial reasons and not as part of a scheme or arrangement the main purpose, or one of the main purposes, of which is the avoidance of tax (ITA 2007, s 165).

The shares

[7.20] There are a number of requirements pertaining to the shares but some of the conditions were relaxed in Finance Act 2012. The shares must be ordinary shares but the definition of qualifying shares has been widened. These changes mirror the changes made for VCT qualifying shares in Finance (No 3) Act 2010 and the definition of qualifying shares for SEIS purposes. Previously, shares under EIS could not include any preferential rights to a dividend. The amendment to ITA 2007, s 173 means investors can subscribe for shares carrying preferential rights to dividends. Shares are not 'qualifying' if (a) they carry preferential rights to assets on a winding-up, (b) the amount or timing of a dividend depends on a decision of a company or another person, (c) the dividend rights are cumulative. The shares cannot carry any present or future right to be redeemed.

Finance Act 2018 has introduced a risk-to-capital condition which means that the company's objective must be to grow and develop its trade in the long term, and that the capital subscribed must be genuinely at risk.

The shares must be subscribed for wholly in cash and be fully paid up at the time they are issued.

Pitfall 1

[**7.21**] In looking at the shares, it is not enough that they are ordinary shares without any preferential rights (subject to the rights now permitted). Care must be taken not to create a preference inadvertently, for example by issuing restricted shares to employees which do not rank *pari passu* on a winding-up. The pre-existing EIS shares would, as a result, have a preferential right on a winding up that could be caught by these provisions. In particular, care needs to be taken in the shareholders' agreement to ensure that the EIS shareholders do not get their money back first in the event of a winding-up, etc.

Pitfall 2

[**7.22**] The issuing of shares involves a process which ends with the entry of the investor's name in the register of members and the issue of a share certificate. For EIS shares to be validly issued, the investor's name must be in the register of members. The date of issue for EIS purposes is the date on which the entry was made. Relief will be denied where the issue process is not completed.

A company can raise no more than £5 million in any one year in respect of venture capital schemes. This is an aggregated amount for all venture capital schemes (EIS, SEIS or Venture Capital Trust (VCT)). This limit is restricted where a company has received any other state-aided capital.

There is an additional cap on the total amount that a company can raise through venture capital schemes; £20 million for a knowledge-intensive company, and £12 million for any other company (s 173AA). A knowledge-intensive company is defined in s 252A.

The relevant shares must be issued in order to raise money for the purposes of a qualifying business activity, and the money raised must be used within two years of the issue of shares or commencement of trade (if later). FA 2012 introduced provisions in ITA 2007, s 175(1A) to prevent the venture capital monies from being used to acquire shares in a company. Such acquisitions do not meet the conditions of employing the money for the purposes of a qualifying business activity.

In order to be able to claim relief, the trade must have been carried on by the issuing company or a qualifying 90% subsidiary for a minimum period of four months ending at or after the time of the issue. Where research and development is involved, this must have been carried on by the issuing company or a qualifying 90% subsidiary, and the research and development must not have been carried on by any other person.

If a company is wound up for genuine commercial reasons before the four-month period has elapsed, relief can, nevertheless, be claimed.

The issuing arrangements for the shares must not include any arrangements with a view to the subsequent repurchase, exchange or disposal of the EIS shares or of any other shares in or securities of the issuing company. In addition, there must be no arrangements in place in connection with the cessation of trade or the disposal of a substantial amount of the assets of the company or of a person connected with the company, or any arrangements designed to protect the investor from anything that would otherwise be a risk of investing in the shares.

This does not prevent the company from indicating to its investors how they might propose realising the shares, for example by seeking a trade sale in three years' time, so long as there are no arrangements in place.

The issuing company

[7.23] The issuing company must satisfy a number of requirements in terms of its structure and its activities. These are set out in ITA 2007, Pt V, Ch IV. Fundamentally, the company must exist wholly for the purpose of carrying on one or more qualifying trades, apart from any activities that have no significant effect (other than in relation to incidental matters) on the extent of the activities of the company in question.

The issuing company can have subsidiaries so long as they are either qualifying subsidiaries (51%) or qualifying 90% subsidiaries. The trade in respect of which the subscription money has been raised must be carried on either by the issuing company or a 90% subsidiary of that company. A company limited by guarantee cannot be a qualifying subsidiary (*Hunters Property plc* [2018] TC06354).

Section 175A introduces a permitted maximum age requirement. If relevant shares are issued after the initial investing period, condition A or B must be met. The initial investment period means, for a knowledge-intensive company, the period of ten years beginning with the first commercial sale, and for any other company the period of seven years beginning with the first commercial sale.

Condition A is that a relevant investment was made in the issuing company before the end of the initial investment period, and some or all of the money raised by that investment was used for the purposes of the relevant qualifying business activity.

Condition B is that the total amount of relevant investments made in the issuing company in a period of 30 consecutive days which includes the issue date is at least 50% of the average turnover amount. The average turnover amount means the average of the turnover in the five accounting periods prior to the share issue.

Qualifying trades

[7.24] The trade in respect of which the money has been raised must be a qualifying trade. A trade is qualifying if it is conducted on a commercial basis and with a view to the realisation of profits and it does not at any time in the period starting with the issue of shares or the commencement of trade if later and ending three years thereafter, consist to a substantial extent of excluded activities. Substantial for this purpose is regarded as 20%.

Excluded activities include the following:

- dealing in land, commodities or futures in shares, securities or other financial instruments;
- financial activities such as banking, money-lending, insurance, debt-factoring and hire-purchase financing;
- dealing in goods other than in an ordinary trade of retail or wholesale distribution;
- leasing or letting assets on hire, except in the case of certain ship-chartering activities;
- receiving royalties or licence fees, except in the case of the exploitation of an intangible asset created by the company or its group;
- providing legal or accountancy services;
- property development;
- farming or market gardening;
- holding, managing or occupying woodlands, any other forestry activities or timber production;
- operating or managing hotels, guest-houses or hostels in which the company carrying on the trade has an interest or which it occupies under licence or any other form of agreement;
- operating or managing nursing homes or residential care homes in which the company carrying on the trade has an interest or which it occupies;
- the generation or export of electricity;
- the generation of heat or subsidised production of gas or fuel; and
- providing services to another company in certain circumstances where the other company's trade consists, to a substantial extent, of excluded activities where the activities have been fragmented between related companies (see ITA 2007, s 199).

Many of these excluded activities are activities which are either heavily asset backed, involve the generation of passive income, or may be regarded as less risky businesses. However, it is still possible to have an EIS qualifying company involved in activities that can give the investor some asset protection, such as children's nurseries or pubs.

It should be noted also that, although insurance underwriting is excluded, insurance brokers may qualify. This is because their revenues consist of commissions rather than underwriting fees. Similarly, many financial advisers will also qualify. Advance assurance is recommended in these cases to give the necessary confirmation that the trade qualifies. HMRC has issued a new form EIS/SEIS(AA) that can be used by companies to apply for advance assurance that their shares will qualify. Although an advance assurance is not statutory, HMRC will normally be bound by the assurances, provided correct and complete information has been given. The advance assurance does not extend to the individual investors.

No disqualifying arrangements

[7.25] The shares must not have been issued in connection with disqualifying arrangements (ITA 2007, s 1278A). These are arrangements where one of the main purposes a person is party to the arrangements is to secure:

- that the relevant company (or its 90% subsidiary) carries on a qualifying activity; and
- the shares are issued to obtain venture capital relief; and
- as a result of the money raised by the issue of shares an amount is paid for the benefit of a party to the arrangements or someone connected with such a party; and /or
- in the absence of the arrangements, it would have been reasonable to expect that the component activities of the relevant business activities would have been carried on by a party to the arrangements or someone connected with such a party.

These provisions are specifically targeted at companies specifically set up for EIS and VCT purposes which have a financing role but have no real commercial substance and where a substantial amount of the trading activities are sub-contracted to another party.

Other requirements regarding the company

[7.26] Throughout the period beginning with the issue of the EIS shares and ending either three years after the issue of shares or three years after the commencement of trade, whichever is later, the issuing company must not be under the control of another company.

Throughout the period beginning with the issue of the EIS shares and ending on the later of three years after the issue of shares or three years after the commencement of trade, the company must remain unquoted, and there must be no arrangements in place for it to cease to be an unquoted company. For EIS purposes, AIM shares are unquoted.

The gross assets of the issuing company together with any subsidiaries must not exceed £15 million before the relevant share issue and must not exceed £16 million immediately after the share issue. Gross assets are measured in accordance with what would be shown on the company's or group's balance sheet immediately before and after the issue. If further shares are to be issued outside the venture capital schemes, it is possible to have a first closing in respect of the shares on which relief is required, keeping that issue within the required parameters, and a second issue after the first has been completed and all formalities in connection with the issue of shares have been attended to.

There is also an overall annual limit of £5 million on the level of funding which a company can obtain from EIS. The issuing company together with any subsidiaries must have less than 250 full-time employees. A just and reasonable fraction is used for part-time employees to arrive at an equivalent full-time employee head count.

Losing relief

[7.27] There are a number of rules which seek to ensure that EIS investors lose relief if they receive value from the company in the period beginning one year before the issue of shares and ending three years thereafter, or three years after the commencement of trade. Withdrawal or reduction of EIS relief is dealt with in ITA 2007, Pt V, Ch VI.

Return of value

[7.28] A return of value can arise where the company:

- buys any of its shares or securities which belong to the investor or an associate, or makes a payment in return for the holder giving up the right to them;
- makes a payment to the investor or an associate for giving up the right to payment of a debt (other than an ordinary trade debt);
- repays a debt owed to the investor or an associate that was incurred before he subscribed for the shares, except, for deferral-relief purposes, where the repayment is not made in connection with any arrangements concerning the share acquisition;
- waives any liability of the investor or an associate to the company, or discharges, or undertakes to discharge, any such liability to a third party;
- lends or advances the investor or an associate money which has not been repaid before the shares are issued;
- provides the investor or an associate with certain benefits or facilities;
- acquires an asset from the investor or an associate for more than its market value, or disposes of an asset to the investor or an associate for less than its market value; or
- makes any other payment to the investor or an associate which is not a 'qualifying payment'.

The investor will also be regarded as having received value where:

- the company (or any company connected with it for corporation tax purposes) is wound up or dissolved and the investor or any associates receive any payment or asset in the winding-up or in connection with the dissolution; or
- anyone connected with the company for EIS purposes buys any of its shares or securities belonging to the investor (or an associate), or makes a payment in return for the right to those shares or securities being given up.

It is possible to make restitution to the company to ensure that value is not regarded as having been received.

Care must be exercised where, for example, the company uses premises which are owned by an EIS shareholder or an associate. If the company pays more than a market rent, the EIS shareholder is likely to be regarded as receiving value from the company. Assume the individual had subscribed £100,000 for EIS shares, on which he had obtained relief of £30,000. The company then paid £20,000 of rent in excess of the market rate, which is the value received from the company. In order to calculate the amount withdrawn, the return of value must first be multiplied by the rate of relief obtained on the investment (30%). If the resultant figure, in this case £6,000, is less than the relief obtained, relief of £6,000 is withdrawn. If the resultant figure is greater than the relief obtained, the whole of the relief obtained when the investment was made is withdrawn.

Withdrawal of relief

[7.29] If income tax relief has been obtained but should not have been given for any reason, it will be withdrawn. The mechanics for income tax relief withdrawal are set out in ITA 2007, Part V, Chapter VI. Income tax relief will be withdrawn in whole or in part if the investor sells his shares within three years of acquiring them or within three years of the commencement of trade, or if the investor or an associate receives any value from the company within the period of restriction.

The amount of relief withdrawn will depend on the circumstances and the quantum of the proceeds or value received. On a receipt of value, the clawback of income tax relief will be the lower of the income tax relief obtained on the subscription and the value received, multiplied by the basic rate of income tax for the tax year in which the relief was obtained.

Where the shares are sold within the relevant period and the disposal is not at arm's length, the whole of the income tax relief is withdrawn.

Where the shares are sold at arm's length within the relevant period, the amount of relief withdrawn will depend on the amount of the consideration received. The amount withdrawn will be the lower of the consideration received, multiplied by 30% and the relief attributable to the shares sold.

Any withdrawal of relief must be notified to HMRC within 60 days of finding out that the relief falls to be withdrawn.

Capital gains tax relief

[7.30] EIS deferral relief is available where an individual has made a capital gain, and qualifying EIS shares are subscribed for within one year before and three years after the gain arose. That gain can be deferred until the EIS shares are subsequently sold, although there are provisions allowing serial reinvestment into EIS shares. It is the gain after any ER which is deferred.

Deferral relief can be claimed in addition to EIS income tax relief, although the capital gains tax exemption does not extend to the deferred gain. It only applies to the gain in excess of the amount subscribed for the shares.

Many of the requirements for the two reliefs are similar, the most fundamental difference being the rules with regard to the connection with the company. For income tax relief, the investor must not be connected with the company. However EIS deferral relief can be available even if the investor owns 100% of the investee company.

Key EIS points

[7.31] Key points to note are as follows:

- income tax relief is available on qualifying investments;
- capital gains tax exemption is available where income tax relief is claimed and not withdrawn;
- capital gains tax deferral is available;
- relief only applies to new shares subscribed, not 'second-hand' shares;
- loans cannot usually be capitalised so as to obtain relief;
- the subscriber must not be connected with the company to get income tax relief;
- money must be used by the company for a qualifying trade;
- the company must be unquoted, although AIM ranks as unquoted for this purpose;
- there are monetary limits that must be adhered to by the company;
- the minimum period of ownership is usually three years;
- relief can be clawed back if any of the EIS conditions is breached, usually within the three-year period.

Seed Enterprise Investment Scheme (SEIS)

[7.32] Seed EIS rules were introduced with effect from 6 April 2012 to incentivise early stage companies. The SEIS is targeted at companies which want to raise funds of up to £150,000. It was introduced for a five-year period but Finance Act 2014 made the relief permanent. It is expected that the SEIS will be used as a precursor to EIS and VCT investment.

Tax relief

[7.33] Under the SEIS, an investor is entitled to income tax relief at 50% (regardless of the individual's own tax rates) on a maximum of £100,000 in any one year. Relief is given as a tax reducer. The investment (or part of it) can be treated as if it was made in the previous year. Any claim for SEIS relief must be made on or before the fifth anniversary of the normal self-assessment filing date for the tax year. So for an investment made in 2015/16 the relief cannot be claimed any later than 31 January 2022. Where the relief is related back to an earlier year the time limit is by reference to that earlier period. A claim for income tax relief can only be made where the company has issued a compliance certificate and this can only be issued where at least 70% of the money has been used by the company for the qualifying business activity. This means that the investor may have to pay the tax and make the claim at a later date. Before issuing a compliance certificate the company must have authorisation from HMRC.

Where income tax relief is available any gain arising on an eventual disposal of the shares will be exempt provided the shares meet the conditions throughout the qualifying period.

With the SEIS there are two relevant periods:

Period A – which begins with the incorporation of the company and ends immediately before the termination date relating to the shares. The termination date is three years from the date the shares are issued.

Period B – which begins with the date on which the shares are issued and ends immediately before the termination date relating to the shares. The termination date is three years from the date the shares are issued.

Any SEIS relief is withdrawn or reduced if there is a disposal of the shares or other disqualifying activity before period B ends. Where the disposal is a transaction not at arm's length the relief is withdrawn in full but where the disposal is at arm's length, the relief is withdrawn using the formula:

$$R \times SEISR$$

Where: R is the amount of consideration received by the investor for the shares, and SEISR is the SEIS rate.

SEIS Qualifying conditions

The investor

[7.34] Neither the investor nor any associate of the investor can be an employee throughout period B but a director is not an employee for these purposes.

The investor cannot have a material interest (broadly a right to acquire more than 30% of the ordinary share capital or the issued share capital or the voting rights of the company or any subsidiary or more than 30% of the assets on a winding-up) throughout period A.

Bona fide

[7.35] The investment must be made for genuine commercial reasons and not as part of tax avoidance arrangements.

Qualifying shares

[7.36] The shares must be subscribed for in cash and fully paid up at the time of issue. The shares must form part of the ordinary share capital of the company and cannot carry any present or future preferential right to dividends (as defined in s 257CA) or to a company's assets on a winding-up or any present or future right to be redeemed.

Finance Act 2018 has introduced the risk-to-capital condition, which means that the company's objective must be to grow and develop its trade in the long term, and that the capital subscribed is genuinely at risk.

Shares may carry limited preferential rights to dividends under s 257CA(3) where the dividend can be varied to any extent by a decision of the company, shareholder or another person or where the dividend right is cumulative. Shares will not qualify for SEIS relief if the preferential right to a dividend is incorporated into the Articles or any other document.

The shares must be issued for the purpose of raising money for a qualifying activity carried on by the company or a qualifying 90% subsidiary. The money raised must be used for the qualifying business activity within period B. Where an insignificant amount is unused or used for different purposes this will not disqualify the individual from obtaining the relief.

Qualifying company

[7.37] The company must be unquoted at the beginning of period B and it cannot control a company that is not a qualifying subsidiary. During period A it cannot be under the control of another company or another company and a connected person.

The company must meet the trading requirement throughout period B. This means that the company (or the group) must exist wholly for the purposes of carrying on one or more new qualifying trades. A new qualifying trade is defined in s 257HF and is one where:

- the trade does not begin to be carried on (by the company or any other person) before the two-year, pre-investment period; and
- at no time before the company begins to carry on the trade was any other trade being carried on by the issuing company or any 51% subsidiary.

The two-year pre-investment period is the two years ending the day before the day the shares are issued.

A qualifying trade takes its meaning from the EIS rules and is one which is conducted on a commercial basis with a view to the realisation of profit and does not consist wholly or substantially of excluded activities.

The total value of the company's assets, or the group's assets if the issuing company is a parent company, cannot exceed £200,000 immediately before the shares are issued. At the time the shares are issued the company together with its subsidiaries must have fewer than 25 full-time equivalent employees.

Value received by the investor

[7.38] Relief will be withdrawn if the investor receives value from the company at any time in Period A. The relief is effectively withdrawn pound for pound in respect of the value received.

SEIS re-investment relief

[7.39] The rules on the SEIS re-investment relief are contained in TCGA 1992, Sch 5BB. Where an individual has a chargeable gain and makes an investment into SEIS qualifying shares the gain is reduced by 50% of the amount of the SEIS investment (FA 2013, s 57). There is no requirement to reinvest the whole of the proceeds to obtain the full relief. Unlike EIS re-investment, the individual must qualify for income tax relief. Where the SEIS conditions are met throughout period B the original gain will remain exempt from CGT. If the SEIS shares are subsequently sold at a gain, there is no claw back of the relief. Where the SEIS shares are eventually sold at a loss the loss will be restricted by the amount of any income tax relief.

Example – reinvesting a gain made in 2012/13 into SEIS shares and making a gain

Sue sold an asset for £150,000 in June 2012 and made a gain of £70,000. In October the same year, she invested £70,000 in SEIS shares and qualifies for reinvestment relief.

In December 2015, Sue disposes of the SEIS shares for £120,000. As Sue has held the SEIS shares for at least three years and all other SEIS conditions are also met, the initial gain of £70,000 made in 2012/13 is exempt from CGT.

The new gain of £50,000 is also exempt from CGT under the SEIS provisions.

Sue must make claims for both SEIS income tax relief and SEIS reinvestment relief because if no relief is claimed for income tax under the SEIS then the disposal will not qualify for exemption from CGT.

If for any reason the SEIS relief is withdrawn or reduced, the SEIS reinvestment relief will also be reduced by the corresponding proportional amount and CGT liability arises to the investor in 2012/13 on the disposal made in that year.

In our example, Sue can claim £35,000 income tax relief (50% of the investment of £70,000 into the SEIS shares) and, assuming entrepreneurs' relief is not available, she will also avoid paying up to £19,600 CGT, (28% × £70,000). This results in a combined relief of 78%.

On the disposal of the SEIS shares Sue will additionally save paying CGT of £14,000 (28% x £50,000) which means in total her relief amounts to £68,600.

If a loss arises on disposal of the SEIS shares the loss is restricted by the income tax relief obtained and relief is not withdrawn in respect of the shares.

Restrictions to SEIS reinvestment relief

[7.40] The CGT exemption is restricted where the amount subscribed for SEIS shares exceeds the maximum subscription of £100,000. The restriction is applied using the formula set out in ITA 2007, s 257AB(2)(b):

SA/TSA × £100,000

Where: SA means the SEIS expenditure, and TSA means the total amount subscribed for shares issued in 2012/13 in respect of which the investor is eligible for and claims SEIS relief for that year.

For example, if an individual subscribes £125,000 for shares in a SEIS company, income tax relief would be restricted to £100,000. The CGT exemption would be restricted to 100,000/125,000 × 100,000 = £80,000. This is a peculiar result, as the more the individual invests in a company (over £100,000), the more the formula reduces the availability of the CGT exemption.

Interaction with EIS

[7.41] A company cannot issue shares under the SEIS scheme if it has already had investment from a VCT, or issued shares in respect of which it has provided an EIS compliance statement (EIS1).

It should also be noted that if a company submits an EIS1 form, this cannot be withdrawn so as to enable the shareholders to claim relief under SEIS relief (*X-Wind Power Ltd v HMRC* [2017]).

For directors who have subscribed for shares under SEIS, ITA 2007, s 169 has been amended to allow the director to make a qualifying investment under EIS within three years of the SEIS investment.

SEIS key points

[7.42]

- income tax relief is available as a 50% tax reducer of the subscription amount up to £100,000;
- CGT deferral relief is available taking the maximum SEIS relief to 78%;
- income tax relief is not available until 70% of the funds raised have been used;
- deferral relief can be claimed before income tax relief;
- investors can go on to invest under EIS or VCT.

Investors' relief

[7.43] A new relief has been introduced by Finance Act 2016 and inserted after TCGA 1992, s 169V, which, although it was introduced as an extension of entrepreneurs' relief, it is best seen as a further relief to facilitate access to funds for private trading companies. Investors' relief (IR) will provide relief where EIS and SEIS are not available.

IR applies to shares in private trading companies subscribed for on or after 17 March 2016, giving a 10% CGT rate so long as the shares are sold after three years or after 5 April 2019 (if later).

There is a lifetime limit of £10 million of gains, which is in addition to the £10 million limit for ER. The relief applies to individuals and to trustees, so long as a number of requirements are met.

The relief is aimed principally at individuals who are not officers or employees of the company, although amendments to the original draft clauses have relaxed this position. Relief will be available where the individual is a 'relevant employee'. A 'relevant employee' is a person who becomes:

(i)   an 'unremunerated director' of the company or a connected company following the purchase of qualifying shares;

(ii)   an employee of the company after 180 days of the share issue, or where there was no reasonable prospect that the person would become an employee at the time of the share issue.

Individuals who hold shares jointly can each claim IR, so long as they each meet the relevant requirements.

Trustees will be able to benefit from IR although their entitlement to relief is linked with an eligible beneficiary. It should be noted that, although the concept is similar to the availability of ER for trustees, the requirements that must be met in relation to the beneficiaries of the trust are different. For ER purposes a 'qualifying beneficiary' is required, whereas for IR an 'eligible beneficiary' for which the criteria are different.

For IR purposes there must be at least one eligible beneficiary, who has had an interest in possession of the qualifying shares for at least three years preceding the disposal, and has not been a relevant employee of the company that issued the shares. Trustees cannot claim IR on the basis of a beneficiary with a temporary life interest, although this is possible in relation to ER.

Where trustees claim IR, this must come out of the eligible beneficiary's entitlement to IR. Where there is more than one eligible beneficiary the gain is apportioned between them. If relief for one or more of the beneficiaries has been used up, IR is not available to the trustees in respect of that proportion of the gain.

IR will be attractive to investors who do not satisfy the requirements for EIS and SEIS, or who have used their lifetime limit for ER. IR will be useful for unquoted trading companies who do not meet the requirements for EIS or SEIS, but are seeking to attract external investment.

Business investment relief for non-domiciliaries

[7.44] Historically, it has been thought that many non-domiciliaries have not invested in the UK because they were afraid to remit offshore income and suffer a tax charge. The Government has recognised this and since 6 April 2012 non-domiciled investors have been able to bring foreign monies onshore to invest in the UK without triggering a tax charge on the remittance.

The relief is available where foreign income or gains are brought onshore to invest in a qualifying investment and where that remittance would otherwise give rise to a taxable remittance. A claim must be made for the relief to apply. Where the relief applies the income or gains are treated as not being remitted to the UK.

In order to qualify for the relief an investment must be made into a qualifying company by a relevant person, who does not receive a reciprocal benefit.

Investment

[7.45] An investment may be made by the issue of shares or by making a loan. Where there is an issue of shares, the shares may be ordinary shares or preference shares. The purchase of shares from a third party will not qualify for relief.

Qualifying company

[7.46] The investment must be made in a private company. The company may be resident in the UK or abroad. Investments in LLPs and other forms of partnership will not qualify for relief. The company must be either:

- an eligible trading company;
- an eligible holding company; or
- an eligible stakeholder company.

For this purpose trading includes anything which is a trade for corporation tax purposes and a business carried on for generating income from land. This includes investing in property investment companies. An eligible holding company will qualify for relief where it is a member of an eligible trading group. An eligible stakeholder company will qualify for relief where it exists wholly for the purpose of making investments in companies which carry on qualifying activities and holds at least one investment in an eligible trading company.

Relevant person

[7.47] A relevant person includes:

- the individual;
- his spouse (or civil partner);
- his minor children and minor grandchildren;
- a close company (or subsidiary) in which a relevant person is a participator;
- a foreign company which would be close if it was UK resident in which a relevant person is a participator;
- a trust where a relevant person is a beneficiary or any entity connected with that trust.

No benefit

[7.48] Relief will be withdrawn if any relevant person either directly or indirectly receives a benefit. A benefit includes anything that is provided to a relevant person by the company that is not in the ordinary course of its business or on arm's length terms. So, for example, a yacht provided to a relevant person at no charge by a boat hire company in which they had made an investment would be a benefit. Commercial returns such as dividends and interests are not benefits for this purpose.

Other conditions

[7.49] Funds must be invested within 45 days of the foreign income or gains being brought into the UK. The target company must then be operational within two years of the qualifying investment being made and remain operational from that date. Where there is a disposal of all or part of the holding in the target company or a repayment of the loan, the investor will have a grace period of 45 days to take the disposal proceeds offshore or to reinvest them. The clock starts ticking from the day the disposal proceeds become available to the relevant person.

Investment possibilities

[7.50]

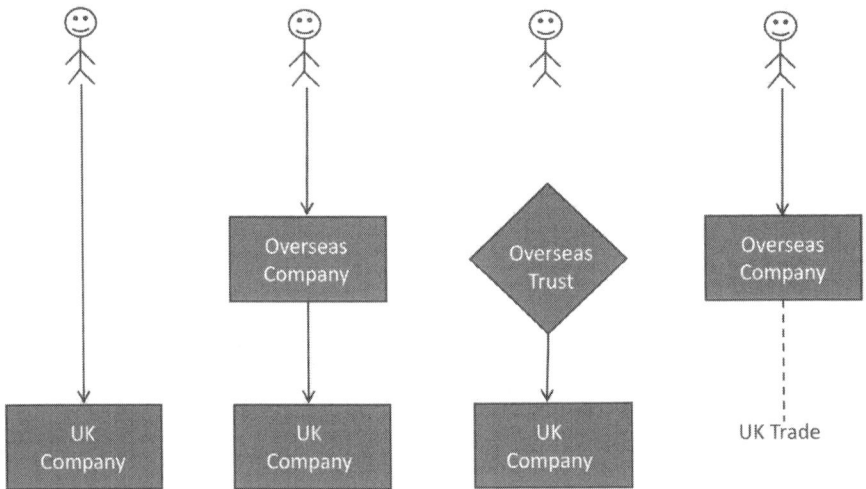

Planning point

[7.51] This new relief will give owner managed businesses access to another source of funds.

Loan relationships for companies

[7.52] For companies, the loan-relationship provisions contained in CTA 2009, ss 292–569 provide a statutory basis for the tax position of loans to and from the company. A loan relationship is defined in CTA 2009, s 302 and exists wherever:

'(a) the company stands (whether by reference to a security or otherwise) in the position of a creditor or debtor as respects any money debt; and

(b) that debt is one arising from a transaction for the lending of money.'

This means that straightforward trade debts are not loan relationships. However, interest charged on late payment of a trade debt falls within the loan-relationship legislation. The fact that interest payments fall within the loan-relationship legislation does not remove the obligation to deduct income tax from interest payments. However, a trade debt can fall within the loan relationship legislation by virtue of CTA 2009, s 479 where an impairment loss arises to a company in respect of an 'unpaid business payment'. A 'business payment' is a payment which is brought into account as a receipt of trade, UK property business or overseas property business carried on by the company.

For most third-party transactions, the tax treatment of loan relationships will follow accounting treatment, assuming the company has prepared accounts in accordance with Generally Accepted Accounting Principles (GAAP). As a result, interest deductions are normally allowed when accrued, and interest is taxed on an accruals basis. Loans provided for or written off are deductible for lenders and taxable for borrowers.

Exceptions from accounting treatment — parties with a connection

[7.53] There are a number of situations where accounting treatment is not followed. Most exceptions arise because the parties to a loan relationship are connected. CTA 2009, s 348 introduces the concept of 'connected companies relationships' and makes it clear that only companies can be parties with a connection for loan relationships purposes. Section 466(2) defines the circumstances in which companies are connected:

'There is a connection between a company ("A") and another company ("B") for an accounting period if there is a time in that period when –

(a) A controls B,

(b) B controls A, or

(c) A and B are both controlled by the same person.'

Control for the purposes of loan relationships is defined in s 472 and means:

' . . . the power of a person to secure that the affairs of the company are conducted in accordance with the person's wishes.

(i) by means of the holding of shares or the possession of voting power in or in relation to the company or any other company, or

(ii) as a result of any powers conferred by the articles of association or other document regulating the company or any other company.'

Notwithstanding the potential width of the definition of control in s 472, the situations in which a company is connected with another person are less common than was the case under the previous definition of parties with a connection for the purposes of loan relationships.

Crucially, two companies that are not in a group relationship will only be regarded as having a connection if they are controlled by the same person. If two companies are controlled by two individuals exercising control together, the companies will not necessarily be regarded as having a connection, even though they may be associated companies for other purposes.

Most often, the question as to whether two companies are connected arises where one of the companies has lent money to the other and now intends to write off that loan. If the two companies have a connection for loan-relationship purposes, the loan can be written off without giving rise to a tax charge for the borrower or a deduction for the lender.

Care must be exercised where a loan has been acquired from an unconnected company, and as result of that acquisition the debtor and creditor become connected. CTA 2009, ss 361 and 362 can impose a corporation tax charge on the write off of the debt or where the creditor's rights are subject to an impairment adjustment in the period before connection is established.

Where debt is acquired by a new creditor company which is itself connected to the debtor or where previously unconnected creditors and debtors become connected, Finance Act 2012 introduced a new anti-avoidance rule to ensure that existing rules relating to deemed releases of pre-existing debt on becoming connected are not circumvented. In such circumstances, a deemed release is imposed on the debtor if the debt has been acquired at a discount by a connected creditor or the debt is impaired when the relevant companies become connected. There are some arrangements which exploit the rules and in doing so gain a tax advantage by avoiding the tax charge which would normally arise in circumstances described above. This new anti-avoidance rule prevents such arrangements from achieving the tax avoidance and applies to arrangements in existence at 1 December 2011.

Late-paid interest

[7.54] Where a company pays interest more than 12 months after the end of the accounting period in which it is accrued, and the company receiving the interest is in a 'non-qualifying territory', relief is given when it is paid rather than when it is accrued in the following situations:

(1) where there is a connection between the debtor company and the person to whom the interest is payable;

(2) where the debtor company is a close company and the person to whom the money is owed is a participator or an associate of a participator in the debtor company, or the money is owed to a company controlled by a participator or an associate of a participator;

(3) where the creditor company has a major interest in the debtor company or the debtor company has a major interest in the creditor company; and

(4) certain arrangements involving occupational pension schemes.

A 'non-qualifying territory' is defined in TIOPA 2010, s 173, and broadly means a territory with which the UK does not have a double taxation agreement (DTA) or the DTA with the UK does not contain a non-discrimination provision.

When interest payable is accrued in the accounts of the 'debtor company' the corporation tax deduction will follow the accounts, regardless of the connection between the companies, except where interest is payable overseas. Where interest is payable overseas the treaty position must be considered.

A major interest is defined in CTA 2009, s 473 and applies where company A and one other person (X) together have control of company B, and the rights company A holds represent at least 40% of the combined rights of company A and X.

For example, if company A has 25% of company B and X has 30% of company B, company A would have a major interest in company B because it has more than 40% × (25% + 30%) = 22%.

Treatment of loan-relationship debits and credits — relief for losses

[7.55] The relief available for loan relationship debits depends on whether the company has a trading or non-trading loan relationship. A company has a trading loan relationship where the relationship is for the purposes of a trade it carries on (CTA 2009, s 297(1)). CTA 2009, s 298 further clarifies the meaning of a trading loan relationship:

> ' . . . a company is taken to be party to a creditor relationship for the purposes of a trade it carries on only if it is a party to the relationship in the course of activities forming an integral part of the trade.'

Any other loan relationship will be treated as a non-trading loan relationship, dealt with in accordance with CTA 2009, ss 456–463.

Where the company has a trading loan relationship, the resulting loan relationship debits and credits are treated as part of the company's trading results. Relief for losses will, therefore, follow the normal rules for setting off corporate losses.

Where the company has a non-trading loan relationship, any loan-relationship credit will be taxed under CTA 2009, s 299 and any loss will be relieved in accordance with CTA 2009, ss 457–459.

A non-trading loan relationship deficit is carried forward and set off against non-trading profits (which includes gains) in future years, unless a claim is made either to surrender the deficit under group relief or under s 459.

Under s 459 a company can claim to set off the non-trading loan relationship deficit against total profits of the deficit period or against profits of accounting periods ending in the previous 12 months after giving every prior relief (s 463).

Although the profits against which non-trading loan-relationship deficits can be offset are restricted, there is flexibility in terms of allocating the loss in a particular period. It may be appropriate to leave profits of the current period in charge if there are tax credits attaching to them (for example foreign income) or to maximise the use of the small-companies' rate of corporation tax.

Key points regarding interest

[7.56] Key points to note are as follows:

- Income tax is deducted from interest payments in certain situations:
    - where individuals pay interest to non-residents (subject to treaty relief);
    - where companies pay interest to any individual; or
    - where companies pay interest to non-residents (subject to treaty relief).
- Withholding taxes do not apply to dividends paid by a UK company.
- For individuals, interest is deductible against other income in accordance with ITA 2007, s 392, subject to the cap of either 25% of income or £50,000, whichever is the greater.
- For companies, interest is deductible in accordance with loan-relationship provisions. Usually, this is on an accruals basis, except for late-paid interest in certain relationships where there is a connection.
- Interest paid by a business is deductible if it is incurred wholly and exclusively for the business.

Failed ventures

[7.57] When businesses are established, there is the optimism that everything will go according to plan, but a large number of new businesses are not successful. There are statistics for the number of failed ventures in particular industry sectors, but it is impossible to know the real number of businesses that never make it. For the founders and investors, one of the key questions when it all fails is whether there are any tax reliefs available. Fortunately, there are some reliefs available to private companies. For unincorporated businesses, the relief comes in the form of trading losses. Losses incurred in the first four years of a trade can be offset against income in the three years prior to the loss year, taking the earliest year first. Apart from that, there is no other relief available.

For incorporated businesses, there are two reliefs available:

(1)   ITA 2007, s 131 – share loss relief; and
(2)   TCGA 1992, s 253 – relief for loans to traders.

Share-loss relief

[7.58] Where an individual incurs a capital loss on the disposal (or deemed disposal) of qualifying shares, he can make a claim for the loss to be deducted in calculating his net income in the year of the loss or for the previous tax year or both tax years. The rule on capital losses is that they can only be offset against capital gains, so this provision is an exception to the main rule.

Qualifying shares are those which have EIS relief or those in a qualifying trading company which were subscribed for by the individual. Shares are subscribed for by an individual if they are issued to the individual by the company in exchange for money or money's worth (ITA 2007, s 135(2)).

Therefore, second-hand shares will never qualify for relief unless they were transferred from a spouse or civil partner and the spouse or civil partner had originally subscribed for the shares. The parties need to be living together at the time of the transfer but do not need to have been living together at the time of the subscription.

The Upper Tribunal decision in *HMRC v Drown (as executors of Leadley Deceased)* [2017] UKUT 111 highlights an issue that can arise where the individual who made the investment dies holding shares that are of negligible value. In this case the executors are not able to make a negligible value claim when completing the deceased's tax returns up to the date of death.

Dyer v Revenue & Customs [2016] UKUT 381 demonstrated the importance of valuation where loans are capitalised into shares. In this case, as the company did not have any legal entitlement to exploit trademarks and there was no contract of employment with the key employee on whom profits depended, the company was found to have had little value when loans were capitalised into shares. As a result there was no negligible value claim.

A qualifying trading company is one which meets each of the conditions A to D as set out in ITA 2007, s 134.

Condition A

[7.59] The company must meet one of the following tests:

- *One.* At the date of disposal, the company meets the trading requirement, the control-and-independence requirement, the qualifying-subsidiaries requirement and the property-managing-subsidiaries requirement.
- *Two.* At the date of disposal, the company has ceased to meet any of the requirements in one above within the previous three years and it has not since that time been an excluded company, an investment company or a trading company.
- *Trading requirement.* The company exists wholly (ignoring incidental purposes) for the purposes of carrying on one or more qualifying trades, or the company is the parent company and the business of the group does not consist wholly or to a substantial extent of the carrying on of non-qualifying activities. Qualifying trades are in accordance with the EIS legislation, and these are detailed in section **[7.24]**. Substantial is taken to mean 20%. Incidental means purposes having no significant effect. In the old business-expansion-scheme legislation, HMRC took insignificant to mean 2%, so this could perhaps be a guideline here.
- *Qualifying subsidiary.* This is a 51% subsidiary.
- *Control and independence.* The company must not control any company which is not a qualifying subsidiary. For the independence part of the test to be met, the company must not be a 51% subsidiary of another company; neither should it be under the control of another company or of another company and a person connected with it. Furthermore, no arrangements must exist which could result in the company becoming under the control of another company.

- *Property-managing subsidiaries.* Any property-managing subsidiary must be a 90% subsidiary.

Condition B

[7.60] The company must either:

- meet the requirement mentioned in condition A for a period of six years ending with the disposal; or
- meet each of the requirements in condition A for a shorter continuous period ending with the date of disposal or, at the date of disposal, not have been an excluded company, an investment company or a trading company before the beginning of that period.

Condition C

[7.61] The company must meet the 'gross-asset-requirement' test both immediately before and immediately after the issue of the shares which are the subject of the loss-relief claim and must also meet the 'unquoted' test at the relevant time.

Gross assets must not exceed £7 million before the share issue and £8 million after the share issue. This has not been increased to match the new EIS limits.

Condition D

[7.62] The company must have carried on its business wholly or mainly in the UK throughout the period beginning with the incorporation of the company, or, if later, 12 months before the shares subject to the loss claim were issued, and ending with the date of disposal.

Wholly or mainly is taken to mean 51%.

A disposal arises when:

(1)   there is a sale of the shares in an arm's-length transaction;
(2)   there is a distribution in the course of dissolving or winding-up a company;
(3)   there is a disposal within TCGA 1992, s 24(1) — this refers to the entire loss or extinction of an asset; or
(4)   there is a negligible-value claim under TCGA 1992, s 24(2).

A negligible-value claim is made where the shares have become of negligible value. With a private company, this is normally proved by showing that the company has become insolvent. In making a claim, the taxpayer is treated as disposing of the shares and immediately reacquiring them at the negligible value. This gives rise to a loss. An earlier time may be specified in the claim if the claimant owned the asset at that earlier time and the asset had become of negligible value at that earlier time, and that earlier time is not more than two years before the beginning of the year of assessment in which the claim was made.

How the claim works

[7.63] The individual:

(1) deducts the loss in calculating the income for the tax year of the loss or of the previous year; and
(2) where a claim is made in relation to two tax years, any part of the loss not deducted in one is taken against the other income for the other tax year.

The claim must be made by the first anniversary of the filing deadline for the tax year in which the loss arose. This relief is also restricted by the cap on reliefs for individuals.

Share loss relief: ITA 2007, section 131

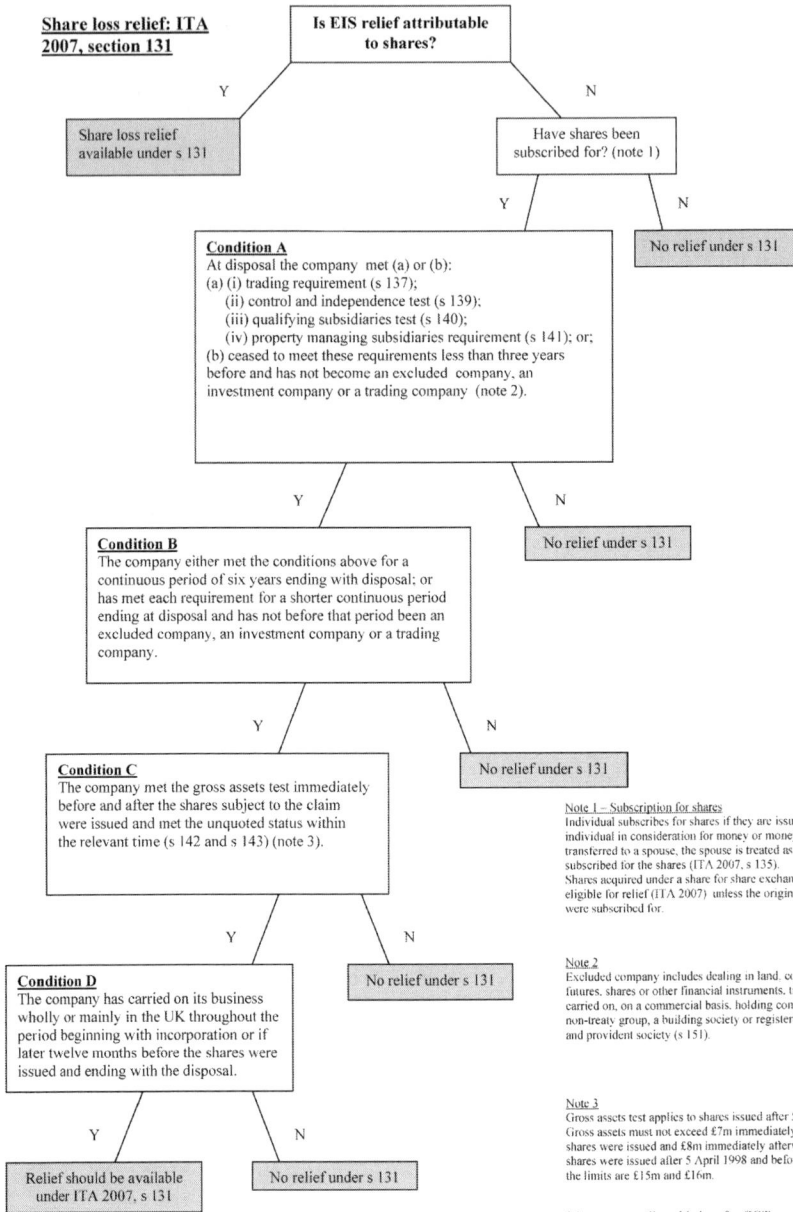

Is EIS relief attributable to shares?

Y → Share loss relief available under s 131

N → Have shares been subscribed for? (note 1)

   Y → **Condition A**

   N → No relief under s 131

Condition A
At disposal the company met (a) or (b):
(a) (i) trading requirement (s 137);
   (ii) control and independence test (s 139);
   (iii) qualifying subsidiaries test (s 140);
   (iv) property managing subsidiaries requirement (s 141); or;
(b) ceased to meet these requirements less than three years before and has not become an excluded company, an investment company or a trading company (note 2).

Y → **Condition B**

N → No relief under s 131

Condition B
The company either met the conditions above for a continuous period of six years ending with disposal; or has met each requirement for a shorter continuous period ending at disposal and has not before that period been an excluded company, an investment company or a trading company.

Y → **Condition C**

N → No relief under s 131

Condition C
The company met the gross assets test immediately before and after the shares subject to the claim were issued and met the unquoted status within the relevant time (s 142 and s 143) (note 3).

Y → **Condition D**

N → No relief under s 131

Condition D
The company has carried on its business wholly or mainly in the UK throughout the period beginning with incorporation or if later twelve months before the shares were issued and ending with the disposal.

Y → Relief should be available under ITA 2007, s 131

N → No relief under s 131

Note 1 – Subscription for shares
Individual subscribes for shares if they are issued to the individual in consideration for money or money's worth. If transferred to a spouse, the spouse is treated as having subscribed for the shares (ITA 2007, s 135).
Shares acquired under a share for share exchange are not eligible for relief (ITA 2007) unless the original shares were subscribed for.

Note 2
Excluded company includes dealing in land, commodities, futures, shares or other financial instruments, trade not carried on, on a commercial basis, holding company of a non-treaty group, a building society or registered industrial and provident society (s 151).

Note 3
Gross assets test applies to shares issued after 5 April 1998. Gross assets must not exceed £7m immediately before the shares were issued and £8m immediately afterwards. Where shares were issued after 5 April 1998 and before 6 April 2006 the limits are £15m and £16m.

*Assumes an allowable loss for CGT purposes (s 131)

Relief for loans to traders

[7.64] Relief for loans to traders is available under TCGA 1992, s 253. The general rule for loans is that they are exempt for capital gains tax purposes, but this relief overrides that to provide relief in certain circumstances.

Where money is lent to a UK-resident borrower wholly for the purposes of a trade and that loan becomes irrecoverable, the lender can make a claim for a capital loss.

The individual can only make a claim if:

(1)   the principal has become irrecoverable;
(2)   the claimant has not assigned the right to recover that amount; and
(3)   the claimant and the borrower are not spouses or civil partners or companies in the same group when the loan was made or at any subsequent time.

A loan becomes irrecoverable where there is no prospect of recovery. HMRC's Capital Gains Manual at 65950–65958 gives examples of circumstances where there may be an issue over recoverability. For example, where the borrower continues to trade, HMRC will want to see evidence that there is no prospect of recovery in the future. Where the lender makes further loans, HMRC will seek to challenge claims for earlier loans where these claims have already been made. Relief for loans only extends to the principal amount.

Where an individual has guaranteed a loan and that guarantee is called upon, relief may also be available. TCGA 1992, s 253(4) provides relief for certain payments made by guarantors of qualifying loans to traders, where the payments are made under the guarantee in consequence of the loan having been irrecoverable from the borrower. The loan must have been of money, and it must have been used wholly for the purposes of the borrower's trade (which does not include the lending of money) or used for the purposes of setting up the trade, provided the trade is actually carried on at some stage. The relief for a payment under a guarantee is broader than relief for a loan in that a claim can be made for both the principal and any interest.

Key points

[7.65] Key points to note are as follows

- Loan capital and preference shares may be appropriate alternatives to ordinary share capital in some circumstances.
- Watch the special definition of connected companies for loan relationship purposes.
- Corporation tax relief may have to be deferred where interest is paid more than 12 months after the end of the accounting period in which it is accrued.
- Individuals can obtain income tax relief for a capital loss on the disposal of shares in a qualifying trading company for which they have subscribed.
- Capital gains tax loss relief is available in respect of irrecoverable loans to traders.

Chapter 8

Reliefs Available to Businesses

Introduction

[8.1] This chapter sets out two key reliefs to businesses: capital allowances and relief for intangibles. Many businesses do not take full advantage of the reliefs available. While tax should not be a driving factor in business purchasing decisions, it is certainly one of the key points which should be considered. All of the reliefs below warrant a book of their own, but in line with the theme of this book we will focus on the key points and any planning opportunities available.

Capital allowances

[8.2] For many owner-managed businesses, the decision and timing of capital expenditure is influenced by commercial need rather than the availability of capital allowances. However, following some major reforms recently introduced to the capital allowance regime, including significant increases in the level of allowances, there may be significant opportunities to mitigate tax liabilities by maximising claims on capital expenditure. It is therefore important to consider both classification and timing of expenditure to ensure that maximum allowances are obtained. Additionally, vendors and purchasers should ensure that transactions are planned to ensure that capital allowances are part of their tax structuring.

Revenue and capital expenditure

[8.3] A business typically incurs two types of expenditure: revenue and capital. Revenue expenditure will be deductible in calculating the business's taxable profits if it is incurred 'wholly and exclusively' for business purposes and is not specifically excluded by statute or case law. Revenue expenditure generally covers the day-to-day running of the business. Capital expenditure is usually that which is incurred for the longer-term benefit of the business and is commonly referred to as the fixed capital of the business. Capital expenditure is not defined in the tax statutes. However, tax cases over the years have established that expenditure is capital in nature if it has an *enduring benefit* for the business, ie it will continue to benefit the business for several years. Capital expenditure is not deductible in calculating a business's taxable profits (unless the business is small and has adopted the cash basis).

Particular problems arise in relation to buildings and repair work. This is a contentious area, and the distinction between repairs to an asset and replacement of an asset has been derived from case law. A repair is restoration by renewal or replacement of subsidiary parts of a whole asset. Renewal, as distinguished from repair, is reconstruction of substantially the whole asset. A renewal is capital expenditure. Where it is established that there are repairs, these will only be deductible against profits where they are not improvements. Take, for example, a roof of a building. If this is replaced with a roof of similar quality, this amounts to a repair, but if the roof is raised and improved, this would amount to capital expenditure. Where there is an element of improvement and this is sufficiently small so as to be incidental, HMRC does accept that a full deduction is available for the repair. Where there is a replacement of an asset in its entirety, no notional allowance is available for what would have been the cost if instead the asset had been repaired.

HMRC accepts that where an improvement is only as a result of changing technology, it should still qualify as a repair. This is best illustrated by their acceptance that replacing single glazed windows with double glazed equivalents is allowable revenue expenditure.

The types of expenditure which normally qualify as repairs for tax purposes include:

- routine maintenance, eg exterior painting which recurs every two years;
- repairs to equipment;
- damp and rot treatment;
- repairing broken windows, doors, lifts, etc, painting and decorating;
- replacing roof tiles/slates, flashing and gutters; and
- stone cleaning.

In the absence of other capital indications, the following replacements are also deductible as revenue items:

- wooden beams with steel girders;
- lead pipes with copper or plastic pipes; and single-glazed windows with double-glazed windows.

Expenditure that would normally qualify as revenue expenditure may sometimes be treated as capital under the integral features provisions contained in the Capital Allowances Act (see **8.8** below).

What are capital allowances?

[8.4] Capital allowances provide a tax deduction for capital expenditure and are usually given on a reducing-balance basis. Capital allowances are generally only available to the owner of an asset or where there is an entitlement to acquire an asset (eg under hire purchase arrangements). A lessee is not usually entitled to capital allowances (subject to the long funding lease provisions introduced in FA 2006). Section 8.6 below considers allowances available to lessors and lessees.

Expenditure on plant and machinery is generally 'pooled', and a writing-down allowance (WDA) of 18% can be claimed as a capital allowance. The remainder of the pool – the written-down value (WDV) – is carried forward to the next period. The WDA for this next period is calculated at 18% on the balance brought forward, having added any new expenditure on plant and machinery and deducted the proceeds (limited to original cost) from any disposal.

To avoid having to carry forward small pools of unrelieved expenditure, a pool can be written off where the value is not more than £1,000.

An annual investment allowance (AIA) is available to businesses, whether unincorporated or incorporated, and regardless of size. Further details are provided at **8.9** below. Over the last five years, here have been a number of changes to the level of allowances, ending with a permanent allowance of £200,000. Special 100% First Year Allowances (FYAs) are available for expenditure on new cars with CO_2 emissions not exceeding 50g/km (75g/km pre-April 2018) and on certain other environmentally friendly assets (see **8.14** below).

Timing of expenditure

[8.5] For capital allowance purposes expenditure is incurred on the date on which the obligation to pay it becomes unconditional (Capital Allowances Act 2001, s 5 (CAA 2001)). This is important in determining in which accounting period or fiscal year writing down allowances can be first claimed on the expenditure and the availability of appropriate allowances, such as first year allowances.

In most cases the date on which the expenditure is actually paid is irrelevant. However, a notable exception is where the actual payment is not made until more than four months after the unconditional obligation. In this instance the expenditure is added to the capital allowance pool on the date that it is incurred.

Leasing

[8.6] Special rules apply to leased equipment. Capital allowances are generally only available to the owner of an asset or where there is an entitlement to acquire an asset (eg under hire purchase arrangements). A lessee is therefore not generally entitled to capital allowances, as this type of arrangement does not entitle him to ownership. Before entering into any finance or operating lease agreement it is worth taking time to consider the tax implications, in particular eligibility to claim capital allowances.

A lessee is able to claim capital allowances for expenditure on long funding leases. CAA 2001, s 70A onwards deals with this in detail, however, in principle a long funding lease includes leases which are longer than five to seven years. Where properties and their contents are leased, 'background plant and machinery' is excluded from this regime and do not qualify for capital allowances. Background plant and machinery includes the majority of items you would expect to find in a property eg air conditioning, electrical systems, lifts.

Plant and machinery

[8.7] Capital allowances are available in respect of capital expenditure on plant and machinery, which is defined mainly by case law.

The first case that considered the meaning of plant was *Yarmouth v France* (1887) 19 QBD 647. Interestingly, this was a non-tax case. In that case, Lindley LJ said that:

> 'In its ordinary sense it includes whatever apparatus is used by a businessman for carrying on his business – not his stock-in-trade which he buys or makes for sale, but all goods and chattels, fixed or movable, live or dead, which he keeps for permanent employment in the business.'

Accordingly, the asset must be used in the permanent employment of the business to qualify as plant. The concept of permanent was explored in the case of *Hinton (Inspector of Taxes) v Maden and Ireland Ltd* [1959] 3 All ER 356, where it was found that knives, used by a shoemaker, which had an average life of three years, were plant. HMRC instructs its inspectors to accept that an asset which has a life of two years or more is sufficiently durable to be plant.

Where something is installed because it is needed in the business (for example, shelves, counters, etc), it is likely to be plant. If it is needed to allow a building to be used for any purpose at all (for example, walls, doors, windows, etc), it is not plant. This introduces the function and setting test. Does the asset have a *function* in the business or is it part of the *setting* in which the business is carried on?

Office equipment such as computers, furniture, etc qualifies for capital allowances as machinery. Also, security cameras, fire and burglar alarms, smoke detectors and illuminated signs qualify for capital allowances in the same way as plant. But there are a number of difficult areas. Lighting systems and electrical wiring will normally be treated as integral features (see **8.8** below). However, electrical wiring for a particular item of equipment will be plant.

It is therefore necessary to determine the split between plant, integral features and premises on an item-by-item basis to ensure appropriate allowances are being claimed.

The difficulties in allocating expenditure can be illustrated by the case of *Wetherspoon (J D) Ltd v Revenue and Customs Comrs* (2007) SpC 657 which was heard by the Special Commissioners and subsequently the first tier tribunal in 2009. The parties could not agree on whether 120 categories of expenditure qualified for capital allowances. Two sample pubs were selected and the tribunal concentrated on a small number of items to address points of principle. The first tier tribunal had to decide whether:

(a) certain fixtures qualified as plant and machinery;

(b) certain building alterations qualified as incidental to the plant and machinery; and

(c) overhead expenditure or preliminaries, including professional fees, such as those of structural engineers, can be attributable to direct costs.

Points to emerge from this case include:

(i) kitchen tiles did not have sufficient nexus to cookers to be able to be categorised as plant and machinery;

(ii) partitions and doors to cubicles did have sufficient nexus to toilets to enable them to be categorised as plant and machinery;

(iii) where there is a multitude of indirect costs such that a detailed assessment would be too time consuming, a pro-rata apportionment is reasonable in principle;

(iv) where splashbacks are required behind sinks they should qualify for capital allowances to the extent that they are specific (rather than part of a larger wipe clean surface);

(v) HMRC will accept global apportionment of preliminaries and professional fees that do not relate to specific items.

Integral features

[8.8] Expenditure on features that are integral to a building will qualify for a WDA of 8%. An integral feature is any of the following items (CAA 2001, s 33A):

* an electrical system (including a lighting system);
* a cold water system;
* a space or water heating system;
* a powered ventilation, air cooling or air purification system;
* a lift, escalator or moving walkway; and
* external solar shading.

Care should be taken when analysing expenditure as some items may include items which fall within the integral features regime and some which may benefit from higher allowances.

Where reparation expenditure of more than 50% of the replacement cost of an integral feature is incurred over any twelve month period, the expense is not eligible for an immediate tax deduction. A claim for capital allowances as an integral feature can however be made, giving an 8% annual deduction (CA 2001, s 33B). This effectively defers relief for the expenditure. It should be noted that the twelve month period is not dependent on accounting periods but on the actual dates when the expenditure is incurred.

Planning point — tax issues

Subject to commercial considerations, it may be appropriate to delay or stagger expenditure on repairs to integral features over a period greater than 12 months.

Example

> Brown Ltd has air conditioning which was originally installed in its headquarters in 2013. On 31 January 2018, the company paid £25,000 to repair the air conditioning. At the time, it would have cost £60,000 to replace the air conditioning.
>
> In December 2018, the air conditioning needed to be repaired again for an additional £5,001. If this expenditure was incurred immediately, the full £30,001 would be disallowed as a revenue deduction. Delaying this repair until after January 2019 would enable revenue deductions to be made.

In the above example, it may be possible to delay the expenditure by a month, without having an impact on the business. If the initial expenditure was incurred in August 2017, and the system subsequently broke down in July 2018, being summer, it may not be possible to delay its repair without impacting on the business.

The annual investment allowance (AIA)

[8.9] An AIA of £200,000 is available to all qualifying businesses in relation to qualifying expenditure incurred in the period from January 2016. For periods 6 April 2014 to 31 December 2015, the AIA level was £500,000. 100% of the cost of assets can be claimed, up to this limit. The AIA is increased or reduced for accounting periods that are longer or shorter than 12 months.

Example

> Consider a company with 12-month accounting period ending 31 March 2016.
>
> **The maximum AIA entitlement is:**
>
> (A)   1 April 2015 to 31 December 2015 9/12 × £500,000 = £375,000.
> (B)   1 January 2016 to 31 March 2016 3/12 × £200,000 = £50,000.
>
> Maximum AIA A+B = £375,000 + £50,000 = £425,000.
>
> **AIA caps for the notional periods**
>
> The overall maximum AIA is £425,000 but claims for expenditure in the period 1 January 2016 to 31 March 2016 are limited to £50,000.

Where an asset costs more than the upper limit, a WDA is available on the balance of the cost in the chargeable period of acquisition. The AIA can be used in relation to assets that belong to either the 18% or 8% pools.

Planning point

As the taxpayer can choose how to allocate the AIA. In order to maximise deductions, the AIA should be allocated to expenditure on items with the lowest allowances first, such as integral features or long life assets.

Businesses should ensure that they maximise the use of the AIA those planning to spend more than their AIA limit should maximise the use of short-life asset elections (see **8.16** onwards).

Qualifying AIA expenditure

[8.10] Most types of asset qualify for AIA, but the following are excluded (CAA2001, s 38B):

*   Cars.
*   Assets that have been subject to a change of use:
    *   The use for a qualifying activity of plant or machinery that was a gift or that was provided for other purposes;
    *   The use for other purposes of plant or machinery that was provided for long funding leasing.
*   Assets on which expenditure was incurred in the following circumstances:
    *   During the chargeable period in which the qualifying activity is discontinued;
    *   In connection with a change in the nature or conduct of a business carried on by another person, where a main benefit of the transaction was to obtain the allowance;
    *   For the purposes of a ring fence trade where a supplementary tax charge is payable.

AIA and a FYA cannot be claimed in respect of the same expenditure.

Businesses qualifying for the AIA

[8.11] The following persons qualify for an AIA (CAA 2001, s 38A):

*   an individual;
*   a partnership of which all the members are individuals; and
*   a company.

It should be noted that a partnership which has a company as a member or partner would not qualify for an AIA.

An AIA will be available to every unincorporated business and singleton company. Companies in a group must share one AIA, which can be allocated in any way between group companies.

There are anti-avoidance rules designed to prevent the fragmentation of businesses into separate entities in order to claim multiple AIAs. Only one AIA is available to two or more unincorporated businesses, companies, or groups of companies that are controlled by the same person and that are also related to one another. For these purposes, businesses or companies are related if their qualifying activities are carried on from the same premises, or if more than 50% of their turnover is derived from the same class of qualifying activity (as defined by EC NACE classifications) (CAA 2001, ss 51A–51 N).

In addition, an AIA will not be available if a person enters into an arrangement designed to obtain an AIA to which they would not otherwise be entitled.

The car regime

[8.12] Prior to April 2009, the treatment of cars was dependent on their cost. Each expensive car, (costing more than £12,000) was held in a separate pool with annual capital allowances capped at £3,000 per car. Expenditure on cheaper cars went to the general pool. No FYAs were available.

For cars acquired since April 2009, the rules have been radically changed and the rate of WDA is based solely on the vehicle's carbon dioxide (CO_2) emissions. FYAs are available on either electronically propelled or a low emission car that does not exceed 50g/km. In addition, a main rate car for the purposes of CAA 2001, s 104AA will now include expenditure on cars with CO2 emissions that do not exceed 110g/km (previously 130g/km).

The following table illustrates how the available WDAs are linked to emissions:

CO_2 emissions	CA pool	WDAs
≤50g/km	Main pool	100% FYAs
≤110g/km	Main pool	18% per annum
>110g/km	Special rate pool	8% per annum

If a business has any cars dealt with under the old rules, these should have been transferred to the general pool with effect from April 2014.

Unincorporated businesses are able to maintain separate pools for cars with a private use element. This means that a balancing allowance would be available if the car is sold for less than its tax written down value.

Car leasing

[8.13] For some businesses, it may be more effective to lease vehicles. As a lessee never owns the asset, he is unable to claim capital allowances (which are claimed by the lessor). However, deductions are available on the lease rental expense, with a possible restriction based on CO_2 emissions. Cars with emissions of 110g/km or less will now receive a full deduction for lease rentals in computing taxable profits. There will be a simple 15% disallowance of lease rentals for cars with emissions greater than 110g/km.

Enhanced capital allowances (ECAs)

[8.14] Expenditure on approved energy-saving or environmentally-beneficial plant attracts a 100% FYA (CAA 2001, ss 45A–45H). The full approved lists of energy-saving and environmentally-beneficial products are contained on the Energy Technology Product List (ETPL) at www.gov.uk/etpl. This is not an exhaustive list of qualifying technologies and for more information, readers are directed to www.gov.uk/government/publications/enhanced-capital-allowa nce-scheme-for-energy-saving-technologies and www.gov.uk/guidance/energy-technology-list.

Where a company has an otherwise unusable loss that is attributable to expenditure on energy-saving or environmentally-beneficial plant, it can surrender the loss in return for a payable tax credit equal to 19% of the loss. The credit is limited to the greater of the company's PAYE and NIC payments in the loss period or £250,000. The credit will be clawed back if the plant is sold within 4 years of the end of the period in which the credit was paid. This credit is only available to companies (CAA 2001, Schedule A1).

Designated Assisted Areas

[8.15] 100% first year capital allowances are available for companies in respect of plant and machinery, where the plant and machinery is used primarily in an area that is a 'designated assisted area'. The level of allowances is subject to a limit of €125 million for a single investment project. A 'designated assisted area; is one which has been designed by an order made by the Treasury. Currently there are approximately 25 areas within the UK.

In order to qualify for the 100% capital allowances, the expenditure must be incurred in the period from 1 April 2012 to 31 March 2020 and must also meet the following conditions set out in CAA 2001, s 45(K):

- The company must be within the charge to corporation tax;
- The expenditure must be incurred for a qualifying trade or a qualifying business such as mining or quarrying;
- The expenditure must be incurred either for a new business undertaken by the company or an expanded business or represent a start-up activity which relates to a fundamental change;
- The plant or machinery must be unused and not second hand; and
- The expenditure must not be replacement expenditure

For expenditure incurred since 17 July 2014 qualifying under the fundamental change condition, there are restrictions applied, based on the level of relevant expenditure incurred in the previous three year period.

Business Premises Renovation Allowance

[8.16] This allowance is available until 31 March/5 April 2017. Where a property has been vacant for at least a year in a designated disadvantaged area, 100% relief may be available for capital expenditure on conversion or renovation work. (CAA 2001, s 360A onwards). The expenditure must be in order to bring the building back into business use. No allowances are available for the cost of acquiring land or extending a building. The rules were tightened up in FA 2014 to restrict relief to specific costs of construction and building work and to put a cap of 5% of the total expenditure for associated costs incurred such as project management.

Rather than claiming a 100% initial allowance, allowances can be spread over four years on a straight line basis. Once the building has been held for more than seven years after first use, there is no claw back of the allowances previously claimed. This was reduced to five years with effect for expenditure incurred on or after 1 April 2014 for companies and 6 April 2014 for unincorporated businesses. Care will therefore need to be taken to ensure that a balancing event, such as a disposal, does not occur within seven years.

Designated disadvantaged areas are Northern Ireland and those designated for these purposes by the Assisted Areas Order 2007.

The full list can be viewed at the following address www.legislation.gov.uk/c y/uksi/2016/751/made.

Land Remediation

[8.17] Where a company incurs expenditure on the remediation of contaminated land, it may be entitled to a deduction of 150% of the qualifying expenditure or receive a tax credit equal to 16% of any qualifying loss.

The company must incur qualifying expenditure on qualifying land. Broadly this means land that was contaminated prior to acquisition and the remedial expenditure would not have been incurred had the land not been in a contaminated state.

The definition of land in a contaminated state (CTA 2009, s 1145) restricts contamination to anything present as a result of industrial activity. This definition has been modified by Statutory Instrument to cover contamination by arsenic, radon or Japanese Knotweed.

Land remediation tax relief is a corporate relief and is not available to individuals or non-resident companies paying income tax. This relief does not require the land to be held as a capital asset so will also be available to property traders.

Details of this relief are contained in CTA 2009, Part 14.

Claiming capital allowances

[8.18] Capital allowances must be claimed (CAA 2001, s 3). Most capital allowances are claimed in the tax return. For income tax purposes, capital allowance claims are made in the self-assessment return. The time limit for making a claim or amending a claim is the normal time limit for making or amending a tax return: the first anniversary of 31 January following the year of assessment. Where a business is carried on in partnership, it is the partnership that claims the capital allowances and not the individual partners.

For a company, the claim is made in the corporation tax self-assessment return, and the usual time limit for making an amendment applies.

Capital allowances do not have to be claimed in full or even at all. Any unclaimed amounts will remain in the pool as part of the balance on which capital allowances may be claimed in future periods. This facilitates planning to delay a claim for allowances to ensure that relief is obtained at the highest possible rate.

Short-life asset elections

[8.19] A short-life asset is one with an expected working life of no more than eight years from the end of the chargeable or basis period in which the expenditure was incurred. However, not all assets can be short-life assets, and the legislation specifically lists those which do not qualify (CAA 2001, ss 83–89):

(i)   most cars (unless hired out to persons receiving certain disability allowances or mobility supplements);
(ii)   ships;
(iii) assets which are hired out otherwise than in the course of a trade or other qualifying activity (although leasing is a qualifying activity in respect of claiming allowances on plant and machinery, other than that provided for use in a dwelling-house or flat);
(iv)   assets acquired partly for the purposes of a trade or other qualifying activity and partly for other purposes;
(v)   assets which are the subject of a partial depreciation subsidy (a non-taxable sum to take account of the depreciation of plant or machinery resulting from its use in the recipient's trade or other qualifying activity);
(vi)   assets brought into use for the trade following non-business use, or received by way of gift;
(vii) assets leased overseas such that they attract only an 8% WDA;
(viii) assets which are leased to two or more persons jointly where CAA 2001, s 116 applies;
(ix)   assets within the long-life asset provisions; and
(x)   assets which are categorised as integral features.

Normally, expenditure on assets (other than assets not used wholly for business purposes) is included in a 'general pool'. Here, when an asset is sold, the disposal proceeds (limited to cost) are subtracted from the WDV of the pool. If this leaves a residue of expenditure, any balancing allowance will only be available when the trade ceases. This may be many years after any individual asset is sold.

Contrast this with the position if a short-life asset election is made. Where such an election is in place, this expenditure is included in its own separate pool. WDAs are still available, but there is a difference in the treatment when the asset in question is sold or scrapped. Because an asset which is the subject of a short-life asset election is allocated its own separate pool, when it is disposed of there is a balancing adjustment equal to the difference between the pool's WDV and the disposal proceeds received. The business therefore receives allowances for the whole net expenditure incurred over the life of the asset.

The benefit of a short-life asset election is best illustrated by way of an example.

Example

Mark (a higher-rate taxpayer) has been running his sole-trader software-development business for a few years. In May 2013, he purchased a new computer for use in his business for £3,000. Mark prepares his accounts to 31 March each year. The WDV of his general pool at 1 April 2013 is £10,000. In the next few years, Mark makes no further acquisitions or disposals, other than scrapping the same computer in July 2015 to replace this with the latest model.

The AIA is ignored for the purposes of this example.

The allowances that Mark would receive if (a) no short-life asset election is made, and (b) such an election is made are as follows:

	No election	With election	
	General pool	General pool	Short-life asset
	£	£	£
Y/e 31 March 2014			
Balance b/f	10,000	10,000	
Additions	3,000		3,000
WDA @ 20%	(2,600)	(2,000)	(600)
c/f	10,400	8,000	2,400
Y/e 31 March 2015			
WDA @ 20%	(2,080)	(1,600)	(480)
c/f	8,320	6,400	1,920
Y/e 31 March 2016			
Balancing allowance on sale			(1,920)
WDA @ 18%	(1,498)	(1,152)	
Balance c/f	6,822	5,248	Nil

Summary of allowances:

Tax year		No election	With election
2013–14		£2,600	£2,600
2014–15		£2,080	£2,080
2015–16		£1,498	£3,072

Using the short-life asset election, Mark can achieve a tax saving in 2015/16 of £630, ie (£3,072 – £1,498) × 40%.

In future years, Mark will receive WDAs on the carried-forward WDV of the general pool in both cases.

Over the life of the business as a whole, the capital allowances obtained will be the same regardless of whether or not short-life asset elections are made; the use of these elections gives a cash flow advantage.

How is the election made and by when?

[8.20] An election (which is irrevocable) needs to be made in writing to HMRC and must specify:

(i)   the plant or machinery subject to the election;
(ii)   the qualifying expenditure incurred; and
(iii)   the date on which the expenditure is incurred.

From a practical point of view, for individual sole traders, this election could be included in the 'Additional information' box in the self-employment pages of the signed self-assessment return.

For companies, the election could be included in the supporting computation to the CT600 return, with reference made to the fact that this is a Schedule to the signed return.

For income tax purposes, the election needs to be made by 22 months following the end of the tax year in which the chargeable period ends. For example, if the chargeable period ends in 2015–16, the election needs to be made by 31 January 2018.

For corporation tax purposes, the deadline is two years after the end of the chargeable period. Therefore if the chargeable period ends on 31 December 2016, the election needs to be made by 31 December 2018.

Where a short-life asset has not been sold or scrapped by the end of the eight-year period, then at the beginning of year nine its WDV is transferred from its separate pool to the general pool, where it will continue to be written down as normal.

Where a business holds assets in very large numbers and either (a) individual identification is impossible (for example, tools or linen), or (b) individual identification is impracticable (for example, calculators or amusement machines), one short-life asset pool may be maintained for the aggregate expenditure on a particular type of asset in a given chargeable period.

In the case of (a), it would be necessary to agree with HMRC the average working life for each category of asset. In such cases, a balancing allowance will normally be available for the last year of the agreed life of the assets.

In the case of both (a) and (b), it would be necessary to keep a record of the number of assets in a particular category bought and sold in each particular chargeable period, as, unless disposal proceeds can be attributed to a particular batch of assets, the guidance states that a first-in first-out basis can be used.

Statement of Practice 1/86 includes two useful worked examples.

Interaction between capital gains and capital allowances

[8.21] The way the capital allowances system and the capital gains system interact is that relief is usually given twice; firstly as WDAs and secondly as a deduction in the capital gains tax computation as part of the base cost. The provision in TCGA 1992, s 41(1) states:

> 'Section 39 shall not require any exclusion from the sums allowable as a deduction in the computation of the gain of any expenditure as being expenditure in respect of which a capital allowance or renewals allowance is made . . . '.

However, there is a restriction in respect of losses. TCGA 1992, s 41(1) goes on to say, 'but the amount of any losses accruing on the disposal of an asset shall be restricted by reference to the capital allowances'.

Section 41(2) provides that expenditure is to be excluded to the extent to which any capital allowance has been made in respect of it. The effect of this is:

- to reduce the amount of the loss; or
- to restrict the loss to nil.

These provisions cannot convert a loss into a gain.

The interaction does not change, whether or not there is a clawback of capital allowances through a balancing charge or otherwise.

Planning with second-hand properties

[8.22] Where businesses acquire second-hand properties, there is often a chance to claim capital allowances using a CAA 2001, s 198 election to transfer the fixtures eligible for capital allowances at a particular price. CAA 2001, s 187A places a restriction on the availability of a section 198 election (which could previously be made at any time based on a valuation of assets qualifying for capital allowances).

Section 187A applies where a person acquires property in respect of which a previous owner has previously pooled the qualifying assets for capital allowances on fixtures, and requires a s 198 election to be made within two years of the transaction date. Failure to do this will prevent the purchaser (and any subsequent owner) from claiming capital allowances in respect of those fixtures although there is nothing preventing the purchaser claiming allowances on new fixtures.

Where allowances have been claimed and the parties cannot agree within the two year window post sale, there is a tribunal mechanism. Based on how HMRC and the Valuation Office interpret and apply the legislation on fixtures apportionments, the purchaser is likely to benefit from the tribunal and sellers could lose all allowances where a property is sold at a gain. There is a partial clawback if the property is sold for a loss. It is therefore important that well drafted capital allowances elections are agreed as part of the sales contract.

The price fixed by the parties must be arrived at in accordance with item 1, 5 or 9 of the Table in s 196, which broadly means that the apportionment will need to be market value or some lower amount agreed between the parties. It should be noted that a s 198 election can only be made on fixtures and no other type of plant and machinery.

To be valid, the election must include:

- the amount fixed by the election;
- the name of each person making the election;
- information sufficient to identify the fixtures;
- information sufficient to identify the land;
- the interest being acquired;
- the tax district references of each person making the election.

As these elections are made jointly between vendor and purchaser, ideally they should be made at the time of the transaction in order to prevent either a dispute over the transfer value or further negotiation between the parties. At the very least, an agreed mechanism as to how the value is to be determined should be included and in addition following changes outlined, a similar mechanism should be included in relation to the new pooling requirement.

As well as the requirement to fix the capital allowance value of the fixtures within two years of the transfer, since April 2014 a mandatory pooling requirement has also come into effect. For transfers after this date the seller must have either pooled or claimed allowances on fixtures where they are entitled to do so otherwise a purchaser will be denied allowances. Purchasers are likely to want this issue covered specifically in any sale contract. For those owners intending to sell commercial property in the future, it is important to start collating the capital allowances history now, if any value is to be obtained from these allowances, even if they choose not to claim the allowances themselves. A review of the history may in itself prove a good opportunity to identify whether such claims should be made.

Relieving excess capital allowances

[8.23] Planning to obtain capital allowances is one thing, but ensuring that they are relieved in the best possible way is another. Where there are excess capital allowances, these can be relieved in a number of ways.

For individuals the normal trading loss rules apply where a loss is created or increased by the claim for capital allowances.

Losses available for individuals include:

- ITA 2007, s 64 — relief against general income;
- ITA 2007, s 71 — extension of losses under ITA 2007, s 64 so they can be offset against gains;
- ITA 2007, s 72 — relief for losses in the first four years of a trade;
- ITA 2007, s 83 — trading losses carried forward against future trading profits; and
- ITA 2007, s 89 — terminal loss relief.

The extent of any loss relief will be subject to the new capping rules as outlined at **[1.5]**.

For companies, again the normal trading loss relief rules would apply:

- CTA 2010, s 37 — losses offset against income of any description for the accounting period or the previous period;
- CTA 2010, s 97–110 — surrender of loss as group relief; and
- CTA 2010, s 45 — losses can be carried forward against future trading income.

Property income

[8.24] For income tax purposes, property losses cannot be used against other income. However, where the loss consists of capital allowances, the amount of the loss attributable to the capital allowances can be set against:

- other income in the year in which the loss arose (subject to loss cap); and
- other income in the following year.

FA 2010 introduced anti-avoidance legislation that restricts sideways relief for individuals incurring property losses as a result of capital allowance claims from AIAs.

Property businesses

[8.25] The capital allowance position for a property letting/investment business is principally determined by the type of property held or whether the business is a qualifying holiday let business, in accordance with Income Tax (Trading and Other Income) Act 2005, s 325 (ITTOIA 2005). Where the property is commercial or the business is a qualifying holiday let business, capital allowances are available on the same basis as other trading businesses.

However, no capital allowances are available in respect of expenditure within residential properties/dwellings, in accordance with CAA 2001, s 35. In such instance, capital allowances would only be available in respect of any qualifying expenditure within communal areas eg lifts/reception desks.

Instead of capital allowances, it has historically been possible to claim, where the property has been let on a furnished basis, either a deduction for the actual expenditure within the property under ITTOIA 2005, s 308 or more frequently claim a wear and tear allowance. This allowance, set out in ITTOIA 2005, ss 308A–308C/CTA 2009, ss 248A–248C, was broadly calculated as 10% of rents minus any council tax/rates paid.

For unfurnished residential property, there were limited options available to claim relief for the provision of furnishings, particularly since HMRC withdrew ESC B47, which historically had allowed a renewals basis to be claimed. Relief in such circumstances was limited to the renewals allowance for tools under ITTOIA 2005, s 68 and CTA 2009, s 68.

Since April 2016, the above wear and tear allowance has been abolished and replaced by a new replacement relief, as set out in ITTOIA 2005, s 311A/CTA 2009, s 250A. Under this new regime, relief is available for the provision of furniture within a residential property regardless as to whether it is let on a furnished or unfurnished basis. The relief is restricted to the replacement cost of providing such items and no deduction is available for the initial outlay. Landlords in this sector therefore need to make sure that there are clear detailed inventories to ensure that they can easily identify when items are replaced and that the expenditure on a like for like basis.

Intangible fixed assets

[8.26] CTA 2009, ss 711–906 (Part 9) deals with the tax treatment of intangible fixed assets held by a company. It is one of the growing number of areas where the corporation tax regime differs fundamentally from the tax position of unincorporated businesses.

What are intangible assets?

[8.27] Section 712 defines what types of asset are included within the provisions, stating that 'intangible asset' has the meaning it has for accounting purposes and includes any intellectual property.

Intellectual property means:

'(a)   any patent, trade mark, registered design, copyright or design right, plant breeders' rights under section 7 of the Plant Varieties Act 1997,

(b)   any right under the law of a country or territory outside the United Kingdom corresponding to or similar to a right within paragraph (a),

(c)   any information or technique not protected by a right within paragraph (a) or (b) but having industrial, commercial or other economic value, or

(d)   any licence or other right in respect of anything within paragraph (a), (b) or (c).'

Intangible fixed asset means 'an intangible asset acquired or created by the company for use on a continuing basis in the course of the company's activities'.

Section 715 states that the provisions of the Schedule apply to goodwill as to an intangible fixed asset, except where otherwise indicated.

Sections 800–816 set out various intangible assets that are excluded, generally because they fall within their own specialist regime. They are not, therefore, termed intangible fixed assets for the purposes of Part 8. These include rights over tangible assets, because these would generally fall within capital gains legislation, assets on which capital allowances have been claimed, assets in specialist industries such as oil, films and sound recordings. Also excluded are assets that are held by the company for non-commercial purposes.

Intangible assets held by the company to the extent that they represent expenditure on research and development are also excluded from the provisions of Part 8.

Start date for the Intangible Assets provisions

[8.28] Section 882 also excludes intangible assets that were created or acquired by the company before 1 April 2002, and also assets acquired after 1 April 2002 from a related party who created or acquired the asset before that date. Goodwill is treated as having been created before 1 April 2002 if the business in question was carried on at any time before that date by the company or a related party (s 884).

The latter point is relevant to incorporations. Where a trade is incorporated after 1 April 2002, but the trade was carried on by the proprietor or a related party prior to that date, the company is not able to claim relief for the acquisition of goodwill. If the business was commenced by the proprietor after that date, and the business is subsequently incorporated prior to 3 December 2014, relief under Sch 29 would be available to the company based on the lower of the price paid and the market value of the goodwill acquired by the company.

For incorporation of businesses on or after 3 December 2014, unless the transfer had been unconditional before that date, no relief under the intangibles provision will be available in accordance with CTA 2009, ss 849B–D. It is worth noting that this restriction not only applies to goodwill but also other intangibles such as unregistered trademarks and any licence arrangements for such items. There does remain some scope to claim a deduction where such an intangible asset was acquired from a third party prior to the incorporation and is transferred to the company as part of the business transfer (see CTA 2009, s 849B(4)(5)).

Where goodwill was created before 1 April 2002 any disposal by the company will be dealt with under capital gains principles. This means that if there is a base cost, an indexation allowance will be available, and capital losses could be used to offset against the gain. Also, provisions introduced in Finance Act 2011 allow CGT assets to be hived down to a new trading subsidiary and if that subsidiary is sold and substantial shareholdings exemption is available, the gain on the goodwill can be wrapped into the SSE claim. This relief is not available in respect of goodwill created after 1 April 2002, as the provisions only apply for capital gains purposes.

Where an intangible was created or acquired on or after 8 July 2015 and that intangible consists of certain intangible assets, then no deductions are available in respect of that asset under the intangible regime in accordance with CTA 2009, s 816A. The intangible assets affected are:

(a)   goodwill;

(b)   an intangible fixed asset that consists of information which relates to customers or potential customers of a business;

(c)   an intangible fixed asset that consists of a relationship (whether contractual or not) between a person carrying on a business and one or more customers of that business;

(d)   an unregistered trade mark or other sign used in the course of a business; or

(e)   a licence or other right in respect of an asset.

A company can therefore have a number of different tax treatments depending on exactly what intangible the company has and when it was created/acquired, as outlined in the table below:

Goodwill created before 1 April 2002	No deduction for amortisation. Treated as a capital asset.
Goodwill and unregistered trademarks created after 1 April 2002 and incorporated with business prior to 3 December 2014	Amortisation available, depending on market value and price paid
Goodwill and unregistered trademarks created after 1 April 2002 and incorporated with business after 3 December 2014	No amortisation possible but amortisation still available for third-party acquisitions
Goodwill, customer databases, unregistered trademarks and licence acquired after 7 July 2015	No amortisation available

Companies therefore need to be careful in tracking what type of intangible they are dealing with.

Accounting treatment for intangibles

[8.29] The key to the relief is that the treatment of qualifying intangible fixed assets follows accounting treatment so long as that treatment is in accordance with GAAP, referred to in the legislation as 'correct accounts'. If the HMRC accountant is of the view that correct accounts have not been drawn up, ss 716 and 717 ensure that relief is available on the basis that if the accounts had been drawn up correctly, with any adjustments that may be regarded as necessary to reflect the 'correct' position.

In most situations, therefore, a corporation tax deduction is available for the amortisation or impairment of qualifying intangible fixed assets shown in the accounts. As an alternative the company can irrevocably elect that a qualifying intangible fixed asset is written down at a fixed rate of 4% on cost.

However, the write down is available only if it is in respect of the amortisation of actual costs incurred by the company on the creation or acquisition of the intangible fixed asset. Any debit that arises from a previous revaluation is excluded.

Following changes to the accounting treatment under FRS 102, goodwill is likely to be written off over a much shorter period than at present and as a result, a greater tax deduction will be seen soon after purchase of the asset.

Income from intangibles

[8.30] Income arising from intangible fixed assets is included as a credit, recognised as it accrues. Where there is an upwards revaluation of an intangible fixed asset, the credit is brought into the charge to tax only in so far as it claws back previous debits that have been claimed in respect of the asset.

Negative goodwill

[8.31] Where the company's accounts recognise negative goodwill, where the value of the separable assets is greater than the aggregate price paid by the company for the business, so much of the credit represented by negative goodwill as is apportioned on a just and reasonable basis to intangible fixed assets will be brought into account for corporation tax purposes.

Debits and credits — trading and non-trading intangibles

[8.32] The treatment of debits and credits depends on the nature of the intangible fixed asset from which they derive. Where assets are held for the purposes of a trade, the debits or credits form part of the trading results of the company. Where assets are held for the purposes of a property business, the debits or credits form part of the results of the property business.

Where assets are not held for either of these or for mining or transport undertakings, the debits or credits are 'non-trading debits' and 'non-trading credits'. Any net non-trading credit is treated as a non-trading gain under s 751. Any net non-trading debit can be set off against total profits or group-relieved in the year, or carried forward as a non-trading debit of the subsequent year.

Realisation of intangibles

[8.33] On realisation of an intangible fixed asset, an adjustment is likely to be necessary to take into account any debits or credits previously taken into account for corporation tax purposes in respect of the asset sold.

For example, if a company purchased an intangible fixed asset in 2008 for £100,000 and in 2012 it sold the asset for £110,000 when its book WDV was

£55,000, the credits on disposal would comprise the claw back of relief previously given of £45,000 and the profit of £10,000. The whole amount would form part of the company's trading profit for the year of disposal, assuming that it used the asset for the purposes of a trade carried on by it.

It is vital to identify whether the company is disposing of pre-April 2002 or post-April 2002 goodwill. If the goodwill existed before April 2002, the company will be treated as making a capital disposal. As a result, trading losses brought forward will not be available to offset against any gain on that disposal. However, any capital losses could be offset.

Following changes made in the Finance Act 2015 and Finance (No 2) Act 2015, where intangibles have been acquired other than through incorporation from a related party, for example, customers or trade lists or any non-qualifying intangible created after 8 July 2015, no amortisation debit is given for those items and in accordance with CTA 2009, s 849(6) any debit on the disposal of these assets will be a non-trading debit. Any excess which can be relieved against current year trading profits will be carried forward and may be of limited use, as it cannot be used against future non-trading profits.

Reinvestment relief

[8.34] Where an intangible fixed asset is realised, it is possible to claim reinvestment relief, the provisions of which are set out in CTA 2009, ss 754–763. In many respects, this relief is similar to roll-over relief for replacement of business assets, but with some important differences.

In order to claim full reinvestment relief, a number of requirements must be met with regard to the old asset and its realisation, and with regard to the expenditure on new assets (referred to as 'other assets' in Sch 29).

The old asset must have been an intangible fixed asset of the company throughout the period of ownership, or there must have been a disposal of another intangible asset that falls within the capital gains code (in other words, the old asset must have been an intangible asset acquired before 1 April 2002, or an old-style asset acquired from a related party after that date).

There must be a gain over original cost on the realisation of the old asset and not simply an accounting profit represented by the claw back of amortisation claimed previously.

The investment in new assets must take place between one year before and three years after the disposal of the old asset, the investment must be in new intangible assets that are debited to the company's balance sheet on acquisition and the new asset must not have been acquired from a related party.

Example

The computation of the reinvestment relief is set out in the following example.

Assume that the old asset cost £10,000, in respect of which amortisation of £2,000 has been claimed. The old asset is sold for £18,000, and other assets are acquired for £19,000.

First, the amount available for relief is calculated: £18,000 – £10,000 = £8,000.

Note that the amortisation clawed back is not available for relief. The gain on the realisation is £18,000 – £8,000 = £10,000.

The tax base cost of the other assets is calculated as £19,000 – £8,000 = £11,000.

As a result, the gain on the realisation is reduced by the amount available for relief, leaving £2,000 chargeable to corporation tax in the year of realisation. This represents the amortisation clawed back.

The cost of the asset acquired is reduced to £11,000, and it is on this reduced figure that the allowable amortisation is based. This means that if the amortisation in the accounts for this asset is £1,900 a year, the allowable amount will be £1,100. The reinvestment relief is recouped over the life of the new asset acquired. This differs from capital gains tax roll-over relief, where the cost of the new asset is reduced and the gain clawed back when the new asset is sold.

Where the amount of qualifying expenditure is less than the gain on realisation of the old asset, the amount available for relief is the amount by which the qualifying expenditure on other assets exceeds the cost of the old asset.

Thus, if in the above example the company spent £12,000 on other assets, the relief would be restricted to £12,000 – £10,000 = £2,000. The proceeds of realisation would be reduced to £16,000, and the cost of the other assets would be reduced to £10,000.

Provisional entitlement to reinvestment relief

[8.35] There are provisions to allow a company to make a declaration of provisional entitlement to relief where the company has the intention of reinvesting the proceeds of realisation of the old asset. This provides relief in the interim period, with any adjustments that may be necessary if the reinvestment does not take place as intended being made when the declaration is withdrawn or when it expires four years after the end of the accounting period in which the realisation took place.

Roll-over relief on disposal of old goodwill

[8.36] As old (pre-FA 2002) goodwill is not within CTA 2009, the disposal of an intangible owned before 1 April 2002 falls within the capital gains tax provisions. However, s 898 provides for the application of the intangibles roll-over provisions to assets existing at the commencement date so that the assets which for all the other intangible provisions are not included are included in the roll-over provisions. This means that the proceeds of an intangible existing on 1 April 2002 can only be rolled into another intangible. For all other purposes, the asset is within the capital gains tax rules – ie any profit is a capital gain. Therefore, where old goodwill is sold, it is possible to roll the gain into new intangibles, but not into any other type of asset.

Planning reminder

[8.37] Unincorporated businesses do not fall within the CTA 2009 provisions. A sole trader selling goodwill is able to benefit from the full roll-over provisions starting at TCGA 1992, s 152.

Related-party provisions

[8.38] The related-party provisions in Part 8 embrace a wider range of situations than would be caught simply by importing more familiar connected party provisions found elsewhere in the Taxes Acts. Transactions between related parties are dealt with in ss 844–849. Related parties are defined in s 835.

A person (P) is a related party in relation to a company (C) if:

(1)   P is a company and controls or has a major interest in C (or vice versa);

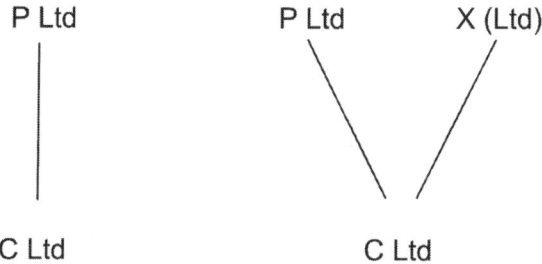

P Ltd   P Ltd   X (Ltd)

|
|
|

C Ltd   C Ltd

(2)   P is a company, and P and C are under the control of the same person;

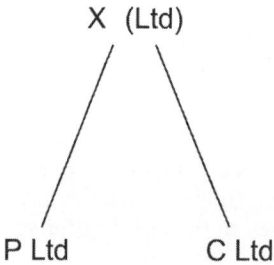

X (Ltd)

P Ltd   C Ltd

(3)   C is a close company, and P is a participator, or an associate of a participator, in C, or a participator in a company that controls or has a major interest in C;

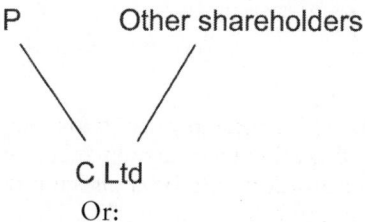

P   Other shareholders

C Ltd

Or:

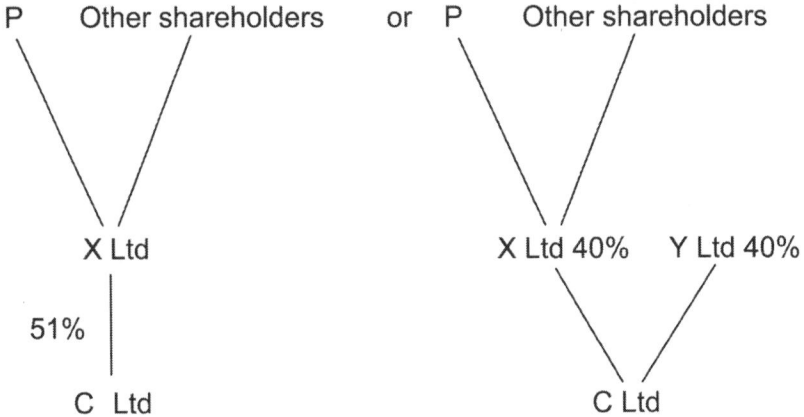

(4)   P is a company, and C is another company in the same group.

Where related-party transactions are relevant

[8.39] Related-party transactions are relevant in the following situations:

(1)   Transactions between related parties must take place at market value.
(2)   There are restrictions to the availability of reinvestment relief.
(3)   A pre-1 April 2002 asset acquired from a related party remains outside the CTA 2009 provisions.
(4)   Incorporation of a business with goodwill or other intangibles.

When dealing with groups and intangible fixed assets, there are provisions that broadly mirror the capital gains group provisions, with broadly the same definition of a group. A group comprises a company ('the principal company of the group') and all its 75% subsidiaries. The group will also include 75% subsidiaries of subsidiaries, so long as those companies are also effective 51% subsidiaries of the principal company of the group.

The principal company of the group cannot be a 75% subsidiary of another company. Intangible fixed assets can be transferred between group companies without incurring a corporation tax charge, but any gain that would have accrued will crystallise if the recipient company leaves the group within six years of the intra-group transfer.

There are also provisions that provide relief on company reconstructions. These apply where there is a scheme of reconstruction within the meaning of TCGA 1992, s 136 and assets transferred in the course of the reconstruction include intangible fixed assets.

In this case, the assets can pass to the transferee on a 'tax-neutral' basis, under CTA 2009, s 818.

These provisions apply only if the reconstruction is effected for bona fide commercial reasons and does not form part of a scheme or arrangement of which the main purpose, or one of the main purposes, is avoidance of liability to corporation tax, capital gains tax or income tax.

Clearance should be applied for in accordance with CTA 2009, s 832 at the same time as applying for clearance under other relevant provisions for the reconstruction.

Key points

[8.40] Key points to note are as follows:

- Use the AIA in relation to assets on which 8% WDAs are available in preference to those on which 18% WDAs are available.
- Take advantage of special 100% FYAs wherever possible. In particular, consider selecting cars with CO_2 emissions of not more than 75g/km.
- Businesses with substantial capital expenditure should consider short-life asset elections to reduce the impact of the new rules.
- Try to spread costs of repairs to integral features over different 12-month periods.
- Maximise the allocation of costs to integral features when a second-hand property is acquired.
- Owners of commercial property should start to collate records on the capital allowance history of fixtures within the property and recognise them within their capital allowance pools to comply with the pooling rules. At the same time review whether claims should be made.
- Reinvestment relief can be claimed in relation to the replacement of intangible fixed assets.
- Ensure evidence is maintained to track exactly when and what intangibles are created and acquired to maximise the availability of any intangible deductions. Depending on the form and when acquired will determine whether any deductions are available and also the treatment on disposal of the asset.

Chapter 9

Creativity and innovation

Introduction

[9.1] In this chapter we will look at some of the main tax issues that affect the creative industries and reliefs that are available to promote innovation in the UK. In particular we will cover some of the issues that can arise where writers, artists and musicians receive a lump sum for rights and where they incorporate their business. We will also look at the relief available to film and TV production companies and video game producers.

The UK Government are keen to promote technological innovation. As a result relief for qualifying research and development expenditure is available and income derived from qualifying IP can benefit from a reduced rate of corporation tax under the patent box.

Writers, artists and musicians

[9.2] Writers, artists and musicians will often begin to carry on their business as a sole trader. Profits and losses will be computed in the same way as any other business, and an income tax deduction will be available for expenses incurred wholly and exclusively for the purposes of the trade or profession.

There is a facility to average fluctuating profits derived wholly or mainly from creative works, which is set out in ITTOIA 2005, ss 221 to 225 as amended by Finance Act 2016. Profits of five consecutive years can be averaged if the volatility condition in s 222A is met. The volatility condition is that:

(a)   one of the following is less than 75% of the other –
   (i)   the average of the relevant profits of the first four tax years to which the claim relates;
   (ii)   the relevant profits of the last of the tax years to which the claim relates; or
(b)   the relevant profits of one or more (but not all) of the five tax years to which the claim relates are nil.

This relief is useful only if the marginal rate of tax is different for each of the years.

Where a writer, artist or musician carries on a trade or profession, rather than deriving income from those activities on an occasional basis, all receipts in connection with the exploitation of what they have created will form part of their trading receipts. This will include capital sums for the disposal of rights to a work as well as the sale of manuscripts (*Wain v Cameron* 67 TC 324), prizes, awards or bursaries.

This treatment is supplemented by the sales of occupation income anti avoidance provisions in ITA 2007, ss 773 to 789. These provisions impose an income tax charge where a capital sum is received in respect of arrangements made to exploit the earning capacity of an individual in an occupation, and the main object or one of the main objects of the transactions or arrangements is the avoidance or reduction of liability to income tax.

There is an exemption in s 784 for sales of going concerns, but this is restricted by s 785 where the value is derived to a material extent from prospective income or receipts derived directly or indirectly from the individual's activities in the occupation. This means that if an unincorporated business is incorporated, and the value is confined to the infrastructure of the business taken over by the company including any goodwill, if relevant, the disposal will be subject to capital gains tax. Care should be taken to exclude any personal goodwill, which would be a significant feature of any business which derives its profits from the creative talents of an individual. However, if the value includes rights that generate an income stream, the profit on the sale of those rights would be subject to income tax.

Where a right to an income stream is transferred to another person, without transferring the underlying asset, the anti-avoidance provisions contained in ITA 2007, ss 809AZA to 809AZG may need to be considered. Under these provisions any amount received in return for the right to the income stream will be taxed as income rather than as a capital gains tax receipt.

Where there is no income tax avoidance motive and the disposal is of the entire business capital gains tax is likely to apply rather than income tax. This will depend on what rights are transferred and whether the seller retains any right to exploit his creative works in the future.

An artist can give away their work. In the case of *Mason v Innes (44 TC 326)* Hammond Innes gave his rights to a new novel to his father. The Inland Revenue (now HMRC) sought to assess him to income tax based on the market value of the rights, on the principle established in *Sharkey v Wernher* (36 TC 275) that brings into account the value of stock when it is extracted from the trade. However, although the writing of the novel and the disposal of the rights took place as part of Hammond Innes' profession, those rights were not stock in trade so *Sharkey v Wernher* did not apply.

Where a creative business is incorporated the intangible fixed assets provisions in part 8 CTA 2009 need to be considered. This legislation applies to intangible assets, which includes copyright or design rights (s 712(3)(a)). There are special rules which apply to transactions between related parties. The basic rule is that the transfer of an intangible asset is treated for all purposes of the Taxes Acts as being at market value (s 845(1)). This suggests that if a creative business is incorporated in order to save income tax on an income stream, the interaction between CTA 2009, s 845 and ITA 2007, s 776 could mean that an income tax charge arises on the market value of the rights transferred to the company even though the decision in *Mason v Innes* does not impose market value under the *Sharkey v Wernher* principle. However, if the creative business started after 1 April 2002 the company should be able to claim a corporation tax deduction for the amortisation recognised in the accounts, notwithstanding the changes in CTA 2009, s 816A which denies a corporation tax deduction in respect of amortisation of goodwill.

Many celebrities and entertainers transfer their image rights to an image rights company (IRC) often for a gross payment. It is common for the IRC to exploit the individual's 'image rights' by licensing third parties to use an aspect of the individual's image in return for royalty payments. The individual is often employed by the IRC and paid a salary and/or dividends. The capital gains tax treatment of the transfer has always been a contentious area.

HMRC's Capital Gains Manual (CG68405-68440) sets out their view on what constitutes an 'image right' for tax purposes, on whether it can be assigned or licensed to a third party, how it should be valued and the associated tax consequences. Broadly speaking, HMRC takes the view that an image right is only separable from the celebrity and capable of transfer if the celebrity is already in the business of exploiting their 'image' on a commercial basis and to a substantive extent.

Creative industry tax reliefs (CITR)

[9.3] There are five creative industry tax reliefs which are available to companies. These are:

- Film tax relief (FTR);
- Animation tax relief (ATR);
- High-end television tax relief (HTR);
- Video games development relief (VGR);
- Theatre tax relief; and
- Orchestra relief.

The common features of all of the reliefs are that:

- Relief is only available if the production is certified as 'British'; and
- A minimum level of UK core expenditure is met.

Where relief is claimed the company will be entitled to an additional tax deduction for qualifying UK core expenditure and if the company is loss making it should be able to surrender the loss for a cash payable tax credit.

A summary of each relief is given below.

Relief for film production

[9.4] Film Tax Relief (FTR) is set out in CTA 2009, ss 1180 to 1216. This relief is available only to a film production company that incurs qualifying expenditure on film production. It is not available to unincorporated businesses, but can be claimed by EIS/SEIS companies, making the investment particularly attractive to qualifying shareholders.

FTR deems the making of each film will be treated as a separate trade which commences when the film production company (FPC) begins to incur pre-production expenditure, or when any income from the film is received if earlier. FTR applies to a British film that is intended for theatrical release, and on which at least 10% of core expenditure is incurred on goods or services used or consumed in the UK.

A qualifying FPC can claim an additional deduction in computing taxable profits, and where the additional deduction produces a loss it can surrender the loss for a payable tax credit.

The additional deduction and the payable credit are calculated as a percentage of UK core expenditure up to a maximum of 80% of the total core expenditure incurred by the FPC.

For a limited-budget film (whose core expenditure is £20m or less) the additional deduction is 100% of core qualifying expenditure and for other films it is 80%.

With effect from 1 April 2014, the distinction between limited budget films and bigger budget films has been removed. Relief will be available on all films at the rate of 25% on the first £20 million, regardless of the budget of the film.

A number of key terms are defined in the legislation.

Film Production Company (FPC)

An FPC is the company that actually makes the film. In order to qualify as an FPC in relation to a film, the company must be responsible for the pre-production, principal photography, post production, and delivery of the film on completion. This does not mean that the FPC is prevented from using third parties to undertake some of these activities, although it must have some involvement in each of the stages of production. It cannot simply commission the entire production of the film from someone else without having an active engagement itself.

There can be no more than one FPC for any film. Where more than one company meets the requirements for qualifying as an FPC, the company most directly engaged in the production will be treated as the FPC. If none of the companies involved in the film meets the requirements of an FPC, there will be no FPC for that film.

A company can elect that it does not satisfy the conditions of an FPC, so that it would be taxed according to normal principles and would not be eligible for FTR. A company might want to do this if it has losses brought forward which would not be available to offset against profits from the film in question, which is treated as a separate trade.

British film

A British film is a film which is certified as such by the Secretary of State for Culture, Media and Sport. A film can qualify as British either by:

- Satisfying the cultural test set out in SI 2006/3430 the Films (Definition of a British Film) (No2) Order 2006; or
- Meeting the terms of one of the UK's bilateral co-production treaties; or
- Meeting the terms of the European Convention on Cinematic Co-Production.

Theatrical release

In order to qualify for FTR the film must be intended for theatrical release (which is exhibition to the paying public at the commercial cinema) at the end of the accounting period, and that it is intended that a significant proportion of the earnings from the film should be obtained from this source. 'Significant proportion' is not defined, but HMRC accepts that 5% of total estimated income is a significant proportion of the earnings of a film.

Core expenditure

Core expenditure comprises expenditure on pre-production, principal photography, and post production. It does not include expenditure on development, distribution, or other non-production activities.

UK expenditure

UK expenditure is defined as 'expenditure on goods and services which are used or consumed in the United Kingdom' (CTA 2009, s 1185). It is important to establish where goods and services are consumed. Services can be consumed in different countries, in which case it is necessary to apportion the costs to establish UK core expenditure. For example, where actors are paid on the basis of time spent on the film it should be straightforward to identify costs in relation to services consumed in the UK. However, in the case of lead actors who are paid a fee independent of time, the FPC will need to consider a reasonable apportionment of the fee.

The calculation of profits and losses

[9.5] Expenditure on film production is treated as revenue expenditure for the purposes of FTR, which means that expenditure will often be recognised earlier than it would have been under normal accountancy principles, especially where the FPC retains the film rights and capitalises the costs of producing the film.

Rules to establish the timing of expenditure recognition are set out in CTA 2009, ss 1189 and 1192. These sections ensure that costs are recognised when they are represented in the state of completion of the film. This means that prepayments (payments made in advance of goods or services to be supplied) are not recognised until the work has been done and deferrals (services supplied for a promise of future payment) are recognised earlier so long as the obligation for future payment is unconditional.

High-end Television productions and animations

[9.6] Similar reliefs were introduced by Finance Act 2013, inserting Part 15A into CTA 2009. These reliefs apply to a television production company (TPC) which produces a qualifying television programme. For the purposes of this relief a television programme is any programme which is produced to be seen on television (including internet), so long as it is a drama, documentary, or animation, and does not fall within any of the following:

- Advertisements;
- Current affairs;
- Entertainment shows;
- Competitions;
- Live performances;
- Training programmes.

In substance, the reliefs work in the same way as the film tax relief. The calculation of the additional deduction is contained in ss 1216CF to 1216CH. Essentially, these provisions give an enhancement of 100% of the qualifying UK core expenditure, up to a maximum of 80% of total qualifying expenditure, although there are provisions to take into account additional deductions in previous periods.

Losses can be surrendered in return for a payment of 25% of the loss surrendered up to the amount of the enhanceable expenditure.

Video Games Tax Relief

[9.7] Another similar relief has been inserted into CTA 2009 at s 1217A by FA 2013. This relief has many similarities with the film and high end TV reliefs, and applied to the production of British video games.

Theatre Tax Relief

[9.8] Budget 2014 announced that Theatre Tax Relief is available from 1 September 2014. This relief will support the production of plays, musicals, opera, ballet and dance at a rate of 25% for touring productions and 20% for other theatre productions.

Detailed guidance on the creative industries tax reliefs, including how the relief is calculated, is available in the Film Production Company and Television and Animation Production Company manuals.

Patent box

[9.9] The patent box regime was introduced in Finance Act 2012 in response to industry lobbying that companies holding and exploiting patents in the UK faced higher overall effective tax rates than their foreign competitors. Whilst the government did not seek to mirror the reliefs available in other countries, it recognised that reform was required to prevent movement of IP offshore and to encourage companies to locate high-value jobs associated with the development, manufacture and exploitation of patents in the UK and maintain the UK's position as a world leader in patented technologies.

The original form of patent box relief continues until June 2021 for companies that entered the scheme on or before June 2016. A new patent box has been introduced to replace the earlier regime, which applies to new entrants to the scheme on or after 1 July 2016, and to all schemes with effect from accounting periods beginning on or after 1 July 2021. The rules in relation to the new patent box have been inserted into Corporate Tax Act 2010, ss 357BF to 357BQ (CTA 2010) by Finance Act 2016.

The following paragraphs apply to the patent box scheme that applies for entrants up to 30 June 2016, and for those companies will continue to apply until June 2021. The new scheme is broadly similar to the rules set out below, with two main differences. Firstly, income from patented products will need to be streamed, and secondly, a closer nexus with research and development will need to be demonstrated, such that the patented products will need to benefit from R&D carried on by the company or group.

The patent box is a very generous relief as:

- It offers qualifying companies an effective rate of corporation tax on patent related profits;
- Qualifying profits include those from product sales, licence fee income and gains on the disposal of the IP;
- Existing patents and exclusive licences qualify, not just new ones;
- A patent held on just one component of a product will enable the profits from the entire product to qualify;
- The patent does not need to be held in the UK where the claimant company is part of a qualifying group;
- The patent box regime is available to both large companies and SMEs; and
- Companies can access it alongside R&D tax relief allowing companies to benefit from both regimes.

The relevant legislation is set out in CTA 2010, ss 357A to 357GE, and the transitional provisions phasing in the relief are set out in FA 2012, Sch 2, paras 7 and 8.

Entry level tests

[9.10] In order to be able to elect into the patent box, a company must:

- Be liable to UK corporation tax;
- Hold qualifying IP rights or an exclusive licence over them in one or more territories;
- Be exploiting those rights with a view to making a profit; and
- Have undertaken qualifying development by making a significant contribution to the creation or development of a patented invention, or a product incorporating the patented item.

These criteria are considered in greater detail in the sections that follow.

Qualifying IP rights

[9.11] In order to elect into the patent box, a company must hold a qualifying IP right or an exclusive licence over that right in at least one territory.

A list of qualifying IP rights is set out in CTA 2010, s 357BB and includes patents granted under the Patents Acts 1977, patents granted under the European Patent Convention and equivalent rights granted under the law of a specified EEA State. The list of equivalent rights is then set out in HMRC manual CIRD210160.

Where the company holds an exclusive licence, the licence holder must also have either the right to bring infringement proceedings without the consent of the proprietor or to receive the whole or the greater part of any damages received in respect of any infringement.

The following example in CIRD210140 illustrates when a licence would and would not qualify for the patent box:

'A company develops and patents an active ingredient that can be used medicinally in the treatment of cardiac problems in adults. Recognising that other companies may wish to develop other applications, it grants a license to another company to develop the product for the use in treatment of cardiac problems in children. It also grants a separate licence allowing another company to use the ingredient in the treatment of head injuries.

As each application is distinct the licensees will be treated as having an exclusive licence.

A licence that retains rights for the owner to licence others to sell the same mixture under a different brand name (or to do so itself), or with minor differences, but to use for essentially the same application, would not provide exclusive rights over the patented invention. Here the rights in relation to the invention would be substantially the same: to use the compound in a mixture with substantially the same outcome.'

Where a company is a member of a group, HMRC recognises that the internal licence arrangements may not mirror those with an independent third party. Consequently the patent box will not be denied to a company which holds the exclusive rights to exploit a patent but where the right to bring infringement proceedings is held by a fellow group company.

Patents pending

[9.12] If a company has applied for a patent but has not yet been granted patent rights it may still elect into the patent box regime. The company will receive the patent box relief for the profits generated during the application period in the accounting period when the patent is granted. The company may only benefit from a patent pending period of up to a maximum of six years, and will not receive Patent Box benefits arising before 1 April 2013.

Qualifying development

[9.13] To satisfy the qualifying development condition the company must create or significantly contribute to the development of the qualifying IP or perform a significant amount of activity in developing the qualifying IP or any item or process incorporating it.

There is no definition of 'significant', however in HMRC manual CIRD210190 there are a number of useful examples as to what HMRC considers significant and the following general rule:

The following example in CIRD210140 illustrates when a licence would and would not qualify for the patent box:

> 'Whether activity is significant will be determined in the light of all the relevant circumstances ...
>
> A contribution could be significant by virtue of the costs, time or effort incurred. Alternatively, it could be significant due to the value or impact of the contribution.'

Where the company is part of a group and the R&D or qualifying development is carried out by another group company it is still possible for the company holding the qualifying IP rights to elect into the patent box as long as it satisfies the active ownership condition, ie the company performs a significant amount of management activity in relation to the rights. Management activity in this context means formulating plans and making decisions in relation to the development or exploitation of the rights. (CTA 2010, s 357BE).

Calculating the relief

[9.14] Whilst the patent box is often described as entitling the company to a 10% rate of corporation tax, the relief operates as a deduction in the corporation tax computation for an amount calculated as follows:

RP x ((MR-IPR)/MR)

Where:

- RP is the relevant IP profits of the trade;
- MR is the main rate of corporation tax; and
- IPR is the special IP rate of corporation tax (ie 10%).

The patent box regime was phased in over five years. Consequently the appropriate percentage of RP that can be included in the above calculation is modified as follows:

Financial year	
2013	60% of RP
2014	70% of RP
2015	80% of RP
2016	90% of RP
2017 and thereafter	100% of RP

Example

For a company with a 31 March 2015 year end and relevant patent profits (RP) of £60,000 the calculation would be as follows:

| Patent Box Deduction | $= (£60,000 \times 70\%) \times (21-10)/21$ |
| | $= £22,000$ |

There are a number of steps set out in s 357C, which need to be followed to arrive at 'relevant IP profits', which form the basis of the claim.

Step 1: Calculate the total gross income of the trade, as defined in s 357CA. This includes not only the gross income of the trade but also compensation, proceeds from intangible assets, and profits from patent rights.

Step 2: Calculate the percentage ('X%') given by the formula:

$$(RIPI / TI) \times 100$$

Where RIPI is relevant IP income (see **[9.8]**), and TI is the total gross income of the trade in the accounting period.

Step 3: Calculate X% of the profits of the trade for the accounting period.

Step 4: Deduct the routine return figure (see **[9.9]**), which gives the 'qualifying residual profit' (QRP). If the qualifying residual profit is not greater than nil, go to step 7.

Step 5: If the company has elected for the small claims treatment (s 357CM), calculate the small claims amount in relation to the trade. The company can use the small claims treatment if its QRP does not exceed £1m, or its QRP does not exceed £3m (divided by the number of associated companies) and it has not used step 6 in any previous accounting period beginning in the previous 4 years. Under the small claims treatment broadly speaking 25% of the QRP is assumed to relate to marketing assets and is therefore deducted from the qualifying profits calculated so far. If the company has not elected for the small claims treatment, step 6 is used instead.

Step 6: Deduct from QRP the marketing assets return figure, which is calculated in accordance with ss 357CN and 357CO, unless the company has elected into the small claims treatment (see **[9.10]**).

Step 7: If the company has elected that profits arising before the grant of the right are to be included in the calculation under s 357CQ, this amount is added to the amount given by step 5 or 6.

Relevant IP income

[9.15] The company then has to identify the profits that can benefit from the patent box regime. The first step is to identify how much of the company's total gross income includes 'relevant IP income' (RIPI), which is income derived from its qualifying patents.

Principally, the relevant IP income will be income arising from the sale of items in respect of which the company holds a qualifying IP right; items which incorporate one or more qualifying items; or packaging designed to hold the item for sale and which performs a function, for example protecting the item.

RIPI includes not only income from sales of patented items, but also licence fees from rights granted by the company out of its qualifying patents, amounts received from the sale of rights, and compensation, damages, insurance proceeds in respect of qualifying patents.

HMRC gives a number of examples of what can be included in sales for the purpose of establishing RIPI at CIRD 220190:

'Example 1

A patented printer cartridge is designed to be inserted in a printer and once installed not to be removed until empty, at which point it will be replaced. The printer cartridge will be incorporated in the printer. Income from the sale of a printer including the printer cartridge (whether the cartridge is installed or included separately in the box with the printer as part of a single package) can therefore qualify as relevant IP income, even if there were no patent over the printer itself.

Example 2

Conversely, if the printer includes a patented invention and the printer cartridge does not, then sales of the cartridges on their own (by the company holding the relevant patents) will qualify as items wholly or mainly designed to be incorporated into the printer provided that they are bespoke to that printer.

Example 3

In contrast, a patented DVD may be designed to work with a wide variety of DVD players and after each use is intended to be removed. So it is not incorporated in the DVD player, or designed to be incorporated.

So unless the DVD player is patented or includes a patented invention, including a patented DVD with it in a sale will not qualify the income from the player as relevant IP income (it is unlikely that the non-qualifying income would be trivial in this). Similarly, if the DVD player is patented and DVDs are not, sales of the DVDs will not produce relevant IP income.

Example 4

A company sells patented razor blades along with a non-patented handle, as a single item and for a single price. The handle is designed to incorporate the blade. As a result, the item is treated under S357CC(5) as a single item incorporating a patented item, and all income is relevant IP income.

Example 5

A non-refillable medical inhaler may include a sleeve, a canister and the active ingredient plus gas and other contents inside the canister to ensure an effective and measured dose of the active ingredient is administered. It may be that each of these items the sleeve, the canister and the contents of the canister are patented.

But even if this is not the case, income from sale of the sleeve, canister and contents together will be within head 1 if any one of the components is patented. The packaging rule will not exclude either the sleeve or the canister, because they fulfil an essential function in the proper administration of the drug and therefore do not need to be considered as separate items.

Example 6

A company sells sandwiches in patented packaging that significantly extends their life on the supermarket shelves. The purpose for which the sandwich is intended to be used is human consumption. HMRC would not accept that extending the shelf-life of the sandwich is essential for that use. The income attributable to the packaging only, computed on a just and reasonable basis, would qualify.

Example 7

A company holds a patent over a system that consists of a number of individual items. Although the items are not all physically incorporated together they are functionally incorporated by virtue of a wireless/ infra-red connection. The company sells the system as a single unit for a single price. The item is the entire system and the income from the sale of the system would fall under Head 1.'

A company can choose between two routes to calculate how much of its profits derive from qualifying income. It can either apportion its total profits according to the ratio of RIPI to total gross income, or apportion expenses between streams of income to arrive at a profit derived from its RIPI stream.

Routine return

[9.16] Having calculated this profit, which should exclude any additional deduction for R&D expenditure, there are two further stages before completing the calculation.

The first is to remove a routine return on certain specified expenses leaving 'Qualifying Residual Profit' ('QRP'). The purpose of this deduction is to eliminate the return on certain items that might be expected if there were no special IP related to the products.

The routine return is calculated as 10% of a number of heads of expenditure, which are set out in s 357CJ. These are:

Head 1: any capital allowances claimed under CAA 2001.

Head 2: any deductions in respect of any premises occupied by the company.

Head 3: any deductions in respect of any director or employee of the company or any externally provided worker.

Head 4: any deductions in respect of plant or machinery used by the company, which includes leasing, maintaining, servicing and operating the plant or machinery.

Head 5: any deductions for legal services (other than IP related services), financial services including valuation or actuarial services, services in connection with the administration or management of the directors or employees, and any other consultancy services.

Head 6: any deductions in respect of the supply of water, fuel and power, telecommunications, computing, postal, transportation of any items, and the collection, removal or disposal of refuse.

Therefore, expenses that are generally included in the routine return calculation relate to personnel, premises, audit fees etc whereas R&D expenses, the cost of goods for resale, finance expenses and licence fees paid to use patents or trademarks would normally be excluded.

A useful list of routine deductions can be found in HMRC manuals CIRD220460.

Marketing assets return

[9.17] Finally, a notional marketing royalty for use of any marketing assets (such as trademarks, customer lists and the goodwill of the business) held by the company is removed from the QRP.

The deduction is calculated as:

NMR – AMR

Where:

- NMR is the notional marketing royalty in respect of the accounting period; and
- AMR is the actual marketing royalty in respect of the accounting period.

The notional marketing royalty is an appropriate percentage of the relevant IP income which the company would pay a third party for the exclusive right to use the marketing assets if the company were not otherwise able to exploit them.

Alternatively a company with QRP of less than £3m can elect to use a small claims treatment which reduces QRP by 25%. This election should, however, be considered carefully as it could result in a greater deduction from qualifying profits that would be the case if a full evaluation of the value of the marketing assets were made.

The resulting profit is called Relevant IP Profits (RP). These profits are included in the calculation of the patent box deduction set out in **[9.14]** and benefit from the reduced rate of corporation tax.

If the Patent Box RP produces a negative figure there is no change to the company's normal corporation tax computation. However, the negative RP must reduce other RP of the company derived from a different trade, of other group companies, or future RP of the company or other group companies.

Other considerations

Electing into the regime

[9.18] The company must notify HMRC in writing of the first accounting period of the company for which a patent box election is to have effect. The election is made on a trade by trade basis and applies to the period specified in the notice and all subsequent accounting periods of the company.

The election must be made by the last day on which the company would be entitled to amend its tax return, under FA 1998, Sch 18, para 15, for the first accounting period to which it is intended to apply.

> 'There is no special form of words for an election. A corporation tax computation including a deduction for relevant IP profits will be taken to be an election where it is clear that this is what is intended; provided it is made within the time limit.' CIRD260100.

In addition a company does not have to be a qualifying company either at the time it makes the election or for the accounting period for which the election first has effect. Consequently a company can elect into the regime during a patent pending period and qualify for the patent box on the profits generated during the patent application period in the accounting period in which the patent is granted.

The company may revoke an election by notifying HMRC in writing of the first accounting period for which the revocation is to have effect. However, a new election does not effect in relation to any accounting period of the company that begins before the end of the period of five years beginning with the day after the last day of the accounting period specified in the notice. CTA 2010, s 357GA.

Anti-avoidance

[9.19] The legislation includes anti-avoidance provisions to stop commercially irrelevant patented items being included in a product to enable income to qualify under the Patent Box regime. Also, in certain circumstances RP in the first four years for which the company qualifies may be reduced by additional deemed R&D expenditure where the actual R&D expenditure is less than 75% of the average R&D expenditure over the four years immediately prior to electing into the Patent Box.

Pitfalls and planning points

[9.20] The new Patent Box regime will be very attractive to any company which is actively involved in developing or producing patented products, but these companies should be aware of a number of possible pitfalls and planning points.

- Seek advice from a patent attorney up front as patent applications must be made before a new product or invention is publically disclosed.
- A patent need not be over the entire product – a small but integral component may be more patentable and will still give access to the patent box.
- Ensure any licensing arrangements satisfy the exclusivity test.
- Elect into the patent box regime as soon as the patent application is filed to maximise the benefits of the reduced rate of corporation tax.
- Consider carefully where patents are held to ensure the qualifying development and active ownership tests are met.

- Even if a company qualifies for the small claims treatment, don't automatically assume that this will be beneficial.
- Make sure adequate accounting records are maintained in order to carry out the complex calculations.
- The patent box only applies to companies.

Research and development

[9.21] Enhanced relief for research and development is available for companies but not for unincorporated businesses. The relief is available for qualifying expenditure on research and development (R&D) incurred by a company or any other entity within the charge to corporation tax so long as the R&D is relevant to the trade carried on by that entity. If the expenditure is incurred by an overseas permanent establishment of a UK company or the UK permanent establishment of a foreign company, the R&D must be relevant to a trade that is within the charge to corporation tax.

There are three schemes currently in place:

- The SME scheme;
- The large company super-deduction scheme; and
- Above the line (ATL) tax credits.

ATL credits were introduced in Finance Act 2013 for research and development expenditure incurred on or after 1 April 2013. The ATL credit runs alongside the existing large company super-deduction relief for expenditure on research and development under CTA 2009, Part 13, but replaces the super-deduction for large companies from 1 April 2016. It is also available to SMEs who previously only qualified for R&D super-deductions under the large company scheme, for example because the R&D was subsidised.

This means that until 1 April 2016 large companies had the choice whether to claim under the super-deduction scheme or the ATL credit regime. SMEs who qualified for super-deductions under the SME scheme are largely unaffected.

What is R&D?

[9.22] For accounting purposes, R&D is defined in SSAP 13, or, if the company has adopted international accounting standards, IAS 38. However, expenditure included for accounting purposes is unlikely to equate with expenditure that is allowable as R&D expenditure for the purposes of the enhanced R&D tax relief. This may relate to the type of activity that is treated as R&D activity and also to the categories of expenditure that can form part of a claim for tax relief. Any company claiming relief should also refer to the BIS (Department for Business Innovation and Skills) guidance issued in 2004, which sets out the type of expenditure that is R&D expenditure for tax purposes, and to the legislation (in CTA 2009, ss 1039–1142) which determines what categories of expenditure qualify.

The first step is to establish whether a company has incurred expenditure on R&D that will qualify for relief. This will require examining what exactly was done, keeping in focus a number of key but basic requirements.

The R&D project

[9.23] First, it is necessary to identify the R&D project. This is likely to be part of a larger project to develop a new product but is unlikely to embrace the whole of that project. An R&D project is a clearly defined project to solve a scientific or technological uncertainty which extends the bounds of knowledge in that particular area. In solving the problem, the company must adopt a systematic approach, although it is not necessary that a solution is found in order to qualify as R&D.

The objective of the project cannot be intended to solve uncertainties or a lack of knowledge peculiar to that company. Its objective must be to extend the bounds of knowledge within the scientific or technological community dealing in that area of expertise. It must extend beyond something that a reasonably competent professional working in that field could have deduced from existing knowledge.

However, paragraph 21 of the BIS guidelines states that:

'Overall knowledge or capability in a field of science or technology can still be advanced (and hence R&D can still be done) in situations where

- *several companies are working at the cutting edge in the same field, and are doing similar work independently; or*
- *work has already been done but this is not known in general because it is a trade secret, and another company repeats the work; or*
- *it is known that a particular advance in science or technology has been achieved, but the details of how are not readily available.'*

A claim for relief is likely to fail if the R&D project cannot be defined. In order to support the claim, the company is likely to require input from the head of R&D in terms of explaining clearly what the project was, what uncertainty they were trying to resolve, how they planned to go about resolving the uncertainty, what the test results were, what conclusions were reached and how the new knowledge could be applied.

The project might, for example, involve the creation of a prototype. It is necessary to be able to recognise when the R&D activity comes to an end with this type of project, as a prototype can be subject to many revisions and changes. Broadly, the R&D project ends when the company has a prototype that functions in a way that resolves the technological or scientific uncertainty that it had identified and that can form the blueprint for models that can be incorporated into the larger development project. Development of the aesthetic qualities of the prototype, or testing the marketability of the product created as a result of the R&D, will not qualify as part of the R&D project. If certification from an independent body is required, for example, this may serve to mark the end of the R&D project.

Expenditure on prototypes that will be made available for sale will not qualify for enhanced relief, as the prototype will not be regarded as having been 'created or adapted solely for use in R&D'.

Science and technology

[9.24] Research and Development must relate to science or technology. It cannot extend to humanities or design projects, although it might be possible to have an R&D project within a design-led objective if, for example, a new type of material needed to be developed to satisfy aesthetic needs.

Software development

[9.25] Software development is encountered regularly in the context of claims for R&D tax relief. Simply being involved in software development does not mean that the relief is available. The same criteria apply in terms of identifying a project that extends the bounds of scientific or technological knowledge. Replicating a manual process in software form or adapting software for a particular application is unlikely to amount to R&D. On the other hand, developing a new type of interface or algorithm, or developing a new type of search engine using a new type of analytical logic are likely to involve R&D. Again, however, it is vital to identify the R&D project within the larger development project.

The development of user functionality for a piece of software is unlikely to be R&D, as this is more likely to be product development or marketing aesthetics, although there may be elements within this that do qualify.

Expenditure on R&D — is the company an SME or large company?

[9.26] Having established that the company has carried out R&D projects, it is necessary to establish what expenditure can be included in the claim. It is here that it becomes important to establish whether the company is an SME or a large company, which is determined by the Commission Recommendation 2003/361/EC of 6 May 2003, as amended by CTA 2009, s 1120. The most important of these amendments redefine the size limits for an SME, which is an enterprise:

- employing less than 500 persons and either
- with a turnover of less than €100m;
- or a balance sheet total of €86m.

The position is straight-forward for an 'autonomous enterprise'.

Care must be taken, however, when considering the term 'enterprise' in the context of the Commission Recommendation, which essentially means that the Recommendation should be looked at closely whenever 25% or more of the share capital of the company is owned by another enterprise (upstream enterprise) or the company is owned by another enterprise (downstream enterprise). These are broadly termed 'partner enterprises'.

In addition, 'linked enterprises' have to be considered in order to ascertain the size of the claimant company for the purposes of the Recommendation. An enterprise is linked if it has the power to control or have a dominant influence over another enterprise.

Article 3 of the Recommendation, headed 'Types of enterprise taken into consideration in calculating staff numbers and financial amounts', should be considered in full whenever partner or linked enterprises are involved. The full text is as follows:

'1   An "autonomous enterprise" is any enterprise which is not classified as a partner enterprise within the meaning of paragraph 2 or as a linked enterprise within the meaning of paragraph 3.

2   "Partner enterprises" are all enterprises which are not classified as linked enterprises within the meaning of paragraph 3 and between which there is the following relationship:

- an enterprise (upstream enterprise) holds, either solely or jointly with one or more linked enterprises within the meaning of paragraph 3, 25% or more of the capital or voting rights of another enterprise (downstream enterprise).

   However, an enterprise may be ranked as autonomous and thus as not having any partner enterprises, even if this 25% threshold is reached or exceeded by the following investors, provided that those investors are not linked, within the meaning of paragraph 3, either individually or jointly to the enterprise in question:

   (a)   public investment corporations, venture capital companies, individuals or groups of individuals with a regular venture capital investment activity who invest equity capital in unquoted businesses ("business angels"), provided the total investment of those business angels in the same enterprise is less than €1250000;

   (b)   universities or non-profit research centres;

   (c)   institutional investors, including regional development funds;

   (d)   autonomous local authorities with an annual budget of less than €10m and less than 5000 inhabitants.

3   "Linked enterprises" are enterprises which have any of the following relationships with each other:

   (a)   an enterprise has a majority of the shareholders' or members' voting rights in another enterprise;

   (b)   an enterprise has the right to appoint or remove a majority of the members of the administrative, management or supervisory body of another enterprise;

   (c)   an enterprise has the right to exercise a dominant influence over another enterprise pursuant to a contract entered into with that enterprise or to a provision in its memorandum or articles of association;

   (d)   an enterprise, which is a shareholder in or member of another enterprise, controls alone, pursuant to an agreement with other shareholders in or members of that enterprise, a majority of shareholders' or members' voting rights in that enterprise.

   There is a presumption that no dominant influence exists if the

4

5

investors listed in the second subparagraph of paragraph 2 are not involving themselves directly or indirectly in the management of the enterprise in question, without prejudice to their rights as stakeholders.

Enterprises having any of the relationships described in the first subparagraph through one or more other enterprises, or any one of the investors mentioned in paragraph 2, are also considered to be linked.

Enterprises which have one or other of such relationships through a natural person or group of natural persons acting jointly are also considered linked enterprises if they engage in their activity or in part of their activity in the same relevant market or in adjacent markets.

An "adjacent market" is considered to be the market for a product or service situated directly upstream or downstream of the relevant market.

Except in the cases set out in paragraph 2, second subparagraph, an enterprise cannot be considered an SME if 25% or more of the capital or voting rights are directly or indirectly controlled, jointly or individually, by one or more public bodies.

Enterprises may make a declaration of status as an autonomous enterprise, partner enterprise or linked enterprise, including the data regarding the ceilings set out in Article 2. The declaration may be made even if the capital is spread in such a way that it is not possible to determine exactly by whom it is held, in which case the enterprise may declare in good faith that it can legitimately presume that it is not owned as to 25% or more by one enterprise or jointly by enterprises linked to one another. Such declarations are made without prejudice to the checks and investigations provided for by national or Community rules.'

Having established which other entities are either partner or linked enterprises, it is necessary to aggregate the figures for head-count, turnover and balance-sheet totals in order to find out whether the SME thresholds have been breached. For partner enterprises, only a proportion of the figures (based on the proportionate interests) are brought into the calculation, but for linked enterprises the total of those linked enterprises is taken into account.

It is not uncommon for a company that believes itself to be an SME to discover that it is a large enterprise when the Commission Recommendation provisions are taken into account. However, it is not until the threshold is breached for a second consecutive year that the company will need to change which R&D scheme it claims under. This is illustrated in the following examples from HMRC manual CIRD 92000:

'If company A has 480 employees in year one but goes up to 510 employees in year 2 it will remain a SME for year 2. If however it still has at least 500 employees in year 3 it will be a large company for year 3.'

Similarly:

'Taking a demerger situation as an example, in year one company B is large by virtue of its membership of a group of companies which results, on aggregation, in it exceeding the staff headcount. In year two company B leaves the group and at its balance sheet date it meets the staff headcount and financial thresholds, however it will still be a large company for that year. It will attain SME status in year three if its meets the SME threshold tests for a second year in succession.'

The two schemes

[9.27] The reliefs available to SMEs and large enterprises differ in a number of respects.

In most circumstances an SME is able to claim an enhanced deduction in respect of qualifying R&D expenditure of 230%.

Large companies and SMEs who do not qualify for the SME super-deduction can only claim relief under the ATL regime.

The SME scheme

[9.28] SMEs can claim a super-deduction equal to 230% of the qualifying R&D expenditure.

In addition loss making SMEs can surrender the lower of their enhanced R&D expenditure and loss for the period for a cash tax credit of 14.5% of the enhanced deduction included in the loss. There is a per project limit to the relief an SME can claim where expenditure on a project exceeds €7.5m, the computation of which is set out in CTA 2009, ss 1113 to 1115.

Above the line tax credits

[9.29] ATL was introduced in Finance Act 2013 for qualifying R&D expenditure with effect from 1 April 2013. The regime applies to large companies wishing to obtain relief for R&D expenditure as well as to SMEs with certain categories of expenditure or which have received subsidies. The relevant legislation is contained within CTA 2009, s 104A et seq.

The relief operates by crediting to profit and loss account an R&D expenditure credit, which is calculated as 11% of the company's qualifying R&D expenditure. This R&D expenditure credit is chargeable to corporation tax, but is available either as an offset against the company's corporation tax liabilities or, subject to a number of steps which are set out in the legislation, as a repayment to the company.

For large companies the categories of qualifying expenditure are the same as those set out above that form the basis of the super-deduction. For SMEs expenditure qualifies under the ATL credit where it falls within one of the categories set out in ss 104C to 104I. These comprise expenditure on sub-contracted R&D, subsidised expenditure, and capped expenditure.

Where a company seeks a payment from HMRC of the R&D expenditure credit there are seven steps set out in s 104N to establish how much of the credit can be claimed. The 'set-off amount' (the amount to which the company is entitled in respect of the R&D expenditure credit is applied as follows:

Step 1: in discharging any corporation tax liability for the accounting period.

Step 2: if the amount remaining after step 1 is greater than the set-off amount net of corporation tax on that set-off amount, the amount remaining after step 1 is reduced to the net value of the set-off amount.

Step 3: if the amount remaining after step 2 is greater than the PAYE and NIC on remuneration paid to workers engaged wholly or partly on R&D, the set-off amount is reduced to that figure. The amount by which the set-off amount is reduced by step 3 is treated as an amount of R&D expenditure credit in the next accounting period.

Step 4: the amount remaining after step 3 is used in discharging the company's corporation tax liabilities for any other period.

Step 5: if the company is a member of a group, it may surrender the whole or any part of what remains after step 4 to any other member of the group.

Step 6: the amount remaining after step 5 is used in discharging any other outstanding tax liability of the company eg PAYE, VAT etc.

Step 7: any amount remaining after step 6 can be repaid to the company, so long as the company's latest published accounts were prepared on the basis that the company is a going concern, and there is nothing in those accounts indicating that they were prepared on that basis because of an expectation that the company would receive R&D expenditure credits.

In claiming this relief, the R&D expenditure credit will need to be recognised in its profit and loss account, which means that the claim will have to be addressed before the financial statements are prepared. The relevant accounting standards under UK GAAP and IFRS are respectively SSAP 4 and IAS 20, 'Accounting for Government Grants'.

ATL example

[9.30] Company A, a large company, has qualifying R&D expenditure of £100,000 in the year ended 31 March 2018. The company pays corporation tax at 19%.

	£
Turnover	400,000
Qualifying R&D expenditure	(100,000)
ATL credit	11,000
Other expenditure	(100,000)
Profit	**211,000**
Taxable profit	**211,000**
Tax at 19%	(40,090)
ATL credit	11,000
Tax payable	**29,090**

If company A was loss making then ATL would be even more valuable as assuming the company has sufficient PAYE / NIC liabilities the R&D credit may be repayable.

Understanding the R&D activities

[9.31] The key to maximising a claim for R&D tax relief is understanding the company's activities in the context of what is required to fall within the relief. The case of *BE Studios Ltd v Smith and Williamson Ltd* [2005] EWHC 2730 (Ch) considered what was required in order to substantiate a claim for R&D tax relief. It was held not to be sufficient to take all the expenditure classed as R&D expenditure for accounting purposes and then exclude marketing costs. The analysis of the expenditure must be systematic and may involve discussions with the R&D department to establish what exactly they did and applying that to the DTI guidance.

What expenditure can be claimed?

[9.32] The categories of expenditure that can qualify for R&D relief are set out in CTA 2009, ss 1051–1053 and can be summarised as follows:

- Staffing costs (s 1123);
- Expenditure on externally provided workers (s 1127);
- Subcontracted R&D (ss 1134–1136);
- Software and consumable items (s 1125).

Staff costs

[9.33] Most R&D claims will comprise, to a large extent, staff costs.

The first step is to identify which staff can be claimed for and then which of their costs qualify.

Step 1 – Which staff

Employees included in the claim must be directly and actively engaged in the R&D activities, which means that they must be hands-on. Costs in respect of clerical or administrative staff cannot be included in the claim. HMRC sets out criteria that are likely to be relevant, and activities are likely to include one or more of the following:

- preparing equipment and materials for experiments and analysis, but not maintaining equipment;
- experimentation and analysis;
- recording measurements, making calculations and preparing charts and graphs of the results; and
- performing work with respect to engineering or design, operations research, mathematical analysis, computer programming, data collection.

Some employees may not be fully engaged on R&D projects, either because not all projects carried on by the R&D department are R&D projects within the BIS guidance or because they have other activities to carry out, such as non-technical management. In this situation, the staff costs must be apportioned, and it is vital to keep time sheets to enable this exercise to be carried out. As part of the R&D claim, staff members have to be identified so that the hours worked on the projects can be rationalised.

The following example is given in CIRD 83000

'Doctor X heads a small nanotechnology research team within a larger company. All the team's current work is on a project to develop a new motor technology (this is the advance being sought by the project). Doctor X spends much of her time directly and actively engaged on activities that directly contribute to seeking this advance. The remainder of her time is spent directly and actively engaged on other activity within the project that falls within the categories of qualifying indirect activities. 100 per cent of her costs can qualify for relief.

Mr M in her team also works full time on this particular project. He checks the Internet for information on other related studies, ensures the lab is clean, checks that the equipment is in good working order and reports it to the maintenance team if it is not. Mr M's costs can qualify, because he is directly and actively engaged in activity within the project that falls within the categories of qualifying indirect activities.

The relevant portion of the maintenance engineer's time (i.e. that part spent repairing the research unit's equipment being used specifically and solely for the R&D project) forms part of the project and can be qualifying indirect activity in which the engineer is directly engaged. The part of the engineer's time spent on maintaining any other equipment on the same site cannot.

Secretarial and administrative work in the company's maintenance department would not qualify, as this is not part of the R&D project. So while the staff costs attributable to the time Mr M spends filing experimental results as part of the R&D project could qualify, the costs attributable to the time a clerk in the Maintenance department spends filing completed maintenance job sheets would not.

Suppose that the work is promising, and the team is to expand. Dr X therefore spends time interviewing to recruit an extra scientist to work on the project. Dr X's time on this can be a qualifying indirect activity, but support Dr X receives from the Corporate HR Department is not.

Similarly, time Dr X spends on line management of Mr M can qualify, but not the Corporate HR Department's support of her line management activities. If Dr X is responsible for managing the project budget, this could qualify, but not the activity of the corporate finance department to prepare accounts or audit project expenditure.'

Step 2 – Which costs

Not all staff costs qualify for R&D relief. The main categories of qualifying costs are salaries, bonuses, pension payments and employers NICs.

Benefits given to staff working on the R&D do not qualify for R&D tax relief.

Revised guidance was published by HMRC on 18 July 2017, which makes it clear that qualifying reimbursed expenditure includes any out of pocket expenses incurred by an employee in enabling him or her to carry out their duties of employment. Previously, HMRC had taken the view that reimbursed expenses had to fall within one of the categories of qualifying expenditure (which would include contractual costs of employment). This may mean that R&D qualifying expenditure has been under-claimed, so in-time returns may need to be amended.

Groups

Where the company concerned is part of a group, it is necessary to identify which company in the group employs the R&D staff. This can usually be established by reference to their contract of employment. If the staff are employed by another group company, with a recharge to the company carrying out the R&D expenditure, there is a danger that the ability to include the staff costs could be restricted because the staff may be regarded as externally provided workers. If the company is seeking to claim a payable tax credit under the ATL regime, there may be insufficient PAYE paid by the claimant company to support the refund.

Externally provided workers

[9.34] Expenditure on externally provided workers is incurred where a staff provider is contracted to provide staff to the claimant company. It does not extend to recruitment fees or any other services that might be provided under the contract. The workers must be directly and actively engaged in the R&D activity, and costs can be apportioned if they do not spend the whole of their time on such activities.

Where staff are provided by an unconnected staff provider, 65% of the amount paid to the staff provider is potentially available as part of the R&D claim. The company and the staff provider can jointly elect that for the purposes of this relief they are treated as connected.

Where the provider is connected with the claimant company, the quantum of the eligible expenditure can be enhanced as follows.

Where the connected staff provider includes:

- all the payment that the company makes to it for provision of staff;
- all of its relevant expenditure in paying the externally provided workers in its accounts (for a period ending not more than 12 months after the end of the accounting period in which the company claiming the R&D allowance makes the payment); and
- does so in accordance with GAAP,

then the company can claim R&D tax credit on the lower of:

- the qualifying payment for staff that it makes to the staff provider; and
- the amount that the staff provider includes as relevant expenditure in its accounting periods ending not more than 12 months after the end of the company's accounting period in which the payment was made (CIRD84050).

The staff provided in this way must be employees of the staff provider. Where the provider provides self-employed consultants, the costs do not fall within these provisions. It may be possible to treat the expenditure as subcontracted R&D.

Subcontracted R&D

[9.35] In order to qualify for relief, subcontracted R&D must be directly undertaken on behalf of the company. The subcontractor must do the work itself, not further subcontract it to a third party.

The subcontracted expenditure that is within this category of qualifying expenditure is different for the SME scheme and the ATL or large-company scheme.

SMEs

An SME is able to subcontract activities that are part of its R&D activities, even if the activities carried on by the subcontractor do not, in themselves, constitute R&D. The company might, for example, subcontract the analysis of test results that arise from its R&D activities, or it might need to subcontract activities that require specialist machinery.

Where the SME subcontracts ancillary activities, as with externally provided workers, where the subcontractor is unconnected with the company, 65% of the payment to the subcontractor can be included in the R&D claim. Where the parties are connected, or jointly elect to be connected, the quantum of the claim can be increased so long as the payment to the subcontractor and the subcontractor's expenditure are brought into account under rules similar to those that apply to staff providers.

For the purposes of analysing the expenditure incurred by the subcontractor, the expenditure must be neither capital nor subsidised and must be incurred in carrying on the subcontracted activities. The expenditure must be on:

- staffing costs;
- externally provided workers;
- consumable items or software (see below); and
- subjects of clinical trials (subject to Treasury Order).

Where an SME subcontracts the main R&D project, the R&D tax relief will depend on who the party is subcontracted to.

If it is to another SME, the subcontracted party will be able to claim R&D tax relief under the large company or ATL scheme.

If the R&D is subcontracted to a large company, the SME will be able to claim R&D relief for 65% of the costs incurred on a similar basis to the subcontracting of ancillary activities set out above.

Large companies

For large companies, expenditure on subcontracted R&D is generally not allowable. However, it can be qualifying expenditure if it is revenue expenditure on relevant R&D and the company contracts for work to be directly undertaken by:

- a qualifying body (which includes a charity, an institution of higher education such as a university, a scientific-research organisation or a health-service body);

- an individual; or
- a partnership, each member of which is an individual.

Where a large company has been contracted to carry out R&D activities it will only be able to claim R&D relief if the work has been commissioned by either:

- a large company; or
- a person otherwise than in the course of a trade, profession or vocation.

Software and Consumable items

[9.36] Revenue expenditure incurred on consumable items used for R&D purposes can be included in the claim for relief. This can include a wide variety of 'consumable or transformable materials' that would fall into the generality of this wording. It would include water, fuel and power used for R&D projects, together with materials consumed in the R&D project. The key is that the items are consumed, either because they are destroyed or subsumed into something larger, or because they have been converted into something that is no longer usable, for example where a chemical has been spent and in the course of which another compound has been produced. The fact that this by-product can be sold for scrap or used for recycling does not mean that it has not been consumed for the purposes of claiming relief. It may be necessary to apportion expenses when the cost is not entirely referable to an R&D project.

Revenue expenditure incurred on software directly used in an R&D project will be qualifying expenditure for the purposes of this relief. Software that is used indirectly, for example software used for secretarial functions in the R&D department, will not fall within qualifying expenditure. Where software is used partly for R&D purposes, an apportionment may be appropriate. Claims for expenditure on software should be supported by literature from the providers detailing specifications of the software and a description of how the software is used in the R&D process.

Subsidised expenditure

[9.37] An SME cannot claim relief for expenditure that has been subsidised. However, if the expenditure would otherwise qualify for relief, the company may be able to make a claim under the ATL scheme, for which there is no restriction for subsidised expenditure.

Where an SME has received any funding which is a notified State Aid, no expenditure on the project in question can be included in a claim for enhanced relief. If the grant or subsidy is not notified State Aid, any expenditure in excess of the grant can be included in a claim under the SME scheme. The remainder may be claimed under the large company or ATL scheme.

Other issues to consider

[9.38] In order to be able to claim the enhanced relief or to claim relief for pre-trading expenditure under s 1045, the company must be able to prepare its accounts on a going concern basis (s 1046).

FA 2004, s 53 allows expenditure to be deducted when it is incurred irrespective of whether it appears as a deduction in the profit and loss account so long as:

- Expenditure is recognised either as a deduction in computing the profit or as an intangible asset; and
- The expenditure is not prevented from being an allowable deduction in calculation of profit of that period (eg it is capital expenditure), and
- The expenditure is incurred during the accounting period.

(CIRD81450)

A claim for enhanced R&D relief must be made within two years of the end of the accounting period in which the expenditure was incurred (FA 1998, para 10, Sch 18).

Possible pitfalls and planning points

[9.39] Key points to note are as follows:

- As with the patent box enhanced R&D relief applies only to companies.
- The relief available differs between SMEs and large companies, so know which size of company you are dealing with.
- The time limit for claiming relief is two years.
- The IP does not have to be held within the company claiming relief.
- Watch out for subsidies and subcontractor relationships.
- Ensure claims include qualifying indirect expenditure.
- Capitalised revenue expenditure can also be claimed.
- 100% capital allowances may be available on assets including buildings and cars used for R&D, but not enhanced reliefs.

How to present the case to HMRC

[9.40] Presentation of the project cannot be underestimated. HMRC will expect to see a good résumé of the R&D projects carried out by the company during the year. This will include a description of the project, what scientific or technological uncertainty the company sought to resolve, what testing was carried out, how this was documented and what the outcome was.

Details of who worked on the projects and the time devoted to the projects will also be required and possibly what materials were used in the projects.

If a claim is made for software, the specification and purpose of the software should also be set out.

Key Points

[9.41]

- Writers, musicians and artists need to take care whenever selling rights to creative works, as there are a number of provisions under which capital receipts can be taxed as income.
- The Patent Box provides a low rate of corporation tax on profits attributable to patented products. Companies seeking to claim this relief need to ensure that their accounting records provide sufficient information to be able to prepare the required computation of qualifying residual profit.
- Relief for research and development can apply to a wide range of projects carried out by a company. It is important to be able to identify where there has been an advance in scientific or technological knowledge in the field in which the company operates and which indirect activities can be included in the claim for R&D relief.
- Above the line credit for R&D expenditure is available for large companies, and will replace the 'super-deduction' for large companies from 2016.

Chapter 10

Employee Benefits and Shares

Introduction

[10.1] Employee benefits and equity reward play an important part in the remuneration package of employees.

This first section looks at the provision of benefits to employees. The general rule is that benefits are subject to tax and Class 1A NICs. However, where the benefits comprise readily convertible assets (RCAs), these will be taxed as earnings, which means that the tax must be accounted for under PAYE and both employee's and employer's NICs are payable. Also, where benefits are provided by voucher or the payment of an employee's debt, the benefit will usually be taxed under PAYE and employer's Class 1 NICs will be payable. The rules for taxable benefits in kind are contained in Income Tax (Earnings and Pensions) Act 2003, Pt 3 (ITEPA 2003). The second section below examines the issue or transfer of shares to employees and how this can be achieved in a tax-efficient manner. The third and final section will cover the provisions aimed at tackling arrangements used for the purpose of disguising remuneration in order to avoid or defer income tax or national insurance contributions.

Employee benefits

[10.2] It is beyond the scope of this book to look at all the benefits which can be provided to employees. The authors have instead focused on the most popular ones. Tax-free benefits can be popular with both the employer and the employee, especially where these can be provided as part of a salary sacrifice scheme. They are detailed in ITEPA 2003, Pt 4, and include the following benefits.

(1)   Mileage allowance payments are approved for 'business travel' up to set limits where the employees use their own vehicles, as follows:

Kind of vehicle	Rate per mile
Car or van	45p for the first 10,000 miles in any tax year
	25p thereafter
Motorcycle	24p
Cycle	20p

Where an employee is paid *less* than the approved amount, he is entitled to deduct the difference from his taxable earnings in his tax return (ITEPA 2003, ss 229–232). It would therefore follow that where an employee is paid in excess of the approved amount, the excess is reported as earnings from employment income.

(2) There are also advisory fuel rates for employees with company cars. As these are only fuel rates, they are lower — there is no wear-and-tear element. They apply where the employer either:

- reimburses employees for business travel in their company cars; or

- requires employees to repay the cost of fuel used for private travel.

There is no taxable benefit where the employer reimburses employees for business travel at the rates below or where the employee repays the cost of private travel fuel at the rates below:

Engine size	Petrol – amount per mile	LPG – amount per mile
1400cc or less	11 pence	7 pence
1401cc to 2000cc	14 pence	8 pence
Over 2000cc	22 pence	13 pence

Engine size	Diesel – amount per mile
1600cc or less	9 pence
1601cc to 2000cc	11 pence
Over 2000cc	13 pence

Hybrid cars are treated as either petrol or diesel cars for this purpose. These rates apply from 1 March 2018. The rates are not statutory. Therefore, they are not binding. HMRC simply says it will not treat the employer as having paid for private fuel where these rates are applied. If the employer unjustifiably reimburses employers at higher rates, any excess is treated as earnings subject to PAYE and NIC. However, where an employer can demonstrate that the cost of business travel in company cars, in the fleet, concerned is higher than the advisory mileage rates then higher rates can be paid. The example given in HMRC's Employment Manual at EIM30057 is where employees need to use particular types of car such as 4 x 4s to cover rough terrain.

If the employee repays the cost of the fuel used for private travel at the advisory rate but drives a very large-engined company car, or unjustifiably pays a lower rate, HMRC may argue that a higher repayment rate should apply in order to avoid any taxable benefit arising.

Similarly, the advisory rates will not be binding where an employer can demonstrate that employees cover the full cost of private fuel by repaying at a lower rate per mile.

Details regarding the advisory fuel rates for employees with company cars can be found on the HMRC website at www.gov.uk/government/publications/advisory-fuel-rates/advisory-fuel-rates-from-1-march-2

016. HMRC's previous guidance clearly stated that it 'will always accept that the guideline rates can be used to calculate the amount that the employee must make good where the engine size is three litres or less'.

(3) 'Passenger payments' are available where an employee or volunteer carries one or more passengers in a car or van for business purposes. Here, it does not matter whether the vehicle is the employee's own or a company vehicle. The approved amount is 5p per mile per passenger. However, if the employer does not pay this amount, then, unlike the mileage allowance payments, the employee cannot take it as a deduction against taxable earnings in his tax return (ITEPA 2003, ss 233, 234).

(4) The provision of parking spaces for cars, vans, motorbikes and bicycles at or near the employee's workplace, or the reimbursement of expenses for such parking, is tax-free (ITEPA 2003, s 237).

(5) The provision of a works bus (seating capacity of 12 or more) or minibus (seating capacity of 9, 10 or 11) to transport employees to and from work is also tax-free, as are employer subsidies for the use of public bus services.

The service must be open to all employees, and, where the service is not a local bus service, it must be available to the employees on no more favourable terms than those available to other passengers.

Where a public bus service subsidy is provided, tax-free treatment will only apply to travel on a specific supported bus route, and not to area bus passes (ITEPA 2003, ss 242, 243).

(6) The use of an employer's bicycle and/or bicycle safety equipment is exempt where the benefit is made available to all employees and the bicycle or safety equipment is used mainly for 'qualifying journeys'. The ownership of the equipment cannot be transferred to the employee (ITEPA 2003, s 244).

A 'qualifying journey' is a journey between the employee's home and workplace, or between one workplace and another.

Some employees may not be able to take up the offer of this benefit as part of a salary sacrifice scheme due to National Minimum Wage or Consumer Credit Act implications. However, HMRC has confirmed that tax-free treatment will be preserved for all employees if a separate pool of bicycles is made available for ineligible employees. An adult may act as a guarantor if an employee is aged under 18 and wishes to enter into a cycle salary sacrifice arrangement but is prevented from doing so because of the Consumer Credit legislation. Further commentary can be found in HMRC's employment income manual at EIM21664.

Where bikes are offered to employees after the end of the loan period for less than their market value, the amount underpaid will be treated as earnings liable to both tax and NIC.

(7) The payment of an employee's travelling costs by way of taxi or similar road transport to get home is tax-free where he is required to work later than usual and at least until 9pm or later and there is no public transport available or it would be unreasonable to expect him or her to use it.

This benefit ceases to be exempt if such transport has been provided on 60 or more previous occasions in the tax year. Occasions where the employee works until 9pm or later must be irregular (ITEPA 2003, s 248). A detailed record must be maintained to demonstrate that all four conditions have been satisfied.

(8) Use of a company pooled car or van is tax-free. Here, a car or van is classed as a pool vehicle if:

- the vehicle is made available to and used by more than one employee by reason of employment;
- the vehicle is not used by one employee to the exclusion of others;
- any private use is incidental; and
- the vehicle is not normally kept overnight at any of the employees' homes unless it is kept on the premises of the provider of the vehicle (ITEPA 2003, ss 167, 168).

(9) The provision of, payment for or reimbursement of work-related training is exempt (ITEPA 2003, s 250). Work-related training means:

'a training course or other activity designed to impart, instil, improve or reinforce any knowledge, skills or personal qualities which:

- are likely to prove useful to the employee when performing the duties of the employment or a related employment; or
- will qualify or better qualify the employee:
  - to perform those duties; or
  - to participate in any charitable or voluntary activities that are available to be performed in association with the employment or a related employment.'

(ITEPA 2003, s 251).

Where the training has a mixed purpose, part reward and part genuine training, the amount needs to be apportioned and the non-training part taxed as a benefit.

The provisions of ITEPA 2003, s 250 do not give employees tax relief for the costs of self-financed training where the cost of training is not reimbursed by the employer. Relief for employees meeting their own costs are only deductible if they are incurred wholly, exclusively and necessarily in the performance of duties. The Courts have taken a very restrictive approach. In *Nolder (Inspector of Taxes) v Walters* (1930) 15 TC 380, Rowlatt J commented at p 387 that the phrase means: 'in doing the work of the office, in doing the things which it is his duty to do while doing the work of the office'.

Therefore, to satisfy this test, the expense must be incurred in actually carrying out the duties of the job. It is not sufficient for the expense to be relevant or related to the employment. This is very much based on fact a point which was particularly pertinent in the case of *Revenue and Customs Comrs v Banerjee* [2009] EWHC 62 (Ch), [2009] 3 All ER 915, [2010] 1 WLR 800. In that case, Dr Banerjee was employed by the NHS under a training contract which required her to attend meetings, courses and conferences, the cost of which was met by her directly for which a claim was made. Because of the requirement under her contract of employment, the case was found in her favour.

(10)   The provision of sports and gym facilities is tax-free, provided these are not made available to the public (ITEPA 2003, s 261).

(11)   Staff events (for example, the Christmas party) are exempt where the cost of all parties in the tax year totals £150 (inc VAT) or less per head. In calculating the cost per head, the total cost of each function is divided by the total number of people who attend (including guests who are non-employees). Where the cost of the event is not exempt, employees are taxable on the full cost per head (not just the excess over £150), in respect of:

- themselves; and
- any members of their family and household who attend as guests.

Where a company holds two events (open to all employees) in a tax year and the cost of each one is below the £150-per-head exemption limit but the total combined cost exceeds £150 per head for the employees who attended both events, they will be chargeable only on the benefit of the lower costing event. (The allowance is set against the cost of the more expensive event.) Employees who only attended one of the events will not receive a taxable benefit (ITEPA 2003, s 264 and Employment Income Manual at EIM21690 — Particular benefits: annual parties and other social functions).

The costs per head include the total cost of providing any transport or accommodation incidentally provided for persons attending plus VAT.

(12)   Relocation costs totalling up to £8,000 are exempt where the employee needs to move as a result of his taking up the employment or as a result of a change in the duties or the place where these are carried out (ITEPA 2003, ss 271–289).

(13)   The provision of free or subsidised meals in any staff canteen *or* on the employer's business premises is tax-free, provided these are offered to all staff and are on a 'reasonable scale'. So, if a sandwich van turns up on the employer's premises daily, the employer could buy sandwiches for all the employees without providing a taxable benefit. This benefit will not be tax-free where it is provided as part of a salary sacrifice scheme (ITEPA 2003, s 317).

(14)   On-site crèches and nurseries are exempt where the facilities are made available to all employees. The premises on which the care is provided must not be a private residence. The employer must provide the premises or, where the employer runs the nursery jointly with others, the employer must contribute to the provision of the premises and have some responsibility for managing and financing the provision of the childcare (ITEPA 2003, ss 318–318D). For employees who had entered a childcare scheme prior to 6 April 2011, the provisions by employers of 'qualifying childcare' vouchers are exempt from both tax and NIC to the extent of £55 per week. Where an employee joins a scheme on or after 6 April 2011, the level of relief available will depend on the rate of tax paid by the employee.

(15)   Regarding the provision of a mobile phone, only one per employee is tax-free (ITEPA 2003, s 319). Revenue & Customs Brief 02/12 clarified the treatment of smartphones, confirming that they can qualify as mobile phones.

(16)   Employer-suggestion-scheme awards of up to £5,000 are exempt where it is not the employee's job to come up with the suggestion. The award must be 'for a suggestion relating to an improvement in efficiency or effectiveness which the employer has decided to adopt and reasonably expects will result in a financial benefit'. The maximum exempt amount is the lower of:

(a)   £5,000;

(b)   half the financial benefit reasonably expected to result from the adoption of the suggestion for the first year after its adoption; or

(c)   one-tenth of the financial benefit reasonably expected to result from its adoption for the first five years after its adoption.

(ITEPA 2003, ss 321, 322).

(17)   Long-service awards for employees who have worked at the company for 20 years or more, provided that they have not received any similar award within the last 10 years and that the award does not exceed £50 for each year of service (ITEPA 2003, s 323).

(18)   Low interest or interest-free loans for any purpose where the amount lent does not exceed £10,000 at any time during the tax year, for example a loan to help purchase a season travel ticket (ITEPA 2003, s 180).

(19)   Employer contributions to a registered personal pension scheme. Contributions exceeding £40,000 may give rise to a tax charge on the employee. Further details on pension tax relief are provided in Chapter 6 (ITEPA 2003, s 308).

(20)   Third party entertainment provided to employees by reason of their employment where the entertainment is not provided or procured by the employer or someone connected to the employer and is not provided in recognition for services past, present or future during the course of the employment (ITEPA 2003, s 265).

(21)   Employer provided periodic medical check-ups (ITEPA 2003, s 320B). An annual check-up or health screening provided by the employer will not give rise to a taxable benefit in kind charge for the employee.

(22)   Medical treatment or an insurance policy for the same for directors and employees working overseas is not a taxable benefit in kind (ITEPA 2003, s 325). This extends to any costs incurred by a director or employee and reimbursed by the employer.

(23)   Zero emission cars. Until 5 April 2015 there was a nil benefit in kind charge for cars and vans which did not produce CO_2 emissions when driven. After 6 April 2015, these vehicles are treated in the same way as other vehicles with CO_2 emissions of less than 50g per km.

Where an employer provides trivial benefits to an employee, this may be exempt from tax if all of the following conditions are met:

•   it costs the employer less than £50 to provide the benefit;

•   the benefit is not in the form of cash or a cash voucher;

•   the benefit is not given as a reward for work or performance; and

•   the employee has no contractual entitlement to the benefit.

This exemption is not available for the directors of close companies and is not applicable to benefits provided under a salary sacrifice arrangement entered into on or after 6 April 2017.

The rules on benefits in kind now allow employers to payroll benefits in kind under the real-time information (RTI) system. The only exceptions to this are the benefit in kind arising from employer-provided living accommodation and beneficial employment-related loans, which must be included in the employee's P11D. Further guidance can be found at www.gov.uk/guidance/ payrolli ng-tax-employees-benefits-and-expenses-through-your-payroll.

Salary sacrifice

[10.3] In the past effective salary sacrifice arrangements between employee and employer have been very tax- and NIC-efficient, providing savings for both employee and employer. In the 2017 Spring Budget, the government brought forward legislation that has significantly restricted the effectiveness of salary sacrifice arrangements.

The legislation means that, where an employee has sacrificed salary in exchange for the provision of benefits, the employee is taxed as if they had been paid in cash; the rules on the taxation of benefits in kind are effectively over-ridden.

For existing salary sacrifice arrangements there is a degree of transitional relief:

- salary sacrifice arrangements that were entered into before 6 April 2017 remained effective for tax purposes until 6 April 2018; and
- salary sacrifices for cars with CO_2 emissions above 75g/km, accommodation and school fees that were entered into before 6 April 2017 will remain effective until 6 April 2021.

For a limited number of benefits, salary sacrifice will remain effective:

- pension contributions and pension advice;
- childcare vouchers;
- workplace provided childcare and nurseries;
- cycle to work; and
- cars with CO_2 emissions of less than 75g/km.

The terms of the arrangements which ideally should be made in writing are that the employee agrees to give up part of their salary, due under existing contractual arrangements in return for a benefit or benefits of the types described above.

An effective salary sacrifice arrangement needs to be in place before entitlement to the salary to be sacrificed arises. Evidence of this change in terms, which usually run for 12 months, should be retained and made available for HMRC scrutiny on request.

Equity participation

[10.4] It has become increasingly important for employees in a company to participate in the equity, giving them a stake in the future growth of the business. Owning shares in the company has the added bonus of being able to reward employees in capital form chargeable to capital gains tax on which the top rate is 28% which is more attractive than a 40% or 45% income tax rate.

The rules found in ITEPA 2003, Pt 7 on 'employment-related securities' are complex and wide in application. The rules apply to interests in shares or securities (including outright ownership) acquired by an individual by reason of their own or someone else's employment. In this context, employment includes holding an office, such as a directorship, and extends to current, former or prospective employment.

The purpose of the legislation is to tax value given to employees (or given to someone associated with an employee), either when shares are acquired by them or if something is done to artificially increase the value of securities that they already hold. Tax charges that arise on employment related securities will always be levied on the employee, even if the securities themselves are acquired or held by another person.

Example

John is employed by Bucolin Holdings Ltd. Bucolin Holdings Ltd intends to issue 10 shares to John to reward him for his hard work during the year and his loyalty to the company. John asks if the company can give the shares to his friend Michael instead of him. Michael has acquired shares from an opportunity made available by reason of John's employment. His shares are therefore employment-related securities, and ITEPA 2003, Pt 7 will apply. Any charges which fall due are chargeable on John, as the opportunity was made available by reason of his employment.

The legislation limits the scope for individuals to argue that shares are not employment related securities, ITEPA 2003, s 421B(3) states that:

'a right or opportunity to acquire securities or an interest in securities made available by a person's employer, or by a person connected with a person's employer, is to be regarded for the purposes of subsection 1 as available by reason of an employment of that person unless:

(a)   the person by whom the right or opportunity is made available is an individual; and

(b)   the right or opportunity is made available in the normal course of the domestic, family or personal relationships of that person.'

With one exception, the effect of this provision is to treat any shares issued or transferred by an employer to any employee as employment-related securities, irrespective of the motives or intentions of either the issuer or the employee. The exception to this rule arises where shares are made available by an individual in the course of family and domestic personal relationships. HMRC has said that where shares in a family-controlled company are newly issued, they will be treated as having been made available by an individual where the 'family and domestic' test is being applied. The exception for transactions between family members does not apply where the shares are, as a matter of fact, provided by reason of employment.

Example

> Robert is issuing 5% of the share capital in Bucolin Holdings to each of his four board members, one of whom is his daughter Catherine. In this case, it would be difficult to put forward the argument that the shares are in the course of 'family and domestic personal relationships', as all the directors are receiving shares at the same time.
>
> Where shares are made available to both family and employees, these should be dealt with separately; where the family shares are provided out of love and affection and as part of future succession planning, this needs to be clear and preferably recorded. It may be that the shareholder provides shares to children working in the business and children not working in the business or, with the latter, they are given another gift of similar value. This strengthens the connection of the gift with the parental relationship.

Shares only cease to be treated as employment-related securities on the seventh anniversary of the date on which the individual ceases to be an employee or on the death of the individual.

These rules, taken as a whole, mean that, in the majority of cases where shares are issued or transferred to employees, they will be caught by the rules contained in ITEPA 2003, Pt 7.

Special care is required in relation to internationally mobile employees, due to the effect of the rules in ITEPA 2003, Part 2, Chapter 5B. Guidance is provided in HMRC's Employment-related Securities Manual at ERSM160000 onwards.

An outline of all of the rules contained in Pt 7 is beyond the scope of this book. However, it is important to alert the practitioner to the fact that there are eight chapters, imposing some 19 chargeable events!

Chapter 2	Restricted securities
Chapter 3	Convertibles
Chapter 3A	MV artificially depressed
Chapter 3B	MV artificially enhanced
Chapter 3C	Acquired for less than market value
Chapter 3D	Sold for more than market value
Chapter 4	Special benefits
Chapter 5	Securities options

The chapters most commonly encountered by practitioners in dealing with owner-managed businesses are those in relation to:

- shares acquired for less than market value;
- restricted securities;
- MV artificially enhanced;
- shares sold for more than market value; and
- securities options.

PAYE and NIC

[10.5] Whether tax arising under the rules on employment related securities is collected through self-assessment or a PAYE withholding obligation will be dependent on the shares' status as Readily Convertible Assets (RCAs). If there is a PAYE withholding obligation then a NIC liability will also arise.

If shares are not RCAs, tax will be payable via the individual's self-assessment return and the amount is included on the share-scheme section of the additional information pages of the return (SA101). It is not included on the P11D as a benefit in kind, therefore it is not subject to Class 1A NICs.

However, where the shares are RCAs or the event giving rise to a tax charge is the disposal of shares for cash or RCAs, income tax will be payable under PAYE and both employer and employee NICs will arise. ITEPA 2003, s 702 will determine whether or not shares are RCAs.

There are ten separate tests, many of which are of little practical significance. Since April 2003, shares are always RCAs if they do not meet the criteria set out in the rules on corporation tax deductions under CTA 2009, Pt 12 (previously FA 2003, Sch 23).

For private companies, the most common situations where shares will be RCAs are where there are arrangements in place to sell the shares (eg impending listing or sale) or where the shares are in a subsidiary company.

HMRC takes the view that shares will be RCAs if the company is being marketed and treats the appointment of a corporate finance team with a sale mandate as the start of that process (irrespective of whether a sale actually goes through). However, the author's experience is that shares will not be treated as RCAs during the period before a company is marketed: the preparation of an information memorandum on its own is not enough to make the shares RCAs.

Share valuation

[10.6] Income Tax (Earnings and Pensions) Act 2003, s 421 specifies that the market value of shares for the purposes of ITEPA 2003, Pt 7 should be calculated in accordance with Taxation of Chargeable Gains Act 1992, Pt VIII (TCGA 1992). This refers to TCGA 1992, s 272, which defines market value as 'the price which those assets might reasonably be expected to fetch on a sale in the open market'. This may mean that the market value of shares for the purposes of charges to tax under ITEPA 2003, Part 7 will be different to the values calculated for the purposes of ITEPA 2003, s 62, which will be calculated using a 'money's worth' valuation, which has different evidential requirements.

It is generally not possible to agree share values with HMRC. Before March 2016 it was possible to agree share values under either the post transaction valuation check facility or by using the PAYE valuation check service, but both of these facilities have been withdrawn and are no longer offered by HMRC. HMRC is willing to agree valuations in advance in relation to an award of shares under one of the statutory schemes (eg EMI or CSOP) and, once a valuation has been agreed, companies generally have sixty days in which to grant awards at that value.

Shares acquired for less than market value

[10.7] Owner-managed businesses often arrange to transfer or issue shares to employees without the employees making an immediate payment for the shares.

In this situation, two interlocking sets of rules need to be considered:

- A charge will arise under ITEPA 2003, s 62 on the difference between the market value of shares that are awarded to employees and the price payable by the employees for those shares; and
- Supplemental charges can arise under ITEPA 2003, Pt 7, Chapter 3C on any part of the value of the shares in respect of which the employee has an obligation to make a payment, but the payment is deferred until some date in the future.

Under ITEPA 2003, s 446V, any amounts that have been taxed under s 62 are deducted from the value on which charges under Chapter 3C are calculated. This means that where an employee has an obligation to pay an amount for shares at a date in the future, but the amount payable is less than the market value of the shares, charges to tax can arise under both sets of rules.

While s 62 imposes an immediate charge on the date that shares are acquired by employees, Chapter 3C operates by treating the value of the unpaid consideration as a loan, which is taxed under the rules on beneficial loans (ITEPA 2003, Part 3, Chapter 7).

Example

John is issued with shares worth £10,000 from Bucolin Holdings Ltd by reason of his employment. He is not required to pay for the shares. John is therefore taxed under ITEPA 2003, s 62 on earnings of £10,000.

At the same time, shares worth £10,000 are issued to Carol, but she is required to pay for the shares, and it is agreed that she will pay for them in three years' time. Carol is deemed to have incurred a notional loan of £10,000 under ITEPA 2003, s 446Q.

On the same day, Mike is issued shares worth £10,000 on terms that Mike will pay up the £1,000 nominal value of the shares before he sells them. Mike will be taxed under s 62 on £9,000 (the difference between the shares' market value and the amount that Mike will have to pay in the future) and will be treated as having a notional loan of £1,000 on the unpaid nominal value of the shares.

Where Chapter 3C treats a notional loan as arising, tax will be charged on the value of the notional loan if it is discharged or if the shares are sold before the unpaid consideration has been paid by the employee.

The notional loan is treated in the same way as any other employment-related beneficial loan: an annual tax charge on the benefit in kind of the notional loan can arise under ITEPA 2003, Pt 3, Chapter 7. The value of the benefit is calculated using the official rate, which is currently 3%.

The annual tax charge will not arise if either:

- the aggregate value of the employee's indebtedness to the company, including the value of the notional loan arising under Chapter 3C is less than the £10,000 de minimis level set out in ITEPA 2003, s 180; or
- under ITEPA 2003, s 178, income tax relief under ITA 2007, s 393 could have been claimed on interest arising on an actual loan taken out by the employee to purchase the shares.

Relief under ITEPA 2003, s 178 will be due where the shares are in a close company (but not a close investment holding company) and the employee meets the full-time working condition or the material-interest condition.

The full time working condition applies where the employee spends the greater part of his time in the actual management or conduct of the company or an associated company. This condition is much more difficult to satisfy than it appears at first glance. The use of the words 'management or conduct' suggests that the employee has to be at a senior level in the company. The Savings and Investment Manual at SAIM10230 states that the terms 'management' and 'conduct' should be given their strict meanings: the employee must have a real input in the running of the business. It goes on to say:

> 'Relief is limited to those who have a significant stake, whether as shareholder or by a combination of shareholding and the possession of significant managerial or technical responsibility in the company. A shareholder will normally be regarded as meeting the "full time working condition" if they are directors of the company or have significant technical or managerial responsibilities. The shareholder must be involved in the overall running and policy making of the company as a whole. Managerial or technical responsibility for just one particular area will not be sufficient, so claims by employees (other than directors) without such significant responsibilities should be refused. Whether or not an individual satisfies the "actual management or conduct" test is a question which can only be answered by consideration of the full facts of any particular case.'

For the material-interest condition to apply, the employee and his associates must be the beneficial owners or be able to control (directly or indirectly) 5% of the ordinary share capital of the company, or be entitled to such rights which would, in the event of a winding-up, entitle them to receive more than 5% of the assets for distribution among the participators.

Relatives or partners and trustees of certain settlements are treated as 'associates' for these purposes and derives from ITA 2007, s 253. A planning point is that where there are a number of employees receiving shares and none of them meet the material interest test, they could make themselves associated by entering into a partnership: this would eliminate any benefit-in-kind charge!

Restricted securities

[10.8] The articles of association of most owner managed businesses place restrictions on the free transfer of shares and often contain clauses compelling employee shareholders to sell shares when they leave the company – often at less than market value if the employee becomes a 'bad leaver', other restrictions may be imposed by shareholders' agreements or subscription agreements that employees enter into. Where such provisions apply shares held by employees will be treated as 'restricted securities' and subject to a regime of tax charges set out in ITEPA 2003, Pt 7, Chapter 2.

ITEPA 2003, s 423 stipulates that employment related securities will be treated as restricted securities where:

'(1) . . .

 (a) there is any contract, agreement, arrangement or condition which makes provision to which any of the subsections (2) to (4) applies, and

 (b) the market value of the employment-related securities is less than it would be but for that provision.

(2) This subsection applies to provision under which:

 (a) there will be a transfer, reversion or forfeiture of the employment-related securities, or (if the employment-related securities are an interest in securities) of the interest or the securities, if certain circumstances arise or do not arise,

 (b) as a result of the transfer, reversion or forfeiture the person by whom the employment-related securities are held will cease to be beneficially entitled to the employment-related securities, and

 (c) that person will not be entitled on the transfer, reversion or forfeiture to receive in respect of the employment-related securities an amount of at least their market value (determined as if there were no provision for transfer, reversion or forfeiture) at the time of the transfer, reversion or forfeiture.

(3) This subsection applies to provision under which there is a restriction on:

 (a) the freedom of a person by whom the employment-related securities are held to dispose of the employment-related securities or proceeds of their sale,

 (b) the right of that person to retain the employment-related securities or proceeds of their sale, or

 (c) any other right conferred by the employment-related securities,

(not being provision to which subsection 2 applies).

(4) This subsection applies to provision under which the disposal or retention of the employment-related securities, or the exercise of a right conferred by the employment-related securities, may result in a disadvantage to:

 (a) the person by whom the employment-related securities are held,

 (b) the employee (if not the person by whom they are held), or

 (c) any person connected with the person by whom they are held or with the employee,

(not being provision to which subsection 2 or 3 applies).'

The First-tier Tribunal in *Sjumarken v Revenue and Customs Comrs (No 2)* [2015] UKFTT 375 (TC), [2015] SWTI 3242 held that, for the purposes of the legislation, a share that is expressed to be free of restrictions will still constitute a restricted security if there are de facto restrictions on disposing or transferring it: in the Sjumarken case, the rules of a share scheme said that a holding period would be waived on cessation of employment and the employee would be free to sell shares, but the company secretary refused to permit the shares to be sold until the end of the original holding period.

Many of the restrictions set out above will have been imposed for genuine commercial purposes – usually to protect the interests of founder or majority shareholders and also to add an element of 'stick' to the 'carrot' of employee share ownership.

As a minimum, the majority of private companies retain the right to veto a transfer of shares and therefore almost all shares in private companies will be 'restricted securities'.

Many restrictions will be personal to a shareholder and only apply by reason of his or her status as an employee, which should suggest that they have no impact on the fiscal value of shares: as set out above, the valuation rules in TCGA 1992, Part VIII apply to all of the charges arising under ITEPA 2003, Pt 7; this valuation standard explicitly disregards features of a share that are personal to the shareholder, because the value is set by reference to a hypothetical third party purchaser at arm's length and such a purchaser would not be affected by restrictions personal to an employee shareholder. This is an element of the incoherence in the legislation in ITEPA 2003, Pt 7 that was criticised by the courts in *Grays Timber Products Ltd v Revenue and Customs Comrs* [2010] UKSC 4, [2010] 2 All ER 1, [2010] 1 WLR 497 (which is discussed in more detail at **[10.10]**), and, in order to make the legislation in ITEPA 2003, Pt 7, Chapter 2 work, taxpayers and HMRC has cooperated in treating personal restrictions on the rights of a share can be as depressing the value of that share; whether this approach would withstand the scrutiny of the courts is debatable.

A distinction needs to be drawn between securities that do not intrinsically possess a right and shares that possess a right which is restricted. An example would be to compare shares that do not carry a right to vote and shares that ordinarily carried a right to vote, but that right was limited under the terms of a shareholders' agreement: the former would not be restricted securities within the meaning of ITEPA 2003, s 423, while the latter would be.

The basic premise of the legislation is that:

- the value that is treated as employment income when an employee acquires shares should be reduced to take into account any restrictions on those shares;
- this reduction in the taxable value of the shares only defers the tax charge on the difference between the restricted and unrestricted market value of the shares — when the shares are sold the restricted securities rules treat a proportion of the sales proceeds as taxable employment income;
- under ITEPA 2003, s 428 the proportion of the sales proceeds that would be subject to income tax is based on the percentage difference between the restricted and unrestricted market value of the shares at the date of acquisition.

There is a risk that tax charges will arise on significantly larger values on future dates, than would be the case if the restricted securities rules did not apply. This is because the rules can capture an element of the growth in the value of a company, not just the company's initial value, as is shown in the following example.

Example

John is awarded shares in Bucolin Holdings Ltd when the UMV is £1. John does not pay anything for the shares. There are restrictions attaching to John's shares such that the value is reduced to £0.80. If John does nothing, he will pay tax on the restricted value now. The proportion subject to the restricted securities rules will be 20%, ie (£1 – £0.80)/£1.

If the shares are sold in the future for, say, £10, 20% of the proceeds will be subject to income tax and national insurance. The rest will be subject to capital gains tax.

At the same time, James buys shares that have the same restrictions attaching to them and pays £1 for them. Because James has paid more than UMV to acquire his shares, no future charges can arise under the restricted securities rules, whether or not James makes an election.

As can be seen from the example, the future income tax charge could be high. However, this could be avoided by the employer and employee entering into a joint election in accordance with ITEPA 2003, s 431. This provision allows the employee to elect to be taxed on the UMV on day one, which ensures that the future growth is subject to capital gains tax.

The making of elections under s 431 has advantages from an employer's perspective:

- once an election has been made, the employer should not, unless one of the other charges under ITEPA 2003, Pt 7 is triggered, have to consider future obligations to withhold PAYE and NIC in respect of the shares;
- the making of elections can significantly simplify a company's reporting obligations under ITEPA 2003, s 421J; and
- on a future disposal of the company, s 431 elections will feature prominently in any due diligence process undertaken by a prospective purchaser.

For these reasons many employers demand that employees enter into elections under s 431, as a condition of participation in equity incentives.

The election needs to be signed within 14 days of the share issue or transfer. The election does not need to be submitted to HMRC, although elections are reviewed during PAYE audits and it is not unknown for HMRC Shares & Assets Valuation to request sight of them before agreeing share values.

When advising an employee who has been given a choice as to whether to make an election, the employee will need to have an estimate of the UMV and AMV and will need to form their own view as to the likely potential growth in the value of the shares. Because the decision is essentially weighing up the risks and rewards of making an election, it will normally be an investment decision; non-FSA regulated practitioners should take particular care that they are not seen to be giving investment advice. It should perhaps be viewed as analogous to the old betting duty – pay your tax on your bet or on your winnings.

In the example above, if John had entered into the election, he would have paid tax on £1 at the outset, and this would have the effect of leaving 0% chargeable to income tax in the future. If John does not make an election the initial tax charge will arise under ITEPA 2003, s 62. Because, as set out above, charges under s 62 are calculated by reference to a different valuation standard to that applying to ITEPA 2003, Pt 7 it can be the case that the 'restricted value' may be greater than UMV; where this is the case, no charge will arise under the restricted securities rules irrespective of whether or not an election is made.

Where the shares are issued on a share-for-share exchange, extra caution is needed. Further details on this are explained in **CHAPTER 14**.

Forfeitable Securities

[10.9] Where an employee receives shares or other securities in a company on terms that mean that the individual could be forced to sell or otherwise dispose of the shares for less than their market value if a condition is not met (for example, a performance condition is not met or the employee ceases employment) they are said to have received forfeitable securities.

If the provision for forfeiting the shares is time-limited and the risk of forfeiture lifts within five years from the date that the employee acquires the shares, then ITEPA 2003, s 425 provides that the tax point for the acquisition of the shares will not be the point at which they were acquired, but, instead, will be when the shares cease to be forfeitable securities.

Example

Charlotte is awarded shares in Bucolin Holdings Ltd and does not pay anything for them. If Charlotte leaves employment with Bucolin Holdings Ltd before the third anniversary of the date that she acquired the shares she will have to sell them back to the company for a nominal consideration. The shares are worth £3,000 when they are acquired by Charlotte.

Charlotte does not pay any tax when she receives the shares, because they are forfeitable securities.

On the third anniversary of the date on which Charlotte received the shares the forfeiture condition lifts. The shares are now worth £30,000. Charlotte is treated as having received £30,000 of taxable employment income.

The Supreme Court reviewed the legislation on forfeitable securities in *UBS AG v Revenue and Customs Comrs; DB Group Services (UK) Ltd v Revenue and Customs Comrs* [2016] UKSC 13, [2016] 3 All ER 1, [2016] 1 WLR 1005, SC. The case concerned two similar schemes that involved employees receiving shares in 'money-box' companies. The shares were structured as forfeitable securities, with forfeiture conditions that lifted after a matter of months had passed, at which point it was argued that the shares fell within an exemption in the legislation, which would have meant that the lifting of the forfeiture condition did not give rise to tax. The Supreme Court held that the forfeiture conditions were arbitrary and not material; and should be disregarded in interpreting the legislation, only material forfeiture clauses should be treated as deferring the tax point.

If the employee had paid anything for the shares, then the amount subject to tax when the forfeiture condition lifts will be limited to the proportion of the value that is the same as the proportionate difference between the value of the shares when they were acquired and the amount paid to acquire them.

Example

> If Charlotte had paid £1,000 to acquire the shares then she would have been treated as having received £20,000 of taxable employment income when the forfeiture condition lifted (ie £30,000 x (£3,000 – £1,000) ÷ £3,000).

This tax treatment is beneficial where employees are receiving shares and there is a genuine risk that they may lose them in the future and postpones the tax point to the time when they should be able to dispose of the shares and raise the cash to pay the tax.

Income Tax (Earnings and Pensions) Act 2003, s 425(3) provides that an employee may agree with their employer to waive this tax treatment, which would mean that they would be taxed when they received the shares under the ordinary restricted securities rules. An election under ITEPA 2003, s 431(1) would also have the effect of disapplying the forfeitable shares rules, as well as the restricted securities rules.

Shares sold for more than market value

[10.10] Where an employee disposes of shares for more than the market value, Chapter 3D treats the excess as employment income. Care needs to be taken in cases where the Articles or Shareholders' Agreement uses a formula or other pre-agreed basis such as 'fair value' to buy out an existing shareholder, as this could result in an amount in excess of market value being paid for the shares. HMRC recognises that there is a potential mismatch between the value calculated by a formula and the market value of the shares for tax purposes, but will seek to tax any 'excess' arising.

An important case highlighting this provision, which practitioners should review is the case of *Grays Timber Products Ltd v Revenue and Customs Comrs* [2010] UKSC 4, [2010] 2 All ER 1, [2010] 1 WLR 497. The crucial aspect in this case was whether the managing director who had under a shareholders' agreement a right to a greater than pro-rata share of the sale proceeds, had received more than market value for his shares following the sale of the company. The case went to the Supreme Court where the judges found in HMRC's favour.

The important aspect highlighted in this case was that the rights under the shareholders' agreement were personal to the taxpayer and were not intrinsic to the assets acquired by the purchaser. Therefore their value could not be taken into account for the purposes of Chapter 3D.

Post-acquisition benefits

[10.11] The provisions on post-acquisition benefits are contained in ITEPA 2003, s 447, which states:

'(1) This Chapter applies if an associated person receives a benefit in connection with employment-related securities by that person or another associated person.'

Benefit is not defined, so the scope of the charge is potentially very wide. However, during the debate on the legislation, the Paymaster General made it clear that 'benefit' in this context is employment reward:

'A reference to benefits in the context of the schedule means the employment reward: the passing of value to an employee in return for the employee's labour. Where investors are carrying out their normal investment transaction, this charge will not affect them.' (Standing Committee B, Clause 12, 21 June 2005)

The burning question in connection with private companies is whether the payment of a dividend could be a benefit for the purposes of this legislation.

Normal dividends are unlikely to be charged under these provisions, as announced in a Ministerial statement on 21 June 2005 by the Paymaster General (Dawn Primarolo):

'These arrangements are devised to deal with the minority of cases where there are complex, contrived arrangements to avoid paying Income Tax and National Insurance on employment rewards. The Government have made clear their intention to close that activity down permanently.

There has been some debate about whether small businesses are caught by the provisions, so I am grateful to have the opportunity to offer small businesses some reassurance.

A change being made to Chapter 4 of the Income Tax (Earnings and Pensions) Act 2003 will remove, where avoidance is involved, the provision that automatically exempts benefits received in connection with securities from a full Income Tax and National Insurance charge, if Income Tax has been paid elsewhere. I am aware, from representations made directly to me and my Department, that professionals have expressed concern about the possible scope of the change. I want to make it clear that this change does not bring all benefits derived from securities into a tax and National Insurance charge. A reference to benefits in the context of the schedule means the employment reward – the passing of value to an employee in return for the employee's labour. Where investors are carrying out their normal investment transaction, this charge will not affect them.

The purpose test introduced in Section 447 of the 2003 Act has been carefully designed to target complex, contrived avoidance arrangements that are used mainly to disguise cash bonuses. If taxpayers use contrived arrangements to get round anti-avoidance legislation – to avoid paying the proper amount of tax and National Insurance – they cannot expect to be excluded from the charge. However, it will be absolutely clear from what I say about the purpose test that this measure will not affect the taxation of those small businesses that do not use contrived schemes to disguise remuneration to avoid tax and National Insurance.'

HMRC has gone on to say in its manual:

'Where an owner-managed company, run as a genuine business, pays dividends out of company profits and there is no contrived scheme to avoid Income Tax or NIC on remuneration or to avoid the IR35 rules, HMRC will not seek to argue that a Chapter 4 benefit has been received by the directors because of the exclusion provided by ITEPA 2003, s 447(4).' (HMRC Employment-Related Securities Manual ERSM90060.)

Concerns were raised that the line between employment income and dividend income would be blurred following the Court of Appeal's decision in *HMRC v PA Holdings Ltd* [2011] EWCA Civ 1414, in which it was held that bonuses paid in the form of dividend distributions to employees should be taxed under Schedule E and not under Schedule F, notwithstanding the provisions in the Taxes Act which gave priority to the Schedule F charge. The case was decided on the law as it stood before ITEPA 2003 was enacted and dealt with a complex arrangement that involved employees receiving shares in a 'money box' company that received cash from the employer company that it distributed as dividends to the employees.

The taxpayer in the Upper Tribunal case of *James H Donald (Darvel) Ltd and others v Revenue and Customs Comnrs* [2015] UKUT 514 (TCC), [2016] STC 616 10.10 took this form of planning even further, with the entire workforce having their employment transferred to a 'money-box' company, being awarded shares in the 'money-box' company and then being remunerated through dividend payments made by that company. The running of the various plans adopted by the taxpayer straddled the introduction of ITEPA 2003 and the tribunal found in favour of HMRC that the payments to the employees should be treated as taxable employment income. The decision was based entirely on a consideration of the substance of the payments to the employees, which overrode the legal form that they had been shaped into, Chapter 4 was not discussed or raised in the case.

There is little comparison with an owner managed trading company, the assets and distributable reserves of which will be dependent on the trading performance of the business, not simply a function of the amounts promised to employees by way of bonus payments, and there has been little evidence to date of HMRC more frequently seeking to apply Chapter 4 to dividend payments.

Partly paid shares

[10.12] The use of partly paid shares has become increasingly popular with private companies over the past few years. Where partly paid shares are used the employees are issued with shares at the market value at the date of issue but only part of the share price is called up. The uncalled amount is taxed under the ITEPA 2003, Pt 7, Chapter 3C rules outlined at **10.5** above.

Given the current beneficial interest rate, for a 40% or 45% tax payer, an annual tax charge will arise of 1.2% or 1.35% of the uncalled balance. Class 1A NIC is payable by the company on the benefit. As set out in 10.5, above, the annual tax and Class 1A NIC charges will not arise if the value of the notional loan falls below the £10,000 de minimis limit or if the notional loan qualifies for relief under ITEPA 2003, s 178.

This means that the shares are acquired by the employee without any immediate tax charges. The shares could have the same rights as fully paid up shares and dividends could be paid in respect of these shares. The dividends could be used to pay off the uncalled balance. Alternatively, the uncalled amount could be paid off shortly before a sale. If the uncalled amount is released or written off a tax charge would arise on the employee, based on the uncalled amount released at that time.

There is a commercial risk for the employee in that if the company becomes insolvent the liquidator will call up any uncalled share capital. In addition, only the paid-up element of the shares will be counted towards the employee's holdings of ordinary share capital for the purposes of Entrepreneurs' Relief, which can mean that an employee's partly paid shares could constitute a large percentage, by number, or the shares in a company, but a small percentage of the ordinary share capital, resulting in the relief not being available when the employee comes to sell his or her shares.

There is no charge under CTA 2010, s 455 as there is no actual loan to the employee shareholder; it is merely a notional loan.

Employee shareholder status (ESS)

[10.13] Until 23 November 2016, employers were able to offer new and existing employees a different employment status, that of 'employee shareholder'. In exchange for an award of shares, employees had to give up a number of their employment rights, but benefitted from an exemption from capital gains tax when they came to sell the shares.

Where an employee holds shares that were issued under ESS on or before 16 March 2016, any growth in the value of the first £50,000 of shares, measured at the time of acquisition, will be exempt from capital gains tax when the shares are eventually sold.

Example

> Peter entered into an employee shareholder agreement with Bucolin Holdings Ltd on 15 March 2016 and was gifted shares worth £60,000, in respect of which he made an election under ITEPA 2003, s 431. When Peter was awarded the shares he was treated as having received taxable employment income of £58,000 (ie £60,000 minus the £2,000 he is deemed to have paid for them by the legislation).
>
> Peter subsequently sells the shares making gains of £600,000 and £500,000 (ie 600,000x50,000/60,000) will be exempt from capital gains tax. The remaining £100,000 of gains will be taxable under the capital gains tax rules in the normal way.

Finance Act 2016 introduced a lifetime limit for the ESS tax relief: an individual can only claim the exemption on £100,000 of gains arising from the disposal of shares issued to him or her under ESS after 16 March 2016.

Example

> Raveen entered into an employee shareholder agreement with Bucolin Holdings Ltd on 17 March 2016 and received the same size of award as Peter.

Raveen also sells the shares making gains of £600,000, but Raveen is subject to the lifetime limit and a maximum of £100,000 will be exempt from capital gains tax. The remaining £500,000 of gains will be taxable under the capital gains tax rules in the normal way.

The last date that ESS shares could be validly transferred to an employee was 1 December 2016 (by a concession, if the employee had received their legal advice on the morning of the Autumn Statement – ie before 1:30pm on 23 November 2016 – they were given an extra day's grace to receive the award of shares).

The rules on ESS are now mainly of interest to practitioners dealing with the tax affairs of the individual employees, but remain relevant to companies which have made awards of ESS shares and which are proposing to undertake transactions, as there is a risk that employees may miss out on a valuable relief if there is a transaction such as the interposition of a new holding company. This is because the ESS legislation disapplies TCGA 1992, s 127, which prevents reorganisations of share capital from being treated as a disposal of shares; there is a risk that a change affecting the ESS shares could be treated as a disposal at market value (which would be exempt from tax/partially exempt under the ESS rules) and then the acquisition of a new shareholding that does not benefit from the protection of the ESS legislation – although such a change will effectively 'rebase' the capital gains tax base cost of the shares, the likelihood is that there will still be a significant tax exposure for the employee on selling his or her shares.

Example

Paul also entered into an employee shareholder agreement with Bucolin Holdings Ltd on 5 March 2016 and received the same size of award as Peter and Raveen.

Shortly after Raveen and Peter sell their shares, Bucolin Holdings Ltd inserts a new holding company, Bucolin Group Holdings PLC, and all of the shareholders exchange their shares in Bucolin Holdings Ltd for new shares in Bucolin Group Holdings PLC.

Although TCGA 1992, s 127 treats the other shareholders as having not made a disposal, Paul is treated as having disposed of his ESS shares at their market value of £600,000 and then acquired his new shares in Bucolin Group Holdings PLC for £600,000. Paul's gain is not subject to tax.

Paul later sells the shares for £1,000,000, which gives him gains of £400,000, which are subject to tax. Had the reorganisation not taken place, all of Paul's gains would have been exempt from tax.

Securities options

[10.14] Non-statutory options (commonly referred to as 'unapproved options') are often used by private companies, for instance, they can be used where the company or the employee in question does not meet the criteria for options to be granted under one of the statutory share schemes and are often used by UK subsidiaries of foreign parented groups, which do not necessarily consider that the expense of implementing a statutory share scheme is justified.

Non-statutory options can be very tax efficient where an individual wishes to dispose of shares to an employee and does not want the employee to pay market value. This is probably best explained by way of an example.

Example

Robert wants to allow John to purchase 10 shares from him in two years' time, but he only wants him to pay today's market value. The shares are worth £200 each today, and it is expected that the shares will be worth £400 each in two years' time.

Without a non-statutory option

John acquires shares worth £4,000 for £2,000, so he has taxable income of £2,000. As a 40% taxpayer, the charge is £800.

Robert makes a disposal, and, as it is not a bargain at arm's length, the market-value rule applies, so his proceeds are deemed to be £4,000, and he pays tax on the gain. If full ER is available, his tax (ignoring any base cost or possible gift relief claims) will be £400. If ER is not available his tax is £800.

The overall tax cost is £1,200 with ER or £1,600 without ER.

With a non-statutory option

John acquires shares worth £4,000 for £2,000, so he has taxable income of £2,000. As a 40% taxpayer, the charge is £800.

Robert has a disposal for £2,000 and, based on the same assumptions as above, a tax charge of £200 with ER or £400 without ER.

The overall tax cost is either £200 or £400 less (depending on the availability of ER) when the non-statutory option is used.

Where the value of the shares is likely to increase, it is beneficial to structure the share reward as an option.

In the example given above, for Robert, although there is a bargain not at arm's length, this is overridden by the option rule in TCGA 1992, s 144ZA(1), which states that:

'(a)   . . . the grant or acquisition of the option and the transaction resulting from its exercise are treated as a single transaction, and

(b)   section 17(1) ("the market-value rule") applies, or would apply but for this section, in relation to:
   (i)   the grant of the option,
   (ii)   the acquisition of the option (whether directly from the grantor or not) by the person exercising it, or
   (iii) the transaction resulting from its exercise.'

Subsections (2) and (3) continue on to say that the market-value rule does not apply.

For the employee, the only advantage of the non-statutory option is that he has a right to acquire shares in the future; a mere promise would not give the same security. For tax purposes, there are no advantages, as the gain on exercise will be chargeable to income tax (and NIC if the shares are RCAs). For ER purposes, the one year holding period commences on exercise.

Reporting

[10.15] Employers have an obligation to register all of their statutory and non-statutory share plans to HMRC using an extension to their online PAYE service.

All chargeable events need to be reported to HMRC using the online service. In addition, employers are now obliged to use the service to self-certify that their statutory share schemes meet the requirements of the relevant legislation for them to benefit from the specific tax advantages set out in ITEPA 2003, Pt 7. This obligation to register plans and to self-certify their status extended to employers who had statutory share schemes which were approved by HMRC under the old rules, the self-certification should have been completed by 6 July 2016.

The electronic forms used in the online system ask for significantly more information than the old paper forms, including details about the valuation of shares, and this, together with the need to register schemes, including unapproved arrangements, (not to mention reliability issues with the online service) makes online reporting onerous.

The information must be submitted to HMRC by 6 July following the tax year in which the chargeable event arose. The responsibility for submitting the information rests with any one of the responsible persons who are:

- the employer;
- the 'host' employer;
- the person from whom the securities (or interest therein) were acquired; or
- the person by whom the securities were issued, unless the securities are excluded securities.

The regime of fines and penalties that supports the reporting regime has historically been something more threatened than enforced. However, it is now reported that HMRC is applying automatic penalties to companies that have registered share plans but failed to make year-end reports before the filing deadline.

If a company has registered an arrangement with HMRC which it does not intend to use in the future, for example a one-off award of shares to an employee under ESS, it may be advisable to register the arrangement as closed by entering a 'final event date' onto the HMRC system, as returns will be needed in every year that the arrangement remains 'live' on the system.

Company share option plan (CSOP)

[10.16] This is a statutory scheme where an employer can grant options over its shares to employees, the options must have an exercise price that is at least equal to the market value of the shares when the option is granted. There is a £30,000 individual limit for the approved options. There is no tax and NIC on exercise of a CSOP option, provided the options are exercised between three and ten years from when the option is granted and the option still meets the requirements of the CSOP Code of ITEPA 2003.

Until recently, the legislation did not allow CSOP options to be granted over shares that had restricted rights. A significant simplification was introduced in Finance Act 2013, allowing CSOP options to be granted over any class of ordinary shares, provided that shares of that class met certain ownership criteria - the intention is to prevent CSOP options from being granted over an 'employee class' of shares with limited rights.

Until 5 April 2014 any new CSOP had to be approved by HMRC before options could be granted to employees. Since then, the approval process has been abolished and companies must instead use HMRC's online system to self-certify that their plan meets the requirements of the CSOP Code of ITEPA 2003.

The changes introduced in Finance Act 2013 and Finance Act 2014 greatly increase the flexibility of CSOP and reduce the cost and complexity of introducing a CSOP plan. As a result, we are increasingly seeing owner-managed business turn to CSOP if they do not meet the requirements for the other types of share plan.

EMI

[10.17] The use of an enterprise management incentives (EMI) scheme is still, in the authors' opinion, the most tax efficient share option scheme for many owner-managed businesses. EMI was introduced in July 2000 specifically for small and medium trading companies and has been designed to help attract and retain key people. It is therefore worth spending a little time outlining the qualifying criteria and the tax implications arising from granting EMI options.

To qualify as an EMI option, the right to acquire the shares must comply with all the requirements of ITEPA 2003, Sch 5 at the time the option is granted and the option must be notified to HMRC using their online service within 92 days of the grant. An EMI option gives the employee a right to acquire shares at a future date. Unlike the other statutory share schemes, an EMI option need only take the form of a bilateral contract between the grantor and the option holder. The option must be granted for commercial reasons in order to recruit or retain an employee in a company and not as part of a scheme or arrangement the main purpose, or one of the main purposes, of which is the avoidance of tax.

To date, challenges to the qualifying status of an EMI option based on the motive test have been rare and most often raised by potential purchasers of a company, and not HMRC. However, the ER legislation, which makes ER easily accessible where shares are acquired on the exercise of EMI options, may mean that we should expect to see more activity in this area; in particular, the author is aware that HMRC regards as suspect arrangements that see options exercised very shortly after they have been granted.

On 4 April 2018, HMRC released Employment Related Securities Bulletin No 27, which highlighted that the EU State Aid Exemption that EMI had operated under since August 2008, expired on midnight 6 April 2018. It is understood that a renewal of the State Aid Exemption has been applied for, but, at the time of writing, it is unclear when the renewal will be granted. For practical purposes, the tax advantages attaching to EMI options granted after 6 April 2018 have been suspended. Hopefully, by the time that this book has gone to press, the position will have been favourably resolved.

Individual limit

[10.18] There is a limit of £250,000 per employee on the market value of the shares over which the option can be granted (£120,000 for grants prior to 16 June 2012). If the employee holds unexercised CSOP options at the time the EMI is granted, this will reduce the £250,000 limit. Where an employee has been granted EMI options over shares with a total value of £250,000, the rules in Sch 5, para 6 state that no further option can be granted to him under EMI within three years of that grant. However, if, for example, options were granted over shares within an initial market value of £249,999 and those shares subsequently fall in value so that the option is under water, the provisions of para 6 do not prevent the release of that option and the grant of a new option within three years of the original grant. The reason para 6 does not restrict further grants is that the first option was over shares with a market value of less than £250,000. However, the purpose test outlined above should not be overlooked.

Overall limit

[10.19] The company cannot have unexercised EMI options exceeding £3 million outstanding at any time. Where the limit is exceeded, the excess is treated as a non-qualifying option.

In valuing the options for the purposes of complying with this limit and the individual limit set out at **10.18**, the valuation is based on the unrestricted market value of the shares subject to the option.

Eligibility of grantee

[10.20] An individual is only eligible for an EMI option if:

- he is an employee of the EMI company or of a qualifying subsidiary;
- he satisfies the requirements as to the commitment of working time; and
- he does not have a material interest in the company.

Commitment of working time

[10.21] The committed working time for the employee must amount to at least 25 hours a week or, if less, 75% of his working time. Working time includes time spent on remunerative work as an employee or a self-employed person.

Material interest

[10.22] An employee is not eligible under the EMI rules if at the time of grant he already has a material interest in the company. A material interest is the ability to control directly or indirectly 30% of the ordinary share capital of the company, or, where there is a close company, possession over entitlement to acquire rights to 30% of the assets available for distribution.

The 30% test is applied at the date of grant. Therefore, if an employee already has 29% of the company, there is nothing to stop a grant of 22% of the shares, which would give the employee control of the company. Provided the value of the EMI shares is within the £250,000 limit, control can be passed.

In determining whether an employee has a material interest, the rights of associates are included. In relation to an individual employee, this includes husband or wife, parent or remoter forebear, ie grandparent, great grand-parent, child, grandchild or great grandchild. Relatives for this purpose do not include brother or sister. Where family companies wish to grant options to employees, including, perhaps, their own children, the employees may qualify for EMI options whereas the children will not, due to the shares held by associates.

Shares over which an EMI option may be granted

[10.23] The shares under an EMI option must be fully paid-up non-redeemable shares which form part of the ordinary share capital of the company (ITA 2007, s 989). This gives a lot of flexibility with EMI shares, in that they can have restricted voting, dividend or capital rights.

Eligible company

[10.24] To be a qualifying company under the EMI rules, the company must satisfy four tests, as to:

(a)   independence;
(b)   limit on gross assets;
(c)   the status of its subsidiaries; and
(d)   the requirements as to trading activities.

The independence test

[10.25] The company must not be a 51% subsidiary of another company or, where the company is not a 51% subsidiary, under the control of another company either acting alone or acting with people connected with that other company. Control is as defined in ITA 2007, s 995. The term 51% subsidiary is defined in CTA 2010, s 1154.

Particular problems can arise where a venture capitalist is involved. The venture capital fund may be a corporate which controls the company, or it may be a partnership with a corporate general partner – in which case the corporate general partner would be connected with all of the other members of the venture capital fund. Where, for example, a husband and wife own a company and they transfer a small part of the share capital to a corporate trustee or an investment holding company to which they are connected, this will result in the corporate trustee or investment holding company being treated as controlling the company together with the husband and wife.

Special care needs to be taken where certain rights are contained in the Articles of Association or Shareholders' Agreement. Based on the shareholdings themselves, it may seem that no corporate has control of the company, but you need to consider any rights given in the Articles or Shareholders' Agreement; the rights could include the entitlement to have the greatest number of directors on the board or 'swamping rights', which are rights to take control of a company if certain conditions, for example banking covenants, are breached.

A further point to note is that HMRC applies these rules by looking at the legal ownership of shares, disregarding beneficial ownership; this can be problematic where significant shareholdings are held in trust with a company acting as trustee.

Gross-asset test

[10.26] The gross assets of an EMI company must not at the time of grant exceed £30 million. Statement of Practice 2/06 gives some guidance on how the gross-asset test should be measured. The general rule is that the value of a company's gross assets at any time is the aggregate of the values of the company's gross assets as shown in its balance sheet if one were drawn up at that time, where the balance sheet is prepared in accordance with normal UK accounting practice. Therefore, if there is substantial off-the-balance-sheet goodwill and it would not be usual to include this goodwill as it is internally generated, it need not be included for the purposes of this calculation.

Qualifying subsidiary

[10.27] In order to be a qualifying subsidiary, the company must be a 51% subsidiary of the EMI company. Where a company has control of any other company, it must be a qualifying subsidiary. For the purpose of applying this test, control has its broader meaning as given in CTA 2010, s 450. This means that where shares are held both by the EMI company and by the shareholders of an EMI company, the EMI company itself must have 51% of the ordinary share capital. Where the subsidiary is a property-managing subsidiary, a 90% test needs to be met. Where the EMI company is party to any joint venture with an unconnected party, the EMI company cannot have control of the joint venture company. Again, control is as per the CTA 2010, s 450 definition.

Trading activities

[10.28] A stand-alone company must exist wholly for the purpose of carrying on one or more qualifying trades. Where the company is a parent company, the activities of the group taken together must not consist to a substantial part in the carrying on of non-qualifying activities and at least one company must be carrying on a qualifying trade or preparing to carry on such a trade. 'Substantial' in this case is taken to mean 20%.

The following activities are disregarded in applying the 20% test:

- holding shares in or making loans to other group companies;
- holding or managing property used by a group company for the purposes of a qualifying trade;
- carrying out research and development from which a qualifying trade will be derived; and
- other activities which meet the trading-activities test of a single company.

A trade is a qualifying trade for EMI purposes if:

- the company has a permanent establishment in the UK. Prior to changes introduced in Finance (No3) Act 2010, the trade had to be carried on wholly or mainly in the UK (further guidance on this is contained in Statement of Practice 3/00);
- it is conducted on a commercial basis with a view to the realisation of profits; and
- it does not consist wholly or to a substantial part in the carrying on of excluded activities.

Where there is a group of companies, it is necessary for only one group company to carry on a qualifying trade in the UK. However, the group itself must not have substantial non-UK trade.

Excluded activities

[10.29] There is a list of excluded activities, and these include the traditional 'safe' trades:

(a)   dealing in land and commodities or futures or in shares, securities and other financial instruments;

(b)   dealing in goods otherwise than in the course of an ordinary trade of wholesale or retail distribution;

(c)   banking, insurance, money-lending, debt-factoring, hire-purchase financing or other financial activities;

(d)   leasing (including letting ships on charter or other assets on hire) or receiving royalties or licence fees;

(e)   providing legal or accounting services;

(f)   farming or market gardening;

(g)   holding, managing or occupying woodlands or any other forestry activity or timber production;

(h)   operating or managing hotels or comparable establishments, managing property used as a hotel or comparable establishment;

(i)   operating or managing nursing homes or residential care homes or managing property used as a nursing home or residential care home; and

(j)   providing services or facilities for a business carried on by another person if that other person's business consists to a substantial extent of excluded activities and a controlling interest in the business is held by a person who also has a controlling interest in the business carried on by the company providing the services or facilities.

The above are self-explanatory. However, it is worth having a quick look at some activities which may be borderline.

The above list excludes insurance as an EMI activity. However, insurance broking is generally accepted as an EMI activity. This is because the broker does not take any underwriting risk but generates its income from commissions. The same is true for some other financial activities — for example, a financial-adviser company may qualify. Although hotels are an excluded activity, restaurants do qualify under EMI. In relation to the leasing restriction, this can cause difficulty where assets are hired out to third parties. HMRC's Tax Bulletin in August 1995 gave HMRC's view that the hiring of chauffeured cars does not fall into the excluded trades (this was in relation to EIS) even though it involves an element of leasing of assets. The relevant part reads:

> 'in cases where the customer is not free to use the property as his own – for example the hire of chauffeured cars . . . – the person using the property is the trader not the customer. This is not regarded as leasing.'

However, it has become known that HMRC now considers that the article in the Tax Bulletin is wrong in respect of chauffeured cars. HMRC considers this to represent an excluded leasing activity.

Care needs to be taken where the company has mixed activities. If there is any doubt as to whether or not a company is eligible to grant options under EMI, seeking advance assurance from HMRC should be considered. Such clearance can be obtained from the Small Companies Enterprise Centre.

Tax treatment of EMI option

Grant of an EMI option

[10.30] There is no tax charge on either the company or the employee on the grant of an EMI share option.

Exercise of an EMI option

[10.31] Where an EMI option is exercised within ten years of grant and the exercise price is equal to the market value as at the date of grant, no tax charge arises on exercise. Where the option is exercisable at a discount, income tax is charged on the amount of difference between the market value of the shares at the time of grant and the amount paid by the employee. If the market value of the shares has fallen and does not exceed the amount paid for the shares, no tax is charged. Where the market value is less than the value as at the time of grant but more than the exercise price paid, then tax is charged on the difference between the market value of the shares at the time of exercise and the amount paid for them. Where the shares are RCAs, the tax charge will be payable via PAYE and will include a National Insurance charge (see **10.33** below).

Difficulties can arise where the shares subject to the option are restricted securities. ITEPA 2003, s 431A provides that if an EMI option is exercised where there is no liability to income tax, the employer and employee are treated as having made an election under s 431(1), so that no additional income tax charges arise on the employee under the restricted securities rules. However, where the options are exercised at a discount, there is no deemed s 431 election. The employee needs to decide whether an election would be appropriate. The following examples illustrate the effect of making a s 431 election where the shares are exercisable at a discount.

Example

John is granted an EMI option over restricted shares in Bucolin Holdings Ltd.

At grant, the actual market value of shares is £12.

The amount payable on exercise is £5.

At exercise, the actual market value is £7.

The unrestricted market value at exercise is £9.

Without an election, the amount chargeable to income tax will be £2 (£7 – £5).

With an election, the amount chargeable to income tax will be increased to £4 (£9 – £5).

Disqualifying events

[10.32] Where there is a disqualifying event and the option is not exercised within 90 days after the event, the relief from income tax and National Insurance will be limited. The following are disqualifying events.

(a)   Loss of independence.

(b)   The company ceasing to meet its trading-activities requirement.

(c)   The option holder ceasing to be an eligible employee.

(d)   The employee ceasing to meet the working-time requirement.

(e)   A variation of the option terms that increases the market value of the shares or a variation that means that the requirements of the legislation are no longer met.

(f)   Any alteration to the share capital of the company which affects the shares under the option. This includes:

    (1)   the creation, variation or removal of the rights relating to any shares in the EMI company;

(2)   the imposition of restrictions relating to any such shares; or

(3)   the variation or removal of a restriction to which any such shares are subject.

If the effect of the alteration is to increase the market value of the shares to which the option relates and either:

(a)   it is not made for commercial reasons; or

(b)   the main purpose for making it is to increase the market value of those shares,

the alteration will be treated as a disqualifying event.

(g)   Conversion of the shares into shares of a different class, unless it is a conversion of shares of one class only into shares of one other class only and all the shares of the original class are converted into shares of the new class and one of the following conditions are met:

- That immediately before the conversion of the majority of the company shares of the original class, these shares are held otherwise than for the benefit of:

    (1)   directors or employees;

    (2)   an associated company; or

    (3)   directors or employees of an associated company.

- That immediately before the conversion, the relevant company is employee controlled as a result of holdings of shares of the original class.

Capital gains tax

[10.33] Capital gains arising from the disposal of shares acquired via EMI options are liable to capital gains tax. Entrepreneurs' Relief will usually be available for employees selling shares derived from an EMI option:

- The 12-month qualifying period for ER starts from the date the options were granted.
- The usual 'personal company' test for ER does not apply and there is no need to hold 5% or more of the nominal share capital and the shares do not have to carry votes.

If ER is not available the CGT rate of 10% or 20% applies.

For shares acquired from the exercise of EMI options before 6 April 2012 different rules applied and the shares will only qualify for ER if the 'personal company' test is met.

Where an option is exercised more than 90 days after a disqualifying event, the shares will not automatically qualify for ER, in which case an employee would only benefit from ER on a sale of the EMI shares if his other holdings in the company meant that he already qualified for ER.

Corporation tax relief

[10.34] Historically, there was no statutory corporation tax deduction for shares given to employees. Many companies generated corporation tax deductions by routing their share schemes through EBTs. It was mainly large companies that benefited, as they could afford the necessary trust structures; this was felt to be unfair to smaller private companies and there was a growing discomfort in government about the use of EBTs.

Since 2003, a statutory relief has been available and is now contained in CTA 2009, Pt 12. Relief is given when employees acquire shares, chargeable events arise in connection with restricted or convertible securities and on the exercise of options.

For the relief to be available, there are four sets of tests to satisfy.

- *The business.* The employing company must be carrying on a business for which the award of shares is made, and that business must be within the charge to corporation tax.
- *The kind of shares acquired.* The shares must be ordinary shares that are fully paid up and non-redeemable.
- *The company that has issued the shares.* The issuing company must either be (i) a quoted company, (ii) a company that is not under the control of another company or (iii) a company that is under the control of quoted company.
- *The company.* The shares must be in the employing company or in a parent company.
- *The income tax position of the employee.* The employee must be chargeable to income tax or would be chargeable to income tax but for an exemption.

The relief is given for the accounting period during which the shares are acquired; this is when the employee acquires a beneficial interest rather than when the legal title passes (if both do not happen at the same time).

For the deduction to be available, the shares can be new or existing shares. This means that relief is available where an existing shareholder transfers shares to an employee.

The employer gets tax relief on the difference between the market value of the shares when the employee acquires them (for example, on the date that the employee exercises an option) and the amount, if any, paid by the employee.

Company takeovers

[10.35] Older share plans often stipulate that options can be exercised after a takeover. Normally this would be problematic, as the shares acquired by an option holder would be shares in a company controlled by another company, which would not ordinarily qualify for relief. For this reason, CTA 2009, s 1016(1A) allows the relief to be given if an option is exercised within 90 days following the date of a takeover.

Example — Interaction of reliefs

Bucolin Extra Ltd is a trading company. Richard, the sole shareholder and director of the company, originally acquired his shares at a cost of £1 per share. Bucolin

Extra Ltd wants to incentivise and retain one of its key employees, Sam, and arranges for Richard to grant her a qualifying EMI option to purchase 1,000 of his shares in the company at the then market value (as agreed with HMRC) of £10 per share, giving her a 5% stake in the company. The options are granted over shares held by Richard.

There will be no tax payable by Bucolin Extra Ltd, Sam or Richard on the grant of the share options.

Five years on and Sam has helped the business grow substantially. As a result, the share price has risen to £100 per share. Richard has received an offer to sell all the shares in Bucolin Extra Ltd to a larger company. Sam therefore exercises her options to acquire all 1,000 shares in order to sell these to the acquiring company. Under the terms of the options, Sam only pays £10 per share, ie £10,000 in total (1,000 × £10).

As the options were exercised within ten years of grant and the price paid was not lower than the market value at the time of grant, Sam pays no tax on exercise.

Bucolin Extra Ltd is entitled to claim a deduction for corporation tax purposes equal to the market value of the shares at the date of exercise less the price paid for the shares, ie £90,000 (£100,000 − £10,000. This will save corporation tax of £18,000 (£90,000 @ 20%).

Richard will make a capital gains tax disposal on the transfer of his shares to Sam. Normally, the transfer of shares at undervalue results in a capital gain with the proceeds being the market value at the time of transfer under TCGA 1992, s 17. However, the market-value rule does not apply where the employee is granted an option (TCGA 1992, s 144ZA). Instead, the proceeds on the disposal are the exercise price of the options, ie the price actually paid for the shares by the employee. The capital gain made by Richard is therefore:

	£
Disposal proceeds (1,000 × £10)	10,000
Less: cost (1,000 × £1)	1,000
Gain	9,000

As this gain will be wholly covered by Richard's annual exemption, if Richard has no other disposals in the year he would not need to claim ER and he would leave his lifetime limit of £10 million intact.

When Sam sells her shares to the acquiring company, Sam will make a capital gain on the sale as follows:

	£
Disposal proceeds (1,000 × £100)	100,000
Less: amount paid for the shares (1,000 × £10)	10,000
Less: amount paid for option:	Nil
Gain	90,000
CGT at 10%	9,000

Sam has held the ordinary share capital for 12 months prior to disposal therefore ER is available.

Example — Interaction of reliefs with a twist

Contrast this with the result if Richard, the sole shareholder and director of Bucolin Extra Ltd, had sold 1,000 shares to Sam for £10 per share five years earlier.

The capital gain that would have been made by Richard on the sale of the shares is the same as in the example above.

Sam's capital gains when she sells the shares to the acquiring company would also be the same as in the above example. As she held 5% of the ordinary share capital for the 12 months prior to disposal ER should be available.

However, in this case, there is no corporation tax deduction available.

The table below compares the tax payable in each of the examples:

	EMI options granted £	Shares transferred £
Sam (employee)		
Income tax:	Nil	Nil
NICs (employee's):	Nil	Nil
Capital gains tax:	9,000	9,000
Bucolin Extra Ltd		
NICs (employer's):	Nil	Nil
Corporation tax saving:	(18,900)	Nil
Richard (sole shareholder/director)		
Capital gains tax (covered by AE)	Nil	Nil

By granting options under the EMI scheme rather than transferring shares straight to the employee, there is an overall tax saving. Also, if Richard had sold the shares to Sam, he would have run the risk of her leaving employment with the shares and would, at the very least, have had to consider the corporate governance implications of having a minority shareholder. With the EMI option, Richard kept control but Sam still benefited!

Example — Interaction of reliefs – a comparison

If Sam had been granted a non-statutory option and if the option was being exercised shortly before the sale of Bucolin Extra Ltd, the company would still have benefitted from corporation tax relief, but would have incurred a charge to employer NIC when Sam exercised her options. This is illustrated in the table, below:

		Non-statutory Option £	EMI Option £	Shares Transferred £
Disposal proceeds	A	100,000	100,000	100,000
Option Exercise Price/ Share Purchase Price	B	10,000	10,000	10,000
Value subject to income tax (A-B)	C	90,000	N/A	N/A
Value subject to capital gains tax (A-(B+C))	D	0	90,000	90,000
PAYE & NIC (Cx(45%+2%))	E	42,300	0	
CGT (Dx10%)	F	0	9,000	9,000
Net benefit to Sam (A-(B+E+F))	G	47,700	81,000	81,000
Employer NIC (Cx13.8%)	H	12,420	0	0
CT Relief (Cx20%)	I	18,000	18,000	N/A
Total cost to Richard ((A+H)-(B+I))	J	84,420	72,000	90,000
Cost to Richard of providing £1 benefit to Sam (J÷G)		£1.77	£0.89	£1.11

The cost to Richard is calculated on the basis that, as sole shareholder before the award to Sam, the costs and reliefs due to the company would flow through into the proceeds of disposing of Bucolin Extra Ltd.

Employment income provided through third parties

[10.36] Provisions were introduced in Finance Act 2011 (now contained in ITEPA 2003, Pt 7A) to deal with cases where payments are made by third parties and these payments are allegedly remuneration from an employer. The purpose of these provisions according to the Treasury is to end the practice where '*highly paid employees offered tax-free, lifetime loans that are never repaid*'.

For most practitioners these rules will be relevant where client companies have employee benefit trusts (EBTs) or Employer Financed Retirement Benefit Schemes (EFRBS), or where their client is eligible to receive or actually receives a benefit from an EBT/EFRBS.

Since the introduction of the rules on disguised remuneration, the Supreme Court has ruled on the proper tax treatment of contributions to EBT structures, in the case of *RFC 2012 (in Liquidation) (formerly The Rangers Football Club plc) v Advocate General for Scotland* [2017] UKSC 45 – better known as the 'Rangers Big Tax Case'.

In broad terms, the court has ruled that a payment made to one person ('B') in respect of the employment of another ('A') remains the taxable employment income of A.

The judgment outlines three situations in which a payment made to a third party would not constitute taxable employment income in the hands of the employee:

- gratuities, profits or incidental benefits (perquisites or perks in the language of the pre-Income Tax (Earnings & Pensions) Act 2003 legislation) that are not convertible into money;
- the payment by the employer of money to a third party to provide a benefit in kind which the employee cannot convert into money, which could fall to be taxed under the Benefits Code of ITEPA 2003 or, possibly, Part 7 (employment related securities) or Part 6 (income which is not earnings or share-related); and
- payments that give an employee a contingent interest in assets, instead of an absolute interest in them – the judgment cites the situation in *Edwards v Roberts* (1935) 19 TC 618, where an employer paid money into a trust for the employee, which would only be paid out if the employee had remained with the company for five years or was a 'good leaver'.

The court held that the structure adopted by Rangers did not fall within any of these exceptions, and it seems unlikely that the courts will be sympathetic to arguments that other EBT/EFRBS contributions will fall outside the scope of the judgment.

The decision in the *Rangers* case seems to render the legislation on disguised remuneration largely redundant. However, while they remain on the statute book, they need careful consideration, as they are far wider reaching than EBT and EFRBS arrangements. HMRC's internal guidance on disguised remuneration rules are contained in the Employment Income Manual at EIM45000.

An arrangement will not give rise to a Pt 7A charge on income unless it 'comes through the section 554 gateway', which broadly covers the five components outlined below. Where the five components are present the value of the cash or assets subject to the relevant step is taxed as employment income. Further details on this charge are set out later.

The tax charge (section 554 Gateway)

[10.37] The provisions contained in ITEPA 2003, Pt 7A can be divided into five components which, if all are present, result in a tax charge unless one of the exemptions applies.

(1) A person ('A') is an employee, or a former or prospective employee, of another person ('B'); and

(2) There is an arrangement ('the relevant arrangement') to which A is a party, or which otherwise (wholly or partly) covers or relates to A; and

(3) It is reasonable to suppose that, in essence—

    (a) the relevant arrangement, or

(b)   the relevant arrangement so far as it covers or relates
to A,

is (wholly or partly) a means of providing, or is otherwise concerned
(wholly or partly) with the provision of, rewards or recognition or
loans in connection with A's employment, or former or prospective
employment, with B; and

(4)   A relevant step is taken by a relevant third person, and
(5)   It is reasonable to suppose that, in essence—
    (a)   the relevant step is taken (wholly or partly) in pursuance of the
relevant arrangement, or
    (b)   there is some other connection (direct or indirect) between the
relevant step and the relevant arrangement.

When does a tax charge arise?

[10.38]

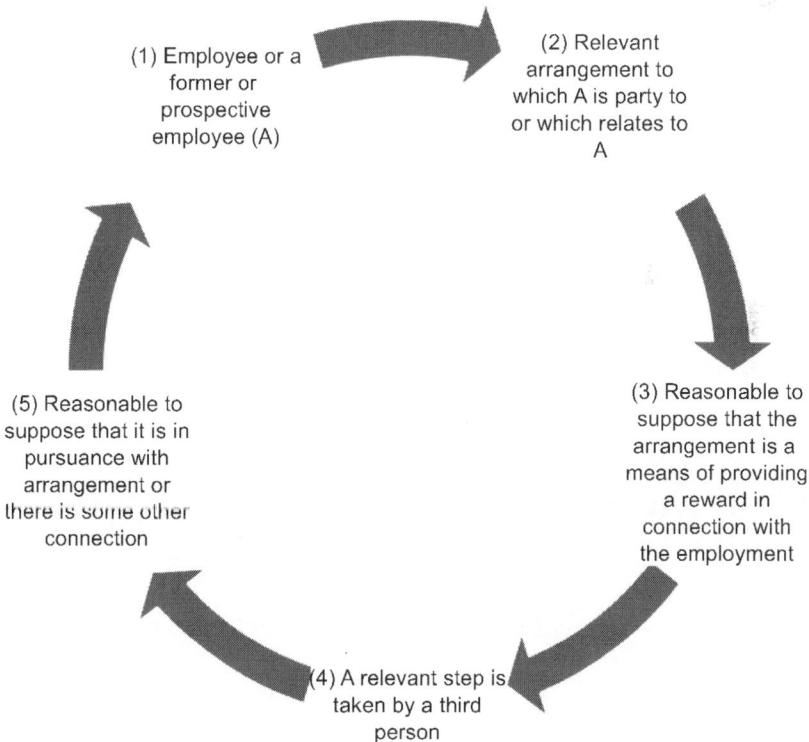

(1) Employee or a former or prospective employee (A)

(2) Relevant arrangement to which A is party to or which relates to A

(3) Reasonable to suppose that the arrangement is a means of providing a reward in connection with the employment

(4) A relevant step is taken by a third person

(5) Reasonable to suppose that it is in pursuance with arrangement or there is some other connection

Relevant third person

[10.39] A relevant person as per s 554A(7) means:

- any person other than the employer and the employee;
- an employee acting as trustee; or
- an employer (or group companies) acting as trustee.

Thus there will not be a Pt 7A tax charge in relation to a step taken by an employer provided he is not acting as a trustee. For the purposes of these rules any company in the same group as the employer at the time of a relevant step is treated as if they are the employer, unless there is a tax avoidance purpose. A group company for these purposes is defined by reference to TCGA 1992, s 170(2)–(11), except substitute 51% for 75% (s 554Y). If the employer is an LLP a third party excludes any wholly-owned subsidiary of the LLP (s 554A(9)). In limited circumstances the employer can be a relevant third person in their own right.

Relevant step

[10.40] There are three classes of relevant steps which can trigger an employment income tax charge where the step is taken by a third party.

- Earmarking (or quasi-earmarking) a sum of money or an asset, eg use of EBT sub-funds, with a view to taking a relevant step at a later date (s 554B).
- Payment of a sum of money (including loans) or transfer of an asset or taking a step by virtue of which a person acquires a relevant asset (this includes grant of options) (s 554C).
- Making an asset available (s 554D).

Earmarking (s 554B)

[10.41] No formality is needed to trigger earmarking; it does not matter that the details of the later relevant step are not fixed. Earmarking could arise from details included in the minutes of a board meeting. HMRC has said that where shares are held to satisfy awards to employees generally and the EBT has not got the names of the employees and the individual numbers of shares then there is no earmarking at that stage.

Payment of a sum of money (s 554C)

[10.42] The important point is that the step can be taxable even though the employee does not benefit from it. Tax charges can arise as a result of something which may happen in the future and there is limited scope for a repayment. For example, where a loan is advanced to an employee and that loan results in a tax charge under these provisions, the repayment of the loan does not entitle the employee to a refund of the tax.

Making an asset available (s 554D)

[10.43] Making an asset available will be taxable under s 554D where either:

(a)   it is made available in a way that is substantially similar to ownership; or

(b)   where the asset is made available at or after the end of the relevant period.

In relation to (a) above what is meant by substantially similar to ownership is covered as part of EIM 45080.

> 'the key question to ask is: "Suppose the relevant person was the outright owner of the asset. What difference would that make to the way in which that person benefited from it?"
>
> The normal provision of company cars on short term leases to employees for their private use would not be a relevant step under Section 554D. Nor would the occasional non-exclusive use of a holiday home while in employment.'

So for example, if the trustees buy a house for an employee to live in there will be a relevant step when the house is made available, even if the trustees retain ownership of the property.

In relation to (b) a relevant step will be taken where the asset is made available at or after the end of the relevant period. The relevant period is the two year period starting on the day on which A's employment with B ceases.

Tax charge

[10.44] Income tax and NIC is due under PAYE when the relevant step is taken. The amount taxed is the value of the relevant step. It is treated as earnings and counts as employment income for the tax year in which the step is taken unless it is in a case of prospective employment and then it is treated as earnings in the tax year in which the employment commences. The value of the relevant amount is the sum of money or the market value of the asset. There are some overlap rules to prevent a double tax charge.

For internationally mobile employees who have left the UK there is still a potential charge if the relevant step is taken after they have left the UK. The amount taxed depends on what can be attributed to UK duties.

The value of the relevant step can be reduced in some circumstances including:

•   if consideration is given by A before, or around the time of the relevant step the value of the relevant step is reduced by the market value of the consideration given (s 554Z8) (this is subject to a tax avoidance test);

•   the exercise price of options can in certain circumstances reduce the value of the relevant step (s 55Z7);

•   if there are two relevant steps in relation to A's employment in respect of the same sum or asset, the value of the later relevant step is reduced by the value of the first (s 554Z5(2));

•   where the relevant step is also taxed as earnings the value of the relevant step will usually be reduced by the same amount (s 554Z6).

Where an employee does not make good, within 90 days, any tax paid by the employer a further charge may arise under ITEPA 2003, s 222.

The relevant step is also subject to NIC.

Exclusions

[10.45] There are a number of exclusions and as with many reliefs the detail should be examined carefully where the reliefs are being relied on. The detailed provisions are contained in s 554E to s 554Y. In summary, the exemptions include:

Steps taken under certain schemes

• Steps taken under certain approved share schemes; EMI, CSOP, SIP and SAYE (s 554E).
• Arrangements solely for the provision of benefits in respect of ill health, disablement or accidental death during service (ITEPA 2003, s 393B).
• Registered pension schemes and arrangements solely for the purpose of making authorised payments under such schemes.

Commercial transactions

• Loans made on ordinary commercial terms where a substantial proportion of the lender's business is with the public.
• Transactions other than loans must be on similar terms as similar transactions with members of the public.

Employee benefit packages

Employee benefit packages are not caught by the new rules where:
• there is no tax avoidance purpose;
• the transaction is in the ordinary course of business;
• if the step is making of a loan, a substantial part of the business involves loans to the public and the loan is part of a package of benefits which is available to a substantial (50%) proportion of B's employees;
• if the step is not a loan, then the transaction with A must be part of a package of benefits which is available to a substantial (50%) proportion of B's employees or a substantial proportion of B's employees who have the same status level.
• the terms of the package are sufficiently generous to enable substantially all of B's employees who want to take advantage to do so;
• the terms of the transaction are substantially the same as the terms of similar transactions with B's other employees;
• a majority of employees to whom the package is made available have 5% or less interest in the employer's business.

Deferred remuneration

Earmarking of deferred remuneration is excluded where:

- the deferred remuneration will be provided on a specified vesting date no more than five years after the award date;
- the award will be revoked if specified conditions are not met on or before the vesting date and at the date of grant, there is a reasonable chance that the award will be revoked on this basis;
- if the remuneration were provided on the award date, it would be 'employment income' for income tax purposes;
- The asset or money which is 'earmarked' represents only the deferred remuneration in question;
- There is no connection with any tax avoidance arrangement.

Employment-related securities

There is no charge under the new rules where there is earmarking for employee share schemes where certain conditions are met. There is also an earmarking exemption for 'exit event' shares but there is a very short time limit for making the awards – only three months after the earmarking.

Other exclusions

- Employee car ownership schemes (s 554O).
- Construction industry holiday schemes (s 554E(1)(e)).
- Benefits which would be exempt as employment income (s 554P).
- Income arising from earmarked sum or asset (s 554Q).
- Acquisitions out of earmarked sums or assets (s 554R).
- Employee pension contributions (s 554S).

Transitional rules

[10.46] Where amounts in EBTs and EFRBS were earmarked before 9 December 2010, these earmarked funds will not give rise to tax charges under these rules unless they are the subject of a relevant step after 6 April 2011.

Schedule 11 to F(No 2)A 2017 enacted a new tax charge on loans that were advanced to beneficiaries of EBTs and EFRBS after 6 April 2019. If those loans are still outstanding on 6 April 2019, the trustees will be deemed to have taken a relevant step on that date, with a value equal to the amount owed (F(No 2)A 2017, Sch 11, para 1). The employer company or the trustees will be obliged to operate PAYE and NIC when the charge arises. There is also a reporting obligation on the company and the trustees to notify HMRC that the loan charge has arisen.

The loan charge operates by looking at the sterling value of the loan when it was first advanced and then seeing how much of that value has been repaid (para 6). The conversion into sterling is intended to prevent the loan charge from being avoided through the use of depreciating currencies (para 10).

EBTS and share plans

[10.47] If it is intended to use shares held in an EBT to satisfy employee share awards, it is generally considered good practice to structure the arrangements so that they do not result in the EBT being seen as having earmarked the shares, rather than relying solely on the exemptions in the legislation for employee share schemes. The company should deal with any details of the share offer and make a recommendation to the trustees of the EBT that the trustees should fulfil the proposed share offer on the assurance that the participants are all within the EBT's beneficial class, without specifying details of individual awards or the identities of the participants. Full details of the participants and the share numbers should be kept vague until close to the transfer date.

Employee Ownership Trusts

[10.48] Finance Act 2014 introduced a new form of indirect employee share ownership, under which shares in a company are held in a trust (an Employee Ownership Trust 'EOT') for the benefit of the employees of the company and its subsidiaries. The rules on whether an EOT will qualify under the new legislation are set out in more detail at **[13.16]**, below.

Unlike other forms of employee share ownership, there is no intention to distribute shares to individual employees - instead the intention is that the majority of the shares in the company shall be held by the EOT and that all of the employees will benefit from the shares.

Under ITEPA 2003, Part 4, Chapter 10A, the main benefit to companies and employees from the Employee Ownership rules is that where a company is under the control of a qualifying EOT, bonus payments of up to £3,600 can be made to each employee without charges to income tax arising. Broadly speaking, to qualify for relief a bonus payment must be offered as part of a scheme open to all employees and there is only limited scope for the payment to be varied from employee to employee. Although the new rules exempt qualifying payments from income tax, there is no parallel provision to exempt them from NIC and both employer and employee NIC will arise.

VAT on employee benefits

[10.49] Employers can be liable to an output VAT charge if the provision of a benefit to an employee qualifies as a supply by the employer. Whilst it might be clear that VAT should be charged when an employee purchases an asset (eg computer, stock, etc) from the employer on which input VAT has been claimed, the employer's VAT liability is perhaps less obvious in salary sacrifice schemes.

In *Astra Zeneca UK Ltd* (C 40/09), the ECJ ruled that the salary sacrificed by the employee constituted consideration for the supply of retail vouchers. As the employer had recovered input VAT when it purchased the vouchers from the retailer, the employer was required to account for output VAT when the vouchers were provided to the employee as a benefit.

Key points

[10.50] Key points to note are as follows.

- PAYE must be operated where readily convertible assets are provided to employees, or where benefits are provided by a voucher or payment of an employee's debt.
- Consider providing tax-free benefits, where possible.
- Watch wide-ranging tax charges on employment-related securities.
- CSOPs enable options to be granted over shares worth up to £30,000 per employee, free of income tax and NIC.
- EMI arrangements enable options to be granted over shares worth up to £250,000 per employee every three years, with no income tax charge unless the exercise price is less than the market value of the shares at the date of grant.
- Partly paid shares are a useful alternative to approved option schemes.
- Where employees have been granted employee shareholder status in the past, care needs to be taken when any changes are proposed to the company's share capital that might strip them of their CGT benefit.
- Companies are entitled to corporation tax relief when employees acquire shares or securities, provided all qualifying conditions are met.
- Provisions to tax employment income provided through third parties are contained in ITEPA 2003, Pt 7A, and tax loans and other benefits from EBTs and EFRBS as well as taxing more innocent transactions.

Chapter 11

Company Reconstructions and Purchase of Own Shares

Company reconstructions

[11.1] There are a number of reasons why the shareholders may want to split a company into separate parts. The separation is referred to as a reconstruction or a demerger. In essence, it involves a company or a group of companies separating out parts of the business so that they can be operated from separate companies and be run by separate management structures. Reconstructions can be a successful alternative to a dividend in specie, one shareholder buying another out, the disposal of assets out of a company or the purchase of own shares by a company. There are a number of reasons why a demerger may be undertaken, and the most common are:

- separation of two businesses with the intention to sell one;
- creating the right platform for an employee share scheme;
- break-up of a company where shareholders have fallen out;
- separation of divisions which do not share a common strategy;
- separation of divisions where one division places a financial burden or high level of risk on the other;
- separation of business activities followed by a management buy-out;
- splitting out an investment business from a trading business;
- preserving tax reliefs — ER and BPR; and
- separation of profitable parts of the business from the non-profitable parts.

Where the transaction is carried out for bona fide commercial reasons, there are tax reliefs that will prevent any tax charges arising. Without these reliefs, a number of tax charges would be triggered, including:

- income tax on any distribution to shareholders;
- capital gains tax on any return of capital to the shareholders;
- stamp duty on transfer of shares;
- stamp duty land tax on the transfer of any properties;
- TCGA 1992, s 179 charges where assets have been transferred intra-group;
- intangible asset exit charges where assets have been transferred intra-group; and
- corporation tax on gains triggered in the company on the disposal of any assets.

There are a number of ways to effect a demerger, and the structure will determine the tax reliefs available. The most common structures involve:

- the transfer of shareholdings in a subsidiary or subsidiaries to one or more of the shareholders or to one or more new companies owned by the shareholders;
- the transfer of one or more trades or businesses to one or more new companies owned by the shareholders; and
- the liquidation of the existing company or holding company and the transfer of the shares in subsidiaries or the business to new companies owned by the shareholders.

In dealing with company reorganisations, the adviser will come across a number of terms which are used interchangeably. The common terms are as follows below.

- *Reconstruction.* This involves the transfer of the whole or part of one company's business to another company without a substantial change in ownership.
- *Partition.* This is a special type of reconstruction involving the separation of a company's business between different groups of shareholders.
- *Demerger.* This is a statutory term describing types of reconstruction and partitions to which demerger relief applies. Demerger relief is the relief available where the transaction is carried out under CTA 2010, ss 1073–1099. These are referred to as statutory demergers.

Three types of demergers are permitted under the Taxes Acts (CTA 2010, ss 1073–1099). These take the form of exempt distributions so that the shareholders are not subject to income tax.

In dealing with any of these reorganisations the employment-related securities provisions should be considered to ensure that no inadvertent tax charges are triggered and any necessary elections are made. The possible application of transactions in securities legislation should also be considered whenever a reconstruction is being planned.

Statutory demergers

[11.2] The purpose of the provisions is to facilitate the division of the trading activities carried on by a single company or group into two or more companies not in the same group or two or more groups.

Type I demerger

[11.3] This is where shares in a subsidiary are distributed to the shareholders of the distributing company. The reliefs are found in CTA 2010, s 1076.

Demerger type I

Pre-demerger   **Post-demerger**

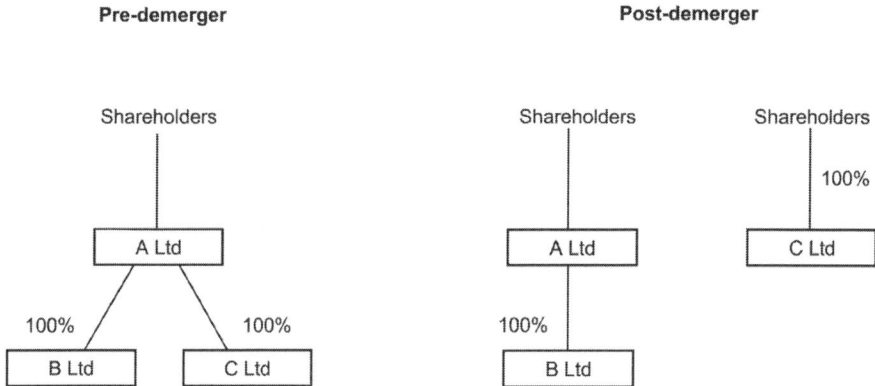

A Type I demerger involves the distribution of the shares in A Ltd directly to the shareholders. Without any form of relief, these transactions could trigger the tax charges as set out below.

- Tax on the distribution to the shareholders. For a higher-rate taxpayer, this works out at 32.5% of the value of the shares in B Ltd. For an additional rate taxpayer this works out as 38.1%.
- If there has been a transfer of assets within the last six years from A Ltd to B Ltd, a TCGA 1992, s 179 charge would be triggered, forming part of the disposal consideration for the shares in A Ltd. A degrouping charge is triggered where there has been a transfer of an intangible asset in the past six years, although in this case the charge would arise in A Ltd.
- Where the value of B Ltd at the time of the disposal is greater than the original cost, a taxable gain will arise on A Ltd.

However, as the transaction falls within CTA 2010, s 1076, there is relief available against some of the tax charges provided conditions A to F in ss 1081 and 1082 are met and if the company making the distribution is a 75% subsidiary; conditions L and M in s 1085 must also be met.

Condition A: Each company involved in the transaction must be EU resident.

Condition B: The distributing company must be a trading company or a member of a trading group, and the demerged 75% subsidiary or subsidiaries must be a trading company or companies, or a member or members of a trading group.

Condition C: The distribution must be made wholly or mainly for the purpose of benefiting some or all of the trading activities which are carried on by a single company or the group and after the distribution will be carried on by the two or more companies or groups.

Condition D:

The distribution must not form part of a scheme or arrangement for:

- the avoidance of tax;
- the making of a chargeable payment;
- making what would be a chargeable payment if it is in pursuance of any arrangements with another company or any of its main participants;
- a change of control; or
- the sale of the company or trade, or the liquidation of the trade after the distribution.

A change of control refers to anyone other than members of the distributing company obtaining control. However, a statutory demerger can be used to partition trading activities between different groups of shareholders.

Condition E: The shares must constitute the whole (or substantially the whole) of the subsidiary company's ordinary share capital and confer the whole (or substantially the whole) of the voting rights, and must not be redeemable.

Condition F: After the demerger, the distributing company must be either a trading company or the holding company of a trading group. However, this does not apply if the distributing company distributes shares or trades to two or more transferee companies (in the case of a Type II or Type III demerger) or there are two or more subsidiaries transferred (in the case of a Type I demerger) and the distributing company is dissolved. This is provided there were no net assets to distribute following the demerger. Extra-Statutory Concession C11 allows a company to retain enough funds to meet the liquidation costs and a negligible amount of share capital. A negligible amount of share capital for these purposes is £5,000 or less.

Condition L: The group to which the distributing company belongs at the date of distribution must be a trading group. If there is more than one group it is the largest group which is looked at.

Condition M: The distribution must be followed by one or more other distributions which are a transfer of shares in one or more companies which are 75% subsidiaries. The members of the holding company must become members of the transferee company or the distributed company, CTA 2010, s 1085.

Tax reliefs

The distribution is exempt from tax. Under TCGA 1992, s 192, there is relief from capital gains tax where the distribution falls within s 1076. Without this relief, the distribution would be treated as a part disposal for capital gains tax purposes. Furthermore, the provisions of TCGA 1992, s 127 apply so that the new shares take on the history and base cost of the old shares. The ER history is therefore transferred to the new shares.

No stamp duty is payable as a distribution in specie is free of stamp duty as a voluntary disposition.

Any exit charge under TCGA 1992, s 179 is exempt from tax by TCGA 1992, s 192(3), which prevents the charge arising where a company ceases to be a member of a group by reason only of an exempt distribution.

The one tax charge which can remain is in A Ltd. The disposal proceeds for the transfer of the shares is deemed to be the market value. This is the connected-party rule – where there is a transfer between connected parties, the market value is substituted for actual proceeds. Any gain arising in A Ltd on the transfer of the shares is not exempt from tax, so it will be taxable unless it is covered by SSE. This is covered in detail in **CHAPTER 5**.

Type II demerger

[11.4] This is where the distributing company transfers its trade or trades to one or more new companies and, in return, those new companies issue shares to the members of the distributing company (CTA 2010, s 1077(1)(a)(i)).

Demerger type II

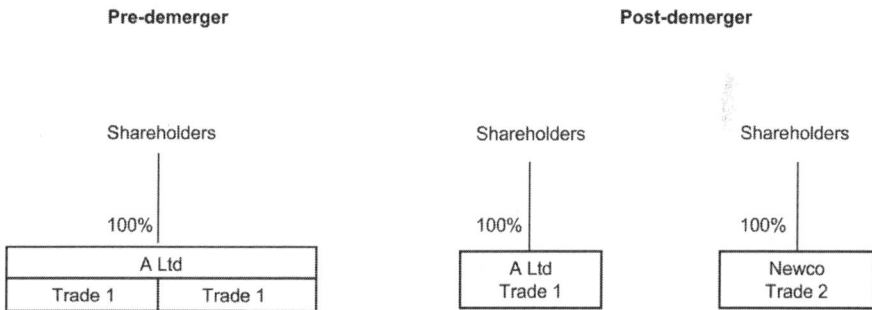

Pre-demerger		Post-demerger	
Shareholders		Shareholders	Shareholders
100%		100%	100%
A Ltd		A Ltd	Newco
Trade 1	Trade 1	Trade 1	Trade 2

The possible tax consequences are:

* tax charges on the transfer of a trade arising from the permanent discontinuance of a trade and the commencement of a new trade (including capital gains and balancing allowances/charges);
* stamp duty land tax charges on the transfer of any properties;
* tax on capital gains on any assets transferred to the new companies;
* income tax on the shareholders in respect of the distribution;
* capital distribution in respect of shares.

However, as the transfer falls within s 1077(1)(a)(i), relief is available. The distribution is exempt from tax by virtue of CTA 2010, s 1077(2), so no income tax charge arises on the shareholders. From a capital gains tax perspective, the shareholders are treated as exchanging their shares in one company for shares in another company so that the share-for-share exchange rule in TCGA 1992, s 135 applies. Therefore, no capital gain arises; the new shares simply take over the history and base cost of the old shares.

Conditions A to D and G, I J and K must be met. If the company making the transfer is a 75% subsidiary conditions L and M must also be met.

Conditions A to D and L and M are outlined under Type 1 demerger above.

Condition G: Where a trade is transferred the distributing company can only retain a minor interest. Minor is taken as being around 10% or less as per SP 13/80. A trade for these purposes does not include dealing in shares, securities, land or commodity futures.

Condition I: The only or main activity of the transferee company or companies following the distribution must be carrying on the trade or the holding of shares transferred to it.

Condition J: The shares issued by the transferee company:

(a)   must not be redeemable;

(b)   must constitute the whole or substantially the whole of its issued ordinary share capital, and

(c)   must confer the whole or substantially the whole of the voting rights in the company.

Condition K: The distributing company after the distribution must be either a trading company or the holding company of a trading group except:

(a)   if the distributing company is a 75% subsidiary of another company; or

(b)   there are two or more transferee companies each of which has had a trade or shares transferred to it and the distributing company must have had no net assets following the distribution.

The transaction is treated as a reconstruction under TCGA 1992, s 139 as it involves the transfer of the whole or part of a business. This means that any transfers of assets within the capital gains tax regime are treated as if the assets included in the transfer were acquired by one company from the other company for a consideration of such amount that neither a gain nor a loss arises.

The transfer of the trade will fall within CTA 2010, s 939. This applies where there is a transfer of a trade without a substantial change in the ownership. Where a company ceases to carry on a trade and another company starts to carry on that trade and:

•   at any time within two years after that event, not less than 75% belongs to the same persons as it did at some time in the year before the event; and

•   the trade is carried on by a company within the charge to corporation tax,

these special succession rules apply. The trade is treated as not being permanently discontinued for the purposes of capital allowances (CTA 2010, ss 948, 949) and trading losses (CTA 2010, s 944(3), (4) and 945(i), (4), (5)). A trade carried on by a company is treated as belonging to the shareholders for these purposes in their shareholding ratio (CTA 2010, s 942).

Many Type II demergers will involve the transfer of a property or properties to new companies. To prevent a stamp duty land tax charge arising on reconstruction, there is an exemption under FA 2003, Sch 7, para 7. Reconstruction is not defined for the purposes of this legislation, but it is usually accepted that where HMRC is satisfied that there is a reconstruction under TCGA 1992, s 139 for the capital gains tax reliefs, then the stamp duty land tax relief will be available. This is subject to the anti-avoidance legislation where there is a change in control of the acquiring company before the end of the period of three years beginning with the effective date of the transaction (or arrangements made within that period) and, at the time control changes, the company (or an associated company) holds a chargeable interest that was acquired using reconstruction relief.

Type III demerger

[11.5] A Type III demerger is where the distributing company transfers shares in one or more of its 75% subsidiaries to a new company or companies and that new company or companies issue shares to some or all of the members of the distributing company.

Demerger type III

Pre-demerger

Post-demerger

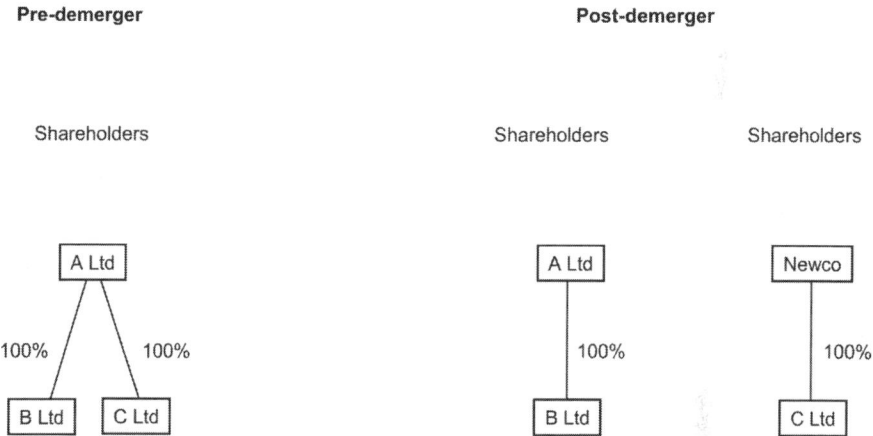

The possible tax consequences are as follows:

* Tax on the distribution to the shareholders. For a higher-rate taxpayer, this works out at 32.5% of the value of the shares in B Ltd and for an additional rate taxpayer this works out as 38.1%.
* Stamp duty at 0.5% on the transfer of shares from A Ltd to the shareholders.
* If there has been a transfer of assets within the last six years from A Ltd to B Ltd, a TCGA 1992, s 179 charge would be triggered. A similar charge is triggered where there has been a transfer of an intangible asset in the past six years.
* Where the value of B Ltd at the time of the disposal is greater than the original cost, a taxable gain will arise on A Ltd.

Where the distribution falls within CTA 2010, s 1077(1)(a)(ii) the following reliefs are available.

* The distribution is exempt from tax.
* No capital gains tax on the return of capital.

- New shares take on the history of the old shares.
- Any exit charge under TCGA 1992, s 179 is exempted from tax by TCGA 1992, s 192(3).

However, there is an added relief in that the gain on the disposal of C Ltd is exempt from tax because the transaction is a reconstruction in accordance with TCGA 1992, s 139. Section 139 prevents a taxable gain arising on a reconstruction. The reason that a Type I demerger cannot qualify for a s 139 relief is because the assets (ie the shares) are not transferred to a company (s 139(1)(a)).

Conditions A to M (excluding condition G) must be met. These are outlined above, with the exception of condition H.

Condition H: Where shares in a subsidiary are transferred those shares must represent the whole or substantially the whole of the distributing company's holding of ordinary shares and voting rights.

Case study

[11.6] If we examine this in relation to Robert's position on the basis that he would like to keep Bucolin Books Ltd in the longer term so there is a need to separate it from the rest of the group, we could look at a Type I or Type III statutory demerger. This means that the shares in Bucolin Books Ltd can be transferred out without triggering a tax charge on either Robert or the company and the shares can be held by Robert directly (Type I demerger or via a new company Type III).

To carry out a statutory demerger, the company will need sufficient distributable reserves, ie the distributable reserves must be equal to the net book value of the assets transferred.

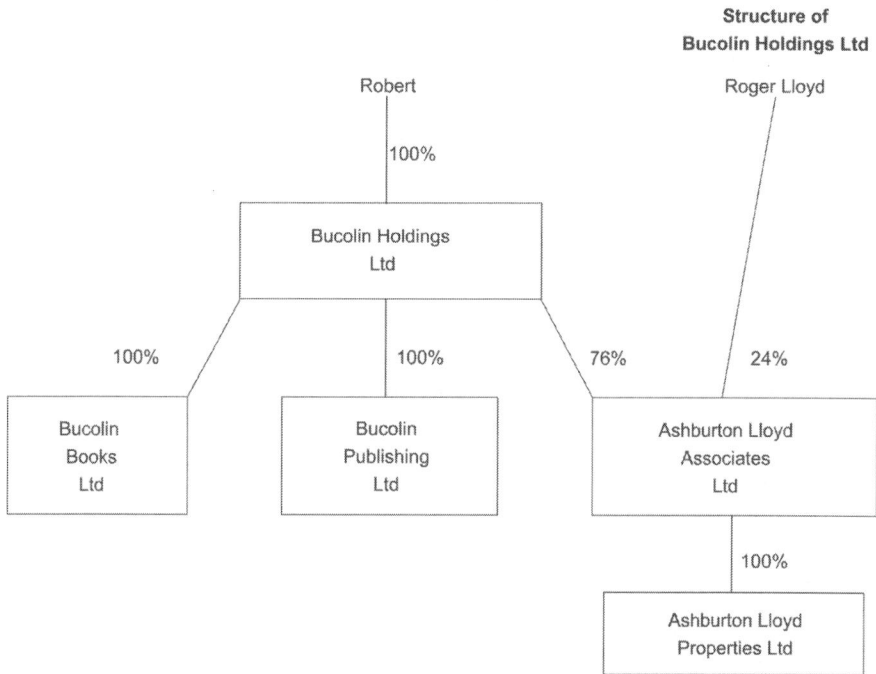

**Structure of
Bucolin Holdings Ltd**

Chargeable payments

[11.7] If within the five years of making an exempt distribution there is a chargeable payment, the amount or value of the payment will be treated as income of the shareholder. A chargeable payment is any payment made otherwise than for a bona fide commercial reason or which is part of a scheme or arrangement the main purpose, or one of the main purposes, of which is the avoidance of tax. The purpose of this rule is to deal with situations where the exempt transfer could end up being treated as a capital transaction and the shareholder will have obtained a tax advantage.

Chargeable payments are payments in money or money's worth to the members (directly or indirectly). They do not include distributions, exempt distributions or payments made for genuine commercial reasons. A chargeable payment is taxable on the recipient. The payer is required to deduct tax at basic rate, ITA 2007, s 928. The payment is not a deductible expense for the company, CTA 2010, s 1087.

A chargeable payment is a payment which meets each of the following conditions.

Condition A: The payment is an exempt distribution.

Condition B: The payment is made in connection with the shares in the company making the payment, the shares of any other company concerned with the exempt distribution or in connection with any transaction affecting those shares.

Condition C: The payment is not made for genuine commercial reasons or forms part of a tax avoidance scheme.

Condition D: The payment is not a distribution or an exempt payment and is not made to a company that belongs to the same group as the company making the payment.

Or it is a chargeable payment by virtue of CTA 2010, s 1089:

'(2)   The payment is a chargeable payment if it meets each of conditions B1 to D1.

(3)   Condition B1 is that the payment is made—

    (*a*)   in connection with the shares in the company (if it is a company) making the payment,

    (*b*)   in connection with the shares in any company concerned in the exempt distribution, or

    (*c*)   in connection with any transaction affecting the shares mentioned in paragraph (*a*) or (*b*).

(4)   Condition C1 is that the payment—

    (*a*)   is not made for genuine commercial reasons, or

    (*b*)   forms part of a tax avoidance scheme.

(5)   Condition D1 is that the payment (if made by a company)—

    (*a*)   is not a distribution or an exempt distribution, and

    (*b*)   is not made to a company that belongs to the same group as that company.'

Clearances and returns

[11.8] Before carrying out a statutory demerger, advance clearance can be obtained from HMRC. This clearance is obtained under CTA 2010, s 1091. At the same time, it is advisable that clearance is obtained under the transactions in securities legislation, contained in ITA 2007, s 701. In respect of the exchange of the shareholders' shares, clearance should be obtained under TCGA 1992, s 138. These clearances can all be dealt with in one letter to HMRC. Further details are contained later in **CHAPTER 14.**

Following the statutory demerger, the company must, within 30 days, make a return to HMRC giving details of the exempt distribution and the circumstances by reason of which it is exempt (CTA 2010, s 1095). If clearance has already been obtained, it is sufficient for the company to send a letter to HMRC confirming that the payment has been made and enclose a copy of the clearance confirmation. A return must also be made where a chargeable payment is made within five years of the exempt distribution.

Non-statutory demergers

Section 110 liquidation reconstruction

[11.9] There are many situations when a statutory demerger may not be appropriate. There are strict tax and legal conditions for statutory demergers which can prevent companies from using them. Non-statutory demergers tend to be used where the following applies.

- There is a separation of an investment and trading business or of two investment businesses. This could include property letting or a separation of a large property business.
- There is an intention to sell off one or more of the demerged businesses.
- The company has insufficient distributable reserves to make the exempt distribution under the statutory demerger provisions.

A non-statutory demerger is carried out by way of a members' voluntary liquidation in accordance with the Insolvency Act 1986, s 110. It is this section that gives a company the power to reconstruct its business whereby the liquidator transfers the assets of the company to a new company or an LLP in exchange for shares in the new company or an interest in the LLP. These shares or LLP interests are then distributed among the shareholders of the old company such that the shareholders of the old company become holders of shares in the new company or members in the new LLP. This method can only be used by a solvent company. A reconstruction under s 110 involves a liquidation of the company and the transfer of the company's assets and liabilities to new companies owned by the original shareholders.

Reconstruction under IA 1986 s 110

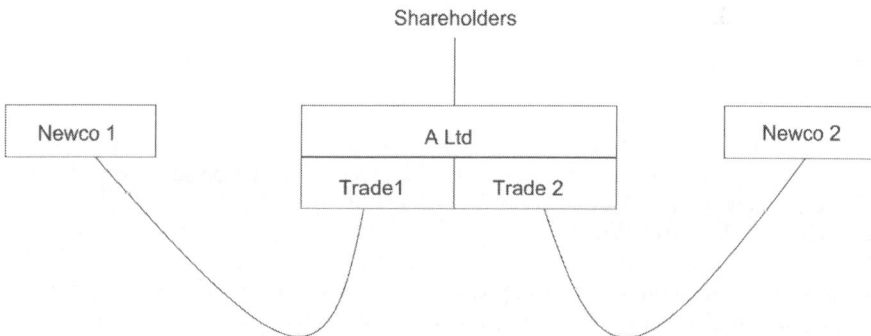

Direct transfer of trade and assets to two stand-alone companies during liquidation of the original company in exchange for issued shares in the two stand-alone companies

There are a number of potential tax charges that could arise on this transaction.

- A gain could arise on the disposal of any subsidiaries.
- A gain could arise on the transfer of any properties or other chargeable assets from A Ltd.
- A stamp duty land tax charge could arise on the transfer of the properties.
- A stamp duty charge could arise on the acquisition of shares in subsidiaries by the new companies set up to facilitate the demerger.
- The shareholders could be taxed on the distribution.
- The business of A Ltd could be treated as ceasing, giving rise to balancing allowances or charges and a loss of any losses carried forward.
- A gain could arise on the disposal of shares from A Ltd.

However, there are some reliefs available for both the shareholders and for the company where the liquidator transfers the assets to a company. There is no relief available where the assets are transferred to an LLP. For the shareholder, relief is available under TCGA 1992, s 136. This applies where there is an arrangement between a company (Company A) and the shareholders and that arrangement is part of a scheme of reconstruction which involves another company (Company B) issuing shares to the shareholders of Company A and the shares in Company A are retained by those persons or are cancelled. In the case of a liquidation reconstruction, the shareholders receive shares in a new company and, as the old company is liquidated, their old shareholdings cease to exist. Therefore, the provisions of TCGA 1992, s 136 apply so that the shareholders are treated as exchanging their holdings in Company A for the shareholdings in Company B. The new shares take on the base cost and ownership period of the old shares.

A scheme of reconstruction must meet certain conditions as per TCGA 1992, Sch 5AA. The legislation lists four conditions, and the restructuring must meet the first and second and either the third or fourth of the conditions.

The *first condition* is that the arrangements involve the issue of ordinary share capital to holders of the shares in the original company. The *second condition* is that under the arrangements the shareholders are entitled to shares the same as all shareholders of that class. The *third condition* is that there must be a continuity of the business. This means that the business or substantially the whole of the business carried on by the old company must be carried on by one or more successor companies. Where there are two or more successor companies, this could include the original company. The *fourth condition* is that the arrangements are carried out under the Companies Act as a compromise or arrangement with members. Most reconstructions of private companies will meet conditions one, two and three.

The relief under TCGA 1992, s 136 is subject to a 'bona fide commercial reason' test together with the rule that the arrangements cannot be for the purpose of tax avoidance. Where any company issues shares in exchange for shares in another company, the share-for-share relief rules will not apply unless the exchange or the scheme of reconstruction is effected for bona fide commercial reasons and does not form part of a scheme of arrangements the main purpose, or one of the main purposes, of which is the avoidance of liability to capital gains tax or corporation tax. As with standard share-for-share exchanges, the bona fide test and anti-avoidance test does not apply where a shareholder holds less than 5% of any class of shares in the company. In the case of a s 110 liquidation reconstruction, this means less than 5% in the company being reconstructed.

For the company, relief is available under TCGA 1992, s 139. This section applies where any scheme of reconstruction involves the transfer of the whole or part of a company's business to another company (and the company acquiring the assets is resident in the UK or the assets are chargeable assets for UK corporation tax purposes both before and after the transaction) and no consideration is received for the transfer otherwise than by the other company taking over the whole or part of the liabilities of the business and the two companies then being treated as if the assets were transferred on a no gain/no loss basis. This prevents any chargeable gains arising on the disposal of the subsidiaries or on the transfer of any chargeable assets, including properties, from the company being liquidated.

In relation to stamp duty land tax, two reliefs are available: reconstruction relief and acquisition relief.

Reconstruction relief is provided for in FA 2003, Sch 7, para 7. This relief allows land and buildings to be transferred between two companies without any charge to stamp duty land tax where the transfer is a transfer of undertaking in exchange for shares and there is no change of ownership. This requires mirror-image shareholdings, so it is available where all the shareholders are receiving shares in the new companies in proportion to their shareholdings in the company being reconstructed.

Acquisition relief, FA 2003, Sch 7, para 8, provides a relief which reduces the stamp duty land tax charge to 0.5%. This is available where there is a partition of the business ie where all the shareholders are not receiving shares in all the new companies. This relief applies where property is transferred as part of the acquisition of an undertaking of another company in exchange for shares and no more than 10% cash.

Unlike reconstruction relief acquisition relief is not available for all businesses. The trade for the purposes of acquisition relief cannot be wholly or mainly in dealing with chargeable interests. This excludes investment businesses and some land dealing activities.

Reconstruction relief is available where all the following conditions are met.

- The consideration for the acquisition must consist wholly or partly of the issue of non-redeemable shares in the acquiring company.
- The shares must be issued to all shareholders of the target company.
- The shareholders of the acquiring company must all be shareholders of the target company after the acquisition.
- Each shareholder must have received shares in proportion to their shares in the original company.
- The acquisition must be for bona fide commercial reasons and not form part of a scheme or arrangement the main purpose, or one of the main purposes, of which is the avoidance of liability to tax.

Where there is a partition of a company between the shareholders, reconstruction relief will not be available. In this case, the company will be looking at using acquisition relief. However, acquisition relief is not available where an undertaking acquired by a company involved in the reconstruction consists wholly or mainly of dealing in chargeable interests. Chargeable interests are defined in FA 2003, s 48, and broadly include estates or interests in land. This means that where a section 110 reconstruction is used to separate property investments and the interests of the shareholders after the transaction do not mirror their respective interests before the transaction SDLT exemption will not be available.

Both reconstruction relief and acquisition relief will suffer a clawback charge where the transferee company is sold within three years of the reconstruction. If arrangements are put in place within three years which would result in a change of control after the period of three years, this would also cause a withdrawal of the relief.

Where the reconstruction is across the board, with the same shareholders taking interests in the new companies in exactly the same proportions as their shareholdings in the old company, stamp duty exemption under FA 1986, s 75 should be available, subject to application for adjudication. If there is a partition as a result of the section 110 liquidation reconstruction it is likely that stamp duty will apply to the acquisition of the subsidiaries involved in the reconstruction.

The reconstruction relies on the succession provisions within CTA 2010, s 939 to enable any trading losses to be carried forward and for the tax WDV of plant and machinery and other assets to be carried over into the transferee company. The common 75% beneficial-ownership test needs to be met — ie at any time within two years after that event, not less than 75% of the business belongs to the same persons as it did at some time in the year before the event.

The liquidation of the distributing company is required under this type of reconstruction demerger to prevent the shareholders from incurring a distribution income tax charge on the assets distributed. Amounts received during the course of a winding-up do not constitute an income distribution by virtue of CTA 2010, s 1030.

The VAT consequences of any business transfers also need to be considered. In many cases, it should not attract any VAT, since the transfer-of-going-concern provisions should apply.

The use of a demerger by liquidation agreement involves the dismantling of a group or a company, with the result being that the shareholders of the old company hold shares in two or more new companies which hold the separated trades or activities.

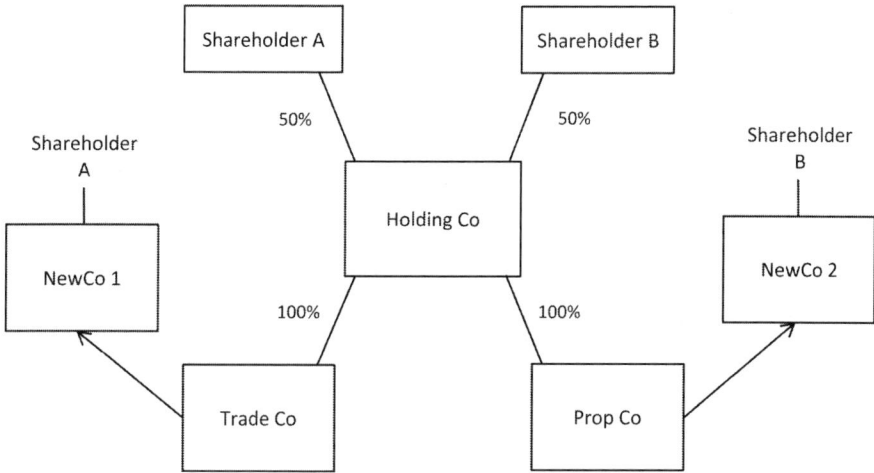

The example above illustrates a common situation whereby the shareholders want to break up the group with one taking the trade and the other the property company. It is assumed that both are of equal value. Using a non-statutory s 110 demerger, the following steps would occur.

- The shareholdings in the Holdings Co would be split into A shares and B shares. The A shares would represent the holding in Trade Co and the B shares would represent the interest in Prop Co.
- Two new companies, Newco 1 and Newco 2, would be formed.
- The holding company would be liquidated in accordance with provisions of the Insolvency Act 1986. This involves an agreement between the liquidator and Newco 1 and Newco 2 that their part of the undertaking of Holdings Co is transferred to each of these companies and that they discharge the liabilities of the parts transferred to them.
- Newco 1 and Newco 2 agree to issue shares to the liquidator, who then distributes them to the original shareholders of Holdings Co in proportion to their existing shareholdings in that company.

Reconstruction trap

[11.10] Where the shares are not split into the different share classes before a liquidation demerger, HMRC will argue that the second condition in TCGA 1992, Sch 5AA, para 3 is not met:

'The second condition is that under the scheme the entitlement of any person to acquire ordinary share capital of the successor company or companies by virtue of holding relevant shares, or relevant shares of any class, is the same as that of any other person holding shares or shares of that class.'

If short cuts are taken and the shares are not split into the different classes, the reliefs could be denied with the result being substantial tax charges on the shareholders.

Capital Reduction demergers

[11.11] A capital reduction demerger is a non-statutory demerger where the parent of a group of companies (distributing company) reduces its capital and transfers the shares of the demerging subsidiary to a Newco, which, in consideration, issues shares to the parent's shareholders. There is no income distribution as the parent reduces the paid up capital on the shareholders' shares so that no distribution arises. This is the case provided the amount reduced is equal to the value of the business that is demerged to the shareholders. To achieve this the capital reduction demerger is typically preceded with the creation of a new holding company to ensure that there is sufficient share capital.

The steps are usually:

- A new company (Newco 1) is incorporated and inserted on top of the group by way of a share for share exchange. This happens at market value.
- Newco 1 re-designates its shares into two classes. One class represents the interest in the subsidiary to be demerged (Sub 1) and the other class represents the remaining interest.
- Sub 1 is transferred to Newco 1.
- Another new company (Newco 2) is incorporated.
- Sub 1 is transferred to Newco 2 by way of a share transfer and a capital reduction of one class of shares in Newco 1.
- Newco 2 issues shares in itself to the shareholders of Newco.

The tax analysis outline above in relation to s 139 applies.

Interaction of s 179, TCGA 1992 with reconstructions

[11.12] Since the s 179 rules were amended in FA 2011 there can be a favourable result in relation to reconstructions.

Under the revised rules the asset that is the subject of the s 179 disposal is re-based immediately after the intra-group disposal by reference to which the s 179 charge arises ie the asset is disposed of and re-acquired at market value.

Any chargeable gain or allowable loss is then transposed to the disposal of shares that gives rise to the de-grouping. This means that any chargeable gain is added to the consideration for the disposal and any allowable loss is added to allowable expenditure (s 179(3D)). Where s 139 applies it is specifically provided in s 139(1A) that the no-gain/no-loss treatment of s 139 overrides the transposition. Therefore any gain transposed to the shares is not charged to tax or carried forward. The shares are simply treated as disposed of and acquired on a no-gain/no-loss basis.

Clearances required

[11.13] Clearances for the transaction should be sought under TCGA 1992, s 138 in respect of the share reorganisation and under ITA 2007, s 701 or CTA

2010, s 748 in respect of the transactions in securities. The splitting of the shares into different classes is a transaction in securities.

Professional fees

[11.14] The professional fees involved with company reorganisations can be high, in particular where an Insolvency Act 1986, s 110 liquidation is carried out. Whether tax relief is available will depend on the facts of the particular case. Dealing with any share reorganisation is a capital cost, so no relief is available for this element. The same goes for the transfer of capital assets — for example, the shares in subsidiaries. The costs will be capital expenditure. Likewise, the initial advice on the structuring and on the ownership is unlikely to be deductible as it is not incurred wholly and exclusively for the purposes of the business. HMRC's view on the deductibility of expenses are contained in their Company Taxation Manual at 17320, 'Distributions: Demergers: legal costs'.

The table below shows the suitability of a statutory demerger or a s 110 reconstruction in particular situations:

	Statu-tory de-merger	*Section 110 reconstruc-tion*
Separating two trading activities with a view to continuing both	√√	√
Separating two trading activities with a view to selling one		√√
Partitioning two trades between different groups of shareholders	√√	√
Separation of trading and investment activities with or without a view to selling one		√√
Partitioning of trading and investment activities between two groups of shareholders		√√
Separation of investment businesses		√√
Separation of businesses where distributable reserves less than book value of assets being distributed		√√
Separation of business activities followed by a management buy-out		√√

Purchase of own shares

[11.15] The purchase of own shares by a company is probably one of the most common ways of dealing with an exiting shareholder. The remaining shareholders do not need to personally raise the funds to buy out the shareholder. A company repurchase can work well where a controlling shareholder wants to exit the business and the minority shareholders want to buy him out. For the exiting shareholder, a company purchase of own shares is acceptable where he qualifies for capital treatment as this gives him a 10%/20% tax rate. For higher/additional rate taxpayers, if ER is available the tax rate falls to 10%. For the remaining shareholders, their shareholdings automatically increase as the repurchased shares are cancelled.

The company can borrow the money for the repurchase, and any interest paid will be treated as a non-trading loan-relationship deficit. The loan-relationship provisions deny relief where the money is used for an unallowable purpose, but it was confirmed in Hansard at the time the legislation went through Parliament that the repurchase of own shares by a company is an acceptable purpose.

The general rule where a company purchases shares from a shareholder is that the shareholder is charged to income tax as if he had received a distribution. For a higher-rate taxpayer, this is 32.5% of the amount received; for an additional rate taxpayer this is 38.1% of the amount received.

There are strict company law conditions that need to be adhered to in the repurchase of own shares by a company. The most important conditions are:

- the shares must be fully paid;
- the company must have authority in its Articles to purchase the shares;
- the company must have sufficient distributable profits (unless there are proceeds available from a fresh issue of shares);
- a capital redemption reserve is created where the repurchase is out of distributable profits. The amount credited to the capital reserve is the nominal value of the shares being repurchased; and
- payment of the sum for the shares must be made on completion and cannot be deferred or in kind.

HMRC's view, as confirmed in Tax Bulletin 21 is that the consideration 'must be paid in money'. However, in the non-tax case of *BDG Roof-Bond Ltd v Douglas* [2000] 1BCLC 401 an obiter dictum was that payment can be made in specie. HMRC to date has not accepted this view. Obiter dicta are not binding and are only persuasive.

Repurchase as a distribution

[11.16] Where the repurchase is taxed as a distribution, the amount of the distribution is the difference between the proceeds and the amount subscribed for the shares. Where the shares were acquired second-hand, the calculation will be the same — there is no relief in calculating the distribution for amounts paid over and above the subscription price. The subscription price includes the nominal value and any share premium.

If the shares subject to the repurchase were acquired on a share-for-share exchange, the subscription price is the value of the shares acquired on the exchange at the time they were issued.

Example

In March 2009, Robert exchanged his shareholding in Bucolin Ltd for shares in Bucolin Holdings Ltd. The terms of the exchange were such that the conditions of TCGA 1992, s 135 were met, so no tax charge arose (ie for capital gains tax purposes, there was a share-for-share exchange). At the time of the exchange, his shares in Bucolin Ltd were worth £100,000. The acquisition by Holdings would be accounted for using merger relief under Companies Act 2006, s 612 so he would be issued with 100 £1 shares in Bucolin Holdings Ltd. The balance of £99,900 could be reflected in a merger reserve in the holding company's accounts. It is possible to capitalise the merger reserve into a share premium account. In 2016, Bucolin Holdings Ltd repurchases the shares for £150,000, at which point the share capital comprises 100 £1 ordinary shares and a share premium account of £99,900. The amount to be taxed as a distribution on Robert is £149,900, not £50,000, as the creation of share premium out of the merger reserve would fall under CTA 2010, s 1004 as securities issued other than for new consideration. There will be a capital gains tax charge on the remainder, based on the original base cost of his shares in Bucolin Ltd, but hopefully he will have the benefit of ER.

However, if, instead, Holdings issues 100,000 £1 ordinary shares as consideration for the shares in Bucolin Limited, and the shares are later repurchased for £150,000, the amount of the distribution would be £50,000. The remaining £100,000 would be treated as a return of capital. Again, there would be a capital gain on the disposal of the shares, based on the original base cost of his shares in Bucolin Limited.

As there is a disposal of shares by the shareholder, the capital gains tax implications also need to be considered. The amount taxed as a distribution is excluded from the capital gains tax charge (TCGA 1992, s 37(1)). In the majority of cases, where the repurchase is taxed as a distribution there will be no capital gains tax implications. However, where the shares have a March 1982 value, are second-hand or were acquired on a share reorganisation, there may be a capital loss. As the shareholder is connected with the company, it may be considered that this is a connected party loss so cannot be used against gains other than those arising from transactions with the company. However, that is not the case. The rules on connected party losses are contained in TCGA 1992, s 18, which states:

'(1) This section shall apply where a person acquires an asset and the person making the disposal is connected with him.

(2) Without prejudice to the generality of section 17(1) the person acquiring the asset and the person making the disposal shall be treated as parties to a transaction otherwise than by way of a bargain made at arm's length.

(3) Subject to subsection (4) below, if on the disposal a loss accrues to the person making the disposal, it shall not be deductible except from a chargeable gain accruing to him on some other disposal of an asset to the person acquiring the asset mentioned in subsection (1) above, being a disposal made at a time when they are connected persons.'

As the shares are cancelled on a repurchase, the company does not make an acquisition. Therefore, there is no restriction on the use of the loss. Where the loss is in an unquoted trading company, it may be possible to convert the capital loss into an income loss by virtue of ITA 2007, s 131 — share-loss relief.

Capital treatment

[11.17] Provisions contained in CTA 2010, s 1033 onwards mean that a share repurchase must be treated as capital where certain conditions are met. For many years, practitioners looked to break the conditions to take advantage of the distribution treatment, but with the favourable CGT rates and the availability of ER most taxpayers now want capital treatment.

In order to get capital gains treatment for a purchase of own shares the company must be an unquoted trading company (CTA 2010, s 1033(i)(a)) and either Condition A or Condition B is met.

Condition A

- the purchase must be made wholly or mainly to benefit the trade of the company or of one of its 75% subsidiaries, and
- the repurchase is not part of a scheme or arrangement to allow a shareholder to participate in the profits of the company without receiving a dividend or a scheme for the avoidance of tax.

Condition B

The shares are purchased from personal representatives (PRs) and the amounts are being used to pay an inheritance tax liability. The PRs must also show that the liability could not otherwise have been settled without causing undue hardship.

(1)   The shareholder whose shares are being repurchased must be resident in the UK in the year of the repurchase (CTA 2010, s 1034).

(2)   The shareholder must have owned his shares for the past five years. Where there has been a reorganisation of share capital, the ownership period applies to the original shares (CTA 2010, s 1035).

(3)   Where the shares were inherited, the holding period of the deceased can be counted and the requirement for the ownership period is reduced to three years (CTA 2010, s 1036).

(4)   The vendor's shareholding must be substantially reduced after the share repurchase. The vendor's interest after the repurchase cannot be more than 75% of the interest before the repurchase (CTA 2010, s 1037).

(5)   The vendor shareholder cannot be connected with the company after the share repurchase. A 30% test applies, and the interests of associates are taken into account (CTA 2010, s 1042).

For the purposes of the purchase-of-own-shares legislation, 'associate' has a narrower meaning than that for close companies. An associate is defined in CTA 2010, s 1059 as including an individual's spouse or civil partner, minor children and any trust created by the individual/spouse/civil partner.

Benefit to the trade

[11.18] For capital treatment the purchase of own shares by the company must in some way give rise to a trading benefit. Usually it is necessary to demonstrate that if the shareholder remains in the company he will have a detrimental effect on the trade. This could be as a result of families falling out, shareholders having completely different views on the future of the business or simply the next generation wanting to take over and develop the business. HMRC accepts that any unwilling shareholder can have a damaging effect on the trade. Statement of Practice 2/82 sets out HMRC's view:

'The "trade benefit test"

1   The Company's sole or main purpose in making the payment must be to benefit a trade carried on by it or by its 75 per cent subsidiary. The condition is not satisfied where, for example, the transaction is designed to serve the personal or wider commercial interests of the vending shareholder (although usually he will benefit from it) or where the intended benefit for the company is to some non-trading activity which it also carries on.

2   If there is a disagreement between the shareholders over the management of the company and that disagreement is having or is expected to have an adverse effect on the company's trade, then the purchase will be regarded as satisfying the trade benefit test provided the effect of the transaction is to remove the dissenting shareholder entirely. Similarly, if the purpose is to ensure that an unwilling shareholder who wishes to end his association with the company does not sell his shares to someone who might not be acceptable to the other shareholders, the purchase will normally be regarded as benefiting the company's trade.

Examples of unwilling shareholders are:

* an outside shareholder who has provided equity finance (whether or not with the expectation of redemption or sale to the company) and who now wishes to withdraw that finance;
* a controlling shareholder who is retiring as a director and wishes to make way for new management;
* PRs of a deceased shareholder, where they wish to realise the value of the shares;
* a legatee of a deceased shareholder, where he does not wish to hold shares in the company.

3   If the company is not buying all the shares owned by the vendor or if although the vendor is selling all his shares he is retaining some other connection with the company – for example, a directorship or an appointment as consultant – it would seem unlikely that the transaction could benefit the company's trade, so the trade benefit test will probably not be satisfied. However, there are exceptions; for example, where a company does not currently have the resources to buy out its retiring controlling shareholder completely but purchases as many of his shares as it can afford with the intention of buying the remainder where possible. In these circumstances, it may still be possible for the company to show that the main purpose is to benefit its trade. Also, the Board do not raise any objection if for sentimental reasons it is desired that a retiring director of a company should retain a small shareholding in it, not exceeding 5 per cent of the issued share capital.'

The 'benefit to the trade' test was considered in *Allum v Marsh (Insp of Taxes)* [2005] STC (SCD) 191. In this case, the company acquired the shares from the two main shareholders (a husband and wife) leaving their son as the remaining shareholder. The company had sold its premises, the proceeds from which were used for the repurchase of shares. The company could not find alternative trading premises and carried on its trade from shared premises, which severely limited its ability to supply its services. The Special Commissioner found in this case that the purchase of own shares by the company had not been made wholly or mainly for the purpose of benefiting the trade but to facilitate the retirement of the taxpayers. Therefore, capital treatment was not available. Statement of Practice 2/82 cites retirement as one of the benefits to the trade accepted by HMRC. However, in this case it was combined with the winding-down of most of the company's activities, and it was this that prevented the test being met.

Substantial reduction

[11.19] Following the share repurchase, the vendor's interest (including associates) must be substantially reduced. Substantially reduced is less than 75% of the previous entitlement.

For example, if John owns 50 shares out of an issued share capital of 200 shares, the minimum amount which would need to be repurchased is 16. This is calculated as follows:

$$\frac{S \times C}{4C - 3S} \rightarrow \frac{50 \times 200}{800 - 150} = 15.38 \text{ rounded up to 16 shares}$$

S is the shareholding of the vendor before the repurchase.

C is the issued share capital before the purchase.

This covers the nominal-value test (s 1037), but in addition to this the vendor's interest in the distributable profits must also be substantially reduced (s 1038). This test is very often overlooked.

Entitlement to profits – the vendor's entitlement to profits must also be substantially reduced. The purpose of this test is to prevent a shareholder selling his shares back to the company and continuing to benefit from a disproportionate amount of profits. It is often assumed that once the nominal value test above is met then this test is also met. This test can be a trap for the unwary.

In applying the test the profits are increased by £100 and if any person is entitled to periodic distributions the profits are also increased by that amount.

> Example 3
> Bucolin Limited has 100,000 ordinary £1 shares and 5,000 10% preference shares in issue. These shares are held as follows:
>
> | John | 20,000 £1 ordinary shares and 5,000 preference shares |
> |---|---|
> | Colin | 50,000 £1 ordinary shares |
> | Ken | 30,000 £1 ordinary shares |
>
> Whether this test is met depends on the price of the repurchased shares and the level of distributable profits.
> The intention is for Jordan Limited to acquire 9,000 shares from John for £15,000.

If the distributable profits were £20,000 before the purchase the profits for the purposes of the test would be:

Distributable profits	£20,000
Statutory addition	£ 100
Preference dividend	£ 500
	£20,600

John's entitlement prior to the purchase is:

Preference dividend	£ 500
20% of the balance of £20,100	£4,020
	£4,520

This is 21.94% of the total.

After the purchase the profits available for distribution are £5,100, John's entitlement is:

Preference dividend	£ 500
12.09% of the balance of £5,100	£ 617
	£1,117

This is 19.95% of the total which does not represent a substantial reduction so **this test is failed**.

Connected test

[11.20] The vendor must not, immediately after the repurchase, be connected with the company making the purchase (CTA 2010, s 1042). A person is connected with the company if he is entitled to more than 30% of:

- the ordinary issued share capital;
- the loan capital and the issued shares capital; or
- the voting power of the company.

In determining the rights, any interests of associates are included. Again, for these purposes, 'associates' takes the narrower definition which only includes a spouse or civil partner and children under 18 as well as any trust created by the individual/spouse/civil partner.

Why a repurchase of shares by the company?

[11.21] As mentioned earlier, where a shareholder is exiting the company, a repurchase by the company is often a more attractive proposition than a purchase by the remaining shareholders. The reasons for this are as follows:

- The company gets a tax deduction for the interest.
- The shareholder does not have to raise finance to buy the shares.

- The repurchase is in effect funded out of future profits.
- The individual shareholders do not have to finance loan repayments out of post-tax income.
- The existing shareholders do not lock money into the base cost of their shares.

Borrowing money to fund the repurchase

[11.22] Where a shareholder borrows money to lend to the company to buy out another shareholder, the availability of relief for the interest needs to be examined closely. This issue must now be addressed in light of the cap on income tax reliefs, as a result of which in many situations it may be preferable to structure borrowings in favour of corporation tax loan relationship provisions rather than relying on relief against personal income.

The rules on loans to a company are covered in **CHAPTER 13**. The rules state that the funds must be used 'wholly and exclusively' for the business. The question is whether the buy-back of the shares is for the purposes of the business. There is no guidance on this outside the legislation. In dealing with a repurchase, the closest that we have is the 'benefit to the trade' test and HMRC accepting that buying out a retiring director or a dissident shareholder is acceptable as a benefit to the trade. For a company under the loan relationship rules, HMRC has confirmed that borrowing to acquire shares is an allowable purpose. The company will get relief for the interest under the loan-relationship provisions — a non-trading loan-relationship deficit. It will have to deduct tax at 20% on any interest on the payments to the shareholder.

Where the company has insufficient funds to pay for the purchase of shares in a single payment it may be appropriate to structure the purchase of shares as a single contract with multiple completion to acquire shares from a departing shareholder. This follows ICAEW Technical Release 745. It is important to ensure that the transaction is structured such that the shareholder foregoes any voting or dividend rights in respect of shares he continues to hold pending completion of the contract. In this respect, it may be advisable to alter the rights of the shares to demonstrate that the shareholder holds no possible rights.

Where it is not possible to undertake a repurchase of own shares, for example because one of the conditions above is not met, then an alternative maybe to consider is the use of a management buyout structure. This would involve the formation of a new company which acquires all the shares in the target company with exiting shareholders receiving cash or loan notes and remaining shareholders receiving additional shares in Newco (share for share). This type of reconstruction is covered in more detail in **CHAPTER 13**.

Valuation issues

[11.23] For all of the situations outlined above, establishing the value of the shares or businesses to be transferred is of paramount importance. In many circumstances, the transaction will be deemed to be between connected parties and therefore market value will be substituted for any amount actually paid.

The case law principles of valuing companies and shareholdings for tax purposes are complex, and entire books are devoted to consideration of this subject. However, a key issue will be the level of discount, if any, applicable to the valuation of minority shareholdings. The range may vary considerably, depending on the size of the shareholding, the purpose of the valuation and the company's circumstances at the valuation date, and expert advice should be sought in respect of this.

Pre-transaction agreement to a valuation is only available in respect of the approved share schemes discussed in **CHAPTER 10**. The disclosure of proposed transaction prices as part of a wider tax clearance which may be agreed subsequently is no guarantee that HMRC's Shares and Assets Valuation division will agree that the figures represent market value for tax purposes. Therefore, for any transaction of potentially significant value, it may be beneficial to seek a professional valuation which will identify the range within which the tax value is likely to be agreed.

It should also be borne in mind that any transaction effectively sets a benchmark price for any subsequent transactions in a company's shares. For example, the price at which a departing shareholder is bought out may then become the starting point for the value of shares awarded under an incentive scheme.

Reduction of share capital

[11.24] The Companies Act 2006 contains provisions which enable a private company to reduce its share capital using a solvency statement procedure without having to enter into any court-based procedure.

The tax implications differ depending on how the share capital being reduced came into existence. There are a number of possibilities:

(1) a subscription or rights issue for cash;
    (a) cash paid on reduction
    (b) no payment on reduction
(2) a bonus issue created out of P&L reserves;
(3) a share for share exchange.

Also, the tax position will be different depending on whether the capital reduction is represented by available assets and is satisfied, usually, by cash, or whether the capital reduction is not represented by available assets and is done to eliminate a deficit on P&L reserves.

1a. Reduction of share capital where shares were originally subscribed for — payment for shares

For example, where a limited company has share capital of 100,000 £1 ordinary shares which were subscribed for at par, and wishes to reduce its share capital to, say, £25,000, by repaying £75,000 to its shareholders, the tax position is as follows.

(a) capital gains tax

As the company is simply repaying share capital of £75,000 pro rata to its shareholders, the transaction is dealt with under capital gains tax principles. Assuming all the shareholders were original subscribers there would be neither a gain nor a loss for capital gains tax purposes, unless they acquired their shares under EIS for example, in which case any deferred gain would come back into charge.

If they are not original subscribers a gain or loss could arise, for example if an individual had acquired the shares from the original subscriber for an amount that is more or less than par.

If there is a loss, it is not considered that this could be a clogged loss under TCGA 1992, s 18(3) as there is no acquisition by the company (see TCGA 1992, s 18(1)), even if the company is connected with the shareholder under TCGA 1992, s 286(6).

(b) income tax

Under CTA 2010, s 1000 a payment by a company to its shareholders can in many situations be taxed on the shareholder as income in the form of a distribution. 'Distribution' is defined in s 1000(1), and includes 'any dividend paid by the company, including a capital dividend'.

However, in the case of a capital reduction the repayment will not be treated as a distribution, following the exception in CTA 2010, s 1000(1), which defines 'distribution' as meaning:

> ' . . . any other distribution out of assets of the company in respect of shares in the company, except however much (if any) of the distribution, represents repayment of capital on the shares . . . '

However, if the shareholders receive more than the amount originally subscribed the excess would be treated as a distribution, unless that amount is 'when it is made, equal in amount or value to any new consideration received by the company for the distribution' (CTA 2010, s 1000(1)B(b)).

(c) accounting entries

The journal entries in the accounts to reflect the reduction in capital in this situation (being no additional amounts to the shareholders) would be:

		Dr	Cr
Dr	share capital	£75,000	
Cr	cash		£75,000

A capital redemption reserve is not required, as would be the case where the company is effecting a purchase of own shares, as the redemption does not require a maintenance of capital.

(d) bonus issue following repayment of capital

If, following the repayment of share capital the company makes a bonus issue of shares paid up otherwise than by the receipt of new consideration, typically out of the P&L reserve, the amount so paid up (up to the value of the previous repayment of capital) will be treated as a distribution under CTA 2010, ss 1022–1023. This applies to bonus issues where there has been any repayment of share capital after 6 April 1965.

1b. Reduction of share capital where shares were originally subscribed for — no payment for shares

A company may have a large share capital which is not represented by the net assets of the company, so that there is also a deficit on P&L account. The company can eliminate this deficit by reducing the share capital. In this case there would be no payment to the shareholders, although the number (but not the percentage) of shares that each shareholder has in the company will be reduced pro rata to their shareholdings.

(a)   capital gains tax

Here the reorganisation rules will come into effect. TCGA 1992, s 126 refers to a reorganisation as including a reduction of share capital. This means that where there is a reduction of share capital through an adjustment to P&L reserves, the base cost per share of the remaining shares held by the shareholders will be increased. The total base cost will remain the same.

This follows TCGA 1992, s 127 which says:

> 'a reorganisation shall not be treated as involving any disposal of the original shares or any acquisition of the new holding or any part of it, but the original shares (taken as a single asset) and the new holding (taken as a single asset) shall be treated as the same asset acquired as the original shares were acquired.'

This means that there will be no disposal by the shareholders. Indeed this is as would be expected as the asset (in the form of shares) held by each of the shareholders has the same value before and after the reduction in share capital.

Using the earlier example but assuming that there was a negative P&L reserve of £75,000:

	£
Position before reduction	
Share Capital	100,000
Profit and Loss	(75,000)
Net Balance Sheet Value	25,000
Position after reduction	25,000
Share Capital	
Profit and Loss	0
Net Balance Sheet Value	25,000

(b)   treatment of future profits and dividends paid by the company

By reducing share capital through P&L reserves, the deficit is eliminated. This means that future profits credited to P&L are available for distribution to the shareholders, whereas before the reduction in share capital those profits would be used to reduce the P&L deficit, and therefore would not have been available for distribution.

If, as a result of the capital reduction, the deficit on P&L reserve is eliminated and a credit balance created, for accounting purposes this reserve is treated as a realised profit as per Companies Act 2006 (Commencement No 7, Transitional Provisions and Savings) Order 2008. From an income tax point of view, if the credit balance that is created is subsequently distributed to the shareholders it would seem that this would be taxed as a dividend, as the capital amount is included in the base cost as per the reorganisation rules.

2. Reduction of share capital arising from a bonus issue

The company's share capital may comprise shares that were subscribed for and paid up by new consideration in the form of cash or assets, and also shares that arose as a result of a bonus issue capitalising P&L reserves, with no further subscription by way of new consideration.

CTA 2010, ss 1024–1028 will apply so as to treat a repayment of share capital which was created otherwise than by new consideration as a distribution. This means that the shareholders will be subject to income tax on the repayment insofar as it is in respect of the shares issued as a bonus issue.

Any repayment of share capital in excess of the original bonus issue will be treated as a capital gain in accordance with 1(a) above.

3. Reduction of share capital arising from a share for share exchange

The situation envisaged here is that Mr A owns A Ltd and B Ltd, and A Ltd acquires B Ltd issuing further shares to Mr A as consideration for his shares in B Ltd.

Clearance would have been obtained under TCGA 1992, s 138 and ITA 2007, s 701 for the share exchange (at this point there would have been no mention of a capital reduction as it was not in contemplation).

(a)   capital gains position following the share exchange

On the basis of clearance having been obtained, Mr A would have received shares with a base cost equal to the original shares in B Ltd, following TCGA 1992, s 127, and applying s 135. For A Ltd, the base cost of the shares in B Ltd would be the market value of those shares at the time of the share exchange.

For income tax purposes the subscribed value would be the market value at the date of the exchange.

(b)   treatment of capital reduction, where cash paid to shareholder

If A Ltd were to reduce its share capital with a payment to Mr A, would that payment be treated as a distribution or as proceeds for capital gains tax purposes?

The position with regard to whether a payment for a reduction of share capital should be treated as a distribution is considered in 1(b) above. In addition, the provisions of CTA 2010, ss 1024–1028 need to be considered. These sections deal with the treatment of shares issued otherwise than by the receipt of new consideration, where there is a repayment of share capital, and broadly seeks to tax such payments as distributions.

(i)   new consideration

New consideration is defined in CTA 2010, s 1115(1), and means:

> 'consideration not provided (directly or indirectly) out of the assets of the company, and in particular new consideration does not include amounts retained by the company by way of capitalising a distribution; . . . '

CTA 2010, s 1115(3) deals with share capital issued at a premium, where the share premium account is subsequently applied in paying up new share capital, and confirms that this will be treated as new consideration for the new share capital unless the share premium account has been used previously under CTA 2010, s 1025(2) to enable a distribution to be treated as repayment of share capital.

Subsection (4) says that 'no consideration derived from the value of any share capital or security of a company, or from voting or other rights in a company, is to be treated for the purposes of this Part as new consideration . . . '

This might suggest that where the consideration received for the new issue of shares in A Ltd is the value of shares in B Ltd, the share for share exchange is caught, with the result that the new shares are not new consideration. Thus, if those shares are subject of a capital reduction, s 1025 would treat the amount paid to Mr A as a distribution.

However, in CTM15140, HMRC's view is:

> 'CTA 2010, s1115(4) to (6) only restrict new consideration derived from share capital in or securities of the same company. It is possible for a company to recognise as new consideration the full value of shares in another company which are received in exchange for the issue of fresh capital or securities.'

It would appear, therefore, that a payment in respect of a reduction of share capital which arose from a share exchange would not be treated as a distribution under CTA 2010, Part 23.

(ii)   transaction in securities

However, if, following the share exchange, A Ltd effects a capital reduction in respect of the shares issued on the acquisition of B Ltd, would HMRC seek to issue a counteraction notice under ITA 2007, s 698?

Transactions in securities are dealt with in **CHAPTER 14**. In the context considered here a shareholder may be liable to a counteraction charge because the 'person receives relevant consideration in connection with . . . the direct or indirect transfer of assets of one close company to another close company . . . .' (ITA 2007, s 685(2)(c) as amended by FA 2010, Sch 12).

'Relevant consideration' is defined in ITA 2007, s 684(5) as consideration 'which consists of any share capital or any security issued by a close company and which is or represents the value of assets which are available for distribution by way of dividend by the company [or] would have been so available apart from anything done by the company.'

Mr A is likely to be regarded as having received an amount in connection with a distribution that would be available in respect of distributable reserves of B Ltd that could otherwise be paid as a dividend to him. As a result, the amount received by Mr A under the capital reduction would be taxed as a distribution rather than as proceeds for capital gains tax purposes.

(iii)   anti avoidance under TCGA 1992, s137

Notwithstanding the likely issue with ITA 2007, s 698, if the capital reduction was in contemplation when the share exchange took place TCGA 1992, s 137 could deny the application of TCGA 1992, s 135, as the transaction is not likely to be regarded as being effected for bona fide commercial reasons. As a result, the shareholders would not benefit from the 'stand in the shoes' provisions of TCGA 1992, s 127, so that a capital gain would crystallise on the share exchange.

(iv)   non-close companies and small shareholders

For non-close companies where the shareholders each hold less than 5% of the shares, it seems feasible to carry out a share for share exchange, issuing B shares to the shareholders, and then effect a capital reduction in respect of the B shares.

(v)   capital reduction not involving a payment to the shareholders

If a capital reduction following a share exchange does not involve a payment to the shareholders, but is intended to eliminate a deficit on P&L perhaps in respect of a write down in the value of the shares acquired, there would be no tax impact on the shareholders. The treatment of this situation is considered in 2 above.

VAT and company reconstructions

[11.25] Company reconstructions may have VAT implications which need to be carefully reviewed and dealt with in the most tax-efficient manner. For example but not limited to the following:

- Selling part of the business or acquiring a business. The treatment of supplies made and whether the transfer of going concern conditions would apply, capital goods scheme adjustments if property is involved, asset sales, the segregation of business activities; effect on any partial exemption (VAT Act 1994, s 49);
- Restructuring of a VAT group, anti-avoidance provisions, eligibility and control requirements, including/removing companies from VAT groups, partial exemption issues (VAT Act 1994, Sch 9; VAT Act 1994, Sch 9A);
- Acquisition/disposal of companies and claiming the VAT on costs attributable thereto; issue sale and purchase of shares and attributable VAT on expenditure (s 49; VAT Act 1994, Sch 9).

Key points

[11.26] Key points to note are as follows:

- Where possible, try to ensure that a demerger qualifies as a statutory demerger in order to obtain the available tax reliefs.
- Consider a s 110 liquidation or a capital reduction reconstruction if a statutory demerger is not possible or appropriate.
- SDLT relief may be clawed back where a transferee company is sold within three years of a reconstruction.
- Consider a share repurchase by the company instead of a purchase by remaining shareholders.
- Companies can obtain tax relief on interest paid on a loan to buy back their own shares.
- Where a share repurchase can be treated as capital this will always be more beneficial with the lower CGT rates and the possibility of ER.
- A reduction of share capital is more straightforward since the introduction of new provisions in the CA 2006.
- Valuation issues should be addressed from the outset.

Chapter 12

Incorporation and Disincorporation

Introduction

[12.1] There are many reasons why the owners of an unincorporated business may wish to move to a corporate structure. Having made the decision, the proprietors need to consider how this can be achieved in the most tax efficient way.

Incorporation will involve a disposal

[12.2] Whichever way an incorporation is carried out and whatever the business comprises, there will be a disposal for capital gains tax purposes. With a typical business, this is likely to involve goodwill and possibly real property. In most cases, because the proprietor and the new company will be connected persons for capital gains purposes, TCGA 1992, s 18 imposes market value on this transaction regardless of what consideration passes between the company and the individual.

This means that if a sole trader decided to cease trading as a sole trader on 31 March and open for business on 1 April in a corporate form, he would be treated as making a disposal of goodwill to the company at market value. It is important to plan the incorporation so that any capital gains arising can be managed.

Where property is transferred to a company on incorporation, even though it is possible to minimise the CGT exposure, for SDLT purposes FA 2003, s 53 deems the transaction to have taken place at market value where the company is connected with the transferor. Where the business is transferred to a company by a partnership, the partnership provisions in FA 2003, Sch 15 take precedence over s 53, which could mean that in some cases no SDLT is payable on incorporation by virtue of the 'sum of lower proportions' provisions. However, the anti-avoidance provisions in s 75A would prevent a business being transferred to a partnership prior to incorporation with a view to using the more favourable SDLT rules that apply to partnerships.

TCGA 1992, s 162

[12.3] TCGA 1992, s 162 provides a statutory relief for incorporation, which is automatic so long as a number of requirements are met and the taxpayer does not elect under s 162A for s 162 not to apply.

Section 162 applies where an individual transfers a business to a company as a going concern, including all the assets of the business except cash, in exchange for shares issued by the company.

As a result, the company will be treated as acquiring the assets at current market value, and the base cost of the shares issued to the proprietor will be the market value of the assets transferred to the company less the gain on the disposal of the assets. The proprietor's capital gain is, therefore, held over until he sells his shares in the company.

Before applying incorporation relief, it is necessary to ascertain that the requirements of TCGA 1992, s 162 are met and identify whether there are any inherent planning opportunities.

What is a business?

[12.4] The legislation refers to a 'business' rather than a trade. There is no statutory definition of 'business', although the question has been considered by the courts. A business includes a trade but might extend to, for example, a property portfolio, so long as it is not held as a passive investment. The First-tier Tribunal decision in *Elizabeth Moyne Ramsay* TC 01871 disallowed section 162 relief in relation to a property letting enterprise on the basis that there was no business being carried on, even though the owners spent significant time managing the property, which comprised a large house divided in to a number of flats. The Upper Tribunal reversed this decision, concluding that the activities carried on by Mrs Ramsay did constitute a trade (2013 UKUT 0226 (TCC). In their decision, the Upper Tribunal indicated that 'business' should be afforded a broad meaning and commented:

> ' It is the degree of activity as a whole which is material to the question whether there is a business, and not the extent of that activity when compared to the number of property or lettings'.

In recent years there has been an increase in the number of property business incorporations. Whether they constitute a business for s 162 purposes will depend on the individual facts. A landlord with one investment property is unlikely to have a business whereas a landlord with a number of properties which are actively managed is likely to have a business. Before embarking on an incorporation exercise this point would need to be considered carefully.

The case of *American Leaf Blending Co Sdn Bhd v Director General of Inland Revenue* [1979] AC 676, also provides some authority on the meaning of the term:

> 'In the case of a private individual it may well be that the mere receipt of rents from property that he owns raises no presumption that he is carrying on a business. In contrast, in their Lordships' view, in the case of a company incorporated for the purpose of making profits for its shareholders any gainful use to which it puts any of its assets prima facie amounts to the carrying on of a business . . .

> The carrying on of a 'business', no doubt, usually calls for some activity on the part of whoever carries it on, though, depending on the nature of the business, the activity may be intermittent with long intervals of quiescence in between. In the

instant case, however, there was evidence before the Special Commissioners of activity in and about the letting of its premises by the company during each of the five years that had elapsed since it closed down its former tobacco business. There were three successive lettings of the warehouse negotiated with different tenants; there was the removal of the machinery from the factory area which made it available for use for storage and a separate letting of that area to a fresh tenant; and as recently as October 1968 there was the negotiation of the letting to a single tenant both of the factory area and the warehouse.'

The business transferred to the company must be a 'going concern', which means that it cannot simply be a collection of assets that could be consolidated into a business by the new company. This was considered by the First-tier Tribunal in the case of *P Roelich v HMRC* [T03704], where the only asset that was recognised on the balance sheet following the transfer was the right to income from an existing contract. The First-tier Tribunal were satisfied that there were wider opportunities transferred and these were not so personal to Mr Roelich to prevent the application of s 162.

Transferring the assets of the business under TCGA 1992, s 162

[12.5] To use TCGA 1992, s 162, all the assets of the business (except cash) must be transferred to the company. Often, when a business is incorporated, the proprietor prefers not to transfer certain assets to the company. Commonly, this involves freehold or leasehold property and private vehicles, because of the possible disadvantageous tax position that would result from holding those assets in the company.

It is possible to extract those assets from the business balance sheet prior to incorporation, but HMRC points out in their manual CG65710 that it is a question of fact whether assets extracted from the business prior to incorporation remain business assets. Forward planning is required, and it is advisable to extract assets that are not to pass to the company well before incorporation so that the business can prepare a revised balance sheet at its normal reporting date before incorporation. Extraction of assets from a business balance sheet is not a disposal for CGT purposes, except where property is taken out of a partnership otherwise than in accordance with the partnership capital sharing ratio, in which case the CGT and SDLT position would need to be considered.

The legislation does not require the transfer of liabilities to the company, although in practice this usually happens. Strictly, where the company takes over liabilities, this constitutes of consideration otherwise than in the form of shares, which restricts the availability of TCGA 1992, s 162 relief (see below). Following Extra-Statutory Concession D32, HMRC say at CG65745 that it would not usually take this point because there is a corresponding reduction in the value of the shares issued as consideration for the business. This only applies to business liabilities. The acquisition cost of the shares can only be reduced to nil or negligible value.

D32 is however a discretionary concession and HMRC may choose not to take this view if, for example, a highly geared property portfolio is transferred to a company, on the basis that the liabilities are more personal rather than business. The adviser would need to take a view on any transaction that appears to fall outside a standard incorporation of a trading business.

Property businesses with bank borrowings can cause difficulties. If the liabilities are not transferred and instead the new company takes out loans and repays the borrowings owed by the individual or partners this will constitute consideration. The borrowings should be transferred and then refinanced or refinanced by the individuals/partners prior to incorporation and then transferred as part of the business transfer.

Consideration for the business under TCGA 1992, s 162

[12.6] Where consideration for the business comprises anything other than shares – for example, the creation of a director's loan account, or cash – the relief is restricted. For this purpose, 'shares' is defined in TCGA 1992, s 288 as including stock, and is not confined to ordinary shares. In some circumstances, therefore, it may be appropriate to issue preference shares which may also be redeemable.

Where the whole of the consideration is in the form of shares, the whole of the gain can be rolled over. Where the consideration is partly in the form of shares, the TCGA 1992, s 162 relief is restricted. Let us assume that the balance sheet of the business that is being incorporated is as follows:

Balance sheet at 31 December 2017	£
Equipment	5,000
Current assets	19,000
Current liabilities	−8,000
Net assets	16,000
Value of assets on incorporation:	
Goodwill (pre-1 April 2002)	75,000
Equipment	4,000
Net current assets (current assets less current liabilities)	11,000
Value of assets transferred	90,000

The base cost of the shares

[12.7] The gain on the disposal of goodwill, assuming there is no base cost, is £75,000. If the new company issues 10,000 ordinary shares as consideration for the business, which have a total value of £90,000, the base cost of those shares for any future disposal would be £15,000 (ie £90,000–£75,000). For the company, the base cost of the goodwill would be £75,000. If the gain is larger than the value of the business being transferred, then the full gain cannot be rolled over. In these cases, this is usually an indication that the proprietor's capital or current account is overdrawn and has been financed by the bank overdraft or loan so a careful review is required.

This result may be particularly attractive for individuals owning a property portfolio which, as noted in **12.4** above, can be treated as a business. It would be possible to incorporate the portfolio, gain an uplift in the base cost of the properties, and then sell the properties without triggering a tax liability on the gain accruing up to the date of incorporation. The company can then reinvest the gross proceeds. If the consideration comprises shares and a director's loan account of £60,000, the consideration would be apportioned. This is achieved by calculating the proportion of the gain that is attributable to the shares, and the balance of the gain remains chargeable to capital gains tax.

The first stage is to establish the cost of the new assets (the shares received as consideration). In this example, the cost of the shares will be £90,000 – £60,000 = £30,000.

The next stage is to calculate the gain attributable to that cost, using the fraction A/B, where A is the cost of the new assets and B is the value of the whole of the consideration received by the transferor in exchange for the business.

The proportion of the gain attributable to the shares is £75,000 × £30,000/ £90,000 = £25,000.

As a result, £50,000 of the gain remains chargeable to capital gains tax, and the base cost of the shares is £5,000 (£30,000 – £25,000).

The SDLT position should always be considered as the transfer of properties to a company by a connected person will trigger an SDLT liability based on the current market value of the properties. Where the unincorporated business is a partnership the Sum of Lower Proportions provisions will apply in calculating the SDLT. For a family partnership the SDLT should work out as zero. For non-family partnerships the calculation typically results in SDLT unless the parties are acting together to control the company.

Preparation for a sale

[12.8] TCGA 1992, s 162 can be used in appropriate circumstances as a precursor to a sale of the business to a third party. On incorporation there is an uplift in the base cost of the business, which can then be sold by the company without triggering an immediate charge to tax on the gain. The proprietors can use the company as a way of deferring tax liabilities on the disposal of the business in a number of ways, depending on their aspirations and objectives. The company could be used to continue a new trade, to be later sold or liquidated with the benefit of ER, or used as a conduit to drip the proceeds from the sale of the trade by means of dividends over a number of years. The vendors are able to secure a deferral of tax liabilities which would not have been available had they simply sold the trade.

Entrepreneurs' relief (ER) and TCGA 1992, s 162

[12.9] The ER position following an incorporation under TCGA 1992, s 162 needs to be considered because the 12-month look back period restarts when the business is transferred to the company in exchange for shares. After 12 months of the transfer, so long as the company is a trading company and the other requirements for ER are met by the shareholder, ER would be available in respect of the shares.

If s 162 is disapplied by s 162A, a disposal will be treated as taking place at the time the assets were transferred to the company. The base cost of the shares and the chargeable assets acquired by the company would not be reduced by the roll-over of the gain under s 162 and normal capital gains tax would be payable. The tax due date will follow the incorporation date.

Most disposals of goodwill from 3 December 2014 onwards in relation to incorporations do not qualify for ER. Finance Act 2015 amended TCGA 1992, by introducing s 169LA to remove goodwill disposed to a related company from the definition of a relevant business asset for the purposes of ER. There are two exceptions to this rule, which were introduced in FA 2016, although taking effect from 3 December 2014. The first is where the person disposing of the business has a small (5% or less) interest in the acquiring company; the second is where the incorporation is followed within 28 days by a disposal of the company to a third party.

In addition, it should be noted that companies are no longer able to claim a corporation tax deduction in relation to goodwill or other customer-related intangibles acquired on or after 8 July 2015, by virtue of Corporation Tax Act 2009, s 816A (CTA 2009). These changes make incorporation much less attractive where trading businesses are concerned, although this route will continue to be used for the incorporation of property investment businesses, for example.

Relief for losses following incorporation

[**12.10**] Where a business is incorporated under s 162 and losses from that business remain unrelieved, ITA 2007, s 86 allows those losses to be carried forward and set off against future income from the company, whether by way of dividend or otherwise.

In these circumstances, it may be appropriate for the company to pay the individual a salary, and for that individual to claim relief under s 86 so as to obtain a refund of the income tax deducted under PAYE. There are a few reasons for this.

First, the company would obtain corporation tax relief on the payment of a salary whereas dividends would be paid out of post-tax profits.

Second, the Employers Allowance of £3,000 per annum would cover any Secondary Class 1 National Insurance up to those levels. It should be noted, however, that the allowance is not available for one-man companies.

Third, salary counts towards an individual's net relevant earnings for the purposes of personal pension contributions and attracting tax relief on those contributions.

With the abolition of the dividend tax credit and the changes to the rates of dividend taxation which came into force as from 6 April 2016, the considerations for profit extraction and s 86 loss relief will likely alter, depending on the level of losses to be relieved as well as the taxpayer's individual circumstances.

Incorporation by way of sale of the business to a company

[12.11] With the increase in the lifetime limit for entrepreneurs' relief to £10m from 6 April 2011, businesses were often incorporated by way of a sale to a company. This was achieved by debiting the company balance sheet with goodwill and the sundry net assets of the business and crediting the director's loan account with the consideration. The aim was to generate a disposal liable to capital gains tax which was then reduced by ER, leaving an amount that could be drawn down from the company without any further tax liabilities for the individual proprietor as profits accrued to the company. This method became even more attractive when the stamp duty charge on goodwill was removed.

With ER now being denied on most disposals of internally generated goodwill on incorporation on or after 3 December 2014, incorporations have become less attractive as gains on the disposal of goodwill could now be subject to CGT at 20% (or even 28% in relation to disposals of residential property). Further details can be found in CHAPTER 3.

The valuation issue

[12.12] If the above route to incorporation is implemented, the value at which the goodwill is transferred to the company must be considered very carefully, and HMRC will challenge any valuation which appears excessive. Any valuation will be determined on the facts of any particular case, but there are some general questions that need to be considered when a business is incorporated.

(1)   Is there an industry norm for valuing the type of business?
(2)   Does the business have separable goodwill, or is it personal to the proprietor?
(3)   Does goodwill exist separately from the premises from which the business is being carried on? This is a pertinent issue with, for example, a care home or a restaurant/bar.
(4)   Is the method of valuation reasonable, bearing in mind the longevity of the business, future profit expectations, market changes etc?

If the business has been overvalued and the director's loan account has been drawn down, the amount overdrawn could be treated as remuneration on which income tax under PAYE and NIC would be due (along with interest on late payments), or it could be treated as a deemed distribution under CTA 2010, s 1000 and taxed accordingly.

It might be possible for the proprietor to repay the loan account and to revise the amount of consideration received for the goodwill but this would only usually be possible if the original disposal of goodwill to the company included an adjuster clause in respect of the consideration. In practice, this is rare, but it should always be included as part of the documentation supporting the incorporation of the business. Where HMRC believes that the valuation has not been done professionally or there is negligence, unwinding the situation will not mitigate the tax. HMRC will seek to tax the relevant amount as salary or a dividend.

One piece of potentially good news is the clarification of HMRC's position regarding 'adherent' goodwill in trade-related properties. Previously, HMRC resisted the possibility that a business of this nature generated any transferable goodwill apart from that which related to the premises from which the business was carried on. However, in a practice note published in 2009, HMRC has recognised that there is likely to be an element of free goodwill within the business in addition to that contained within the property. The practice note, issued in conjunction with the Royal Institution of Chartered Surveyors, also sets out examples of the way in which goodwill might be calculated for this type of business.

Incorporation using TCGA 1992, s 165

[12.13] The third method of incorporation is by means of TCGA 1992, s 165. The proprietor transfers the chargeable assets of the trade to the company by way of gift. The other net assets that are not chargeable to capital gains tax are usually transferred by crediting the director's loan account with the net value.

Under s 165, the gain on the asset is held over on the transfer to the company. This means that the gain is deferred, with the company taking over the asset at market value less the held-over gain. In the longer term, this route is unattractive because the proprietor holds shares with a base cost equal to the amount subscribed, and the company usually has a low base cost for the assets acquired on incorporation. This route would not be efficient if a sale of the business to a third party is foreseeable.

Section 165 might be used if incorporation is required for commercial reasons but the gain on disposal of the goodwill is prohibitive, either because of the value of the goodwill or because ER is not available following the December 2014 changes. Section 165 is more restrictive than s 162 in terms of the type of asset that can be transferred. Section 162 extends to businesses that are not necessarily trades. In order to obtain relief under s 165, the asset must be used for the purposes of a *trade* carried on by the transferor (or his personal company). Section 165 cannot therefore be used to incorporate a property business.

Section 165 cannot be used to transfer shares to a company, although it can be used to make gifts of trading-company shares to individuals or trustees. Further details on s 165 are contained later in this chapter.

Finally, it should be borne in mind that if, as part of an incorporation under s 165, property is transferred to a company, stamp duty land tax would be chargeable. The normal rule that no stamp duty land tax is payable in relation to a gift does not apply when the gift is made to a company. Instead, stamp duty would be payable in relation to the market value of the transferred property.

Entrepreneurs' relief and TCGA 1992, s 165

[12.14] Once the shares in the trading company have been owned for one year, and the other conditions for ER have been met, relief can be claimed on a future disposal of the shares in the new company.

Other issues

Cessation of the old business

[12.15] Whichever route is chosen for incorporation, there is an array of other issues that have to be addressed. From a tax perspective, the unincorporated business ceases, so normal cessation provisions apply and these may skew the timing of tax payments until the transition to the company has been completed. On cessation, any (transitional) overlap relief will be available to offset against the profits assessable for the final period. However, unless incorporation takes place at the normal year end of the business, more than 12 months' profit may fall into charge.

In addition, there may be balancing allowances or charges in respect of capital allowances. Where appropriate, it may be advantageous to consider a disposal of plant and machinery at a price which gives rise to a balancing allowance or at least avoids a balancing charge. Alternatively, the sole trader or partners and the company may jointly elect within two years after the transfer date for assets to be treated as transferred at the tax written-down value.

Careful consideration must also be made where property is transferred in respect of fixture and fittings capital allowance pools in order to ensure that the availability of these capital allowances is maintained. Since Finance Act 2012, the availability of capital allowances on fixtures within a property was made conditional on (i) previous business expenditure on qualifying fixtures being pooled before a subsequent transfer on to another person, and (ii) the value of the fixtures being established formally within two years of a transfer. The first condition applied to all transfers since April 2014, whilst the requirement to fix a value has been in place since April 2012. In the event that these conditions are not met, the capital allowances on such assets will be lost permanently.

Transfer of stock

[12.16] A transfer of stock has to be considered in the context of ITTOIA 2005, ss 177–178. These sections apply where stock is sold to a connected person who carries on or intends to carry on a trade in the UK and is entitled to deduct the cost of stock as an expense in calculating the profits of the trade. ITTOIA 2005, s 177 imposes an arm's length market value to the stock in this situation.

Section 178 applies where the value of the stock determined under s 177 exceeds both the acquisition value and the sale proceeds and enables a joint election to be made so that the value of the stock is taken to be the acquisition value or, if greater, the sale proceeds. The election must be made by the first anniversary of the normal filing date for the personal tax return covering the incorporation of the business.

The transfer of stock provisions are likely to be of particular relevance for businesses such as property development or antique dealing, where the value of stock may be significantly different from the cost shown in the business accounts.

Transfer of employees

[12.17] The employees of the business will be transferred to the company under TUPE provisions. This will necessitate the issue of P45s and the establishment of a new PAYE scheme for the company. Employment law issues will also have to be dealt with.

Incorporation and BPR

[12.18] Often, the business being incorporated will qualify for inheritance tax BPR (see **CHAPTER 3**). In these circumstances, the owner of the business will want to know whether his interests in the new company will also qualify for BPR.

The two-year rule

[12.19] The general rule in relation to BPR is that the property qualifying for relief needs to have been owned by the person claiming the relief for a period of two years before the relief becomes available.

When a business is incorporated, in the majority of cases a new company (Newco) will be formed. Will the owner of Newco then have to wait for two years from its creation before BPR will be available? The answer – perhaps unexpectedly – is that it seems to depend upon how the qualifying business is incorporated.

Replacement business property

[12.20] Where one qualifying business asset replaces another, the periods of ownership of the two assets can be considered together (IHTA 1984, s 107). Thus, if the first asset has been owned for two years or more, any qualifying replacement asset will immediately qualify for BPR.

Therefore, if, on an incorporation, the shares in Newco can be said to have 'replaced' the old business assets (and assuming the old business and Newco would otherwise qualify for relief), those Newco shares can qualify for BPR immediately upon the incorporation. Whether or not this will be the case, however, will depend upon the way in which the business is incorporated. The three typical methods of incorporation referred to in the previous part of this chapter are considered below:

1.   TCGA 1992, s 162 roll-over incorporation

[12.21] If the entire assets of the original business are exchanged for shares in Newco, the Newco shares would clearly have replaced the original business assets. In this case, BPR should be available immediately on the Newco shares if the business assets were held for two years.

2.   Incorporation by way of sale for debt

[12.22] By contrast, if a business is incorporated by the owners, (1) first creating Newco; and (2) then selling the assets of the business to Newco in exchange for (typically) a director's loan account, the position is different.

In this scenario, the original business will have been replaced by the amount due on the loan account and not by the Newco shares. Thus, the shares in Newco will need to be held for a period of two years before they qualify for relief. Meanwhile, the loan account, while replacing the original business, will not itself qualify for relief because a debt due under a loan account would not normally qualify for BPR (but see further below).

It is perhaps worth noting that the lack of any immediately available BPR in relation to the Newco shares is potentially an academic point, because the shares in Newco would, in any event, have little initial value as the company would be encumbered by the loan account. If, however, the company were to grow in value significantly during the two years following incorporation, thereby increasing the value of the Newco shares, the loss of BPR for that two-year period could be significant.

3.   TCGA 1992, s 165 hold-over incorporation

[12.23] The third method of incorporation involves the creation of Newco, followed by the 'gift' of the original business to Newco by the original owner, who would then claim gift relief from capital gains tax under TCGA 1992, s 165.

This method of incorporation is the most difficult of the three to analyse. On the one hand, the value in the old business is immediately reflected in the value of the Newco shares, leading to the conclusion that those shares could be said to have *replaced* the old business. On the other hand, for a gift to have been made to Newco, the Newco shares must have existed at the same time as the old business (ie immediately prior to the gift) and therefore how could those shares have replaced the old business? Likewise, isn't the concept of making a gift at odds with the notion of replacement? When an individual gives something away, he does not replace it with anything.

Although this is something of a grey area, it is the authors' experience that HMRC would not resist a claim that the Newco shares have replaced the old business in these circumstances. Further (and as discussed above), the imposition of stamp duty land tax on a gift to a company has severely reduced the attractiveness of this method of incorporation, so, again, the point may be academic.

Further BPR points

[12.24] In the examples used above, the Newco shares immediately replace the old business. In fact, the inheritance tax rules allow relief where the old business and Newco shares have been owned for 'at least two years falling within the five years immediately preceding', which, in practice, allows for a gap of up to three years between the sale of one business and the acquisition of another. This is most often of significance where an individual sells one business to a third party and acquires a new business from a third party. It can, however, be important in an incorporation context too, for example:

- if an individual incorporates Newco using the proceeds of sale of a qualifying business sold within the previous three years in exchange for share capital, the Newco shares would qualify for BPR immediately; or
- if a business had been incorporated by the 'sale for debt' method, the director's loan account could be repaid at any time during the three years following incorporation and the cash repaid used to acquire Newco shares, which could then qualify for relief immediately (as qualifying under the 'two out of five year' rule vis-a-vis the originally incorporated business).

Finally, the general rule is that the amount of any BPR in relation to the replacement property 'shall not exceed what it would have been had the replacement . . . not been made' (IHTA 1984, s 107(2)).

Planning points

In the case of a 'sale for debt' (ie a credit to the director's loan account) incorporation, the loss of BPR on the Newco shares for two years is unlikely to be significant unless the owner is particularly elderly. Nevertheless, a two-year-term assurance policy to cover the risk of death within that period might be worth considering in certain circumstances.

The (indefinite) loss of relief in relation to the director's loan account is likely to be the more significant issue, and, in circumstances where inheritance tax mitigation is a high priority (again, where elderly owners are involved), the following might be considered.

While the credit balance on a simple director's loan account cannot qualify for BPR, 'securities of a company which are unquoted and which either by themselves or together with . . . any unquoted shares so owned gave the transferor control of the company . . . ' will qualify for 100% relief (IHTA 1984, ss 104(1)(a), 105(1)(b)). Consideration might therefore be given to the sale of the business in exchange for a

---

security with some voting rights attached rather than for a simple book debt. It is important to note, however, that the votes have to 'give' the owner control so that if a person already has control of a company through the votes attaching to his ordinary shares, the voting securities will not attract BPR.

- Alternatively, the original loan account might be exchanged for new shares in the company – these could be ordinary shares or preference shares possibly of a redeemable nature.

VAT and incorporation

[12.25] When incorporating a business, the following VAT issues may arise:

- dealing with the VAT on pre-incorporation expenditure;
- issues in relation to the transfer of going concern provisions and the capital goods scheme;
- VAT attributable to the sale and purchase of shares;
- VAT and capital introductions;
- partial exemption and property transactions (VAT Act 1994, s 49, Schs 9 and 10; Notice 706).

Key points on incorporation

[12.26] Key points to note are as set out below.

- There are broadly three methods of incorporation: TCGA 1992, s 162, sale of the business to a company and TCGA 1992, s 165.
- TCGA 1992, ss 162 and 165 afford the possibility of complete deferral of the gain on incorporation.
- Sale of the business triggers a gain, in respect of which ER may not be available on the disposal of goodwill from 3 December 2014 onwards.
- The decision to incorporate must involve consideration of the practical issues and whether it is the right decision commercially.
- Generally TCGA 1992, s 162 relief will be effective for BPR purposes in terms of the ownership period of assets. In certain circumstances, it may also be possible to obtain a similar favourable result using s 165 relief.
- In the case of a 'sale for debt' where IHT mitigation is paramount, some relevant planning should be considered to exchange director's loan accounts for assets qualifying for BPR.

Disincorporation

[12.27] This relief ceased to be available on 31 March 2018 and no similar relief has been proposed. There were instances where proprietors wished to bring a company to an end and to continue the trade in an unincorporated form. FA 2013, ss 58–61 introduced a disincorporation relief that was available to small companies disincorporating between 1 April 2013 and 31 March 2018. The relief applied where a company transferred its business to some or all of its shareholders and the transfer of the business was a qualifying business transfer. A transfer was a qualifying business transfer as defined in FA 2013, s 59 if the following conditions were met:

(A)   The business is transferred as a going concern.

(B)   The business is transferred together with all of the assets of the business (cash can be excluded).

(C)   The total market value of the qualifying assets (goodwill and property not held as stock) of the business included in the transfer does not exceed £100,000.

(D)   All the shareholders to whom the business is transferred are individuals (which includes partners of a partnership, but not members of an LLP).

(E)   Each of those shareholders held shares in the company throughout the period of 12 months ending with the business transfer date.

A claim for disincorporation relief must be made jointly by the company and all the shareholders to whom the business is transferred, and is irrevocable.

The effect of the election is to hold over the gain on the qualifying assets, including pre and post 1 April 2002 goodwill. The provisions do not address the tax position on the transfer of plant and machinery or stock, for which there are already reliefs in CAA 2001, s 266 and CTA 2009, s 167. Furthermore, there is no relief for the individual shareholders, who would have to consider their income tax and capital gains tax position on disincorporation.

If a company ceased to trade and passed the business to its shareholders, an accounting period comes to an end. This may be relevant if the company had trading losses in the period to cessation but has an asset it has yet to sell and on which a gain will arise. It may be appropriate, therefore, to delay the transfer of the business until that property has been sold.

Transfer of goodwill on disincorporation

[12.28] The transfer of the business itself would have given rise to a disposal of any chargeable assets transferred, and where goodwill was involved, there would have been a disposal of an intangible asset if the goodwill was created between 1 April 2002 and 8 July 2015. These transfers will be treated as having taken place at market value if the company and the transferee were connected (which was usually the case). The former will be treated as a capital gain, so any previous capital losses brought forward can be offset. The latter will form part of the trading results of the company if the intangible asset was acquired after 1 April 2002, so trading losses brought forward are likely to be available for offset.

On the disincorporation of a business, the transferee is likely to be a shareholder and a director of the company. The transfer of assets could be treated either as a distribution or as a benefit in kind if the company continued after the disincorporation of the business. If the company was being wound up in the course of the disincorporation, the transfer of the assets would be treated as proceeds for the transferee's shares in the company. This will give rise to a capital gain and, assuming the company was a trading company for at least one year before the disincorporation, ER should be available.

TCGA 1992, s 165 hold-over relief

[12.29] The transfer of assets at undervalue or to a connected party triggers the market-value rules in TCGA 1992, ss 17, 18. This means that the transfer is treated as happening at market value, with the gain calculated accordingly. This can leave the transferor with a taxable gain and no proceeds. Where, however, the assets transferred are business assets, a hold-over relief is available under TCGA 1992, s 165. This means that no tax charge arises on the transfer and the gains are effectively passed on to the transferee. Where there is a sale at undervalue (ie *some* proceeds are received but not full market value), partial hold-over relief is available.

The relief works as follows.

Example 1

Suppose Robert gifts a business asset to his daughter Catherine and the market value at the date of the gift is £100,000. The original cost of the asset was £25,000 in March 1982.

	£
Deemed proceeds	100,000
Cost	25,000
Gain	75,000
Gain held over under s 165	75,000
Gain taxable on Robert	Nil
Catherine's base cost	
Market value at transfer	100,000
Gain held over under s 165	75,000
Base cost going forward	25,000

What qualifies for gift relief?

[12.30] For a gain to be held over under TCGA 1992, s 165, there needs to be:

(1)   a transfer by an individual otherwise than by way of a bargain at arm's length;
(2)   the asset transferred must meet the conditions of the legislation; and
(3)   a claim must be made by the transferor and the person who acquired the asset (or where the transferee is a trust the transferor alone) for the hold-over relief to apply.

The key point is that the transfer needs to be made by an individual, but it can be made to any person – and a person can include a company (except where shares are being transferred).

Qualifying assets

Shares

[12.31] Shares or securities qualify where they are shares or securities in a trading company (or in the holding company of a trading group) and the company is unlisted or the company is the transferor's personal company. The transferor's personal company is one in which the shareholder holds 5% or more of the voting rights. A trading company and a holding company of a trading group are defined in TCGA 1992, s 165A. A trading company is one 'carrying on trading activities whose activities do not include, to a substantial extent, activities other than trading activities'.

Trading activities, as per TCGA 1992, s 165A(4), include:

'activities carried on by the company:
(a) in the course of, or for the purposes of, a trade being carried on by it,
(b) for the purposes of a trade that it is preparing to carry on,
(c) with a view to its acquiring or starting to carry on a trade, or
(d) with a view to its acquiring a significant interest in the share capital of another company that:
   (i)   is a trading company or the holding company of a trading group, and
   (ii) if the acquiring company is a member of a group of companies, it is not a member of that group.'

TCGA 1992, s 165A(8) defines a trading group as a:

'group of companies:
(a) one or more of whose members carry on trading activities, and
(b) the activities of whose members when taken together do not include substantial non-trading activities.'

So, in establishing whether the company or group is trading, the 80:20 (trading: non-trading) test needs to be met. However, that is not the end of the matter. Where the company has non-business assets, there can be a restriction on the hold-over relief. The restriction operates where the transferor has held at least 25% of the voting rights in the 12 months prior to the disposal, or at any time within the 12-month period it was the transferor's personal company, ie the transferor was able to exercise at least 5% of the votes. The voting rights are those attributable to the individual so do not include any rights held by associates or other connected parties.

The restriction operates by reducing the held-over gain by the following formula:

$$\frac{\text{Market value of chargeable business assets}}{\text{Market value of chargeable non-business assets}}$$

An asset is a business asset for a company or group where it is used for the purposes of a trade, profession or vocation carried on by the company or a member of the group. An asset is a chargeable asset in relation to a company or a group where any gain accruing on a disposal would be a chargeable gain. This would include assets standing at a loss as the legislation is looking at the treatment in the event it is sold at a profit. In applying the test, plant and machinery are included even though these seldom give rise to a chargeable gain. Cash will never be a chargeable asset. Therefore, excess cash can only affect gift relief if it causes the 80:20 test to be breached.

The treatment of goodwill in this context needs to be considered carefully. If the trade existed before 1 April 2002, goodwill will be treated as a chargeable asset for the purposes of this calculation. However, if the trade started or was acquired from an unconnected party after 1 April 2002 (and before 8 July 2015), goodwill is an intangible asset for CTA 2009 purposes, but is not a chargeable asset. This can give rise to an unwelcome result. Where for instance, a company owns post April 2002 goodwill and £1 of chargeable non-business assets there would be 100% restriction of the relief.

Example 2

Supposing that in Example 1 above the asset was 10 shares in Bucolin Holdings Ltd (Robert's personal company). The balance sheet of the group at the date of the gift was as follows:

	£
Freehold business offices	700,000
Investment property	500,000
Goodwill (pre-1 April 2002)	600,000
Plant and machinery (cost £40,000)	10,000
Trade debtors	110,000
Cash	100,000
Sundry net assets (all non-chargeable)	50,000
	2,070,000

Chargeable assets and chargeable business assets are:

	Chargeable assets	Chargeable business assets
	£	£
Freehold business offices	700,000	700,000
Investment property	500,000	–
Goodwill	600,000	600,000
Plant and machinery (cost £40,000)	10,000	10,000
Total	1,810,000	1,310,000

Hold-over relief is restricted to 1310/1810 of the gain.

The gain is £75,000.

The amount held over under TCGA 1992, s 165 is 1310/1810 × £75,000 = £54,281.

The gain taxable on Robert is £20,719.

ER will be available on this gain.

If the goodwill is a chargeable intangible asset for CTA 2009 purposes, goodwill would not feature in the calculation. The relevant fraction would become 710/1210 × £75,000 = £44,008. Thereby reducing the held over gain.

Other assets

[12.32] Other assets qualify for relief under TCGA 1992, s 165 where they are used for the purposes of a trade, profession or vocation being carried on by:

(1)   the transferor;
(2)   his personal company – ie one where the transferor holds at least 5% of the voting rights; or
(3)   a member of a trading group of which the holding company is the transferor's personal company.

As with shares, there is a restriction, but in the case of other assets applies where the assets were not used by any of the above throughout the whole period of ownership. The gain available for hold-over is restricted to:

$$\frac{\text{Days in the period the asset was used in a business by one of the list above}}{\text{Total period of ownership}}$$

In looking at the period of ownership, any period before March 1982 must also be included.

Where the asset is a building or structure and, over the period of ownership or any substantial part of that period, part of the building or structure was not used for the purposes of the trade, profession or vocation, an adjustment must be made to the held-over gain. There is no guidance on what is substantial in this context. The adjustment is done on a just and reasonable basis, which for many buildings would be floor space.

Where relief is to be restricted both by reference to periods of non-business use and by reference to partial non-business use, the time restriction should be applied first (HMRC Capital Gains Manual at 66952).

Residence of transferee

[12.33] Relief under TCGA 1992, s 165 can only apply where the transferee is UK-resident.

Where a gift is made to a transferee who subsequently becomes non-resident less than six years after the end of the year of assessment in which the relevant disposal is made, gift relief is revoked. This condition is relaxed:

- where the transferee is an individual;
- the reason for becoming non-resident is employment abroad;
- the individual becomes resident in the UK again within a period of three years; and
- during his absence from the UK, he did not dispose of the asset.

Where the gain is assessed on the transferee because the transferee is non-resident, this will be assessed on the transferor where it remains unpaid 12 months after the date it became payable by the transferee. Any transferor claiming relief under TCGA 1992, s 165 should therefore consider how the tax might be paid and compensation recovered from the transferee in these circumstances.

Where some proceeds are received

[12.34] Where the transfer is not an outright gift but instead a sale at undervalue, the transferor will have a chargeable gain to the extent that the proceeds received exceed the base cost (and any other amounts deductible under TCGA 1992, s 38).

Spouses and civil partners

[12.35] Transfers between spouses and civil partners generally happen on a no gain/no loss basis, as per TCGA 1992, s 58. However, where there is a separation, this rule only applies to the end of the year of assessment in which they separate but prior to the divorce decree absolute or prior to the final dissolution order. Any transfers after this date need to be on an arm's length basis. Where business assets are transferred as part of a divorce settlement, s 165 hold-over relief is available only where there is recourse to the courts. HMRC accepts that this is where a court makes an order:

- for ancillary relief under the Matrimonial Causes Act 1973 which results in a transfer of assets from one spouse to another;
- for property adjustment under the Civil Partnership Act 2004; or
- formally ratifying an agreement reached by the divorcing parties or by the civil partners of a dissolved civil partnership dealing with the transfer of assets.

In all other cases, HMRC argues that the transfer is in return for giving up rights and these rights are valid consideration so that the hold-over relief is restricted, as consideration has been given.

However, some planning can be done between spouses and civil partners.

Planning point

Supposing Robert has a building with a shop on the ground floor and a flat on the first floor. The shop is used by Bucolin Holdings. For the past five years, the flat was let out, but in the last year it has been used by the

---

shop for storage. Robert would like to gift the shop to Catherine, but he has been advised that a gain will be triggered as the full amount cannot be rolled over because of the non-business use. Is there anything Robert can do?

Robert could gift the property to his wife, Susan (she owns 15% of the shares in Bucolin Holdings). Susan could at a later date gift the property to Catherine. On the gift to Susan, no tax arises as the transfer is at no gain/no loss (TCGA 1992, s 58). When Susan gifts the property to Catherine, there is no restriction on the hold-over, as the asset had business use throughout her period of ownership.

Time limit for making the claim

[12.36] The gift-relief claim must be made within four years after the end of the year of assessment in which the gift was made.

Revoking the claim

[12.37] One of the common questions which arises is whether the hold-over claim can be revoked once it has been made. It is not clear in the legislation. However, when amendments were being made to the TCGA 1992, s 165 rules in respect of settlor-interested trusts, the Paymaster General was recorded in Hansard as saying:

'This is a claim, not an election, so I am advised that sections 165 and 260 are claims-based sections and the normal rules relating to the withdrawal of claims apply. Thus, a claim cannot be withdrawn or amended after it has become final.

Within the time limit for amending the claim, it may be withdrawn at any time. If a claim is made within a return and the window for amending that return is closed, the settlor cannot undo the position, so they are stuck with the consequences of the decision they made when they made the claim. Likewise, if a claim is made outside a return and the window for amending the claim has passed – 12 months from the date when the claim was made, for example: the settlor cannot undo the position. Again, he is stuck with the consequence of his decision to make a claim.'

This makes it clear that the 'five year ten months' rule does not apply to revoking or amending a claim under either TCGA 1992, s 165 or s 260.

Gifts to settlor-interested trusts

[12.38] Where assets are transferred to a settlor-interested trust or there are arrangements under which the settlement will or may become a settlor-interested trust, s 165 relief is not available on the transfer. These rules were introduced in FA 2004 to counter anti-avoidance and they are very widely drawn. There are only limited exceptions from the rules such as maintenance of a historic building or a property used for the benefit of a disabled person.

Part III

Succession

Chapter 13

Selling the Business

Introduction

[13.1] The sale of a business is probably the biggest transaction the share-holder or owner will undertake during his lifetime. Planning is important to ensure that there are no nasty surprises. Many vendors will be expecting a tax rate of 10% assuming they have the benefit of ER, but for various reasons this may not be the case. This is covered in more detail under **CHAPTER 3**. In any event, with the availability of a 20% CGT rate (for disposals on or after 6 April 2016), vendors can look forward to a lower tax payment on the disposal of their business. The purpose of this chapter is to examine how a sale may be structured and the different forms the sale consideration can take. In view of recent ER changes and anti-avoidance, it is imperative that advisers work with their clients to review their existing business structures.

Sale of a sole trade or an interest in a partnership

[13.2] The sale of a sole trade or an interest in a partnership is relatively straight-forward. Where the business is sold outright in exchange for an agreed sum of cash, either payable up front or on deferred terms, the gain is calculated in the year in which the disposal takes place. Where the disposal is a qualifying business disposal for ER purposes the £10m lifetime limit will be available provided it has not been fully utilised by the vendor. Therefore, any goodwill or other assets within the capital gains tax rules will benefit from either ER or the 20% CGT rate. In regards to the transfer of other assets, these need to be dealt with under the usual trading rules. Remember that partnerships (and LLPs) are transparent for tax purposes.

Deferred consideration is brought into the CGT computation at the time of the sale without any discount for the fact that the consideration is deferred. Where part of the deferred consideration is structured as an earn-out, this needs to be valued at the date of sale and brought into the CGT computation in the tax year of disposal. The full rules on deferred consideration and earn-outs (commonly referred to as '*Marren v Ingles*' type consideration (*Marren (Inspector of Taxes) v Ingles* [1980] 3 All ER 95) or a 'chose in action'), are described in further detail below.

Where an unincorporated business is disposed of in exchange for shares, usually no form of deferral relief is available and the full amount becomes taxable in the year of disposal. However, it may be possible to structure the sale as an incorporation so that the rules under Taxation of Chargeable Gains

Act 1992, s 162 (TCGA 1992) would apply. This would effectively defer some or all of the gain depending on the type of consideration received for the sale.

Planning point

Instead of receiving shares, the vendor could receive cash and could subscribe for new shares in the takeover company. If the company qualifies under the EIS rules, deferral relief would be available to the vendor. Provided there is no requirement or contract dictating that the vendor has to invest the proceeds, the deferral should be achieved. The situation has been improved with the changes introduced in Finance Act 2015 so that vendors no longer have to choose between claiming ER in the year of sale or deferring the gain under the EIS rules and paying tax at 20% when the deferred gain comes into charge. A gain can now be deferred and benefit from ER when that gain comes back into charge.

Sale of a business where there is a company

[13.3] A common question is whether the shareholder should sell the shares in the company or the assets out of the company. The conflict between the two has somewhat disappeared now that companies no longer benefit from a corporation tax deduction on the acquisition of 'customer related' intangibles. Prior to 8 July 2015 a company purchaser usually wanted to buy the assets of a business as a tax deduction was available for the goodwill under the rules for intangibles (even though the acquisition of property gave rise to a Stamp Duty Land Tax (SDLT) charge). A corporation tax deduction is still available for the write-off of other (non customer-related) intangibles. If a company acquires shares, there is no scope for a write-off for intangibles. Stamp duty is payable on the shares at a rate of 0.5%. Sometimes, where the purchaser is a company, the shares qualify under the SSE rules and where the purchaser thinks that there may be a future sale of the shares at a later date, they may be interested in acquiring the shares so that SSE will apply on that later sale. For the purchaser who has already thought of planning, they may want to acquire the assets and obtain a write-off for the non-customer related intangibles and at a later date transfer the business into a subsidiary company which could eventually be sold, thereby obtaining SSE. This gives the best of both reliefs — a write-off for the non customer-related intangibles and no tax on future gains, Where trade-related assets are transferred to another group company, the period for which the investing company is treated as holding a substantial shareholding for SSE purposes in the company invested in is extended by the period of time during which these assets were held and used by the group (TCGA 1992, Sch 7AC para 15A) provided the following conditions apply:

- That, immediately before the disposal, the investing company holds a substantial shareholding in the investee company, and
- that at the time of the disposal, the asset is being used for the purposes of a trade carried on by the investee company, and

- at the time of the transfer of the asset to the investee company by the investing company (or any other company) they were all members of the same group, and
- the asset was previously used by a member of the group, other than the investee company, for the purposes of a trade carried on by that member when it was a member of the group

It is important to note that in the capital gains tax manual, HMRC expresses the view that it does not consider that TCGA 1992, Sch 7AC para 15A applies unless a 'group' existed for the requisite qualifying SSE period. So, for example, if a single stand-alone company establishes a new subsidiary and transfers trade-related assets to that subsidiary, HMRC's view is that para 15A does not operate to deem the period the trading assets were held by the parent company to be a qualifying period for SSE purposes. Conversely, where a group had been in existence for more than 12 months, a transfer of trade-related assets to a newly formed subsidiary benefits from these provisions.

The changes to these SSE rules coupled with the reform of the s 179 exit charge rules make it possible to transfer a trade to a subsidiary and sell the subsidiary without a TCGA 1992, s 179 exit. At the same time, SSE is available on the disposal of the shares.

These changes are limited to capital gains and do not extend to the equivalent provisions dealing with intangible fixed assets. This is particularly important in the context of goodwill acquired or created after 1 April 2002 which will be treated as an intangible fixed asset. For intangibles, the transfer of goodwill intra-group is on a no gain/no loss basis, but if the transferee leaves the group within six years, there is an exit charge.

The vendor will typically want to sell the shares in the company. This is because ER may be available, and if the gain is less than £10 million the effective tax rate will be 10%. Whereas if the company sells the business, gains will arise in the company and another layer of tax is charged on the extraction of the proceeds. For many owner-managed businesses, there will be a substantial gain on goodwill (chargeable to corporation tax) as it is likely to have been internally generated, so it will not have a base cost. Once the company has sorted out its own affairs, the next step is most likely a liquidation of the company to distribute the proceeds to the shareholders. If done correctly, the shareholders could be eligible for ER on the distribution. However, the company will already have suffered a layer of tax. This results in double tax, which gives an effective tax rate of 27% (assuming the company pays tax at 19%), compared to 10%, which would be the case if the shares had been sold for the same price where ER is available. Where ER is not available the effective tax rate would be 35% compared to the 20% CGT rate available if the shares were sold. The exposure to stamp taxes should also be taken into account. Finally, the liquidation of the company following the sale of the business could be caught by the TAAR (aimed at 'phoenixing') which applies to transactions on or after 6 April 2016. If the shareholder carries on a trade or similar activity within a period of two years from the date of the liquidation distribution, the TAAR could apply meaning that the shareholder would be liable to income tax on the distribution.

The usual way to deal with these conflicts is by way of negotiation. Many purchasers now take the tax position of the vendor into account and will offer a different price for the assets or the shares. In most cases, this should resolve the tension. While the sale of shares might seem the easiest, the shareholders will have to commit to warranties and indemnities in relation to the historic activities of the company.

For the shareholder who sells his shares, the consideration can take a number of different forms.

Immediate cash consideration

[13.4] Where the sale of shares is in return for immediate consideration, the gain is calculated in the year of the disposal and the tax becomes due on or before 31 January following the tax year in which the disposal takes place. As the sale is likely to be under contract, this is the date the contract becomes unconditional. This is probably the most straight-forward transaction and only occurs in a small number of cases.

Deferred consideration

[13.5] The most common form of consideration is deferred consideration. This can fall into two different categories: ascertainable and unascertainable.

Ascertainable

[13.6] Where the sales consideration is ascertainable, it is taxable in full in the year of disposal. There is no discount available to the shareholder for the fact that the consideration is deferred. This means that the shareholder could find himself paying tax on consideration he has not yet received. TCGA 1992, s 280 does provide for an instalment option:

> 'If the consideration, or part of the consideration, taken into account in the computation of the gain is payable by instalments over a period beginning not earlier than the time when the disposal is made, being a period exceeding 18 months, then, at the option of the person making the disposal, the tax on a chargeable gain arising on the disposal may be paid by such instalments as the Board may allow over a period not exceeding 8 years and ending not later than the time at which the last of the first mentioned instalments is payable.'

When this provision was introduced in 1972, it was recorded in Hansard that the purpose of the provision was to deal with cases of undue hardship. In deciding whether or not there is undue hardship, HMRC would consider any resources made available by the transaction. So for the taxpayer to use TCGA 1992, s 280, the consideration had to be received in instalments and the taxpayer had to satisfy the Board of HMRC that payment of the tax in one sum would cause undue hardship. Since self-assessment was introduced, the consideration simply needs to be paid in instalments. There is no requirement to prove undue hardship. The taxpayer needs to make the application to his

Inspector. Once the Board has agreed the instalment payments, the taxpayer will receive a letter confirming that the payment by instalments is appropriate and that each instalment must be paid on or before the due date of each instalment and interest will be payable on any late payments. Thirty days before the due date of each instalment, HMRC will send the taxpayer an application for payment. The instalment option will not be available where the taxpayer has agreed to leave the amount outstanding, which is sometimes the case with management buy-outs.

The key point in respect of ascertainable deferred consideration is that no discount is available to the taxpayer for the fact that the consideration is deferred.

The instalment option is only available for ascertainable consideration. Where a maximum figure is put on unascertainable consideration that does not make it eligible for the instalment option.

Unascertainable

[13.7] The other form of deferred consideration is unascertainable consideration. This is consideration which cannot be calculated with absolute certainty at the date of the transaction because of some variable or contingency. This is usually referred to as a 'chose in action' and is calculated in accordance with the principle established in the case of *Marren (Inspector of Taxes) v Ingles* [1980] 3 All ER 95.

The decision in this tax case applies where the sale involves some right to future consideration and this cannot be calculated with certainty. The consideration to be brought into account is based on the valuation at the time of disposal. This is added to any other consideration received as part of the transaction. Tax immediately becomes payable on that combined total to the extent that a gain arises. This right to future income is in itself a new asset. When the right is subsequently satisfied, the amount received is treated as a capital sum derived from assets (TCGA 1992, s 22).

The difficulties in dealing with these kinds of payments are:

- *The valuation.* A value needs to be put on the right to acquire the future consideration.
- *Entrepreneurs' relief.* Where ER is available on a sale, there is an expectation that ER will be available on the future sum. This will not be the case. ER may be available on the gain arising on the initial calculation but it will never be available if there is an open gain when the chose in action is satisfied. The satisfaction of the right cannot be 'a material disposal of a business asset'. However, the 20% tax rate (28% for disposals prior to 6 April 2016 for a non-basic rate taxpayer) will apply.

Example

Robert sold shares in Bucolin Ltd in 2011/12 for £2m, with a further sum being payable dependent on Bucolin Ltd's results. HMRC agreed that the contingent right was worth £100,000 at the date of the disposal.

In 2015/16, £300,000 becomes payable to Robert under the right. In 2011/12, Robert is taxed on £2m plus £100,000. In 2015/16, a gain arises on the 'chose in action' amount received £300,000.

Value of right when received = £100,000.

Gross gain = £200,000 (£300,000 – £100,000), taxable in 2015/16

What if Robert had received £300,000 of cash in 2011/12 plus a contingent right of up to £2m? If the right was valued at £1.7m at the date of the disposal, the consideration for 2011/12 would be the £300,000 initial payment plus the market value of right to future consideration of £1,700,000.

Total consideration = £2,000,000 (£300,000 + £1,700,000).

Suppose that in 2015/16 the amount ultimately received for the contingent consideration was £1m. A capital loss would arise.

Amount received = £1,000,000 (value of right of £1,700,000 – loss of £700,000).

Under TCGA 1992, s 279A if a loss arises on a *Marren v Ingles* type transaction an election can be made for the loss to be treated as if it had arisen in the year in which the disposal was made. This means that the taxpayer can go back and recalculate the gain and obtain a refund of tax.

The lack of ER on this contingent consideration has already been referred to above. Where there is a disposal of shares and the future consideration is contingent, there is the temptation to knock down the value of the right to that future sum so as to reduce the tax at the outset. However, where the consideration is brought into the calculation in the year in which the disposal is made, ER on the disposal will apply. Therefore, if the share disposal is a qualifying business disposal, this will apply to the value placed on the contingent consideration. The right to that future consideration is a new asset so ER will not be available when it is subsequently satisfied. Therefore, the valuation needs to be considered very carefully. The assumption that the earnout is an arbitrary figure could lead to an increase in the tax rate. Conversely, using an abnormally inflated valuation to maximise ER entitlement may be challenged by HMRC.

> **Planning point**
> A proper valuation should be carried out on the earnout to ensure that the benefit of ER is maximised.

Contingent liabilities

[13.8] Where there are contingent liabilities on a sale, these cannot be brought into the capital gains tax computation at the time of the disposal. TCGA 1992, s 49 states that no deduction can be taken for a contingent liability. However, where a contingent liability subsequently becomes enforceable, a claim can be made for an adjustment to the computation so that a tax refund can be made. The most common type of adjustment is where a payment is made under a warranty or an indemnity by the vendor. Their disposal consideration should be adjusted and the tax refunded to the vendor. No time limit is specified in s 49 so the default time limit of four years applies. For example, if there is a contingent liability adjustment for a sale in 2017/18 the taxpayer has until 5 April 2022 to make a claim. This is relevant as most sale and purchase agreements have a six-year window for claims meaning that there is a possibility that relief may not be available for a contingent liability.

Consideration becoming irrecoverable

[13.9] Where consideration which was deferred becomes irrecoverable, the vendor can revise the original proceeds to reflect the fact that the consideration is irrecoverable TCGA 1992, s 48. Under self-assessment, the taxpayer needs to demonstrate that some part of the consideration has become irrecoverable. If any part of the consideration proves to be irrecoverable and the claim is made, the taxpayer can get a refund of tax. Where consideration is payable in foreign currency, that currency is brought into account at its value as at the date of the disposal. Where the value of the currency subsequently falls, so that the amount received is actually less than the value brought into account, the shortfall is not irrecoverable consideration and no claim can be made under TCGA 1992, s 48.

Planning point

Structuring a sale where part of the consideration is ascertainable but deferred and contingent on results, can be a more straightforward way to proceed with a sale than using an earn out which requires a valuation. Relief under TCGA 1992, s 48 can be considered for any consideration which ultimately becomes irrecoverable due to results.

Deductibility of payments

[13.10] In the case of *Blackwell*, the deductibility of payments came under scrutiny. The FTT had originally allowed a deduction under TCGA 1992, s 38(1)(b) for a payment of £17.5m in computing Mr Blackwell's capital gain on the disposal of his shares in Blackwell Publishing (Holdings) Limited ('BP Holdings'). The UT overturned this decision and the Court of Appeal agreed with the UT.

In 2003, following an unsuccessful takeover attempt by the Taylor and Francis Group plc ('Taylor and Francis'), Mr Blackwell entered into an agreement with Taylor and Francis to promote their offer in return for £1m.

In 2006, following a much more attractive offer from John Wiley & Sons Inc ('Wiley'), Mr Blackwell paid £17.5m and Wiley paid £7.5m to Taylor and

Francis to be released from certain obligations he had undertaken in 2003 in relation to his shares in BP Holdings. This was done in order to avoid any potential litigation from Taylor and Francis and in order for the Wiley deal to go through.

Shortly after making that payment he disposed of those shares to Wiley. In the FTT HMRC argued that the £25m claimed by Mr Blackwell as a deduction from the consideration received on the disposal of his shares in BP Holdings was not allowable under TCGA 1992, s 38(1)(b).

The Tribunal considered that the £17.5m had been incurred on the shares for the purpose of enhancing their value. Mr Blackwell believed that the payment would enhance the value of his shares because it would enable the higher bid to be accepted.

The Tribunal also found that, although the expenditure had not changed the 'nature' of the shares (as the rights attaching to them remained the same), it was reflected in the 'state' of the shares and so that the conditions of s 38 were satisfied. The argument was as to whether the £17.5m payment was allowable for capital gains tax purposes, focused on breaking down s 38(1)(b) of the TCGA 1992 into 'two limbs'.

The first limb relates to expenditure being reflected in the state or nature of the asset. The second limb relates to the establishment, preservation or defence of title to, or to a right over the asset.

The UT considered that when taking into account the 'first limb' of s 38(1)(b), that at the time of the disposal, the state or nature of the shares did not reflect the money paid under the 2006 agreement. Since the shares were not changed by the 2006 agreement, its state or nature could not have altered.

When considering the 'second limb' of the legislation, the UT concluded that Mr Blackwell did not establish, preserve or defend any right over the shares. The 2006 agreement enabled Mr Blackwell to exercise rights relating to his shares but it did not create or establish such rights and as such, the 'asset' remained the same. The appeal was therefore allowed, and the expenditure incurred by Mr Blackwell was not deductible for CGT purposes. The Court of Appeal dismissed the taxpayer's appeal and agreed with the UT that the asset was the bundle of rights and obligations that a buyer acquired, not the bundle of rights and obligations personal to the seller. The exclusivity agreement was personal to the taxpayer therefore the payment was not reflected in the state or nature of the shares (*Blackwell v Revenue and Customs Comrs* [2017] EWCA Civ 232, [2017] 4 All ER 188, [2017] 4 WLR 164).

The deductibility of expenditure for CGT purposes was also considered (among other points) in the case of *John Arthur Day and Amanda Jane Dalgety v HMRC* [2015] UKFTT 139. The taxpayers sought a deduction for painting and decorating as enhancement costs under s 38. HMRC accepted that the costs had been incurred but did not accept that the costs were reflected in the state or nature of the property at the time of disposal. The Tribunal did not accept HMRC's view and found that on the balance of probabilities that the state of the walls and woodwork was such that the painting and filling of the walls etc contributed to increasing the market value of the property.

On the sale of a business the nature of any expenditure incurred to facilitate the sale will need to be considered carefully to ensure that it falls within the provisions of s 38(1)(b) of the TCGA 1992.

This decision could have an impact on transactions where the state or nature of an asset is not changed as a result of the expenditure, and does not have any impact on the owner's rights in relation to the asset in question.

Consideration other than cash

[**13.11**] Paying cash for a business is high risk, and many purchasers will opt for payment in shares or in loan notes. Where shares or loan notes are given in exchange for the sale of shares, the gain can be deferred by the vendor if the conditions of TCGA 1992, s 135 are met. TCGA 1992, s 135 applies where a company issues shares or debentures to a person in exchange for shares or debentures in another company.

The share-exchange rules apply in the following circumstances:

(1)　where company B holds, or, as a result of the exchange, will hold, more than 25% of the ordinary share capital of company A;

(2)　where company B issues shares or debentures in exchange for shares as a result of a general offer made to members of company A or any class of members of company A and the offer is made on a condition such that, if it were satisfied, company B would have control over company A;

(3)　where company B holds, or, in consequence of the exchange, will hold, the greater part of the voting power of company A.

Where one of the above three circumstances is met, the rules on share reorganisations within TCGA 1992, ss 127–135 apply such that the shares received by the vendor take over the history of the shares given up by the vendor. The rules on the share-for-share exchange cannot apply if the transaction is not effected for bona fide commercial reasons or if one of the main reasons for the transaction is the avoidance of liability to capital gains tax or corporation tax. For this reason, it is important that the decision for loan notes is driven by the purchaser rather than the vendor. In relation to a person who does not hold more than 5% of the shares in the vendor company, the bona fide and tax-avoidance tests do not apply.

Where the shares are exchanged for shares in another company, the key point for a shareholder will be whether or not a future disposal of the shares will be a qualifying business disposal for ER purposes. The ER rules give some flexibility. If the disposal of the original shares would have qualified for ER but the gain on a later disposal may not qualify, TCGA 1992, s 169Q allows the taxpayer to make a claim so that the shares for share rules do not apply so the disposal comes into charge with the benefit of ER. A claim is likely to be made where the vendor shareholder will hold less than 5% of the issued share capital in the takeover company and is not going to be an employee in the business.

There is no definition of an employee within the ER legislation. The rules merely state that 'the individual is an officer or employee of the company, or (if the company is a member of a trading group) of one or more companies which are members of the trading group (TCGA 1992, s 169I(6)(b). The legislation does not use the terms full-time or part-time employee, so there is no minimum requirement as to the number of hours the individual must work per week in the company. In other tax provisions, HMRC has used the term 'full-time working officer or employee', and this is taken to be somebody required in their capacity as an officer or employee to devote substantially the whole of his time to the service of the company. HMRC practice has taken this to be at least three-quarters of normal working hours. If the legislation meant full-time, this would have been included within the definition. Also, there is no requirement for the role to be at senior or management level. So, provided the employment is genuine, the employee test for ER will be met. It is very important that the vendor has a real role within the business and is seen as an employee or officer by both staff and outsiders. The best way to deal with the employment situation is for the purchaser to put an employment contract in place, and this should detail the work which the employee must carry out. Where the shares received on a takeover are restricted, there may be a requirement for the shareholder to enter into a ITEPA 2003, s 431 election. Further details on this are below.

Where the shares are exchanged for loan notes, the question is whether or not the loan note is a qualifying corporate bond (QCB) or a non-qualifying corporate bond (non-QCB). A QCB is exempt from capital gains tax in accordance with TCGA 1992, s 115. A QCB is defined in TCGA 1992, s 117 as 'any asset representing a loan relationship of a company'. This generally means securities which were issued by a company to raise debt finance. The corporate bond will be treated as a security provided:

(a)   the debt represents and has at all times represented a normal commercial loan; and

(b)   the loan is expressed in sterling and no provision has been made for a conversion into, or redemption in, a currency other than sterling.

Where QCBs are issued to the shareholder in exchange for shares, they are excluded under TCGA 1992, s 135, but hold-over is available under TCGA 1992, s 116. Section 116 applies the reorganisation rules. The effect is that the capital gain is deferred until the QCBs are redeemed. Where the QCBs become worthless, the shareholder could find himself having to pay a capital gains tax liability without receiving any cash. For this reason, many vendor shareholders will only accept QCBs where these are bank guaranteed.

It is not possible to claim ER and defer a gain – the vendor must choose between claiming ER and paying tax at 10% upfront, or deferring the gain and paying tax at 20% when the deferred gain comes into charge.

Non-QCBs are loan notes that do not meet the conditions for a QCB. A common way to convert a QCB to a non-QCB was to have a currency-conversion clause or an option to convert the loan note into shares. However, following the decision in *Astall & Edwards v HMRC* [2009] EWCA Civ 1010, it is possible that HMRC could challenge the effectiveness of a currency conversion clause, so specialist advice should be taken. The advantage of taking a non-QCB is that it is treated as a security so that the non-QCB takes on the history of the original shares. This means that there is the possibility of ER on a future redemption. Unlike a QCB, if the non-QCB subsequently becomes worthless, the shareholder will receive no proceeds and it is likely a loss will arise.

Whether the shareholder opts for the QCBs or non-QCBs will depend on a number of things, including the effective tax rate and the commercial risk associated with the loan notes.

It may be better to receive non-QCBs where:

- the shares in the old company have been held for less than one year and a future disposal could qualify for ER; or
- there is any doubt that the loan notes will not ultimately be redeemed in full — if QCBs are received, even if the full amount is not received on redemption, the whole frozen chargeable gain remains taxable. This is particularly the case where the loan notes are unsecured. With non-QCBs, the proceeds are what are actually received on ultimate redemption.

Where non-QCBs are taken on a transaction the vendor may want to elect under TCGA 1992, s 169Q to disapply the reorganisation rules and trigger the gain now to obtain ER.

As mentioned above, it may be possible to convert a QCB into a non-QCB by the inclusion of a foreign-currency clause in the loan agreement. In *Harding v Revenue and Customs Comrs* [2007] SWTI 1437, SCD the taxpayer tried to argue that the non-QCBs which were received on a sale became QCBs following the lapse of a foreign-currency option in the original loan notes. The taxpayer was unsuccessful in arguing that the loan notes had become QCBs. Had he been successful, this certainly would have changed the way in which loan notes were used, as the redemption would not have given rise to a tax charge and there would be no deferred gain to come into charge.

Shares or loan notes can also be used to satisfy an earn-out. Cash earn-outs were discussed above, and the main point was that any deferred cash consideration is taxable in the year of disposal. Where the earn-out is to be satisfied in loan notes or in shares, TCGA 1992, s 138A applies the rules of s 135 so that no immediate gain arises on the shareholder. The application of the rules is automatic, but the shareholder can elect for the rules not to apply. The vendor shareholder is likely to make this election if ER is not likely to be available on a future disposal.

Sample wording for s 138A election:

On [date] I sold my holding of [x] ordinary shares in [company name] to [purchaser] for consideration that included the right to an earn-out, to be calculated by reference to future profits and to be satisfied in [ordinary shares OR loan notes] in [purchaser] on [dates].

In accordance with the provisions of section 138A of TCGA 1992, I elect to disapply section 127 of TCGA 1992 in relation to the earn-out right. I wish to bring the value of the earn-out right (estimated at £x) into the computation of the gain on disposal of my shares and claim entrepreneurs' relief on that gain.

Please acknowledge receipt and acceptance of this election by signing, dating and returning the enclosed copy.

A pitfall to watch out for on these earn-outs is that in relation to employment-related securities. Where the earn-out is clearly part of the sale consideration, there should be no risk that the amounts will be brought into charge as earnings from employment. HMRC has listed a number of key indicators which it considers important in determining whether an earn-out is for the sale consideration rather than remuneration.

- The sale agreement demonstrates that the earn-out is part of the valuable consideration given for the shares in the old company.
- The value received from the earn-out reflects the value of the shares given up.
- Where the vendor continues to be employed in the business, the earn-out is not in any way linked to him continuing in the employment.
- Where the vendor continues to be employed, the earn-out is not conditional upon future employment beyond a reasonable requirement to stay to protect the value of the business being sold.
- Where the vendor continues to be employed, there are no personal performance targets included in the earn-out.
- Non-employees or former employees receive the earn-out on the same terms as employees remaining.

Therefore, it seems that where the earn-out is not in any way linked to employment, there is no risk that the amounts will be taxed as employment income. HMRC accepts that it may be necessary for the vendor to continue to be employed within the business and will not link the earn-out where the period for which he must remain as an employee is reasonable. There is no clarification by what is meant by reasonable, however. Each business would have to be looked at according to its own facts, and the length of time would vary accordingly. Some businesses would have a longer hand-over period than others.

In addition to the points listed above, other factors which HMRC cites as being relevant include:

- negotiations between the seller and buyer as to the level of the earn-out;
- any clearances obtained which demonstrate the bona fide nature of the transactions; and
- any evidence that future bonuses or remuneration would be rolled into the sales consideration.

If it transpires that the earn-out is partly deferred consideration for the shares and partly linked to remuneration and the reward for services, an apportionment will need to be made. HMRC accepts that this can be on a just and reasonable basis.

Clearances are required under TCGA 1992, s 138 in respect of the exchange of shares and in addition, where cash is involved, clearance is required under the transactions in securities legislation (ITA 2007, s 701).

Planning point

Where the vendor has taken loan notes and it transpires that the full amount may not be redeemed, the taxpayer can gift them to charity and prevent the deferred gain coming into charge. The rules for transferring assets on a no gain/no loss basis to charity are contained in TCGA 1992, s 257. Revenue Interpretation 23 extends these rules to cover situations where non-QCBs are gifted. For the taxpayer, doing this with QCBs can eliminate a tax charge which would become payable irrespective of the fact that the vendor has not received the proceeds.

Management buy-outs

[13.12] The sale of the business will not always take place to a third party. In many cases, the management will carry out a management buy-out to obtain control of the business. The vendor shareholder may stay involved with the business and hold some shares going forward. A management buy-out is achieved by the management establishing a new company. The new company makes an offer to acquire the shares in the existing company. Where the management have shares in the existing company, they would exchange their shares, while the exiting shareholder would take cash or perhaps cash and shares. In many cases, the main shareholder will not be exiting completely and will obtain a percentage in the new company. Where the vendor is not stepping back completely from the business, it is important that the full level of involvement and the extent of the shareholding is detailed in the clearance application for the transaction. Where HMRC believes that the vendor is not giving up sufficient interest, they may give clearance under the share-for-share exchange provisions while refusing clearance under the transactions in securities provisions. For example, where a vendor shareholder has 100% of the business and a new company is set up by management so that the management may take 20% of the company with the vendor shareholder having 80% in the new company, HMRC is highly unlikely to give clearance for this under the transactions-in-securities rules, particularly now with the fundamental change of control test which has been amended with effect for transactions on or after 6 April 2016. However, if the vendor shareholder was reducing his interest to below 50%, HMRC is more likely to give clearance. However, there must be some degree of stepping back by the vendor shareholder and he should give up some control or at least have contracts in place to give up this control in the future. Transactions-in-securities does not apply to circumstances where after the transaction the shareholder holds directly or indirectly 25% or less of the company.

The new company can borrow money to effect the transaction, and this can be borrowed from either the shareholders or from a third party, usually a bank.

Where the money is borrowed from a bank, the new company will have a loan and the repayments may be financed by dividends from the old company. This creates an active company for the purposes of the associated company rules. Loans from the target company to the new company should be avoided as this can trigger a tax charge under the loan to participator rules as outlined in Chapter 2 'Loans to shareholders'. Where there is only bank interest being paid out of the new company, this company will have a non-trading loan relationship credit. This can be group relieved against the old company where there is a 75% relationship.

When a management buy-out is carried out, the intention is often to hive up the business of the old company to the new company to get around the associated companies point. The normal sequence of events is that the company is acquired and the trade is hived up immediately. Although this could be within a matter of minutes (or seconds), HMRC is very insistent that those companies would be associated during the period even though one was only active for a few moments. Management buy-out teams need to be aware of this point in their first year of taking over the business. With the reduction in the full rate of corporation tax this will become of less significance.

Where there is a hive up of the business there is a loss of tax relief for the amount paid for the shares.

Borrowings by the employees

[13.13] Where the management of the company borrow to put money into the business, they will seek to have interest relief for the amounts borrowed. Interest relief will only be available where the employees have:

- a material interest in the company; or
- they work for the greater part of their time in the actual management or conduct of the business of the company.

The rules on the interest relief are contained in ITA 2007 ss 392–395 in relation to relief for loans taken out to acquire an interest in or make a loan to a close company. Where the loan is to acquire an interest in or make a loan to an employee-controlled-company, the rules are contained in ITA 2007 ss 396, 397.

A material interest is defined as controlling 5% of the ordinary share capital of the company. This takes into account the rights of any associates.

Many employees will seek to get relief because they spend the greater part of their time in the actual management or conduct of the company. This test is very narrow and is applied at the highest level. The terms are interpreted strictly; the shareholder must have a real say in the running of the business. The idea is that the relief is limited to those who have a significant stake, whether as a shareholder or by having significant managerial or technical responsibility in the company. The key point is that the shareholder must be involved in the overall running and policy-making of the company as a whole. Managerial or technical responsibility in one particular area is not sufficient.

The cap for income tax reliefs may restrict tax relief on the borrowings where large sums are borrowed.

Employee Ownership

[13.14] Finance Act 2014 introduced a new, beneficial tax regime to apply to qualifying disposals to a new class of Employee Ownership Trust ('EOT'). These rules offer business owners who are not necessarily looking for a third-party purchaser an attractive exit route, which offers them the opportunity to realise value from their companies without incurring tax charges.

Qualifying criteria

[13.15] TCGA 1992, s 236H sets out a number of criteria that must be satisfied before a disposal can qualify for relief under this regime.

At the beginning of the tax year in which the disposal is made, the EOT must not have had a 'controlling interest' (defined in TCGA 1992, s 236M as ownership of more than 50% of the ordinary share capital or 50% of the economic rights) in the company which issued the shares in respect of which relief is being claimed ('the Issuer'). For relief to be claimed, the EOT must have a controlling interest at the end of the tax year. In addition, from the point at which the EOT first acquires a controlling interest in the Issuer, the EOT must continue to hold that controlling interest until the end of the tax year.

At the time of the disposal and for the remainder of the tax year after the disposal is made, the Issuer must be a trading company or the holding company of a trading group and the trust which purchases the shares must meet the 'all employee benefit requirement' set out in TCGA 1992, ss 236J to 236L.

In addition to the relatively standard requirement that the Issuer is a trading company, the legislation also stipulates that the make-up of the workforce must be balanced away from people who are participators in the Issuer or are connected to participators (in this context, 'participator' takes the wider meaning set out in CTA 2010, s 454, but is limited to participators holding or entitled to more than 5%, and 'connected' has its usual meaning). In order for the Issuer to meet these requirements TCGA 1992, s 236N stipulates that the ratio of employees who are participators, or are connected with participations, to employees who are neither must be less than 2:5.

Finally, the relief is a one-off: it can only be claimed in one tax year: if the transferor or any person connected with the transferor has disposed of shares in the Issuer or in any company that is a member of the same group as the Issuer and claimed relief under the Employee Ownership rules in a previous tax year, no further claims can be made in future years.

The EOT

[13.16] If a company wishes to set up a new trust to act as an EOT, the deed must meet a number of conditions:

- the trust must only apply assets of the trust in such a way that benefits eligible employees on the same terms;
- the trustees must not have the power to use the trust assets to create a new trust or to transfer the assets to another trust (although there is an exception for transfers of assets to other qualifying EOTs);
- the trustees must not have power to make loans to beneficiaries; and
- the trust's powers of amendment must prevent changes to the trust which would mean that it no longer met these conditions.

The restrictions on the making of loans and the creation of new trusts seem understandable in the light of the rules on Disguised Remuneration, which were aimed at stopping the widespread use of EBTs for tax planning involving loans and the creation of sub-funds.

In the context of the legislation, an eligible employee will be any person who is an officer or employee of either the Issuer or a company that is part of the same group as the Issuer, other than an 'excluded participator'.

The new legislation follows the IHT rules in IHTA 1984, s 13 at this point and defines an excluded participator as someone who is entitled to more than 5% of any class of shares that are part of the ordinary share capital or who would be entitled to more than 5% of the proceeds on a winding up. In addition, persons connected with a 5% participator are also excluded from benefit. As with the IHT legislation, the rules contain a 'look back' provision, which excludes anyone who was a participator in the ten years preceding the date on which assets became comprised in the trust.

The rules in TCGA 1992, s 236K, which determine whether benefits are provided on the same terms, also have an origin in existing legislation, in this case the rules on Share Incentive Plans in the SIP Code of ITEPA 2003: the provision of benefits may be varied from employee to employee only by reference to each individual's remuneration, or to their length of service, or to the hours that they work. If the trustees use any other criteria to discriminate between employees, then they will not meet the requirements of the test.

It is possible for existing trusts to be treated as meeting the all-employee benefit requirement. TCGA 1992, s 236L allows dispositions to existing trusts to qualify for relief provided that on 10 December 2013:

- the trust was already in existence;
- IHTA 1984, s 86 applied to the trust; and
- the trustees were entitled to more than 10% of the ordinary share capital of the Issuer, were able to exercise at least 10% of the voting rights and their economic entitlement to dividends and capital represented at least 10% of the total (and there were no arrangements in place to take these rights away without the trustees' permission).

If the trust meets these requirements, then a disposal to the trust can qualify for relief provided that in the twelve months before the disposal, the trustees have not:

- used any of the trust property for the benefit of employees, unless their use of the trust assets would have met the terms set out in TCGA 1992, s 236K;

- created a new trust using any of the existing trust's assets or transferred assets to another trust;
- made loans to beneficiaries.

For existing trusts, the 10 year look-back period to determine whether someone should be treated as a participator, based on historic shareholdings, is not linked to the date on which the trust was first funded, but instead runs to 10 December 2013.

In practice, many of the EBTs established by OMBs which hold shares go for long periods without undertaking any transactions at all; it may not be difficult for a disposal to an existing trust to qualify for relief under these rules.

The relief

[13.17] The EOT regime offers a number of tax reliefs: shareholders who make a qualifying disposal to an EOT are treated as having disposed of their shares on a no-gain, no-loss basis, effectively exempting them from CGT. The IHT rules are also relaxed in relation to transfers of property to a qualifying EOT, making it possible to fund the EOT to make share purchases. There are also benefits that can accrue to the workforce of working for an EOT controlled company, which are discussed at **[10.48]** above.

There is an important caveat: the likelihood is that many shareholders in the OMB environment will be exposed to the rules on employment related securities in ITEPA 2003, Part 7; if the shares that are sold to the EOT are restricted securities, or if they are sold for more than their market value, the new legislation on EOTs will not prevent charges from arising under the ITEPA rules.

It should be borne in mind that the legislation also contains claw-back provisions; under TCGA 1992, s 236O the relief is withdrawn if, during the tax year following the year in which the disposal of shares took place:

- the Issuer ceases to meet the trading requirement;
- the trust ceases to meet the all-employee benefit requirement or loses its controlling interest in the Issuer;
- the trustees use the trust assets in a way that breaches the all-employee benefit requirement; or
- the ratio of employees or office-holders who are treated as participators and those who are not increases to more than 2:5.

If one of these 'disqualifying events' occurs, the original disposal of shares will need to be re-calculated as if it was an ordinary sale of shares (albeit, that it may be necessary to consider whether TCGA 1992, s 17 should apply).

The objective behind these claw-back provisions is to ensure that, as far as possible, transferors are genuinely giving up their control of the company and leaving behind a viable company, not an enterprise so stripped of cash and assets that it fails in the next year.

In the author's view, the EOT rules provide an interesting alternative for business owners who wish to exit, but see no third party purchaser coming forward within a reasonable time-scale. The combination of reliefs for transferors and for employees of EOT controlled businesses may make this an attractive approach for both companies and their owners and advisers should ensure that this approach to seeking an exit is raised with owners in the future.

Options

[13.18] Sometimes, instead of selling the company outright, the owner may decide to grant an option over his shares. At the same time, an option could be put in place — a put option, by which he could place his shares on the purchaser at some date in the future. An exchange of options does not constitute a disposal for capital gains tax purposes. The disposal happens on the exercise of the share option in accordance with TCGA 1992, s 144. Where this is combined with an intention to leave the UK, HMRC will seek to treat the arrangements as a sham and argue that the disposal was at the time the cross option arrangements were entered into.

Share-for-share exchanges and employment-related securities

[13.19] When dealing with a share-for-share exchange, the common mistake is to focus on the capital gains tax position and the roll-over position. Very often, the income tax position is forgotten or ignored. Where the shares being exchanged (or received) are restricted securities, tax charges could inadvertently be triggered for the employees and for proprietors, who may not consider themselves exposed to the employment related securities regime. If the employees have not received any cash on the deal, this can be a big shock.

The income tax implications depend on whether an election has been made: if valid elections have been made under ITEPA 2003, s 431(1) the restricted securities rules should not give rise to any tax charges.

No charge will arise if the share exchange falls within either ITEPA 2003, s 429 or s 430A. To qualify for relief under s 429 if a complete class of share is exchanged and either:

- the company is employee controlled by shares of that class; or
- the majority of shares of that class are not owned by employees.

ITEPA 2003, s 430A provides a more generous measure of relief where restricted securities are disposed of and at least part of the consideration given for the old securities is represented by new restricted securities. Provided that the unrestricted market value of the new shares does not exceed the unrestricted market value of the new shares at the time of the exchange of shares, the exchange will not be treated as a chargeable event for the purposes of the restricted securities rules and any future tax charges will be calculated as if the employees still held the old securities.

Where the consideration for the restricted securities is made up of a combination of new restricted securities and either cash or unrestricted shares, the transaction will be treated as two separate transactions: one transaction where the consideration is wholly restricted securities, to which s 430A will apply, and a separate transaction where the consideration is wholly cash or unrestricted securities, to which s 427(3)(c) will apply.

Separate rules apply to shares that were acquired before 16 April 2003.

Exchange scenario 1

[**13.20**] Restricted shares acquired on or after 16 April 2003 are exchanged for new restricted shares with no election on the old shares.

Provided that the UMV of the new shares is not greater than the UMV of the old shares, s 430A will apply and no chargeable event will arise.

Exchange scenario 2

[**13.21**] Restricted shares were acquired on or after 16 April 2003 and an election under ITEPA 2003, s 431(1) was made. The shares were exchanged for new restricted shares. Although s 430A would prevent a charge arising, the fact that the election has been made means that, ITEPA 2003, ss 425–430 do not apply, and no charge would arise under the restricted securities rules.

This assumes that the exchange is for the same value of shares. However, if the value of the new restricted securities is more than the value of the shares given up, there is likely to be a tax charge, and the employee needs to decide whether another s 431 election should be made.

Exchange scenario 3

[**13.22**] Conditional shares acquired before 16 April 2003 are exchanged for new shares:

- if the roll-over provisions for company reorganisations in TCGA 1992, s 127 apply, no charge will be crystallised unless the new shares are unrestricted – in which case a charge can arise under ITEPA 2003, Part 7, Chapter 4, as originally enacted, will arise;
- in any other case, the disposal of the old shares creates a charge under the old TA 1988, s 140A provisions. If the new shares are restricted securities, consideration will need to be given to making an election under s 431 within fourteen days of the exchange of shares.

Planning point

Where the vendor has sold the business and realised the cash and then wants to provide for his family, he may want to set up a trust. If a trust is settled with cash, a lifetime charge of 20% will arise to the extent that the amounts settled exceed the nil-rate band (assuming this is available — if not, the whole amount settled could be subject to a lifetime charge). Instead, the vendor could use the proceeds, or some of the proceeds, to

---

invest in assets qualifying for BPR. Those assets could be transferred into the trust, and BPR would be available. The trust can then immediately sell the assets and the shareholders will have established a trust without incurring a tax charge.

Key points

[13.23] Key points to note are as follows:

- deferral relief is not available where an unincorporated business is sold to a company in exchange for shares so consider the use of incorporation relief;
- ascertainable deferred consideration is taxable in full in the year of disposal, but an instalment payment option may be available;
- ER is not available on future sums where deferred consideration is unascertainable;
- contingent liabilities cannot be taken into account at the time of disposal, but a tax refund can be claimed when the liability becomes enforceable;
- watch the tax avoidance test where a vendor dictates the use of loan notes;
- watch the possibility of earn-out consideration being treated as remuneration if not correctly structured; and
- in management buyout situations it is important not to overlook the employment-related securities position for employees and to make elections where appropriate in respect of restricted shares.

Becoming non-resident

[13.24] Quite often the vendor of a business will be planning to retire abroad once the sale is completed and a question is often raised whether becoming non-resident in the UK before the sale is undertaken would lead to a substantial tax saving. The rules on breaking UK tax residence are governed by the statutory residence test.

The Statutory Residence Test

[13.25] Below is an overview of the Statutory Residence Test (SRT).

The first step in determining an individual's residence position is to establish whether they are an arriver or a leaver. These are defined as follows:

- Arriver – Someone coming to the UK who **was not** resident in the UK for any of the previous three years.
- Leaver – Someone leaving the UK who **was** resident in the UK for any of the previous three years.

Often the rules in relation to arrivers are slightly more relaxed than those for leavers.

The SRT is designed in three parts, and works sequentially so once a condition is satisfied and the status is determined then there is no need to progress any further. Each test is to be applied to a single fiscal year only. The three arms of the test are outlined below.

The Automatic Overseas Test (AOT). The conditions are:

- not UK resident in any of the last three years and less than 46 days in the UK in the current year (the First AOT);
- resident in the UK in any of the last three years and less than 16 days in the UK this year (the Second AOT); and
- works sufficient hours overseas (the Third AOT).

The First and Second AOTs are fairly straight-forward. The Third AOT is more complex. In order to meet the Third AOT an individual must:

- work sufficient hours overseas (broadly 35 hours per week);
- have no significant breaks from overseas work during the year;
- the number of days on which he does more than three hours work in the UK is less than 31;
- spend less than 91 days in the UK; and
- not be subject to the exclusion for some transportation workers eg some workers on ships and aircraft.

A significant break from overseas work occurs where at least 31 days go by and not one of those days is a day where the individual does more than three hours overseas work or is a day on which he would have done more than three hours work had he not been on annual leave, sick leave or parenting leave.

The Automatic UK Test (AUT). The conditions are:

- present in the UK for 183 days or more in the current year (the First AUT);
- only on main home or homes in the UK (the Second AUT); and
- in full-time employment in the UK (the Third AUT).

Like the day count tests in relation to the AOT, the First AUT is fairly straight-forward. The Second and Third AUTs are more complex.

In order to meet the Second AUT the individual must meet the following conditions:

- have a UK home during all or part of the year;
- spend 30 days in that home during the year; and
- there is a period of 91 consecutive days in respect of which:
  - the individual has that home;
  - at least 30 days of that period fall within the year; and
  - throughout that 91-day period the individual has no home overseas.

In order to meet the Third AUT the individual must meet the following conditions:

- the individual works sufficient hours in the UK assessed over a period of 365 days (broadly 35 hours per week);
- the individual is not within the exception for certain transportation workers;
- during that period he has no significant breaks from UK work;
- all or part of the 365-day period falls within the relevant year;
- more than 75% of the individuals' work days are in the UK (a work day being one where he does more than three hours work); and
- at least one day which falls within the 365-day period and within the relevant tax year is a UK work day.

In a similar vein to the Third Automatic Overseas Test, a significant break from UK work occurs where at least 31 days go by and not one of those days is a day where the individual does more than three hours UK work or is a day on which he would have done more than three hours work had he not been on annual leave, sick leave or parenting leave.

Where conditions in both of the AOT and AUT are met then the AOT takes precedence.

The Sufficient Ties Test only applies if neither of the above tests are satisfied.

This test works on the basis of a combination of days present in the UK and satisfying certain factors which tie a person to the UK. In essence the greater the days in the UK the fewer factors need to be satisfied to acquire residence. The factors are:

- family is UK resident;
- accommodation is accessible in the UK and is used in the tax year;
- substantive work is done in the UK;
- UK presence in previous years (91 days or more in either of the previous two years); and
- more days spent in the UK than in any other single country in same tax year.

When considering the applicable factors Arrivers can ignore the last tie.

Even if non-UK residence is attained, a tax liability may still arise if prior to departure steps have been taken to avoid any liability to tax and as part of these arrangements non-UK residence is essential to the planning. Two examples of a liability arising are:

(1) a transaction is entered into prior to becoming non-UK resident, which does not give rise to any liability at the time and subsequently HMRC successfully invokes the Transactions in Securities rules to charge the transaction to income tax; or

(2) a disposal of shares is exempted from tax under the provisions of TCGA 1992, s 135 such that new shares or securities are acquired in exchange for the original shares – this exemption may be revoked if the individual then goes non-UK resident and disposes of the shares whilst overseas as seen in the case of *Snell v Revenue and Customs Comrs* [2006] EWHC 3350 (Ch), [2007] STC 1279, 78 TC 294.

On the assumption that residency is broken before any sale of the business occurs, there are still pitfalls to be wary of both in the UK and in the new jurisdiction of residence. UK tax liabilities may still accrue to an individual who has successfully broken their UK fiscal residence and subsequently sold their business. The most likely trap to be caught by is that of realising a gain in the year of departure. The SRT does allow split year treatment to be applied in limited circumstances so that any gains arising after the date of departure are not taxable in the UK. These limited circumstances apply where an individual leaves the UK to:

(1)   Work full time overseas (case 1)
(2)   Accompany their spouse or partner who is leaving the UK to work full time overseas (case 2)
(3)   Set up their only home overseas (case 3).

In relation to each case, there are a number of anti-avoidance rules in place to restrict the circumstances in which split year treatment will apply and careful consideration should be given in each case before relying on split year treatment.

If an individual has successfully broken residence and sold their company in a tax year after the year of departure then the next problem that may arise is that of an early return to the UK. TCGA 1992, section 10A is designed to prevent individuals from leaving the UK temporarily for the sole purpose of realising a tax free capital gain. Section 10A will seek to charge to tax any capital gain realised in a year of non-UK residence on an asset owned by that individual before they departed if their return to the UK is within five years following the year of departure. Any gain caught by this rule is deemed to arise in the year of return, which can give rise to a loss of entrepreneurs' relief.

Planning point

To avoid the loss of Entrepreneurs' Relief (ER) any non-UK resident who realises a gain which qualifies for ER should lodge a protective claim with HMRC by 31 January following the year of realisation. If subsequently they return to the UK and a charge to capital gains tax (CGT) may arise then they may claim the ER in the year the gain is charged to tax. Whilst ER will apply to qualifying shares as well as other assets the avoidance of CGT on the disposal of assets used in a trade in the UK or a UK branch of a foreign trade carried on by an individual will remain subject to CGT on their disposal even where the individual is non-UK resident at the time of disposal. Therefore to avoid this particular problem any unincorporated business should be incorporated before the sale, ensuring that the provisions of TCGA 1992, s 162 are satisfied in the process.

VAT on disposal of a business

[13.26] The VAT consequences of disposing of a business vary considerably according to the way the business is sold. For example:

•   Disposal of shares in the company:

Such a disposal is usually exempt. However, zero-rating might apply if the shares are sold to a purchaser belonging overseas, entitling the vendor to recover VAT on costs of disposal such as professional fees. In many cases, though, the one-off disposal of shares (eg by a family member) will not constitute a business activity for the shareholder and will therefore fall outside the scope of VAT.

- Sale of assets by the business:
  Such supplies are subject to the normal VAT rules and most assets will be subject to VAT at the standard rate. Selling to overseas customers can attract zero-rating in certain circumstances.
- Transferring the assets of the business as a going concern:
  If the assets amount to a going concern and if the transaction meets all the relevant criteria, the sale will qualify as a transfer of going concern (TOGC) and will automatically fall outside the scope of VAT. Anti-avoidance rules apply where property is transferred as part of the assets.

Key points

[13.27] Key points to note are as follows:

- Any individual who spends less than 16 days in the UK in a tax year will be non-resident.
- A non-UK resident individual will not be taxable on capital gains, but temporary non-residence rules apply to crystallise a tax charge in relation to capital gains where the individual returns to the UK within five complete tax years.
- To avoid the loss of ER a non-resident who qualifies for ER should lodge a protective claim with HMRC by 31 January following the year of realisation.

Chapter 14

Transactions in Securities and Clearances

Introduction

[14.1] The transactions in securities legislation is designed to attack situations where a shareholder benefits from no tax or pays capital gains tax instead of income tax or, in some cases, corporation tax on distributions from a company. In this book we will not consider the transactions in securities legislation relating to corporates, as this is not generally of concern to OMBs. The rules in relation to countering income tax advantages were revised in FA 2010 and again in Finance Act 2016. The number of circumstances was reduced to two; with the old circumstances D and E becoming A and B. The escape clause which previously had a bona fide commercial test and a *no tax avoidance* motive was streamlined so now obtaining a tax advantage must not be the main objective of the transaction. More specifically, the provisions are limited to close companies and there is a let out from the rules where there is a fundamental change of ownership. The provisions for non-corporates are set out in ITA 2007, ss 682–713. (The rules for corporates are contained in CTA 2010, s 731 onwards.) All the references in this chapter are to individuals and ITA 2007.

This anti-avoidance legislation gives HMRC the authority to issue a counter-action notice under s 698 to cancel a tax advantage where there is a transaction in securities. There are some basic requirements which must be met in order for a counteraction to be made:

- the person must be party to a transaction in securities (or two or more transactions);
- the circumstances are covered by s 685 and are not excluded by s 686;
- the main or one of the main purposes of the transactions is to obtain a tax advantage;
- an income tax advantage is actually obtained.

It is clear that the tax advantage must be obtained as a result of the transaction in securities.

What is the purpose of s 698?

[14.2] In general, where there is an income tax advantage, the legislation is designed to treat the consideration on the sale of shares as though it was a distribution.

If there is a charge under s 698 the income received (with no deduction for base cost) is treated as a dividend.

For the purposes of the legislation a person obtains an income tax advantage if the amount of income tax which would be payable on the consideration exceeds the amount of CGT. Historically, income tax rates have been higher than CGT rates and this trend is likely to continue given the proposed increases in the tax on dividends and the reduction in the rates of CGT which took effect from April 2016.

What is a transaction in securities?

[14.3] Transactions in securities are defined in ITA 2007, s 684 as transactions:

' . . . of whatever description, relating to securities, and in particular–

(a) the purchase, sale or exchange of securities,
(b) issuing or securing the issue of new securities,
(c) applying or subscribing for new securities,
(d) altering or securing the alteration of the rights attached to the securities,
(e) a repayment of share capital or share premium, and
(f) a distribution in respect of securities in a winding up.'

Securities include shares and loan stock, and where a company is not limited by shares it includes the interest of a member whatever form that interest should take.

Finance Act 2016 made some fundamental changes to the types of transaction that are treated as transactions in securities, and now includes distributions on winding up a company. Historically, a liquidation on its own was not a transaction in securities. This was supported by case law in *IRC v Laird Group plc* [2003] UKHL 54, [2003] 4 All ER 669, [2003] STC 1349 at 1359, where Lord Millet said:

'The distribution of the undistributed profits of a company in liquidation to its shareholders is not a transaction relating to securities because neither the shares themselves nor the rights attached to them are affected by a payment which merely gives effect to the shareholders' rights; they receive only what is already theirs.'

However where a liquidation was combined with a pre-liquidation agreement or the alteration of share rights it was a transaction in securities. Also the combination of a liquidation and the issue of shares in another company which continues to carry on the business of the liquidated company was a transaction in securities.

Following the changes in Finance Act 2016, even an ordinary liquidation in which a company is wound up once it has completed its business or transferred its business to an unconnected person is within the scope of the transactions in securities anti-avoidance provisions. This means that the persons involved in the transaction have to demonstrate that the main purpose of the transaction is not to obtain an income tax advantage and that no one obtains an income tax advantage as a result of the transaction.

However, as mentioned, the rules can apply to counteract a tax advantage where there is a transaction in securities together with a liquidation. This is what HMRC tried to argue in the case of *Ebsworth v Revenue and Customs* [2009] UKFTT 199 (TC), [2009] SFTD 602 as described below but were unsuccessful as the trade had been sold to an existing company.

HMRC's Company Taxation Manual at 36850 gives some examples, and although these have now been changed, the following example that used to be included gives an indication of the type of transaction that is likely to be caught.

Example

A is the sole shareholder of trading Company X, which has £1m cash representing its undistributed profits. A subscribes for shares in new company, Company Y. Company X transfers its trade and assets (but not the cash) to Company Y, which continues to carry on the trade.

Company X is put into liquidation and the cash paid as a capital distribution to A. This transaction is caught by s 684 so that the cash etc received by A in the liquidation (except to the extent that it represents the return of the amount subscribed for the share capital in X) can be taxed as a distribution.

In the courts, a transaction in securities has been held to include:

- the redemption of securities (*IRC v Parker* [1966] AC 141, [1966] 1 All ER 399, HL);
- the alteration of rights attaching to shares (*IRC v Joiner* [1975] 3 All ER 1050, [1975] 1 WLR 1701, HL); and
- loans by a company to individuals who subsequently acquired the company (*Williams v IRC* [1980] 3 All ER 321).

The following were found not to be transactions in securities:

- payment of a dividend (*RC v Laird Group plc* [2003] UKHL 54); and
- liquidation (*IRC v Joiner* [1975] 3 All ER 1050) (although this has now been superseded by the Finance Act 2016 changes to the definition of transaction in securities, which inserts s 684(2)(f)).

Types of situation

[14.4] The types of situation that would invoke a notice are set out below.

- The payment of a substantial dividend by a company prior to sale of shares in that company together with an agreement whereby some or all of the shareholders waive all, or part of, their dividend rights and in return receive a greater share of the sale proceeds.
- The sale by a significant shareholder in a close company of part of the holding to the trustees of a pension scheme of which he is a member or to the trustees of an EBT where it is funded by contributions from the company.

- The transfer or sale by a company of its assets or business to another company having some or all of the same shareholders followed by a liquidation of the other company whose assets have been acquired. This is particularly in point for shareholders who have tried to cash in on ER by using phoenix arrangements. Such arrangements have also been targeted in Finance Act 2016 by the introduction of a TAAR in Income Tax (Trading and Other Income) Act 2005, s 396B (ITTOIA 2005).

- Receipt of capital consideration by shareholders of a company or group following a demerger or a scheme of reconstruction from the sale or liquidation of one of the demerged companies.

Ebsworth v R&C [2009] FTT 199 (TC)

[14.5] This First-tier Tribunal case concerns a counteraction notice under the predecessor legislation. Mr and Mrs E were separating and Mrs E wanted to exit the business after the trade had ceased. The company was liquidated and the remaining trade (which was virtually worthless) went to Mr E's new company for £1 and the cash in the company was distributed. HMRC sought to tax the amounts received by Mr E as dividends.

The liquidation of the company was not a transaction in securities but HMRC argued that the setting up of the new company was a transaction in securities. As for the tax advantage, HMRC said that there should have been a purchase of own shares to remove Mrs E and then Mr E could have paid a dividend. HMRC denied that the then escape clause applied. HMRC's line of attack was challenged on all parts of s 684 as was:

- as there was no comparator there was no tax advantage;
- if there was a tax advantage it was not as a result of a liquidation and a transaction in securities;
- there was a bona fide commercial reason for the transaction.

HMRC lost on all points. It was found that this was a normal liquidation and not comparable to *IRC v Joiner* [1975] 3 All ER 1050 where there had been a liquidation agreement with a change in share rights.

Circumstances when the legislation applies

[14.6] The circumstances to which the legislation applies in respect of consideration received in connection with a distribution by or assets of a close company are contained in s 685 to the extent that they are not excluded by s 686.

Circumstance A

[14.7] If as a result of a transaction (or transactions) in securities a person receives consideration in connection with:

(a)   the distribution, transfer or realisation of assets of a close company;

(b)   the application of assets of a close company in discharge or liabilities; or

(c)   the direct or indirect transfer of assets of one close company to another close company,

and no income tax is paid on the consideration.

The most common situation caught by Circumstance A is where there is a sale of one company to another company without a fundamental change of control such as that in the case of *CIR v Cleary*, (44 TC 399).

Circumstance B

[14.8] In circumstance B:

•   a person receives consideration in connection with the transaction in securities;
•   two or more close companies are concerned in the transactions, and
•   the person does not bear income tax on the distribution.

Income tax advantage

[14.9] A person obtains an income tax advantage where the amount of income tax which would be payable on the relevant consideration if it was a distribution is more than the CGT arising on that consideration.

Relevant consideration is:

(a)   the value of assets which are available for distribution by way of a dividend by the company;
(b)   or the value of what would have been available apart from anything done by the company; or
(c)   consideration representing the value of trading stock of the company.

Where there is an exchange of shares for loan notes or shares, relevant consideration means any share capital or security issued by a close company which represents the value of assets which are available for distribution or would have been available for distribution but for something done by the company or represents the value of the trading stock.

Maximum charge under s 698

[14.10] ITA 2007, section 687 provides:

'(1)   For the purposes of this Chapter the person obtains an income tax advantage if—

    (a)   the amount of any income tax which would be payable by the person in respect of the relevant consideration if it constituted a qualifying distribution exceeds the amount of any capital gains tax payable in respect of it, or

(b)   income tax would be payable by the person in respect of the relevant consideration if it constituted a qualifying distribution and no capital gains tax is payable in respect of it.

(2)   So much of the relevant consideration as exceeds the maximum amount that could in any circumstances have been paid to the person by way of a qualifying distribution at the time when the relevant consideration is received is to be left out of account for the purposes of subsection (1).'

The provisions in effect provide guidance on the calculation of the income tax advantage by reference to distributable reserves. However at which point should the reserves be looked at? In *CIR v Parker* 43 TC 396 it was the date of redemption to ascertain whether there was a tax advantage. This means that where loan notes are issued, the redemption of the loan notes can be caught even if there were no distributable reserves when the loan notes were issued.

In working out the amount of consideration to be taxed as income the group distributable reserves at the time of the transaction are calculated (s 685(7B)). There is no offset for profit and loss deficits in subsidiaries. The amount taxed as a distribution cannot exceed that amount.

Excluded circumstances

[14.11] The only excluded circumstance is where there is a fundamental change of ownership. This safe haven is for cases where there is a 'real' change of ownership and was introduced to reflect existing HMRC practice. However practitioners will be aware of cases where retention of ownership at much higher levels were accepted by HMRC. Indeed such cases can still get clearance that there will be no counteraction notice where the motive of the transaction is not tax avoidance.

Fundamental change of ownership

[14.12] If immediately before the transaction in securities the person holds shares or an interest in shares in a close company and there is a fundamental change in ownership then the transaction will not be caught by the anti-avoidance provisions. Finance Act 2016 rewrote the fundamental change of ownership provisions by inserting new sub-ss (2) and (3) in place of the former sub-ss (2) to (5).

The key requirement is set out in the new sub-section 3, where the condition to be met is that the original shareholder or original shareholders taken together with any associate or associates:

(a)   do not directly or indirectly hold more than 25% of the ordinary share capital of the close company;

(b)   do not directly or indirectly hold shares in the close company carrying an entitlement to more than 25% of the distributions which may be made by the close company; and

(c)   do not directly or indirectly hold shares in the close company carrying more than 25% of the total voting rights in the close company.

These changes mean that there must now be an economic change in ownership in order to be able to benefit from the automatic let out.

Under the old provisions there was a fundamental change in ownership where the following conditions were met as a result of the transaction and continued to be met for a period of two years.

Condition A: At least 75% of the ordinary share capital of the close company is held beneficially by a person(s) who is/are not connected with the party (and was/were not connected within the previous two years).

And

Condition B: The shares in the close company held by the person/persons carry an entitlement to at least 75% of the distributions which can be made by the company.

And

Condition C: The shares carry at least 75% of the voting rights in the company.

For the purposes of applying this exception the definition of connected in ITA 2007, s 993 (which includes spouse, civil partners, relatives and trustees of particular trusts) and the definition of control in CTA 2010, s 450 should be applied.

This meant that where a company was acquired by a new holding company, and that holding company was not controlled by anyone who was a shareholder of the target company the transactions in securities legislation would not apply to any cash received by the shareholders of the target company as a result of the acquisition by the new holding company.

HMRC has now recognised this weakness in the old legislation and have introduced new provisions, with a single condition in s 686(3). Now, there is a fundamental change of ownership of a close company if, as a result of the transaction, the original shareholder or original shareholders taken together with any associates do not directly or indirectly hold more than 25% of the ordinary share capital of the close company, and do not have a direct or indirect entitlement to more than 25% of the distributions or votes in relation to that company.

As a result, the provisions look through corporate shareholdings to establish the old shareholders' effective interest in the company; there must be a real change in ownership in order to be able to fall into the automatic excluded circumstances.

The commercial test which applied under the legislation prior to the 2010 changes is no longer a let out. This can make it much easier for restructuring which is driven by the purchaser.

Clearances

[14.13] Clearance is available, for any transaction to which the rules may apply, under ITA 2007, s 701. The application can be made before or after a transaction has happened. (Note — this is different to a clearance under TCGA

1992, s 138, which can only be obtained in advance.) Ideally, the clearance should be obtained in advance, because if there is a problem, there is the opportunity to restructure the transaction. If the fundamental change of control test is met no clearance should be submitted as the test is a question of fact.

The legislation which enables the Board to counteract tax avoidance in consequence of a transaction in securities can only be invoked by the Anti-Avoidance Clearance and Counteraction team. Following receipt of the application, HMRC has 30 days in which to respond or request further information. If such further information is not provided within a further 30 days from the notification, or such further time as allowed by HMRC, no further response will be provided by HMRC.

Cancellation of the tax advantage is not part of the self-assessment enquiry regime. The downside of this is that the cancellation can be made within six years after the chargeable period to which the tax advantage relates. The 12-month period under self-assessment does not apply. A discovery assessment does not have to be made under TMA 1970, s 29; neither does negligence have to be proved for the Board of HMRC to invoke a counteraction. This means that an individual taxpayer should complete their returns on the basis which they consider to be correct without having any regard to the transactions in securities provisions.

The change in the rules has shifted the burden of proof; under the old provisions the taxpayer had to prove that the transactions were for bona fide commercial reasons; under the new provisions it is for HMRC to prove that one of the main purposes was to secure a tax advantage.

Getting the clearance application right is key to any transaction. The clearance needs to ensure that the tax reliefs applied for are obtained, and it should provide the instructions to any advisers acting in the transactions. HMRC receives thousands of applications per year, so advisers should make it as straight-forward as possible to provide something that is self-explanatory and provides all the necessary information. The authors have read many clearances over the years which do not provide information on how a transaction is going to be carried out — some have received positive clearance from HMRC. However, any clearance is only as good as the facts which are disclosed, so if material facts are missing, this invalidates the clearance. Similarly, if the clearance letter has a list of steps, it is important that advisers follow these steps. Taking shortcuts can cause tax reliefs to be lost.

In addition to the statutory clearances HMRC has a non-statutory clearance facility which enables businesses to obtain clearance both pre and post transactions. (For pre-transaction, evidence must be supplied to show that the transaction is seriously being considered.) For HMRC to consider the application there must be 'material uncertainty' about the transaction or event, and that the issue must be 'commercially significant'. Essentially the adviser has to dig a hole and then climb out!

This non-statutory clearance facility is intended to be the first port of call for business queries. It is irrelevant whether the technical issue is in connection with the last four Finance Acts or relates to much older legislation. COP 10 applications are still available for non-business matters (ie for the last four Finance Acts). This facility does not replace the statutory clearance mechanism currently available.

For the clearances that are referred to in this book, only one single application is necessary as they are handled on an integrated basis. For example, on a management buy-out there may be clearances for a share-for-share exchange and for transactions in securities.

Clearances should be sent to:

HM Revenue and Customs
CTIS Clearance
S0483
Newcastle NE98 1ZZ

By e-mail: reconstructions@hmrc.gsi.gov.uk.

Where clearances are market sensitive they should be marked as such.

The clearances can be submitted by email; fax – 03000 589802; or by post. A clearance application should only be submitted once. So, for example, if it is faxed or sent via email, another copy should not be sent by post.

Where the application is emailed, the letter should contain a suitable acceptance that the client accepts the risks associated with emails. The appropriate wording is included below in the sample letter.

This sample clearance letter outlines the points which should be included.

Sample clearance letter

[14.14]

HM Revenue and Customs
CTIS Clearance
S0483
Newcastle NE98 1ZZ

Dear Sir

List all the companies involved and abbreviations used in the letter

Applications for advance clearances under:

Section 701 Income Tax Act 2007

Section 748 Corporation Tax Act 2010

Section 1091, 1092 Corporation Tax Act 2010

Section 1044 Corporation Tax Act 2010

Section 138 Taxation of Chargeable Gains Act 1992

We have been instructed by XYZ limited *[add other companies if relevant — for example on a takeover]* and its shareholders to apply for advance clearance under the provisions of section 701 Income Tax Act 2007 ('ITA 2007') *[change section as relevant]* and section 138 Taxation of Chargeable Gains Act 1992 ('TCGA 1992') *[change section as relevant]* in connection with the transactions proposed below.

The proposed transactions are intended as a means of separating the businesses of . . . . /bringing together the businesses of . . . . / exiting a disruptive shareholder . . . . /facilitating a management buy-out etc. *[state what the transaction is trying to achieve]*

In essence the proposals involve the liquidation of . . . . /the exchange of shares . . . . /the acquisition of shares . . . . *[give a brief description of the transaction]*

Clearances are accordingly sought under:

(1)   Section 138 TCGA 1992 *[change section as relevant]* as regards the disposal of shares in XYZ Ltd by the shareholders . . . . in exchange for the issue of shares in Newco; and

(2)   Section 701 ITA 2007 *[change section as relevant]* as regards the transactions in securities under which . . . . all above shares will be disposed.

1 Companies and background

Give background to all the companies and who started them, family involved etc. Give highlights of shareholdings, eg 50% are held by the Smith family and 50% are held by the Adams family.

Keep details of tax references and precise shareholdings to the appendices.

2 The directors' deliberations

Give details of what the issues were for the directors and how they have reached their decision, ie what the problem is and the different ways in which they have thought about solving it.

The Board of Directors believes it is now an appropriate time to restructure the various activities highlighted above. The key reasons for this decision . . . .

The Board has decided that their preferred option would be . . . .

3 Proposed transaction

Give full details of the proposed transactions and all the steps involved. Make reference to the appendices, which should show the proposed transaction in diagram form.

4 Purpose and benefits

Reiterate the purpose and benefits.

5 Clearances sought

We consider that the transactions described above will be carried out for bona fide commercial reasons and that none of them has as their main objective, or one of their main objectives, to enable a tax advantage to be obtained. We seek clearance in accordance with TCGA 1992, s 138 that s 137(1) should have no effect so TCGA 1992, s 135 will not be prevented from applying to the share for share/loan notes, etc, exchange.

We seek clearance under ITA 2007, s 701 that no counteraction notice will be served under ITA 2007, s 698 as the main purpose, or one of the main purposes of the transaction(s) is not to obtain an income tax advantage.

We seek clearance under CTA 2010, s 748 that no counteraction notice will be served under CTA 2010, s 746 as the transaction(s) are effected for genuine commercial reasons and that enabling corporation tax advantages to be obtained is not the main object or one of the main objects of any of the transactions.

We confirm that our client understands and accepts the risks associated with email and that they are happy for you to send information concerning their business or personal details to us by email. We also confirm the email address that we want you to contact us is . . . .

Should you require any clarification on any of the points above or any additional information please contact . . . . on the email or number above.

Yours faithfully.

Appendix 1	Diagram of the group before the transaction
Appendix 2	Diagram of the transaction during the transactions
Appendix 3	Diagram of the transaction after the transaction
Appendix 4	Company details
Appendix 5	Shareholder details (including relative shareholdings and consideration)
Appendix 6	Accounts

Is there a counteraction risk?

- Is the person a party to one or more transactions in securities?
- Will the person obtain an income tax advantage in consequence of the transaction(s)?
- Is either condition A or B outlined above satisfied?
- Is obtaining an income tax advantage the purpose or one of the main purposes of the transaction(s)?

If yes to all the above, does the fundamental change of ownership exception apply? If no then there is a counteraction risk.

Key points

[14.15] Key points to note are as follows:

- the anti-avoidance rules only apply where there is a transaction in securities, in prescribed circumstances, resulting in an income tax advantage;
- the anti-avoidance rules will not apply if it can be shown that there was no tax avoidance objective, or if HMRC takes no action following a statutory declaration, or if a tribunal rules that there is no case for further action;
- clearance applications must contain all relevant information for a clearance to be binding.

Chapter 15

Succession Planning and the Family Business

Introduction

[15.1] If a business is not to be sold during the owner's lifetime, the issue of succession will need to be addressed. Sometimes, the succession route will be clear and a particular child or children will be identified as the future owner/manager. For others, the succession strategy will be less apparent.

A discussion of the practical 'family' issues that would need to be addressed in identifying a successor and, for example, ensuring that he has the ability to manage the business while at the same time ensuring 'equality' with other family members is beyond the scope of this book. What this chapter addresses are the *tax* issues which need to be considered when planning for succession.

The issues will be addressed in the following order:

*   the pros and cons of lifetime gifts of business assets;
*   if a decision is made to retain assets until death, what testamentary strategies are available;
*   if a lifetime gift is to be made:
    –   an understanding of the BPR clawback rules;
    –   the pros and cons of gifts into a trust;
    –   the different types of trust which might be used;
    –   the avoidance of capital gains tax and income tax on gifts; and
    –   the particular problems in relation to gifts of investment businesses.

For ease of reference, the term 'business' will be used generically in this chapter to refer to sole trades, partnerships *and* companies.

Lifetime gifts — the 'cons'

[15.2] The principal downside in making a lifetime gift of business assets is the loss of any capital gains tax 'uplift' on death (TCGA 1992, s 62). Although, gift relief may be available to defer some or all of the gain under TCGA 1992, s 165.

This is particularly acute in relation to a gift of business assets qualifying for 100% BPR, because, for such assets, retaining them until death is especially attractive. Not only is there a capital gains tax uplift but, in addition, there is also no inheritance tax to pay. Thus, the recipient of such assets under the terms of a will or intestacy has the best of all possible worlds — he has no immediate tax liability on the death *and* no further tax liability on any sale of those assets either (assuming no increase in value since death).

Why, then, take steps – making a lifetime gift – which could leave the potential beneficiary in a worse position?

Lifetime gifts — the 'pros'

[15.3] When dealing with business assets qualifying for BPR, the only conceivable *tax* motivation for making a lifetime gift of such assets is the concern that BPR may not be available at 100% or 50% in relation to relevant business assets at the date of death.

There are two main reasons why this might be the case:

• the nature of the business may change in a way which would cause the relief to be restricted or denied; or
• there could be adverse legislative change.

A typical example of the first reason would be where a trading business has been using its profits to accumulate 'investments' to such an extent that it is getting close to becoming 'mainly' an investment business or, alternatively, where a positive decision has been made to sell the trade and use the proceeds to acquire investments.

In relation to the second reason, the fear is of politically motivated change. BPR has been available at 100% only since 1992, and, for example, between 1992 and 1996, relief in respect of 'non-controlling' unquoted shareholdings was available at only 50%. There may be a concern that the rate of relief will return to levels of less than 100% at some future point.

In its 1994 policy document 'Tackling tax abuses – tackling unemployment', the Labour Party (then in opposition) identified 100% BPR as being overly generous, and in the early months and years following Labour's 1997 election victory there was an expectation that a reduction in the rate of BPR would be quickly forthcoming. In fact, no such reduction was ever made during Labour's 13 years in office and neither has any reduction in the rate been effected by subsequent governments since Labour left office in 2010.

It is probably fair to say that, for the moment, the odds on there being a reduction in the rate of BPR have lengthened with the Conservative Party – which originally introduced the 100% rate – now being in power. In future, the position could again become more uncertain if there is a government which does not include the Conservative Party.

Lifetime gifts — weighing the alternatives

[15.4] In both of the above cases, fear of a future loss of relief would motivate a taxpayer to make a lifetime gift of business assets so as to ensure that BPR was 'banked' while available at 100% (the extent to which relief is *actually* banked when a gift is made is considered below in relation to the BPR 'clawback' rules). There is nevertheless a difference between a taxpayer having a concern about a loss of BPR because of facts known about a business's likely future strategy and a concern about possible future legislative change.

A concern about the former will generate a far more pressing need to bank the relief — the potential fear of 40% inheritance tax applying to the entire value of the business on death being significantly more detrimental than a potential loss of capital gains tax uplift (particularly if the business is likely to be continued rather than sold after the death).

Acting upon a concern about future legislative change is more of a gamble. If the rules don't change and BPR remains available at 100% until death, a capital gains tax uplift will have been foregone for no advantage.

In the authors' experience, during the last Labour administration, where a business owner had reached a stage in life where he no longer required an income from the business nor wished to receive any part of any future sale proceeds, and/or where it was likely that the business would continue in the hands of the donees (such that the potential loss of a capital gains tax uplift was largely academic because no future disposal was likely), there was little to be lost in making a lifetime gift and a lot to be gained in terms of a 'hedge' against possible future legislative change. If the odds of such legislation change have lengthened under the Conservative governments and now the coalition, the value of such a 'hedge' will have reduced in the short- to medium-term. When the next election in May 2022 nears, perhaps the value will increase again?

In relation to businesses *not* qualifying for BPR, the advantage of making a lifetime gift is, of course, far more apparent. Retaining the assets could ultimately (on the death of the owner) trigger a 40% inheritance tax charge. Thus, the standard inheritance tax strategy of making a gift with the intention of surviving for a period of seven years becomes as important in relation to these assets as for any other assets owned by the taxpayer. The specific planning issues faced by a taxpayer in relation to a gift of such an 'investment' business are addressed at the end of this chapter.

Testamentary planning with business assets — an outright gift to the surviving spouse

[15.5] If a taxpayer decides to retain business assets until death, a similar issue will arise as to whether or not to try to bank any BPR available on death.

Of course, if the taxpayer is not survived by his or her spouse (any comments in relation to spouses would be equally applicable to 'civil partners' but for, ease of reference, 'spouse' will be used throughout the rest of this chapter), BPR will apply automatically to reduce the potential inheritance tax liability.

Where, however, the taxpayer is survived by his or her spouse, if the business assets are left outright to the spouse, the gift will be fully exempt anyway because of 'spouse exemption' (assuming the restriction on gifts between domiciled and non-domiciled spouses contained in IHTA 1984, s 18(2) does not apply). Thus, in these circumstances, where no specific advantage can be taken of BPR, the surviving spouse should consider entering into a Deed of Variation within two years of death to redirect the assets to a 'non-exempt' individual.

Why should it matter whether it is BPR or spouse exemption which reduces the inheritance tax liability in these circumstances?

The answer is that it is not so much that it is of advantage to attract a particular sort of relief, rather that there may be a longer term advantage in keeping the business assets outside the surviving spouse's estate — to ensure that those assets do not then become liable to inheritance tax on the death of the surviving spouse in due course.

As described in **CHAPTER 3**, a surviving spouse would always inherit his or her deceased spouse's period of ownership and could therefore immediately qualify for BPR upon inheriting qualifying business assets — ie notwithstanding that he or she had not owned those assets for two years (IHTA 1984, s 108). Longer term, however, it is not inevitable that BPR will continue to apply.

After the death of the first spouse, it is often the case that the surviving spouse would not wish to continue to run the business. In these circumstances, the business may be sold, in which case, the proceeds of sale would not attract relief in the surviving spouse's estate (unless used to acquire 'replacement' BPR property). Likewise, the rate of BPR could fall following the first death. In both cases, assets which were entirely free from inheritance tax on the first death could become subject to a charge on the death of the surviving spouse.

Testamentary planning with business assets — a trust for the surviving spouse

[15.6] Rather than leaving assets qualifying for BPR directly to the surviving spouse on the first death, it may be sensible for such assets to be left to a discretionary trust where those assets (and any proceeds of sale should they be sold) would be held outside the spouse's estate whatever the future circumstances. Under the terms of the discretionary trust the surviving spouse would be named as one of the 'potential beneficiaries' who could then benefit from the income and capital of the trust assets at the discretion of the trustees, but those assets would not be treated as forming part of the surviving spouse's estate on his or her death.

What if the intention was for the surviving spouse to continue the business after the first death? Subject to the comments below (about discretionary trusts and dividend income), there would be no reason why the business could not continue with the business assets held by the trustees. Once the trustees had owned the business assets for two years they would also qualify for BPR in their hands.

Furthermore, if the surviving spouse wished to continue the business and was otherwise wealthy enough to *purchase* the business assets from the trustees, this could provide a simple means by which the surviving spouse could convert chargeable assets in his or her hands (eg cash) into assets qualifying for relief — thereby reducing the future inheritance tax liability still further. In these circumstances, there would, of course, be stamp taxes to pay on the purchase and possibly capital gains tax to be paid by the trustees if the business assets had increased in value between death and the date of sale, but these tax charges are likely to be relatively modest.

The following additional points need to be mentioned in relation to the strategy of leaving assets to a discretionary trust on the first death:

- leaving the business assets to the discretionary trust is not an entirely 'free lunch'; discretionary trusts are themselves potentially subject to periodic inheritance tax charges on each ten-yearly anniversary of the trust ('ten-yearly charges') and when assets leave the trust ('exit charges'). For as long as the business assets qualify for BPR in the hands of the trustees (and the trustees would need to hold them for two years before relief becomes available), these charges will not apply. As soon as relief disappears, however, – eg on a sale – the assets would become subject to a charge of, at most, 6% every 10 years. This 6% charge every 10 years needs to be compared to the alternative of a 40% charge on the death of the surviving spouse if he or she had inherited the assets directly. It will depend upon the likely life expectancy of the surviving spouse as to whether a 6% charge every ten years is preferable to a one-off 40% charge on death. For younger spouses, this may not be the case as the 'net present value' of a 40% tax charge some distance in the future may not be that great.

- If the business in question is carried on through the medium of a company with shares left to the trustees, it is important to appreciate that there are disadvantageous rates of income tax (discussed further below) that can apply to the dividend income received by the trustees if it is intended for it to be distributed (for example) to the surviving spouse. This problem can be overcome by the conversion of the discretionary trust to an interest-in-possession trust for the spouse once two years have elapsed since the date of death. Any conversion within the two-year period would be 'read back' to the date of death, with the effect of bringing the assets back within the surviving spouse's estate for inheritance tax purposes.

Again, where the business assets concerned do not attract BPR, they would need to be left to the surviving spouse in order to attract spouse exemption. It should be remembered, however, that the surviving spouse may then be in a much better position to consider making a lifetime gift of these assets because the capital gains tax uplift on the deceased spouse's death will have removed the possibility of a significant capital gains tax charge in relation to a gift of those assets by the spouse. The possibility of such a charge is – as discussed below – often the main impediment to the making of a gift of such assets.

Equalisation

[15.7] The opportunity to take advantage of BPR on the death of the first spouse offers a possible inheritance tax saving opportunity; however, if all the business assets are held by one spouse, that opportunity would arise only if the spouse owning those assets is the first to die.

In such circumstances, and so as to ensure that the strategy can be adopted regardless of which spouse dies first, an equalisation of business assets between spouses might be considered, with one spouse making a lifetime gift to the other.

Would the 'receiving spouse' then qualify for BPR immediately, not then having owned the business assets for two years?

As the receiving spouse would not, in these circumstances, have inherited the assets on the death of his deceased spouse, the transferor's period of ownership would not be automatically acquired, and it would therefore *not* be true to say that the recipient would qualify for BPR in *all* circumstances.

However, the reason for making the inter-spouse gift would be so that the receiving spouse could take advantage of BPR if he were to die first, and there is a separate rule – previously referred to in **CHAPTER 3** – which would ensure that the recipient spouse did attract relief in these circumstances. This rule, contained in IHTA 1984, s 109, provides that where there are two transfers, one of which is on death, the period of ownership of the first transferor can be counted as part of the period of ownership of the second transferor. Here we are envisaging one lifetime transfer from the first spouse to the second followed by a second transfer to a discretionary trust on the death of the second spouse, and therefore the conditions for relief would be met.

The same rule would apply where one spouse transfers *all* the business assets to the other. This might be the case where the recipient spouse was terminally ill and therefore almost certain to predecease the transferor.

The BPR clawback rules

[15.8] The planning strategies referred to above rely on banking BPR by making a gift of business assets at a time when they qualify for 100% relief.

It is important to understand, however, that in relation to a *lifetime* gift simply because an asset qualifies for relief at the time of the gift, that does not necessarily mean that the gift will always be free from inheritance tax. BPR can be 'clawed back' if:

(1)   the donor fails to survive the gift by a period of seven years; *and*
(2)   in the meantime, either:
        (a)   the gifted assets have ceased to be owned by the donee; or
        (b)   (in the case of all business assets other than unquoted shares) the assets have ceased to qualify for relief in the hands of the donee.

Thus, for example, if unquoted shares qualifying for relief are given away and within seven years of the gift the shares are sold by the donee (and not replaced by other qualifying business assets) *and* within seven years of the gift the donor dies, inheritance tax is calculated in relation to the gift as if no BPR had been available. In relation to a gift in excess of a donor's nil-rate band, an inheritance tax charge would then arise broadly in the same way as if the donor had made a 'failed' potentially exempt transfer.

In the case of unquoted shares, the legislation is particularly generous. For other business assets – and using the same example – the clawback rules will be triggered if the assets cease to qualify for relief prior to the donor's death within seven years (for example, where a business changes from one of trade to investment). In relation to unquoted shares, the clawback will be triggered *only if* those shares cease to be owned by the donee. Thus, if shares in a trading company are given away and within seven years of the gift the donor dies, the company having in the meantime ceased its trade, and become an investment company, there would be *no* clawback.

In the case of a gift of unquoted shares, therefore, BPR is more securely 'banked' and far less easily clawed back than for other business assets.

Planning point

While it is important to be aware of the possibility of a clawback of BPR, in planning terms no immediate steps need to be taken at the date of the gift.

If either the donor survives for seven years following the gift, or dies within the period and the gifted assets are at that time still being owned by the donee (and, in the case of assets other than unquoted shares, still qualifying for BPR), there will be no clawback.

The donor can therefore adopt a 'wait and see' approach. For as long as the assets remain held by the donee (and in the case of assets other than unquoted shares still qualifying for relief), there will be no clawback even if the donor dies within seven years of the gift. If one of these factors changes, the donor would know that if he were then to die within seven years of the gift, there would be a clawback of relief. In such circumstances, the donor or donee could *then* insure against any possible inheritance tax liability arising as a result of the clawback by the use of a life assurance policy (taken out on the donor's life) for the remainder of the seven-year term.

The use of trusts

[15.9] Where a taxpayer has made the decision to make a lifetime gift of business assets – perhaps to bank BPR or simply to set the seven-year 'clock' running on a gift of non-qualifying investment assets – the next logical step to consider is to whom should the gift be made?

Should an outright gift to, say, a child or grandchild be made or should a gift into some form of trust be considered? Further, if a trust is to be used, what type of trust should it be?

Trusts offer potential advantages and disadvantages. On the positive side, trusts offer the possibility of the following.

- *Control.* The donor, as one of the trustees of the recipient trust, can retain some control (in a fiduciary capacity) over the gifted assets. In the case of business assets, this can be particularly attractive where the donor is not yet ready to pass control of the business to others.
- *Flexibility.* The terms of any trust would be likely to include powers for the trustees to change the identity of the beneficiaries from time to time. Thus, a donor could give away assets to a trust knowing that he wished to remove the assets from his estate but not yet knowing who – say, from among a class of his children and grandchildren – should ultimately benefit.
- *Protection.* Donors are often concerned that their intended donees will divorce or become insolvent with the assets gifted then potentially falling in the hands of donees' former spouses, or creditors. While trusts are by no means a complete protection from the claims of divorcing spouses or creditors, they do enable the assets to be 'one step removed' from potential claimants — potentially making any claims upon them more difficult.

On the negative side, however, trusts are often perceived to be as set out below.

- *Complicated.* They involve abstract legal concepts which are often difficult to understand for those without legal training.
- *Expensive.* The *Bleak House* scenario, whereby all the assets of a trust are ultimately exhausted in legal fees, is the most extreme caricature of this view.
- *Uncertain.* The radical overhaul of trust taxation by the last Labour government in 2006 was an extreme example, but historically trust taxation has been subject to significant legislative change. This is often motivated by a governmental desire to curb the tax advantages offered by trusts.

Different donors will, of course, take radically different positions on these issues. Some individuals simply refuse to contemplate the use of trusts in relation to their personal financial affairs. Others will do anything they can to retain control of gifted assets so as to keep them out of the control of profligate donees.

What type of trust to use — an income tax issue?

[15.10] Where a decision has been made to make a gift into trust, the two main types of trust which might be chosen are:

- an interest-in-possession trust, where there is a named beneficiary or beneficiaries with a fixed right or fixed rights to the trust income; or
- a discretionary trust, where the income of the trust is distributed at the trustees' discretion among a class of beneficiaries, and where the trustees can accumulate any trust income (ie add it to the capital of the trust) not distributed.

In relation to both types of trust, the trustees would usually retain an absolute discretion over capital distributions together with a power to amend the trusts and, for example, convert an interest-in-possession trust to a discretionary trust or vice versa. The main difference between the two types of trust, therefore, is the way that income is dealt with by the trustees. This, in turn, gives rise to a significant difference in the income tax treatment which is particularly acute in relation to dividend income.

In relation to an interest-in-possession trust, a beneficiary is entitled as of right to any income payable to the trustees (and, for this reason, the trustees of such a trust will often mandate the trust's income direct to a beneficiary). In these circumstances, the beneficiary (broadly speaking) is liable to income tax on the income as if he had received it directly. Thus, if the trustees are entitled to dividend income, the beneficiaries receive it as dividend income and the beneficial rates of tax for dividend income are available to them.

From 6 April 2016, trustees pay tax on dividend income at the basic rate of 7.5% and on other income at the basic rate of 20%. Under current legislation non- and basic-rate taxpayers would pay 7.5% tax on any dividend they receive, a higher-rate taxpayer would pay tax at 32.5% of the net dividend received and an additional rate taxpayer would pay 38.1%. The beneficiaries would be entitled to the 7.5%/20% credit as appropriate. In addition, the beneficiaries would also be entitled to a 0% rate on the first £5,000 (£2,000 from 6 April 2018) of dividend income and potentially a Personal Savings Allowance of up to £1,000. From a practical point of view, it may be preferable for income from a life interest trust to be mandated directly to the beneficiaries, as access to the 0% on dividends would be accessed directly by the beneficiaries, and the trustees would not need to account for income tax on dividends or deposit interest which is paid gross with effect from 6 April 2016.

Where income is received from a discretionary trust, because it is payable at the discretion of the trustees, it is treated as general *non-savings income from a trust* in the hands of the beneficiary rather than as the particular form of income arising to the trustees. Thus, the dividend tax rates *cannot* be claimed by the beneficiaries. Instead, when distributing the income to the beneficiaries, the trustees need to make sure that they have paid and accounted for 45% income tax to HMRC, and the beneficiaries therefore receive only 55% of the net dividend originally received by the trustees (together with a 45% tax-deduction certificate). In these circumstances, if the beneficiary is a non-taxpayer, he can make a tax-repayment claim for the full 45%. A basic-rate taxpayer can recover 25% (to take them to 20% net), a higher-rate taxpayer can claim back 5% (to take them to 40% net) and an additional rate taxpayer can reclaim nothing. Neither trustees nor beneficiaries receive a Personal Savings Allowance for discretionary trust income.

Thus, comparing the effective tax rate payable in relation to the same dividend received via the two types of trust gives the following result under current legislation:

	Interest in possession[*]	Discretionary
Non-taxpayer	0%	0%
Basic-rate taxpayer	7.5%	20%
Higher-rate taxpayer	32.5%	40%

	Interest in possession[*]	Discretionary
Additional rate tax-payer	38.1%	45%

[*] Assuming that the beneficiary has already used all of the 0% dividend rate.

Thus, where it is likely that dividend income is to be received by a trust and distributed amongst the beneficiaries, basic- and higher- and additional-rate taxpayers are significantly worse off receiving the income from a discretionary trust rather than an interest-in-possession trust. Thus, where a gift of company shares is contemplated, an interest-in-possession trust is usually more income tax efficient in the longer-term than a discretionary trust.

There is an IIP concession such that trustees do not have to declare trust savings income to HMRC where the tax liability is less than £100. This concession only applies where savings income is the trustees' only source of income.

Planning point

Historically, many old discretionary trusts suffer from the income tax problem discussed above.

Following changes introduced to the inheritance tax treatment of trusts in FA 2006, it is now possible subject to the terms of the trust, to convert a discretionary trust to an interest-in-possession trust without any inheritance tax 'exit charge' arising and without any capital gains tax charges (because no taxpayer is becoming absolutely entitled as against the trustees).

Therefore, by the use of such a conversion, it is now possible to improve the income tax position for the beneficiaries of such trusts. Further, the conversion does not have to be irrevocable so that a reversion to a discretionary form (or to an interest in possession trust with different beneficial interests) at some future point would also be possible.

Avoiding capital gains tax in relation to lifetime gifts

[15.11] A gift of business assets will generally constitute a disposal for capital gains tax purposes, and, because it is between 'connected parties', the disposal will be treated as made at market value.

The assets to be gifted may qualify for full ER – see **CHAPTER 3** – in which case, capital gains tax may be chargeable at an effective rate of only 10% in relation to all or part of the gains. Nevertheless, it would usually be sensible for the donor to seek to avoid any immediate tax charge, and therefore some form of hold-over relief would be required so that, effectively, any gains could be passed on to the donees along with the gifted assets.

As explained in **CHAPTER 12**, if the assets gifted comprise trading assets, business asset hold-over relief under TCGA 1992, s 165 could be available to defer any gains. As explained in detail in that chapter, however, that relief can be subject to restrictions, and s 165 hold-over relief would not be available at all in relation to a gift of investment assets.

Where business asset hold-over relief is available in full in relation to a business asset, the availability of relief is not dependent upon the identity of the donee (although no relief is available to settlor-interested trusts see (**12.38**)). Therefore, a donor holding such assets could consider either an outright gift or a gift into trust, and any capital gains tax liability should be capable of being deferred.

Where, however, no business asset hold-over relief is available, an alternative is required.

Where a gift is made into a lifetime discretionary trust or interest-in-possession trust, hold-over relief is always available (subject to the same caveat about settlor-interested trusts) under the provisions of TCGA 1992, s 260.

Thus, a donor wishing to avoid a capital gains tax liability on a gift of business assets not qualifying for business asset hold-over relief is obliged to make a transfer to such a trust if hold-over relief is to be available.

Such a gift into trust is a chargeable transfer for inheritance tax purposes (ie not a potentially exempt transfer), and it can be immediately chargeable to inheritance tax when it is made. Inheritance tax in relation to such a lifetime chargeable transfer is charged at half the rate which would otherwise apply on death (currently 20%) on:

–   the donor's transfer of value – the amount by which the donor's estate is reduced as a result of the transfer;
–   in excess of his available inheritance tax nil-rate band (currently £325,000);
–   after taking account of any BPR available.

Thus, where an individual wishes to make a gift of business assets qualifying for 100% BPR or worth less than £325,000, those assets could be transferred into trust with the chargeable gains held over under TCGA 1992, s 260 and with no inheritance tax liability.

In all other circumstances – ie in relation to an investment business worth more than £325,000 – succession planning becomes much more difficult because the donor is faced with a dilemma. A transfer to a trust will attract a hold-over relief under TCGA 1992, s 260 but will give rise to an immediate liability to inheritance tax and an *outright* gift (ie not in trust) would avoid any immediate inheritance tax gift (as a potentially exempt transfer) but would trigger an immediate capital gains tax liability as no hold-over relief would be available. For such businesses, planning would typically involve working with the donor's nil-rate band, and this is explored further below in the final section of this chapter.

Sole traders

[**15.12**] The following two specific issues arise in relation to sole traders wishing to give away business assets.

First, a gift of all, or an interest in, a personal trading business can qualify for BPR. It was previously believed (see the first edition of this book) that a gift of some of the *assets of* that business would *not* qualify for relief. This view (as put forward by HMRC) was rejected in the High Court in the case of *Revenue and Customs Comrs v The Trustees of Nelson Dance Family Settlement* [2009] EWHC 71(Ch), [2009] STC 802 and BPR was allowed in relation to the transfer of two parcels of land used by a farming business.

Thus BPR can be available in relation to the transfer of the entirety of a sole trader's business; the transfer of an interest in the business (ie by bringing in a partner to the business) *or* in relation to a transfer of some of the assets of the business.

Secondly, the potential for an income tax charge arising as a result of a revaluation of stock needs to be avoided. Ordinarily, a gift of an interest in the business, or of part of the stock, would be accounted for in terms of, first, a transfer of stock to capital (on the ceasing of the trade in relation to that stock) followed by a gift of capital. The transfer of stock to capital would ordinarily give rise to an income tax charge on the inherent profit (market value less cost) in that stock at that time. This income tax charge can be avoided only by making an election in respect of the continuation of the trade, and this can be done whenever there is a transfer between connected parties, ie between the donor and his children or between the donor and a trust that he has created.

Succession planning for investment businesses

[15.13] As explained above, succession planning is particularly difficult in relation to a valuable investment business where neither business asset hold-over relief for capital gains tax purposes nor BPR for inheritance tax purposes is available.

Typically, a strategy of making gifts into trust – with the benefit of s 260 hold-over relief – at a value within the donor's nil-rate band, would be adopted for such businesses.

In the case, for example, of an investment company, this would typically involve the following elements:

- Because an individual's nil-rate band effectively revives every seven years, a long-term plan of making gifts to the limit of the donor's available nil-rate band as soon as the previous gift has been survived by seven years offers the best way to maximise the total amount of tax-free transfers over time.
- Where both spouses own shares in the company, each can make gifts up to their own nil-rate band. Further, spouses can take advantage of the fact that their holdings are related for inheritance tax purposes – as the following example illustrates – to ensure that their respective transfers of value are kept within their nil-rate bands.

Example — *Crossing the control threshold tax-effectively*

Mr and Mrs Fellowes own 51% of the shares in a property investment company, and these shares are worth £400,000. Mrs Fellowes owns 5.1% and Mr Fellowes owns 45.9%.

If Mr and Mrs Fellowes make gifts of their shares on the same day, the reduction in their joint estates of £400,000 will be allocated between them on a pro-rata basis – ie £40,000 to Mrs Fellowes and £360,000 to Mr Fellowes – to arrive at their respective transfers of value for inheritance tax purposes. Mr Fellowes' transfer would therefore be in excess of his nil-rate band.

If, however, they make their transfers on consecutive days, the result is very different.

Mrs Fellowes first makes a gift of her holding. Prior to the gift, her shares were worth £40,000, and she has nothing after the gift, so her transfer of value is still £40,000.

Mr Fellowes now owns 45.9% of the shares, and, as this no longer forms part of a controlling holding with his wife, it will now be worth a lot less than the £360,000 it was worth before his wife made her gift (because of the discount that would be applied to a minority holding). Thus, when Mr Fellowes makes a gift of his shares, his transfer of value will be correspondingly reduced, and it is likely in these circumstances that the minority discount would be enough to bring Mr Fellowes' transfer within his nil-rate band.

Finally, if a donor adopts a long-term strategy of making gifts up to the value of the nil-rate band every seven years, the danger is that his retained shares will increase in value organically over the period (as the value of the underlying investments grow) such that the periodic gifts simply keep the potential inheritance tax liability at a constant level rather than actually reducing it.

To avoid this problem, it is always sensible the first time this strategy is adopted, for a new class of 'growth' shares to be created in the company. The rights attaching to these shares would be drafted to ensure that they carry any future value arising as a result of organic growth. When these shares are created, they would usually have a modest value and could therefore be given away at the same time as representing only a very small part (in value terms) of the first nil-rate band tranche.

Seven years later, any growth in value would already be outside the donor's estate (as reflected in the growth shares already given away), and when the second, third and fourth (etc) nil-rate-band tranches are given away in future years, this would further reduce the potential inheritance tax liability on each occasion.

A more ambitious plan would involve the creation of a new class of shares which automatically increases in value over time ('deferred shares'). Once created, these shares would also be given away and given that their value then accrues over time, the transfer of value at the time of the gift would be minimised (hopefully to less than the transferor's 'nil rate band').

A full analysis of all the tax consequences associated with the creation of either growth or deferred shares is beyond the scope of this book but the following points should be noted:

- The alteration in the share capital of a *close company* or in the rights attaching to the shares is treated as having been made by the participators and can therefore give rise to Inheritance Tax consequences for them. In relation to 'deferred shares', HMRC takes the view that – in addition to any inheritance tax consequences at the time the shares are initially created – there is also an alteration of rights at the point (in the future) when the deferred shares come to rank equally with another class of shares (see Press Release of 11 September 1991 and HMRC Manuals at SVM108280, Example 1). Some advisers question the validity of this view.

  In the authors' view, even if HMRC is correct, it is possible to avoid a large inheritance tax charge at the future point.

- It is also important to consider whether there are any Capital Gains Tax 'value shifting' consequences or Income Tax issues concerning the creation of 'employment related securities', when creating new classes of shares as part of an Inheritance Tax planning exercise.

Disclosure of tax avoidance schemes (DOTAS)

[15.14] The DOTAS regime was extended with effect from 6 April 2011 to include inheritance tax arrangements where the aim of those arrangements is to seek to avoid or reduce the inheritance tax entry charge when transferring property into trust.

This provision was limited as it only applied new schemes created on or after 6 April 2011. Schemes which are the same or substantially the same as arrangements made available before 6 April 2011 were exempted from disclosure.

The government has published further legislation in the Inheritance Tax Avoidance Scheme Regulation 2017 with the intention to 'widen the DOTAS hallmark for IHT to identify more types of IHT avoidance while recognising that reliefs and exemptions are used legitimately by the majority of people'. This now includes arrangements that would have been previously exempted from disclosure under the 2011 hallmark. These will now have to be tested against the new IHT hallmark which takes effect from 1 April 2018.

These measures apply to both lifetime gifts and transfers on deaths. For disclosure, both of the following conditions would need to be met:

- Condition 1: the main purpose, or one of the main purposes, of the arrangements is to enable a person to obtain an inheritance tax advantage; and
- Condition 2: the arrangements are contrived or abnormal or involve one or more contrived or abnormal steps without which a tax advantage could not be obtained.

The Government recognises that the words 'obtaining a tax advantage' may have a wide scope in the context of IHT and in particular with BPR, the Government does not seek to discourage the legitimate use of reliefs and it is intended that non-abusive arrangements should not be caught. The Government will consider whether clarification is required in these areas to confirm that non-abusive arrangements do not need to be disclosed.

The confidentiality and premium fee hallmarks were also extended to cover IHT with effect from 23 February 2016.

Clearance applications

[15.15] Finally, there will be many occasions – particularly in relation to businesses which are part 'trading' and part 'investment' (or where there are very large amounts of retained cash) – where it will not be possible to reach a confident conclusion as to whether, or to the extent to which, BPR will be available in relation to a particular business.

Finding out that BPR is not available or restricted in circumstances where it has been assumed that it is available in full can be costly — eg where shares worth in excess of a client's nil rate band have been transferred during his lifetime into trust, with a 20% inheritance tax charge arising. Likewise, historically such uncertainty will have deterred many from making such transfers.

It is to be welcomed then that since May 2008, it has been possible to apply in advance to HMRC for a non-statutory clearance in relation to BPR. Originally intended as a pilot project for six months, the scheme has been extended and it continues at the time of writing.

Simply put, in relation to a genuinely contemplated lifetime transfer which is 'commercially significant' to a business (for example, the succession of control/management to younger family members) and where there is 'material uncertainty' as to the application of the law, HMRC will now give a ruling in advance of a transfer as to the availability of BPR.

Key points

[15.16] Key points to note are as follows:

• watch loss of capital gains tax uplift on lifetime gifts of business assets;
• consider gifting business assets to a discretionary trust on death, in order to bank 100% BPR;
• consider equalising business assets between spouses;
• lifetime transfers to interest-in-possession trusts are now immediately chargeable to IHT, but this offers CGT hold-over opportunities.

Chapter 16

Ceasing the Business and Winding Up a Company

Introduction

[16.1] There are many reasons why the shareholders will want to wind up the business. However, with owner-managed businesses, the decision tends to be for one of two reasons:

- The business has been sold and the shareholders want to get the proceeds out of the company.
- The shareholders want to cease the business and distribute the assets.

Tax consequences for the shareholders

[16.2] A winding-up involves a formal liquidation of the company. Many shareholders will not want to go down this route; instead, they will seek a dissolution of the company. This involves the cessation of the business, the distribution of the assets to the shareholders and the striking-off of the company.

Distributions made to the shareholders in the course of a winding-up are not treated as a dividend (CTA 2010, s 1000(1)(B)); instead, any receipts are taxed as a return of capital, so the 10% or 20% tax rate applies and in some cases ER is available. With a dissolution, the distributions made are income distributions and are taxed in the same way as a normal dividend.

For the majority of shareholders, it is more beneficial to have capital gains tax treatment rather than income tax treatment. But this may not always be the case. For basic rate taxpayers, from 6 April 2018, the rate of tax on dividends and other distributions from a company will be at 7.5% on amounts exceeding £2,000 (£5,000 from 6 April 2016). This compares favourably to the tax rate of 10% for capital gains tax purposes, although bear in mind the annual exempt amount of £11,700. However, for higher-rate taxpayers with significant gains capital treatment is likely to be preferred, so a formal liquidation is often the best way forward.

There may be some instances where the extraction of funds by way of a pre-liquidation dividend may be more tax efficient as seen above by the rate of tax. This advantage may also remain where the dividends are now subject to income tax at dividend rates, it is simply a case of crunching the numbers. Any planning in this regard should be undertaken prior to the appointment of a liquidator.

Shareholders were able to wind up a company informally, but distributions received by the shareholders in respect of a dissolution of a company will be taxed as dividends unless the total amount paid out by the company in respect of the dissolution does not exceed £25,000 (CTA 2010, s 1030A).

Moreover, the changes introduced by Finance Act 2016 in relation to transactions in securities, and the TAAR in relation to the winding up of companies need to be considered.

With effect from 6 April 2016 a distribution in respect of securities on a winding up has been treated as a transaction in securities, which means that the proceeds could be taxed as a dividend if the purpose or one of the main purposes of the transaction was to obtain an income tax advantage, and any person obtains an income tax advantage in consequence of the transaction.

A winding up is likely to be particularly vulnerable where, for example, the company has been retaining profits in anticipation of a winding up so that the shareholders can extract the funds as part of a capital gain rather than paying income tax on a distribution or on remuneration from the company.

Clearance can be sought under Income Tax Act 2007, s 701 to ensure that HMRC is satisfied that the anti-avoidance legislation should not be applied.

Also with effect from 6 April 2016 a new targeted anti-avoidance rule was introduced, which will need to be considered whenever a close company is wound up and a distribution made to a shareholder who is an individual. The TAAR applies where four conditions set out in ITTOIA 2005, s 396B are met. The conditions are:

'A.   that, immediately before the winding up, the individual has at least a 5% interest in the company;

B.   that the company is a close company when it is wound up, or was a close company at any time in the period of two years ending with the start of the winding up;

C.   that, at any time within the period of two years beginning with the date on which the distribution is made:

    a)   the individual carries on a trade or activity which is the same as, or similar to, that carried on by the company or an effective 51% subsidiary of the company,

    b)   the individual is a partner in a partnership which carries on such a trade or activity,

    c)   the individual, or a person connected with him or her, is a participator in a company in which he or she has at least a 5% interest and which at that time carries on such a trade or activity, or is connected with a company which carries on such a trade or activity, or

    d)   the individual is involved with the carrying on of such a trade or activity by a person connected with the individual;

D.   that it is reasonable to assume, having regard to all the circumstances, that the main purpose or one of the main purposes of the winding up is the avoidance or reduction of a charge to income tax, or the winding up forms part of arrangements the main purpose or one of the main purposes of which is the avoidance or reduction of a charge to income tax.'

The amount of the distribution for the purposes of these provisions takes into account the CGT base cost of the shares. There is no clearance mechanism in relation to these provisions.

These provisions can apply in a wide range of circumstances, and could particularly affect, for example, property developers who may use separate companies for each development they undertake. Such individuals will need to be able to demonstrate that the reason for the winding up is not to avoid or reduce a liability to income tax (Condition D).

Planning point

If the company's capital does exceed £25,000, there are a few options:

- Reregister the company as an unlimited company and have a lawful distribution of the share capital.
- Liquidate the company formally — no *bona vacantia* problem, but there will be liquidators' fees to pay.
- Carry out a reduction of share capital as outlined in CHAPTER 11.
- Consider paying dividends, perhaps over a few years.
- However, the TAAR and the changes to transactions in securities need to be considered.

Winding up and entrepreneurs' relief

[16.3] The ER rules are quite generous where a company has ceased to trade. The disposal of shares (or in this case a distribution on dissolution) will qualify under the rule that the company has within three years immediately preceding the disposal ceased to be a trading company. Therefore where a company is wound up and the total distributions do not exceed £25,000, ER should be available if all the other ER tests as outlined in CHAPTER 3 are met, and where the TAAR does not apply. Where assets available for distribution exceed £25,000 the company must be liquidated formally so that the shareholders can treat the transaction in accordance with CGT principles (again subject to the application of the TAAR).

As the trigger point for ER purposes is the date the company ceases to trade, particular care should be taken to ensure the liquidator can realise the company's assets and be in a position to make distributions to the shareholders within the three-year time frame.

Overdrawn directors' loan account

[16.4] Where there are overdrawn directors' loan accounts, these need to be dealt with. Where the company is solvent, these are usually cleared by a credit which is treated as a distribution on the winding-up. However, if this does not happen, it may simply mean that the loan is written off. Where any part of a loan from a company to a director is not repaid, the director is assessed on it under ITTOIA 2005, s 415 (as if the amount were a net dividend) provided the liquidator formally writes off the unpaid balance. To do this, the liquidator must take an active decision either not to chase the debt or to write it off. Where the liquidator does not take any action in respect of the loan and the liquidation is completed, the amount cannot be assessed on the director under these income tax provisions. Nevertheless, whenever a company is wound up an income tax liability could arise either under the transactions in securities provisions or TAAR, whether or not part of the proceeds on a winding up are used to repay an overdrawn director's loan account.

Indeed, particular care would have to be exercised where the loan account has increased in the period leading up to the winding up of the company, as this could be seen as part of an arrangement to ensure that amounts drawn out by the director are taxed under CGT rather than under income tax rules. This 'arrangement' could be challenged under transactions in securities as a 'money-boxing arrangement', or under the TAAR as a way of reducing a liability to income tax (which would otherwise have arisen if the amount taken as a loan had been treated as remuneration or a dividend).

Tax consequences for the company

[16.5] On a winding-up, the company will cease to trade or carry on a business. Depending on the circumstances surrounding the winding-up, the trade or business may in fact have ceased earlier. For instance, if the trade was sold, the sale would lead to a cessation irrespective of when the company is wound up. A company in insolvent liquidation may have continued to trade up to the point of liquidation.

The cessation of a trade triggers the end of an accounting period and has a number of tax consequences.

Losses

[16.6] Any losses incurred in the last year of the trade can be carried back under CTA 2010, s 39. The company must have been carrying on the trade in the previous periods. The trade itself must not have been carried on wholly outside the UK. If these conditions have been met, the loss can be carried back against total profits (including trading profits) arising in accounting periods falling within the three years ending immediately before the loss-making period begins.

For losses incurred after 1 April 2017, there is greater flexibility in how those losses can be used (subject to conditions). These losses can be carried forward and set off against any future profits of the company, without the need for streaming, and can be surrendered to other group companies in future years. The requirement that trading losses can only be surrendered in the year in which they are incurred does not apply to these losses.

This does mean, however, that pre-1 April 2017 losses will have to be identified, as they will continue to be subject to the old restrictions.

Carried-forward losses that will be affected by the new changes include:

- non-trading loan relationship deficits;
- trade losses carried forward;
- non-trading losses on intangible fixed assets carried forward;
- management expenses carried forward;
- UK property business losses carried forward.

The flexible use of losses carried forward will be subject to a restriction of 50% of profits after in year deductions, that exceeds the £5m maximum allowance.

For example, a company with £12m profit remaining after in-year reliefs and that has access to the maximum £5m deductions allowance will be able to cover only a maximum of £8.5m profits by carried-forward losses (the £5m deductions allowance plus 50% of the remaining profits of £7m). The result of this is that a company will pay tax on £3.5m.

Stock

[16.7] Where a company holds stock when it ceases to trade, the stock must be valued in accordance with CTA 2009, ss 164–167. For unincorporated businesses, these rules are now contained in ITTOIA 2005, s 182.

The rules provide that where the stock is sold or transferred for valuable consideration to a person who carries on (or intends to carry on) a trade in the UK, the amount to be brought into account is:

- the actual price where the parties are unconnected; and
- the market value (arm's length price) where the parties are connected.

Where the parties are connected they can enter into a joint election, within two years of the end of the accounting period in which the trade discontinued, for the transfer price to be the price paid or the original acquisition cost where these are lower than the market value. This election is not available to large companies as transfer pricing rules take precedence.

Debts proving to be irrecoverable

[16.8] Bad debts are usually dealt with under loan relationship principles. Non-lending relationships, which include trade debts, are treated as if they were loan relationships by virtue of CTA 2009, ss 477 to 486. This gives relief for bad debts where there is an impairment under loan relationship principles. Where, unusually, loan relationship rules do not apply non-money debts are released wholly and exclusively for the purposes of the trade as part of a statutory insolvency arrangement a deduction is available under CTA 2009, s 55.

Pre-packaged administrations

[16.9] Pre-packed administrations, or 'pre-packs' as they are known, became popular during the recession. A pre-pack works as follows:

- a limited company is either insolvent or about to become insolvent;
- it has a business or some valuable assets and a prospective purchaser is available;
- an insolvency practitioner (IP) is brought in to assess whether the proposed sale would be acceptable to the IP in the capacity of administrator;
- the purchaser and the company negotiate for the sale but no sale is executed;
- the company is put into administration;
- the IP executes the sale;
- following the sale the company is wound up.

The main tax issue arising in these circumstances is the one of trading losses which may have been accumulating for some time. The best option was if the company itself used losses but this was not always possible. Any profit that arose on the sale of the assets or business was usually in a different accounting period, as the entry of a company into administration triggered a new accounting period for corporation tax purposes. Trading losses pre-1 April 2017 can only be set off against chargeable gains in the same accounting period in which the losses arose. Any gain arising on goodwill would be a credit on an intangible asset, so any trading losses should be available to offset against this profit. Finance Act 2017 (No 2) has reformed loss relief to restrict the amount of loss relief available to businesses with substantial profits, and to allow most carried-forward losses arising from 1 April 2017 to be used in a more flexible manner against total profits (rather than against particular types of profits). Accounting periods straddling 1 April 2017 will need to be apportioned between old rules and new rules.

One way of dealing with the above problem was to have the pre-pack carried out by an administrative receiver rather than an administrator. The appointment of an administrative receiver did not trigger the end of an accounting period.

The preservation of the losses should be considered. If the ownership of the Oldco and the Newco are the same, the provisions in CTA 2010 could be used to transfer and preserve the losses.

An alternative was for the administrator to hive down the trade to a new subsidiary and dispose of the shares to the purchaser. Provided the purchaser continues the business, the losses should be available going forward once again under provisions contained in CTA 2010, which are looked at in more detail below.

Transfer of the business to a connected company

Transfer of the trade without a change in ownership (CTA 2010, s 940A)

[16.10] Where there is a transfer of a trade without a substantial change in the ownership, special rules apply that prevent some of the cessation rules applying. The rules in CTA 2010, s 940A apply where:

- on a company ceasing to carry on a trade another company begins to carry it on so there is a transfer of trade; and
- at the time of transfer or at some time in the period of two years after the transfer 75% of the trade belonged to certain persons; and
- at some time during the period of one year ending immediately before the transfer a 75% interest in the transferred trade belonged to the same persons; and
- the trade is carried on by a company within the charge to corporation tax or income tax.

This legislation provides that the normal cessation rules do not apply for the following.

- *Capital allowances.* In dealing with the computations for the predecessor and the successor companies, any consideration given for the assets transferred with the trade is ignored. This means that the assets are transferred at their tax WDV.
- *Trading losses carried forward.* Any unused trading losses of the predecessor are allowed against the successor's future income from the same trade. The amount available is the loss after any CTA 2010, s 37 or group relief claims have been made. Where the predecessor was insolvent, a restriction will apply.

Restriction on transfer of losses

[**16.11**] Where the company transferring the losses is insolvent, there is a restriction on the losses which can be carried forward. This is referred to as the relevant-liabilities restriction. To calculate the restriction:

(1)   add up the liabilities (excluding share capital and reserves kept by the predecessor);

(2)   deduct the value of any assets kept by the predecessor; and

(3)   deduct any sale consideration given for the transfer.

If the result is a positive sum, that is the amount of the losses which are not available going forward. Where the result is negative, there is no restriction on the losses.

Example 1

Bucolin Red Ltd has sustained heavy losses and agrees to sell its business to Bucolin Green Ltd. Bucolin Green Ltd is not taking over the loan, creditors or cash. Bucolin Red Ltd and Bucolin Green Ltd have a common shareholding of 80% and Bucolin Green agrees to pay £300,000 for the business.

The accumulated trading losses at the date of the transfer are £1m.

Bucolin Red Ltd's balance sheet on the day it ceased to carry on the trade was as follows:

Assets	£	Liabilities	£
Fixed assets	200,000	Loan	750,000
Stock	120,000	Creditors	590,000
Debtors	300,000	Share capital	120,000
Cash	100,000	Profit and loss	(740,000)
Total	720,000	Total	720,000

Relevant liabilities restriction

Liabilities retained:
  overdraft/loan – £750,000
  creditors – £590,000
Less assets retained:
  cash – £100,000
  net – £1,240,000
  less consideration – £300,000
  balance – £940,000
Bucolin Green is limited to losses of £60,000 – that is, £1m – £940,000.

In calculating the relevant liabilities the predecessor's capital is to be treated as a liability of the predecessor so far as it is recently converted capital.

Recently converted capital is capital which arose from a conversion occurring in the previous twelve months.

Planning point

Where a subsidiary owes money to a parent company the parent company could consider capitalising this so if there is a future transfer under CTA 2010, s 940A the relevant liabilities are reduced so the losses available to carry forward are increased.

Pitfall

[16.12] Where there is a phoenix-company arrangement, this is likely to trigger the transactions-in-securities legislation. This means that distributions will be taxed as income so neither the CGT rates nor ER will be available. With lower CGT rates this is something HMRC will be watching out for.

VAT and ceasing the business (VATA 1994, Sch 1)

[16.13] When a business ceases, various VAT situations may arise which require to be addressed including:

- reviewing the position relating to VAT groups;
- VAT charge on stock and assets at date of cessation;
- notification to HMRC;
- post-cessation input tax claims, Notice 700/11;
- dealing with VAT bad debt relief, Notice 700/18;
- reviewing and concluding capital goods scheme adjustments where applicable, Notice 706/2;
- accounting for VAT under the cash accounting, annual accounting and flat-rate schemes, Notices 731, 732 and 733.

A business which ceases to make either supplies or relevant acquisitions is required to cancel its VAT registration. Notification of deregistration must be made to HMRC within 30 days, either online or via the VAT 7 form.

A business is permitted to deregister voluntarily if its supplies or relevant acquisitions fall below the relevant thresholds. Since 1 April 2017, the standard deregistration threshold is £83,000 and the deregistration threshold for acquisitions is £85,000.

Key points

[16.14] Key points to note are as follows:

- In most situations, following the disappearance of ESC C16, a formal liquidation will be appropriate for all but the smallest companies
- Take care with the transfer of a business with substantial losses to ensure these are not restricted.
- Before carrying out a pre-pack make sure that the tax issues have been considered.
- Review the new changes to corporation tax carry forward loss relief including the restrictions.

Part IV

Tax Administration

Chapter 17

Penalties and HMRC Powers

Introduction

[17.1] A comprehensive understanding of the rights and powers available to HMRC in relation to penalties, assessments and information requests is essential in all dealings with HMRC as a professional advisor.

The appeals and Tribunal system are dealt with separately in **CHAPTER 18**.

Penalties

[17.2] The UK tax system is primarily self-assessment based. HMRC has the power to impose a number of different penalties on those who fail to meet their obligations and to penalise those who make errors. Penalties can broadly be divided into the following categories.

- Late filing and failure to file penalties.
- Penalties for failure to keep proper records.
- Tax geared penalties for failure to notify chargeability and for fraud or negligence.
- Tax geared penalties for errors introduced by Finance Act 2007 and extended by Finance Act 2008.
- Additional penalties for failure to meet the 'Requirement to Correct' legislation.

Note also the higher penalties payable for undeclared income and gains arising in relation to overseas assets.

Significant changes to the penalty system were introduced in April 2008 as part of HMRC's ongoing consultation process for 'Modernising Powers, Deterrents and Safeguards'. At the time of writing, legislation has been drafted in relation to the RTC. Enforcement of the legislation has been delayed due to the summer election and is unlikely to be legislated prior to going to print due to the summer recess. Regardless of the party elected, the author believes that given the importance of taxation in politics, the RTC legislation is likely to be enacted. More detail on the RTC can be found at **17.15**.

Fixed penalties — late filing

[17.3] Finance Act 2009, Sch 55 and s 106 and Finance Act 2010 (No 3) Sch 10 and s 26 legislated for a new penalty regime for the late filing of income tax and capital gains tax returns from 6 April 2011. An initial penalty of £100 is charged on the day following the date the return was due. Furthermore, when the return is three months' overdue, daily penalties of £10 per day for a maximum of 90 days can be charged. A further penalty of 5% of the tax liability, or £300 (whichever is higher) is levied if the tax return is six months late. A second penalty of 5% of the tax liability, or £300 (whichever is higher) is charged if the tax return is 12 months late.

HMRC reserves the right to increase the percentage of the second 'further penalty'. They may do this, if, by failing to file the return within 12 months, information was withheld and the person knew that the information would help HMRC establish the correct liability. HMRC will then categorise the 'behaviour' of the person into one of the following: non-deliberate; deliberate; and deliberate and concealed.

The second 'further penalty' will not be increased if the behaviour was 'non-deliberate', which is defined as a person who did not know that by failing to file their tax return on time, information was being withheld from HMRC which would help them establish the correct tax liability.

'Deliberate' is defined as being where a person knew that by failing to file their tax return on time, information was being withheld that would help HMRC establish the correct tax liability.

'Deliberate and concealed' is defined as a person who knew that the information they were withholding would help HMRC establish the correct tax liability and took additional steps to conceal this.

The penalty will be increased dependent upon which category a person falls into.

Paragraphs 17 and 18, Schedule 18 Finance Act 1998 impose a penalty of £100 if a corporation tax return is submitted up to three months late. This increases to £200 if it is over three months late. If the previous two returns were also late the above amounts increase to £500 and £1,000, respectively.

In addition, where the corporation tax return remains outstanding 6 months after the due date a penalty of 10% of the unpaid tax at that date can be imposed. This rises to 20% if the return is outstanding one year after it was due to be submitted.

Penalties are imposed for failure to submit PAYE and P11D forms on time. The penalty is £100 per 50 employees for each month or part of the month the return remains outstanding after the due date. There is also a maximum penalty of £3,000 if a paper return is submitted and the employer is required to file the return online.

Failure to submit a VAT return or pay the VAT by the due date triggers a default surcharge period of 12 months. The surcharges increase for every occasion within the default surcharge period that a VAT return is submitted late, with a maximum surcharge of 15% of the unpaid VAT.

Late payment penalties

[17.4] Finance Act 2009, Sch 56, para 107 provided a new penalty regime for late payment penalties for 2010/11 and later years.

If tax remains outstanding after 30 days of the due date, then a 5% penalty is charged and an additional 5% is charged if the tax is unpaid after six and twelve months from the due date. HMRC has to notify the taxpayer of the penalty and the reason it has been levied. The penalty is payable within 30 days of the penalty notice and there is the right of appeal against both the imposition and amount of the penalty. The late payment penalty applies to taxes under the self-assessment regime and replaced the surcharge provisions on balancing payments up to the 2009/10 tax year.

The 2016 UTT decision in *Donaldson v Revenue and Customs Comrs* [2014] UKUT 536 (TCC), [2015] STC 689 means that the self-assessment reminder form and the SA326D – reminder for a late tax return – constitute sufficient notice for the penalties and HMRC do not need to provide any additional warning.

Fixed penalties — failure to keep proper records

[17.5] TMA 1970, s 12B sets out the records that should be kept by a taxpayer. Essentially records should be kept that enable the taxpayer to make and submit an accurate and complete tax return.

Businesses are required to retain their records for five years after the filing date of the return and private individuals need to retain their records for 12 months after the filing date. If there is an ongoing enquiry or investigation the records should be kept until HMRC confirms they are no longer required.

A penalty of up to £3,000 may be imposed for a failure to keep proper records (TMA 1970, s 12B(5)).

Tax geared penalties introduced by Finance Act 2007 and extended by Finance Act 2008

[17.6] Finance Act 2007 introduced a new regime of tax geared penalties for incorrect tax returns and accounts.

The main objectives of the new penalty regime are to improve compliance behaviour and to encourage full, unprompted disclosure where errors do occur.

The new legislation applies to income tax, corporation tax, capital gains tax, VAT, PAYE, NIC and the Construction Industry Scheme. It generally applies for tax periods commencing on or after 1 April 2008 and where the return submission date is on or after 1 April 2009 (SI 2008/568).

Schedule 40 Finance Act 2008 extended the new regime to Inheritance Tax, Stamp Duty Land Tax and many other indirect taxes and duties. Schedule 41 Finance Act 2008 further extended it to include circumstances where the taxpayer fails to notify chargeability to HMRC and to circumstances where an unauthorised person issues a VAT invoice or supplies a product knowing it will be used in a way that attracts higher duty than was paid to HMRC. These regulations are broadly for tax periods commencing on or after 1 April 2009 and where the return submission date is on or after 1 April 2010 (SI 2009/571).

HMRC has changed its terminology in this area. Instead of 'voluntary' disclosure HMRC is now using the term 'unprompted'. 'Careless' has replaced 'negligent' and 'deliberate' has replaced 'fraudulent'. The method of calculating the penalty has also changed substantially and is more complex as set out below.

Calculating the penalty

[17.7] The calculation of tax geared penalties under the new regime is a five-step process.

Step 1 — identify the behaviour and potential lost revenue

[17.8] Not every adjustment to a self-assessment will result in a penalty. If the error was innocent, ie if reasonable care was taken and information exists to demonstrate this, no penalty is chargeable.

A taxpayer who discovers an error in a return or other document submitted to HMRC and fails to take reasonable steps to correct the position is considered to have been careless up until the point that the inaccuracy is discovered. If the taxpayer does not then take any steps to rectify the error, the revenue lost to HMRC as a result of the continuing error will be deemed to be a result of deliberate behaviour. Likewise, if HMRC makes an error which the taxpayer or their agent identifies and fails to take reasonable steps to correct the taxpayer is considered to have been careless up until the point the error is discovered.

The three behaviours categorised in the legislation are: 'careless', 'deliberate' and 'deliberate and concealed'. There are extensive examples and further explanations of this in the Compliance Handbook from CH81100 to CH81170.

'Careless' is essentially failure to take reasonable care. People with different levels of knowledge and experience are not to be treated in a similar way. For example, a sole trader with no formal tax and accounting training who has only been in business as a hairdresser for three years would be expected to show a lower level of care than a director of a building company who has been in this role for the last 20 years and who has a professional accountancy qualification. The new powers regime in FA 2008 enables HMRC to gather evidence to assist them in assessing each taxpayer's abilities in this respect. Examples of when HMRC considers reasonable care to have been taken are detailed at CH81130.

A 'deliberate' inaccuracy occurs when a person gives HMRC a document that he knows to be inaccurate. This could be due to the omission of bank interest from their tax return or the submission of accounts which are incorrect because they failed to declare all cash sales during the period.

An error is classified as 'deliberate and concealed' when a document that the taxpayer knows to be inaccurate is deliberately submitted to HMRC and the taxpayer takes steps to conceal the inaccuracy eg by holding the bank account in a false name, destroying documentation or creating false documentation.

Where the taxpayer engages a third party and that person makes an error in the tax return or other document submitted to HMRC, a penalty is still chargeable on the taxpayer unless they are able to demonstrate that they took reasonable care to check the return before they signed it. This is demonstrated in recent case *J Gedir v HMRC* [2016] UKFTT 188.

If HMRC has opened an enquiry or the taxpayer is making a disclosure, then each inaccuracy is considered separately. For example, if an enquiry into a family owned limited company involves inaccuracies in the capital allowances claim, legal and professional expenses and director's loan account entries, each of these inaccuracies should be considered separately so as to identify the behaviour that led to each inaccuracy. The amount of tax at stake (including any amount that was erroneously refunded) for each of these inaccuracies must be quantified to enable the penalty to be calculated — this is now called the 'Potential Lost Revenue' (PLR).

Where the error alters the amount of a loss there are different rules depending upon whether the loss has been utilised and whether group relief is applicable. These are included at Paragraphs 7 and 8 of Schedule 24 FA 2007 and in the Compliance Handbook at CH82300.

Calculating the penalty: Step 2 — identify the maximum and minimum penalties

[17.9] The chart shown below depicts the maximum and minimum penalties based on each of the above behaviours.

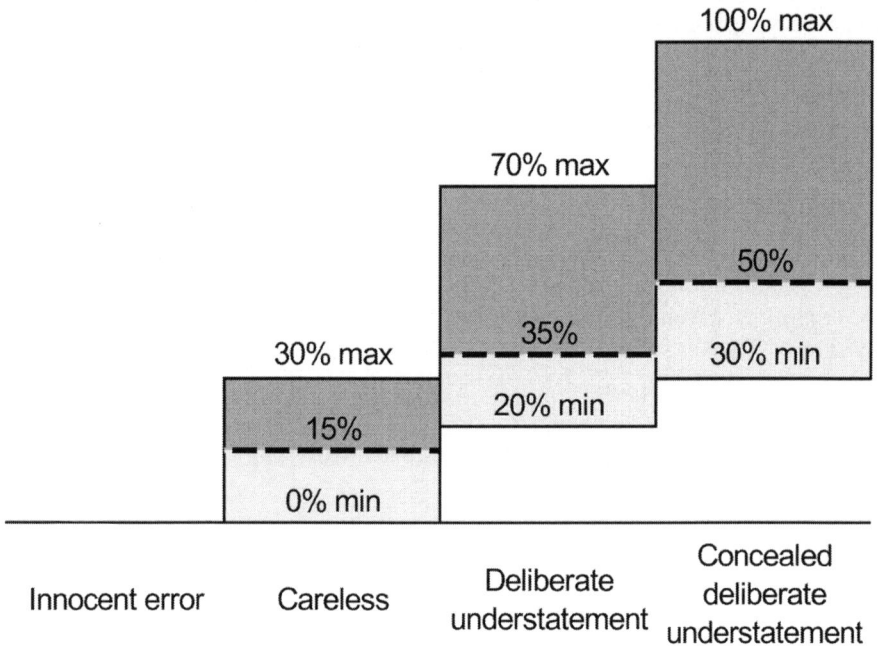

Penalty range for prompted disclosure
Extra reduction available for unprompted disclosure

There is no penalty for cases where it is agreed that the taxpayer has taken reasonable care.

Unprompted disclosures attract lower penalties than prompted disclosures. If a company makes a deliberate understatement in its accounts and voluntarily discloses this to HMRC, the minimum penalty is 20%, compared to 35% if the disclosure was prompted, eg by HMRC opening an enquiry. The maximum penalty in both cases is 70% of the PLR.

The maximum amount by which the penalty can be reduced is calculated by subtracting the minimum penalty from the maximum penalty for the behaviour. In the case of the company making a voluntary disclosure of a deliberate understatement of £20,000 tax, the maximum reduction is 50% (70% – 20%).

Calculating the penalty: Step 3 — negotiate the disclosure reduction

[17.10] The quality of the disclosure made is key in negotiating the penalty reduction. HMRC's Compliance Handbook contains examples of this at pages CH82400–CH82460.

The categories to be negotiated are as follows:

Reduction for disclosure:	Maximum mitigation
Telling HMRC about the inaccuracy	30%
Giving HMRC reasonable help to quantify it	40%
Allowing HMRC access to records so they can ensure that the inaccuracy is fully corrected	30%
Total maximum mitigation	100%

In order to calculate the penalty chargeable, the mitigation percentage is applied to the maximum reduction. So, with the above example, if the total maximum mitigation is 75%, then the total penalty reduction is 42.5% and the applicable penalty would be 32.5% of the PLR.

Within all three of the mitigation categories, consideration needs to be given to the 'quality' of disclosure by considering the timing, nature and extent of the assistance given.

'Telling' includes making a full disclosure, admitting the errors and explaining how and why the inaccuracy arose. In this context, 'timing' relates to making a full disclosure of everything the taxpayer is aware of at the time when the disclosure is made. 'Nature' of the disclosure covers what happened and how willing the taxpayer was to answer questions as well as making a disclosure. 'Extent' takes into account whether the disclosure is full or partial.

'Helping' includes giving reasonable help and actively engaging and assisting in the process of quantifying the disclosure, including volunteering information. 'Timing' relates to how swiftly help and information are provided. 'Nature' covers whether the help was useful and assisted the Officer in quantifying the PLR. When considering the 'Extent', the Officer will reflect on whether help was provided throughout the whole period of the compliance check or only for part of it.

'Giving access' is permitting access to business records, other records and relevant documentation for the Officer to check to ensure that the disclosure is full and has been correctly quantified. When considering the 'Timing' aspect, if HMRC received all information and documentation promptly, without the need to use their formal information powers, then full mitigation should be available. 'Nature' covers whether access was provided at a convenient time and location and whether copies were made available on request of the Officer. If all existing records that are reasonably required for checking the tax position are made available, then full reduction for the 'Extent' of this part of the disclosure should be available.

Clearly it would be helpful to retain evidence gathered during the course of the enquiry or investigation to help substantiate the reductions that are appropriate for penalty negotiations.

Advisers should also reflect on their own part in the conduct of the enquiry. Merely answering HMRC's specific questions may not be enough to obtain full mitigation under the 'helping' category for instance. Volunteering information including background details regarding the operation of a business, for example, that assist the officer in understanding the issues and quantifying any under-declarations of tax should result in a lower penalty. Delays in responding to letters may also have a detrimental effect on the ultimate penalty.

Whilst assisting HMRC with their enquiries, advisers should ensure that the information is reasonably requested and is relevant to the enquiry. Any information provided to HMRC should focus on resolving the matters under enquiry.

Calculating the penalty: Step 4 — calculate the penalty

[17.11] Once the disclosure reduction has been negotiated, the next step is to calculate the actual penalty.

Firstly calculate the actual reduction in the penalty. This is the disclosure mitigation multiplied by the maximum reduction. If we return to our earlier example of a company making an unprompted disclosure of a deliberate understatement, the maximum reduction in the penalty was 50%. Say their agent negotiated the reduction at Step 3 to be 75%, then the actual penalty reduction is 50% × 75% = 37.5%.

The actual penalty percentage can then be calculated by subtracting the reduction in the penalty from the maximum penalty percentage. For the company in our example this would be 70% – 37.5% = 32.5%

The actual penalty is then calculated by multiplying the penalty percentage by the PLR. In our example the penalty payable will be 32.5% × £20,000 = £6,500.

Calculating the penalty: Step 5 — consider suspending the penalty or attribute it to someone else

[17.12] If a penalty is charged due to carelessness it may be possible to have the penalty suspended provided certain conditions are met. This could be valuable in practice as a taxpayer may end up paying no penalty whatsoever. Penalties charged because of deliberate errors, regardless of whether they were concealed, cannot be suspended.

If at the end of the suspension period (up to two years) all the conditions have been met, the penalty will be cancelled. HMRC's guidelines regarding the suspension of penalties can be found at CH83100–CH83220.

The taxpayer or their adviser should discuss with the Officer whether the penalty can be suspended and, if so, the terms of the suspension. HMRC is unlikely to agree that a penalty can be suspended if it derives from a transaction or event that is a one-off eg a capital gain on the sale of a property where the company owns no other properties, however a recent case *Hall v HMRC* [2016] UKFTT 412, suggests that even if the under-declaration of tax is as a result of a one-off transaction, there may still be scope for the penalties to be suspended.

The terms of the suspension should be SMART: Specific, Measurable, Achievable, Realistic and Time bound. It is likely that one of the terms will be an obligation on the taxpayer to submit all returns and pay all tax on time and care should be taken in this respect by those businesses which file a number of returns including corporation tax, VAT and PAYE etc. Should any of these returns be filed or the tax paid after the due date, the penalty will become chargeable.

The conditions must be documented and at the end of the suspension period, the onus is on the taxpayer to demonstrate that all the conditions have been met.

If there is a disagreement the taxpayer may appeal against the amount of the penalty, the decision whether to suspend it and/or the conditions of suspension.

There are provisions for HMRC to pursue individual company officers personally for payment of all or part of a penalty attributable to the company. The option to pursue the individual company officers is likely to be taken when it is established that the officer was involved in the events which led to the deliberate understatement of tax due. This provision is separate to the Senior Accounting Officer regulations in Finance Act 2009.

Penalties for offshore evasion

[17.13] Finance Act 2010, Sch 10 provides for tax geared penalties where there is an offshore link. The new penalties came into force from 6 April 2011 and apply to tax liabilities arising on or after this date

The penalties are described as an 'enhancement' of the penalties for:

- failure to notify;
- inaccuracy on a return; and
- failure to file a return on time.

These penalties will be linked to the tax transparency of the territory in which the income or gain arises. HMRC has categorised countries on the basis of how difficult it is for them to secure information. Put simply, the harder it is to secure information the higher the penalties are.

There are three levels of penalty:

- where the income or gain arises in a territory in 'category 1', the penalty rate will be the same as under existing legislation;
- where the income or gain arises in a territory in 'category 2', the penalty rate will be 1.5 times that in existing legislation – up to 150 per cent of tax;
- where the income or gain arises in a territory in 'category 3', the penalty rate will be double that in existing legislation – up to 200 per cent of tax.

Finance Act 2015 introduced a number of changes to the offshore penalty regime, including the introduction of a new 'category 0', applying to tax evasion linked to the countries considered most transparent, including the UK. To qualify for inclusion within this category, the country in question must have adopted the global Common Reporting Standard (CRS) and must previously have been designated to be a category 1 territory. Further details on the CRS are provided at **17.27**. The maximum penalty rate applying to category 0 is 100%, and the maximum penalty for the new category 1 has been increased to 125% of the PLR.

The Act also introduced an 'aggravated penalty' in relation to those moving the proceeds of tax evasion in order to escape tax transparency, applying to all funds moved after 27 March 2015. In certain cases, this penalty will increase total penalties due by 50%.

The offshore penalty regime was also extended to include inheritance tax and to cover circumstances in which the proceeds of non-compliance are hidden offshore.

Finance Act 2016 legislated a number of measures aimed at tackling offshore tax evasion:

- A strict liability criminal offence for tax evasion – the controversial new measure will introduce a new criminal offence which will remove the need to prove intent to evade tax, for the most serious cases of failure to disclose offshore income and gains. These provisions came into force on 7 October 2017 and have effect in relation to the tax year 6 April 2017 and subsequent years.
- Civil penalties for offshore tax evaders – the government will increase civil penalties in respect of deliberate offshore tax evasion, and will introduce a new penalty linked to the value of the asset on which tax was evaded; naming and shaming of tax evaders is also set to increase. Broadly these have effect from 1 April 2017.
- Civil penalties for those who enable offshore evasion – civil penalties Have been introduced with effect from 1 January 2017 for those who have enabled tax evasion; the 'enablers' will also face publication of their personal details.

Requirement to Correct

[17.14] The RTC is a requirement for taxpayers to review their affairs and correct any offshore non-compliance by 30 September 2018. The RTC relates to income tax, capital gains tax and inheritance tax non-compliance that took place in tax years prior to 6 April 2017. The taxpayer is expected to review and correct prior years in accordance with the time limits for assessment, ie if a taxpayer believes that he has always taken reasonable care, then he only needs to review his tax affairs in the past four years.

There is a provision in the legislation that gives HMRC additional time to assess tax payers and effectively 'freezes time' as at 5 April 2017. HMRC then have until 5 April 2021 to raise assessments in line with normal time limits as though the assessments were raised at 5 April 2017. For example, prior to the RTC, HMRC would have until 5 April 2017 to raise assessments for 2012/13 reasonable care. With the RTC in force, HMRC will now have until 5 April 2021 to raise assessments for the same period.

The reason for the extension is to give HMRC additional time to review the information provided by overseas jurisdictions under the terms of the CRS.

Further penalties will apply where a taxpayer is found not to have complied with the RTC. These range from 100% to 200% of the tax due, in addition to the normal penalties for the initial non-compliance. In the most serious cases of non-compliance with the RTC legislation, where the tax due is in excess of £25,000 for any given year, HMRC can charge an asset-based penalty of up to 10% of the value of the relevant asset.

It is no coincidence that the deadline for the correction of all overseas tax irregularities coincides with the deadline for the implementation of the exchange of information under the CRS (for those countries that are not early adopters). After 30 September 2018, HMRC will have access to unprecedented amounts of information in relation to offshore assets and will no longer be as dependent on voluntary disclosures to recover lost revenues.

Implications of failed tax planning on the amount of a tax-geared penalty

[17.15] Many companies and individuals undertake some kind of tax planning to mitigate their liabilities. There are two main reasons why such planning sometimes fails to achieve the reduction in tax that was intended: failure of the technical advice or a failure in the implementation of the planning.

Failure of the tax advice may occur for many reasons such as an error by an agent in their analysis of the position or a clarification of the law as a result of a court hearing that means the arrangements do not achieve their desired effect.

A failure in implementation generally occurs when the client fails to understand what they are required to do or they do not carry out the adviser's instructions diligently.

If HMRC enquires or investigates the planning and ultimately, whether by negotiation with HMRC or a ruling from the Tribunal, the tax becomes payable, HMRC is likely to consider whether a penalty can be charged.

CH81130 indicates that HMRC considers that if a return is submitted on the basis of a reasonably arguable view of the tax position then if this view is not ultimately upheld no penalty will be chargeable. Similarly, if a taxpayer acts on the advice of a competent adviser which proves to be wrong despite the adviser being given the correct facts then no penalty is due according to HMRC's guidance. Arguably therefore, if the planning fails solely on a technical point then no penalty will be due unless the technical basis of the planning was not reasonably arguable.

However, it is more difficult to anticipate the penalty position where the planning has not been correctly implemented. HMRC is likely to look in detail at what was meant to happen, what actually happened and why the planning was not implemented correctly in order to ascertain whether reasonable care was taken or, if not, whether the error was careless or deliberate.

Tax agents may therefore want to consider what records they need to maintain and whether they check their client's implementation of any planning, however basic, in order to maximise the chances of a successful outcome and minimise any potential penalties that HMRC may seek to charge.

Other consequences of a penalty

[17.16] If a taxpayer is charged a penalty for deliberate behaviour, then HMRC considers there is a higher risk that their tax returns or accounts will be incorrect in the future. To ensure that taxpayers do not continue to understate the tax due on their returns, HMRC introduced in February 2011 its Managing Deliberate Defaulters (MDD) programme for taxpayers who deliberately understated their tax liabilities. Those entered into the programme face further scrutiny of all their tax affairs for a period of two to five years and face unannounced visits from HMRC to check that business records are up to date and complete. In addition, the taxpayers selected for the programme are required to submit additional information with their tax returns and can expect HMRC to cross check the information they obtain with the tax-payer's business records and accounts. This may involve test purchases or checking a supplier or customer's records using their information powers.

In addition, FA 2009, s 94 includes provisions enabling HMRC to publish names and other details of those taxpayers who incur a penalty for deliberate or deliberate and concealed errors leading to PLR in excess of £25,000. The legislation was brought into effect by Treasury Order on 3 March 2010 and applies to failures or wrongdoings for return periods starting on or after 1 April. No details of deliberate defaults committed prior to the legislation becoming effective will be published.

Penalties for deliberate wrongdoing by agents

[17.17] Finance Act 2012, Sch 38 and s 223 detail the legislation targeting dishonest tax agents, which came into force in April 2013 by statutory instrument.

The purpose of Sch 38 is to allow HMRC to take action against agents believed to have been deliberately dishonest. 'Deliberately dishonest' is described as assisting in the preparation of a return, form, information or document that the agent knows is incorrect. A 'tax agent' is defined as anyone who assists clients with their tax affairs in the normal course of their business, whether directly or indirectly.

Should HMRC determine that an agent has been dishonest it has the power to issue a dishonest conduct notice and fine the agent up to £50,000. HMRC can also publish the details of the agent fined under the new rules if the agent does not fully cooperate with HMRC. The agent does have the right of appeal to the First-tier Tribunal against the measures described above.

In addition, HMRC has the power to issue a File Access Notice (FAN) to the agent concerned requiring production of the agent's working papers in order to check the extent of the problem. Once the agent has been put on notice that a FAN is or will be given to them, the agent is guilty of a criminal offence should they conceal, destroy or otherwise dispose of a material document. The offence is punishable on summary conviction by a fine or on indictment by imprisonment of up to two years or a fine, or both.

Key points

[17.18] The key points on penalties are as follows.

- Fixed penalties are imposed for failure to submit a tax return on time.
- If a taxpayer fails to keep proper records then HMRC may impose a fine of up to £3,000.
- Failure to notify chargeability or cases of fraud or negligence for tax periods before 1 April 2008 will attract penalties of up to 100% of the tax lost. It is possible to negotiate abatement of this penalty based on 'disclosure', 'co-operation' and 'seriousness'.
- Taxpayers and advisers will need to carefully identify whether the old or new penalty regime applies and negotiate the penalty using the correct criteria and guidelines.
- A new penalty regime was introduced by FA 2007 and extended by FA 2008. Tax geared penalties will be imposed for cases of carelessness and/or deliberate, concealed errors. Penalties can be reduced based on the quality of disclosure.
- Tax agents and advisers should ensure that files are maintained in a way that captures evidence to substantiate behaviours and factors that could affect penalty negotiations.
- Penalty suspension should be requested for penalties arising as a result of careless behaviour. Subject to successful completion of specific conditions, the penalty will be cancelled.
- Use the new Appeals procedures if you disagree with a penalty decision. This may include asking HMRC for an Internal Review. If unsuccessful at Internal Review, the client can request ADR and/or list the dispute with the Tribunal Service.
- Penalties of up to 200% may apply where there is an offshore link to the potential lost revenue.

Further penalties are chargeable for non-compliance with the RTC.

HMRC powers

[17.19] 'Compliance checks' is HMRC's own term for any intervention that enables it to check whether a person is complying with their obligations under the Taxes Acts. It therefore encompasses:

- HMRC's powers to demand information;
- HMRC's power to inspect business premises, assets and records;
- enquiries;
- discovery powers; and
- investigations.

Information powers

[17.20] The majority of HMRC's information powers are set out in Sch 36 FA 2008. These give HMRC the power to obtain information from taxpayers and third parties. Any statutory references quoted in this chapter relate to Sch

36 FA 2008 unless otherwise stated. Extensive commentary on this legislation is available in HMRC's Compliance Handbook.

FA 2009, s 95 enables the Treasury to alter the legislation by Statutory Instrument at any time, so the latest position should always be checked.

HMRC can use these powers to obtain information at any point — there is no need for an enquiry to be open.

Information can be sought regarding a taxpayer's 'tax position' which is:

• a person's past, present or future liability to pay tax;
• penalties or other amounts that have been paid, are payable or may be payable; and
• claims, elections or other notices that have been or may be made.

Sch 36 enables HMRC to obtain information relating to income tax, capital gains tax, corporation tax and VAT.

FA 2009, s 96(1) extends the above information powers to include inheritance tax and various indirect taxes with effect from 1 April 2010.

If HMRC wishes to use their powers in Sch 36 they need to demonstrate that the information or documentation is 'reasonably required'. Information should be needed to help HMRC decide what the correct tax position is, how an error can be put right or ensure that the correct amount of tax is paid. The request should be reasonable and proportionate and in the taxpayer's possession or power to obtain. If it is not, then you should consider an appeal.

Obtaining information from a taxpayer

[17.21] Paragraph 1 enables HMRC to request information or documents that is reasonably required by the Officer for checking a person's tax position.

The request may initially be informal. It could, for example, be made in a letter that is sent during the course of an enquiry. However, if the information or documentation is not provided then the HMRC Officer can issue an information notice. There is no need for the First-tier Tribunal to authorise the issuing of the notice. A specimen copy of the notice can be found in the Appendix to HMRC's Compliance Handbook at CHApp1.

The notice will specify the deadline for providing the information and documents. It may also specify the following:

• whether an original of the document must be produced (if this is not specified then copies are acceptable); and
• whether the document must be produced for inspection at a specific location at a specific time.

The taxpayer should be given a reasonable period to comply with the notice. There is no minimum time period specified in the legislation but CH23420 does suggest that it is reasonable to expect documents to be provided within 30 days but that longer may be needed at busy periods. If the taxpayer cannot provide the information in the period specified, he should explain why this is the case and propose a new deadline in writing.

HMRC can seek information and documentation that is relevant to the taxpayer's past, present or future tax liabilities. Some examples of information requests are below:

Past: Mr Jones disclosed the sale of a property on his tax return submitted 6 months ago. An enquiry has been opened and HMRC has requested a schedule listing all improvement expenditure over £500 incurred and invoices for all items listed.

Present: Miss Smith made an error on her 2008/09 Tax Return in connection with her garden centre business. An enquiry was opened and the error was corrected. As part of the enquiry, the Officer imposed a tax geared penalty for the error as it was agreed it was careless. Her advisor negotiated with the Officer and it was agreed that the penalty would be suspended subject to Miss Smith satisfying certain conditions over a two year period. The officer has now issued an information notice to obtain access to her current business records so that he can check she is still abiding by the conditions of the penalty suspension.

Future: A small, owner managed group holding company has submitted a clearance application with regard to a proposed restructuring. HMRC would like further details of the proposed transaction before they respond to the application. HMRC therefore issues an information notice.

Obtaining information from a third party

[17.22] HMRC also has the power to obtain information and documents from third parties with or without the agreement of the taxpayer. The ability to ask for 'information' was an extension of HMRC's information powers in respect of third parties. These information notices may name the taxpayer but this is not compulsory.

Third party notices might, for example, be used to obtain details about a company from its tax accountant, from an architect about the renovations carried out to a company's offices or from a company about a supplier or customer.

Notices to obtain information which do not name the taxpayer might be used to obtain details about all the partners in a partnership from the nominated partner, for example. They might also be used to obtain information from a company about employees or contractors.

Whilst third party notices can be issued with the taxpayer's approval, it is anticipated that most will be issued with the approval of the First-tier Tribunal instead. Unless the Tribunal considers it will impede the assessment or collection of tax, the person to whom the notice is addressed will be told that the information or documents are required and given a reasonable opportunity to make representations to an HMRC officer. The officer must then give a summary of the representations to the Tribunal for consideration.

Restrictions on HMRC's information powers

[17.23] There are a number of restrictions on HMRC's power to obtain information. These are set out at Part 4 of Schedule 36.

The primary point is that a person need only produce a document if it is in the person's 'possession or power'. In this context possession means the legal right to possess a document. Power means a legal right to view the document without anyone else's consent, eg electronic data which you can access.

Requests for director's personal documentation eg bank statements, during a corporate enquiry should therefore be considered in this context and with regard to the need to help HMRC in the context of penalty mitigation (see section **17.6**).

In the case of tax advisers and auditors there are some limitations on the documents or information that HMRC can request. Similarly, legal professional privilege continues to be a restriction on HMRC's powers. However, there are some limitations and in particular a tax accountant does need to provide information explaining any documents or information that they have assisted the client in supplying to HMRC.

Appeals against information notices

[17.24] In most cases, it is not possible to appeal against an information notice, as no appeals are permitted against requests to provide information or documents that form part of the taxpayer's statutory records. In addition, no appeals are allowed where the First-tier Tribunal has approved the giving of the notice unless the notice is issued to obtain information from a third party about persons whose identities are unknown.

Statutory records include records of all receipts and expenses, all goods purchased and sold, all supporting documents relating to the transactions of the business, ie accounts, books, deeds, contracts, vouchers and receipts. Records may be retained on a computer.

Appeals must be made in writing to the officer who issued the notice within 30 days of the date of the notice. The grounds for the appeal must be stated.

Once the officer has received the appeal he may request it should be heard by the First-tier Tribunal, which have the authority to confirm, alter the terms or cancel the information notice or any requirements within it. A new deadline will be set by the Tribunal or the Officer for supplying the information and documentation requested in the remaining parts of the notice.

If you disagree with the terms of any information notice you may appeal, providing the notice is not for statutory records or pre-approved by the Tribunal as detailed above.

Failing to comply with an information notice

[17.25] A penalty of £300 will be charged for failure to comply with an information notice. In addition, daily penalties of up to £60 will be imposed if the failure continues after the imposition of the £300 penalty. These penalties can be imposed by any HMRC Officer and appeals can be made to the First-tier Tribunal within 30 days of the notice imposing the penalty.

The above penalties will also be charged to any person who deliberately obstructs an HMRC officer during the course of an inspection pre-approved by the First-tier Tribunal. They also apply to a person who conceals, destroys or otherwise disposes of a document or who arranges for this to occur.

Anyone who receives a notice needs to be aware of the above consequences and of the potential impact on any tax geared penalties.

It may be that the taxpayer has a 'reasonable excuse' (as described at CH26340) for not complying with the notice. If so, the HMRC officer should be informed without unreasonable delay.

In addition, under limited circumstances, a tax geared penalty may be imposed. The legislation also enables a fine or imprisonment to follow if documents are concealed, destroyed or disposed of after a First-tier Tribunal has approved a third party notice.

In order to properly judge the context, it is important to check whether a Schedule 36 Notice has been issued with First-tier Tribunal approval.

Data gathering powers

[17.26] Schedule 23 FA 2011 brought into force new data gathering powers enabling HMRC to gather specific pieces of information about a group of people for use in risk analysis. These data gathering powers differ from the information and inspection powers covered above as they cannot be used for checking the tax position of the data holder. However, nothing in the purpose or scope of the power restricts what the data can be used for. The powers allow HMRC to acquire bulk information which according to their guidance is essential due to the large number of taxpayers and the cost of administering the tax system.

A data holder notice may be issued to a data holder and this is defined as an individual in possession of 'relevant data'. As with the information powers at Schedule 36 there is a limit to how far back HMRC can request data and it must be within the power or possession of the data holder. Also, if the notice has the approval of the Tribunal then there is no right of appeal and penalties will apply for a failure to comply with the notice.

The data-holder notice may specify the 'means and form' in which the data-holder must provide the relevant data, providing that the means and form are reasonable. 'Means and form' includes being able to stipulate the structure and medium through which data is required; so long as the request is reasonable. What is considered reasonable depends on the circumstances and ability of the data holder.

By way of an example, HMRC may use these data gathering powers to require card payment processors to provide data about their customers. The data will be used to check whether businesses have suppressed their income or operated within the hidden economy. The legislation specifies the data available for HMRC to request as credit, debit and charge card sales of the retailer; the retailer's name, address and VAT number if applicable and bank account details.

Other information powers

[17.27] Whilst most powers contained in TMA 1970, s 20 were repealed on the introduction of the powers in FA 2008, some remain: s 20A (power to call for the papers of a tax accountant) and s 20BA (Orders for the delivery of documents from a third party). However, these may be amended as part of HMRC's ongoing consultation on changes to their powers.

In addition, there are some powers for gathering information as a precursor to a criminal prosecution which are contained in the Serious Organised Crime and Police Act 2005, s 144 Finance Act 2000 and the Police and Criminal Evidence Act 1984. The latter also gives officers the power to search or arrest taxpayers.

Finance Act 2012, s 224 expands HMRC's information powers (FA 2008, Sch 36) to allow a formal request to be made to a business or organisation (data holder) to confirm a person's name and address from incomplete information such as a bank account number. The purpose of the new power is to assist HMRC and other tax jurisdictions where they believe that there has been suspicious activity but the person cannot be fully identified. Once the identity of the person is known HMRC can use their information powers to request further information if required. In order to use this power HMRC needs to meet certain conditions:

- the information is reasonably required to check the person's tax position;
- the person's identity is not clear and can be ascertained using the information in HMRC's possession; and
- HMRC believes that the person's details will have been obtained by the data handler in the course of its business.

The amendment follows the OECD report on the UK's ability to exchange information to the international standard.

The change to the information powers came into force on 1 April 2012.

Finance Act 2009, Sch 49 includes new provisions to enable HMRC to obtain contact details from third parties in relation to taxpayers who have outstanding debts with HMRC.

Swiss – UK tax agreement

Finance Act 2012 ratified the agreement between the Swiss and UK governments which came into force on 1 January 2013 and affects UK resident individuals with assets under the management of Swiss banks.

A one-off flat rate tax was charged on 31 May 2013 to regularise the past if the individual could not demonstrate that the Swiss assets had previously been disclosed to HMRC or was not prepared to disclose their Swiss assets. The agreement provides for a levy on the assets of an individual who died on or after 1 January 2013 and had not previously disclosed their Swiss bank account. Those who believe that the one-off payment has been wrongly levied from their account may make a claim to HMRC to have this amount refunded. Written confirmation from their Swiss bank that they will not administer the refund must be obtained before approaching HMRC. Tax case *Vrang v Revenue and Customs Comrs* [2017] EWHC 1055 (Admin), [2017] STC 1192, [2017] All ER (D) 86 (May) confirms that there is no legislative requirement for HMRC to refund the charge even if the tax withheld significantly exceeds the true liability.

Going forward, Swiss banks will automatically withhold tax on income and gains arising on or after 1 January 2013 unless the UK resident individual can confirm the Swiss assets have been declared.

Swiss banks will automatically deduct relevant withholding taxes and pay these over to the Swiss tax authorities, unless the individual discloses the assets to HMRC and provides a confirmation each year stating that they are tax compliant from a UK perspective.

The agreement also allows for HMRC to ask that the 320 Swiss banks exchange information with the UK in relation to UK residents. HMRC will, initially, be allowed to make up to 500 requests per annum for information on a named taxpayer that held or holds an account or deposit with a Swiss bank. There is no need for HMRC to name the bank.

In return, the UK has agreed it will not 'acquire' stolen data concerning UK residents of Swiss banks or prosecute Swiss bank employees linked to tax evasion.

Automatic Exchange of Information

In April 2015 the UK government brought into force new regulations allowing it to automatically exchange financial information with other jurisdictions under its various international agreements. The new regulations give effect to the Multilateral Competent Authority Agreement on the Automatic Exchange of Financial Account Information signed in October 2014, implementing the OECD's Common Reporting Standard.

The new regulations will legislate for UK institutions to disclose information relating to their customers' accounts, including details on account balances, interest payments and beneficial ownership, where those customers are resident outside the UK. The information will then be forwarded to those other jurisdictions which are party to the relevant international agreements. By the end of August 2016, over 100 jurisdictions were signed up to the OECD CRS agreement. In exchange, HMRC will receive information from these other jurisdictions, which will be used to combat offshore tax evasion by UK resident taxpayers.

Financial Intermediaries (FIs) will be required to carry out specified due diligence procedures to identify account holders who are resident overseas and determine each client's tax residency so that their bank account information can be forwarded to the correct jurisdiction. From 1 January 2016, the FIs were required to compile the relevant information in relation to those accounts open as at 31 December 2015 as well as all new accounts opened from 1 January 2016. The implementation timetable saw the first exchange of information in 2017 by the 'early adopter' countries. The remaining signatories to the CRS are expected to begin exchanging information in January 2018.

Amendments were made to the International Tax Compliance Regulations 2015 under the power inserted into s 222 of Finance Act 2013 by s 50 of Finance (No 2) Act 2015 concerning client notification letters about international tax compliance agreements. Under the regulations, advisers are required to notify their clients of the following:

- that HMRC will soon be getting data on overseas financial accounts under the OECD CRS agreement from 2017, allowing HMRC to check that the appropriate levels of tax are levied from those holding overseas accounts;
- that there are opportunities to come forward about your overseas tax affairs if you need to; and
- for those who fail to disclose overseas accounts, HMRC will enforce penalties through the offshore penalty regime, civil penalties for tax evaders and the new criminal offence for failure to declare taxable offshore income and gains.

The legislation came into force on 30 September 2016 and advisers are required to notify their clients by 31 August 2017 or face a £3,000 fine.

Inspection powers

[17.28] Finance Act 2008, Schedule 36 contains powers enabling HMRC to inspect businesses, their assets on the premises and documents. They also enable HMRC to carry out Employer Compliance and VAT visits.

HMRC is now able to deal with income tax, capital gains tax and corporation tax matters via an inspection. They can therefore review the business's records and discuss all tax issues relating to a taxpayer's profits and losses.

There are many reasons why HMRC may choose to inspect an owner managed business. HMRC may carry out a VAT inspection or they may want to follow up on a matter which forms part of an ongoing enquiry. For example, if a company is claiming expense deductions for extensive repairs carried out to a warehouse, the officer may want to visit and view the property in order to help him establish whether the repairs are capital improvements. For VAT or Customs Duties, HMRC may want to inspect specific imported stock.

HMRC can only inspect business premises. They are not permitted to inspect residential homes. If a person operates their business from their home, the officer should seek to arrange the inspection at another venue, eg an HMRC office or their accountant's office.

HMRC will give at least seven days' notice of a visit in most cases. There are examples of inspection notices in the Appendix to the Compliance Handbook at CHApp1. These indicate that HMRC will, in normal cases, issue an information notice with the inspection notice. It is likely therefore that 30 days' notice of the visit may be provided.

Inspection notices should always be checked to ensure that they are reasonable and that the visit is convenient. CH25460 suggests that Officers should visit at a time convenient to the business. Any issues should be raised with HMRC. A restaurant, for example, may request a visit in the afternoon between the lunch and dinner services to avoid disruption to their customers.

Businesses need to prepare for a visit and understand what information needs to be provided. They should plan who will answer the officer's questions and deal with any requests for copies of documents. CH25320 states that HMRC officers can ask questions to obtain information relating to things they inspect.

If the officer is obstructed before or during their visit, then penalties may be charged. These are the same as for failure to deal with information notices.

Unannounced visits are permitted under certain circumstances. If the business manager is not present, HMRC can still enter the business premises if they pin their inspection notice in a prominent position. They cannot force entry under these provisions. Section 114 enables HMRC to inspect computer records.

HMRC may require a company or one of its staff to provide reasonable assistance for the inspection to enable computerised records to be reviewed and to help the Officer copy or print data.

HMRC can remove original documents but should only do so at a reasonable time. They should also keep them for the minimum period possible to complete their review. Businesses need to be aware of this and ask for a receipt for all documents removed. In most cases, HMRC should at least provide a copy of the document if the business needs it.

Enquiries

[17.29] The declaration made by the taxpayer on the face of each Return is that the return is correct and complete to the best of their knowledge. An officer undertaking a self-assessment enquiry will be seeking to establish whether or not the return is complete and correct.

HMRC can open an enquiry providing they give notice of this to the taxpayer. They may enquire into everything in the Return, including claims and elections, and any amount that affects the liability for another period (eg losses carried back) or another company's liability (eg surrender for group relief).

HMRC must open the enquiry within the time limits allowed.

- From 1 April 2008 when a tax return is submitted by the filing deadline, the enquiry window is 12 months from the actual submission date. Where the return is submitted late then the enquiry window closes on the quarter day immediately following 12 months from submission, the quarter dates being 31 January, 30 April, 31 July or 31 October.
- For accounting periods ending after 31 March 2008 the enquiry time limit for single companies and small groups is 12 months from the submission date of the return if it was submitted early or on time. For

other companies it remains unchanged. If the return is late the deadline becomes the 31 January, 30 April, 31 July or 31 October next following the first anniversary of the day on which the return is submitted or the amendment to the return made.

The notice opening the enquiry has to be received by the above deadlines.

Where accounting issues are under enquiry, the investigating officer will liaise with qualified accountants employed by HMRC. This has become more prevalent now that accounting profits are more closely aligned with taxable profits. Consideration of accounting issues is now likely to form part of many corporation tax enquiries.

HMRC may seek to charge penalties at the end of the enquiry and the penalty regulations should be borne in mind throughout an enquiry, to ensure that the responses to HMRC are helpful in maximising the penalty reductions.

If, at any stage in the enquiry, HMRC believes that there might otherwise be a loss of tax, it may amend the taxpayer's self-assessment. This may apply, for example, if there was a possibility of the company being wound up. The taxpayer may appeal against such amendments within 30 days.

The enquiry will not be treated as complete until HMRC issues a closure notice. The taxpayer may apply to the First-tier Tribunal for a direction that a closure notice must be issued in a specified period. A direction will be given unless HMRC can demonstrate that it has reasonable grounds for continuing the enquiry. This is a useful safeguard that is worth bearing in mind if an enquiry appears to have stagnated or there are unreasonable delays.

HMRC also has the power to issue aspect closure notices where they are satisfied that one area of an enquiry is complete. On receipt of the aspect closure notice the taxpayer is required to pay the tax relevant to that aspect if appropriate. Note also that the taxpayer can apply for an aspect closure notice in appropriate circumstances. This allows both the taxpayer and HMRC to concentrate on and settle the key areas of an enquiry.

If the taxpayer cannot agree with HMRC on a particular point and HMRC has issued an amended self assessment then an appeal may be made to the First-tier Tribunal or the case referred for Internal Review by HMRC.

No self-assessment return may be enquired into more than once. This is the case even if the enquiry is started and finished within the period during which the enquiry window would otherwise be open. This does not, however, preclude HMRC from opening Code of Practice 8 or 9 investigations or issuing discovery assessments under certain circumstances.

SP16/91 as clarified by RI 192 (October 1998) states that accountancy expenses incurred as a result of self assessment enquiries will be disallowed if additional tax liabilities are identified as a result of the enquiry which arise as a result of fraudulent or negligent conduct.

Discovery

[17.30] The legislation relating to discovery can be found at TMA 1970, s 29 and at FA 1998, Schedule 18, paras 42–46.

There is no formal definition of the word 'discovery'. However, HMRC may make an assessment where:

- the loss of tax is attributable to fraudulent or negligent conduct by or on behalf of the taxpayer; or
- HMRC could not have been expected, on the basis of the information available to them at the relevant time, to be aware of the potential loss of tax.

In *Revenue & Customs Comrs v Charlton* [2012] UKUT 770 (TCC) (20 December 2012), Judge Roger Berner stated that 'in our judgment, no new information, of fact or law, is required for there to be a discovery. All that is required is that it has newly appeared to an officer, acting honestly and reasonably, that there is an insufficiency in an assessment. That can be for any reason, including a change of view, change of opinion, or correction of an oversight.'

Discovery where the loss of tax is due to fraudulent or negligent conduct

[17.31] The terms 'fraudulent' and 'negligent' conduct are redefined by FA 2008, Schedule 39 as 'deliberate' and 'careless' conduct respectively. These behaviours mirror those described in the new penalty legislation.

Until the new information powers were introduced by FA 2008, HMRC could only issue an assessment using their discovery powers: the legislation does not give them the power to open an enquiry for prior years. The new information powers enable them to gather documents and information so that they can quantify the tax lost.

HMRC most frequently use their powers to issue a discovery assessment when they identify during an open enquiry that the taxpayer's return contains an error which might also apply to earlier tax periods. This may, for example, occur if HMRC identifies problems with the accounting treatment applied in one period, which may have affected the value of expenses claimed in earlier years.

HMRC may allege that the difficulties with the accounting system and analysis of expenses result from negligence, thus enabling them to raise assessments for earlier years.

Discovery where HMRC could not be expected to be aware of the loss of tax

[17.32] This is an area for which there is a significant amount of case law to consider in addition to the legislation, most importantly the case of *Veltema v Langham (Inspector of Taxes)* [2004] EWCA Civ 193, [2004] STC 544. HMRC practice in this area was then clarified by SP1/06. This includes some examples including a case involving a valuation and another where HMRC and the taxpayer take a different view of the technical position of a particular issue.

If a person has fully alerted HMRC to the full circumstances of an entry in a return, HMRC is precluded from making a discovery.

TMA 1970, s 29(6) and FA 1988, Sch 18, para 44(2) confirm that information is available to an officer if it is:

- contained in the taxpayer's return for the period concerned or either of the two preceding periods;
- contained in any claim for the period concerned;
- contained in any accounts, statements or documents accompanying the return or claim or produced in the course of an enquiry;
- information the existence and relevance of which the officer could reasonably be expected to infer from information in the three points above; and
- information the existence and relevance of which has been notified to the officer by or on behalf of the taxpayer.

A taxpayer may therefore be tempted to include significant information with a return in order to attempt to preclude a discovery assessment. However, EM3261 makes it clear that HMRC considers that it is not precluded from issuing a discovery assessment where the volume of information supplied is so extensive that an officer 'could not have been reasonably expected to be aware' of the significance of particular information and the officer's attention has not been drawn to it by the taxpayer or their agent.

Discovery provisions do not apply where liability on a Return has been calculated in accordance with a practice generally prevailing at the time the return was made, even though that practice has subsequently changed. Tax advisers should therefore consider keeping historical technical books and information in order to substantiate they followed the prevailing practice at the time in order to defend their clients against a discovery assessment.

In a further clarification of the legislation in this area, the High Court decided that HMRC is not precluded from raising a discovery assessment merely because it would have been reasonable for an officer, had he thought about it, to initiate an enquiry into a return which could have been expected to reveal the true facts (*Revenue & Customs Comrs v Household Estate Agents Ltd* [2007] EWHC 1684 (Ch), [2008] STC 2045).

It was also clarified that it is not necessary for there to have been an enquiry into a period (or another period) before a discovery assessment is issued (*Kennerley v Revenue & Customs Comrs* [2007] STC (SCD) 188, [2007] SWTI 265).

The more recent case of *Revenue & Customs Comrs v Charlton* [2012] UKUT 770 (TCC), indicated a swing in favour of the taxpayer as the Tribunal decided that HMRC was not entitled to raise a discovery assessment in respect of three taxpayers involved in an avoidance scheme who had declared the scheme on their returns and included the relevant DOTAS number.

Time-limits for discovery assessments and appeals against them

[17.33] The time limits for the issue of discovery assessments are as shown below:

Up to 31 March 2010:	Income Tax, PAYE and CGT	Corporation Tax
Negligent conduct	20 years 10 months	21 years
Fraudulent conduct	20 years 10 months	21 years
Other reasons	5 years 10 months	6 years

From 01/04/2010 (CH53100)	Income Tax, PAYE and CGT	Corporation Tax
Careless understatement	6 years	6 years
Deliberate understatement	20 years	20 years
Other reasons	4 years	4 years

The time limits for assessments for inheritance tax and various indirect taxes were altered by the provisions in Schedule 51 Finance Act 2009.

Appeals against discovery assessments may be made to the First-tier Tribunal.

Disclosures & investigations

[17.34] Investigations are generally carried out by either Local Compliance or in more serious cases by the Fraud Investigation Service (FIS) or Criminal Taxes Unit within HMRC.

The FIS team can investigate cases of suspected serious fraud using Code of Practice 9 which provides the taxpayer with protection from prosecution and enables a civil settlement to be reached out of court. In such cases the taxpayer must make a full disclosure of all irregularities and arrange to settle tax, interest and tax-geared penalties. In return they receive written confirmation of the closure of the investigation. As part of the process HMRC expects to interview all taxpayers. It is wise to ensure that taxpayers are fully briefed and accompanied by a practitioner with experience in successfully handling such investigations.

From 31 January 2012, HMRC introduced the Contractual Disclosure Facility (CDF) which replaces the Civil Investigation of Fraud (CIF) process under Code of Practice 9. There are many similarities between the processes, but it is important to be aware of the differences. The main one being that HMRC does not offer immunity from prosecution for tax fraud unless the individual enters into a contractual arrangement to fully disclose all material matters and makes an outline disclosure under that arrangement. But even then the immunity only covers those taxes which are within the outline disclosure.

Code of Practice 8 is also available. This is for use in cases of tax avoidance and again provides the taxpayer with the opportunity to make a full disclosure and negotiate a settlement with HMRC.

Disclosures can be made to the FIS teams as well as to any local office or the Offshore Coordination Unit (OCU) — the location will depend upon the amount of tax at stake and the issues involved. The process and approach is very different to that of an enquiry so if a taxpayer needs to make a voluntary disclosure to HMRC, consideration should be given to obtaining assistance from practitioners who specialise in cases involving Code of Practice 8 and 9. An experienced practitioner will be able to advise on how to make a disclosure, ensure you avoid the pitfalls and guide you through the process to a successful negotiation of the final liability.

HMRC's 'High Net Worth Individual' Unit (HNWI Unit) was set up from 1 April 2009 to monitor approximately 5,000 of the wealthiest individual taxpayers. Taxpayers dealt with by this unit have Customer Relationship Managers, similar to the arrangement with large companies. CRMs will seek meetings with taxpayers and their agents, acting as a 'one stop shop' for all tax matters. Specialist advice is likely to be required to manage the relationship with HMRC for a taxpayer dealt with by this unit.

The Liechtenstein Disclosure Facility (LDF) provided an opportunity for those with previously undeclared income or gains relating to an offshore asset to make a disclosure to HMRC under certain beneficial terms. The LDF closed for new registrations on 31 December 2015.

At the date of writing, HMRC had introduced a new 'Worldwide Disclosure Facility' due to launch on 5 September 2016. The new facility is a digital disclosure service where the disclosure of all tax, interest and penalties due, is made online. There is expected to be little space available to justify penalty loadings and as such, further communication and negotiation with HMRC may be necessary following disclosure. Prior to submitting a disclosure, the taxpayer must first notify HMRC of their intention to do so. Unlike the LDF and the Swiss-UK Tax Cooperation Agreement, there are no beneficial terms or lower penalties available.

HMRC has not indicated for how long this facility will be available.

Follower notices

[17.35] HMRC has been aware that one of the advantages of being involved in tax avoidance schemes is the cash flow advantage from deferring payment until the case has been heard at the Tribunal and a final decision made, which can take years. To remove the cash flow advantage HMRC has introduced new legislation in Finance Act 2014 requiring those who have used an avoidance scheme to pay the tax in advance if the scheme was similar to one already overturned by the courts to settle with HMRC and pay what is owed.

The taxpayer will be issued with a follower notice, requiring them to amend the relevant return within 90 days of the notice. A follower notice must be issued within 12 months, beginning with the later of:

• The date of the relevant judicial ruling; or
• The date on which the return or claim was received by HMRC; or
• The date on which an appeal was raised.

The notice must state the specific judicial ruling in question and explain why it is relevant to the 'follower'. While there is no right of appeal against the notice, written representations may be made by the taxpayer on one of the following grounds:

- There is no open enquiry or ongoing appeal against an assessment, closure notice or determination;
- There is no tax advantage resulting from the arrangements used;
- A previous follower notice has already been issued;
- The judicial ruling is not relevant to the arrangements; or
- The notice was not issued within the stated time limit

On receipt of any representations made, HMRC must confirm whether they intend to withdraw or confirm the notice.

Failure to take the necessary 'corrective action' within the 90 day time limit (or 30 days following the day on which HMRC confirms their position on the basis of any representations made) will result in the taxpayer becoming liable to a penalty. The maximum penalty is 50% of the value of the denied advantage. The minimum rate, should the full level of mitigation be allowed, is 10%. The penalty may be mitigated on the basis of the quality of co-operation shown by the taxpayer. HMRC must notify the penalty:

- Where there is an open enquiry, no later than 90 days after the closure notice issued;
- Where there is an ongoing appeal, no later than 90 days beginning with the earliest of:
  - The date on which corrective action is taken by the taxpayer
  - The date on which a final judicial ruling is made in respect of the appeal
  - The date on which the appeal is abandoned before it is determined in the courts

An appeal may be raised against the decision to impose a penalty and this must be done within 30 days of the date on which the penalty is notified. The grounds for an appeal may include:

- The same grounds as those for making a written representation against the notice
- That it was reasonable, when taking into account all of the circumstances, for the taxpayers not to have taken the corrective action

Accelerated Payment Notice (APN) and penalties for failure to comply

[17.36] APNs may be issued to those who have used tax planning arrangements and where certain conditions have been met:

- A follower notice has been issued (see above at Section **17.35**);
- They have used a DOTAS (Disclosure of Tax Avoidance Scheme) notifiable arrangement, or

- The planning used is subject to a GAAR (General Anti Abuse Rules) counteraction notice.

The APN legislation also requires that an enquiry has been opened or an appeal raised against a closure notice, assessment or determination before a notice may be issued. As with the follower notices, the return or claim must be made on the basis that a tax advantage has resulted from the use of the arrangements. The notice will require the taxpayer to pay an amount which equates to the disputed tax resulting from their participation in the avoidance scheme.

There is no right of appeal against the APN although written representations may be made within 90 days of the date of the notice. Representations may only be made on one or more of the following grounds:

- There is no open enquiry into the relevant return; or
- There is no ongoing appeal in place; or
- There is no tax advantage arising as a result of the arrangements used; or
- None of the following conditions have been met:
  - A follower notice has been issued
  - The return includes DOTAS notifiable arrangements
  - A GAAR counteraction notice has been issued in respect of the arrangements

Where an APN has been issued and the tax remains unpaid after 90 days of the date of the notice (or within 30 days of the date on which HMRC confirms the notice following any representations made, if later), the taxpayer is liable to a penalty, chargeable as follows:

- 5% of the amount unpaid on the day following the end of the payment period;
- 5% of the amount unpaid five months after the penalty day; and
- 5% of the total amount outstanding 11 months after the penalty day.

An appeal may be made against the late payment penalties and taxpayers may also claim reasonable excuse for the late payment.

Key points

[17.37] Key points to note are as follows.

- HMRC's extensive powers to obtain information are mainly included in Schedule 36 Finance Act 2008.
- The majority of information notices will request statutory records and therefore cannot be appealed. All notices should be carefully reviewed to ensure that the information requested and time period are reasonable. If the taxpayer has a reasonable excuse for not complying this should be put to HMRC in writing.
- Inspection visits can now cover Corporation Tax, Income Tax and Capital Gains Tax as well as VAT and PAYE. Businesses will need to assist HMRC in reviewing computerised records and be prepared to answer the officer's questions.

- Data gathering powers came into force from 1 April 2012 enabling HMRC to acquire specific bulk information from relating to a group of people for the purposes of risk analysis.
- HMRC has retained its powers to enquire into tax returns. Generally, enquiries must be opened within 12 months of the submission of the return. If the enquiry is prolonged, then it is possible to force a closure notice to be issued.
- HMRC can issue and the taxpayer can apply for aspect closure notices during the course of an enquiry.
- HMRC has considerable powers to issue discovery assessments. It can gather information from taxpayers and third parties using its new information powers. Agents should ensure that sufficient disclosure is given on Tax Returns to preclude discoveries where possible.
- Investigations for tax avoidance or tax evasion are generally conducted under Codes of Practice 8 and 9. Assistance should be sought from a practitioner experienced in this area from the outset.
- Data gathering powers came into force from 1 April 2012 enabling HMRC to acquire specific bulk information from relating to a group of people for the purposes of risk analysis.
- High net worth individuals are dealt with by a specialised unit within HMRC and are allocated their own Customer Relationship Manager.
- New powers introduced in the Finance Act 2014 allow HMRC to demand the upfront payment of disputed tax in cases involving certain tax avoidance schemes and arrangements.

Chapter 18

Tax Tribunals and HMRC Internal Reviews

Introduction

[18.1] The reform of the tax tribunal system in April 2009 arose in the context of a wider reform of Britain's entire Tribunal system, undertaken by the Ministry of Justice.

The need to reform the tribunal system was initially set out in a review conducted in 2001 by Sir Andrew Leggett – 'Tribunals for Users – One System One Service'.

This work culminated in the Tribunals, Courts and Enforcement Act 2007 (TCEA 2007). The TCE Act put in place a new, unified and flexible tribunals' structure.

The TCE Act framework creates a new two-tier Tribunal system. A First Tier Tribunal and an Upper Tribunal, both of which are split into Chambers. Each Chamber is comprised of similar jurisdictions, for example tax. Each Chamber operates under rules and procedures tailored to the needs of individual jurisdictions within the Chamber.

Tax tribunals

[18.2] Appeals against HMRC decisions are heard by either the First Tier Tribunal (Tax) or the Upper Tribunal (Finance and Tax). These replaced the General and Special Commissioners, the VAT and Duties Tribunal and the Section 704 of the ITA 2007 and Section 706 of the ICTA 1988 tribunals. The new process was given effect by The Transfer of Tribunal Functions and Revenue and Customs Appeals Order 2009.

The tax tribunals' procedures are governed by The Tribunal Procedure (Upper Tribunal) Rules 2008 SI 2008/2698. The Tribunal Procedure (First-tier Tribunal) (General Regulatory Chamber) Rules 2009 (as amended) and The Tribunal Procedure (First-tier Tribunal) (Tax Chambers) Rules 2009.

Appeals against HMRC decisions heard in the Tax Chamber include:

- Income tax;
- Corporation tax;
- Capital gains tax;
- Inheritance tax;
- Stamp Duty Land tax;

- PAYE Coding Notices;
- National Insurance Contributions;
- Statutory Payments;
- VAT and duties such as Customs duties, excise duties or landfill tax, aggregates or climate change levies;
- The amounts of tax or duty to be paid;
- Penalties; and
- Certain other decisions.

Appeals against decisions in relation to tax credits, child benefits and non-tax child trust fund are dealt with by the Social Entitlement Chamber.

The First Tier Tribunal hears most appeals in the first instance. Decisions of the First Tier Tribunal may be appealed to the Upper Tribunal on a point of law if the First Tier or Upper Tribunal gives permission. The Upper Tier Tribunal replaced the High Court Chancery Division for tax appeals.

Appeals against the decisions of the Upper Tribunal are made to the relevant appellate court on a point of law and with permission (appeals from the Upper Tribunal are not made to the High Court).

Rights of appeal

[18.3] In general, taxpayers have a right of appeal against decisions, assessments, notices and determinations made by HMRC. The law entitles taxpayers to have their appeal considered by a tribunal. This may be at a hearing or on the basis of paper submissions from the parties to the proceedings.

An appeal must be made in writing within the time limit, usually 30 days.

Alternative Dispute Resolution

[18.4] In 2011, HMRC launched two separate Alternative Dispute Resolution ('ADR') pilot schemes to explore the benefits of using ADR as a method of facilitating agreement between HMRC and taxpayers when resolving tax disputes. One pilot covered cases involving larger businesses or taxpayers with complex affairs, and the other primarily involved small and medium-sized enterprises ('SMEs') or individuals.

Following the success of these pilot schemes, ADR has now become another route that allows all taxpayers to attempt to resolve tax disputes with HMRC, potentially without the need for litigation. ADR is available to all taxpayers (both corporates and individuals) where a tax issue is in dispute, whether or not an appealable tax decision or assessment has been made by HMRC.

ADR covers both VAT and direct taxes disputes. Entering into the ADR process will not affect the taxpayer's existing review and appeal rights. ADR runs in parallel with the appeal and review processes, thus for example, a taxpayer can enter the mediation process whilst waiting for his appeal to be heard before the tribunal.

Although ADR cannot guarantee resolution of the dispute, it can by the end of the process provide clarity on the outstanding issues which can aid and focus the litigation process.

ADR cannot be used for the following categories of dispute:

* payments;
* fixed penalties on the grounds of reasonable excuse;
* tax credits;
* PAYE codes;
* HMRC delays in using information;
* default charges; or
* cases dealt with by HMRC's criminal investigators.

How ADR works

ADR normally involves an independent person from HMRC (a 'facilitator'). The facilitator will have mediation training and will not previously have been involved in the dispute. In some instances, an independent third-party meditator may be appointed or joint HMRC/agent facilitators may also be employed. The facilitator will work with both the taxpayer and HMRC's enquiry caseworker to try and broker an agreement between both parties.

The mediation process is normally over one or two days. Both the taxpayer and HMRC participate in the negotiations or can be represented by their advisers. The negotiations are led by the facilitator via a series of meetings involving one or both parties. ADR is a private, without prejudice process that may lead to a confidential agreement to close an enquiry on mutually acceptable terms or clarify the issues that may need to be litigated. The terms of the agreement can cover penalties and the time in which the liability may be paid, as well as agreeing the amount of tax due.

On the day of the mediation there will be initial statements in a joint meeting, including if required, a discussion to agree the key points at issue. After this initial meeting both parties will retire to their respective rooms, where the facilitator will then begin the negotiation process by moving between the taxpayer's and HMRC's rooms, discussing issues and potential solutions.

During the negotiation process, the facilitator may suggest further joint meetings with parts or all of the teams from both sides to discuss specific issues.

At the end of the mediation both parties either make an agreement in principle to resolve the dispute or agree on the next steps, if no resolution is found.

Applying for ADR

In order for a case to be considered for ADR, an application needs to be made to HMRC's Dispute Resolution Unit ('DRU'). For the application form and associated guidance see HMRC's website www.gov.uk/guidance/tax-disputes-alternative-dispute-resolution-adr.

The application form requires the following key information:

- taxpayer's contact details;
- HMRC caseworker's name, office and contact details;
- HMRC appeals officer's name and reference number (if applicable);
- a summary of the details of the dispute, including the relevant years/periods, outstanding issues and tax at stake;
- an explanation of how ADR can help settle the dispute; and
- the taxpayer's agent's details.

The DRU will confirm within 30 days of receiving the application if the case has been accepted for ADR and will notify the relevant stakeholders within HMRC. There is no right of appeal if the case is rejected.

Prior to mediation, both parties will sign a template ADR Facilitation Agreement.

HMRC Reviews

[18.5] From 1 April 2009 taxpayers have a legal right to have appealable decisions or assessments reviewed by another HMRC officer before appealing to the tribunal.

Some matters are not reviewable:

- decisions where there is no right of appeal (eg a refusal to allow a late claim);
- decisions about whether to permit a late review;
- decisions about whether to allow a late appeal;
- refusals to allow postponement or hardship applications; and
- conclusions of a review.

Whilst the option of a review may be a relatively cheap, interim alternative to taking a dispute to tribunal, taxpayers should be aware that there are risks. In particular, the entire matter under dispute is referred to the review officer. Consequently, there is a risk the review officer may conclude that points already agreed in the taxpayer's favour should be revisited and end up being restated in HMRC's favour. It is important to judge carefully whether a review is in the taxpayer's best interests.

The procedures for dealing with a dispute about a decision or assessment should be transparent, objective and consistent in the way they are applied.

Although a taxpayer has a statutory right to a review, it is not compulsory. The taxpayer can decide not to have a review and appeal to the tribunal directly. Alternatively, they can apply for mediation under ADR or appeal to the tribunal after the review if they disagree with the outcome. An appeal cannot be lodged, however, whilst a review is in progress.

The role of the review officer is to check whether the decision or assessment is in line with HMRC legal and technical guidance, policy and practice. Under HMRC's Settlements and Litigation Strategy (see below) HMRC should only pursue sensible cases with good prospects of success. The review officer is obliged to consider whether the case is one which HMRC would want to defend at tribunal. The taxpayer can submit extra information to the review officer, however, if the additional information is substantial, it is likely that the review officer will refer the case back to the caseworker or decision-maker.

The purpose of the review (for HMRC) is primarily to review the decision, not to assess new facts or evidence.

A review can be triggered in three ways:

- HMRC offers a review and the taxpayer accepts HMRC's offer (applies to direct and indirect tax); or
- the taxpayer asks for a review (applies to direct tax only); or
- a third party to a decision asks for a review (applies in the context of indirect tax only).

If a taxpayer is offered a review (direct tax), they will have 30 days from the date of the offer letter within which to accept the offer or appeal to the tribunal. As explained above, ADR may also be a possible alternative, regardless of whether this is specifically highlighted by HMRC. Once an appeal has been notified to the tribunal, it is no longer possible to request a review. If an application is made for ADR, it is advisable to also make an appeal to tribunal in order to protect the taxpayer's right to take the appeal further. If ADR does not resolve the issue, and the deadline for application to the tribunal has passed, then the appeal cannot be pursued. If no response is filed, the matter will be treated as settled in accordance with HMRC's position, subject to any late appeal rights.

Once a review has been requested, the HMRC representative who dealt with the decision or assessment will refer the matter to the appropriate review team. HMRC will consider postponement applications for direct tax liabilities at this stage and will normally arrange for the suspension of indirect taxes pending the outcome of the review.

In the event of a failure to reply to an offer of a review on time, HMRC should consider accepting a late acceptance of its offer. HMRC should accept the late application if there was a reasonable excuse for the delay (eg illness or overseas travel) and a review was requested without unreasonable delay after the excuse ceased. A refusal to accept a late application for review cannot be appealed to the tribunal.

Reviews will be carried out by independent review officers with experience of the subject matter of the appeal. Independence in this context implies that the review officer is independent of the HMRC representative who made the decision being appealed and the decision-maker's line management. If the matter under appeal is large and complex, review officers will work in teams.

Once a taxpayer has asked for a review or accepted an offer of a review, the decision-maker will prepare a report for the review officer. The report should summarise the:

- decision to review;
- facts;
- relevant legislation and practice;

- decision-maker's reasoning;
- taxpayer's argument and evidence; and
- decision-maker's argument and evidence.

The decision-maker is obliged to provide the review officer with all the information necessary for the review.

Although not part of HMRC's published views, if a taxpayer has any concerns about the objectivity of the report provided to the review officer, it is arguable that they have a right to request sight of the papers passed to the review officer by the decision-maker. This is because HMRC has stated publicly that its aim is for the process to be transparent, objective and consistent. This is stated to be an overriding aim of the review process, which is a statutory right afforded to taxpayers.

Once a review is under way the review officer will write to confirm that the review process has commenced and to provide their contact details. Taxes Management Act 1970, s 49E (TMA 1970) provides that the reviews must be completed within 45 days. If the review officer thinks additional time may be needed to complete the review, they may ask for agreement to an extension. Assuming the taxpayer wanted the review to take place in the first place and the extension request is reasonable, it would be practical to agree to the request.

The review officer should invite any additional information or arguments to be provided at this stage.

In judging whether or not the review process proceeds as it should, it is worth bearing in mind what is expected of a review officer. This includes:

- making sure they have all the relevant information;
- making an early estimate about how long the review process is likely to take;
- keeping taxpayers and their advisers informed about progress;
- checking that HMRC's decision was legally and technically valid;
- considering all the facts critically;
- consulting as necessary with taxpayers and their advisers, the decision-maker, HMRC technical specialists (accountants, the Solicitor's Office etc);
- considering whether it would be beneficial to meet with taxpayers and their advisers to progress matters; and
- handling unrepresented taxpayers sensitively.

Review officers are authorised to enter into negotiations to settle a case, albeit within the bounds of HMRC Settlements and Litigation Strategy. This is usually done by instructing the decision-maker to undertake those negotiations in line with the review officer's advice and guidance.

As a rule, review officers should not discuss a case with the decision-maker whilst a review is on-going. HMRC adopts this approach in order that the review officer is and is seen to be independent. Nonetheless, there will in reality be situations where the review officer has to liaise with the decision-maker, for example where they need to seek clarification of the decision-maker's report. Taxpayers and their advisers would be wise to ensure they are kept informed about any such contact and that the entitlement to an offer of equivalent telephone or face-to-face contact with the review officer is respected. Having such input ensures that taxpayers and their advisers have an equal opportunity to make representations to the review officer during the course of the review.

If new information or arguments are provided to HMRC during the course of a review this will normally result in the review officer referring the same back to the decision-maker for them to consider. Unless the new information or arguments are insubstantial, a request from HMRC for an extension of the review period is to be expected.

If HMRC decides that the new information or arguments provided sway them to conclude the matter in the taxpayer's favour, the review process will not need to be concluded. The matter will be settled in accordance with usual procedures, for example under TMA 1970, s 54 for direct tax matters and by way of amended assessments for indirect tax related matters.

A review will be concluded in one of three ways:

* HMRC's decision is upheld;
* HMRC's decision is varied; or
* HMRC's decision is cancelled.

A 'Conclusion of Review' letter will be sent to the taxpayer, their adviser and the decision-maker by the review officer. Taxpayers have 30 days to consider the review officer's conclusions and decide whether to appeal to tribunal.

Note that if HMRC fails to complete the review within the relevant review period, HMRC's decision is treated as upheld (per TMA 1970, s 49E(8)) and the taxpayer then has to consider whether to appeal to the tribunal.

It is not possible to have a decision reviewed more than once. There are two options open to the taxpayer in order to continue their case after a review has taken place: one is to apply for the ADR process; and ultimately, after all other avenues have been exhausted the taxpayer can appeal to the tribunal.

Some key points to note about the review process and its stages are:

* HMRC must complete the review within 45 days, although it is open to the parties to agree a longer period if necessary.
* HMRC must write to the taxpayer with the review decision, and the taxpayer then has 30 days to appeal or notify the appeal to the tribunal.
* Where HMRC does not complete the review within the review period, then the review is treated as upholding HMRC's view of the matter. HMRC must notify the appellant of this as soon as possible. The appellant then has 30 days from when they hear from HMRC to appeal to the tribunal.
* The requirement to pay any disputed tax is normally suspended during the review period.

First Tier and Upper Tribunals

[18.6] The tax tribunals are independent judicial bodies. Cases may be heard by either legally qualified members, non-legal members or a combination of both. The Upper Tribunal consists of specialist judges appointed by The Lord Chancellor. Members of the tribunal are not connected to HMRC.

The administration of the tax tribunals, for example making arrangements for hearings, is carried out by the Tribunals Service which is part of the Ministry of Justice.

Tribunals hearing tax appeals are part of a statutory two-tier structure comprising the First Tier Tribunal and the Upper Tribunal.

Decisions of the First Tier Tribunal may be appealed to the Upper Tribunal on a point of law if the First Tier or Upper Tribunal gives permission. The Upper Tribunal replaced the High Court for tax appeals. Appeals against decisions of the Upper Tribunal are made to the relevant appellate court on a point of law and with permission.

The First Tier Tribunal considers most appeals in the first instance. A small number of appeals categorised as Complex may be heard by the Upper Tribunal in the first instance. The Upper Tribunal will also consider applications by HMRC for tax-geared penalties under FA 2008, Sch 36, para 50(2) (additional tax-geared penalty for failing to comply with an information notice or obstructing an HMRC Inspection) and it can also hear some judicial review cases where these have been delegated to it by the High Court.

The Upper Tribunal is a Superior Court of Record, which means that its decisions create legally binding precedents. It has similar powers to the High Court.

Many tribunal cases will be decided by just one judge whilst more complicated cases may have one or two additional members. Most cases in the default paper or basic categories will be considered by non-legal members of the tribunal.

There is no fee payable for applying for permission to appeal or for appealing to the First Tier or Upper Tribunal. The tribunal will not pay a taxpayer's or their representative's travel expenses for attending a hearing.

The Tribunal Service Central Processing Centre

[18.7] Appeals and applications to the tribunal should be sent to:

First-Tier Tribunal (Tax)
HMRC Courts and Tribunal Service
PO Box 16972
Birmingham B16 6TZ
Telephone: 0300 123 1024 (8:30 am–5:00 pm)

Notice of Appeal Forms can be submitted electronically at taxappeals@hmcts.gsi.gov.uk.

An appeal or application will be allocated to a category. Default Paper and Basic cases will be administered by the office in Birmingham whilst most Standard cases and all Complex cases will be administered by one of the Tribunals

Service's other offices at London, Manchester or Edinburgh. The relevant Tribunals Service's offices perform the role of liaising with the judiciary and the parties to the case in order to make arrangements for the case to be dealt with by the tribunal.

Reviews and appeals for direct taxes

[18.8] Any appeal must be made to HMRC before being sent to the tribunal.

For an appeal to be valid, it must be made in writing, within the time limit, by the appropriate person, against an appealable HMRC decision and contain the grounds of appeal.

It is important that the grounds of appeal are clear and not precluded by law.

HMRC will often provide an appeal form when issuing an appealable decision. Alternatively, appeal forms can be downloaded from the HMRC website or via its order line. An appeal can also be made by letter.

The person named in the decision, a personal representative, a partner acting on behalf of a partnership or an authorised agent can appeal.

At the same time as an appeal is made, the taxpayer should consider making a postponement application under TMA 1970, s 55(3). This will enable payment of any additional tax to be postponed pending the outcome of the appeal. This is not appropriate where accelerated payment notices have been issued (see Chapter 17 for more details on accelerated payment notices and follower notices).

Any application for postponement must be made in writing and within 30 days of the decision or assessment. Late postponement applications are possible on largely the same basis as late appeal applications (see below). If agreement cannot be reached with HMRC, the taxpayer can ask the tribunal to decide the amount of tax to be postponed.

Once an appeal has been made, taxpayers and their advisers can have further discussions with HMRC in order to try to resolve the dispute. Usually such discussions will be with the HMRC representative they have dealt with up to that point.

After sending an appeal to HMRC, the taxpayer can have the matter reviewed by HMRC or notify their appeal to the tribunal. It is important to remember that an appeal cannot be notified to the tribunal until it has been sent to HMRC.

An appeal can be notified to the tribunal at any time after it has been sent to HMRC, unless an HMRC review has been initiated. In the latter case, an appeal to the tribunal can only be made once the review has been completed.

HMRC cannot refer an appeal to the tribunal until an offer of a review has been made. Once an offer of a review has been made by HMRC, the taxpayer has 30 days from the date of the review offer to accept it or notify the appeal to the tribunal.

If after receiving an HMRC offer of a review the taxpayer does not notify the appeal to the tribunal or accept the review offer, the offer lapses and HMRC treats the matter as settled in accordance with its original decision, subject to the taxpayer being able to make a late appeal or late review application.

If the taxpayer does not agree with the outcome of the HMRC review, they will have 30 days from the date of the conclusion of the review to notify the appeal to the tribunal.

Late appeals

TMA 1970, s 49(3) provides for late appeals. HMRC must accept a late appeal if there was a reasonable excuse for the delay and the appeal was made without unreasonable delay after the excuse ceased. The individual facts and circumstances of the specific case will determine whether there was a reasonable excuse for the delay in appealing.

If HMRC refuses a late appeal application, the taxpayer can refer the matter to the tribunal. The tribunal is not limited by the reasonable excuse conditions and can accept late appeal applications if it considers it is in the interests of justice to do so.

Appealing to the tribunal

If and when the taxpayer decides to appeal to the tribunal, they can do so by completing a Tribunals Service appeal form online at www.appeal-tax-tribun al.service.gov.uk. This form can be downloaded in Word and PDF format from the gov.uk website or a copy can be ordered from the tax tribunal helpline on 0300 123 1024.

Taxpayers should ensure they include a copy of the HMRC decision letter, assessment or review conclusion letter that they are appealing against. The Tribunals Service will process the appeal, notifying HMRC that the taxpayer has appealed.

Reviews and appeals for indirect tax decisions

[18.9] When HMRC makes an appealable indirect tax decision, it will make an offer of a review at the same time (usually included with the decision letter).

At this stage, the taxpayer may either:

- accept the decision;
- send new information or arguments to HMRC;
- accept the offer of an HMRC review;
- apply for ADR; or
- appeal to the tribunal.

If the taxpayer wishes to accept the review offer or appeal to the tribunal they should do so within 30 days of the date of the decision letter (unless an extended time limit has been agreed with HMRC where new information or arguments have been submitted).

If the taxpayer accepts the offer of an HMRC review, the review period is again 45 days and the taxpayer may only appeal to the tribunal after receipt of a conclusion of review letter from HMRC or after the review period has expired.

An appeal can be made directly to the tribunal without appealing to HMRC, except in relation to information notices issued under FA 2008, Sch 36. In the latter case, the appeal process follows the direct tax appeal and review procedure regardless of whether the compliance check relates to direct or indirect tax.

Late appeals can be made.

Payment of tax pending the outcome

HMRC will suspend payment of indirect tax where the taxpayer has provided new information after a decision has been issued. In non-Customs cases HMRC is required to consider suspending payment of indirect tax where the taxpayer has requested a review. In Customs cases, suspension of payment is not available.

If the taxpayer appeals an indirect tax decision to the tribunal, the tribunal may only hear the appeal if the disputed tax has been paid to HMRC, unless:

- security is provided (in excise and customs duties cases); or
- HMRC or the tribunal have accepted that to do so would cause the taxpayer financial hardship (VATA 1994, s 84(3B)).

Forms

[18.10] The forms needed to appeal to the tax tribunals are available on the gov.uk website in Word and PDF format.

Categories of tribunal case

[18.11] When the tribunal receives a notice of appeal or application it will allocate the case to one of the following categories:

- default paper;
- basic;
- standard; or
- complex.

The tribunal may at any time decide to reallocate the case to a different category and HMRC or the taxpayer can apply to the tribunal for the case to be allocated to a different category. Basic, standard and complex cases are normally decided at a hearing, but either HMRC or the taxpayer may ask for the case to be considered on the basis of the papers alone. The tribunal has the ultimate discretion over this.

The types of case normally within each category are set out below:

Default paper

- SA and CTSA fixed filing penalties;
- employer end of year late return penalties;
- construction industry late return penalties;
- class 2 NIC late notification penalties;
- income tax surcharges; and
- penalties for failure to make a return.

Basic

- Appeals against penalties for late filing and late payment, including daily penalties;
- appeals against penalties for incorrect returns, except appeals against penalties for deliberate action, cases where an appeal is also brought against the assessment of tax to which the return relates;
- appeals against penalties in indirect taxes where the taxpayer is appealing on the basis of reasonable excuse;
- appeals against decisions on CIS gross payment status;
- appeals against information notices;
- applications for permission to make a late appeal;
- applications for postponement of the payment of tax pending resolution of an appeal; and
- applications for a direction that HMRC close an enquiry.

Standard

- Cases that are not categorised as Default Paper, Basic or Complex by the tribunal.

Complex

- Cases that require lengthy or complex evidence or a lengthy hearing;
- cases that involve a complex or important principle or issue; and
- cases involving a large financial sum.

Once HMRC and the taxpayer have provided the required information, the Tribunals Service will write to both parties with a hearing date and venue, except in Default Paper cases where there is usually no hearing. In Standard and Complex cases, the Tribunals Service will write to the parties asking for dates to avoid before allocating a hearing date.

Both parties are entitled to ask for a Default Paper appeal to be dealt with at a hearing rather than on the basis of paper submissions alone. If either party asks for a hearing the tribunal must hold one.

In Basic cases, if HMRC intends to raise new arguments at the hearing that the taxpayer is not aware of, tribunal rules require it to write to the taxpayer advising them of the new arguments as soon as possible and in enough detail for the taxpayer to be able to respond to those arguments at the hearing.

In Standard and Complex cases HMRC must send a statement of case to the tribunal and a copy to the taxpayer within 60 days of the tribunal notifying them of the appeal or application. Their statement of case must state the legal provision under which the decision under appeal was made and set out HMRC's position on the issues in dispute. Once HMRC has sent the statement of case to the tribunal, the tribunal rules require each party to the appeal or application to send the tribunal and all other parties a list of documents that they intend to rely on or produce at the hearing. This must be done within 42 days of HMRC submitting its statement of case. All parties can see and copy other parties' listed documents unless they are privileged.

Any documents that need to be sent to the tribunal should be sent by pre-paid post or document exchange, delivered by hand or sent by any other method that has been agreed with the tribunal (for example, email). The document must be sent to the address given for the proceedings. The taxpayer should bring copies of all documents submitted as evidence to an oral hearing, assuming one is to be held.

Whilst all the preparatory work before the tribunal is going on, taxpayers and their advisers can still seek to settle the matter by negotiation. If progress is being made in those negotiations, either HMRC or the taxpayer can apply to the tribunal for the hearing to be postponed or adjourned.

The tribunal must give each party entitled to attend a hearing reasonable notice of the time and place of a hearing and it must also give them reasonable notice of any changes to the time and place. Reasonable notice means at least 14 days but the tribunal may give less than 14 days' notice if the parties agree or in urgent or exceptional circumstances.

The tribunal is empowered to make decisions in relation to the management of the appeal proceedings. This is known as 'giving a direction'. These powers flow from the relevant chamber's procedural rules.

If HMRC or the taxpayer fail to comply with a direction, the tribunal can take any action it thinks is just, including waiving the requirement, requiring the failure to be put right, striking out the party's case or restricting the party's participation in the proceedings.

The First Tier Tribunal may also refer to the Upper Tribunal and ask the Upper Tribunal to exercise its power (which may involve a financial penalty) if a person does not comply with a tribunal requirement to:

- attend at any place to give evidence;
- swear an oath in connection with giving evidence;
- give evidence as a witness;
- produce a document; or
- facilitate the inspection of a document or any other thing, including any premises.

The taxpayer can appoint a representative to represent them during the tribunal proceedings, such as a solicitor, accountant, tax adviser or any other person (qualified or not). The representative can do anything on behalf of their client, except sign a witness statement. The tribunal will assume that a representative is continuing to act unless told otherwise. Once a representative has been appointed, the tribunal only has to correspond with that representative.

The taxpayer can also be accompanied by another person at the tribunal hearing, such as a friend or business associate to provide them with moral and practical support. There is no need to notify HMRC or the tribunal in advance that they will be accompanied.

Striking out of a case

[18.12] The tribunal has the power to strike out all or part of an appeal. It must do so if it does not have jurisdiction to hear the case, for example if an HMRC review is on-going.

If a direction is not complied with, proceedings will be automatically struck out if the direction had been issued with the proviso that this would be the consequence of non-compliance.

The tribunal may also strike out all or part of a case if:

- a party to the proceedings did not cooperate with the tribunal to such an extent that it was impossible for the tribunal to deal with the proceedings fairly; or
- the tribunal does not think there is any prospect of a party's case, or part of it, succeeding.

The tribunal may not strike out a case or part of a case without first giving the relevant party to the case an opportunity to make representations. Furthermore, the relevant party can in certain circumstances apply to have their case reinstated. They must apply for reinstatement within 28 days.

The tribunal hearing

[18.13] All parties are entitled to attend a hearing unless the hearing is on a matter where the respondent is not to be given notice of the hearing, for example an application by HMRC to inspect business premises. The tribunal also has the power to direct that a party is to be excluded from a hearing.

The tribunal may proceed with a hearing even if a party does not attend if the tribunal is satisfied that the party was promptly notified of the hearing and if it thinks that to continue is in the interests of justice.

If a party finds that they will not be able to attend a hearing which has already been fixed, they should tell the relevant tribunal office as soon as possible, in writing if time is available, otherwise by telephone. It would be wise to have the tribunal office's telephone number to hand whilst travelling to the hearing, in case of any delays en route.

All hearings will be held in public except where the tribunal gives a direction that the hearing or part of it should be held in private. The tribunal can restrict access to the hearing if it thinks it is justified:

- in the interests of public order or national security;
- to protect a person's right to respect for private and family life;
- to maintain the confidentiality of sensitive information;
- to avoid serious harm to the public interest; or
- because not to restrict access would prejudice the interests of justice.

The tribunal will not accept an application for a hearing to be made in private because the taxpayer finds it embarrassing to have their financial affairs discussed in a public setting. In line with Article 6 of the Human Rights Convention, 'everyone is entitled to a fair and public hearing'. However, if there is a compelling argument, such as a potential safety issue, then the tribunal may rule that a public hearing would not be beneficial. In practice, it is unusual for members of the public to attend tax tribunal hearings.

The tribunal may order that certain documents, information or any matter likely to lead to members of the public identifying anyone the tribunal thinks should not be identified (eg minors) may not be disclosed or made public.

Parties likely to be in attendance at a hearing include the tribunal panel, the tribunal clerk, HMRC representative(s), witnesses, the taxpayer and (if relevant) their representative(s).

Evidence

In addition to the list of documents (Standard and Complex cases), the tribunal may give directions relating to:

- issues on which it requires evidence or submissions;
- the nature of the evidence and submissions it requires;
- whether the parties are allowed or required to provide expert witness evidence and, if so, whether the parties must jointly appoint a single expert;
- any limit to the number of witnesses a party may have in relation to a particular issue or generally;
- the manner in which the evidence or submissions are required, for example orally at the hearing or in writing; and
- the deadline by which the evidence or submissions must be provided.

The tribunal may admit evidence whether or not it would be admissible in a civil trial in the UK and the Upper Tribunal may admit evidence whether or not it was available to a previous decision-maker.

The tribunal may refuse to admit evidence where it was not produced on time, provided in the manner required by the tribunal, or where it believes it would be unfair to admit the evidence.

Witnesses

The tribunal may allow or require a witness to give evidence on oath and may provide an oath to be used.

The tribunal may summon any person, including HMRC decision-makers and review officers, to attend a hearing as a witness. It may do this as a result of an application by HMRC or the taxpayer or on its own initiative.

It can also issue a summons ordering a witness to appear and answer any questions or produce any documents in their possession or control which relate to any issue in the proceedings.

Conduct of hearing

The normal order where the onus of proof is on the taxpayer is that the taxpayer will present their case first. HMRC will then present its case and the taxpayer will have a further opportunity to respond. In cases where the burden of proof is on HMRC (for example, penalties for deliberate behaviour), HMRC will present its case first.

Hearings for cases categorised as Default Paper or Basic will normally be conducted in an informal atmosphere whilst appeals in Standard and Complex cases will tend to be conducted more formally.

At the end of the hearing the tribunal may ask the parties to retire whilst they discuss the case. The judge of the tribunal may then announce their decision. In more complicated cases the tribunal members may consider their decision at length and write to the parties with their decision in due course. In any case, all tribunal decisions will be confirmed in writing.

Costs — generally

In practice, the tribunals tend to only award costs in relatively rare cases.

Costs — First Tier Tribunal

The First Tier Tribunal may award costs in Complex cases but the taxpayer can write to the tribunal within 28 days of the notice of the case category to say that they want the proceedings excluded from potential liability for costs.

The First Tier Tribunal can also award costs if it thinks that one of the parties or their representative acted unreasonably in bringing, defending or conducting the proceedings or in relation to wasted costs (see TCEA 2007, s 29(4)). The tribunal cannot make an order relating to costs without taking into account the taxpayer's means or giving them an opportunity to make representations. The amount of costs can be determined in a number of ways, thought these are beyond the scope of this book.

Costs — Upper Tribunal

The Upper Tribunal can only make an award for costs:

- on appeal from a decision of the First Tier Tribunal;
- where the case has been referred by or on appeal from another tribunal in the same circumstances and to the same extent as the First Tier Tribunal above;

- in judicial review proceedings;
- in proceedings transferred from the First Tier Tribunal;
- if it thinks either party acted unreasonably in bringing, defending or conducting the proceedings; or
- in relation to wasted costs.

The same safeguards as mentioned above for the First Tier Tribunal apply, except that the Upper Tribunal does not have to consider an individual's means if the case before the Upper Tribunal is an appeal against a decision of the First Tier Tribunal.

In appropriate cases, the taxpayer should be aware of the 'Rees Principle' whereby under the terms of a Parliamentary statement, HMRC is willing in appropriate circumstances and in particular where they are appealing against an adverse decision, to consider waiving any claim to costs in cases before the Upper Tribunal or the appeal courts. Influential factors in this regard include the risk of financial hardship to the taxpayer, the involvement of a point of law the clarification of which HMRC believes would be of benefit to taxpayers as a whole or the efficient collection and management of tax revenue.

Outcome of the hearing — First Tier Tribunal

[18.14] Where a case falls within the Default Paper category or the tribunal thinks it can decide the case without a hearing and all parties to the case agree and neither person asks for a hearing, the case will be decided by the tribunal without a hearing.

The tribunal may give its decision orally at a hearing or in writing at a later date.

Whether there has been a hearing or not, the tribunal will send all parties a decision notice within 28 days of making the decision or as soon as possible after that. The decision notice must, unless the parties agree it is unnecessary, include a summary of facts and reasons for the decision or be accompanied by full written reasons for the decision.

If the tribunal does not provide full written reasons for its decision, any party to the proceedings can apply for the full reasons. The application must be made within 28 days of the decision notice.

Outcome of the hearing — Upper Tribunal

[18.15] The Upper Tribunal may decide a case without a hearing. It may give its decision orally at a hearing or in writing at a later date.

The Upper Tribunal will send all parties a decision notice within 28 days of making the decision or as soon as possible after that. The Upper Tribunal must provide full written reasons for its decision unless all parties agree that this is unnecessary or the decision was made with the consent of the parties.

Publication of decisions

[18.16] The tribunal may publish a decision or the reasons for decision. It may also send notice of a decision or the reasons for it to any person. Decisions (including those taken by the tax tribunals' predecessor tribunals) taken since April 2003 are available on the gov.uk website.

HMRC action following the tribunal decision

[18.17] Having reviewed the tribunal decision, the HMRC tribunal case-worker or Solicitor's Office will liaise with other interested parties within HMRC such as policy and technical specialists and Solicitor's Office in order to reach a consensus as to whether to appeal the decision. In doing so, HMRC will act in line with its Settlements and Litigation Strategy (see below).

Asking the tribunal to set aside its decision

[18.18] The tribunal can set aside its decision or part of its decision and remake the decision if it thinks it is in the interests of justice to do so **and** one or more of the following conditions is met:

- a document relating to the proceedings was not sent to or was not received at an appropriate time by a party or a party's representative;
- a document relating to the proceedings was not sent to the tribunal at an appropriate time;
- there has been any other procedural irregularity; or
- a party or party's representative was not present at a hearing related to the proceedings.

If the taxpayer wishes to ask the tribunal to set aside its decision or part of its decision, they must do so within 28 days of the First Tier Tribunal or within one month of the Upper Tribunal sending its respective notice of decision.

Tribunal review of its decision

[18.19] The First Tier Tribunal may review its decision when a party to the proceedings asks for permission to appeal and it is satisfied that there was an error of law in the decision. This enables the tribunal to correct any obvious errors of law and thereby avoid more extensive litigation.

The Upper Tribunal can only review a decision if a party has applied for permission to appeal and when making the decision the First Tier Tribunal had overlooked a provision in law or a binding authority that could have a material effect on the decision, or since its decision a higher court has made a decision that is binding on the Upper Tribunal and which could have had a material effect on the Upper Tribunal's decision if the higher court's decision had been made first.

Appeal to the Upper Tribunal

[18.20] Before being able to make an appeal to the Upper Tribunal the taxpayer must have asked for a full statement of the First Tier Tribunal's reasons for its decision and applied to the First Tier Tribunal for permission to appeal. Appeals can generally only be made on a point of law. The taxpayer has 56 days from the date the First Tier Tribunal provides its full statement of reasons to lodge an application for permission to appeal to the Upper Tribunal.

If the First Tier Tribunal does not grant the taxpayer permission to appeal to the Upper Tribunal, they may apply to the Upper Tribunal for permission to appeal. The appeal form can be downloaded from the gov.uk website or obtained by calling 020 7612 9730 and requesting the 'Permission to Appeal Form FTC1'. An appeal must be made within one month of the First Tier Tribunal's refusal to give permission, although late applications can be made if the taxpayer can provide good reason for the delay.

The contact details of the Upper Tribunal are:

The Upper Tribunal Office (Tax and Chancery Chamber)
Fifth Floor
Rolls Building
Fetter Lane
London EC4A 1NL
Telephone: 0207 612 9730 (9 am–5 pm)
Email: financeandtaxappeals@hmcts.gsi.gov.uk

If the Upper Tribunal refuses permission to appeal or gives permission on limited grounds, the taxpayer may apply in writing within 14 days for the decision to be reconsidered at an oral hearing. A refusal of permission to appeal may be set aside by the Upper Tribunal judge if there has been a procedural irregularity in the proceedings and the judge considers it is in the interests of justice to do so.

HMRC Litigation and Settlements Strategy

[18.21] HMRC policy is to engage with the tribunal system in a way that is consistent with its Litigation and Settlements Strategy (available on the HMRC website). Taxpayers and their advisers should consider the contents of this document, in particular when considering whether and how to approach an appeal involving complex technical issues, large sums and/or points of principle.

Judicial review

[18.22] For most tax matters there are appeal procedures set out in law that enable disputes between the taxpayer and HMRC to be settled. However, in some cases there is no right of appeal to the tribunal against HMRC actions.

This arises mainly where the decision made by HMRC is in relation to a discretionary matter, for example a decision on whether a late claim should be accepted or the application of Extra Statutory Concessions.

Where there is no statutory right of appeal the taxpayer may turn to judicial review to take the dispute forward. A judicial review may be sought if it is believed that an HMRC officer is not carrying out or is delaying in carrying out their duties, has assumed powers to which they were not entitled or did not properly exercise their discretion, for example by refusing to apply an Extra Statutory Concession.

Judicial review may also look at HMRC decisions where the dispute is not about whether the decision is technically correct but where the taxpayer believes that they were misdirected and in consequence suffered disadvantage, for example that a return is wrong, because they relied on incorrect advice received from their adviser or guidance provided by HMRC.

Judicial review may also consider cases where the taxpayer believes that an HMRC officer has not listened properly to their representations or has acted in a way that appears to be unfair.

Finally, the taxpayer may also seek judicial review against the First Tier Tribunal where there is no appeal on a point of law against the tribunal decision, for example where the tribunal has refused a late appeal or refused to review its previous decision.

Judicial review proceedings can be undertaken by the Upper Tribunal but in all cases except those involving judicial review of the First Tier Tribunal's own procedures, an initial application must be made to the High Court who will consider whether it is appropriate to refer the case for a decision by the Upper Tribunal.

Before the taxpayer can apply to the High Court for judicial review, they must send a 'pre-action letter' to HMRC. The purpose of the 'pre-action letter' is to identify the issues in dispute and to establish whether litigation can be avoided. HMRC's Solicitor's Office will review the letter and is normally required to respond within 14 days. The response will typically be dealt with by HMRC's complaints unit.

An application for judicial review must be made to the High Court within three months of the date of the decision the application relates to. Late applications may be accepted, if good reasons are provided.

If the High Court grants permission for judicial review, the taxpayer must provide detailed grounds in support of their case to the High Court in writing within 35 days of the High Court granting permission.

Complaints against HMRC

[18.23] The tribunals cannot deal with administrative complaints about the conduct of HMRC officials. If taxpayers are unhappy about the way HMRC has dealt with their tax affairs, they can refer to HMRC's guidance on how to complain, available on their website at www.gov.uk/guidance/complain-to-h m-revenue-and-customs.

Key points

[18.24] Key points to note are as follows:

- HMRC introduced ADR to assist in resolving disputes between tax-payers and HMRC.
- Whether dealing with an appeal or HMRC review, it is important to respect all relevant deadlines.
- Care should be exercised in judging whether to opt for an HMRC review.
- Consider applying for postponement of direct tax or suspension of the payment of indirect tax and penalties pending the outcome of an appeal.

Appendix 1

Our Top OMB Cases

A reading list for those wishing to learn more

Introduction

This title is intended as a guide through the maze of UK direct tax legislation for practitioners advising owned managed businesses. This is a maze in constant flux and, of course, a practitioner will spend a lot of his or her time reading through the detail of Finance Acts and other tax legislation trying to keep up. This is often a tortuous process involving the application of many 'cold towels' to the head!

The purpose of this short Appendix is to remind readers of the usefulness of a full and careful read of a tax case. Most readers will keep up to date with case law changes from synopses in periodicals or websites but there is an awful lot to be gained from reading the entire case from time to time — principally, the fact that the general tax principles to each case are usually set out in a clear form with at the same time an impression given of how those principles apply to a specific case.

The cases that follow are cross-referenced to the relevant section of the book. For ease of reference shorthand case descriptions have been given but full case names and references are all available in the Table of Cases at the front of the book.

In each case a description of why the case is important has been provided; however, we have deliberately not summarised the details of the case because the intention is that you should read them! Even if you do not, hopefully the list will be useful in those 'what was the name of that case?' moments!

Name of case & year	OMB Tax Area	Why read it?	Cross-reference to book section
Allum v Marsh 2005	Company buy back of own shares	Key case on 'benefit to trade' test.	**11.18**
American Leaf Blending Co 1979	General principles	First point of reference for the definition of 'business'.	**12.4**

Name of case & year	OMB Tax Area	Why read it?	Cross-reference to book section
Astall and Edwards 2009	Company reconstructions	In an example of the move to a purposive interpretation of the legislation by the Courts. Certain terms in the instrument evidencing the creation of a security were disregarded because they had 'no practical reality'.	13.11
Barclays Bank Trust Co v IRC 1998	BPR: 'Excepted Assets'	BPR was restricted because 'too much' cash held to be an 'excepted asset'. HMRC will inevitably refer to this case when arguing for similar reductions in other cases but the facts are very peculiar and it is often not difficult to distinguish other cases from it.	3.51
Birmingham & District Cattle By-Products v CIR 1919	Starting in business	Leading case on the point at which a trade commences.	1.2
Bullock v Unit Construction 1959	Corporate residence	Highlights the importance of looking at the facts to determine the highest level of control and not just the legal arrangements.	1.37
Colley and Hillberg v Clements 2005	Incorporation	Fascinating example of the many ways in which an incorporation can go wrong.	4.18
Cook v Medway Housing 1997	General principles	First point of reference for definition of what constitutes an 'investment company'.	3.48
Copeman v William Flood 1940	Payments to employees	Leading case on the need for payments to employees to be made wholly and exclusively for the purposes of a trade.	1.12
De Beers v Howe 1906	Corporate residence	Early example of company found to be resident in UK by virtue of central management and control.	3.49

Name of case & year	OMB Tax Area	Why read it?	Cross-reference to book section
Farmer v IRC 1999	BPR: 'wholly or mainly' test	Clear example of how the 'wholly and mainly' test should be applied in practice. Includes succinct description of the factors to be taken into account.	3.49
Hinton v Maden and Ireland 1959	Capital Allowances	Case which established that plant must be for permanent use within a trade and have a useful economic life of at least 2 years.	8.7
IRC v Joiner 1975	Transactions in securities	Early case setting out general principles.	14.3
Jackson v Lasker Homes 1956	Deductions against profits	Highlights the circumstances in which a tenant's restoration costs are deductible.	4.4
Jones v Garnett 2007 (aka the Arctic Systems Case)	Settlements legislation	Leading case concerning whether dividends paid to one spouse can be taxed on the other.	1.25–1.30
Laerstate BV v HMRC 2009	Corporate residence	A Dutch company was held to be UK-resident on the basis of the conduct of directors outside board meeting and there was insufficient evidence that the central management and control of the company was exercised at the board meetings, which were held outside the UK.	1.37
Langham v Veltema 2007	HMRC powers	Case which clarified the quality of disclosure required to preclude HMRC from making a discovery assessment.	17.31
Marren v Ingles 1980	Capital Gains Tax	Leading case on the taxation of unascertainable deferred sale of consideration and the creation of a 'chose in action'.	13.7

Name of case & year	*OMB Tax Area*	*Why read it?*	*Cross-reference to book section*
Nolder v Walters 1930	Employee Benefits	Leading case on 'wholly exclusively and necessarily' test in relation to employees' expenses. To be deductible the expense must be incurred in actually doing the job.	9.2
Phillips v HMRC 2006	BPR: meaning of "holding investments"	Extraordinary example of how difficult it is, in cases not involving the 'letting' of land, for HMRC to establish that a company's business is one of holding investments.	3.48
Purchase v Tesco Stores 1984	Company losses	Interesting case on 'change of ownership' issues. The anti-avoidance legislation may be invoked where the change is significant even if it is not fundamental.	1.17
Purves v Harrison 2001	Capital Gains Tax	Salutary case on timing of 'associated disposals'.	3.32
Newfields Developments 2001	"Control" of a company	Useful case examining the meaning of an 'associate' and highlighting the sometimes artificial nature of the concept of company 'control'.	2.5
Yarmouth v France 1887	Capital Allowances	Leading case on definition of 'plant', namely that it is apparatus used in a business for the purposes of his business.	8.7
Grays Timber Products v HMRC 2010	Employment related securities	An enhanced share sale price arrived at under a shareholder's agreement did not represent market value, and the director shareholder was subject to income tax on the excess amount.	10.6
Ebsworth v R&C 2009	Transactions in securities and liquidation of a company	Shareholders liquidated a company, with particular facts. HMRC prevented from issuing a counteraction notice.	14.3

Name of case & year	OMB Tax Area	Why read it?	Cross-reference to book section
Snell v HMRC 2006	Disposal of shares for loan notes and taxpayer subsequently leaves UK before redemption	An application for clearance was made in advance of the transaction but the intention to move abroad was not made clear. Clearance was set aside and the issue of loan notes was treated as consideration for the shares.	
HMRC v PA Holdings Ltd 2011	Treatment of dividends paid to employee/shareholders	A case which demonstrates the scrutiny paid by HMRC to arrangements whereby employees are remunerated in the form of dividends. It was held that dividends paid to employees instead of bonuses were taxable as employment income.	**10.8**
Elizabeth Moyne Ramsay 2013	Incorporation of a property business	Sets useful principles about what constitutes a business for the purpose of section 162 incorporation relief.	**12.4**
Pawson 2013	BPR	BPR denied on a holiday let as insufficient services provided.	**3.46**
The Trustees of David Zetland Settlement 2013	BPR	Services offices denied BPR	**3.46**
Donovan & McLaren 2014	Dividend waivers	Highlights the risks associated with repeated dividend waivers particularly where the company has limited distributable reserves.	
Febrey v HMRC 2014	Director's liability for unpaid PAYE and NICs	Demonstrates the importance of proper record keeping and that responsibility for a company's tax affairs cannot be avoided by delegation.	
MC & LJ Ive Ltd 2014	Benefits in kind	Highlights the importance of checking the letter of the law when an arrangement appears to avoid a tax charge which would otherwise arise.	

Name of case & year	OMB Tax Area	Why read it?	Cross-reference to book section
Mehjoo v Harben Barker 2014	Scope of accountants' duty of care	The Court of Appeal held that practitioners do not have an open-ended duty of care in relation to their clients. However, they do need to ensure that their letter of engagement reflects clearly the services they have agreed to provide to their clients.	
Robert Ames 2015	EIS	Demonstrates the importance of making a claim for EIS relief in order to be able to claim exemption from CGT on disposal of the EIS shares.	
RFC 2012 plc (in liquidation) (formerly Rangers Football Club plc) v Advocate General for Scotland 2017		Contributions to an EBT from which the trustees made loans to employees are to be treated as remuneration. This case seals the fate of many EBTs.	
Blackwell v HMRC 2017		This case looked at deductibility of expenditure for CGT purposes of a payment to release a shareholder from an exclusivity agreement to enable him to sell the shares to another party. It was held not to be deductible.	

Appendix 2

VAT

Introduction

This appendix covers the main VAT changes announced during 2016/17 up to July 2017. It also includes an update on many of the VAT changes previously introduced by the 2016 Finance Act. It is not meant to be a comprehensive guide to VAT but does highlight the major changes.

VAT Registration limits

From 1 April 2016:

- the taxable turnover threshold, which determines whether a person must be registered for VAT, has increased to £85,000;
- the taxable turnover threshold which determines whether a person may apply for deregistration has increased £83,000; and
- the registration and deregistration threshold for relevant acquisitions from other EU member states has also increased from to £85,000.

Thresholds for VAT accounting schemes

Flat Rate Scheme

The Flat Rate Scheme can be used by businesses if the estimated VAT taxable turnover (excluding VAT) in the next year will be no more than £150,000.

Businesses can continue to use the Flat Rate to account for VAT until their total business income exceeds £230,000 (including VAT).

Cash Accounting Scheme

Cash accounting can be used if estimated turnover (excluding VAT) during the next tax year will be no more than £1.35 million.

Once using cash accounting, the business can keep using it until their turnover (excluding VAT) exceeds £1.6 million.

Annual Accounting Scheme

Businesses can use annual accounting if estimated turnover (excluding VAT) during the next tax year will be no more than £1.35 million.

Once using annual accounting, the business can keep using it until its turnover (excluding VAT) is more than £1.6 million.

Businesses using the Annual Accounting Scheme:

- only need to complete one VAT Return at the end of the year,
- make nine monthly, or three quarterly, interim payments during the year, and
- either make a balancing payment or receive a balancing refund at the end of the year.

Retail schemes

Retailers normally can't account for VAT in the normal way, but can simplify their VAT accounting by using either a standard or bespoke retail scheme.

HMRC publishes standard schemes if the business' annual retail turnover - excluding VAT - is under £130 million. Businesses with turnover in excess of £130 million must agree a bespoke scheme.

Standard retail schemes require VAT on sales to be determined by using one of the following methods:

- point of sale
- direct calculation
- apportionment

Where retail turnover excluding VAT is less than £1 million the business can use a simplified direct calculation or apportionment scheme.

Thresholds for payments on account

Businesses which have an annual VAT liability of £2.3 million or more must make interim payments on account at the end of the second and third months of each VAT quarter. A balancing payment must be included for the quarter (the quarterly liability less the payments on account made) with the VAT Return. The level of interim payments that apply for one year is based on the business' VAT liability in the previous year.

If the annual VAT liability falls below £1.8 million the business can apply to stop making payments on account; though a business will automatically be removed from the requirement to make payments on account six months after the year end in which its VAT liability falls below £2.3 million.

Gifts and parties

Gifts

Business gifts cover a wide range of items from brochures, posters and advertising matter to expensive goods of the kind given as 'executive presents'.

VAT on business gifts is reclaimable and no output tax payable where the gifts are made to the same person and the total cost of all the gifts does not exceed £50 in any 12-month period.

Any 12-month period can be used which includes the day on which the gift is made.

Where the total cost of any business gifts made to the same person in any 12-month period exceeds £50 and the business has been entitled to reclaim input VAT, output VAT is required to be accounted for on the total cost value of all the gifts.

Parties and other staff functions

VAT on the cost of providing entertainment for entertaining employees is reclaimable. Where both employees and business contacts enjoy the entertainment, the business can reclaim the VAT on the part of the cost which is attributable to entertaining the employees.

VAT and telecommunications, broadcasting services and electronic/online services

Since 1 January 2015, businesses supplying the following services to non-business consumers in the EC are required to charge VAT in the EC member state where the consumer is located.

- Telecommunication services
- Broadcasting services
- Electronic services (including services provided online)

These services will include downloaded apps, video on demand, gaming, e-books, music downloads, anti-virus software, online auctions and so on. Even the smallest online businesses will be affected by these changes.

A new scheme, the 'Mini One Stop Shop' (MOSS), helps reduce the impact on affected businesses. Instead of registering for VAT in each of the consumers' member states, MOSS-registered businesses report the foreign VAT due in other member states on their UK MOSS VAT returns.

However, this MOSS scheme will only remove the administrative burden of registering for VAT in other member states. Affected businesses must still understand the relevant VAT rates and rules in the consumer's member state and will still suffer the practical difficulties of how to identify in which member state the consumer is located before charging the correct VAT-inclusive price.

For micro-businesses, there are further obstacles with tailored solutions. A business which is not registered for VAT (eg because it is too small) cannot use the MOSS; and HMRC has therefore allowed micro-businesses to register for VAT without charging VAT on their sales in the UK. In addition, HMRC allows micro-businesses to rely on their payment service providers to determine the consumers' locations. However, micro-businesses are still required to register either for VAT overseas or for MOSS (and VAT) in the UK.

Some issues remain unresolved. For example, many businesses have not registered for MOSS and cannot do so retrospectively. They are therefore required to register for VAT in their consumers' countries for the period they were not registered with MOSS, as they cannot take advantage of the local de minimis limits unless they are established there.

Supplies made by service carriers in the telecommunications industry are subject to the reverse charge if the supplies made are wholesale supplies to one of the following in the UK:

- other service carriers;
- network operators to supply users, such as consumers.

The reverse charge can only be used for business to business sales where both businesses are registered or liable to be registered for VAT. However, there are no value thresholds for your sales.

Where the reverse charge applies, the customer will account for the VAT instead of the supplier.

Joint and several liability for internet traders

The government is cracking down on the avoidance of VAT on goods sold online and new rules have been introduced.

The law requires overseas businesses which sell goods in the UK to account for UK VAT.

HMRC have the discretion to direct overseas businesses that should be registered for VAT in the UK to appoint a UK-established VAT representative. The VAT representative would be required to account for the VAT on behalf of the overseas business giving HMRC greater flexibility in relation to the collection of VAT and from whom it can require security of payment for VAT they perceive may be at risk.

HMRC have powers to make online marketplaces jointly and severally liable for the unpaid VAT of overseas businesses who are non-compliant with UK VAT rules.

In addition, the government intends to introduce new requirements for UK fulfilment houses in terms of their due diligence and record-keeping. This is intended to come into effect in 2018.

Brexit

On 23 June 2016, the British public voted to leave the EU.

One thing that's certain is that leaving the EU will require a UK legal basis for VAT after exit.

There remain many questions regarding a post-Brexit landscape.

*   How will the VAT rates be affected?

*   Might the extent of the categories be changed for zero-rated, exempt and reduced-rated supplies?

*   Will import VAT and duty apply to goods traded with the EU?

*   Are international traders in goods guaranteed to lose the EU simplifications such as triangulation, distance selling, MOSS and other ways of avoiding the need to register for VAT in other EC member states?
*   How will the mechanism be affected for recovering VAT incurred in other EC member states?

When planning ahead for a business, particularly in respect of VAT, a close eye should be kept on the developments and negotiations towards Brexit.

Transfer of Going Concerns to VAT Groups

The Upper Tribunal has held that the activities of a company within a VAT group to which a supply of a business had been transferred contributed directly to the economic activity of the group as a whole. The transfer of the business to the company in the VAT group qualified as the transfer of a business as a going concern (TOGC) and outside the scope of VAT.

The businesses within the VAT group had not lost their individual identities despite them being in a VAT group where the supplies between them were ignored for VAT purposes.

VAT groups that have incurred VAT on a TOGC should consider any redress if the VAT could not be fully claimed at the time.

Changed VAT liability of e-books

In addition to the new rules introduced from 1 January 2015 which requires the supply of an e-book (along with other electronically supplied items, broadcasting and television services) which is made to a non-business customer to be subject to VAT in the customer's country, the EU's Court of Justice (CJEU) has also stated that the standard rate of VAT must apply to the supply of e-books.

Previously, some countries such as Luxembourg, France, Italy and Malta had charged reduced rates, including rates (such as 3% in Luxembourg) below the lowest permitted by the EU Principal VAT Directive, on the grounds that an e-book was similar to a physical book. The CJEU disagreed and launched formal infringement proceedings.

However, the EU is now considering permitting member states to set their own rates of VAT, which could even see e-books being zero-rated as currently applies to physical books in the UK.

Work on more than one building

In a Policy Paper published 23 August 2016, HMRC has accepted that a new dwelling can be constructed in more than one building and a conversion can consist in converting more than one building (which were non-residential) into a single dwelling.

Works to these multiple building projects could therefore be zero-rated or reduced-rated accordingly. Where constructors or contractors have charged VAT at the full standard rate, consideration should be made as to whether this was correct. Developers might wish to challenge contractors and can amend errors in the past four years.

When can holding companies recover VAT on purchases?

On 15 May 2017, HMRC issued their long-awaited policy relating to the recovery of VAT on purchases by holding companies.

When a business acquires a new company, it incurs costs such as legal and professional expenses in evaluating the new company, planning the acquisition and implementing it. These costs generally carry a VAT charge which the acquiring business seeks to recover from HMRC.

It might at first appear that the test of whether input tax can be recovered is simple: the input tax is required to have a direct and immediate link to a taxable supply. However, the issue has exercised the courts and tribunals in recent years.

HMRC's policy addresses a number of areas in determining whether input tax is recoverable:

- whether holding shares is part of a taxable business activity;
- whether the holding company is the recipient of the purchase;
- direct, continuous and necessary extension;
- the intention to make taxable supplies;
- contingent consideration;
- attributing purchases to taxable supplies when a holding company joins a VAT group;
- stewardship costs in a VAT group;
- apportioning costs used in mixed economic and non-economic activities.

Of particular interest is HMRC's policy that input tax can, in the right circumstances, be recovered even if there is no taxable supply between the purchasing business and the acquired business. However, there are a number of unanswered questions at this point and caution should therefore be encouraged in applying this new concept. For example:

- Could this approach also result in the recovery of input tax incurred in setting up new subsidiaries?
- Is it only companies to which this policy applies, or also similar circumstances for other entities such as LLPs, sole traders, etc?
- How will HMRC test a business' intention in acquiring shares in another business and whether it is a qualifying extension of the acquirer?

Index